HISTORIES OF HATE

Histories of Hate

THE RADICAL RIGHT IN AOTEAROA NEW ZEALAND

EDITED BY MATTHEW CUNNINGHAM, MARINUS LA ROOIJ AND PAUL SPOONLEY

OTAGO UNIVERSITY PRESS
Te Whare Tā o Te Wānanga o Ōtākou

Published by Otago University Press
Te Whare Tā o Te Wānanga o Ōtākou
533 Castle Street
Dunedin, New Zealand
university.press@otago.ac.nz
www.otago.ac.nz/press

First published 2022

ISBN 978-1-99-004840-1

A catalogue record for this book is available from the National Library of New Zealand.

Published with the assistance of Creative New Zealand.

Editor: Jane Parkin
Indexer: Lee Slater
Design and typesetting: Fiona Moffat

Printed in Hong Kong through Asia Pacific Offset

CONTENTS

ACKNOWLEDGEMENTS

WE DEDICATE THIS BOOK to the memory of the 51 shuhada who died as a result of the terrorist attack on 15 March 2019 – and to all those who have been, and continue to be, targeted by the radical right in Aotearoa New Zealand.

We also acknowledge the survivors of the attack – those brave women, men and children who have found the strength to keep going despite the unimaginable emotional and physical trauma. And who, despite everything, have worked with renewed faith and energy to help build a society that is more tolerant and understanding. It is in acknowledgement of this spirit that we have agreed to donate our royalties to the Sakinah Community Trust: a group of widows, mothers and daughters of the shuhada who have come together to 'fund community initiatives that focus on well-being and bringing communities together for a better future in which we all belong'.* We thought it fitting to end the final chapter of our collection with a quote – indeed, a challenge – from Dr Hamimah Ahmat, Chairperson of the Trust.

We acknowledge Otago University Press for publishing our book. Sue Wootton, Fiona Moffat, Meg Hamilton, Mel Stevens, Lee Slater and the rest of the team – thank you for your tireless efforts in carrying our manuscript through review, editing and production. Our thanks also to Jane Parkin for her amazing copy-editing skills, and the two anonymous peer reviewers who pushed us to make the book a more cohesive whole.

* 'Our Purpose', Sakinah Community Trust: https://sakinahtrust.org/our-purpose/

We thank the staff of the various libraries and archives that have assisted us with our research and provided permission to use their images: the National Library/ Alexander Turnbull Library, Hocken Collections Uare Taoka o Hākena, Archives New Zealand, the Parliamentary Library, the J.C. Beaglehole Room and University of Auckland Library. Thank you also to Fairfax New Zealand, *Salient* magazine, Ross Kettle and Christopher Slane for granting us permission to use your excellent photos and cartoons. The book is infinitely richer for them.

Finally, thank you to all the individuals and organisations who made the time to engage with us as we produced the book. In addition to the wonderful people at the Sakinah Community Trust, we acknowledge Lynette Shum, Anjum Rahman, Murray Stirling of Masjid Al Noor, Juliet Moses of the New Zealand Jewish Council, the Federation of Islamic Associations, the New Zealand Chinese Association and the Pearl of the Islands Foundation.

Every effort has been made to determine the copyright status of the images reproduced in this book, to seek permissions where required, and to include the appropriate acknowledgements. While most were out of copyright, it proved impossible to conclusively determine the status of a few of the old and orphaned items. If notified of any errors or omissions we will be pleased to rectify them at the earliest opportunity.

Introduction

Exploring radical intolerance and extremism in New Zealand

MATTHEW CUNNINGHAM, MARINUS LA ROOIJ AND PAUL SPOONLEY

ON 15 MARCH 2019, a terrorist motivated by extreme right-wing views carried out mass shootings at the Al Noor Mosque and Linwood Islamic Centre in Christchurch, New Zealand.* Fifty-one people were killed, a further 40 received life-changing injuries and countless other lives were forever affected. This horrific atrocity spurred a concerted effort to discover how it happened and to prevent it from happening again. The New Zealand government moved quickly to pass legislation banning semi-automatic firearms and particular types of shotguns, and has begun the process of reforming the laws relating to incitement of hate and discrimination. It also established a Royal Commission of Inquiry to investigate the attack (including the role and actions of public-sector agencies) and recommend changes that could prevent similar atrocities in the future. The final report, which was presented to the governor-general on 26 November 2020, contained 44 recommendations relating to counterterrorism, firearms licensing, the needs of those most affected by the attacks, and how New Zealand should respond to the needs of an increasingly diverse population.[1] Online extremism has come under additional scrutiny: Prime Minister Jacinda Ardern initiated a political summit in Paris in May 2019 (referred to as the 'Christchurch Call'), which resulted in many countries and online service providers signing a non-binding pledge to combat right-wing radicalism online.

* Following the example set by New Zealand Prime Minister Jacinda Ardern, we have chosen not to name the individual responsible for the terrorist attacks in Christchurch. We refer to the individual as 'the 15 March terrorist' or simply 'the terrorist' rather than 'the shooter' (which is more commonly used) or 'the individual' (which the Royal Commission used) as we felt this more accurately described the nature of the crimes he perpetrated.

Discussion of the radical right in Aotearoa New Zealand has grown in scope and sophistication since the attack. News outlets and activist groups have exposed individuals espousing racist and extremist thinking, among them the chief editor of the New Zealand Initiative (a pro-market think tank) and individuals within the New Zealand Defence Force. Their efforts contributed to the arrest of two people who allegedly threatened to bomb the two Christchurch mosques on the second anniversary of the original attack.[2] Academics, too, have sought to understand the terrorist's motivations and draw attention to the risk of copycat attacks.[3] The Australian writer Jeff Sparrow argued that the terrorist 'emerged from a fascist subculture in which he'd previously been a minor and anonymous figure'. Having travelled extensively throughout Europe and interacted with far-right organisations overseas, the terrorist allegedly became frustrated with 'the failure of fascist party-building' and decided upon the course of 'accelerationism'* instead.[4] Defence and security experts John Battersby and Rhys Ball positioned the attack as an example of a series of 'sole actor' terrorist attacks in New Zealand since the 1970s. The terrorist, they argued, did not 'end New Zealand's innocence'.[5] He simply, and tragically, 'reminded New Zealand of its long-standing vulnerability'.[6] The shootings also caused a great deal of national soul-searching about the country's history, driven partially by a concern that the security and intelligence services failed to recognise the growing threat posed by white supremacists.[7] Several media outlets argued that New Zealand has 'a long history of white supremacy' extending back to the signing of Te Tiriti o Waitangi in 1840. Some suggested it extends even further back to the motivations that underpinned the voyages of Abel Tasman and James Cook. The social Darwinistic attitudes of early settlers, state measures to restrict non-white immigration in the late nineteenth and early twentieth centuries, and the dawn raids against Pasifika communities in the 1970s are some of the examples of assumed racial and cultural superiority discussed as part of this long history.[8]

This increased coverage has played an important role in raising public awareness about uncomfortable aspects of our past – that this might not be us, to borrow from PM Ardern's words after the attacks, but there is still a little bit of us in this. However, it has limitations. It implies that an inevitable and relatively straight line can be drawn from disparate aspects of the past to the 15 March terrorist attack. But history is rarely linear or unidirectional. It twists and turns; it branches, ruptures, finds unexpected dead ends or reaches a certain outcome through design or chance. And while the

* Acts of terror intended to destabilise and hasten the collapse of the current democratic system by inciting racial violence.

attention paid to the terrorist and his background has been valuable, it sheds little light on New Zealand's diverse history of radical right extremism and intolerance. In part, this is because the terrorist (an Australian citizen) was largely disconnected from the New Zealand radical right, although he was influenced by the same international ideas and actors. But more importantly, New Zealand's diverse radical right history cannot be explained solely through the lens of 'white supremacy'. It has involved various forms of intolerance, including sexism, anti-communism (as a cover to attack a range of political beliefs), religious bigotry, anti-Treatyism, and opposition to sexual liberation, homosexuality, transgenderism and non-binary gender identification. Nor did white supremacism and the conception of 'whiteness' mean the same thing to different actors in different time periods.

This book argues that New Zealand's radical-right tradition is a complex and multi-faceted phenomenon stretching back to the late nineteenth century. It is a diverse mix of ideologues, organisations, social clubs, politicians, political factions and political parties animated by different causes in different ways and at different times. The contributors to this book have tried to capture some of these many histories while acknowledging that no single book can provide a comprehensive account. We use the term 'histories' quite deliberately, for there is no united history of the radical right in New Zealand: it is a broad church that cannot be simplified into a single activity or ideology. And as horrifying as the 15 March terrorist attack was, it is only one piece of a much bigger picture. Each chapter explores one aspect of New Zealand's radical-right tradition, be it an individual, an organisation (or group of organisations) or an ideological strand. This introduction draws out some common themes in terms of ideology, structure (where the radical right sits within the broader political and social system) and political behaviour. It also identifies the unique aspects of New Zealand's radical-right tradition that distinguish it from its international counterparts – what we have termed the 'Kiwi inflection' of the radical right.

For the first time, we have brought together experts from multiple disciplines to approach this subject: historians, sociologists, political scientists, kaupapa Māori scholars, and experts in religious and media studies. Some are professors with decades of experience in academia who are frequently called upon to provide expert advice in this area. Others are budding new scholars, educators or professional researchers. We invited them to submit to this publication, noting that their contributions do not necessarily reflect the views of other authors or the editors. But we hope that this will stimulate further discussion and debate. Our combined efforts represent the first overarching account of the New Zealand radical right since Paul Spoonley's well-known volume, *The Politics of Nostalgia*, in 1987.[9] It is a sparsely studied area: apart from Spoonley's work, there is only a smattering of books, book chapters, journal articles and theses devoted to specific aspects of the New Zealand radical right, many of which were written by contributors to this volume. While we cannot answer the question plaguing our national psyche – 'how did this happen here?' – we hope to provide information that will help others to approach it.

TERMINOLOGY

RADICAL RIGHT

There is arguably no consensus on appropriate terminology when it comes to describing the radical right either in New Zealand or internationally. Since the end of World War II, international scholars have used several terms to describe different 'waves' of right-wing activity, including neo-fascist, ultra-conservative, extreme right, radical right and far right.[10] This has been further complicated by the increasing electoral success of right-wing and nationalistic parties and social organisations in the last few decades (particularly in Europe and the US), and the rise of accompanying ideological subcultures such as the alt-right and identitarianism. Some scholars use the phrase 'radical right' to describe this increasingly mainstream phenomenon while reserving 'extreme right' for openly racist, neo-fascist and anti-democratic groups that largely remain on the fringes.[11] Others have suggested labels such as the 'populist radical right', 'national populism' or 'post fascism' to describe this contemporary phenomenon.[12] In the New Zealand context, Spoonley used the term 'extreme right' to describe 'new forms of conservative and reactionary expression' that arose in the 1970s and 1980s and were openly racist in outlook.[13] But not all such groups are primarily focused on race.

There are two key reasons why we opted for 'radical right' over other options. First, our book considers a wide range of right-wing ideas, groups, supporters, strategies and behaviours, ranging from beyond the centre-right out to the farthest fringes. Of particular interest is where the radical right has 'jumped the firebreak' from the fringe, and begun influencing mainstream political policy and social discourse. This process of radicalisation is a key area of interest for scholars of the European radical right. Markus Wagner and Thomas Meyer, for example, have demonstrated the rightward shift of both left- and right-wing parties in Europe on issues such as immigration and law and order since the 1980s.[14] 'Radical right', then, is simply our description of views that are *more radical* than those held by the mainstream, including the centre-right.

Over time, what is regarded as radical and right has changed. While this lends itself to some variability as mainstream views have shifted, we argue later in this introduction why this spectrum approach is both necessary and unavoidable to understand the New Zealand radical right.

Secondly, the terms proposed in the literature tend to concern the period *after* World War II, with some focusing specifically on the years from the 1990s to the present. While World War II is an important break point, this book concerns events both before and after the war. There are, however, some limitations to how widely the term 'radical right' can be applied in the pre-war period. Many of the ideas and policies of the pre-war period that are considered extreme by today's standards were uncontroversial at the time. This is not to say that there were no radical right groups during this period, but rather that many of the views that are now considered synonymous with the radical right were once identified with a bipartisan mainstream – and, in some cases, championed by the political left more than the right. As we note below, it is more appropriate to view the pre-war period as having provided a reservoir of ideas, behaviours and strategies from which the postwar radical right drew, rather than retrospectively (and inappropriately) applying the radical-right label. There are also some direct continuities between pre- and postwar actors and organisations on the radical right.

Various other terms are used by our contributors to describe specific aspects of the radical right, including 'white supremacism', 'eugenics', 'neo-fascism', 'neo-Nazism', 'identitarianism' and the 'alt-right'. While we leave it to authors to define these terms in their chapters, two other general concepts that are closely interwoven with the radical right warrant definition here: populism and fascism. While neither has an agreed definition among scholars, the literature provides considerable guidance on how to approach them.

POPULISM

The term 'populism' first emerged at the end of the nineteenth century. It was coined to describe two left-wing agrarian political movements – the People's Party in the US and the *Narodniks* in Russia – both of which appealed directly to 'the people' against an elite who had supposedly monopolised political power for their own ends.[15] Since the 1950s, it has been used in relation to a wide variety of parties, movements and individuals, particularly in Europe and Latin America.[16] Academic interest has grown further since the 1990s, driven by the dramatic increase in left- and right-wing populism.[17] Rovina Kaltwasser and Benjamin Moffitt identified three schools of thought in the literature: the ideational, politico-strategic and socio-cultural (which Moffitt describes as 'discursive-performative').

The ideational approach defines populism as an ideology, albeit a 'thin' one that cannot stand alone: it is always combined with more substantive ideologies, such as liberalism, conservatism and nationalism. The politico-strategic approach views populism as a form of political strategy and a mode of organisation – something that is *done* rather than something that *is*. It focuses heavily on the role of the 'leader' and their supposedly direct, unmediated connection to 'the people'. The socio-cultural approach stresses that populism is, above all, a form of discourse. Not only is language used by populists to describe the conflict between 'the people' and their enemies but it is also used to construct who 'the people' and their 'enemies' actually are.[18] These approaches are complementary rather than exclusive, and they share the common thread of struggle between a virtuous and homogenous 'people' and the corrupt 'elite' that no longer represents its constituents. The desire to combat or exclude an 'other' that is believed to be seeking to usurp the status of the 'people' is another common feature of populism.

FASCISM

The history of the scholarly journey to define fascism can be broadly understood as an ongoing, and often highly contested, debate between ideological and material approaches.[19] In simple terms, the ideological approach involves the attempt to identify a common set of ideas that all fascist movements (or at least the major ones) shared. This is often referred to as a 'fascist minimum' and it has resulted in a wide range of definitions. At one end is Stanley Payne's lengthy set of common fascist characteristics, including shared ideology and goals, a similar style and organisation, and the key ideologies that fascism opposes (the 'fascist negations'). At the other is Roger Griffin's more succinct definition of fascism as a 'palingenetic form of populist ultra-nationalism', or a form of nationalism centred around a myth of national rebirth.[20] The materialist approach, in contrast, explores the conditions out of which fascism arose. It suggests that fascism is a response to economic crisis, often (but not exclusively) described as a stage of capitalist development where the propertied class back a brutally repressive regime to protect their interests against the marauding forces of communism – real or perceived.[21] Secondary themes within the literature include the debate over which movements were – or were not – fascist, and whether fascism might be better classified as 'a form of political behaviour' rather than an ideology or a response to economic crisis.[22]

Few individuals or groups in the history of Aotearoa New Zealand were genuinely fascist. So why is understanding fascism important to an analysis of this country's radical right? First, it helps to cut through the noise generated by the overuse of the term. 'Fascist' and 'Nazi' have long been popular political insults on both sides of the political spectrum, and have been taken to an entirely new level of irrationality by some opponents of the government's Covid-19 public health measures. Journalists and political pundits occasionally use fascism, 'far right' and 'white supremacism' interchangeably. This obscures the important differences between these concepts and the contested nature of their definitions. Secondly, fascism is a key part of the international context that informs the New Zealand radical right. Fascism may have been a negligible force in this country but it was – and remains – a powerful thread within the radical-right traditions of other countries that have influenced the shape of the radical right here, particularly in Europe. Finally, fascism provided a bundle of ideas and strategies that openly neo-fascist and neo-Nazi groups sought to emulate in New Zealand after World War II. While small in number, understanding what these groups were trying to achieve helps us understand the groups themselves.

Payne's set of fascist characteristics, reproduced in Table 1, overleaf, provides a useful summary of common fascist ideas, goals, styles and 'negations'. This model was intended as a 'wide-spectrum description'; individual groups 'might differ somewhat with regard to one or two individual criteria' while conforming generally to 'the overall description or ideal type'.[23] While this allows for some flexibility when considering whether specific groups conform sufficiently to the fascist 'mould', it is important to remember that fascism is only one of many influences on New Zealand's broad and disparate radical-right tradition.

AN INTERNATIONAL COMPARATIVE FRAMEWORK

When writing about the European radical right in 1988, Klaus von Beyme bemoaned the fact that there was 'virtually no comparative literature on the topic'.[24] The explosion of scholarly interest in the subject since then has dramatically reversed this deficiency. Internationally, scholars now generally agree that the postwar radical right is comprised of four 'waves', although there is some debate about the characteristics and time periods of each. Cas Mudde described these waves as neo-fascism (1945–55), right-wing populism (1955–80), the radical right (1980–2000) and the populist radical right (2000–present) (see Table 2, page 17). The latter describes the recent electoral successes achieved by nationalist parties and leaders around the world.[25]

TABLE 1: PAYNE'S DEFINITION OF FASCISM

A. IDEOLOGY AND GOALS

- Espousal of an idealist, vitalist and voluntaristic philosophy, normally involving the attempt to realise a new modern, self-determined and secular culture
- Creation of a new nationalist authoritarian state not based on traditional principles or models
- Organisation of a new highly regulated, multi-class, integrated national economic structure, whether called national corporatist, national socialist, or national syndicalist
- Positive evaluation and use of, or willingness to use, violence and war
- The goal of empire, expansion, or a radical change in the nation's relationship with other powers

B. THE FASCIST NEGATIONS

- Anti-liberalism
- Anti-communism
- Anti-conservatism (though with the understanding that fascist groups were willing to undertake temporary alliances with other sectors, most commonly with the right)

C. STYLE AND ORGANISATION

- Attempted mass mobilisation with militarisation of political relationships and style and with the goal of a mass party militia
- Emphasis on aesthetic structure of meetings, symbols and political liturgy, stressing emotional and mystical aspects
- Extreme stress on the masculine principle and male dominance, while espousing a strongly organic view of society
- Exaltation of youth above other phases of life, emphasising the conflict of generations, at least in effecting the initial political transformation
- Specific tendency toward an authoritarian, charismatic, personal style of command, whether or not the command is to some degree initially elective

TABLE 2: MUDDE'S DESCRIPTION OF THE FOUR WAVES OF THE POSTWAR RADICAL RIGHT

WAVE ONE: NEO-FASCISM (1945–55)

- Comprised of small groups of fascists who remained loyal to wartime fascist ideology
- Backwards- rather than forwards-looking
- Rarely gained popular support and often faced significant state repression
- Rarely contested elections and came well under electoral thresholds when they did
- Outside of Europe, neo-fascism was often represented by East European émigré organisations
- Example: Italian Social Movement

WAVE TWO: RIGHT-WING POPULISM (1955–80)

- The rise of a variety of right-wing populist parties and politicians that defined themselves by opposition to the postwar elite rather than allegiance to fascism
- Revolted against postwar conditions, in particular the marginalisation of the rural periphery and the growth of the welfare state
- Neo-fascism continued into this period, and some former fascists were involved in the new right-wing populist parties
- Example: Poujadism

WAVE THREE: RADICAL RIGHT (1980–2000)

- First significant wave of far-right politics in Western Europe
- Fuelled by unemployment and mass immigration in the 1980s
- Expressed nativism, authoritarianism, populism and anti-globalism / anti-European integration sentiment
- Some were new parties (especially in former communist states), while others were mainstream parties that transformed themselves into radical right parties
- Minor electoral successes in Europe
- Examples: Belgium Vlaams Blok, Croatian Party of Rights, Slovak National Party

WAVE FOUR: POPULIST RADICAL RIGHT (2000–PRESENT)

- Buoyed by three 'crises': the September 11 2001 terrorist attacks, the 2008 Global Financial Crisis and the European 'refugee crisis' in 2015
- Combined existing radical right ideology with a focus on Islamophobia and opposition to 'political correctness'
- Increased mainstreaming – radical right parties regularly achieve electoral success and form majority or coalition governments, and their views have been adopted (often in a more moderate form) by mainstream parties
- Very heterogenous – includes existing radical-right parties and transformed conservative parties as well as a 'dizzying array' of new parties
- Has broken through in countries that were previously resistant, such as Germany, Sweden, Austria and Hungary
- Examples: Fidesz, Jobbik, People's Party – our Slovakia, Law and Justice
- Not limited to Europe – see Trump in the US, Bolsonaro in Brazil and Modi in India

Mudde's descriptions are fairly Eurocentric, despite his attempt (with varying degrees of success) to apply this framework to the US, Latin America and Asia. They also do not capture authoritarian right-wing regimes in the postwar period, such as Pinochet's Chilean military junta. Nevertheless, it provides a useful starting point for comparative purposes when assessing the 'Kiwi inflection' of the radical right.

TRACING THE HISTORIES OF NEW ZEALAND'S RADICAL RIGHT

This book is presented in five parts, each representing an important facet of New Zealand's radical-right tradition. We discuss the chapters in each of these parts below, and place them within their broader historical context. We also outline some of the unique aspects of New Zealand's radical right (the 'Kiwi inflection') by comparing these chapters to the international literature summarised in Mudde's framework.

PART 1: ORIGINS OF THE NEW ZEALAND RADICAL RIGHT IN THE LATE NINETEENTH AND EARLY TWENTIETH CENTURIES

One of the key differences of our work is that we begin our analysis in the late nineteenth century. While we agree that World War II is an important break point, there are two aspects of the pre-war period that, in the New Zealand context at least, are crucial to understanding the postwar radical right. The first, which the chapters in Part 1 consider, consists of ideas and policies that were relatively mainstream in New Zealand in the late nineteenth century and the first half of the twentieth, but which are now largely considered the preserve of the radical right. In Chapter One, Leonie Pihama and Cherryl Smith explore how scientific racism and the application of biological concepts of natural selection to cultural interactions were used to reinforce the notion of British superiority; to portray Māori as savage, inferior and unfit; and to rationalise the dispossession of Māori from their land and other resources. They argue that these were important precursors to the way in which the pseudo-scientific practice of eugenics was adapted to the New Zealand context in the early twentieth century and subsequently influenced the provision of health services to Māori.

In Chapter Two, Stevan Eldred-Grigg and Zeng Dazheng discuss political discrimination against Chinese immigrants from 1880 to 1920. They argue that this cannot be reduced to a singular 'Sinophobia', and can be understood only by looking at the ways various social groups were enmeshed in, and broke through, complex economic and historical patterns already fraught with deeply political fissures. Chapter Three by Marinus La Rooij explores a tragic manifestation of this anti-Chinese prejudice – the murder of Chinese miner Joe Kum Yung by Lionel Terry in 1905 – and the radicalisation process that led Terry to commit this crime.

It would be incorrect to assume that eugenics and Sinophobia were universally supported. As John Stenhouse has shown, while scientific racism clearly existed in the late nineteenth century, it did not totally eclipse older traditions of 'racial harmony and humanitarianism' that had, to some degree, influenced the shape of early colonial politics in New Zealand.[26] The 'dying race' theme – or the commonly held belief that Māori were becoming extinct and that it was incumbent on Pākehā 'as good, compassionate colonists ... to smooth down their dying pillow' – also had several meanings.[27] While some Pākehā saw Māori as doomed to literal or cultural extinction, the state responded to the declining Māori population with various policies designed to ensure their survival through assimilation.[28] Some Pākehā resisted: the Anglican missionaries who founded Te Aute College in 1854 'did not want Māori either to die out or to become nothing more than "hewers of wood and drawers of water" for white settlers'.[29] And while eugenics may have been imbued with notions of racial purity, recent scholarship has demonstrated that it was a much broader phenomenon that encompassed subjects as diverse as 'education, religion, the arts, and popular culture, [and] pro-natalist "positive" practices such as baby contests and marriage counselling'.[30] It also encouraged better standards of health and pre- and postnatal care, although Māori did not have equal access to the resources and services designed to achieve this. Cora Wilding's Sunlight League and Truby King's Plunket Society both grew out of a concern with declining Pākehā fertility and a desire to preserve the quality of the Pākehā 'racial stock'.[31] Prominent Māori figures like Tā Āpirana Ngata and Te Rangi Hīroa (Sir Peter Buck) supported eugenics, albeit through a Māori lens, and expressed concern over potential liaisons between Māori women and their Chinese market-gardener employers.[32]

Racism against Asian immigrants reflected moralistic as well as economic and racial anxieties. Organisations as varied as the Returned Soldiers' Association, Chambers of Commerce and trade unions opposed Asian immigration on the basis that it would undercut white wages and businesses and limit access to land for development. The anti-immigration White New Zealand League was partially a response to Chinese and Indian immigrants leasing and buying land around Pukekohe and supposedly posing a 'sexual threat' to European and Māori women.[33] Nor was state-sanctioned intolerance directed solely against those of Asian (typically Chinese) descent. Indians, Syrians (including Lebanese and Assyrians), Samoans and Dalmatians were likewise targeted by legislation aimed at curbing certain economic activities such as hawking and kauri-gum digging. By 1920, New Zealand had effectively constructed a 'white New Zealand' policy that was overwhelmingly targeted at excluding Asian immigrants and ensuring that immigrants to New Zealand were of 'British' racial stock. Between 1879 and 1920, more than 20 pieces of legislation were passed to restrict Chinese immigration and economic activity. This included a £10 poll tax (later increased to £100) that was not repealed until 1944 (although it does not appear to have been actively levied after 1934), denying Chinese immigrants the ability to become naturalised citizens (not repealed until 1952) and tying the number of Chinese immigrants to the tonnage of the vessels they arrived on. This culminated in the Immigration Restriction Amendment Act in 1920, which gave the minister of customs and his officials significant leeway to deny intending immigrants entry to New Zealand. This was directed primarily against those of Asian and Southern and Eastern European descent.[34]

There are links between these various threads of intolerance. Brian Moloughney and John Stenhouse suggested that 'colonial nationalism', or the desire to build a better Britain in the South Pacific, provided 'the crucial wider context within which an array of phenomena often treated as discrete and unrelated … may comprehensively be understood'. Seen through this lens, Chinese gold miners and vegetable growers, Dalmatian gumdiggers, Assyrian and Hindu (Indian) hawkers, Māori prophets, and the mentally and physically 'unfit' were all threats or impediments to idealistic politicians 'determined to build a better society than anywhere else in the world'. It is not hard to see how such a vision would have appealed to self-professed progressives of all stripes who prided themselves on their novel uses of the state's machinery to achieve better social outcomes. This process of nation-building, Moloughney and Stenhouse argued, transcended racial boundaries to encompass other 'enemies' such as Jews, Irish Catholics and fundamentalist Protestants.[35] Philip Ferguson suggested that it was particularly targeted against the Chinese because they were viewed 'as the group most likely to undermine the process, morality and democracy of the new society and as the least capable of self-improvement'.[36] Colonial nationalism also reflected the overlaps between conceptions of 'whiteness' and 'Britishness'. William Massey, prime minister when the Immigration Restriction Amendment Act was passed in 1920, is well known for having described the Bill as representing 'a deep-seated sentiment on the part of a huge majority of the people of this country that this Dominion shall be what is often called a "white" New Zealand …' Few, however, refer to the end of his sentence: '… and that the people who come here should, as far as it is possible for us to provide for it, be of the same way of thinking from the British Empire point of view – I might have said the Imperial point of view, but I say from the British Empire point of view – and that they shall be people who will be loyal to the Empire, loyal to the Crown, and loyal to this country when they become its citizens.'[37]

This does not detract from the fact that the Act was clearly intended to affect racial exclusion, but it demonstrates the different ways that 'whiteness' has been conceptualised over time. There is a sense of colonial insecurity beneath this nation-building programme – a young Pākehā nation with a limited white population, isolated in the South Pacific, fearful of supposed enemies to the north. It explains the disproportionate fear that New Zealanders had of invasion by Tsarist Russia in the late nineteenth century – a fear that later encompassed the Soviet Union and communism after the Bolshevik revolution.[38]

In Chapter Four, Mark Derby discusses an interesting outlier in this period – the life and works of Arthur Desmond, a New Zealand-born itinerant worker, 'left-wing firebrand' and sometime journalist whose penchant for plagiarism often landed him in hot water. Like many disillusioned syndicalists of his time (including those who helped fill the ranks of the Italian fascist movement after World War I), Desmond came to reject the union movement and embrace a hyper-masculine, overtly racist world-view that glorified individual strength and rejected collective action.[39] Derby demonstrates how *Might Is Right*, Desmond's literary manifesto for intolerance written after relocating to the US, was appropriated in recent decades by white supremacists in New Zealand. Yet *Might Is Right* was not considered right wing when it was written. As Derby points out, sections of the Industrial Workers of the World were among its strongest supporters. The salvaging of Desmond's work from the dustbin of history, and the way it has been deliberately separated from its historical context by contemporary figures, is a cogent example of how late-nineteenth-century conceptualisations of race and gender have been repurposed in support of contemporary white supremacy.

PART 2: THE IDEOLOGICAL CAULDRON OF THE INTERWAR YEARS

The second aspect of the pre-war period that is crucial to understanding New Zealand's postwar radical right is the emergence of several radical groups and ideologues during the interwar years. They emerged in response to a series of events that generated a sense of crisis: the Great War, the Bolshevik revolution (and the accompanying economic and industrial turmoil of the immediate postwar period) and the Great Depression. Chapters Five through Seven explore some key aspects of this 'ideological cauldron'.

In Chapter Five, Elizabeth Ward discusses three fringe anti-communist groups – the Loyal Citizens League, the Protestant Political Association and the Welfare League, all of which arose either in the waning days of World War I or shortly after. What distinguished these groups from mainstream anti-communism was their central belief that local manifestations of labour unrest were part of a wider conspiracy to bring down the British Empire. Ward demonstrates how this more radical form of anti-communism occasionally influenced mainstream views, in both the social and political spheres.

Chapter Six explores the Protestant Political Association through a different lens. By comparing it to the New Zealand Legion that arose during the 1930s Depression, Matthew Cunningham explains why both groups managed to attract an unusually high level of support. Both appeared at times of pronounced crisis – the Great War and the Great Depression respectively – which made people more susceptible to radical alternatives. Both also tapped into long-simmering prejudices that in ordinary times did not animate people to the same extent, and were able to channel these concerns through a skilful blend of organisational and promotional techniques.

In Chapter Seven, Marinus La Rooij examines the rise of antisemitic conspiracy theories during the Great Depression. He demonstrates how antisemitism – which had been fairly limited prior to the Great War – became hardwired into a diverse radical monetary reform movement during the 1930s.[40] The Douglas Social Credit movement was the best known and most longstanding product of this phenomenon, but the works of the journalist Arthur Nelson Field played a more prominent role in the growth of radical monetary reform politics and antisemitism during the Depression. These beliefs sat on the fringe of a broader stream of underconsumptionist economic thinking – the belief that a lack of consumer spending power was preventing economic recovery – which contributed to the backlash against economic orthodoxy that was a crucial factor in Labour's victory in the 1935 General Election.[41]

Field also had a profound effect on the burgeoning Douglas Credit movement, which would play a central role in the New Zealand radical right for the next few decades. It is difficult to determine the number of people who joined Douglas Credit. The movement's journal *New World* claimed there were 60,000 members in May 1933, although the historian Robin Clifton gave a more modest figure of 4000 across 255 branches in 1935. Leading Reform politician and former Prime Minister Gordon Coates suggested that 200,000 monetary reformers supported the Labour Party in 1935, although not all of these would have been Douglas Crediters.[42] Support was spread across the cities but was especially strong in rural areas – particularly in newly broken-in dairy country – unlike the more urban-based Australian Social Credit movement at the time.[43] Clifton described New Zealand Douglas Credit as essentially a middle-class movement representing 'the hopes and fears of small property owners who wish to rise economically, without hazarding their existing social position'.[44] Spoonley described this group as the 'old petty-bourgeois', which consisted of 'small rural producers such as dairy farmers, the smaller retail stores like dairies and those working as independent tradespeople'. Squeezed between political labour on one side and big business/capital on the other, the economic turmoil of the Depression led them to look for 'political alternatives' to the 'dominant political groups'. However, their hopes that Labour might implement Douglas Credit policy after 1935 were dashed, and the remnants of the movement regrouped in the decades that followed.[45]

Why did fascism or right-wing authoritarianism not arise in New Zealand during the interwar years? The answer might have something to do with the stronger democratic traditions of Commonwealth countries and the US, coupled with the lack of a local 'stab-in-the-back' or irredentist myth (the desire to restore lost territories or cultural enclaves to the state). Yet several prominent fascist movements arose in Britain – most notably the National Fascisti, the British Union of Fascists and the Imperial Fascist League – and hundreds of thousands of Australians joined secret paramilitary movements during the Depression in anticipation of a communist uprising or a breakdown in social order.[46] In New South Wales, a paramilitary movement named the New Guard spent the summer of 1931–32 conducting drills and mobilisation exercises and engaging in brawls with communists and the unemployed, and came close to launching a coup d'état against Jack Lang's State Labor government.[47] New Zealand experienced none of this. Active support for fascism was largely limited to the small Italian diaspora, although there was general support among some conservatives for fascism's ardent anti-communism and nationalism. The paramilitary ambitions of the 1920 Loyal Citizens League soon dissipated when a much-feared general strike never eventuated.[48] One crucial difference is that the power of the state was never in jeopardy in New Zealand. Even at the height of the Depression – the crucible that forged the alliance between the German establishment and Nazism – the state, or specifically governing political parties, did not need to turn to dubious alternatives for backing. Indeed, conservative parties held power for the duration of the Depression and responded quickly and effectively to sporadic riots in early 1932. Unlike in Australia, there were no labour bogeymen in power whom conservatives could direct their frustration against. This may explain why so many turned to radical theories for monetary reform instead.[49] In a clear sign of New Zealand's rejection of extremes, the

New Zealand Legion went to great lengths to reassure the country that it was 'not a New Guard' or a 'Fascist group'.[50]

The various radical groups and ideologues that arose during the interwar years were important precursors to the postwar radical right. But they were not universally considered right wing at the time. Anti-communism was a comfortable fit with more mainstream political conservatism, notwithstanding the paranoid and conspiratorial lengths groups like the Welfare League took it to. Antisemitism and monetary reform appealed to parts of the political left as well, with the Labour Party the ultimate beneficiary of these political concerns. It would be more appropriate to view the pre-war period as having provided a reservoir of ideas, behaviours and strategies from which the postwar radical right drew, in some cases through the deliberate appropriation and reinterpretation of the works of specific individuals such as A.N. Field, Lionel Terry and Arthur Desmond. There were also some direct organisational and individual continuities, most clearly in the ranks of the Douglas Credit movement. The crucial difference is that the interwar groups were trying to push a centre *that already reflected their views to some degree* further towards more radical options. The postwar groups, in contrast, generally shared a desire to *wind back the clock* to how they believed things were before the centre shifted from under them. While this proposition does not hold true in all instances, it provides a useful analytical framework, and we return to it in the next section.

PART 3: THE RISE OF THE RADICAL RIGHT AFTER WORLD WAR II

Like the radical right internationally, World War II presents an important break-point for the New Zealand radical right. Antisemitism became, for a time, much less tenable owing to the 'recoil effect' of the mass murder of Europe's Jews in the Holocaust.[51] New Zealand was also experiencing major social, political and demographic changes. Women had entered the workforce in large numbers, the rapidly growing Māori population was relocating to urban areas and becoming more prominent culturally and politically, international politics was being reshaped around the new Cold War dynamic, and the welfare state was now generally the subject of bipartisan consensus. The British Empire was in decline and the United Kingdom was reorienting towards Europe and away from its antipodean colonies.[52] Restrictions against Asian and South European immigration were gradually removed both to meet the increased workforce demands of a booming economy and, in some instances, as part of a more sympathetic response to ethnic diversity.

In short, the centre was shifting. Ideas that had been relatively mainstream in the pre-war period were becoming much less acceptable. The radical right was partially a response to this shift, filling the ideological spaces vacated or neglected by the move towards the centre. But economics played a role as well. Spoonley explained the rise of the radical right in the postwar period as 'a product of the social dislocation that has accompanied industrialisation' as the profitability of the old petty-bourgeois style of production was increasingly squeezed by monopoly capital and finance, big business and large-scale production, and the increasing clout of trade unions.[53] The twin themes of ideological retreat and economic dislocation will continue to be explored below.

It becomes apparent that New Zealand's postwar radical right tradition does not closely align with Mudde's framework for the international radical right. Rather than comprising broadly sequential 'waves', New Zealand experienced a gradual evolution across multiple threads of radical-right intolerance, interspersed with moments of crisis that generated new threads. Two key new threads – religious and cultural intolerance, and the rise of identitarianism and the alt-right – are the subject of Parts Four and Five, and are discussed later in this introduction. Chapters Eight through Ten explore some of the other diverse threads of the postwar radical right, including neo-Nazism and neo-fascism, Empire loyalty, anti-communism, support for the white-minority governments in southern Africa, economic liberalism and skinhead gangs.

Why did New Zealand not experience a wave of 'neo-fascism' in the decade after the war, as many European countries did? Partly this was because there had been no prewar domestic fascist movement for people to look back on with fondness. There were also no sharp economic or political crises after the war to generate a radical-right response as New Zealand experienced relatively uninterrupted economic prosperity until the 1970s. New Zealanders of a radical-right bent also had an existing alternative to invest in – the Douglas Credit movement, which remained haunted by a fringe of antisemites, Empire loyalists and anti-bank monetary reformists. In 1953, elements within the Social Credit Association, the main representative body for Douglas Credit in New Zealand, decided to form a Social Credit Political League to contest the election, and managed to receive between five and 20 percent of the vote in every general election from 1954 to 1987. (This never equated to more than two members of Parliament.) A debate arose within the Association in the 1960s between the 'purist' old guard who demanded fidelity to Douglas's original policies – including his belief in a conspiracy of Jewish international financiers – and a 'pragmatic' younger generation who sought to liberalise the movement. This led the 'purist' faction to split away to form a short-lived New Democratic Party and opened up an ideological space that was filled by the League of Rights.[54]

There were thus few radical right groups in New Zealand in the 1950s and 1960s. However, as Steven Loveridge shows in Chapter Eight, this did not mean that New Zealand experienced an uninterrupted period of political 'golden weather'. Taking a 'tour' of the right-wing fringe from rebellious pranksters adopting Nazi regalia all the way to neo-Nazism, Loveridge identifies a diverse range of fringe-dwellers, including social rebels, disaffected conservatives, isolated cranks, immigrant fascists and native-born neo-Nazis. While most of these groups were short-lived, three warrant mention for their ongoing significance. The first was the National Socialist Party of New Zealand, the first political foray of New Zealand's longest-standing radical-right torchbearer, Colin King-Ansell, who represented the party in several unsuccessful electoral campaigns in the 1970s. The second was the National Front, which was formed via an amalgamation of various radical-right groups in 1967, and has been dissolved and recreated several times since then. The Front has housed many of New Zealand's most renowned radical-right figures, including King-Ansell, Kerry Bolton, Kyle Chapman and Anton Foljambe. The third was the League of Rights, a branch of the Australian movement of the same name whose founder, Eric Butler, was a Douglas Crediter who had been heavily influenced by the works of A.N. Field.[55] The League was officially launched in New Zealand in 1970, and combined fervent British patriotism and racism with the 'purist' Douglas Credit tradition it inherited after the split in that movement. It produced a considerable amount of propaganda – including a steady stream of anonymous letters to major newspapers – and founded or worked with dozens of other radical-right groups before it folded in the early 2000s.[56] These three groups stand out amid the dozens of radical right-wing groups that formed, splintered and dissolved in the 1970s and 1980s.

Chapters Nine and Ten explore specific strands within the postwar radical-right tradition. In Chapter Nine, Sebastian Potgieter and Tyler West discuss support for the white-minority governments in South Africa and Rhodesia. They demonstrate how the issue of sporting contacts with South Africa produced an unusual degree of unity among New Zealand's radical right-wing groups, and garnered them some considerable public support. This complicates the popular narrative that the 1970s and 1980s were a time when greater tolerance and pluralism were being consolidated.

In Chapter Ten, Jarrod Gilbert discusses the rise of skinhead gangs in New Zealand in the 1980s and 1990s. He reveals that the skinhead scene brought together many veteran radical right-wing figures with a younger generation who would play a leading role in the radical right in subsequent decades (notably Chapman). The skinhead scene declined in the late 1990s, but it reminds us that gang formation is a consequence of social conditions rather than ethnicity.

PART 4: RELIGIOUS AND CULTURAL INTOLERANCE

The political centre has continued to shift, and the radical right has continued to fill the spaces vacated or neglected by this ideological retreat. The rise of a variety of social and cultural liberation movements in the 1970s generated new threads of radical-right activity in New Zealand. These movements had the dual effect of driving mainstream opinion towards greater pluralism at the same time as they spurred a radical-right backlash seeking to return to an illusory past.

Chapters Eleven and Twelve explore two important manifestations of this backlash. In Chapter Eleven, Dolores Janiewski analyses the rise of New Zealand's religious right in response to changing social mores concerning gender roles, homosexuality, monogamy, abortion and gender identities. Tracing the evolution of the religious right from 1970 to 2020, Janiewski identifies 'family values' as the key theme uniting the various groups and political parties that appeared in this 50-year period.

In Chapter Twelve, Peter Meihana examines opposition to the growing recognition of rights guaranteed to Māori under the Treaty of Waitangi – a reaction that Richard Hill termed 'Anti-Treatyism'.[57] From its origins in scholarly reappraisals of the Treaty, Māori land and protest movements, and the establishment of the Waitangi Tribunal in the 1970s, the 'Māori Renaissance' has been manifest in areas as diverse as Treaty of Waitangi claims and settlements, the embedding of Treaty principles in legislation and policy, government departments dedicated to Māori development, and local-government representation in the form of Māori wards and constituencies. Yet unlike the 'history wars' that have infected Australia's national politics, media and education system, New Zealand's version has largely been a one-sided battle. With a few notable exceptions, it has been mostly ignored by academics and politicians alike.[58]

PART 5: THE RADICAL RIGHT IN THE TWENTY-FIRST CENTURY

International scholarly attention has recently, and unsurprisingly, focused on Mudde's 'fourth wave' of the radical right. From a cluster of right-wing parties with an 'uneven electoral performance' in 2000, the radical right has grown to include a broad range of political parties, social movements (including intellectual, media and political organisations) and subcultures.[59] Together, they have achieved direct electoral success and a significant degree of influence on mainstream politics in a range of countries. This heterogenous mix encompasses phenomena as diverse as the Hungarian Civic Alliance (Fidesz), the Brexit campaign, Donald Trump, identitarianism and the alt-right. Understanding these diverse international phenomena is crucial to assessing the 'Kiwi inflection' of the radical right that is explored in Chapters Thirteen to Fifteen.

Mudde identified four themes shared by the fourth wave: a fear that mass immigration presents 'an existential threat' to the nation and state; a heightened focus on security and 'law and order'; a populist belief that 'the elite' in politics and business are corrupting the nation with 'postmodernist' and 'cultural Marxist' ideas; and an obsession with nationalism over internationalism or cosmopolitanism (seen as manifest in the actions of the United Nations and the European Union). Their ideological response to this threat – which has been buoyed by the September 11 2001 terrorist attacks, the 2008–2012 Global Financial Crisis and the European 'refugee crisis' of 2015 – revolves around nativism (or support for ethnically homogenous states), Islamophobia, authoritarianism and populism.[60] Assessing recent trends in the literature, Mudde argued that supporters of the fourth wave are motivated both by opposition *to* established parties and support *for* radical-right parties, and are more likely to be driven by anxiety over cultural change than the dislocation caused by economic change. The two are nevertheless closely intertwined, as demonstrated by the popular refrain that immigrants are responsible for taking 'our' jobs.[61]

The fourth wave is clearly more than a fleeting or inconsequential phenomenon. 'National populism', as Roger Eatwell and Matthew Goodwin described it, is 'rooted in very deep and long-term currents' that are unlikely to abate in the near future. In addition to a distrust of the 'political elite' and fear of demographic change caused by 'mass' immigration, the relative deprivation and inequality caused by the neoliberal economic reforms of the 1980s and the de-alignment of traditional political parties from their (formerly) relatively stable class bases have contributed to it.[62] Jens Rydgren emphasised the importance of this process of political de-alignment. Whereas postwar politics 'was dominated by a conflict between different socio-economic positions', the recent convergence of left and right around neoliberalism has thrust socio-cultural issues such as 'values, identity and culture' to the forefront. Rydgren also explained this as 'a delayed reaction to the emancipatory politics that has its origins in the 1960s and 1970s'.[63]

The politicisation of immigration has been central to this process, with Paul Hainsworth concluding that opposition to immigration has replaced anti-communism as the key unifying theme on the radical right since the end of the Cold War.[64] Enzo Traverso described the contemporary radical right as 'post-fascism', in that it represents both continuity and change from interwar fascism and the neo-fascist groups of the postwar period – 'a phenomenon in transition, a movement that is still in transformation and has not yet crystallised'.[65] At a time when free-market capitalism has become the ideological default, the radical right has provided a surrogate for the lack of utopian alternatives.[66] This is perhaps why some on the radical right describe themselves as 'alternative' or 'alt-right'.

There is a growing body of literature concerning the fourth wave in Australia, particularly the rise of One Nation and the mainstreaming of radical-right views by the Howard government from the 1990s.[67] As Andy Fleming and Aurelian Mondon recently noted, One Nation disrupted the bipartisan consensus that had emerged over multiculturalism in the 1970s and 1980s. The Liberal Party subsequently normalised and entrenched One Nation's policies in the late 1990s to such an extent that it undercut One Nation's support base. Several groups emerged in the void created by the near collapse of One Nation, including the Australia First Party and the United Patriots Front, although they struggled to attract even a fraction of the support that One Nation did. Nevertheless, the 2005 race riot in Cronulla and the 'Reclaim Australia' rally in 2015, coupled with ongoing bipartisan support for mandatory detention of asylum seekers, demonstrate the length of One Nation's shadow.[68] Some scholars have drawn parallels between One Nation and the New Zealand First Party, or between its leader Winston Peters and historical New Zealand political leaders of a populist bent.[69] Moffitt concluded that New Zealand First is '*the* populist party in New Zealand' while noting that New Zealand's political landscape is 'comparatively less populist' than Australia's, and Peters is a 'smoother and more effective political operator' than Australian populist politicians like Pauline Hanson and Bob Katter. He also highlighted how New Zealand First's political agenda extends beyond the usual anxieties of the radical right. This has complicated attempts to define where the party sits on the ideological spectrum.[70]

With the tragic exception of the 15 March terrorist attacks, New Zealand's experience of the fourth wave has been minor. Apart from the comparatively mild examples of New Zealand First and the libertarian ACT, no major radical-right political party has emerged, nor has there been a local equivalent to Donald Trump to transform the centre-right National Party from within. Chapters Thirteen to Fifteen reveal how isolated and self-contained the radical right has been in twenty-first-century New Zealand. In Chapter Thirteen, Mark Dunick follows the political career of Chapman and other devotees of the skinhead movement through the brief revitalisation of the National Front and the rise and fall of the Right Wing Resistance movement. But Chapman and his followers are more the exception than the rule in the twenty-first-century radical right, despite his more recent penchant for Covid-19 conspiracy theories.

Chapters Fourteen and Fifteen explore how identitarianism and the alt-right have manifested in New Zealand over the past few years. In Chapter Fourteen, Paul Spoonley and Paul Morris provide an overview of the alt-right and identitarian subcultures, and the local influence of QAnon conspiracy theories, with a focus on the short-lived Dominion Movement and its successor Action Zealandia. They also analyse the wide variety of conspiratorial parties that emerged in 2020, including Advance New Zealand and the New Conservatives, as well as the wave of anti-vaccine, anti-government and anti-mandate protests by a loud but tiny minority after the Covid-19 outbreak in August 2021. In Chapter Fifteen, Michael Daubs explains how the internet has allowed radical-right and white-extremist views to spread internationally through websites, social networks and messaging services. Using Manuel Castells' concept of the 'network society', Daubs explores how the social structures and activities of the international radical right are organised around information networks and technology. He also highlights some of the challenges that regulators and law enforcement face in trying to combat the spread of online extremism, including the ease and speed with which digital content can be replicated and the possibilities of technologies and platforms that can circumvent restrictions.

Why has the contemporary radical right in New Zealand failed to achieve the level of success it has elsewhere? Moffitt argued that the 'strong undercurrent of anti-elitism in both Australian and New Zealand culture' has made it 'difficult for the "obvious" populist actors outside the major parties to differentiate themselves'.[71] Yet, in Australia, the political mainstream was willing to co-opt the views of One Nation to the extent that Pauline Hanson's return to politics in 2016 was received with much less denunciation than her initial appearance in the 1990s.[72] New Zealand First has not shifted the mainstream in the same way, despite having profited electorally from anti-immigrant sentiment.[73] Arguably, its most significant contributions to mainstream politics have been the exaltation of universal superannuation, a bipartisan reluctance to revisit the retirement age of 65, and the SuperGold Card for seniors. Opposition to the recognition of the Treaty and a desire for Māori to return to the margins in New Zealand society have episodically returned to the political stage but are yet to cause a fundamental lasting shift in mainstream political discourse. The lack of domestic 'crises' that could be used to drum up radical-right support may be another contributing factor. New Zealand has not experienced a major Islamic terrorist attack, and it accepts only a very modest number of refugees each year.[74] There is also relatively high trust in the political system and political parties, despite the vociferous backlash against Covid-19 vaccine mandates from a vocal minority. Over 90 percent of the population aged 12 and over received at least two doses of the vaccine.

A more fundamental answer may lie in New Zealand's Mixed Member Proportional (MMP) electoral system and the role played by New Zealand First in that system. Since its introduction in 1996, MMP has allowed a wide variety of third parties to enter Parliament and exercise influence on government – until the 2020 General Election, no single party gained enough seats to govern without the support of one or more third parties. MMP may, therefore, have mitigated the effects of political de-alignment and cultural anxiety experienced in other countries. As voters' allegiances shifted from traditional, class-based allegiances towards a wider variety of values-based allegiances, the relatively permissive threshold of New Zealand's MMP system ensured that third parties have not been 'locked out' of the political system. As a result, there is no large body of disillusioned voters who feel unrepresented by the nation's political 'elites'. MMP has also arguably contributed to New Zealand First's relatively consistent electoral success since its formation in 1993.[75] It may be that Peters' 'lite' form of populism has acted as a 'pressure valve' to let off some of the pent-up steam of potential right-wing radicals while preventing the formation of a more extreme radical-right populist party. Even the Covid-19 pandemic could not disrupt this electoral balance – while some of New Zealand First's vote was undoubtedly picked up by the 'crowded mess' of conspiratorial and radical-right parties on the ballot in the 2020 election, the lack of unity between these groups meant that none came close to the threshold required to enter Parliament.[76]

The sharp rise in anti-vaccination and anti-mandate protests since 2020, culminating in the occupation of Parliament grounds in early 2022, could presage a breakthrough moment for the New Zealand radical right – 'a kind of Trojan Horse for norm-setting and norm-entrenchment of far-right ideologies in Aotearoa New Zealand', as The Disinformation Project put it in November 2021.[77] What is clear is that the speed and spread of mis- and disinformation was 'by order of magnitude greater' than in 2020 and early 2021, and that international 'far right conspiratorial narratives' from the US and Australia in particular have been 'repackaged and re-shared' in New Zealand as part of this process.[78] But radical-right ideas appear to be only one thread in this confused tangle. Issues as varied as gun control, reform of Three Waters infrastructure services and the use of sodium fluoroacetate (1080) to control invasive species have been woven into the mix, all gathered under the loose banner of 'freedom'.[79] Nor, as the Convoy 2022 occupation demonstrated, do the protesters agree on aims and methods. While some of Parliament's protesters claimed to be seeking a peaceful end to vaccine mandates, others refused to leave until the government, judiciary and media were dissolved, put on trial or summarily executed. New Agers and Pentecostals mingled with sovereign citizens and sovereign hīkoi amid a significant undercurrent of QAnon, alt-right and identitarian ideas. A loose parallel could be drawn with the flurry of antisemitic monetary-reform groups that arose during the Great Depression. As La Rooij suggests in Chapter Seven, small groups of 'hardened conspiracists' may continue in their obsession to 'expose' those pulling the strings behind all manner of future events.

WAYS OF UNDERSTANDING THE NEW ZEALAND RADICAL RIGHT

What are we to make of this diverse array of histories? Can we identify any common threads or shared understandings? In attempting to do this in a systematic way, Spoonley's *The Politics of Nostalgia* defined the postwar 'extreme right' as a monist and purist style of politics with an ideology based around conspiracy theory, distrust of democracy, sexism, nationalism and racism. Its adherents support small-scale and owner-operated businesses, private property, the nuclear family, traditional education, militarism, the nation and the 'race', and oppose finance capital, feminism, liberalism, intellectualism and communism.[80] Yet Spoonley acknowledged that his focus was on groups in the 1970s and 1980s that explicitly expressed racism.[81] Andrew Moore provided a similar set of ideological characteristics in his 1995 study of Australian right-wing politics. While admitting that political terminology is often an exercise in 'shuffling [one's] own deck of marked cards', Moore noted that the Australian right wing was typically a more extreme version of mainstream conservatism, embraced conspiracy theory 'as a central organising concept', encompassed an exclusionary form of nationalism – which has shifted over time from imperial patriotism to a nationalist chauvinism – and expressed suspicion or outright contempt for liberal parliamentary democracy.[82] There are clear overlaps between Spoonley's and Moore's works and those of the international scholars discussed above. But one of the key themes that emerges from the chapters in this book is that the radical right cannot be understood on ideological terms alone. It is simultaneously a disparate collection of ideas, a response to structural conditions and a form of political behaviour. We now deal our own shuffled deck of cards into these three piles.

THE RADICAL RIGHT AS AN IDEOLOGY

We have already identified two common characteristics of New Zealand's radical right. The first is that it has no single history: it is a diverse mix of ideas, ideologues, organisations, social clubs and political parties animated by different causes in different ways and at different times. The second is that its adherents' views are more radical than those held by the mainstream or centre-right: they encompass a wide spectrum of ideas ranging all the way out to the farthest fringes. This fluid approach reflects the disparate nature of the radical right and the ideological mutability of the centre. Ideas that were once mainstream have become radical as the centre has shifted, and sometimes vice versa – for example, classical liberalism is no longer a radical position, given the neoliberal shift of the 1980s. More often than not, radical-right ideas have migrated around the socio-cultural spectrum, involving varying degrees of racial, cultural, religious, political, gender and sexual intolerance. When the radical right has expressed views on economic matters, it tends to portray these as being of secondary importance and its views are often fairly centrist or even left-leaning. There are exceptions, of course: the Welfare League, the Country and Liberal Parties, the Tax Reduction Integrity Movement and Zenith Applied Philosophy have all espoused classical liberal views.

Intolerance stands out as the key ideological feature of the radical right. From its roots in late-nineteenth-century mainstream views to its manifestation in the twenty-first century, it has been motivated by a ceaseless struggle to expose, confront and/or expel a dizzying array of 'others' whom it believes pose an existential threat to traditional values and beliefs, the racial and cultural makeup of the nation, or transnational identities such as the British Empire, the 'white race' or 'Western civilisation' – the 'they' in stark contrast to the 'us'. Some of these have remained constant, such as the radical right's consistent fear of Chinese immigrants, its discomfort with Māori assertions of cultural and political influence, and its obsession with communism (or, more appropriately, those they believe to be communist or 'extreme socialist', as the centrist Ardern Labour government has been described by some conspiracy-watchers).[83] The threat posed by 'others' has come and gone, or has experienced surges in 'popularity' amid long-term, low level intolerance: Russians in the 1880s and 1890s; Germans and Catholics in the 1910s; Catholics, Irish and socialists in the 1920s; Jews in the 1930s; secularists and Empire disloyalists in the 1950s and 1960s; Pasifika in the 1970s; Māori 'radicals' in the 1980s–90s; and Muslims in the twenty-first century. With so many insidious enemies plotting against New Zealand in recent history, one wonders how we have managed to escape relatively unscathed. Other facets of the radical right, such as racism, sexism, anti-communism, religious bigotry, anti-Treatyism and opposition to sexual liberation, homosexuality, transgenderism and non-binary gender identification can all be understood as specific manifestations of this intolerance. Contrary to popular belief, not all radical-right groups have been racist, or at least not explicitly so. And while nationalism is a common preoccupation of the radical right, this too can be best understood through the lens of intolerance. The nation the radical right wishes to preserve exemplifies what it seeks to protect from the 'other'. It is typically illusory, a nostalgic representation of what one American historian has described as 'the way we never were'.[84]

The radical right's overwhelming intolerance against the 'other' invariably leads it to adopt a fundamentally conspiratorial world-view. Richard Hofstader's work on the 'paranoid style' of American right-wing fringe groups in the 1960s provides a useful way of conceptualising this world-view.[85] When faced with complex and often rapid social, cultural and economic change, the radical right constructs a deliberate conspiracy that explains the world and brings order to the chaos. Sometimes the believed plot centres on a small, singular group of conspirators, such as a coterie of Jewish bankers; at other times it is an unholy alliance, such as the Catholic Church and communists, or left-wing intellectuals and supposedly corrupt iwi leaders. At other times, the plot is managed by a distant conspiracy of the elite who use other people as its 'shock troops', such as Lionel Terry's fear of being swamped by organised Chinese immigration and the 15 March terrorist's fear of the 'great replacement'. The radical-right commonly argues that the state plays a role in these plots, whether through failing to act against the threat or actively abetting it, leading to strong anti-establishment sentiments. Populism often comes into play in the latter case, as the radical right claims to represent a broader group of people – whether it is the nation, the 'people', the 'white race' or the 'silent majority' – against a corrupt ruling elite who are out of touch with those they claim to represent.

Yet this is not always the case. Neo-fascists and white supremacists are usually well aware that only a tiny minority of fringe-dwellers share their views. They have thus focused their efforts on shifting public opinion rightwards, often by trying to 'accelerate' change through 'entryism' into other political currents that can provide a platform and access to people susceptible to radicalisation, by harassment of perceived adversaries (such as journalists and academics), by promoting misinformation to incite extreme responses to real or perceived events, and, in some cases, by undertaking acts of violence to provoke a destabilising response.

Distrust of democracy is common across the radical right, although it is more nuanced than might seem at first glance. While neo-fascist and neo-Nazi groups openly oppose liberal democracy, other radical-right groups claim to want a *stronger* democracy, and they even suggest policies that might improve some forms of democratic participation (such as binding referenda and greater freedom of speech). The Protestant Political Association promoted a Catholic conspiracy and claimed to stand for 'equal rights to all, special privileges to none'; the League of Rights saw Jews as an existential threat while holding 'the vision of a world that could be one of expanding freedom and security for all'; the New Conservatives promote conservative views on marriage and gender while also standing for 'personal responsibility, limited government, free markets, individual liberty, the importance of family, and a strong national identity'.[86]

Claims from the radical right about protecting freedom and democracy should be treated with scepticism. Democracy is multi-layered. It includes 'the rights necessary for individual freedom' (such as a liberal constitution and an independent judiciary), the rights associated with participating in 'the exercise of political power' (such as universal suffrage) and, since the advent of the welfare state, the right to 'a modicum of economic welfare and security'.[87] In the New Zealand context, one could add the rights encapsulated in the Treaty of Waitangi and its principles, such as self-determination, partnership, active protection and restorative justice/redress. The radical right's distrust of democracy, as it operates in modern society, lies in its inability to acknowledge the validity of these layers, many of which it sees as anti-democratic. Its vision of democracy fixates on some of these layers, and wields them to curtail others. Underpinning this is the radical right's fear that its vision of democracy is under threat. The radical monetary reform movements of the 1930s Depression feared that individual economic rights and sovereign authority over the currency were being threatened by a gigantic plot to enslave the nation through the establishment of the Reserve Bank. The religious right believes that the rights of men, unborn children and religious worshippers are threatened by a permissive, secular state. Anti-Treatyists believe that Pākehā rights are threatened by what they refer to as 'racial apartheid'. They are unable (or unwilling) to see that multiple, complementary visions of democracy can (and do) co-exist and that some of the 'rights' they champion involve repressing the rights of others.

THE RADICAL RIGHT AS A STRUCTURAL RESPONSE

We have noted that World War II represents an important break-point, in that it delineates between interwar groups that wanted to push a centre *that already reflected their views to some degree* further towards more radical options, and postwar groups that shared a desire to *wind back the clock* to how they believed things were before the centre shifted from under them. While this proposition does not hold true in all instances – extreme views such as neo-fascism were never mainstream in New Zealand, for example – it provides a useful analytical framework for understanding both the emergence of the radical right after the war and its subsequent evolution to the present day.

The radical right is the product of ideological retreat (real and perceived) and economic dislocation, filling the spaces vacated or neglected by the centre (particularly the centre-right) as it has shifted over time. These spaces are predominantly socio-cultural rather than economic. However, the radical right's occupation of these vacated spaces has not been a passive rearguard action. Radical-right actors have expressed their views through varying shades of outrage, disbelief and, on rare occasions, violence. They represent a vehement backlash against a real or imagined threat to the values, traditions and identities they claim to defend. More often, what they are really defending are the perceived privileges and entitlements they have exclusively enjoyed, and preventing them from being expanded to include other groups.

The two key shifts of the centre that have fuelled the New Zealand radical right are the social, political and demographic changes after World War II, and the various 'liberation' movements in the 1970s that contributed to an increasingly pluralist society. These shifts have been accompanied by economic change: the postwar period witnessed the embedding of the welfare state and the marginalisation of small producers, and the 1970s and 1980s consisted of a series of economic shocks followed by the rapid liberalisation of the economy. This combination of cultural and economic crises appears to have played a key role in fuelling New Zealand's radical right toward greater prominence and, in some cases, to seep into the mainstream. World War I and the 1930s Depression were similar examples of social and economic crises that spurred radical responses, many of which became the precursors of the postwar radical right. This aligns with an international literature that highlights the role that crises, particularly economic ones, play in opening up the political space for more people to be driven to radical alternatives.[88] But crises do not need to be real or shared by the bulk of New Zealanders to generate a response. The decline of Britain as a global superpower and the increasing socio-cultural liberalisation of the 1970s were seen by many as positive developments, yet they generated specific radical-right responses. The radical right's success depended on its ability to build narratives of crisis around a supposed existential threat posed by a conspiratorial 'other' or 'others'. These narratives allow the radical right to justify its intolerance as a matter of self-preservation.

The lack of similar shifts in the early twenty-first century is one of the reasons New Zealand has not experienced the same dramatic rise of a populist radical right that other countries have. New Zealand's experience of the Global Financial Crisis was comparatively mild and brief. Unemployment peaked at 6.1 percent – compared to 10–11 percent in the early 1990s – and recovery was buoyed by public spending on the Christchurch earthquake recovery and China's growing demand for New Zealand's primary exports. Yet these figures obscure certain disparities. Unemployment for young adults rose to 11 percent by 2009 and remained above 10 percent until 2014.[89] Māori and Pasifika participation in employment was disproportionately affected and took longer to rebound: unemployment rates in 2014 remained at 12.3 percent for Māori and 12 percent for Pasifika, and did not show significant improvement until the 2018 census.[90] Yet there was no resulting surge in radical-right activity. The only such group of any significance in New Zealand at the time was Right Wing Resistance, whose open embrace of neo-Nazism was abhorrent to the vast majority of New Zealanders. Frustrated New Zealanders could of course have emulated the Tea Party movement in the US, but the fact that a centre-right government (which included the fiscally conservative ACT party) was in power may have dampened enthusiasm to do so. With identitarianism and the alt-right still a few years away, there were limited other international alternatives to draw upon.

THE RADICAL RIGHT AS A POLITICAL BEHAVIOUR

How do radical right groups behave, both internally (towards their own members) and externally (towards the groups and systems they hope to influence)? One common feature is an extreme form of social and cultural monism – that is, its dedicated adherents refuse to bend, even when faced with instances of their own illogicality or inconsistency. Purity is preserved by the selective use of evidence that supports their world-view, expanding the conspiracy to encompass evidence that does not, and ejecting members who challenge the group's world-view. This monist style grows stronger the further one moves away from the centre towards the fringes, leading to increased isolation, exclusiveness, and a belief that one is the unique bearer of truth and salvation. Spoonley aptly described such extreme groups as 'sects'.[91] It is one of the main reasons why the radical right is usually so fractured and fractious. As

Chapter Eight notes, even the National Socialist Party of New Zealand and the New Zealand National Socialist Party were 'at loggerheads' in the late 1960s.

Nonetheless, the radical right and its antecedents have influenced mainstream politics at various points. Prior to World War II, many of the ideas later associated with the radical right, such as Sinophobia and 'scientific' racism, attracted widespread support. Radical groups had an influence on both the centre-right and the centre-left – among them the Welfare League's influence on the Reform Party's anti-communism and the Labour Party's selective use of monetary-reform rhetoric. Since the war, the radical right has maintained a desire to influence the mainstream and has often 'jumped the firebreak' into a form of respectability to achieve this. These connections have largely involved ideas that sit closer to the mainstream, such as those of the religious right (in the abortion law reform of the 1970s) and anti-Treatyism (in the foreshore and seabed debates of the 2000s). Less often, connections have been made between the centre-right and the extreme fringe, as was the case with the League of Rights in the 1970s and 1980s, and the National Front's unsuccessful attempts to infiltrate the National Party. Yet despite the occasional blurring of lines, it is important to maintain a distinction between the radical and centre-right.

Finally, the radical right has consistently, and successfully, striven to connect with like-minded groups and individuals overseas. While the internet has provided the contemporary radical right with additional opportunities to develop these connections, the historical radical right was equally committed to building international networks through correspondence, the circulation of various types of literature, speaking tours and countless other forms of connection. The extensive collections left behind by Howard Elliott (National Lecturer of the Protestant Political Association) and A.N. Field contain thousands of letters, pamphlets and books from across the world. Some domestic groups have been wholly transplanted from overseas, such as New Zealand branches of the League of Rights and League of Empire Loyalists, or have modelled themselves on international examples such as the National Front. Less often, New Zealand groups and activists have had considerable influence overseas, such as Arthur Desmond, A.N. Field and Right Wing Resistance. Sadly, the international influence of the 15 March terrorist has been significant: his words and actions now haunt the darker corners of the internet, inspiring others in their intolerance, calls to violence and acts of terror.

CONTINUITY AND CHANGE

We have outlined some of the common threads and shared understandings across New Zealand's radical right. But what about the key differences? Some emerge from the discussion above – the diverse array of 'others', for example, and the general delineation between the focus of pre- and post-World War II groups. But the biggest difference appears to be the kinds of people who have been drawn to the radical right at various times. While data on membership of radical-right groups in New Zealand is thin, there appears to have been a diverse range of 'constituencies' over time, from the young unemployed working-class white men drawn to the skinhead scene in the 1980s and 1990s; to the older 'respectable' professionals and political figures attracted to the New Zealand Legion in the 1930s, and the supporters of white-minority southern Africa governments in the early 1970s; to the predominantly rural, small-producer supporters of Douglas Credit in the interwar and postwar period; and to the younger, tertiary-educated, pseudo-intellectual members of Action Zealandia. Being male and of European descent – a Pākehā New Zealander – appears to be a common factor, but certainly not an exclusive one. Those drawn to the radical right are motivated by a belief that their values, traditions and identities are under existential threat from nefarious groups of 'others'. Major shifts in society's predominant socio-cultural values, combined with rapid economic change and crisis, add fuel to these motivations.

Almost all radical right groups in New Zealand's history have attempted to influence public opinion, with the exception of skinhead gangs in the 1980s and 1990s who were generally more interested in mind-altering substances than ideology. Radical-right groups have spread their views through a variety of strategies and propaganda techniques, including large public rallies, canvassing political figures, conducting campaigns on key issues, distributing international literature, and issuing steady streams of pamphlets, newsletters, letters to the editor and social media. It is difficult to gauge how successful this material has been in influencing hearts and minds. It has clearly failed to shift social and political opinion on a macro scale, although it could be argued that the constant 'saturation' of the public with radical-right views, particularly those closer to mainstream opinion, has helped to keep issues live and build support for particular causes, such as anti-communism and the maintenance of white-minority governments in southern Africa, and opposition to Māori rights under the Treaty. Writing letters to the editor – a strategy begun by the Welfare League and Douglas Credit in the interwar years and perfected by the League of Rights – is a good example of this, and has given the impression that certain views are more widely held than they actually are.[92]

The onset of the internet age and the birth of digitally proficient alt-right and identitarian groups is, in many ways, a continuation of the tradition of propaganda saturation rather than 'a considerable deviation from past far right groups'.[93] However, the reach of these groups has varied considerably. Advance New Zealand and the New Conservatives' shrewd use of social media attracted supporters in at least the tens of thousands (judging by the percentage of their vote in the 2020 General Election), and anti-vaccination and anti-mandate material has spread even more rapidly since August 2021. In contrast, the readership of Action Zealandia's pseudo-intellectual blog posts is likely limited to a few hundred people. Where groups sit on the radical-right spectrum is important to the spread and influence of their message.

Conceptions of 'whiteness' have also changed over time from an exclusive British or Anglo-Saxon racial lineage to a broader, transnational whiteness. Lionel Terry's racially motivated murder of Joe Kum Yung in 1905 and the beliefs of the 15 March terrorist clearly demonstrate this shift. Terry's manifesto was a mixture of Sinophobia, antisemitism and anti-capitalism, and his understanding of whiteness was intertwined with a distinct 'Britishness'. This is quite different from the Islamophobic, global whiteness of an idealised 'Christendom' espoused by the terrorist, whose specific glorification of Serbian nationalists would have sat uneasily with Terry's championing of the Briton over other Europeans and perceived lesser races.[94] As Gilbert cites Kyle Chapman in Chapter Ten: 'If it looks white, acts white, and fights white, then it is white.' It is possibly no coincidence that the broadening of what the New Zealand radical right conceptualises as 'white' coincided with the postwar decline of the British Empire and the rise of a distinctly national identity as the country's economic and patriotic connections with the United Kingdom waned. The ease and speed with which the radical right can forge transnational connections in the digital age has also likely contributed to the rise of a global white identity, as has the general rejection of overt racism in the postwar period. However, the ways in which whiteness, white privilege and Pākehā identity in New Zealand have changed over time remain a relatively understudied field, limiting the conclusions we can draw.[95]

WHERE TO NEXT?

New Zealand's radical-right tradition is, in many ways, a history of abject failure. Since World War II, radical right groups have failed to attract large followings, achieve substantial electoral success or fundamentally shift the centre of politics. Despite this, a lone wolf like the 15 March terrorist was able to carry out a devastating attack that took the lives of 51 innocent people and maimed many others. This shows that we should never be complacent about the risks that the radical right, and extremists more generally, can pose. We have traversed just some of the histories of New Zealand's radical right in this book. Considerable ground remains to be explored, and the arguments we propose need to be unpacked – indeed, challenged – by further research. The story of New Zealand's radical right is also far from over. Shortly after we started writing this book, the world was gripped by a once-in-a-century pandemic that, among other things, caused a dramatic spike in conspiratorial thinking that has revived the fortunes of some of the radical right's most extreme political beliefs. While we have endeavoured to cover some of these developments, the events are still unfolding. This makes it difficult to draw firm conclusions as to the long-term implications. The radical-right tradition will continue to evolve, and scholars of all disciplines must continue to treat it as a topic worthy of serious consideration. We hope this book will serve as a foundation for further discussion in a way that is consistent with the values of an open, democratic and multicultural society.

PART 1
Origins of the New Zealand radical right in the late nineteenth and early twentieth centuries

CHAPTER ONE

He kākano ahau

Colonisation, scientific racism and the construction of racial 'fitness' in Aotearoa

LEONIE PIHAMA AND CHERRYL SMITH

E kore au e ngaro, he kākano ahau i ruia mai i Rangiātea
I will never be lost, I am a seed that was sown in Rangiātea

THIS CHAPTER DRAWS ITS TITLE FROM, and opens with, a whakatauākī (proverbial saying) that speaks to the origins of Māori in the spiritual and ancestral homeland of Rangiātea. It reminds us that understanding whakapapa (ancestral lineage) is central to the way we see ourselves as tangata whenua (people of the land/indigenous people). Whakapapa is at the core of all Māori relationships: with each other, with our tūpuna (ancestors), with our whenua (lands), with our taiao (environment). The importance of recognising our cultural relationships lies in the understanding that any other way of being defined by others is a colonial importation to Aotearoa (known in colonial terms as New Zealand). This includes racial hierarchies and eugenics.

Notions of 'race' or racial hierarchies did not exist for Māori prior to colonisation. Māori society was grounded upon whānau (extended family groups), hapū (subtribes/clan) and iwi (tribal groupings). Societal structures were built around whakapapa and expressed in the ways these collective groups interacted and inter-related. It was at first contact with Pākehā that our tūpuna saw a group of people who looked physically different. This was described by Mohi Turei, of Ngāti Porou, who acted as a scribe for Pita Kāpiti on the sighting of those who arrived with Abel Tasman:

> They were turehu [fairy people], punehunehu [misty looking], ma [fair], ma korako [pale, like albinos], whero takou [red, like ochre] – that was the way their faces looked … The local people knew that these were turehu [fairy people], patupaiarehe [fairies], aparangi [evil gods], atua kahukahu [still-born spirits], kowhiowhio [whistling spirits].[1]

Interestingly, the words used to describe those on board are not associated with humans but rather with wairua, or spiritual beings or forms of spirits themselves. What this tells us is that our tūpuna did not consider there to be distinctive 'races' among people. Such thinking came to Aotearoa with the arrival of colonising forces. Moreover, the ideologies, discourses and practices associated with 'race', including eugenics, that arrived at that time were to be used as both a rationale for, and justification of, violent acts of colonial invasion.

This chapter discusses the impact of eugenics in the context of colonisation and racial hierarchies. Beginning with a discussion of capitalism, 'race' and colonial imperialism, we highlight how the construction of 'race' has had significant impacts on Māori. We then move to a brief discussion of early developments in eugenics theory, and the ways these have been embedded within a range of systems and structures as a justification for colonisation and the dispossession of Māori. We look at the ways eugenics has defined notions of who is 'fit' or 'unfit', and how this has served to maintain and reproduce racism and white supremacy in this country. Such views were far from radical in Aotearoa in the late-nineteenth and first half of the twentieth centuries. They attracted bipartisan societal and political support. Where some may suggest caution in drawing a direct connection between nineteenth-century social Darwinism/early-twentieth-century eugenics and twenty-first-century health services, Māori have long argued that the early underpinnings of 'race', racial hierarchies and the structures of white dominance continue to influence and determine discriminatory and racist practices. One key difference is that, while overt expressions of racism were increasingly relegated to the fringes after World War II, structural and institutional racism have persisted through embedded processes, behaviours and expectations. This has contributed to disproportionately poorer outcomes for Māori across a wide variety of social and economic measures.

The definition of who is 'worthy' of access to resources, including within the provision of healthcare, is an example of this. In 2019, the Waitangi Tribunal highlighted the impact of institutional racism on Māori health, including the widening disparities faced by Māori in respect of access and treatment and the increasing inequitable distribution of resources.[2] This has been further highlighted by the National Māori Pandemic Group, Te Rōpū Whakakaupapa, with regard to the marginalisation of

Māori in the approach taken to the Covid-19 pandemic, and in the vaccine roll-out. Indeed, the Waitangi Tribunal found in 2021 that the Crown's vaccination strategy and its shift to the Covid-19 Protection Framework (or 'traffic light system') breached the Treaty in a number of ways.[3] It is, therefore, appropriate that our final discussion turns to the way eugenics can be seen to have a continued influence on the provision of health services and in responses to the recent pandemic.

CAPITALISM, 'RACE' AND COLONIAL IMPERIALISM

The Western notion of 'race' is constructed within culturally defined ideas that have justified colonial imperialism to serve the interests of some groups over others. Religion has also provided (and continues to provide) justification for the development of racial hierarchies. Gustav Jahoda argued that images of the 'Other' as 'strange', 'exotic' and 'feared' have been a constant feature in European history and have their ideological foundations in early Greco-Roman traditions. The conceptualisation of the 'Other' as foreign and fearsome, and as 'monstrous races', dominated such discourses. This characterisation, Jahoda argued, was located in ideas about the 'ferocious barbarian', who was referred to as physically misshapen and, more often than not, as a 'flesh eater'. Jahoda noted that the biblical stories of Ham and his descendants were seized upon to provide justification for the enslavement of black peoples.[4]

Racially based hierarchies, as they exist in present-day Aotearoa, are a consequence of colonisation. Cherryl Smith has argued that the realisation of the Empire required indigenous peoples to be rendered 'inferior'.[5] The concept of 'discovery' as asserted over indigenous peoples' lands can be viewed in relationship to ideas of ownership, exploitation and oppression.[6] Colonisation, Smith argues, was driven by capitalism, and resulted in the dispossession and subjugation of the indigenous population.[7] Leonie Pihama has highlighted that alongside the drive for capitalist gain, colonisation required an intersection of colonial belief systems of class, gender and 'race':

> Just as forms of Christianity were used to validate the position of white men in gendered order so too do have [*sic*] they been utilised to legitimise white peoples place in the hierarchy just next to a white male god. In discourses of race it is the 'barbaric' 'savage' 'inferior' 'Other' that is racialised, being white is not engaged, rather being white is viewed as the standard from which all other peoples are measured and defined. Adding class to the mix has provided the fundamental economic justification for the foundation and continuance of processes of capitalism that maintain processes of commodification of all things.[8]

The colonisation of Aotearoa was but one element in the universal expansion of the capitalist mode of production as British imperial forces sought to provide new sources of land, raw materials and labour power.[9] The hope was that British colonial settlement would be successful in establishing a new 'little England' through the expansion of British capitalism and by 'physically transplanting a vertical slice of British Society – economics, politics and ideology'.[10] Integral to such transplantation was the social ordering that utilised notions of 'race' centred on beliefs about the 'advanced' nature of Europeans and the 'inferiority' of everybody else.[11] Racial hierarchies and white supremacist belief systems have been powerful discourses over many generations in Aotearoa just as, through a wide range of mechanisms, they have validated the confiscation of lands and the dispossession of resources, the denial of indigenous languages, cultures and knowledge, and the denigration of generations of indigenous peoples around the world.[12]

Alongside the capitalist, racial and class underpinnings of the dispossession of indigenous peoples, the impact of discourses such as eugenics has also been influential. These theories are grounded in Western definitions of 'race' and racial classification over many centuries. Bronwen Douglas provided an extensive discussion of European debates surrounding the term 'race', its changing definitions over time and the disguising of beliefs of white superiority in supposedly 'scientific' explanations of diversity and differentiation. In doing so, she condensed what is described as: 'a major discursive shift associated with the altered meaning of race: the metamorphosis of prevailing Enlightenment ideas about externally induced variation within an essentially similar humanity into a science of race that reified human difference as permanent, hereditary, and innately somatic [relating to the body].'[13]

The means by which the racialisation of peoples serves the interests of dominant groups is not only concealed but also validated through colonial research that provided a rationale for racial dominance.[14] As Ranginui Walker wrote: 'Like its Greek and Roman predecessors, the British Empire portrayed itself as civilised and painted the people it encountered in the New World as savage, uncivilised and inferior. The British racial hierarchy placed Europeans at the top and 'natives' at the bottom … British colonisers saw Maori tribalism and communal ownership of land as a mark of primitive and barbaric people.'[15]

'Race' as a classification gained increasing authority throughout the eighteenth century through works that are described as 'typological thinking'; that is, the defining of people into certain 'types'.[16] This laid the foundations for the next step into classificatory systems of 'race'. Drawing on 'scientific' explanations, 'race' became quickly legitimised as a way to classify peoples and place groups in relationship to each other through the existence of a 'natural' hierarchy. The development of this definition of 'race' was encouraged by Europeans' increased encounters with other peoples and the need to justify exploitative colonial practices.

Alongside the 'scientific' justifications were a range of colonising classifications in religious documents in which indigenous nations were located as non-Christian and less than human. The impact of this was highlighted by Steve Newcomb:

> Under various theological and legal doctrines formulated during and after the Crusades, non-Christians were considered enemies of the Catholic faith and, as such, less than human. Accordingly, in the bull of 1452, Pope Nicholas directed King Alfonso to 'capture, vanquish, and subdue the Saracens, Pagans, and other enemies of Christ,' to 'put them into perpetual slavery,' and 'to take all their possessions and property' ... Acting on this papal privilege, Portugal continued to traffic in African slaves, and expanded its royal dominions by making 'discoveries' along the western coast of Africa, claiming those lands as Portuguese territory.[17]

Onondaga Nation Faithkeeper Oren Lyons highlighted how the Doctrine of Discovery of 1493 defined indigenous people as 'non-people', through which 'Christopher Columbus kicked off a frenzy of transatlantic voyages, [and] native lands "discovered" by European explorers were considered "unoccupied" because the people in those uncharted lands were not Christian.'[18]

The Papal Bulls and the Doctrine of Discovery are significant to Māori as they underpinned and legalised Christian beliefs of white superiority and served as justifications globally for colonisation and the denial of the rights and even the existence of indigenous peoples. As Māori scholar and activist Margaret Mutu noted, the Doctrine of Discovery gave colonisers 'permission to dispossess, enslave and exterminate other races, cultures and religions.'[19]

Charles Darwin was an early contributor to the development of theories of racial hierarchy that were later expanded within the eugenics movement. His studies of the natural world were used to support the proposition that natural selection provided an explanation for the social order of human beings.[20] The process of natural selection, while including a process of genetic adaptation, focused particularly on the concept that the stronger or best adapted of the species would survive.[21] Darwin argued that there is a natural hierarchical order to all species, and from this evolved the concept of natural selection and survival of the fittest.[22] The ideas of social Darwinism were elaborated further by Herbert Spencer who argued that societies, too, were evolving and that it was natural the fittest would survive.[23] Humans were categorised in relation to each other on the basis of their perceived level of civilisation and a hierarchical system of racial classification. Darwin proclaimed that 'each race moves along the ladder of civilization, propelled by natural selection, aided by use – inheritance, with selfish instinct giving way to reason, morality and English customs'.[24] Within such a hierarchy, 'Savages' and 'Negroes' were positioned at the lower or inferior end of the spectrum and Europeans (typically northern Europeans and Anglo-Saxons) in a superior position. It is from this premise that ideologies of white supremacism are derived.

THE RACISM OF EUGENICS

The origins of eugenics go back to the idea of 'breeding good stock' and were found in Roman, Greek, Spartan and other societies. The development of eugenics as a science, however, can be tracked back to Charles Darwin and his cousin Francis Galton, who coined the term eugenics in 1883 from the Greek meaning 'well born'. Galton believed that promoting marriage among those with 'superior' traits would improve the human species over time, referring to this as 'positive' eugenics. According to Garland Allen, Galton saw such people as: '"[T]ruly or well-born," and referred to a plan to encourage the "best people" in society to have more children (positive eugenics) and to discourage or prevent the "worst elements" of society from having many, if any, children (negative eugenics).'[25]

Galton drew extensively upon Darwin's work to emphasise the role of genetics in social organisation, particularly in regard to intelligence. He also sought to validate and expand upon the concept of racial hierarchy by promulgating a theory of the genetically predetermined structuring of intelligence.[26] Intelligence testing became another vehicle by which racial inferiority, or superiority, could be `scientifically' substantiated by legitimising the notion that intelligence was biologically preordained. Eugenics became a key 'scientific' mechanism to support notions of genetic superiority.[27] As J. Daniels and V. Houghton stated: 'The Galton paradigm of a ladder view of society predetermined the climbers moving with different weights given to them at the start of their journey preordaining the final result of the competition.'[28] Within this model, everyone is born with a predisposed genetic makeup that will ultimately determine their 'advancement' up the ladder of society; however, some genetic makeups are superior to others. Those born with the 'right' genetic makeup (i.e. Anglo-Saxons) are inherently physically and intellectually 'superior'. On the other hand, those who have inherited a lesser or 'inferior' genetic makeup carry a heavier burden and, like their forebears, will remain on the lower rungs of civilisation's ladder. Within such a paradigm, we each carry particular genetic baggage that preordains, and ultimately enshrines, our positioning.

Biological and racial superiority was further argued by Darwin in the colonial expansion experience. His visit to Aotearoa in 1835 led to his proclaiming Māori as a 'fearsome people … a more warlike race of inhabitants could be found in no part of the world … [whose] shifty looks betrayed a fierce cunning, and tattooed face revealed a base nature'.[29]

This perception was couched within the doctrine of the 'ignoble savage', which contrasted with the earlier 'romantic' view of French explorer Marion du Fresne who characterised Māori as the 'noble savage'.[30] In working to validate natural selection, Darwin increasingly promoted the British experience as the yardstick by which other 'races' could – and should – be measured.[31] In espousing the inferiority of Māori and what he considered to be their 'warlikeness', Darwin believed that warfare in the colonies was necessary in that it provided a means by which the coloniser could become familiar with the terrain and adapt; it was considered an essential part of natural selection.[32] Within this view, the victor in the 'competition' between the 'races' could be deemed the stronger and, therefore, the superior of the two.

A wide range of modes of 'scientific' legitimation emerged to justify 'race' hierarchies. For example, the practice of phrenology incorporated the study of the size and shape of the skulls of different races as a means to relate 'superiority' to brain size. In the mid-nineteenth century, Arthur Thomson, an early medical observer of Māori, noted:

> It was ascertained, by weighing the quantity of millet seed skulls contained and by measurements with tapes and compasses, that New Zealanders' [Māori] heads are smaller than the heads of Englishmen, consequently the New Zealanders are inferior to the English in mental capacity. This comparative smallness of the brain is produced by neglecting to exercise the higher faculties of the mind, for as muscles shrunk from want of use, it is only natural that generations of mental indolence should lessen the size of the brains.[33]

The so-called 'sciences' of intelligence testing and phrenology are examples of the ways that notions of genetics, biology and 'race' have been used to embed and legitimate notions of white superiority.[34] This has served to provide justification for the maintenance of Pākehā dominance in Aotearoa and the subsequent subordination of Māori, the tangata whenua. Biological determinism, and dominant group constructions of racial hierarchies through paradigms such as social Darwinism, became the means by which the coloniser was equipped with 'scientific evidence' of the 'inferiority' of Māori people. Eugenics became another way not only to assert dominance but also to ensure its maintenance and reproduction.

EUGENICS IN AOTEAROA

Truby King was a key campaigner for eugenics in Aotearoa. King, the founder of the infant health-focused Plunket Society, actively emphasised a 'cult of domesticity' and 'racial fitness' to halt society's 'degeneration'.[35] Māori were not the focus of the Plunket movement at its inception: its key emphasis on maintaining the fitness and purity of the 'race' was directed at Pākehā. As Hilary Stace noted:

> Truby King, Seacliff Superintendent [Seacliff was a psychiatric hospital in Otago], who had a physical impairment, later became Inspector General of Health … He, his wife and supporters were positive eugenists who believed that teaching mothers the strict rules of scientific mothering would increase the fitness of the race. Committees of wealthy middle class women then took the ideology to the breeding populace. King was our local manifestation of the scientific mothering trend, and part of the international tradition of male experts telling women how to parent and then blaming them if anything went wrong.[36]

Promoting the domestication of Pākehā women would, King believed, give 'an enormous benefit to the women, and prospectively to the "race".'[37] Failure to do so would have a significant impact on maintaining the superiority of 'the race', as Erik Olssen pointed out: 'The conjunction of the cult of true womanhood and Spencer's social Darwinism imbued lapses from the ideal conception of womanly behaviour not only with moral significance but with calamitous consequences for the race.'[38]

Eugenics was a widespread ideology that could be found in a range of other organisations and social initiatives. These included health camps, compulsory military training and movements such as Scouts, and had support across a wide spectrum of political positionings.[39] Philip Fleming has argued that eugenics in Aotearoa was more about social Darwinism than a calculated attempt to impose racial purity in the population as a whole. While there was never any legislation designed to limit the birth rate among certain segments of the population, and so enhance the 'fitness' of future generations (although clauses to this effect were almost included in the Mental Defectives Amendment Act 1928), there was widespread concern that degeneracy would see the 'fit' population being overrun if some sanctions were not imposed. Eugenics argued that such 'degeneracy' might cause damage to heredity, resulting in insanity, perversion, and mentally and physically disabled children.[40] Environmental influences that could supposedly give rise to 'weaker stock' included cultural factors, masturbation, prostitution, poverty, crime, personal failings, physical features and climate. Letters published in early newspapers highlight the views of those who considered degeneracy as a 'curse':

> Men and women who know nothing of consequences, nothing of responsibility, nothing of the law of 'As you sow you reap' bring into the world children they do not want. The children become burdens instead of blessings. These babes are a curse, not only to their parents, but to themselves. These unwelcome children born of degenerate parents, fill the prisons, asylums and hospitals. They live by fraud and violence, and worst of all, they marry and bequeath their vices to their children. There is one hope, and that is, ignorance must stop populating the world with failures.[41]

The positioning of Māori, like other colonised indigenous peoples, as inferior and, therefore, 'unfit' can be seen in a range of labels and characterisations, including as primitive, as a lower social order, as lazy, as intellectually deficient and uncivilised. For example, nineteenth-century ethnographer Elsdon Best noted that for work requiring strength or endurance, 'the Maori is not equal to the European settler. The discipline that produces these qualities is the product of more advanced civilizations, and is not a feature of the lower planes of civilization.'[42] In reference to Māori belief systems, missionary and politician William Colenso stated: 'Their moral side was a dark picture; it was relieved by only the faintest gleams of light; selfishness, in some form or other, was the base-line of it. Their conversation was sensual, their ideas filthy, and their language obscene. Chastity was rare, if known at all. They were given to sorcery, witchcraft, murder.'[43]

Another nineteenth-century observer, Edward Markham, stated that the decline in the Māori population after widespread European settlement was, like the decline of other indigenous peoples, an act of God:

> It seems to me that the same causes that depopulated the Indian Tribes are doing the same all over the World. In New Zealand the same as in Canada or North America, and in Southern Africa the Hottentots are a decreasing people

> and by all accounts the Islands of the South Seas are the same. Rum, Blankets, Muskets, Tobacco and Diseases have been the great destroyers; but my belief is the Almighty intended it should be so or it would not have been allowed, Out of Evil comes Good.[44]

There are those who have argued that there is little evidence to show that eugenics was a populist belief espoused widely beyond a group of academics, politicians and biologists.[45] Others, notably Stace, have countered that eugenics went beyond a scientific idea and was entrenched in everyday thinking and rationalisations that became pervasive across many parts of society.[46]

While Māori were not included overtly in discussions about eugenics, there were deep concerns about the need to ensure the fitness of 'the national stock'.[47] This was typically defined as British in origin, and many Pākehā viewed themselves as British or European and, as such, separate from Māori. Māori leaders of the late nineteenth and early twentieth centuries had complex relationships with eugenics. Historian Barbara Brookes noted that both Māui Pōmare and his colleague Āpirana Ngata viewed eugenics through ideas of being 'well-born', noting that this was a notion they were familiar with given their knowledge of whakapapa and the ways relationships are viewed within, and between, whānau, hapū and iwi. Brookes highlighted how this differed from Māori cultural norms in the early nineteenth century:

> From the beginning of European settlement, Māori iwi (tribes) had worked to incorporate the newcomers into their own society and intermarriage was a key means of doing so. By the 1920s, however, men who were themselves products of Māori/Pākehā marriages became increasingly concerned about the implications for 'the race' represented by Māori/Chinese liaisons. What had once been an open attitude of engagement with newcomers constricted as the racial identity of Māori became of national concern. The particular national identity of New Zealand relied on an idea of two peoples, distinct yet harmonious. Māori/Chinese relationships threatened that ideal.[48]

It is important to note that Māori had suffered significantly in terms of population decline due to disease, war and loss of land. Individuals such as Pōmare, Ngata and Te Rangi Hīroa were actively engaged in seeking ways of stemming the decline. Preserving the 'racial fitness' of Māori was seen by these men as one way to do this, alongside improving sanitation and health in Māori communities, support for Māori land development and preserving traditions through support for ethnology and anthropology. It is also reflective of the wider ways in which Pōmare engaged with issues such as the Tohunga Suppression Act 1907, which was designed to discourage the methods of traditional Māori healers. Mason Durie noted that Pōmare 'regarded tohunga as unhelpful and accused them of causing more harm than good, especially in the management of infectious diseases such as tuberculosis'.[49]

EUGENICS AND THE CONSTRUCTION OF THE 'UNFIT' IN AOTEAROA

Psychology professor Tony Taylor noted that post-World War I, an increased interest in the field of eugenics internationally had a direct influence on developments in Aotearoa: 'This was the international climate in which eugenics became an issue in New Zealand. Due to the country's close colonial ties with Britain, many of New Zealand's administrators, health professionals and politicians came from the Mother-country, and the intelligentsia was aware of the eugenics debate that was underway there and elsewhere.'[50]

A focus on heredity and 'bad' breeding as a contributor to 'social ills', underpinned by the widespread concern that 'degeneracy' would see the 'fit' population being overrun unless sanctions were imposed, led to calls for sterilisation, segregation and the restriction of particular classes of immigrants. As a result, the government decided in 1924 to establish a Commission of Inquiry into Mental Defectives and Sexual Offenders. Members of the committee of inquiry were appointed by Māui Pōmare, now minister of health, and included W.H. Triggs (chair), Truby King, Donald McGavin, Ada Paterson, Charles E. Matthews and J. Beck. Of the 92 submissions received by the committee, the majority were from high-profile doctors, medical officers, health inspectors, inspectors of schools, church representatives, women's organisations, and prison and mental home superintendents. Chief Justice and former Premier Robert Stout, a eugenicist, was adamant that 'those who are mentally defective should be kept at some state institution and not be allowed to breed'. While he noted that the US had legislation in place allowing for the sterilisation of sexual perverts, he lamented that 'our people are not yet thoroughly alive to the importance of eugenics'.[51] As a judge, he linked criminality with feeble-mindedness, and characterised a quarter of those appearing before him in those terms. He went on: 'I think they should also be set apart in a home where they will not be allowed freedom from control, but will be looked after and given such happiness as possible, but be subject to confinement.'

Banning marriages of the unfit and certifying people before marriage were suggestions put to the committee. Many submitters advocated sterilisation. Some pointed to social Darwinism as a reason for promoting eugenics and sterilisation: '[W]e have to recognise the inequality of mankind, second, that heredity plays a most important part in the life of our offenders and third that the State has a right to prevent them from breeding.'[52]

A submission made on behalf of the Department of Education expressed great alarm at the overwhelming numbers of 'feeble-minded' children and adults, and suggested they should be prevented from breeding by segregation. The department argued that by not acting, there would be 'serious racial deterioration'. Many of the submitters pointed to an increase in the number of 'defectives', arguing that it had an impact on the 'virility of the race'.[53] Homosexuality was equated with degeneracy and mental defectiveness, and a number of those incarcerated in the country's prisons and psychiatric institutions were counted as 'sexual perverts'. One of the prison doctors testified: '[W]e have three types of sexual offences: homi-sexualism, rape and exhibitionism'; it was suggested that treatment should consist of outdoor activity and hard labour.

The first finding in the inquiry's recommendation summary highlighted the priority of protecting and safeguarding Pākehā racial fitness, stating: 'That the unchecked multiplication of the feeble minded and epileptic is leading to a continually growing addition to the sum of human misery, an ever increasing burden on the state, and the serious deterioration of the race.'[54]

Well-respected organisations such as Plunket and Family Planning, still in operation today, were established in the wake of these wider concerns about racial fitness and purity. Helen Smyth defined eugenics as 'the control of reproduction to produce better offspring', and made the point that 'many of those who lent their support to the birth control movement did so because of their belief in controlled breeding. It was a eugenics society that first offered support to New Zealand's fledgling family planning group.'[55]

While concerns about racial fitness became less of an explicit driving factor after World War II, institutional racism continued to influence the provision of social services. Fertility control is an example of this. In Aotearoa in the 1960s, with rapid Māori population growth and urbanisation, attention began to be focused on contraception for Māori. Māori were having big families and this was considered a 'problem'.[56] The introduction of a new injectable contraceptive saw a disproportionately high number of Māori women being given Depo Provera. This was a direct result of the negative stereotypes related to Māori whānau. As Phillida Bunkle and Judith Ackroyd wrote in 1982:

> Sometimes it seems that Depo is the new eugenics, preventing the breeding of the socially unfit; handed out in prisons and mental hospitals and abortion clinics and given to Maori twice as often as Pakehas. Depo is not accepted as a contraceptive in Australia but is given to Aboriginal women; it is stringently limited in Britain but prescribed extensively for West Indians; it is approved for Black but not White women in South Africa.[57]

More recently, Leonie Pihama argued that deficit notions of 'Māori teen pregnancy' have been shaped through Western discourses of who is fit to have a child:

> In colonial America and Britain, early discourse related to the 'fitness' of a parent, were linked to the wider eugenics movement that determined individuals as 'inferior' or 'superior' based upon genetics. This movement aligned with the wider evolutionary thesis promoted by Charles Darwin, and a key author of eugenics was in fact Darwin's cousin, Francis Galton … Relationships between close relations, i.e. incestuous relationships, were deemed to produce 'degenerate children', and mixed-race marriages in many American states remained unlawful. Other factors that were deemed to define an 'unfit' individual included 'feeblemindedness', 'lunatics', 'idiots', and 'imbeciles', with these being later expanded to include 'the poor or unproductive' … This led to the imposition of forced sterilisation of those deemed unfit. Luker argues that the discourse of 'fitness' was a part of a wider agenda of social control and attempts to control poverty. The economic underpinnings are clearly highlighted in that most sterilisations performed were on the 'poor', and such an approach continued into the 1960s with the focus then turning upon African American women. A clear underpinning assumption is that poor (as well as non-white) people are 'inferior' in intelligence, character, and ability to raise children.[58]

The positioning of Māori as 'deficient' in regard to family size and teen pregnancy continues to influence both public and policy debates and thinking, with particular impacts on a range of health and educational developments for Māori.[59] Risk factors for teenage pregnancy identified by L.J. Woodward et al. reproduced the notion that just being Māori was an inherent 'risk'.[60] These assumptions also inform acts of state violence against whānau whose children are removed and placed into state institutions.[61] The point is that the fundamental assumptions about who is 'fit' or 'unfit' that underpin discourses concerning eugenics impact upon Māori in significant ways across society and over time. Another example of the way eugenics has influenced wider healthcare provision is seen in recent discussions regarding Covid-19.

EUGENICS, HEALTH SERVICES AND COVID-19

As the Covid-19 pandemic raged across the world, it became increasingly clear that systemic racism and failure to provide adequate healthcare services to particular sectors of society meant that death rates were more severe in those populations. The failure is not new. In Aotearoa, it is the outcome of many years of repeat failures to ensure the wellbeing of Māori and, in particular, the Crown's failure to guarantee tino rangatiratanga (Māori sovereignty/self-determination) in the design and implementation of the health system. The extreme population decrease experienced by Māori since contact with Pākehā has been described by Ian Pool as the result of 'disease invasions'.[62] indigenous nations worldwide have experienced 'disease invasions', and they continue to do so today, just as racism and eugenics continue to inform access to healthcare. Rāwiri Tinirau et. al stated: '[R]ace theories became the underlying current that perpetuated racism within Aotearoa by being enacted through legislation and policy. This has led to Māori being predisposed to substandard socio-economic conditions such as poorer housing, employment, access to quality healthcare and being discriminated against interpersonally.'[63]

These ideologies continue to underpin health systems in Aotearoa.[64] Research related to Māori health outcomes highlights that Māori health disparities are attributable to colonisation, racism and cultural invasion.[65] The experiences of many Māori in the health system are shaped by encounters with systemic and structural racism.[66] We should, therefore, not be surprised that Māori experiences of pandemics have not mirrored those of Pākehā. This is highlighted in the analysis of both the smallpox epidemic of 1913 and the influenza pandemic in 1918, during which Māori were severely impacted.[67] Leonie Pihama and Marjorie Lipsham noted: 'Pool (2015) attributes this to factors including access to adequate healthcare; Māori having less immunity to the disease than Pākehā (white New Zealanders); morbidity rates; and the social impact of colonisation. These factors were further exacerbated by systemic racism and the predominance of deficit ideologies that created a context in which Māori did not receive the medical treatment needed.'[68]

In the US, the failure of the health system during the Covid-19 pandemic can be seen as an example of the embedded nature of eugenics among those advocating so-called 'herd immunity'. While Aotearoa did not take the 'herd immunity' route for Covid-19, it is important that we understand how eugenics continues to underpin such approaches. Mark Mosley made the following observations in relation to the notion of 'herd immunity':

> Natural herd immunity is the idea that you just let the virus run its course, and it just keeps infecting whomever until you achieve herd immunity without a vaccine or a partially used vaccine. It is partly a political calculation if you cannot produce a vaccine in time, it is poorly effective, or people on the whole are too hesitant to take it. If this is an intentional plan suggested by your government and its administration, then it allows for a disproportionate number of deaths of the elderly, obese, non-white, poor, homeless, prisoners, institutionalized mentally ill, and those with comorbidities. It is the death of the 'unfit' in exchange for the immunity of the herd made up of predominantly young, wealthy, white, and healthy people.[69]

Early reaction from Māori to the New Zealand government's Covid-19 response argued that the current health system had failed to consider the impact on Māori. It was also clearly noted that the Ministry of Health continued to promote a 'one size fits all' approach that did not 'fit' Māori.[70] If there was a significant Covid-19 breakout in Aotearoa, it would be Māori (and Pasifika) communities who would be most impacted.[71] This appears to have been borne out by the disproportionate number of Māori and Pasifika cases in the outbreaks of the Delta and Omicron variants since August 2021, and in the disproportionate number of hospitalisations and deaths. In December 2021, the Waitangi Tribunal found that the Crown's vaccination strategy and its shift to the Covid-19 Protection Framework breached the principles of the Treaty. The Tribunal argued that the Crown failed to adequately consult with Māori health leaders or address their concerns about the rapid shift to the Protection Framework. It also rejected the advice of some of its own officials regarding the timing of the shift and the need to adjust the age limits for Māori in the vaccine roll-out.[72] The impact of eugenics on Māori health can be seen within the deeply embedded structural racism and the continued failure to deal with the fundamental issues that underpin disparities in the health system.[73]

CLOSING REFLECTIONS

The focus of this chapter has been to track some of the history of eugenics in Aotearoa and its impact upon Māori up to the present. Few people are aware that there was widespread support for eugenics in Aotearoa in the 1920s among key policy makers, academics, and health and education workers. The chapter also highlights how key notions, such as distinctions between the 'fit' and the 'unfit', were built upon early 'race' hierarchies in order to establish and maintain dominant colonial power relationships in this country. Such ideologies have served not only to marginalise Māori in racialised hierarchies but also to underpin the ongoing failure of successive governments to acknowledge Māori as tangata whenua or to adequately provide for their health and welfare.

Māori are rarely written directly into the history of eugenics. In much of the literature, there is an absence of any mention of Māori or indigenous peoples. However, eugenics has been a tool or a manifestation of colonisation in British settler states, including Aotearoa. If we consider colonisation to be the myriad overt and subtle processes by which colonisers actively impose themselves, their institutions and their values on indigenous peoples, then eugenics becomes one of those processes and works alongside others that are embedded in core societal systems such as law, capitalism, religion, warfare, education or health.

Indigenous peoples have been cast as being unfit to maintain sovereignty of their own countries, as speaking unfit languages, as being unfit socially and culturally, and positioned in racial hierarchies that have embedded white supremacy and colonial rule. These are overt consequences of eugenics, but more covert forms underpin and reproduce attacks on Māori (and other indigenous peoples) for having big families, for being considered a burden on the taxpayer, for having children too young and for being neglectful or abusive parents.

Aotearoa has enacted 'positive eugenics', asserting that the purity and fitness of the 'white race' be maintained in order to ensure its dominance and superiority. It has also been enacted through the colonial invasion of these lands based upon capitalist imperatives to dispossess Māori and transplant British imperial rule. For over 200 years this has served to reproduce systems of oppression and justify ongoing acts of racism. Eugenics continues to underpin health service provision and decision-making, as seen in the continued reproduction of health disparities for Māori.

If we are to deal with the impact of eugenics in this country, we must first deal with the fundamental issues of colonisation and the ongoing perpetuation of colonial ideologies and practices that deny Māori our rights as the indigenous peoples of this land. Until this is done, we will not truly dismantle the many forms of racist, xenophobic and colonising practices and structures that dominate this society.

CHAPTER TWO

Anti-Chinese politics in New Zealand, 1880 to 1920

STEVAN ELDRED-GRIGG AND ZENG DAZHENG

HISTORIANS GENERALLY REGARD the years from 1880 to 1920 as marking the high point of an exclusionary policy towards the Chinese in New Zealand. The focus of this chapter is the evolution of that policy in the Pākehā context – a policy that, together with the wider politics of 'White New Zealand', cast a long shadow. However, this is only a part of the history of China and New Zealand, which includes, for example, the politics of race inside China and the relationship between Chinese migrants and tangata whenua. Policy and politics encompass only part of the range of human experience, individually and collectively, of family, friendship, faith, sex, conflict, class, longing, fear, greed, conceit, hope, love and loss. Such experiences are outside this chapter's scope but we have discussed them elsewhere.[1]

Episodes of racial discrimination and, occasionally, open violence against the Chinese during this period will not be recounted here either. These stories, too, have been told elsewhere. Instead, we explore the evolution of racism in relation to changing class politics. By this, we do not mean that racism is simply a manifestation of class. Instead, we see racism as a living thing evolving in its own right, like religion, philosophy or politics. It also evolves in symbiosis or competition with other living things. A wide variety of social and economic variables need to link up – or snap – before conflicts within a state can go one way or another.

THE RISE OF ANTI-CHINESE POLITICS AND THE POLL TAX DEBATE

The poll tax (discussed in the Introduction), for example, is often held up as the key proof of anti-Chinese discrimination. Even a cursory glance at the parliamentary debates on the Chinese Immigration Act in 1881 reveal more than simple-minded prejudice at work. The conservative government that introduced the legislation was in an odd position. It had dismissed an opposition member's comparable Bill a year earlier, and a subsequent international conference on immigration by the seven colonies – several of which were already implementing anti-Chinese immigration policies – provided a convenient opportunity for an about-turn.[2] The government, nevertheless, found more reasons to justify its action. Harry Atkinson was famously prone to liberal fads.[3] He spoke about 'the right … to protect our present form of civilisation' and 'protect our wage-earning-class from competition with foreigners who have a very much lower standard of living' as the principal reasons for the Bill.[4] He was, however, no knight of labour.[5]

Frederick Whitaker, a conservative lawyer and Attorney-General, opened the debate in the Legislative Council (New Zealand's Upper House) by saying that the Bill aimed not to keep out all Chinese but to safeguard order in the colony. He also argued that all the neighbouring colonies were imposing poll taxes and New Zealand needed to do the same. If it did not, the country would attract thousands of Chinese migrants who could no longer get into the other six colonies.[6] A group of moderate conservatives endorsed the government's point of view. James Menzies, landowner, said that 'the Chinese in this colony at the present time are upon the whole beneficial in the way of providing excellent servants, cheap labour, and all the rest of it, to a limited extent', but that they would become a threat to order if their numbers grew.[7] George Waterhouse, merchant and landowner, spoke out against 'bigotry, malevolence, and uncharitableness' towards the Chinese. He nevertheless feared local Chinese might one day spell trouble for little New Zealand as the Chinese Empire was bound to recover as a great power.[8]

Some imagined themselves in the shoes of the white working class: they were not keen for wages in the colony to drop too low. 'I like to see labour as cheap as possible,' said John Peacock, a Canterbury merchant, 'but I do not wish to have Chinese labour in order to grind down the European labourer.'[9] Henry Miller, sheep-farming son of a baronet, saw the Chinese as 'most industrious, persevering'. Nevertheless, he thought the labouring men's need for self-preservation must take precedence over 'general philosophy' and 'chivalry'. He also wondered if married 'Chinamen' should be welcomed as settlers, unlike unattached diggers and 'coolies'.

Others like William Hutchison, liberal journalist and Opposition MP for Wellington, went further. He claimed that he was speaking 'in the interest of the working men' and denounced opposition to the Bill as 'another attempt to continue that poverty and make it permanent in this country'. Hutchison had sponsored the member's Bill shelved a year earlier. Thomas Fraser, a wealthy landowner and friend of gold diggers, talked about the Chinese 'coming here, robbing our land of the gold and our people of bread'.[10] Samuel Andrews, plasterer and gold digger, had little to say other than offering support to the government and telling Parliament that he knew from his experiences on the diggings about the 'horrible diseases' that might be lurking among even the 'most desirable' Chinese.[11] Heinrich Lahmann, storekeeper and former digger, declared that while 'the labouring class' were in favour of restricting immigration, they did not wish to drive away those who were already in New Zealand.[12] Being on the side of the conservative government and its wealthy backers seems to have blunted much of the class politics of the likes of Hutchinson and others.

John Hall, the wealthy conservative premier, observed that many MPs who were 'in the habit of supporting the Government do not care for this bill'. Even those who gave their support begrudgingly protested at the same time. In the House of Representatives (Lower House) William Fox, for example, preached the 'universal large-hearted liberality towards all people of every nation' that he thought was characteristically British. And the voters of the colony, as migrants themselves – or even 'intruders', as another member put it bluntly – 'ought not, because a man is of a different colour from ourselves, to withhold the same right and privilege which we have been accustomed in the Old Country to yield to all who have a claim to the name of man'.[13] Fox's speech was not radical for its colour-blindness. He was merely referring to the current idea of a British Empire that ruled over its 'possessions' and its 'subjects' whatever their ethnic origin.

James Wallis, a conservative Auckland surgeon, agreed that such an open border policy was part and parcel of British imperialism. After all, it was 'the English [who] forced their treaty down the throats of the Chinese'.[14] Only a year earlier, he had spoken against such legislation and extolled industrious and law-abiding Chinese who were 'examples and models of Europeans'. And if the living standard of the labouring class were to be reduced by Chinese immigration, Wallis wondered if that might not be a good thing, given the vice of 'over-feeding'.[15] He could not resist, either, comparing the Bill's supporters to the Luddites of the early nineteenth century. He voted for the Bill in the end, but not before accusing its more committed supporters of 'ingratiating' themselves with 'the loafers of New Zealand'.[16]

Several speakers in the Legislative Council voiced their passionate opposition to the 'rabble-rousing' behind the Bill. De Renzie Brett, landowner, said Parliament was 'acting in a most cruel way'. He argued that the government had brought the 'trashy, abominable' Bill before Parliament for reasons of cynical electioneering: the government feared 'not being elected at the coming election' and hoped to buy votes from the working class.[17] Mathew Holmes, another landowner, spoke just as strongly. 'I never would think of shutting our ports against any people who propose to come here,' he said; 'there is nothing I abhor more than injustice or persecution of any individual or any nationality.'[18] The gentlemanly Henry Scotland stormed: 'I think the people who come after us will be thoroughly ashamed and thoroughly astonished at what their progenitors have done, for it is simply an inhuman and barbarous measure.'[19]

The historian Philip Ferguson, who has done some of the most sustained work on White New Zealand, argued that 'what is most notable about the debate in 1881 is that there were not any coherent political divisions along party or class lines'. This incoherence partly reflects a finer differentiation between groups within the propertied and employing class rather than a straightforward left–right dichotomy. Large landowners and their close friends and cousins were a lot more likely to think Chinese migration acceptable than those who were small or middling traders, or small or middling farmers, or those who claimed to speak for the working class. As Ferguson himself observed: '[W]hat can perhaps be discerned is the beginning of the class alliance between workers and a section of capital'. The section that would forge this alliance was small and middling capital, or what Ferguson called 'the industrial and commercial bourgeoisie'. That class alliance would evolve into the class struggle between the left and the right for much of the twentieth century.[20] For now, however, the class identities central to the struggle were still in the making through such moments as the debates over the Chinese question, and are essential to explain some of the apparent paradoxes.

One paradox is that some of the most virulent anti-Chinese rhetoric came from the left, outside and inside Parliament. It suggests a parallel to the modern-day 'white working-class racism' of Brexit and Trump that has puzzled some on the contemporary left.[21] Working people in 1880 were watching anxiously at the beginning of a prolonged economic crisis, known to historians as the Long Depression. Some working people perhaps had an inkling that their recent victories – manhood suffrage, high wages and mobility – had more to do with the simple laws of supply and demand than their own political clout as the working class. The scarcity of labour and the abundance of colonised land kept up egalitarian appearances, not egalitarian politics.

The truth is that these colonial working people and their political leaders spoke out repeatedly against allowing 'too many' immigrants, of whatever race and origin, into New Zealand. Workers in Wellington reacted angrily to proposals for more immigration in 1879, even if it came from the thousands starving at 'Home'. 'There are families in our own city on the point of starvation,' said one letter writer. 'I hardly think it necessary to increase that number by further immigration.'[22] A crowded meeting of the Working Men's Rights League came to blows over one dissenting jester against the anti-immigration demands. A militant voice denounced 'cold-blooded, diabolical, selfish' capitalists who wanted more cheap labour. More notable, perhaps, were the many who thought, as did the conservative mainstream, that the surplus supply of labour must be balanced by getting more capitalists to New Zealand.[23]

The 'law' of supply and demand was one link between the working people and their small and middling capitalist allies. The enemy of both groups was a 'squattocracy' that seemed to hold one down and crowd the other out – a squattocracy that wanted 'coolie' labour. At the same time, working people had reservations about the sincerity of those who claimed to speak for them. Even the tireless champion of the anti-Chinese cause, William Hutchison, was 'like many others – very profuse with promises before election' but afterwards cared not a bit for the working man on the larger immigration question.[24] In the same year, the press pilloried premier and former governor Sir George Grey for making a secret offer to the imperial government to take 6000 distressed agricultural labourers while promising to check immigration. Even the left rebuked Richard Seddon (then MP for Hokitika) who defended Grey – 'false and hollow', said the *Grey River Argus* – while attacking what they saw as a conspiracy of the right. [25]

The new idea of the nation-state was another link between the working people and their small and middling capitalist allies. The nation-state was to be defined as a remodelled 'British-ness' that broke with the ambiguities of a multi-ethnic British Empire. New Zealand voters who campaigned to keep the Chinese out sometimes saw themselves as defending Britishness. In truth, they were defending a very narrow notion of 'whiteness'. English and Scottish were white, certainly, and at a stretch Germans and Scandinavians, but not Irish or Jews.[26] And being poor could rank lower on the pecking order than being the wrong colour: John Lundon, an Irish migrant made good, declared that 'pauper immigrants' had no place in New Zealand; 'they are worse than the Chinese, because the Chinese go away again'.[27] The working class itself had only recently become 'white'. Middle-class observers as late as the 1880s still spoke of the British urban poor as the dark 'other'.[28]

Working-class people who saw themselves as white sometimes talked about the 'immorality' of the Chinese, foreshadowing a limited and limiting politics of respectability. They seldom talked about religion and culture in a sustained manner as the common bond between the white middle classes. Yet working people often spoke confidently about liberty, democracy and, again, wages – concepts ill-fitted to the idea of race as part of an immutable social order but central to their own revolutionary ideal of a 'better' Britain. 'The Chinaman's wage' was as 'un-British' as his 'yellow' skin. In such ways, working people coded political demands for wages into a racial bottom-line that white employers could not cross.[29] Indeed, it was perhaps the *only* division between the white worker and the Chinese. One group of workers in 1879 said they felt no fear of Chinese coming into the colony; the Chinese worker, they added, was 'an ordinary member of the human family' and Chinese newcomers 'would form worthy co-workers with Britain's sons'. All they asked was that workers, no matter what their race, stick together to safeguard and strengthen hours and pay.[30]

Middle-class people, by contrast, used grand words like civilisation and progress to code racial superiority into the very idea of white Britishness, as evidenced by, among other things, the new-fangled theory of evolutionary biology. While the phrase social Darwinism had only just been coined, the notion of 'the survival of the fittest' was already in common circulation. 'The Caucasian is higher in the scale of created beings than the Mongolian', the *South Canterbury Times* declared in 1881. 'If it is a question of the survival of the fittest, the latter must succumb.'[31] Pseudo-science would mutate into the blind faith of people like the writer and politician William Pember Reeves, for whom the 'repulsive' Mongolian was two rungs down the ladder from the white man.

The survival of the fittest presumed competition, but while it held together an idea of racial superiority, it also undermined the argument for shutting out competition from the Chinese. 'The Chinaman cannot hurt you if you are more fitted than he to survive the struggle for existence', observed one 'Ah Sin' from Napier. 'But in his heart the Englishman does not believe, in his superiority, and he fears, aye, he trembles at the approach of the struggle.'[32] Moreover, the idea of competition showed up the white workers who could not be made into the idealised types of a superior race dreamed up by those who governed the racial state.[33] The ideal white New Zealander for liberal politicians like Seddon was the self-reliant and independent small landholder living 'close to the soil', not the urban working class. Chinese migrants were only one of the obstacles to achieving that ideal.

In fact, from time to time conservative politicians thought some Chinese might fit the bill better than others as potential colonists. Frederick Whitaker, while trying to show the Chinese Immigration Bill was not 'prohibition', argued, for example, 'that we shall have the more respectable class of Chinese coming here … men who are worth having here, men who will work, and who will be induced to come here from the fact that the looser and worse classes are not permitted to land here'.[34] It was not just white politicians who thought so. Peacock noted that 'the intelligent mercantile Chinese of Sydney object to this immigration, because they say that it adds to the number of pauper Chinese, who are already a burden upon the trading Chinese in the colony, and they object to Chinese immigration on that score'.[35]

Those who opposed the anti-Chinese Bill often endorsed the same type of life idealised by Seddon and the liberal politicians in New Zealand. Occasional comment was made about the folly of protectionism on the part of the labouring classes, for immigrant labour was the tide that would float all boats.[36] Henry Chamberlin, an Auckland merchant, did not 'approve of protecting labour … only the protection of local industries'. He also talked about the usefulness of Chinese labour to plant tea and spin silk for Auckland.[37] George Johnson, a lawyer and landowner who opposed the Bill, believed that 'the cry which has been got up against these Chinese comes from men who are not working honestly, and who are not willing to put their shoulders to the wheel to do what it is necessary for them to do'.[38] James Williamson, an Auckland merchant, claimed not to favour low wages, but went on to say that wages had already climbed too high and had become 'fictitious wages'.[39] William Murray, a farmer, preached the 'fullest' of 'the Lord's earth' for the Chinese and Britons alike. He thought that if the Chinese would prove more successful than his own race, 'they would only, after all, carry out the theory as to the survival of the fittest'.[40]

Nor were the opponents of race legislation making a radical break with mainstream conservatism when they challenged popular prejudice against the Chinese. Conservative opinions were as likely to scorn white claims to racial or cultural superiority as to embrace them, depending on who made the claim. The *Press*, for example, disdainfully wrote in 1887 about the 'affected superiority' and 'boasted civilisation' of Europeans.[41] Others among the educated and cosmopolitan spoke of China with genuine admiration. De Renzie Brett, for example, reminded his fellow members of Parliament that the Chinese had been advanced two thousand or more years ago when Britons were 'living in barbarity in the wilds of Ireland, England, and Scotland'. To the slander of the Chinese being unclean, he replied that there could not be a 'dirtier breed on the face of the earth than Scotchmen and Irishmen, and the people of other barbarous nations'; the Chinese, he vouched, bathed regularly whenever they were near water.[42]

Generous sentiments came easy to well-to-do people and their pressmen whose own hours of work and rates of pay would be unaffected by Chinese immigration. Yet their view of the Chinese was often as one dimensional as that of their opponents. The refrain, again and again, was about the 'industrious', the 'docile', the 'thrifty' Chinese. The wealthy were projecting onto the Chinese the features so lacking in the white working class. William Downie Stewart Snr thought 'Chinese and women are the two greatest conservative classes in the world'.[43] It would seem the myth of the Chinese as a model minority has not much changed since the late nineteenth century. Then, as now, the myth denied their agency – which was at least acknowledged by those who saw them as competitors, and is crucial as a basis of common humanity, whatever other differences.

BUILDING THE RACIAL STATE

The progression of White New Zealand appeared linear on the surface but, underneath, kept eddying and swirling, driven by complex forces and radical breaks. The poll-tax Bill squeaked through the Lower House by a majority of one, and 13 to 10 in the Upper House. On this shaky foundation, the racial state would be built gradually over the next 40 years, not only against the Chinese but also against Indians, Arabs and Croatians. Racism seemed to peak around the turn of the century, but continued to be a serious factor in parliamentary politics when a conservative Reform government passed the Immigration Restriction Amendment Act 1920. New Zealand-born Chinese, who hitherto had been shielded from much of the anti-Chinese agitation, now became 'resident aliens'.

The Liberal Party that took power in 1890 under the 'one man, one vote' principle was backed by some business groups, some small farmers, many factory owners and most of the working class, and went on to govern the country for more than 20 years. It was repeatedly accused by its conservative opponents of cynically manipulating working-class voters – not the least on the Chinese question. Any half-aware populist could see, though, that the new government was expected to do much more for its voters than shutting the door to the Chinese. What the Liberal Party promised to deliver was new labour and factory laws and the expropriation, or 'bursting up', of the big landed estates. Labour and factory laws were meant to safeguard wages and conditions by doing away with class conflict. Expropriation of estates was a way to preserve the hope that workers might become small farmers and escape wage labour altogether. A safety net would provide for the deserving poor – Chinese not included – who fell on hard times. New immigration laws were neither here nor there. The 'influx' of Chinese was not a very pressing matter for leaders of the Liberal Party.

Nevertheless, politicians and populists now played the race card more boldly. Seddon, Reeves and some other government leaders would supply the rhetoric and stratagem, as well as convictions and theory. Reeves was the most consistently opposed to Chinese immigration and in 1895 sponsored an anti-Chinese demonstration in Christchurch that was supported by some trade unions. Reeves demanded that the government 'lay down the principle that New Zealand was to be for white people'. He was well received by the raucous crowd, who shouted down a protest by an Anglican vicar. A second Liberal MP, the merchant George Smith, was lukewarm and thought such measures, while justified, must not hinder the work of trying to 'open up markets' in China. After the meeting, when citizens were asked to stay behind to form an Anti-Chinese League, 'only a few' took the trouble.[44] When a Wellington branch of the Anti-Chinese League was formed during the winter, many of the seats were taken by trade union members. Membership of anti-Chinese Leagues stayed very small, however, and they swiftly faded away, as had other similar organisations that had sprung up over the years.

It was difficult to know whether politicians were following or leading popular opinion. In the same year as the Christchurch demonstration in 1895, the Liberal Party introduced a new law to raise the poll tax to £100. Parliament was told that 'the prevention of undesirable persons coming to New Zealand, especially the Chinese, is of great importance as affecting the well-being and purity of our race, and as unduly disturbing our trade and industries.'[45]

The left of the party led the charge. Wages still featured in the debate; one government member went as far as to state that the problem was 'not so much the Chinese but Chinese cheap labour'.[46] But it had few teeth when the charge was not laid upon the villainous runholder, and the point was overwhelmed by discourses on racial purity and superiority. John Rigg, printer, trade unionist and a close friend of Reeves, exemplified this style of anti-Chinese agitation when he railed in the Upper House against 'a nation of thieves, and liars, and of persons of dishonest dealings, and without any knowledge or perception at all of morality'.[47] He belaboured the point by faulting the Chinese for gambling, using filthy language and ripening fruit in their bed chambers. Rigg was somewhat taken aback by the heartfelt reaction of his fellow member, Samuel Shrimski. Polish-born and Jewish, Shrimski asked that the door be kept open for the Chinese: 'I know what it is to be persecuted, and therefore I have that feeling for my fellow-men which I hope and trust they will always extend to me.' Henry Scotland, who had opposed the 1880 Bill, was now indignant about the 'very narrow feeling against foreigners ... This Bill not only wants to heave half a brick, but a whole cart-load of bricks against the unfortunate Chinese' because he worked too hard and was too busy to read penny rags, join trade unions or spout at meetings about things he did not understand.[48]

The conservatives baulked at the anti-Chinese demagoguery for other reasons than personal experience of discrimination. Some were still speaking behind closed doors about bringing in 'coolies' to drag down wages. Ōamaru merchant James Gemmell, for example, secretly proposed to a meeting of landowners and farmers that 500 Chinese workers be shipped into North Otago. 'The only country that we can depend on is China,' he told the meeting. Others spoke publicly. Anna Stout, whose husband Robert Stout was a leading liberal and leader of the Anti-Chinese League, said to the National Council of Women that 'Industrious Europeans had nothing to fear from the Chinese, but the drunken, lazy, and dissolute had everything to fear.'[49]

Conservative opinion more often opposed the populism than the racism. Upon the establishment of the Christchurch Anti-Chinese League, the *Press*, the leading voice of landed conservatism, commented that while it had no hesitation in strongly supporting necessary measures to stop the influx of the Chinese it objected to 'the question being used as a stalkinghorse for the benefit of certain politicians, and ... the public being played with for political purposes'.[50] Conservative politicians toed the same line in Parliament. Some still grumbled that anti-immigrant measures were anti-competitive, yet none would go as far as openly supporting a lowering of wages. Others made concessions to the industrious 'Chinaman'. The majority thought some controls against the influx of Chinese necessary but objected to how the government was going about it. The most substantial criticism focused on the cheap electioneering.[51]

A new approach to the Chinese question was emerging. The conservatives had bigger fish to fry than getting more 'coolies' into the colony or standing up for the industrious, albeit 'undesirable' ones who were already here. Morgan Grace, landowner, made this point, saying that 'the whole future' of the country now depended on wise conservatives in the Upper House acting as brakes on the 'socialist' extremes of the Lower House. 'This Council shall not get into a collision with the House of Representatives on a question of minor importance like the Asiatic Restriction Bill.'[52]

Ten years later, the Liberal Party was again spurred into action in response to popular pressure that one historian argued was set up on the sly to shore up support for the government.[53] A few groups were formed during the winter of 1907 to work towards a White New Zealand. The Anti-Asiatic League in Palmerston North, for example, called for all Chinese to be expelled. A branch was set up in Masterton. The White Race League, another group, sought members from throughout the country. The founder was Thomas McDonald, a doctor; William Lloyd, a public servant, was the dominion leader. The plan, at first, was to set up a league in every city. The limits to intolerance were quickly exposed when it became clear that the phrase 'anti-Chinese' provoked what Lloyd called 'a certain amount of hostility'.[54] He was busy for a few weeks that winter meeting workers, shopkeepers and others to set up the first two branches in the southern provinces. A gathering of white laundrymen and shopkeepers listened, for example, to the goals of the Dunedin league. 'The meeting was crowded,' noted a newspaper, 'and enthusiastically favoured a White New Zealand.'[55] Lloyd followed this with more work in the northern provinces.

Other politicians were also eagerly playing that card – and one group played it with considerable sincerity. James Munro, president of the Independent Political Labour League, spoke on behalf of many socialists when he asked Parliament to 'introduce at the earliest possible moment legislation restricting the entry of Chinese'. The vice-president of the party went still further: together with the president of the Otago Trades and Labour Council, he called for a racial state of unprecedented severity in which intermarriage of whites and Chinese would be 'absolutely prohibited' under law.[56]

The government responded with the Chinese Immigrants Amendment Act 1907, which proposed not a hike in the poll tax but a reading test: prospective Chinese immigrants would have to read and understand a printed text of at least 100 words in English before being allowed entry. The White Race League, within a few brief months of its founding, was heard of no longer. A new regulation the following year turned the screws still more tightly on migration by imposing a standardised system of thumbprinting on Chinese leaving the seaports.

EVOLVING RACISM ON THE RIGHT

Very few conservatives chose to speak against the new law. None spoke against the Bill in the Lower House. Francis Trask was the only voice speaking against it in the Upper House. A butcher and former gold digger, he was the type of citizen most often at the heart of opposition to immigration by Chinese – and yet he opposed the new Bill on the grounds of what he called 'fair play towards man and man and towards nation and nation'. He believed, too, that the Bill would harm New Zealand in the eyes of China.[57]

Party discipline, meanwhile, explained some of the silence among other conservatives. William Massey, leader of the Opposition, had already pledged to support doubling the poll tax; he would 'give place to no man as to the wisdom of preventing the Chinese becoming established in this country'.[58]

A decade later, Massey would bring in his own immigration laws: first, to exclude socialists and other enemies of a right-wing government; second, to stop any 'coloured' migrants. Up until then, Chinese who could afford a poll tax and pass the language test could come and go as they pleased. Massey now wanted to give effect to 'a deep-seated sentiment on the part of a huge majority of the people of this country that this Dominion shall be what is often called a "white" New Zealand … Clearly, we want to keep the race as pure in this Dominion as it is possible to keep it.'[59]

A watershed had been reached between the turn of the century and 1920; the political right would not favour immigration from China again until the 1990s. This watershed partly resulted from the shifting ground of conservatism personified by 'Farmer Bill' Massey. He was a new type of conservative leader, looked down upon by the old gentry. A former wage worker on a southern estate and, afterwards, a northern farmer who toiled in his own paddocks, he disliked the grand manner of landowners as much as he disliked socialists. Massey climbed on to a new rung of political power in 1909 when he founded the Reform Party. Old conservatives took a deep breath and rallied behind what seemed to be the only political body that could win power once more for the right. The Reform leader and many other new conservatives were deeply racist in a way many old conservatives were not.

The new conservatism suited a growing section of the middle class, including white shopkeepers and small farmers. If the Liberal Party represented a united front between the middle and working class against the landed gentry – and against unearned wealth – the Reform Party, led by Massey, offered them an alternative voice that distinguished them from workers by their virtues of hard work, discipline and so on. White shopkeepers and small farmers had also been at the forefront of White New Zealand since the last decade of the nineteenth century.

The eve of the Liberals' election to power had seen the first alliance of workers and shopkeepers on the 'Chinese Question'. Wellington, home to the biggest cluster of Chinese outside Otago, was the setting for a meeting between delegates from the Master Grocers' Association and the Trades and Labour Council. Together, they agreed that 'steps' needed to be taken 'to put a stop to Chinese trading in the city'. All unions affiliated to the Trades and Labour Council were to order members and their families to stop buying 'groceries, fruit, vegetables, and other goods from Chinese storekeepers in the City'. Vigilance committees would police the boycott.[60] A similar boycott movement was talked over in other towns from time to time throughout the last decade of the nineteenth century, but always the outcome was lacklustre. Most white working-class or middle-class women, it turned out, were keen to buy their fruit and vegetables where they were cheapest – at the Chinese greengrocers – rather than to fork out more pennies to make some sort of racial point. They did not take too kindly, either, to some vigilance committee of men telling them where and what to buy. Nor did many men carry out any kind of vigilance. And the Anti-Chinese Leagues, for all their organising talents, failed, in the words of Anna Stout, 'in growing even a two-penny cabbage'.[61]

As time went on, there was a dawning awareness among white shopkeepers that the labour movement was no longer their wholehearted ally. Sydenham shopkeepers were dismayed by the new point of view when they held a meeting of people in their borough and were told by Alfred Hart, painter and former president of the Canterbury Trades and Labour Council, that it was thanks to Chinese fruit shops that the white 'poor man' was now able to afford fruit. Chinese shopkeepers, by selling good fruit at a good price, were stopping white shopkeepers from tying up the trade in 'fruit rings'. George Good, leader of the shopkeepers, hardly knew what to say. 'It is the working people who are to blame,' he tried gamely. 'These working people have their unions and their federations to secure better pay, and quite right too, and yet it is these people who support the Chinese.' Shopkeeper Charles Munro added: 'It is a Chinese puzzle to me how Labour men can stick up for the Chinamen.'[62]

Despite the imposition of further restrictions in the 1920 Act, when another attempt was made at rallying the 'White Race' in 1926, it was a group of potato farmers in Pukekohe, rather than wage earners or workers, who led the charge against the 'Hindus' as well as the Chinese, though they did attract some union support.[63] The White New Zealand League demanded protection from 'unfair' competition for profit, as well as wages – a somewhat uncomfortable position for anyone who saw themselves as market entrepreneurs rather than exploited workers. The League had no more success in gathering public support than those who came before, and soon languished in much the same way.

CHANGING ATTITUDES ON THE LEFT

Working people feared Chinese immigration for the same reasons an earlier generation did. Wages and standards of living remained at the centre of the issue. And no anti-Chinese meetings could have held their attention without at least paying lip service to the protection of wages and conditions from 'unfair competition'. But working people also discovered that the 'Chinese Question' could be used against their interests by small and middling employers, as well as by the landed gentry. In the mid-1890s, carpenters and cabinetmakers listened attentively to scaremongering about the influx of cheap Chinese furniture manufactured in Victoria.[64] They were to be told in the Arbitration Court only two years later that for the very same reason their employers could not possibly concede to their demand for a minimum wage.[65]

Working people's feelings about the Chinese were often complex and contradictory, and many resolved to live with the contradictions rather than trying to work them out in words or theory. Working people who worried about a somewhat abstract invasion of workers driving down wages frequently drew a careful and intuitive distinction between the would-be newcomers and those who were already here and were part of their daily lives. A small but easy-going democracy of enjoyment inside gambling houses, sly-grog shops and brothels drew many of the sportier or merrier whites to mix and mingle with Chinese. Hundreds, from 'all walks of life', came through the year to play in Haining Street, Wellington.[66] 'I am not a man to regard a Chinaman as other than human because he is a Chinaman,' wrote a white worker in that city.[67] 'I never heard anyone complain that in this district the Chinese were encroaching on the avenues of industry,' wrote another in Reefton.[68] Bullying was frowned on as 'wrong and unkind' even by the cheap newspapers that fought immigration from China.[69]

Very few working people left any records of their feelings, even while leading figures in the labour movement often spoke heatedly. The Wellington Anti-Chinese League was led, for example, by Allan Orr, a gold digger and union leader, 'ever ready to espouse the cause of anyone who is wronged or oppressed' but with a glaring blind spot when it came to the Chinese.[70] Marianne Tasker, formerly a servant, was another labour leader who was secretary of an Anti-Chinese League.[71] Labour leaders like them were told by the Liberal Party not just to dwell on wages and conditions but to think about the destiny of 'the race'. Reeves, as minister of labour, beseeched the Wellington Anti-Chinese League to look upon the issue not as a 'mere unionist question' or even 'a mere matter of £ s d, but as a high and a national duty which they were doing not only for themselves but for … their children and their children's children'.[72]

Not all spokespersons of the working people felt this way. Amery Daldy, wife of a shoemaker and a leading figure in the women's suffrage and temperance movements, took it as a matter of principle to vote against her colleague, Marianne Tasker, at a meeting of the National Women's Council.[73] 'We Britishers somehow seem to think we have a right to the whole world,' she said. 'We have gone to India and China, and by forcing opium on the Chinese and in other ways have done them as much injury as they are likely to do us. The Chinese must live somewhere. I think it would be more becoming for us to abolish slums.'[74]

A new voice now began to be heard, too – the voice of an international socialism and a young labour leadership. Socialist internationalism had been hinted at as early as the immigration debates of the 1890s when a few on the left of the Liberal Party wrote or spoke against White New Zealand. One was the dogged Patrick O'Regan, child of a gold-digger family, who wrote under the name 'Horny Hand'. He walked out of the Liberal Party after the turn of the century and, as a journalist and independent MP, spoke up for the rights of all workers everywhere in the world. He also opposed dominion imperialism in the Pacific and New Zealand involvement in World War I. O'Regan did his best to stop the poll tax being lifted to £100. When Chinese householders signed a petition protesting police powers under the opium laws, he brought the document before the minister of justice.[75]

Socialists were struck by how Chinese workers backed white workers during the 1913 Great Strike as angry standoffs between labour and capital occurred up and down the country. Chinese crews at several seaports told employers they would not unload cargo. One crowd of workers 'greeted with cheers' a troop of Chinese stokers at Lyttelton, praising them as 'good fellows' for not being 'scabs'.[76] Chinese shopkeepers, too, were praised for boycotting fruit unloaded by white scab workers from ships in Wellington. 'Chinese are the greatest strikers and boycotters,' wrote a socialist editor. 'They have, without the asking, taken their stand with the white striker.'[77]

Socialist internationalism was linked on the left with a strengthening feeling that there was no racial hierarchy. Whites were not superior to other races. Whites who laboured for wages were the workmates of anybody and everybody who laboured for wages – or for no wages – anywhere in the world. The Chinese were not an enemy of the white working class; capitalism and imperialism were the enemies of the worldwide working class. Socialists attacked white shopkeepers, white market gardeners and other small capitalists as hypocrites when they spoke out against Chinese coming into the country to make money. 'Come to think of it, that's about all the British merchants and military instructors go to China for' ran an editorial in the socialist and internationalist weekly, *Maoriland Worker*.[78]

Internationalism breathed new life into the bones of socialism and the labour movement. Labour leaders and working people would go on worrying about immigration and hold onto racist or more broadly xenophobic language for another generation or so out of a deep-seated fear about the impact on their hard-won power

– not the least because the political right wanted it that way. The Reform government under Massey would carry on the policy of assisted immigration from Britain that was good for White New Zealand. Working people, and their representatives, saw this policy as another attempt to shift the balance of power. Peter Fraser, who would become prime minister for the Labour Party, spoke against the policy to bring out immigrants from the 'motherland': 'I am not in favour of any inundation of black or white labour if it will reduce the standard of living of the workers in this country,' he told Parliament. 'I am not in favour of penalising anybody because of race, or creed, or blood.'[79] The Labour Party 'lost interest in agitating around White New Zealand', noted one historian, and, along with worker unions, 'showed little enthusiasm when overtures were made towards them by middle class dominated white race groups'.[80] A new policy on the political left was to try to get Chinese workers into the labour movement so that all could work together for better conditions and pay. The New Zealand Workers Union, for example, agreed in 1921 to welcome Chinese. 'We are not responsible for their presence in this country,' wrote labour leader James Thorn, 'and when they are brought here or allowed in by the exploiter, it is up to us to organise them.'[81]

We have now come a full circle, in a sense. In 1880, the old internationalism of the British Empire that would go anywhere, exploit anyone and sell anything for a profit was on the way out. Now the working people had worked out an internationalism of their own. By 1920, a clear political consensus that Chinese immigration was 'undesirable' was backed by a legal framework that discriminated based on race. Yet, not 30 years later, this legal framework began to be dismantled. Overt anti-Chinese discrimination, once uncontroversial, largely drifted to the political fringes. It was picked up in earnest by the radical right from the 1990s as the government's enticement of wealthy immigrants led to a significant increase in Asian immigration.[82] Chapter Ten explores how this resentment fuelled the growth of skinhead groups in the 1990s, and Chapter Thirteen traces this renewed Sinophobia through the revitalisation of the National Front in the early 2000s. Ironically, the National Front showed how far the country had come by praising the anti-Chinese stance of New Zealand politicians in the late nineteenth and early twentieth centuries. This is perhaps one of the clearest examples of the contemporary radical right idolising and adapting formerly mainstream views into new contexts.

CHAPTER THREE

Lionel Terry

Radicalisation, Revolution and the 'Great Replacement' Myth

MARINUS LA ROOIJ

IN SEPTEMBER 1905, Joe Kum Yung, an elderly Chinese man who had lived and toiled legally in New Zealand for decades, was murdered by Englishman Lionel Terry in the heart of Wellington's Chinatown. The murder and subsequent trial created a sensation, making newspaper headlines around the world. Today, the common view of Terry's motive for murder was simply to awaken New Zealanders to the peril of Asian immigration. Yet Terry's radicalisation was much more profound than this. He committed murder to draw public attention to the imagined life-or-death crisis facing the British people and their empire. Terry argued in his manifesto *The Shadow*, written in the months leading up to the crime, that there was a coordinated global super-conspiracy by powerful Jews to destroy the Empire and replace racial Britons through mass alien immigration.

Terry's crisis narrative mirrors that of today's white supremacist 'identitarians' who believe a global super-conspiracy is dedicated to replacing white people and destroying 'European culture'.[1] These beliefs have spread over the last 20 years in the recesses of the internet, and more recently appeared in the political mainstream – notably in Charlottesville, Virginia, in August 2017 when hundreds of far-right extremists marched, chanting 'Jews will not replace us!'[2] Belief in this 'white genocide' super-conspiracy, or great replacement myth, has been used to promote the notion that the established democratic political order is fundamentally corrupt, and to justify violence and terrorism against racial and religious minorities, immigrants and white people deemed 'undesirable'.[3]

The parallels between Terry's views and the 'great replacement' believers of today are striking. While much has been written about Terry, his crime, the sympathetic public response and his later years in a mental asylum, little attention has been paid to his political ideas.[4] Most of what has been written about Terry dismisses him as a lunatic, a 'white supremacist' acting outside the norms of British society in his time. It is perhaps a comforting approach to view Terry's crime and beliefs as an historical outlier. But to understand the process of radicalisation taking place among some in the far right today, it is opportune to critically re-examine Terry's beliefs, their development and context. This chapter explores Terry's life before he came to New Zealand, his radicalisation pathway, his emerging belief in a 'great replacement' super-conspiracy – and his desire to trigger a revolution of British working people across the Empire.

EARLY YEARS

Edward Lionel Terry was born in Kent in 1873. His family were descended from yeomen farmers who had worked the lands of south-east England for generations. Later tales told by Terry, likely emanating from his eccentric father Edward, included fanciful stories of the family being descended from aristocratic refugees from revolutionary France or, paradoxically, from Emperor Napoleon Bonaparte himself.[5] His Anglo-Saxon and Church of England pedigree was apparently insufficient: the desire to be someone more significant was an important feature of Lionel Terry's life.

In the 1880s, following success in the corn trade, Edward senior moved his family to London, where he aspired to middle-class respectability. Lionel Terry, without his father's knowledge, joined the Royal Artillery in 1892, his occupation noted as 'artist'. The following year, he was stationed at Windsor Barracks, having transferred to the Royal Horse Guards known as the 'Blues'.[6] His service with the prestigious Blues was short: Terry's father paid to free him of his 12-year term of service.[7] It is likely that Terry had become bored with the discipline and routine of army life – two or three years would become the maximum time he applied himself to anything. Terry made much of his service with the Blues, yet only a few years after his departure inquiries by a London newspaper found that none of the officers of the regiment could recall him.[8]

Seeking adventure, Terry left England in October 1895 to join the Matabeleland Mounted Police stationed at Bulawayo in present-day Zimbabwe. His arrival there coincided with the infamous Jameson Raid that attempted to overthrow the independent Boer republic of the Transvaal. For imperial patriots like Cecil Rhodes, who orchestrated the raid with the tacit support of the British Colonial Office, the continuing expansion of the Empire was logical to allow access into the African interior and the gold inconveniently located within the Transvaal.[9] British public sentiment also favoured imperial expansion in Africa. Terry played his part, serving in the British military response to the so-called Second Matabele War of 1896–97, during which the once dominant Ndebele people sought to reclaim their sovereignty, lands and way of life following the blood-soaked British victory in the First Matabele War. Serving in the Matabeleland relief force under the command of Sir Frederick Carrington, Terry was involved in several engagements as the sieges of British settlements were lifted. However, his contribution was mostly unremarkable.[10] It is possible that during his time with the British South Africa Company's private army he was, as he later boasted, able to 'make an intimate friend of Cecil Rhodes, who thought very highly of him'.[11] More significantly, his time in South Africa likely reinforced Terry's views of British racial superiority and the manifest destiny of the Empire's expansion over 'lesser' peoples like the Ndebele and the 'dop-guzzling' Afrikaners he despised.[12] It is also possible that the killing of British settlers by the Ndebele in the early stages of the rebellion hardened his world-view. For him, the right of British working people to toil and profit from the lands they rightly conquered was a recurring theme.

SINOPHOBIC RADICALISATION IN CANADA

After only a few years, Terry left Africa and returned to London, where his father unsuccessfully tried to settle him into the family business. His desire for adventure and his inability to settle into a mundane life saw him set off again. In 1900, he reached Vancouver Island in British Columbia and found work as a coal miner in the small settlement of South Wellington, Nanaimo. There was high demand for labour in western North America owing to the rapid growth of railways and steamship travel and the increased coal production this required. Wages and conditions were poor, however, making the political environment in British Columbia radicalised and racially charged over the question of where this labour might be sourced.[13]

The question of admitting Chinese and Japanese immigrants, and the competition this created with white workers (predominantly British or American), had been hotly debated for decades before Terry arrived.[14] Intertwined with the politics of race and immigration was the question of labour and capital, and the degree to which business should be regulated and the rights of workers (notably wages and safety) protected.

During Terry's time in British Columbia came daily news of the South African war, where the might of the British Empire was set to crush the independent Boer republics of the Transvaal and Orange Free State. Terry's identity as self-proclaimed champion of the British working man and his fanatical hatred of Asians appears to have been forged during these years. Later, he was remembered as having 'achieved considerable notoriety in this province' as 'a labor agitator' and 'the Socialist who was known at Wellington mines'.[15]

VANCOUVER ISLAND LABOUR ACTIVIST

Terry's radicalisation occurred during a labour dispute, when his role as secretary of the Alexandra Miners' Union placed him in the middle of the struggle. The Alexandra Mine where he worked was owned by the Hon. James Dunsmuir, the provincial premier recently elected on a ticket opposing Asian immigration. But Dunsmuir, a British Columbian of Scottish ancestry, struggled to find enough British men to work his mines, particularly men prepared to do so at the price he was prepared to pay to make the coal profitable. He needed Chinese and Japanese labour to make up the shortfall. Early in 1900, Dunsmuir had attempted to bring 200 Scotsmen out to Canada, but the effort left him out of pocket, as most of the miners baulked at the low wages and absconded for better opportunities in Seattle.[16] In late 1900, when coal prices were falling, Dunsmuir decided to concentrate production on mines with lower costs and higher-quality coal. This included trying to lift the Alexandra Mine's productivity by increased coal production and cutting costs, sparking a miners' strike in December, with Terry demanding that Dunsmuir back down.[17]

Dunsmuir responded by locking the miners out and closing the mine. The premier was well known for his ruthlessness in politics and business; even the future Canadian Prime Minister William Lyon Mackenzie King described him privately as a 'selfish millionaire [who] has become something of a tyrannical autocrat'.[18] Earlier in the year Dunsmuir had relocated coal-mining activities from the old company town of Wellington down to Ladysmith. This decision meant that the five thousand residents of Wellington had to abandon their homes to find work elsewhere. One local paper described this as nothing less than a 'tyrannous exercise of authority which had deprived [the miners] of the property in which the savings of years had been invested and was nothing less than the denial of the rights of freemen'.[19] Dunsmuir had also successfully divided miners along racial lines, using Chinese workers to break strikes and build the railway allowing coal to be rerouted from Wellington.[20]

Dunsmuir's move to put mostly British men out of work at the Alexandra Mine put him on a path for conflict with the idealistic union secretary. 'I have a great perhaps morbid-love of justice and fair play,' Terry wrote.[21] He took every opportunity to attack Dunsmuir, and showed tactical nous in timing an open letter to him to cause maximum embarrassment while Dunsmuir was in the Canadian capital meeting the prime minister. Published in the *Ottawa Citizen*, Terry's letter denounced the premier's treatment of the workers: 'Nearly 200 men, many with wives and families, are thus thrown out of employment in the depth of winter, and as the mine has now been closed down for six weeks, the bare necessities of life are beginning to be regarded as luxuries.'[22]

The long and ultimately futile Alexandra strike would have a profound radicalising effect on Terry, fuelling a burning hatred for Asians (Chinese and Japanese, derisively described in Canada as 'Mongolians') and the capitalists who sought to profit from them. At first Terry's campaign was focused on Dunsmuir and the economics of the struggle, including that British Columbians were now buying American rather than Canadian coal. But as the strike ground on, Terry's public pronouncements became more passioned and personal against Dunsmuir, and made increasing reference to Asian immigration as the main problem. In one blistering open letter to Dunsmuir in February 1901, Terry denounced the 'inordinate greed of the Premier of British Columbia, who would conceal beneath his much-vaunted anti-Mongolian mask a despicable scheme to force, by means of poverty and starvation, the men on whom future generations of Canada depend, to accept Chinamen's wages.'[23]

Most white miners in the province believed they could not compete with Asian workers simply because the latter were prepared to work in worse conditions, for less money and longer hours. For Dunsmuir, the matter was one of economics: the Alexandra Mine was not profitable, and he claimed there was work available at his other mines.[24] While publicly he made the right noises to reflect popular sentiment in favour of restricting further immigration, as a businessman he had fought the government's restrictions on hiring Asians in court. Dunsmuir even recovered the cost of these legal proceedings by deducting a monthly sum from the wages of his Chinese workers.[25] Unsurprisingly, Dunsmuir was the largest employer of Asian labour in British Columbia, and his focus on minimising costs and maximising output meant his mines were among the most dangerous in North America.[26]

The feud between Dunsmuir and Terry escalated dramatically on 15 February when the Dunsmuir-owned No.6 pit in Cumberland exploded, entombing over 60 white and Asian men and boys. Instead of using the disaster to widen the strike to other mines and attack Dunsmuir's failings as an employer, Terry instead blamed the presence of Asians for what had happened. Writing at length to the local newspaper, he raged that:

> [T]he immigrants of China and Japan, employed in coal mines in this province, represent the lowest class of the people of those nations, we submit that the employment of those immigrants constitutes a grave menace to the safety of the mining community of this province. With regard to the fatal explosion at Cumberland … we submit that better precautions would have been adopted by management if the men employed in No.6 mine had been all white men, and we believe the explosion would not have occurred had no Mongolians been working in the mine.[27]

INCREASED ANTI-ASIAN ACTIVISM

This loss of British life radicalised Terry further, and his focus shifted from the economic viability of the Alexandra Mine to seeing Asian immigration as the pre-eminent question. By March, his racial views were so unrestrained that he caused an uproar while addressing a meeting of the Extension Mine Union at Ladysmith. Though he was there to gain support for the Alexandra miners, he was less interested in winning friends than in the opportunity to racially taunt Chinese miners in the audience.[28] By April, Terry was openly talking about a larger struggle to keep the wealth of British lands in British hands. Writing to the local newspaper, he advocated his vision of the Empire as a racially pure domain – won by British blood for the exclusive betterment of racial Britons:

> I am a British subject and a patriot, as were my fathers. I do not take any credit for having fought and bled for my country; it was my duty. I will not submit to a policy [of Asian immigration] which threatens to pollute the blood of the Empire. For the blood of the Empire is the strength of the Empire. And the white man's might is the white man's right to the flag of a thousand years.[29]

While he was a racial-imperialist, Terry's view of Asian immigration as an existential threat to British Columbia's future was shared by his fellow Alexandra miners and a large portion of the province's white population. Asian immigration was a volatile political question in British Columbia, often bringing the province into conflict with Canadian and imperial policy.[30] Responding to this local agitation, the dominion government in Ottawa initiated the Royal Commission to Investigate Chinese and Japanese Immigration (known as the Oriental Commission).[31] Terry appeared before the commission in April, submitting on behalf of the Alexandra Miners' Union. Despite his strong views, one newspaper described him as looking 'every inch "a soldier of the Queen" as he sat in the witness box'.[32] Using his height and soldier's posture, Terry calmly explained that among other evils the 'presence of Mongolians in this province is a great factor in keeping white men of all classes from settling [here], and we believe it is also the cause of many white men leaving …' Importantly, Terry asserted that unless 'rapid action is taken with a view to expelling them from this province the white man will leave this province in possession of Chinese and Japanese immigrants'.[33] The commission would go on to recommend against further Asian immigration, as the Chinese were considered 'unfit for full citizenship'. The recommendation was supported by the Nanaimo Trades and Labour Council that urged the rest of the labour movement to join it and oppose the 'Horrible Yellow scourge.'[34]

While Terry's fears for the Empire's future grew, the Alexandra strike ground on. Terry appears to have retained the confidence of the miners, and his efforts were described as 'Herculean'.[35] But he was a hothead and an individualist. A series of personal feuds with fellow miners and unionists had to be reined in by the union's leadership. One lengthy spat during May was with antagonist Arthur Ramsdale, secretary of the Extension Miners' Union. In March, on hearing that the Extension Union's officials were not prepared to support a combined mass meeting of all the Nanaimo miners, Terry wrote to Ramsdale expressing his 'disgust'.[36] Matters escalated when Ramsdale denounced Terry for openly attacking the Extension miners at a union meeting in Ladysmith.[37] Terry retaliated by publicly calling on the Extension miners not to be 'blinded by falsehood and corruption – drive forth the traitors from your ranks'.[38] Ramsdale responded in kind: 'It seems to me that [Terry] cannot rest unless he is denouncing or characterising someone. He reminds me of a bladder that is filled with obnoxious gasses. The least prick it gets it gives vent to the corruptible odour that is generated inside, owing to the odious disposition of Mr Terry he is hurting the cause of the South Wellington men.'[39]

MOVE TO NEW ZEALAND

The Alexandra miners were little helped by this feud, and went back to negotiate with Dunsmuir after he signalled the mine might reopen if profitable terms were reached. Yet their union secretary had no role in the negotiations; Dunsmuir refused to attend any meeting where Terry was present.[40] Now blacklisted from Dunsmuir's mines and with the strike seemingly over, Terry decided that life would be better in New Zealand. Explaining his move to another settler outpost on the extreme verges of the Empire,

Terry said: '… the life led by the colonists in New Zealand is in favourable contrast to that lived on this side of the ocean, particularly amongst the Americans, who make life a thing very unpleasant to contemplate by reason of their excessive working hours, shortening their lives and utterly failing to understand what is meant by the pleasure of living.'[41]

It is possible that Terry chose New Zealand because of stories circulating within the international labour movement about the progressive conditions for working people in the colony. He may also have been influenced by Hugh McAllen, a resident of Nanaimo who had formerly mined coal in New Zealand. Like Terry, McAllen presented to the Oriental Commission, stating that New Zealand's coal miners were better paid than in Canada and were white.[42] Along with his wanderlust, seeking a British workers' paradise was possibly the main factor in Terry's decision.

While Terry had only a momentary impact on the politics of British Columbia, the province had a radicalising effect on him. His anti-Asian and socialist views were intense, but they reflected British Columbia's highly charged politics of race and class. Years later, after Terry's crime in New Zealand was known, opposition to Asian immigration continued to grow and culminated in a September 1907 protest organised by the Asiatic Exclusion League in Vancouver City. The protest soon degenerated into a violent rampage that targeted Chinatown and saw James Dunsmuir, now Lieutenant-Governor, burnt in effigy by a cheering mob of some 25,000 people.[43] So while his time in southern Africa provided Terry with his identity as a soldier of the Empire, in Canada he became the champion of the British toiling masses and their defender against the Asiatic hordes seeking to usurp their lands. His feud with Dunsmuir had also convinced him that the Empire's capitalist class was itself a threat, the enabling power that facilitated Asian immigration and the dispossession of racial Britons.

UNMASKING THE CAPITALIST ENEMY WITHIN THE EMPIRE

The New Zealand that Terry arrived at in 1901 had also been dominated by the Asian immigration question. The Liberal government under Premier Richard Seddon vigorously opposed Asian immigration, introducing a poll tax in 1893 and other measures that discouraged arrivals and encouraged Chinese to return home (as discussed in Chapter Two). Seddon's opposition was based on his loathing of the Chinese and understanding that opposing Asian immigration was a vote winner – particularly among working-class Pākehā.[44] Just as in Canada, the New Zealand labour movement was vocal in its opposition to Asian migration.[45] When Terry arrived, the Asian population in New Zealand was declining and the immigration question largely moot – albeit still useful for Seddon to mobilise his working-class base.[46]

Terry found work as a surveyor with the Lands and Surveys Department in Mangonui, Northland. Camped in remote bush country, he worked by day and wrote at night, producing his first major attack on the British capitalists whom he believed were corrupting the Empire. Over seven long pages, the poem *God or Mammon?* served to characterise the British Empire as a racial domain, hard won by Britons – for their exclusive benefit. Terry was not particularly religious, but he used numerous metaphors from biblical and Christian tradition, as well as the well-known New Testament pronouncement that you cannot serve God and 'Mammon', the evil personification of wealth and false object of worship.[47] *God or Mammon?* describes how the British people created a vast global empire by sacrificing their blood and 'seas of gore' to vanquish their despised European foes – the Spanish, French and Russians. Yet, it went on, 'Mighty Britain' now 'strains and struggles in the toils of shameful doom'.[48] This calamity was caused by debased Britons whose '[b]ribery and foul corruption rampant rage throughout the land'. Their greed was placed above national interests by bringing in race aliens to toil on the Empire's conquered lands and 'Gather in the white man's harvest, reap the fruits by white man sown':

> See, advancing, grim, relentless, as a scourge sent forth from hell,
> Comes the blighting curse of Mammon, in the white man's land to dwell;
> Mongol, Ethiop, nameless horror, human brute from many a clime,
> Vomited from earth's dark pest holes; bred of plague, disease, and crime.
> Swathed in rags and noisome odours, gaunt and fleshless, dwarfed of limb,
> Visaged like the grisly jackal seeking dead, midst shadows dim;
> See the horde of drug besotten, sin begotten, fiends of filth,
> Swarming o'er thy nations bulwarks; pillaging thy nations wealth.[49]

The poem ends with an appeal to King Edward VII to rise up and 'purge thy country; drive the alien from thy shores!' and claims that this is a struggle of '*life* or *death*!'[50]

Terry's 'spirited verse' was 'tastily printed in pamphlet form' during June 1902, with the influential *New Zealand Herald* believing it 'makes the strongest possible poetic case for the racial purity of "all the Britains"'.[51] Dunedin's evening newspaper described it as a 'vigorous bit of writing, and worth reading'.[52] While the pamphlet had modest circulation, Terry printed as many as he could afford, the poem was reprinted in the widely read *New Zealand Illustrated Magazine*.[53]

TREACHERY IN THE TRANSVAAL

God or Mammon? assumes that 'those who hold the reins of power' and are 'spurred by wolfish lust for gold' are British, albeit corrupted by greed to trade away 'their brother's birth right'.[54] As his thinking further metastasised during 1904, the idea of a corrupted British capitalist class was strengthened by his growing outrage at events in the newly conquered territories of southern Africa. Following their catastrophic defeat, the Boer republics were subsumed into the Empire as Crown colonies with limited self-government.[55] The franchise extended only to those the British trusted, including the mine owners of the Transvaal who sought Chinese workers to fill the labour shortage and restart gold production. The move to bring Chinese to work the Witwatersrand (Rand) mines created an outcry around the Empire, notably in New Zealand.[56] Under Seddon's leadership, New Zealand was an enthusiastic participant in the effort to crush the 'barbarian' Boers, with around 6500 men volunteering to fight.[57] Like Terry, most New Zealanders believed that with the Boers defeated and more than 40,000 Afrikaner and African civilians dead, the wealth of the conquered territories belonged to Britons. Seddon summed up this view, believing it was important to reap the spoils of war by repopulating the new colonies with racial Britons, particularly from the Australasian colonies. He also argued that such a resettlement would be a 'means of preventing trouble in the future' by keeping the hated Boers in check.[58] As he wrote in February 1903: 'It would be a grave mistake to countenance the introduction of Asiatics or Coolies [Indians] to work the South African gold mines; that the British white population from Australia and New Zealand and elsewhere was bound to increase [in the Transvaal], and the mine owners need not be anxious.'[59]

Seddon's many protests during 1903–04 against the importation of Chinese labour into the Transvaal enhanced his status, particularly in Australia and Britain where he became a household name.[60] His stand was also widely supported in New Zealand, particularly within the labour movement. The Liberal-aligned *New Zealand Times* summed up the popular mood in January 1904:

> Mr Seddon deserves the support of every right-thinking man in the community for the firm stand he is taking against the introduction of Asiatic Labour [into the Transvaal] … [that colony] owes its existence to the bone and sinew, the blood and the treasure poured into it from all round the Empire. The [military] intervention was undertaken for a purpose – the purpose of holding the country for the Empire and of preventing an alien race from setting up a foreign flag of independence there.[61]

Importantly, Seddon used his populist opposition to Asian immigration to attack his conservative opponents, including those in the Legislative Council, which had passed a motion that New Zealand should keep out of the business of another self-governing British colony. Seddon responded that New Zealand's war service gave it a voice in the matter and that the Transvaal's limited democracy was little more than a joke. The labour movement threw its support behind Seddon's crusade, with most of the Trades and Labour Councils passing motions in support.[62] The Transvaal controversy seemed also to re-energise the labour movement's opposition to Chinese immigration generally, with the Independent Political Labour League reaffirming its pledge to a White New Zealand as part of its socialist vision.[63]

Later in January 1904, Terry joined the debate, echoing the sentiments of the labour movement and expressing his disgust to the *New Zealand Times* at the importation of Chinese workers, but going further than most in calling for violence. He expressed his regret that the 45,000 electors of the Transvaal who had supported Chinese labour were not 'included in the late killing match' of the war. He suggested a new contingent of colonial soldiers might be needed to 'assist in securing the new sister colony' and 'meet the Mongol on his arrival'. After it was 'effectively demonstrated that South Africa is the property of the British and not the Chinese Empire', Terry mused as to whether 'further purification might be effected by the extinction' of the Transvaal electors. He finished with: 'I opine that most of the late contingenters will recollect what kind of white creatures they are who haunt that blood-bought shadow land.'[64]

THE SINO-SEMITIC PERIL UNMASKED

This last sentence was a reference to the large number of Jews who lived and worked in and around Johannesburg, having arrived over previous decades from Britain and the Russian Empire to seek their fortune in the gold mines and escape Tsarist persecution.[65] Some of these Jewish immigrants had indeed found their fortune, and were now influential mine owners – nicknamed 'Randlords'. While the so-called Randlords had influenced the path to war, they soon became the focus of a growing anti-war movement in the United Kingdom as the initial optimism of the Anglo-Boer War was followed by a series of British defeats. This opposition grew more vocal as the fighting ground on and stories circulated about the devastating death toll among Boer civilians from British scorched-earth tactics and use of concentration camps rife with hunger and disease. In Britain, the anti-war movement rationalised the debacle by exaggerating the role of the Jewish mine owners in the onset of the war. This was despite the fact that the absorption of the Boer republics into British South Africa was a longstanding feature of imperial policy, with men like Cecil Rhodes, Leander Starr Jameson and Secretary of State for the Colonies Joseph Chamberlain playing more crucial roles in the path to war.[66] After the war, the idea of a Jewish conspiracy instigating the conflict, and now also controlling policy in the conquered territories, became a pervasive feature of liberal and left-wing criticism of Britain's southern African policies. In New Zealand, the pro-Liberal Wellington *Free Lance* complained:

> Briton and Colonial have saved the Rand mines – for the Hebrew and the coolie. They cannot run the richest mines in the world with profit if they pay decent wages, so they propose to flood Johannesburg with Asiatics … Why not Chinamen or Hindoos for the Waihi mines, coolies in Coolgardie, blackfellows at Ballarat and Bendigo?? Bankruptcy? Fudge![67]

In January 1904, the newspaper again bemoaned that the Rand 'gold bugs' wanted to use Chinese labour to enrich themselves and put the 'British worker to extinction' in South Africa.[68] The view that Jewish interests were behind the Chinese labour scheme even became a talking point for the Liberal government. During a protest rally in Wellington organised by the Trades and Labour Council in February that year, Prime Minister Seddon, senior government ministers and the mayor of Wellington denounced the proposed importation of Chinese labour to South Africa. From the platform senior Liberal stalwart and Legislative Councillor Thomas Kennedy MacDonald thundered that 'powerful financial interests' lay behind the importation of Chinese labour: '… the great capitalists connected with the Rand mines, men who were practically foreigners, the great bulk of whom had not a drop of British blood in their veins, and who had no sympathies with British interests … These men wanted cheap labour and care nothing for creating a home for the British people.'[69]

William Naughton, president of the Trades and Labour Council, shared similar sentiments, arguing that while the war was fought 'for the purpose of painting South Africa red' for the British Empire, a group of rich 'German Jews, who had no sympathy with British aspirations', were now painting the Transvaal 'yellow'.[70] Lionel Terry was living in Wellington at the time and was likely to have been among the 500 people attending the protest. His thinking certainly demonstrated a parallel evolution, with Seddon's campaign part of the authorising context for his subsequent actions.

Days before the protest, the *New Zealand Times* published a column by Terry, who had cultivated a relationship with the paper and impressed it with his 'expertise' on the immigration question and his travels in southern Africa and around the Empire. The column reflected not only Terry's belief that alien immigration was the most urgent and catastrophic question but also his bewilderment at the lack of public reaction to it: 'It is strange, in view of the tremendous and ever-increasing influx of aliens into every part of the Empire, how few people recognise the terrible importance of this subject.'[71]

THE JEWISH SUPER-CONSPIRACY

For Terry, the introduction of non-British peoples would inevitably make the 'white man's' position 'unbearable', leading to violence and the need for military force to restore order. Reflecting on his time in British Columbia, he noted that this racial tension had led to the formation of the Oriental Commission that recommended against further immigration. Yet Terry's conundrum was why this advice was heeded neither in Canada nor in South Africa, and why the British Empire was not pursuing British racial interests as a matter of policy. He asked:

> In view of such cases as these, one might easily be persuaded to believe that a conspiracy existed between the Imperial Government and the capitalist classes to settle for ever the great labour problem by crushing the white man under the heel of the alien … [This] demonstrates the tremendous power possessed by Mammon, when it is able to come before the world and solemnly propose to rob the white man of his birth right and hand it over to the scum of the earth, disguised beneath the white cloak of a professedly Christian Government.[72]

Crucially, Terry concluded by stating that the greater danger facing the Empire came from within. It was difficult to rationalise how his beloved Empire could be so seemingly rotten, pursuing the interests of alien enemies at the expense of racial Britons. To resolve this, he turned to the notion of a Jewish super-conspiracy.[73] This was, he believed, more than just a small circle of Jews in Johannesburg subversively influencing imperial policy in southern Africa. Rather it was a coordinated and sophisticated operation controlling critical parts of British and imperial government and society, with thousands of people working in tandem to usurp control of the Empire. On his return to Northland in mid-1904 to work for the Lands and Surveys Department, Terry dived deep into conspiracy research, with the *Free Lance* remarking: '[H]e has received information indicating that the Rothschilds have been for many years "the private advisers of the British Cabinet." He wants to know what remuneration the Rothschilds get for acting as private directors of Imperial policy, and asserts that the great financiers were prime movers in the [Jameson] raid, the [Boer] war, and the [Transvaal] Chinese slavery outrage.'[74]

This final step in Terry's radicalisation was likely influenced by J.A. Hobson, an antisemite and leading English liberal critic of the Boer War. Among his attacks on sinister Jewish influences, Hobson's book *The War in South Africa* accused the Rothschilds and other Jewish interests of being its likely architects.[75] Hobson's conspiracist views became influential in liberal and left-wing circles within Britain, then percolated through the Empire. The book circulated widely in New Zealand in 1904, and one Dunedin war sceptic cited Hobson as evidence that the clique of Randlords was behind the war, dragging Britain 'into the position of shame and degradation it now occupies'.[76] The Adelaide *Herald* certainly picked up Hobson's argument in January 1904, noting that the Transvaal had fallen into 'the hands of a small group of international financiers, chiefly German in origin and Jewish in race'.[77] Terry may also have been influenced by *Munsey's Magazine*, an American glossy that published a lengthy and upbeat article late in 1903 on the world's most successful Jews, including the Rothschild family.[78] Copies of that issue circulated in New Zealand, with the *Herald* exclaiming with unrestrained and wild exaggeration that '[a]ll over the world, in all ranks and professions, at the very top is the Jew'.[79] The *Christchurch Star* and the *Lyttelton Times* followed up with a positive account of the 'Money Kings of Europe', suggesting that the Rothschilds had a positive influence on Britain's interests.[80]

THE JEWISH SHADOW OVER THE EMPIRE

Terry saw no such positive influence, and in July 1904 he self-published his political manifesto and poetic epic of the Jewish super-conspiracy – *The Shadow*. Dedicated to his 'Brother Britons', the booklet contained what Terry had envisaged as an apocalyptic call to arms, with an introduction that shares all the hallmarks of the antisemitic and conspiracist propaganda produced over the following decades by radicalised British patriots who lost faith in the established order and wanted to accelerate its collapse.[81] In this view, British democracy, the courts and government ministries were all under the control of hidden and malevolent forces; Terry himself declared 'that the Government of the British Empire is Jew-ridden and corrupt'.[82] Comparing the British establishment to a criminal enterprise, and citing notorious scandals of the time, he argued that the United Kingdom's most important institutions, from the army, Royal Navy, Parliament and the 'corrupt press', were agents of the conspiracy.[83] Continuing the metaphor of a corrupt company, the British Empire had as its 'managing director a Jew', and the conspirators were driven by the 'natural hatred existing between the various races of the world'. With aliens, notably Jews, allowed to live in the heart of the Empire, the racial struggle, Terry believed, had unleashed this criminal enterprise: 'The chief imports of the company include undesirable aliens, cheap labour, poverty, misery, crime, vice, disease, plague, and gold. Its chief exports are truth, purity, honour, health, justice, patriotism, and British blood.'[84]

REVOLUTIONARY CALL TO PURIFY THE EMPIRE

Canada features prominently in the stream-of-consciousness that is *The Shadow*'s introduction. Clearly not writing primarily for a New Zealand audience, Terry described Canada as 'undoubtedly' the Empire's 'most important colony'. But it had an 'internal rottenness' concealed by its dishonest newspapers, which explained why the 'truth' of the super-conspiracy was not known by the British people. He used the Transvaal labour question as further evidence that the British labouring classes – the Empire's 'lifeblood' – faced enslavement, the unnatural horrors of race-mixing and eventual 'slaughter'. To avert this apocalypse, Terry called for a revolution led by the King in which 'swift measures be taken to exclude and eradicate the alien element'.[85] Terry's belief in the need for a British racial revolution was longstanding. When appearing before the Oriental Commission in 1901, he 'dropped the remark' that he 'rather favoured revolutions' as a method to settle the 'Mongolian question'. He gave the Jameson Raid as an example of a justified revolution, an attempt to impose righteous British rule over the inferior Afrikaners.[86] For Terry, all that was lacking was a spark of awareness: 'And revolution is inevitable when Britons awaken to the peril which threatens them – provided that Britons [still] exist.'[87]

The Shadow failed to be the spark Terry longed for, despite his posting copies to newspapers around New Zealand. The *Mangonui County Times* was supportive in selling the pamphlet on his behalf, writing '[w]e strongly advise all Britons … to invest in a copy'.[88] But Terry's views were too much even for the anti-immigrant *Waikato Times*.[89] Hoping to incite an Empire-wide rebellion, Terry sent copies of *The Shadow* overseas. A newspaper in Sheffield reviewed it as a 'poetic profusion against alien immigration'.[90] An enthusiastic reviewer in Gundagai, rural New South Wales, recommended *The Shadow* as '… worth a place in your library. If you haven't got a library get the book and put it in company with the family prayer book. It is good reading for young Australians!'[91]

In Sydney a less sympathetic review described Terry's 'very jaundiced and bitter obsession, the effect of too much dwelling upon a thing which has its special evils, but does not dominate the body politic. Yet there is a certain power in it.'[92] But *The Shadow*'s power proved insufficient to prompt a strong following, mainly because Terry's views were more extreme than the public mood, which by 1905 had cooled somewhat over the Transvaal question. Nor were most New Zealanders ready to embrace the idea that their beloved Empire was corrupt. Dunedin's *Evening Star* reflected this divergence in temperaments: 'Mr Terry's chief fault is that he overstates his case. The world is not so bad nor so black as he paints it; all rich men are not scoundrels, and the labouring man is not, as far as we can discover, the very life of the Empire.'[93]

MARCH ON WELLINGTON

Frustrated by a lack of a public awakening, Terry decided to take more direct action. In July 1905 he abandoned the comfort of winterless Northland and embarked on foot for a two-month journey south, promoting *The Shadow* on his way. It is likely that Terry had already decided to commit some dramatic act in the capital. On reaching the Waikato, Terry was interviewed as to what had prompted his walk. After a lengthy discussion of *The Shadow*, the journalist commented: 'We are not going to tackle the task of criticising the book, but we should like to express the opinion that if what information it contains is true, and Mr Terry assures us that it is true, it is high time that the country woke up.'[94]

Terry's murder of Joe Kum Yung on 24 September was well thought out, and designed to provoke this racial awakening. Terry's knowledge of the media and politics, obtained in British Columbia, is evident in his planning for the murder four years later. Just as he sought to embarrass Dunsmuir, he likely timed his crime to influence the General Election set for 6 December 1905. Having stalked Chinatown for three days, he selected Yung, who was old and frail – someone who was low risk for fighting back, and whose death he believed would not offend public sensitivities. Terry's planning assumed that in the wake of the murder, the coronial inquiry, criminal trial and, especially, his inevitable sentencing to death by hanging would create a sensation. He knew that the execution of a Briton for the murder of a Chinese man would create outrage and stir public passions in the weeks before the election. As he had planned, the trial put the 'yellow peril' back into the forefront of political debate. Perhaps he also hoped that the publicity would strengthen Seddon's hand in the fight against the Sino-Semitic peril across the Empire, and trigger the racial revolution he believed was needed.[95] On the day of the murder, Terry wrote to the governor:

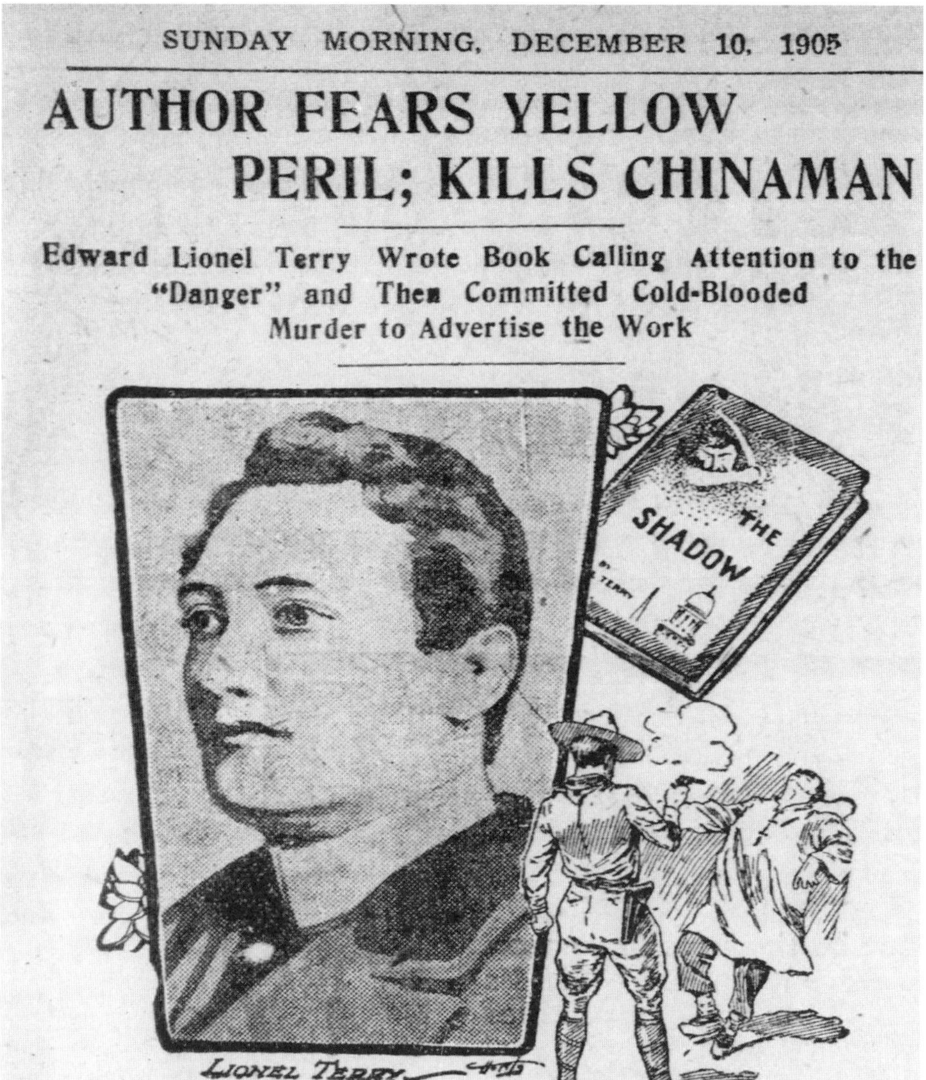

SUNDAY MORNING, DECEMBER 10, 1905

AUTHOR FEARS YELLOW PERIL; KILLS CHINAMAN

Edward Lionel Terry Wrote Book Calling Attention to the "Danger" and Then Committed Cold-Blooded Murder to Advertise the Work

Lionel Terry's murder of Joe Kum Yung was sensationalised by the international press, with this image featuring across the US. *Pittsburgh Press*, 10 December 1905, p. 5. www.newspapers.com

> I have decided to bring the matter before the public eye in a manner which will compel the attention it demands. I will not, under any consideration whatever, allow my brother Britons to be jeopardised by alien invaders, and to make this decision perfectly plain, I have this evening (Sunday) put a Chinaman to death …[96]

The next day, Terry handed himself in to the police to await a martyr's death – the spark to ignite the British workers' revolution and racial cleansing he longed for. But the Seddon government, anxious to avoid a public backlash, commuted his death sentence to life imprisonment. Its rationale was that Terry suffered from 'monomania', a fashionable diagnosis for obsession where the sufferer is said to be completely sane except for one topic that sends them into a 'craze of the most profound order'.[97] While the diagnosis was politically useful in neutralising the embarrassment of the crime, it infuriated Terry who in the years ahead staged 'one-man riots' in protest at his incarceration as a madman and not a political prisoner. By 1913, after years in solitary confinement, Terry had completely lost faith in the British people and the Empire, and wished for its destruction. For him, the 'Dodo Empire' with its 'manifold stupidities' did not deserve to survive, and because they had not heeded his warnings the British people and their King deserved to perish along with it.[98]

AFTERMATH

The Liberal government had contained the embarrassment caused by Terry's crime, but his trial had further charged the political landscape. While Terry had not been active in New Zealand's embryonic labour movement, he was seen by it as a kindred spirit. The *New Zealand Worker*, newspaper of the Independent Political Labour League, repeated Terry's claims that the British government had been manipulated to start a war with the Boers and then bring in Chinese workers – with the culprits being a 'horde of foreign Jews'.[99] The newspaper also combined its loathing of Jewish capitalists with a horror of Chinese disease and competition, calling for the exclusion of 'Chows' from the country and an economic boycott of those already here to protect the wages and businesses of racial Britons.[100] As a result, the movement was very sympathetic to Terry's plight, arguing that he should be acquitted in his murder trial and the crime classed as 'justifiable homicide', and even that the jury should pass a vote of thanks to Terry for his display of 'true patriotism'.[101]

While escaping the noose, Terry's rationale for murder – a Jewish super-conspiracy to ruin and replace the British people – would remain a thread of radical political

THE SOUTH AFRICAN RAND-LORDS' HARD LUCK.

'The South African Rand-Lords' Hard Luck'. The caption to this cartoon read: *Rand-Lord Bullenstein: Mine goodness gracious, Henry Bannerman! Vot in Himmel vos you do? How dare you rob me and ze uzzer British beoples of our cheap Chinese labour? Is zis ze way to dreat me—me vot 'as shed ze blood of my brodder vor you?*
While Terry was deemed insane and conveniently moved out of the headlines, the idea of a Jewish-Chinese menace to the British Empire remained popular.

New Zealand Free Lance, 20 January 1906, p. 7. https://paperspast.natlib.govt.nz

discourse in New Zealand in the coming decades. While he received decreasing and increasingly infrequent mention in the newspapers until his death in 1952, and was completely forgotten by the radical antisemitic movement that arose during the 1930s economic crisis, this amnesia ended in the 1980s. This was when New Zealand white supremacist Kerry Bolton extolled Terry in the British National Front's newspaper, describing him as a trailblazer of 'racial nationalism in New Zealand' whose manifesto 'continues to provide a sound basis for contemporary NZ nationalism, with its call for white world revolution'.[102] More recently, Bolton published a hagiography of Terry, praising him for exposing the capitalist conspiracy against white people, while also greatly embellishing his hero's backstory in an effort to salvage his reputation.[103] But while Bolton shares Terry's belief in the idea of a malevolent super-conspiracy against white people, he does not explain why, after more than a hundred years of trying, the plotters (or presumably their great-grandchildren) are struggling to bring their fiendish plans to fruition.

CONCLUSION

Terry's revolutionary racial socialism developed in distinct stages in his life. His radicalisation was generated by the contradictions of a global British Empire that had engulfed, conquered or drawn in many other races and cultures. For Terry and others, this success saw the British elite reap the rewards of free enterprise in exploiting the Empire's wealth. But he believed that this great wealth was gained at the expense of the ordinary British people who had fought for and worked the lands conquered, and that those who should be enjoying the dividends of Empire were becoming marginalised, vulnerable and struggling to survive. This contradiction led him to adopt conspiratorialist thinking and, as his views hardened, his rhetoric became more violent. Increasingly, he described his imagined racial enemies in non-human terms.

Importantly, Terry was no mere outlier. His views were widely held, and in New Zealand their evolution was likely encouraged by the Seddon Liberal government, whose anti-Asian and antisemitic opposition to the Transvaal question likely provided an authorising context for Terry's final stage of radicalisation. His last step into extremism saw him espousing the need to destroy the existing order through a racial revolution, the spark for which would be his martyrdom. In this Terry was a portent of things to come. The decades ahead would see others radicalised by similar beliefs in super-conspiracies and shadowy racial struggles. It was for this complex rationale, and not a mere racial hatred, that Joe Kum Yung was murdered.

CHAPTER FOUR

'Devils are in demand'

Arthur Desmond's 'Might Is Right' and its present-day influence on the far right

MARK DERBY

THE PROTO-FASCIST MANIFESTO *Might Is Right*, first published in the late nineteenth century, is, according to a leading US researcher of the far right, today 'widely popular … among ethnocentric white nationalists of all levels, from suit-and-tie white supremacists to neo-Nazis'.[1] Another researcher has described *Might Is Right* as 'required reading' among white supremacist organisations, particularly neo-Aryan groups on the far right, since at least the 1980s.[2] The manifesto gained sudden notoriety with the wider public in July 2019, when 19-year-old Santino Legan urged his Instagram followers to 'Read *Might Is Right*.' He then travelled to the Gilroy Garlic Festival in California, an annual celebration of the town's main crop. Legan fired an automatic weapon into the crowd, apparently at random, killing three people and wounding 17.[3] The US technology company Amazon withdrew all editions of *Might Is Right* from sale in early 2020, presumably in response to this shooting.

The first edition of *Might Is Right* appeared in Chicago in 1896 under the title *The Philosophy of Power* and the nom-de-plume Ragnar Redbeard. The author's real identity has been much debated and is still not conclusively established. However, this remarkably enduring document was almost certainly written by a former farm worker from Hawke's Bay, New Zealand, who then went by the name Arthur Desmond. He later moved to Australia and eventually to the US, where his book acquired a degree of acclaim in its author's own lifetime, when it appealed primarily to groups on the far left of the labour movement.

After Desmond's death in 1929, *Might Is Right* sank into obscurity for several decades. Since the 1980s, however, it has been widely disseminated in both hard-

THE SPEAKER OF THE EVENING.

copy and digital formats as an *urtext* for elements of the extreme right, especially within neo-pagan/Aryan groups. New editions appear almost annually. *Might Is Right* is distributed and discussed on far-right websites such as 4chan, Stormfront and The Daily Stormer. One group, the Redbeard Right, is explicitly 'dedicated to the dissemination of The Philosophy of Power as articulated by Ragnar RedBeard and dissident thinkers'.[4]

OPPOSITE: A tall man with a red beard believed to be Arthur Desmond, 'declaiming on the subject "Might Is Right"' in Chicago's Union Square auditorium, 1896.
Chicago Chronicle, 26 April 1896, p. 3. www.newspapers.com

This chapter will present evidence for Arthur Desmond's authorship of *Might Is Right*, and trace the passage of the book's ideological influence from one extreme of the political spectrum to the other.[5]

'REPRESENTATIVE OF THE SMALL SETTLER AND THE WORKING MAN' – EARLY YEARS IN NEW ZEALAND

Practically the only assertion about the so-called Arthur Desmond that can be made with full confidence is that he was a deliberately mysterious character who systematically concealed aspects of his identity and his past, including the year and country of his birth and his original given name. Nevertheless, it appears highly likely that he was born around 1860 of Irish and English parentage, and was raised in New Zealand from a young age. By the 1880s he was working as a drover, shepherd and musterer on sheep stations in Hawke's Bay, and calling himself Arthur Desmond. Under that name, and aged about 25, he contested the parliamentary seat of Hawke's Bay in the 1884 General Election as 'a representative of the small settler and the working man'.[6]

In a succession of fiery speeches and wordy pamphlets, Desmond campaigned for a capital gains tax, state expenditure on public works, votes for women and an eight-hour working day for farm labourers like himself. The public response to his candidature ran from admiration to ridicule, and Desmond was roundly defeated and then lost a court case over his unpaid election expenses.[7] Undaunted, he put himself forward at the next election three years later, again failing to take the Hawke's Bay seat but increasing his vote and broadening his reputation as a left-wing firebrand.[8]

Two years later, in 1889, his public image took an unexpected turn. The prophet and former guerrilla leader Te Kooti, newly pardoned by the government, proposed to visit his followers in the small Hawke's Bay settlement of Te Karaka. A handsome new meeting house was built there to welcome him and his cavalcade of unarmed supporters, but the visit was vehemently opposed by the non-Māori settler community who recalled atrocities committed in the district by Te Kooti and his troops 20 years earlier. At packed and noisy public meetings, the only voice raised in support of Te Kooti's right to return to Hawke's Bay was Desmond's.[9] Eventually the settlers prevailed, and Te Kooti was arrested before he could reach Te Karaka.[10]

The disheartened Desmond composed a defiant 'Song of Te Kooti', which was published in the prestigious Sydney magazine the *Bulletin*. One stanza reads:

> They tried to enslave us, to trample us down
> Like the millions that serve them in field and in town
> But the sapling that's bended when freed will rebound
> Exult for Te Kooti – e ha![11]

Te Kooti remains one of the most controversial figures in New Zealand history – a superb guerrilla fighter and military leader who also ordered, and perhaps participated in, the murder of unarmed men, women and children, Māori as well as Pākehā. Desmond himself was very young when those events took place, but he would certainly have learned of them, perhaps from Māori workmates on the Hawke's Bay sheep stations where he worked. He appears to have revered Te Kooti not only in his latter-day persona as a prophetic leader but also as the much younger bush fighter and brutal opponent of the Crown.

Desmond is far from the only Pākehā New Zealander to idealise Te Kooti's actions – well-regarded academics have also done so, although from the safer stance of historical distance. Desmond, perhaps uniquely among Pākehā, openly and courageously championed Te Kooti in the rebel's own lifetime. It seems very possible that it was Te Kooti's uncompromising ferocity that inspired this alienated, impressionable and ambitious young farm worker to develop a political philosophy that justified and advocated for sheer physical violence to overcome personal as well as political repression.

The furore aroused by Desmond's support for Te Kooti forced him to abandon his local political aspirations and drift north to work in the timber industry in the King Country and Northland. From tented camps in the bush, he wrote poems, articles and letters incessantly, especially for the newly formed cultural journal *Zealandia*. Its June 1890 issue published his essay 'Christ as a social reformer', which begins with conventional Christian socialist arguments and ends with the strident declaration that: 'What the world wants today is a MAN – a heroic champion of the right – a ruthless demolisher of age-old shams … whose clarion call shall ring around the world, inspiring millions to enlist beneath the standard of a new crusade and go forth to battle unto death for the rights of man – for the cause of the poor.'[12]

This and other writings of Desmond's attracted the support of Sir George Grey, a former governor and premier of New Zealand, and by 1890 a radical backbencher. Desmond exploited this celebrity endorsement for all it was worth.

When the 1890 maritime strike erupted in Auckland, Desmond emerged in that city as a hardened labour organiser and propagandist. The *Auckland Star* printed his prediction of the dispute's outcome in terms that now regularly recurred in his work: 'The army of labour is wheeling and concentrating in mighty battalions ... But the World Leader, the Messiah of the poor and oppressed, has not yet appeared. Nevertheless, he will come when the hour has tolled, and the decisive blow has to be struck ... He shall be a true king ... a champion of the 'held in bondage', a smiter of falsehood, a demolisher of wrong.'[13]

In this period, Desmond is believed to have produced 25 copies of a typewritten pamphlet titled *Might Is Right – logic of to-day* under the nom-de-plume Redbeard ('Ragnar' would be added a few years later.)[14] He claimed elsewhere that his book began to take shape even earlier, in the sour aftermath of his failed 1887 parliamentary bid.[15]

By October 1890, Desmond succeeded in launching a professionally produced radical weekly journal, the *Tribune*, supplying most of the content himself. Eight vociferous issues appeared before the paper collapsed following his ignominious ejection from the Queen Street editorial office he had been occupying illegally. By then he had also suffered a succession of other self-inflicted misfortunes. His essay 'Christ as a social reformer' was shown to have been largely plagiarised from a US journal. He forged documents to implicate a high-profile politician in corruption, who then sued him for libel. The would-be labour journalist was, therefore, forced to flee New Zealand for Australia. Just before he left the country, disgraced, dispirited and 'down and out', he handed a set of back copies of the *Tribune* to the Liberal MP William Tanner for safekeeping until he could reclaim them 'in happier times'. Tanner recalled him as 'genuinely able, poetic, ardent and Irish'.[16]

Desmond never returned to New Zealand to collect those back issues, but he eventually encountered happier times elsewhere. Over the next 20 years he realised his ambition to be recognised as an influential writer, and acquired a degree of renown, if not wealth. In that period he also underwent an ideological transformation, from a left-liberal champion of the working class and dispossessed Māori to a vehemently antisemitic, racist and misogynist autocrat. This progression was gradual, and not as

THE TYRANNY OF CAPITAL AGAIN.
Eviction of Desmond by Ewington. The tripe-boom in danger of bursting.

Desmond, editor of the short-lived *Tribune* newspaper, is unceremoniously ejected from his squatted editorial office, in this cartoon from a popular weekly.

Observer, 22 November 1890, p. 16. https://paperspast.natlib.govt.nz

diametrical as it might now appear. Desmond never repudiated the views he espoused in New Zealand – rather, he refined and intensified them, and retained many of his early supporters as he traversed the political spectrum.

'A POET AND A DWELLER IN BOHEMIA' – DESMOND IN AUSTRALIA

From New Zealand Desmond first travelled to Sydney, hoping to outrun the reputation he had acquired in Auckland as a dishonest and unreliable loudmouth. He soon became a central figure among the writers, radicals and visionaries who gathered at William McNamara's socialist bookshop in Castlereagh Street. They included Billy Hughes and Alfred Deakin, both future Australian prime ministers; William Holman and Jack Lang, both future premiers of New South Wales; and Harry Holland, later a leader of the New Zealand Labour Party. Another habitué of the bookshop, who became a close friend of Desmond's, was Henry Lawson, at that time a prolific but little-known writer and journalist. Hughes described Desmond as: 'in appearance every inch a poet and a dweller in Bohemia. He was a stout figure of a man and might have stepped straight out of the Latin Quarter with his fresh complexion, blue eyes and beautiful brown beard; he always affected one of those black, broad-brimmed flop hats … He was a fine poet, and when sober a most entertaining fellow.'[17]

Within months of arriving in Sydney, this literary chameleon was contributing well-informed articles on local financial dealings to the *Bulletin* and other papers. When the *Bulletin* stopped publishing him for fear of libel suits, Desmond founded his own muckraking scandal sheet, *Hard Cash – a magazine of finance, politics and religion*, which tracked the string of business collapses then afflicting the city. Scheming Jews, Desmond wrote, were at the root of the financial crisis. His antisemitism was blatant even by the standards of his day, yet it probably lost him no support among his readers. Such views were regrettably common among nineteenth-century radicals in Australia and elsewhere.

Desmond's admiration for an imagined all-powerful leader, untroubled by conscience, led him to declare in *Hard Cash* that 'the majority of men are cowards – therefore they are slaves. That is heresy, but it's true.'[18] In parallel with his prolific journalism, he continued to expand the personal manifesto he had first sketched in Auckland. An Australian colleague, Julian Stuart, recalled that, 'I ridiculed Desmond for wasting his time writing "Might Is Right" and begged him to keep on writing poetry instead.'[19]

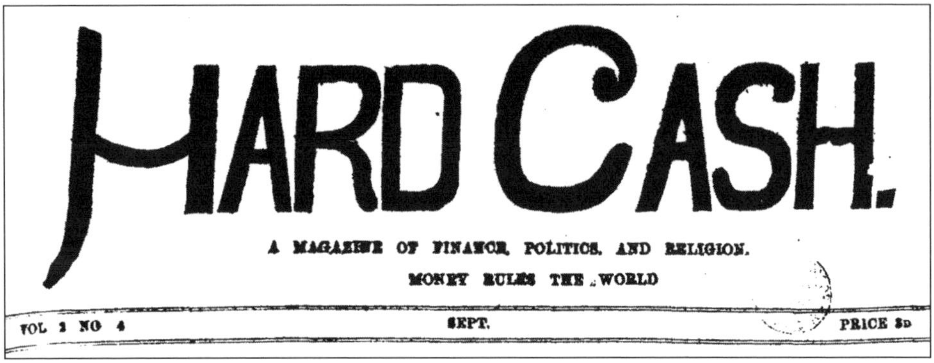
HARD CASH.

A MAGAZINE OF FINANCE, POLITICS, AND RELIGION.

MONEY RULES THE WORLD

VOL 3 NO 4 SEPT. PRICE 3D

Crudely produced and scabrous but remarkably influential – Desmond's self-published Sydney magazine of 'finance, politics and religion'. *Hard Cash*, vol. 3, September 1893. www.reasoninrevolt.net.au

Desmond's earlier socialism had now transmuted into a despotic strain of anarchism, strongly influenced by Nietzsche but particularly by Max Stirner, a more obscure German philosopher. Stirner's major work, *Der Einzige und sein Eigentum* (*The ego and its own*), first published in 1844, employed the phrase 'Might is right' as an expression of its author's 'egoist' world-view. Stirner may, therefore, have given Desmond the title and much of the ideological underpinning for his own magnum opus.

The police succeeded in shutting down *Hard Cash* in late 1893, and Desmond returned to the street-level agitation he had practised in Auckland during the 1890 strike. In Sydney, he led theatrical protests by the city's army of homeless and unemployed citizens, and provided for them by managing a hostel and soup kitchen. According to Australian author Vance Marshall, in this period Desmond's 'finger was traceable in every decisive movement associated with the working class'.[20] Throughout 1894 he also continued to exercise his talents for scabrous journalism and incendiary verse. He served as the in-house poet for the journal *Justice*, was a frequent contributor to other radical publications, and founded two more short-lived financial journals. Inevitably, however, the threat of multiple libel suits and imminent arrest drove him to again flee overseas.

'MIGHTY MEN OF VALOR' – DESMOND IN THE UNITED STATES

Arthur Desmond's movements and enterprises in the years after he left Australia shade swiftly into pure conjecture. He is most reliably traced through surviving copies of his later publications, and even these are contestable since he wrote under a bewildering collection of pseudonyms and repeatedly republished the same work under a new title. He appears to have travelled first to England, where he published various inflammatory verses, before sailing to the US and, by 1896, finding a new home in Chicago. In that year the first edition of *Might Is Right* (re-titled *The Survival of the Fittest, or the Philosophy of Power*) was published in Chicago under the neo-Viking pseudonym of Ragnar Redbeard, which Desmond had used periodically since his days in Sydney.[21] The name almost certainly derives from *ragnarök*, the apocalypse of Norse mythology. A revised edition under the title *Might Is Right* appeared in London in 1898. The author was then given as Arthur Uing, a variant of Desmond's mother's maiden name, Ewing. At least three further editions appeared in the author's lifetime, each one a substantial revision of the last.

Finally free to publish without editorial constraints or charges of libel or plagiarism, Desmond produced a cascade of bile, an incoherent doctrine of individual will and sublime force. As Ragnar Redbeard, he argued that true egalitarianism cannot exist and that the white race is innately biologically superior to other races. This is the doctrine of social Darwinism, the idea that certain races or ethnicities are inherently better equipped for survival than others. Racial equality is dismissed as an 'ignoble slave-shibboleth', and Redbeard instead glorifies the 'battle-blooded,' the 'destroyers of false hope,' 'they who believe in nothing.'[22]

Might Is Right, in each of its successive manifestations, incorporated and extended Desmond's large body of earlier writings and speeches, and studded them with fragments by other writers, poets, philosophers and political leaders he admired, often without attribution. Many of these quotations reveal the author's inadequate understanding of his sources, especially in his simplistic rendering of scientific principles in fields such as anthropology. Much of this remarkable work is written in the form of bombastic prose-poetry. *Might Is Right* celebrates the actions of 'mighty men of valor, great destroyers; destroyers of all that is vile, angels of death ... He who would rule the coming age must be hard, cruel, and deliberately intrepid, for softness assails not successfully the idols of the multitude.'[23] Those discredited idols, its author repeatedly avers, include all established religions but particularly New Testament

Christianity. He dismisses Christian ethics as 'oriental legerdemain' and declares, 'We are sick unto nausea of the "good Lord Jesus" … We are tired to death of "Equality." Gods are at a discount, devils are in demand.'[24]

Seeking the celebrity by association that he had once acquired from Sir George Grey, Desmond sent a copy of the first edition of *Might Is Right* to the towering literary figure of the age, the saintly Christian anarchist Leo Tolstoy. He was rewarded with a horrified précis in Tolstoy's 1898 essay collection *What is Art?* Although the pacifist Russian was openly appalled at the 'denial of morality and the laudation of vice' in Desmond's work, this recognition surely represents the apotheosis of the one-time drover's literary ambitions.[25]

Other early readers of the book were less prominent but more adulatory. In Desmond's own lifetime, sections of the Industrial Workers of the World, an obstreperous transnational labour movement also known as the IWW or the Wobblies, were among his most ardent admirers. A New Orleans Wobbly newspaper, *The Voice of the People*, displayed the term 'Might Is Right' on its masthead. In a 1913 issue that gave news of strike actions around the world, including in far-off New Zealand, the paper offered Desmond's book for sale at 50 cents a copy, describing it as 'one of the most tremendous books ever printed. Boldly, aye, savagely, Redbeard challenges the maudlin sentimentality and hypocrisy of the slave-made world, proclaiming … "The race IS to the swift, the battle to the strong."'[26] Elements of the anarchist and far-left labour movements offered other tributes to *Might Is Right* throughout the 1910s and 1920s, causing the historian Rachel Barrowman to conclude that Arthur Desmond 'may claim to be the only New Zealander to have exerted an ideological influence on the international labour movement'.[27]

That ideological influence, paradoxically, centred on a disdainful rejection of mass action. *Might Is Right* proclaimed that collective organisations such as unions appealed only to the sheep-like, and that the conscience-free hyper-male the book celebrated should deal with them as does the butcher or the wolf. This vitriolic totalitarianism has led several writers to conclude that the Chicago-based Desmond entirely renounced the progressive opinions of the plucky Hawke's Bay underdog, the champion of Auckland's proletariat and the crusading Sydney journalist of his past. Yet several common threads can be traced from even his earliest writings, and other political movements and philosophies of the same period demonstrate a similarly unfortunate regression. Across the English-speaking world, a series of crushing political defeats for the militant labour movement in the early twentieth century led some deeply disillusioned radicals to move so far to the left that they dropped off the edge. These embittered intransigents came to regard the mass of the union movement with the contempt shown by their most extreme opponents, and *Might Is Right*'s toxic bigotry and pathological grandiosity evidently offered them a redemptive credo.

Although his book went through at least five editions in his lifetime and he acquired a measure of notoriety as a galvanising literary voice, Desmond does not appear to have prospered from his writing. He was employed variously in later life by a Chicago confectionary company, as a freelance advertising salesman and as owner-manager of a second-hand bookshop. As always, he concealed and enhanced his circumstances by inventing a gaudy public persona. He awarded himself a doctorate in law from the University of Chicago, and cultivated rumours of his courage, wealth and political influence. He was said to have fought in the Boer War, reported for a New York paper on the Russo-Japanese War, and owned a vast hunting estate in Montana.[28] These myths flourished and intertwined until very little about his final years could be believed. Some claimed he was killed in Mexico with Pancho Villa in 1911; others nominated Palestine while serving with General Allenby during World War I. The most plausible and prosaic version of his death is from a stroke in 1929 while running his Chicago bookshop.

DESMOND'S PRESENT-DAY INFLUENCE

Following its author's death, *Might Is Right* fell into obscurity for several decades. It resurfaced in the late 1960s in a milieu far removed from the boisterous, aggressively proletarian and insurrectionary world of the Wobblies and their middle-class partisans. As an enthusiastic plagiarist himself, Desmond may have appreciated the irony that his work was plagiarised by the occult entrepreneur and fabulist Anton LaVey for his best-selling *The Satanic Bible*, first published in 1969.[29] In haste to meet a publisher's deadline, LaVey took sections of 'an obscure, turn-of-the-century political tract' (apparently the 1910 edition of *Might Is Right*) and used these, without attribution, as the prologue to his own book.[30]

The modish San Francisco Satanists who first read *The Satanic Bible* may have missed the connection with Desmond and his work, but its influence soon spread to other netherworld denizens such as neo-Viking cultists. By the 1980s LaVey himself was said to be 'flirting with the trappings of Nazism and the Ku Klux Klan' and 'drawing heavily on the Nietzschian concept of the *übermensch* as the idealized Satanist'.[31] Several new editions of *Might Is Right* appeared in the 1970s and 1980s as it gained a reputation within the more esoteric realms of the far right.

By the early 1990s a symbolic landmark was reached when Desmond's manifesto returned to the country where he first began declaiming in print. In 1992, New Zealand's most prominent propagandist of the far right, Kerry Bolton, published a local edition of *Might Is Right* under his own imprint, Realist Publications. He dedicated it to 'this emerging generation of "Iron Youth," that they may grasp the opportunity to take the Future, and to History's warrior elite of all nations'.[32] Bolton had been attracted to neo-Nazi and similar movements since his teenage years, and joined groups such as the New Zealand National Front in the 1970s. By 1981, he lived in Christchurch where, together with former National Front leader David Crawford, he founded the New Zealand branch of the Church of Odin, described as exclusively for whites 'of non-Jewish descent'.[33] This transition from purely political movements of the far right, such as the National Front, into those which emphasised mystical and occult experiences led him to mentors such as LaVey, who had reached the same standpoint from the opposite direction. Bolton eventually formed a New Zealand branch of LaVey's neo-Satanist cult, the Order of the Left Hand Path, largely due to 'the potential that Satanism had for disseminating neo-Nazism'.[34]

To a diligent apostle of reaction such as Bolton, *Might Is Right* may have seemed the ideal synthesis of far-right and neo-pagan doctrines. In his self-published magazine *The Heretic*, which also carried advertising for an English neo-Nazi Nordic/satanic group, Bolton described *Might Is Right* as standing alongside Nietzsche's best-known works, and as one of 'the most heretical works of the last one hundred years … Herein are challenged and demolished all the sacred cows of Desmond's and our own time: Christianity, humanitarianism, pacifism, egalitarianism.'[35]

Arthur Desmond and his latter-day disciple Kerry Bolton have several intriguing features in common. One is a predilection for exotic pseudonyms – like Desmond, Bolton published work under various, often Nordic-sounding names such as Wulf Grimwald. Both men were compulsively literate, and promulgated their opinions in print at every opportunity, usually through self-published and short-lived periodicals for want of better outlets. Unlike Desmond, however, Bolton appears to have reassessed some of his critical judgements in later life. In early 2020, on the white nationalist website 'Countercurrents', he described *Might Is Right* as '[a] work of stunning banality. Holding this up as any kind of philosophical background for the Right is appalling. Nihilism and misanthropy … haven't we got enough of that in society already?'[36]

AUTHORSHIP

One significant feature of *Might Is Right* that Bolton seems never to have queried is the identity of its author. Perhaps prompted by nationalist fellow-feeling, he accepted without question that Ragnar Redbeard was a nom-de-plume for Arthur Desmond, a New Zealander. Other readers of the book, especially those in the US and the United Kingdom, have speculated at length that Ragnar Redbeard was actually the pen name of a more distinguished writer. Desmond's lifelong practice of concealing and reinventing his identity laid fertile ground for such speculations.

One suggested candidate for the book's authorship is Ambrose Bierce, the US author of celebrated works such as the satirical *Devil's Dictionary* and much fiercely partisan journalism. His greatest literary output coincided with the first publication of *Might Is Right*, and he led the adventurous life Arthur Desmond aspired to, vanishing mysteriously in 1913 while accompanying Pancho Villa's insurrectionary forces in Mexico.[37] Some admirers of *Might Is Right* have maintained that its author suffered a similar fate, furthering claims that Bierce wrote the book. However, while Ambrose Bierce was a fervent agnostic, he did not share Ragnar Redbeard's other fixations and was evidently a much more elegant and witty writer.

Another US writer, the novelist, radical socialist and antisemite Jack London (real name John Chaney), is at first sight a somewhat stronger candidate for the authorship of *Might Is Right*. According to Rodger Jacobs, an authority on London's literary output, after this suggestion first appeared in the early twentieth century, 'the canard spread with the tenacious fury of an urban myth and it continues to be repeated to this day'.[38] In 1999, the canard appeared in a 'Millennial Wotansvolk' edition of *Might Is Right* edited by Katja Lane, the wife of Ku Klux Klan and Aryan Nations leader David Lane who was then imprisoned for several racially motivated crimes including murder.[39] In her introduction to that edition, Ms Lane acknowledged that Ragnar Redbeard's true identity 'remains an enigmatic issue'. Nevertheless, it became 'convincingly clear' to her while editing the book that substantial portions were written by Jack London, whom she described as 'a purely artistic genius'.[40]

In a 1999 essay, Jacobs convincingly debunked that conclusion. He dismissed *Might Is Right* itself as 'a silly love poem to the idea of social Darwinism … favored by anarchists, white supremacists, Stalinists, socialists, Satanists, and high school outcasts toting automatic weapons in their backpacks'.[41] He noted that in 1896, when the book was first published in Chicago, Jack London completed his first and only year of university – in California. He had yet to find his own literary voice and was writing 'embarrassingly bad triolets, humorous verse, and sonnets that newspapers and magazines were rejecting as fast as he was submitting them … Couple all of this with the fact that young Jack London had yet to explore the worlds of Fredric Nietzsche and Herbert Spencer and it's not too difficult to arrive at the irrefutable conclusion that London was not Ragnar Redbeard.'[42]

On the other hand, evidence for Arthur Desmond's authorship of *Might Is Right* is abundant and compelling. In addition to the biographical evidence given earlier, the text is riddled with references to Māori custom and traditions, a subject Desmond was known to have studied in some depth. Māori, in fact, appear to be the only non-white race *Might Is Right* addresses with respect, albeit in condescending terms, such as this defence of the practice of ritual cannibalism:

> Very intelligent New Zealand aboriginals may still be found, who describe with much apparent gusto, how (in comparatively recent dates) they satiated their ravenous hunger, by banqueting all night upon the grilled flesh of foemen they had tomahawked during the day. Neither is it uncommon to hear tattooed old veterans tell how war-captives were penned up like cattle and fattened upon each other, until required for the tribal oven (formed of red-hot stones, paved into an oval hollow in the ground) … The Maoris also have a tradition that if a man kills and eats his enemy, he by doing so, absorbs all the dead man's vitality, strength and courage.[43]

Desmond's unacknowledged quotation from a poem, 'In the Days When the World Was Wide', by his old friend and admirer Henry Lawson, whose work was little known beyond Australasia when *Might Is Right* first appeared, is likewise indicative of his authorship.[44]

Of the entire body of Arthur Desmond's published work, undoubtedly impressive in quantity if not in quality, *Might Is Right*, despite its shambling grandiloquence, is the only example that continues to be read today. It has remained in print for over a century through the dedication of a succession of publishers working well outside the literary mainstream. As the US researcher Kitty Shropshire noted, the work 'has found an audience amongst three niche print cultures: individualist anarchists, occultists, and white nationalists'.[45]

While best known today for its influence among the last of these groups, all three continue to admire, reproduce and circulate Desmond's magnum opus. As recently as 2019 the Union of Egoists, dedicated to the writing and ideas of right-wing or 'egoist' anarchism, published a heavily annotated 'authoritative edition' of *Might Is Right*.[46] Among occultists and white nationalists, the book's following appears to be growing stronger, especially with young, male and socially alienated members of far-right groups in the US and elsewhere. Shropshire has found that *Might Is Right* 'seems to have been particularly influential amongst those who identified with neo-paganism/Aryanism' such as the neo-Nazi National Alliance, which offers the book for sale through its website.[47]

Shropshire noted that some sections of this disparate readership found the ideological proximity of others uncomfortable. Katya Lane's introduction to the 1999 'Millennial Wotansvolk' edition, she found, 'downplayed *Might Is Right*'s historic association with anarchism and instead emphasised the racist nature of its social Darwinism, suggesting that reading *Might Is Right* would help "Aryan" men rediscover their "Nature-ordained manhood".'[48] Others have succeeded in presenting the book to more than one of its ultra-marginal constituencies simultaneously. US Church of Satan member Shane Bugbee published the 1996 'centennial edition' complete with commentaries by super-Satanist Anton LaVey and neo-Nazi Katya Lane. Bugbee then reprinted this edition in 2003 and promoted it on the online radio station radiofreesatan.com, alongside a founder of the White Aryan Resistance and a member of the white power band RaHoWa ('Racial Holy War'), whose 1995 album *Cult of the Holy War* includes lyrics derived from passages in *Might Is Right*.[49]

Amazon's recent decision to cease distributing Desmond's book is unlikely to restrict its availability. Innovations in digital publishing have seen new editions appear almost every year in the twenty-first century in hardcover, paperback and through print-on-demand. Self-produced audiobook versions are available, as are German, Finnish, French, Spanish and other translated editions. Far-right internet communities such as 8chan and Stormfront supply PDF copies for digital download, along with unintentionally hilarious analyses of the book's relevance to the present day. Among their favoured chat-room topics is Ragnar Redbeard's ultra-misogynist attitude towards women, who he contends 'must be held in thorough subjection'.[50] This stance aligns with that of the modern Incel ('involuntary celibate') movement, and may provide young men with intellectual justification for misogynist anger, violence against women and even acts of terrorism.

Santino Legan's endorsement of *Might Is Right* immediately before the 2019 Gilroy Garlic Festival shooting drove other admirers of the book to hastily qualify their approbation. Legan's Facebook posts included messages forwarded from the Redbeard Right website, along with passages quoted directly from *Might Is Right*. The Redbeard Right group responded that they 'do not disavow his actions but we are not responsible for the actions of those who read our posts. We do not encourage our readers to commit violence. We do not condone what he did – his actions contributed nothing to our cause of white wellbeing.' This unusually equivocal reaction to a random mass shooting may still be read on the group's website.[51]

CONCLUSION

Almost a century after his death Arthur Desmond remains an intriguing, contradictory figure, and large parts of his life story are uncertain and disputed. His authorship of *Might Is Right*, however, in all its various editions and alternative titles, seems indisputable to this writer. The only one of Desmond's many publications that is still read and reprinted today, this book has become a primary text and inspiration for the white nationalist movement in the US and elsewhere.

What is known of its author's life reveals that he was a serial plagiarist and fabulist with a long record of dishonesty, bankruptcy and betrayal. He failed to live up to the image he celebrated in *Might Is Right* of an all-conquering, fearless and ruthless *übermensch*. It is hoped that by linking *Might Is Right* to its real author and his unimpressive personal history, readers of Desmond's preposterous magnum opus will be less inclined to regard it as a manual to live by.

PART 2
The ideological cauldron of the interwar years

CHAPTER FIVE

'Under Which Flag?'

Radical anti-socialist groups in the interwar period

ELIZABETH WARD

IN JUNE 1914, the cover of the Reform Party newspaper, *Light and Liberty*, was emblazoned with the heading 'Under Which Flag?' Drawing on the Great Strike at the end of 1913, editor E.A. James was posing the question: did voters want to live under the New Zealand and British flags of order and freedom, or the revolutionary flag of the Red Federation and its allies, the Wardite Liberals?[1] This implied that the connection between the Liberal Party and the more radical parts of the labour movement had sinister undertones. However, the events of World War I, including the formation of the New Zealand Labour Party in 1916 and the Bolshevik revolution in October 1917, led some across the conservative political spectrum to believe that the question 'Under Which Flag?' had wider implications. They claimed, often with no shortage of hyperbolic language, that those who wanted to bring New Zealand under the 'revolutionary' flag of socialism were part of a wider international conspiracy. Radical anti-socialists believed that socialists wanted not only to cause turmoil in New Zealand but also to bring down the entire British Empire, endangering everything that had been gained from winning the Great War. For them, the idea of 'Under Which Flag?' took on a deeper meaning. The fight was about much more than keeping the Labour Party out of office. For these groups, the choice was clear: tolerate socialism and New Zealand would be forced under 'the "Red Flag" of anarchy and terrorism'.[2]

Although anti-socialism, and anti-communism specifically, are most often associated with the early Cold War period, radical anti-socialist groups also flourished between the wars. During this period, socialism was used as a by-word for supposedly dangerous and revolutionary elements in society. It was not necessarily linked to the political theory of socialism or communism; instead, radical anti-socialist groups believed that what they called socialism was a front for a wider revolutionary plot. Therefore, they saw any movement that challenged the status quo as being 'socialist'. If the movement did not outwardly declare socialism, then radical anti-socialists accused them of hiding it. Given that the interwar period was one of social instability and change, radical anti-socialist groups were able to stoke public fears by exploiting an established distrust of socialism built by events before World War I, such as the Great Strike of 1913. The stability of the British Empire was generally thought to be important to New Zealand, where the memory of the great personal sacrifices made on behalf of the Empire during the war was still fresh. The use of the term 'Empire' by radical anti-socialist groups, therefore, symbolised order, freedom and democratic government. The Empire was also economically important, with Britain providing a preferential market for a significant proportion of this country's primary produce. New Zealand's identity also rested on its place in the Empire, with most New Zealanders still considering Britain the centre of culture.[3] The idea that socialists had a hidden agenda to destroy the British Empire thus found fertile ground.

When the Labour Party was formed in 1916, there was some genuine puzzlement at the need for a party that represented 'labour'.[4] Both the Liberal and Reform parties claimed to represent 'sane labour' and decried the idea that any 'special' representation of labour was needed.[5] The question then arose: if workers were adequately represented by existing political parties and other interest groups, why was the Labour Party needed? The answer from radical anti-socialist groups was that the Labour Party was not what it appeared to be. As the interwar period progressed, radical anti-socialist groups also targeted various unions, the Communist Party and anti-war movements, and often grossly inflated their influence. The actual beliefs or size of these movements were irrelevant. They believed that agents of these international movements could appear at any time, so were alert to what they described as 'socialist tendencies'. These had very little to do with socialism as a theory or political movement: they were a symbol of the corruption of postwar society, seditious activity and, ultimately, world revolution. Because there was already popular suspicion of socialism, radical anti-socialist groups were able to influence mainstream political discourse – notably in publicity material produced by the governing Reform Party.[6] Such efforts to sow fear and intolerance were so successful that in 1935 Robert Masters, the chief whip of the outgoing coalition government, burned many government papers because he distrusted the motives of the incoming Labour Party.[7]

This chapter examines three New Zealand groups that promoted radical anti-socialist ideas. Two of them, the Protestant Political Association (PPA) and Loyal Citizens League, were most active between 1919 and 1921. The New Zealand Welfare League, the longest-running and most effective radical anti-socialist group of the interwar period, will be the main focus of discussion. All of them believed that socialism was more than a political theory, and all of them established international connections. The transnational nature of radical anti-socialist movements was evident from the outset.

Despite their influence on mainstream political discourse (particularly the Welfare League), there has been little research on radical anti-socialist groups in New Zealand. An article published in 1969 discussed the Welfare League, and a thesis on the early years of the PPA was completed in 1966.[8] Most scholars have studied radical anti-socialist groups as part of a wider interwar radical right, or as part of the interwar political framework. Matthew Cunningham and Marinus La Rooij have researched interwar radical anti-socialists, while Barry Gustafson mentioned the Welfare League's role in the 1919 election and the PPA's anti-Labour Party stance.[9] However, the connection that the PPA drew between socialism, the Labour Party and the Catholic Church is usually mentioned within the context of sectarianism rather than anti-socialism.[10]

The basis for the distrust of socialism by some interwar New Zealanders can be traced back to the middle of the first decade of the twentieth century when several aspects of a growing, more vocal socialist movement were causing disquiet.[11] Class harmony was highly prized in New Zealand, and many believed that socialists were creating 'class conflict' by portraying the employer as the enemy of the worker.[12] Those socialists who favoured direct industrial action were seen as an even greater danger. The Industrial Workers of the World (IWW) or Wobblies, which set up a branch in New Zealand in 1907, epitomised these fears.[13] Founded in Chicago in 1905, the IWW believed that '[t]he working class and the employing class have nothing in common.'[14] For them, the overthrow of capitalism through parliamentary change was impossible; instead, they believed that direct action in the form of workplace strikes and eventually a general strike would bring a proletarian revolution.[15] The activities of groups like the IWW led some to believe that socialism itself had sinister motives.[16]

One flash point was the question of land nationalisation. Between 1907 and 1911, farmers and homeowners became increasingly concerned about land tenure. This had been a political issue since the election in 1890 of the Ballance Liberal government, which had a policy of buying and leasing out rural land. Farmers in particular saw this as a threat to their ability to freehold land and as a possible Trojan horse for the eventual government ownership of all land in New Zealand.[17] However, it was the formation in 1904 of the Independent Political Labour League, with its explicit policy of land nationalisation, that increasingly linked land nationalisation to socialism.[18] Furthermore, Ward's attempts in 1907 to settle the debate between the leaseholders and freeholders in the Liberal Party achieved the opposite, igniting a fierce defence of freehold by farmers.[19] These trends were expressed by Opposition leader William Massey in February 1908 in a speech to a large gathering of supporters. He said that:

> [The last] two years had seen demands put forward by people who believed in the socialistic theory that the country should be run on socialistic lines, land should be nationalised, that all industry should be nationalised and that people should be divided into two classes … He (Mr Massey) was not in the habit of speaking soft platitudes or of endeavouring to arouse needless alarm and he would not speak as he did if he did not think the danger was very real.[20]

The feeling that 'the danger was very real' was heightened by the formation of the New Zealand Federation of Labour in 1909. The Federation quickly became known as the 'Red Feds' owing to their commitment to using strikes as the main form of industrial action.[21] In 1912, the New Zealand Federation of Labour conference voted to adopt the preamble to the IWW constitution, which called for the overthrow of capitalism.[22] Even the *Lyttelton Times*, a newspaper known to favour a moderate socialist outlook, thought the Federation's decision to model its constitution on the IWW was 'strange', and described the IWW as 'responsible for alarming outbreaks of mob violence and apparently senseless attacks upon property'.[23] The editor of the pro-Reform *Press* said the Federation of Labour had brought a 'menacing position of affairs into the industrial world'.[24] These concerns appeared to be validated by the 1913 strike. Although it was short-lived and largely confined to Wellington and Auckland, its episodes of violence and disorder reinforced the fear that socialists would bring anarchy to New Zealand.[25] The idea that the strike would lead to 'mob rule' was common in newspaper reports.[26] A letter to the *Dominion* summed up popular feeling: 'Shall a small section of the community, which believes in mob rule, terrorise their fellows?'[27] The Reform Party seized the initiative, and used the

OPPOSITE: From the cover of the *New Zealand Home Pictorial* in 1931, this image illustrates the exaggerated fear that communism will overtake the country unless the population is vigilant. This paranoia about domestic Bolshevism was a key concept promoted by radical anti-socialist groups.

New Zealand Home Pictorial, 12 August 1931. S-L-1724-cover, Alexander Turnbull Library, Wellington

Registered at the G.P.O. for transmission as a newspaper.

44 -Page

Vol. 1.—No. 37.

AUCKLAND, WELLINGTON, 6d CHRISTCHURCH AND DUNEDIN.

PICTURES STORIES ARTICLES

"FOR EVERY MEMBER OF THE FAMILY"

THE N.Z. HOME PICTORIAL

WEDNEDAY, AUGUST 12th, 1931

disorder seen during the strike to discredit Labour and the Liberals during the 1914 election campaign.[28] Its promise of 'sane, safe and progressive policy' seemed to resonate with voters, and it received 47 percent of the vote.[29]

The beginning of World War I diverted public and political attention away from socialism. However, the formation of the Labour Party in 1916 served as a reminder that socialists were still active. When the party's platform was released in July 1916, the *Press* described it as 'a jumble of Socialism and nonsense'.[30] There was already some suspicion about Labour's loyalty to Britain after five of the six Labour members refused to join the wartime coalition government.[31] Opposition to conscription, the issue that united the previous disparate labour groups, led to further accusations that the Labour Party, and socialists in general, were seditious and undermining the Empire's war effort. This image was reinforced when several dozen party members were imprisoned for sedition in 1917 for their anti-conscription stance.[32] The editor of the *Manawatu Standard* captured the mood of the press when it described the Labour Party as 'class-conscious anti-nationalists who masquerade as champions of Labour, that name will not be one to conjure with among a people whose abiding characteristic is loyalty to law and the Imperial idea'.[33]

The Russian Revolution added to socialism's anti-Empire reputation, and introduced the notion that the Labour Party could be a front for Bolshevism. Prior to World War I, Russia had been seen as a key threat to New Zealand's and the Empire's safety.[34] The revolution and the subsequent withdrawal of Russia from the war meant 'Russian' and 'Bolshevik' became synonymous with 'traitor' and 'extremist'.[35] Pro-revolution statements from prominent Labour Party members added to the belief that socialism and the Labour Party wanted to undermine the Empire and had pro-Russian objectives. Harry Holland stated at a public meeting in December 1918 that he was personally prepared to take the name Bolshevik and 'The Bolsheviks were the socialist party'.[36] During his campaign for the 1918 Palmerston by-election, Labour candidate Alex Galbraith described himself as a 'New Zealand Bolshevik', and Peter Fraser said that 'the Labour Party has but one flag … the Red Flag'.[37]

THE WELFARE LEAGUE

The gains made by the Labour Party in the series of 1918 by-elections greatly boosted its morale.[38] But this also led to a growing concern among some sectors of society that Labour might be an ascendant force in New Zealand politics. It was against this background that the first radical anti-socialist group emerged. The New Zealand

Welfare League was formed in Wellington on 12 March 1919. Some of its founders had also been involved in the Federation of New Zealand Patriotic War Relief Societies and the National Efficiency Board, suggesting that its formation owed something to contacts made during the war.[39] The League's main purpose was 'to oppose the propaganda and activities of those sections of the community which openly espouse Bolshevik and revolutionary principles'.[40] But it was its broad interpretation of 'those sections of the community' that made it a radical anti-socialist group. Throughout its existence, the League maintained that local manifestations of political labour and industrial unrest were part of a coordinated international conspiracy to bring down the British Empire rather than a response to local conditions. The League included the Labour Party among this group.

The Welfare League proposed to counter 'revolutionary propaganda' in two ways. First, it would support responsible candidates for Parliament and stable government who favoured 'no one class of the community'.[41] Second, it would 'educate public opinion'.[42] Arthur Harper, the League's secretary, was the son of an establishment Christchurch family; his father was the first Anglican Bishop of Christchurch.[43] During the rest of 1919, he travelled the country to drum up support, so that by the time of the 1919 election the four main centres and some towns had League branches.[44] As the election approached, the League began to send articles to newspapers as part of its 'educative' role. By late November and early December these were appearing in newspapers throughout the country – including the radical socialist *Maoriland Worker*.[45] It would appear that even the *Worker* was prepared to accept material that was explicitly against socialism if the advertiser was prepared to pay.

At first there was some confusion about the Welfare League's purpose. With an election looming, many believed that the League was the beginning of another political party – part of the redrawing of party lines in response to the emergence of Labour.[46] The *New Zealand Times* thought it was a splinter group of Reform.[47] From the outset, its leader Charles Skerrett stressed that the League was not a political body.[48] Yet the rumours persisted, and in September Skerrett met with several MPs for what the *Dominion* reported as an attempt to form a party.[49] The outcome of this meeting is unknown, but given that the League began its campaign of publishing propaganda in newspapers in October 1919, it is likely that it recognised its campaign against socialism was best served as an interest group rather than a political party.[50]

The lead-up to the 1919 election cemented the Welfare League's main preoccupation for the next 20 or so years of its existence: providing 'educational propaganda' to newspapers for publication.[51] This was chosen as its main area of activity because it was much more cost effective than platform work.[52] The expense of publishing was mitigated by the fact that many newspapers published their material for free.[53] In 1920 the League claimed to have published more than 200 articles in 50 separate newspapers.[54] In a speech given at the 1921 Welfare League national conference, Skerrett claimed that the League was regularly published in 30 newspapers and occasionally in a further 40.[55] It provided twice-weekly articles on current affairs or educative matters, as well as articles on specific local issues and answers to critics.[56] In its 1931 annual report, the League stated that it was sending out weekly articles to about 60 newspapers, of which somewhere between 60 to 70 percent were published.[57] Another feature of the Welfare League's work was to reply to 'dangerous propaganda' in the form of letters to the editor.[58] This low level, cost-effective and consistent stream of propaganda allowed the League to influence public opinion. It is hard to measure how effective their propaganda was, but it is fair to assume that it would have had some effect on public perceptions and discourse.

The Welfare League initially focused on discrediting the Labour Party, which it saw as the principal vehicle for socialism in New Zealand. Its main aim was to cast doubt in the public's mind about the real origins and motives of the party. The most common way it did this was by prefacing the name 'Labour Party' with a negative adjective – the word 'red', for example.[59] This linked the Labour Party to communist Russia and suggested that there was potentially a Labour group that was not 'red' – what the Welfare League referred to as 'sane labour'. Another method was to use the term 'so-called Labour Party', implying that the party secretly represented someone else.[60] Then in 1923 came the term Socialist-Labour or Labour-Socialist Party.[61] This became the League's most common descriptor for the Labour Party.[62] Again this implied that the party was not actually representing workers but instead was working to bring socialism (and, therefore, Bolshevism) to New Zealand, in alliance with other forces that wished to destroy the British Empire.

The Welfare League also suggested that the Labour Party and its politicians were lying to cover their true identity. In the early 1920s, it published articles asking such 'questions' of Labour and its members as 'did [they] support Lenin's Labour policy?'[63] It asked MP for Christchurch South Ted Howard if he had 'informed electors as you recently did members of the House, that you were opposed to the whole system of parliamentary government, or did you follow

OPPOSITE: Appearing in the *Dominion* on 1 December 1919, two weeks before the 1919 election, this cartoon illustrates the Welfare League's message that the Labour Party was a front for revolution.

Dominion, 1 December 1919, p. 2. https://paperspast.natlib.govt.nz

"Riding for a Fall."

The Official Labour Candidate's Dilemma—"Where is he Going ?"

(Published by Arrangement for the N.Z. Welfare League.)

the course of hiding your true sentiments until the election was over?'[64] Labour's deception, the League argued, was that it was trying to present an acceptable face while holding to socialist doctrine. After a speech by Labour leader Harry Holland in Wellington in 1922, the League accused Labour of 'having two programmes – one which they publish and present to the public and the other which they hold in reserve to use if they should ever gain control'. The article ends: '[W]e are confident that his [Holland's] party is not the true Labour Party but one that is deceiving people'.[65]

As the Labour Party began to moderate its platform from 1924, the League began to accuse the party of further hiding its true intentions. Typical of these efforts was a 1924 article entitled 'Socialist menace: Where the chief danger lies'. The League contended that it was a mistake to think that danger came just from those who wanted armed revolution. It came from 'the so-called moderate socialists who use all the methods of espionage, camouflage, and false professions which are calculated to hoodwink and disarm their opponents'.[66] A 1928 article described socialists as having undergone 'Dress Reform' to cover up their socialist doctrine:

> [Labour's] socialism is not so naked as it was a few years back. The word 'revolution' they have discarded for the time being. Their red shirt of pronounced sympathy with the Bolshevik comrades of Russia has been covered with a blue overcoat of Liberal professions … The view taken by us is that it may have some connection with the approaching general elections – who knows?[67]

In other words, Labour's desire to broaden its appeal – a tactic common to all political parties – was nothing more than an underhanded attempt to trick the electorate into voting for them. Once ensconced in power, its politicians would surely shed their blue overcoats and welcome back their Bolshevik comrades with open arms.

The Labour Party was not the only group condemned as part of the plot. The Alliance of Labour (the successor of the Federation of Labour), and the union movement in general, were also accused of being enemies of New Zealand and the Empire. This was a feature of the League's material during the months of industrial action in the early 1920s. It sought to explain both the mood of disorder and the economic slump of 1921–22 by placing the blame on syndicalists and those connected with the IWW within the union movement. In August 1920, a series of articles appeared that claimed that New Zealand unions had been corrupted by IWW ideas and that there were 'mischief-makers' acting behind the scenes.[68] In September the League argued that, because strikes supposedly hurt workers, the intention was really to cause disorder and ferment revolution.[69] As the industrial situation began to settle, the number of articles targeting unions and the Alliance of Labour decreased. However, socialist infiltration of the union movement continued to be discussed in League articles. In 1926 the League warned against 'Revolutionary Trade Unionism', and in 1932 it argued that unions could be a front for communist activity.[70] In reality, the communists were few in number, largely unsuccessful and posed little threat.[71] However, the Welfare League saw the communists' attempts to influence the union movement as an example of a well-organised, international conspiracy against the Empire.

In the mid- to late 1920s, the Labour Party distanced itself from the more radical aims of socialism, and in 1925 members of the New Zealand Communist Party were excluded from membership of the Labour Party.[72] Initially, the League continued to link the two parties. A 1928 article titled 'Socialism and communism: Which?' claimed that socialism and communism were the same, except that 'Socialism's gate is adorned with flowers, communism's with blood'.[73] A 1930 article about the dangers of the communist 'red hand' ended with a reminder that the Labour Party was socialist and, therefore, aligned with communists rather than workers.[74] This idea became progressively untenable in the early 1930s as the Communist Party began to stand candidates against Labour in general elections.[75] Public scepticism about the conflation of Labour and Communist parties was epitomised in a 1928 letter to the *Manawatu Standard* in which the writer asked the Welfare League to stop 'bunching' Labour and the communists together.[76]

By 1930, the League had turned most of its attention to the Communist Party.[77] In 1931 it was claiming that 'we have never branded [Labour] as Communistic – nor are we responsible for branding them as Socialistic'.[78] It also highlighted the differences between the two parties.[79] This change of focus was most likely caused by the deepening economic depression and fears that communists were at work among the unemployed.[80] As it had in the early 1920s when industrial unrest was heightened, the Welfare League explained the disorder caused by the Depression as part of a wider conspiracy. In 1931 it wrote that the Third International, an international organisation headed by the Soviet Union and advocating for global communism, had 'discovered a few years ago that British people were not suitable material for working up into a bloody revolution'. Instead, it was using communist agents to stir up industrial disorder and cause economic collapse, believing that this would lead to revolution in New Zealand and ultimately bring down the British Empire.[81] The League was particularly concerned about the Unemployed Workers Union, linking it to the Communist Party and the Red International Labour Union.[82] It warned relief workers that they were being targeted and would be 'cannon fodder' in the planned revolution.[83] There was anxiety, too, about communism influencing young minds. The League published several articles appealing to youth in 1932.[84] And in 1933 it warned that schools and universities had been infiltrated by communists, sparking considerable controversy centred on Victoria University.[85]

During the 1930s, the League also increased the attention it gave to the disarmament and anti-war movements. This built on its longstanding concerns about Labour's internationalist stance.[86] The League believed attempts to base international relations on a multinational approach undermined the Empire, and that those advocating for internationalism must have ulterior motives. It was convinced that these movements were part of a communist conspiracy to disarm Britain and the Empire.[87]

The Welfare League's message became increasingly insignificant after the election of the Labour Party in 1935. It published a pamphlet in 1938 claiming that Labour was directing New Zealand toward socialism.[88] But the Labour Party was re-elected that year in a landslide, suggesting that radical anti-socialist rhetoric was losing its appeal. The League continued to sporadically publish in newspapers, and in 1940 produced a series of articles attacking communists as a potential 'fifth column'. The New Zealand Communist Party was opposed to the war, in line with the Soviet Union's position at the time.[89] By 1942 the League had stopped publishing altogether, ending 23 years of radical anti-socialist activity.[90]

LOYAL CITIZENS LEAGUE

At the beginning of October 1920, reports began appearing in newspapers about the formation of a clandestine new organisation named the Loyal Citizens League, the League of Loyal Citizens or the Loyalty League. The timing and objectives of these organisations suggest they were one and the same. The Loyal Citizens League differed from the Welfare League and PPA in that its main objective was to organise a secret 'citizen army' to defend New Zealand from a socialist revolution. Unlike the other two groups, it appears that much of the Loyal Citizens League activity was initiated by the government.[91] Nevertheless, the degree of civilian involvement reflects the influence of radical anti-socialist perceptions among concerned professionals, businesspeople and primary producers at the time of an international 'red scare'.[92]

The genesis of the Loyal Citizens League lay with the Defence Department and Brigadier-General George Richardson, the general officer in charge of administration.[93] From the beginning of 1920, the Defence Department had been concerned about the possibility of an economically crippling general strike. These fears took on new urgency in September and October 1920 after a series of short-lived coal miners' strikes and a dispute on the Wellington waterfront.[94] In late September, Richardson prepared a series of memoranda, which recommended the formation of a 'Citizen's Protection League' to protect life, property and trade in the event of a general strike.[95] His proposal drew on the Defence Department's desire to avoid military involvement in industrial disputes, its experience with managing the special constables the government had employed to break the 1913 Great Strike, and its belief that a similar body of 'loyal citizens' should be organised in readiness for the next great strike. This culminated in the formation of a Loyal Citizens League in Wellington on 13 October when several citizens interested in 'maintaining law & order in the event of industrial strife' met and formed a secret organisation with the blessing of the prime minister.[96]

The first newspaper report on the formation of Loyal Citizens League was not so secret. In early October, an article appeared in the *Manawatu Standard* about a Loyal Citizens League branch being formed in Hawera.[97] It claimed that those who called the meeting were motivated by a recent statement from the leader of the Miners Union, J. Arbuckle, in which he said the workers 'must take charge of industry'.[98] It seems that this meeting was not tied to the Wellington league or to Richardson, but was rather the initiative of a prominent member of the PPA named Ewen McGregor who 'had embarrassed the Govt. to some extent by his actions'.[99] Not only was he not connected to the government's covert efforts, but he was far more public than the government would have liked. However, McGregor's actions did not prevent the government-sanctioned Wellington league from touring the country and forming branches. The papers of the Wellington Loyal Citizens League note that members travelled to several 'counties' to canvass support in case of 'industrial strife'.[100] This is further corroborated by the diary of Leslie Adkin, a Levin farmer, who recorded that on 22 October 1920 he attended a meeting at which 12 farmers signed up to the 'Loyalty League' because they were so concerned about 'industrial strife'.[101] There were also reports of meetings taking place in Eltham, possibly Greytown, and mention of a Palmerston North branch and a Gisborne group called the 'Poverty Bay Industrial Emergency Committee'.[102] The latter believed the Loyal Citizens League was the rebirth of the 'Employers, Farmers and Citizens Defence

Committees', an organisation that had represented employers and farmers during the 1913 Great Strike by dealing with government agencies, fundraising and recruiting scab labour.[103]

The Loyal Citizens League was short-lived. The secret nature of the group makes it difficult to know when it dissolved, although it is probable that the calming of the 'red scare' and a decrease in industrial action played a role. The only hint comes from the *Evening Star,* which connected the 'Loyal Citizens League from 1921' with a new group that arose in Dunedin local body politics in 1923 called the Citizens League.[104] It is highly unlikely that they were directly linked.[105]

PROTESTANT POLITICAL ASSOCIATION

The PPA was formed in 1917 by members of the Loyal Orange Lodges.[106] Although the main aim of the PPA was to combat what it perceived as undue Catholic influence in New Zealand, it occasionally expressed radical anti-socialist views. Chapter Six explores the PPA's anti-Catholicism in more depth, including its origins and the events that led to a flare-up of sectarian tensions during World War I. This section focuses primarily on the PPA's (mis)understanding of socialism, and the sinister connections it believed existed between the forces of socialism and the Catholic Church.

Like the Welfare League, the PPA thought the Labour Party was controlled by international forces that wanted to bring down the British Empire. However, the PPA believed that the Catholic Church, rather than Bolshevism, sat at the centre of the conspiracy. Following the Easter Rising in 1916 and the Anglo-Irish Treaty in 1921, the Labour Party's support for an Irish Free State was clear. The *Maoriland Worker* supported Sinn Féin, and Labour Party leader Harry Holland, who was the editor at the time, took a special interest in the 'Irish question'.[107] Other Labour MPs like Peter Fraser and Ted Howard also publicly supported the establishment of an Irish Free State.[108]

The supposedly dangerous connection between Labour and the Catholic Church remained a staple of PPA material during the 1920s. The PPA claimed that the New Zealand Labour Party was controlled by Catholics and was a danger to New Zealand and the wider Empire.[109] A political statement from the early 1920s opened with the suggestion that Sinn Féin was a 'section' of socialism.[110] Howard Elliott, the PPA's National Lecturer, claimed in 1920 that the real menace in New Zealand was 'the [Red] extremists and the Church of Rome' and that '[t]he Red and Green were marching in unison in Australia and Ireland and would do so here.' At a 1922 meeting in Wellington, Elliott said that '[t]he Bolsheviks and Rome were both against the

British Empire and only a combination of the two made it possible for either to get into power.'[111] In Dunedin in 1925 he declared 'that there was a tacit and practical alliance between these movements [socialism and communism] and the Roman Catholic Church'.[112] The PPA saw no contradiction in claiming that a political sect often connected with atheism was secretly controlled by the Catholic Church. After 1925, Elliott's public speeches focused more on opposing state support for Catholic schools and the danger of Catholics in the public service.[113] It is not clear why the PPA shifted away from positioning socialism as part of a Catholic conspiracy. Labour's efforts to distance itself from more overt expressions of socialism from the mid-1920s may have been a factor. The PPA was also reorganised in 1925, and this may have had some effect on the topics it emphasised at public meetings.[114]

In 1925 a booklet titled *What is the Red Menace?* was published by a group calling itself the Loyalty League.[115] It first appeared in late September, and was possibly inspired by the upcoming election. The Loyalty League claimed that socialism was a conspiracy that originated with deceitful men who worked through the Illuminati, a group supposedly founded by an ex-Jesuit priest yet controlled by Jews. The Illuminati apparently had German origins, was behind the French and Russian revolutions, and was undermining the British Empire. The inclusion of Russia and Germany in the socialist plot targeted two traditional enemies of New Zealand. Linking socialism to international Jewry also tapped into antisemitic conspiracy theories circulating in Britain during the 1920s. A more familiar theme was that socialism was a trick and that the Labour Party 'had quite a different origin and the working class only figure in the light of dupes'.[116]

Little is known about the Loyalty League, yet there are several hints that it was connected to the PPA. The ideas expressed in *What is the Red Menace?* can be found in the PPA overseas pamphlet collection held by Auckland University Library.[117] The PPA also published a pamphlet called 'The Communist Germ' that summarised the ideas in *What is the Red Menace?*[118] It is undated, but it was produced after 1925 because it mentions the refusal of the New Zealand Labour Party to accept members of the Communist Party.[119] Like *What is the Red Menace?* it linked communism with the Illuminati and suggested the Labour Party was controlled by international forces, particularly the Soviet Union.

After publishing *What is the Red Menace?* the Loyalty League was not heard of again until it was revived in 1929. At the beginning of that year Elliott resigned from the PPA, and in early September the PPA issued a statement saying that it had no connection with attempts to revive the Loyalty League, despite having 'fostered [it] at its inception.'[120] In mid-September it was announced that the Loyalty League had been reorganised and that Elliott was its secretary.[121] This incarnation of the Loyalty League attracted little press coverage and left behind sparse documentation, so it is difficult to ascertain whether it was similar to the 1925 version. However, its attempted revival, connections with Elliott and similar rhetoric suggest that there may be some connections between the PPA and the 1925 and 1929 versions of the Loyalty League.

NEW ZEALAND RADICAL ANTI-SOCIALISTS AND THEIR INTERNATIONAL CONNECTIONS

Publications like *What is the Red Menace?* that expressed ideas similar to those of groups in other countries highlight the international connectedness of New Zealand radical anti-socialist groups. Both the PPA and the Welfare League appear to have had regular contact with like-minded groups in other countries. The PPA's contacts were mostly with anti-Catholic groups, yet its leaders' extensive collection of international literature shows a strong vein of anti-socialism. The PPA pamphlet collection includes material from Australia, Britain and the US.[122] Connections with Australia are reinforced by the fact that Elliott was an Australian who came to New Zealand with well-developed anti-Catholic beliefs.[123] This was illustrated in 1922 when the PPA brought Rev. R Ditterich, the president of the Australian Protestant Federation, to New Zealand for a speaking tour to highlight the ambition of Catholics to replace the British flag with that of the papacy.[124] Elliott was also invited to give a speech to the Victorian Loyalist League in 1921.[125]

However, it was the Welfare League that was the most actively connected with radical anti-socialist groups in other countries, and was connected with groups in Australia, Canada and Britain from the outset.[126] In 1921, Dave McLaren, one of the League's speakers, told an audience in Stratford that the League was in 'constant correspondence with that organisation (a similar one in Britain) and with others in Australia the US and Canada'.[127] A copy of the League's 1921 interim report is in the Australian National Library.[128] There were also newspaper reports of League material reaching London.[129] At the end of 1921, Skerrett made a trip to the Northern Hemisphere, and in Britain had 'taken a keen interest' in two groups that were similar to the Welfare League.[130] It appears that these international contacts were maintained, as they are mentioned in the League's 1932 annual report.[131]

According to the Welfare League, the groups that were part of its network all arose about the same time without any coordination between them. In 1921 Harper noted the 'interesting part of this Empire-wide feeling is the fact that without previous consultation of any sort, these movements sprang up at the same time'.[132] He also described an organisation called 'Golden Rule Clubs', which had begun in the US and had similar principles to the Welfare League.[133] The main purpose of these international networks was to keep each other informed of socialist activities in other countries. Contacts appear to have been informal and cultivated by a shared interest in combating socialism. In the Welfare League's 1931 annual report, for example, information from the wealthy Labour Research Department of England is mentioned in the 'Dangerous Propaganda' section.[134] The fact that the League was able to become part of this network within 18 months of its foundation, and maintained the connections for much of its existence, demonstrates the significance of an active international informal exchange of radical anti-socialist material.

The Welfare League joined an organisation known as the International Entente against the Third International (IAE) sometime in the mid-1920s.[135] This group was founded in Switzerland in 1924, reflecting the desire of radical anti-socialist groups to coordinate their activities. It was mainly active in Europe but had affiliates in all the countries in which the Welfare League also claimed to have contacts. The main work of the IAE was to produce publications like books, bulletins, magazines and reports on communist activities.[136] In this regard it had much in common with the Welfare League, although it is difficult to judge how much influence it had on the League. In 1925 and 1926 the League published articles on communist activity in China.[137] Yet these mainly focused on the potential curtailing of British activity in China and the threat this posed to the Empire. The League was also concerned about socialist activity in South Africa and India, but this too was filtered through the lens of the danger to Empire rather than international instability.[138] While it cultivated international connections, the Welfare League's core belief that the British Empire was in danger from socialism led it to focus more on activity in Britain than in other countries in the Empire or the wider world.

RADICAL ANTI-SOCIALISM AND THE REFORM PARTY

The Reform Party was the dominant political party in New Zealand during the interwar period.[139] Its ideology placed it on the centre-right of New Zealand politics, and after the rump of the Liberal Party collapsed in the early 1920s it regarded the Labour Party as its main political opponent. Reform propaganda targeted Labour policy for electoral purposes but was not averse to drawing upon radical anti-socialist ideas about the party's alleged hidden agenda. The general public may not have actively read material produced by the PPA or the Welfare League, but Reform was the governing party between 1912 and 1928. This suggests that the groups' material probably had a wider public appeal.

From 1920 until 1928, Reform published a newspaper called *The Newsletter.*[140] Its main purpose was to present a positive picture of the Reform government and its policies while attacking the Opposition parties. *The Newsletter* would often dissect Labour policies and directly attack Labour leaders. It also published material on Labour parties in other countries, particularly in Britain and in Australian states where Labor was in power during the 1920s. For the most part, these attacks focused on policies, and can be seen as part of the general cut and thrust of politics. They did not suggest that the Labour Party was a front for any anti-New Zealand or anti-Empire movements. Instead, they focused on trying to discredit Labour by exposing the failure and dangers of its policies.

However, *The Newsletter* did at times use rhetoric that drew on some of the ideas of radical anti-socialists, suggesting that Labour, some unions and, in later years, the Communist Party were a front for German, Russian or international socialist conspiracies. The first edition published in 1920 included an article entitled 'The Labour Party and the World Revolution', in which the writer claimed the New Zealand Labour Party was linked to the Alliance of Labour, the IWW and Soviet Russia.[141] This theme occurred about two or three times a year in the early 1920s.[142] In September 1921 the editor declared that '[t]he paper is frankly and unreservedly against Labour extremists, Bolsheviks and disloyalists generally.'[143] By 1923 *The Newsletter* had moderated some of its language, although it began using a similar tactic to the Welfare League by trying to demonstrate that Labour was not being upfront with the public. In March 1924 it suggested that Labour was trying to gain the votes of farmers by not being honest about its land policy.[144] In November it called Labour 'pink' and claimed that its 'paleness' was a camouflage of its real position.[145]

In February 1926, *The Newsletter* published its most radical anti-socialist edition. Its aim was to show how Labour and the communists were linked. It used terms from radical anti-socialists like 'Labour-Socialist Party' and 'so-called Labour Party'. It traced

OPPOSITE: The October 1925 edition of the Reform Party's newspaper *The Newsletter* focused on the upcoming election. This full-page advertisement is an example of the way Reform used radical anti-socialist ideas for electioneering purposes. It appeared after an article about the 'Labour-Socialist Party' and its links to Russia.

The Newsletter, 10 October 1925, p.8. S-L 91-8, Alexander Turnbull Library, Wellington

The Red Menace is Here in New Zealand

The Agents of the Third International, directed from Moscow, are at work in New Zealand today, as witness the Shipping Strike

Your Country or Trotsky's?

The Russian Communists order their New Zealand agents to use every means, legal or illegal, to foment disorder and revolution

IN THE RED PROGRAMME THERE IS—

No Constitutional Government
Neither Free Speech nor Free Press
No Trade Unions
No Private Property

THE RED OBJECTIVE IS—

An Armed Rising
Government by Force
Confiscation of Property
Proletariat Dictatorship

"I am positive that Moscow has ordered this strike, and that it is directed entirely against Britain's oversea trade. I have discovered that the activities of the Reds in America and Canada are solely against Britain. It is curious that German, Greek, and other European shipping, paying half the British wages, are left entirely alone."—Mr. J. Havelock Wilson, Secretary of the British Seamen's and Firemen's Union, in an interview on 30th September.

WHAT IS IT TO BE—

NEW ZEALAND
As you would like it

OR

NEW ZEALAND
As Russia would make it

the 'evolution' of the pre-war 'Red' Federation of Labour to the contemporary Labour Party, and drew upon material from the radical-right and conspiracist British newspaper *The Patriot*.[146] Given that the Labour Party had become the official Opposition after the 1925 election, it is probable *The Newsletter*'s editor was concerned about Labour's growing popularity and used such radical material to sow doubt about its credibility. *The Newsletter* continued to use the term Labour-Socialist to describe the Labour Party, particularly in the lead-up to the 1928 election.[147]

These examples show that Reform was not above using radical anti-socialist rhetoric to discredit its political opponents. Reform was different from the radical anti-socialist groups covered in this chapter in that its first goal was to win elections against the Labour Party. It did not appear to hold the deeper belief that Labour, and socialism in general, was a front for sedition, social disorder and revolution. Even so, it seems that via *The Newsletter* radical anti-socialist ideas did periodically filter into mainstream political discourse in an effort to generate distrust in the Labour Party.

CONCLUSION

The interwar period saw a surge in radical anti-socialist activity in New Zealand. The three groups examined in this chapter expounded a message that the Labour Party, some unions, communists, and the peace and disarmament movements were all dangerous and part of a wider socialist conspiracy to bring down the British Empire. This intolerance was built on an established distrust of socialism and a strong loyalty to Empire, particularly in the aftermath of the sacrifices of the Great War. The groups believed they needed to educate New Zealanders about this socialist menace, and this was reflected in their focus on publishing propaganda. The PPA and the Welfare League had a high profile during this period. The league was a prolific publisher, supplying newspaper articles that enabled it to feed the public a consistent diet of radical anti-socialist material – a slow and steady approach designed to infiltrate and influence opinion over a long period. To a certain extent the PPA followed a similar line to the Welfare League, except it saw the Catholic Church as being the force behind socialism.

Radical anti-socialist groups became less accepted as the interwar period progressed.[148] By the early 1930s, the PPA and Loyalty League had ceased to have any public presence. The Welfare League continued to publish articles, but became progressively interested in rebutting Douglas Social Credit ideas and providing commentary on economic matters. This shift is illustrated by its reaction to the election of the Labour government in 1935. The League stated that it seemed Labour had 'a more general constructive policy to meet the problems of the day'.[149] Labour's victory demonstrated that for most New Zealanders the fear that the country would submit to a red flag was baseless. The socialist bogeyman failed to materialise upon Labour's rise to power, and the Welfare League increasingly focused on communism from the early 1930s. Its legacy can be seen in the anti-communist rhetoric of the postwar period.[150]

CHAPTER SIX

Conservative populism between the wars

The Protestant Political Association and the New Zealand Legion

MATTHEW CUNNINGHAM

THIS CHAPTER SEEKS TO COMPLICATE ONE OF THE THEMES that emerges from many of the chapters in this volume: that the radical right does not, nor has it ever, attracted significant support in New Zealand. It focuses on two large organisations that arose during the interwar years. The first, the Protestant Political Association (PPA), was an anti-Catholic and anti-socialist movement founded in July 1917 that reached its peak around 1920 before a prolonged decline over the following decade. The second, the New Zealand Legion (NZL), was a laissez-faire, anti-party movement that appeared and grew very rapidly in early 1933 only to decline just as fast from the latter half of that year. While very different in many fundamental ways, the two organisations achieved a degree of significance that the myriad other organisations that have emerged, dissolved, reformed, splintered and fused on the radical right in New Zealand have not. They both achieved the (admittedly fluid) threshold of mass membership: the PPA claimed a dubious figure of 250,000 members in August 1920, whereas the NZL claimed a more believable figure of 'in excess of 20,000' in August 1933.[1] They both attracted significant national attention, being covered extensively by the press, discussed by MPs and vigorously criticised by their opponents. They also had a degree of influence on mainstream politics, whether in the form of tangible political outcomes (such as election results and legislation) or indirect influences (eight former NZL members were selected as National Party candidates in 1938, and one – Sid Holland – became prime minister in 1949).[2]

How did the PPA and the NZL manage to attract significant support when other radical right-wing organisations have failed to do so? Before considering this question, it must be acknowledged that the phrase 'significant support' is contestable, depending on how one defines the threshold of significance. For example, the mainstreaming of what Cas Mudde described as the 'populist radical right' across Europe, the US and elsewhere since 2000 arguably demonstrates an important measure of significance: the ability to build lasting political machines – or to capture existing political machines – that achieve enough electoral success to form governments or to be seen as a potential coalition partner.[3] Neither the PPA nor the NZL accomplished this, despite both organisations considering the option of putting up their own parliamentary candidates.[4] Likewise, for communities that have been the target of abuse or violence by the radical right, the term 'significance' assumes much more immediate meaning – it is a lived experience that often leaves a deep and indelible impact. Notwithstanding these important semantic differences, the metrics listed above – membership, national attention and degree of mainstream political influence – constitute three measures of significance that, arguably, no other organisation to the right of the centre-right in New Zealand has achieved wholesale. This chapter compares various facets of the PPA and the NZL to determine how they managed this feat. In particular, it relies on the distinction drawn by Jens Rydgren between demand-side explanations that focus on 'changing preferences, beliefs, and attitudes', and supply-side explanations that address 'political opportunity structures and party organisational factors'.[5] Let us turn first to the demand side.

THE POWER OF POPULISM

A struggle between a virtuous majority and a nefarious 'other' lay at the core of both the PPA and the NZL world-view. While the players in this struggle were different for each organisation, the struggle itself was the same: the 'other' was attempting to gather more power to themselves while depriving the majority of their 'rights, values, prosperity, identity, and voice'.[6] For the PPA, the struggle was between Protestants and Catholics – they believed the latter were trying to secure privileged treatment for themselves, undermine the Great War effort and bring New Zealand under the control of the Papacy. The mantle of this 'other' also extended to the Labour Party, which the PPA believed had been thoroughly subverted from within by the Catholic conspiracy – and, increasingly after October 1917, by the forces of international communism centred in Moscow. Chapter Five explored the PPA's anti-socialism in more detail. For the NZL, the struggle was between the citizens – those loyal, decent, hard-working men and women in the political centre who were supposedly unmoved by the posturing of the left and right – and political parties and their sycophantic politicians who had tarnished the democratic process, used political power and the public purse for their own selfish interests, and sapped the spirit of individualism through excessive borrowing and 'socialistic' policies.

The populist struggles that animated the PPA and the NZL did not emerge in a vacuum. Both anti-Catholicism and anti-partyism were long-simmering prejudices that, in ordinary times, did not animate people to the extent they did during times of crisis. This lent the struggles a legitimacy that they might otherwise not have possessed: it allowed the leaders of the two organisations to point to a legacy of events that 'proved' their struggles were real. The PPA emerged from a long history of low level sectarianism in New Zealand that was influenced in part by more bitter sectarian strife in other parts of the Anglo world such as Britain, Australia, Canada and the US.[7] While domestic sectarianism was fairly muted prior to World War I, tensions occasionally arose on matters of public policy, particularly education. The Education Act 1877 introduced a secular education system in New Zealand while still allowing space for religious denominations to establish their own private schools. This drew criticism from Protestants and Catholics alike. Catholic authorities worked strenuously to establish separate denominational schools and lobbied the government for public funding to support their efforts. Some Protestant churches and the Loyal Orange Institution (LOI) – an international Protestant order that had first been brought to New Zealand in the 1840s – opposed Catholic requests for public funding and pushed repeatedly to make Bible instruction in state schools mandatory. Catholic authorities supported the secular status quo for state schools, given that those Catholics who were unable to attend denominational schools would otherwise have been subjected to Protestant Bible instruction.[8] Tensions also occasionally arose over the claim that Catholics were over-represented in the public service, particularly after Joseph Ward – of Irish Catholic descent – became prime minister in 1906.[9] The ongoing question of Irish Home Rule, along with the 1907 papal *Ne Temere* decree that sought greater Church regulation of inter-faith marriages, added further fuel to the occasional sectarian flare-up.[10]

It took what Harold Moores described as 'three great controversies' to ignite a blaze from these sectarian embers: the revival of the education question in 1910, the 1916 Easter Rising, and debates about conscripting Catholic clergy for the Great War.[11] The renewed debate over Bible instruction in state schools led to the formation of the Catholic Federation, a permanent organisation to champion Catholic political and social interests structured around parishes and dioceses. The federation continued to agitate for public funding of denominational schools during the war, which led to some furious clashes with the minister of education.[12] The outbreak of rebellion in Dublin in April 1916 was at first met with mixed opinions by Irish New Zealanders; however, the increasingly brutal tactics adopted by the British government to suppress the rebellion hardened attitudes in favour of the rebels.[13]

The debate over conscription was particularly acrimonious. Catholic authorities sought to protect Catholic priests, theological students and members of the order known as the Marist Brothers (who were not ordained but had taken vows and served as teachers at Catholic schools) from conscription, except for providing chaplains.[14] While these groups were not exempt under the Military Service Act 1916, the government privately agreed with Catholic authorities that, if they were called up in one of the conscription ballots, it would certify that it was not in the public interest for them to be conscripted. However, the unwillingness of some military boards to accept these certifications led Catholic bishops to publicly accuse the government of reneging on its agreement.[15] Domestic tensions were fanned by the two failed referenda to introduce conscription in Australia – these were vigorously opposed by Australian Catholics and most of the Labor Party – and a general strike in 1917 across eastern Australia.[16] Future PPA leaders kept abreast of the events unfolding across the Tasman, and were avid collectors of the propaganda being produced by Australian anti-Catholic groups such as the Loyalist League.[17] All of this contributed to a growing feeling among some Protestants that Catholics were failing to do their share for the war effort and were agitating for special privileges. It laid the groundwork for the PPA to claim that the loyalty of Catholics lay with Rome rather than Britain, and that they might even be actively undermining the British Empire.

The NZL emerged from a similarly lengthy history of low level anti-political party sentiment in New Zealand. Like sectarianism, opposition to party politics was common across many countries in the Anglo world. In Australia, it emerged in the late nineteenth century in response to the formation of political labour parties in the states that later united under the banner of a Federal Labor Party in 1901. Not only did many Australian conservatives view political labour as illegitimate but they also expressed concern over its organisational unity. In each electorate Labor pre-selected candidates who swore to uphold its official platform – a process that may seem uncontroversial today but was considered by many conservatives to be an intrusion on the freedom of MPs to vote according to their consciences.[18] As a united Labour Party was not formed in New Zealand until 1916, anti-party ire was originally directed at the Liberal Party – the country's first official political party, which governed from 1891 until 1912. In all but four years between 1893 and 1912, conservatives introduced 'elective executive' Bills from the Opposition benches which, if enacted, would have given Parliament the authority to elect the prime minister and Cabinet. These Bills, while unsuccessful, represented a broader sense of dissatisfaction with the Liberals' style of government, as the notoriously anti-party *Otago Daily Times* summed up:

> Sooner or later party government will give place to something better. One move in this direction, no doubt, will be the election of the Executive by Parliament, which will free Ministers from any temptation to conciliate individual members and constituencies ... The chief advantage, however, of abolishing party government would be the restoration to the representatives of the people of their independence. They would not have to choose between the call of the party whip and their own conscientious convictions.[19]

The Liberals, in turn, directed the same criticism of 'machine'-style politics against the newly formed Reform Party – particularly during the 1911 election – although the steady flow of elective executive Bills dried up after a victorious Reform took office in 1912.[20] Anti-party sentiment was revived briefly in early 1919 in the form of a short-lived 'Anti-Party Political League', which sought 'to abolish party government and to support only those who pledge themselves to vote for measures and not for men'.[21] Conservative pressure groups continued to use similar language throughout the 1920s, albeit with less vehemence. The anti-communist propaganda organisation named the Welfare League (discussed in Chapter Five) proclaimed that it sought to 'place the National or Community interests before those of any Party, Section, or Individual'.[22]

The onset of the Great Depression did not immediately inflame this anti-party sentiment. This was partially because non-labour governments were in power until 1935: the liberal-rump-turned-laissez-faire United Party (with support from Labour) from 1928 to 1931, and a United–Reform coalition from 1931 to 1935. These governments generally kept to the traditional dictums of 'sane finance' to reduce public expenditure, although they were willing to introduce limited experiments in state intervention to address growing insolvency and unemployment. This conservative approach, along with the Depression not reaching its nadir in New Zealand until 1933, dampened initial attempts to generate a populist backlash against the political establishment.[23] A New Zealand National Movement that was formed by dissatisfied members of the Reform Party in mid-1932 failed to generate widespread support, despite an extensive tour of the South Island.[24]

It took a galvanising event similar to the 'three great crises' during World War I to rouse disconcerted conservatives to action – the government's decision in January

1933 to devalue the currency against the British pound to boost farmers' export earnings. The benefits that this decision accrued to farmers had the opposite effect on import-dependent businesspeople, who had to pay more for the products on which their enterprises were based. It also increased private and public debt on the London market. For these conservatives, already feeling a sense of inchoate discontent on account of the parlous economic situation, the idea that MPs were kowtowing to the whims of their parties rather than voting in the interests of all New Zealanders suddenly seemed less far-fetched.[25]

The decision to devalue the currency also animated those who believed in limited government and free markets. While New Zealand's laissez-faire tradition was never as purist as that of British conservatives and liberals in the nineteenth century, it was an undercurrent in centre-right politics from the late nineteenth century, particularly after the advent of the Liberal Party. It was mediated by the pragmatic intervention of the state in colonial economic development across Australasia, which scholars have variously described as 'colonial socialism' or 'progressive colonisation'.[26] From the beginning of the 1920s, many laissez-faire conservatives, particularly urban businessmen, began to express dissatisfaction with the Reform Party's increasing willingness to intervene in the economy to support the primary sector. The government's attempt to introduce fixed prices and common marketing to the Dairy Board in 1926 aroused heated opposition, particularly from a pressure group called the Free Marketing League.[27] Laissez-faire tensions were kept in check during the initial years of the Depression by a government that generally adhered to traditional deflationary methods designed to reduce expenditure and 'deflate' the overall economy. Devaluing the currency unleashed those tensions virtually overnight.

While the fears that fuelled the PPA and the NZL were galvanised by specific events, these occurred within the context of broader crises – the Great War and the Great Depression. Crises have a habit of breeding political volatility: they raise tensions, magnify prejudices and push people to turn to solutions they would not normally consider. Peter Gourevitch's aptly named *Politics in Hard Times* demonstrated how three major economic crises – the Long Depression of the 1890s, the Great Depression of the 1930s and the 'wide gyrations of the 1970s and 1980s' – drove 'masses of voters desperate for some sort of change' in several Western countries to turn to political parties that were willing to make deals 'that took them away from their traditional political as well as policy attachments'. These crises, he argued, 'opened the system of relationships, making politics and policy more fluid' until 'a resolution was reached, closing the system for a time, until the next crisis'.[28] The Great War and the Great

Depression generated a similar sense of crisis-driven discontent. While New Zealand entered into the war with much patriotic fanfare and a degree of national unity, the quick realisation that it would not be 'over by Christmas', coupled with early German advances and the defeat at Gallipoli, made it clear that this was to be a protracted and bloody conflict.[29] Political and societal tensions rose on the home front over issues such as conscription and the rise of political labour, albeit not to the same extent as they did in Australia. Patriotic and xenophobic organisations looked for enemies at home: Germans and Austro-Hungarians, pacifists and conscientious objectors, socialists and labour politicians alike were painted as disloyal and disruptive, or as part of a fifth column in league with the Kaiser. The loosening of social mores and cost-of-living increases added another layer of domestic pressure to these tensions.[30]

The Great Depression generated a similar sense of discontent. It hastened an economic plunge that had begun in 1929 with a decline in export prices, especially in the wool market. By 1933, export prices had declined by 45 percent from their 1929 level, the volume of imports had decreased by 40 percent and unemployment had reached 12 percent of the registered workforce.[31] A series of riots in the first half of 1932, coupled with the perception that the government was insensitive to the plight of the unfortunate, and incapable of enacting the reforms necessary to restore prosperity, added to the sense of uncertainty. Unorthodox economic ideas gained in popularity, ranging from the developing work of economists like J.M. Keynes to the less reputable theories of Major C.H. Douglas and other monetary reformers (these are discussed in more detail in Chapter Seven). The following recollection of Sir Douglas Robb, a surgeon inspired to join the NZL, captures this sense of general discontent:

> [W]e were interested in the depression & the effect on our new-born practices, and on our friends, particularly farmers. There were also street riots to be feared. The Govt. of the day seemed as confused as we were and we heard the self-appointed saviours professing new economic doctrines, particularly Social Credit & Major Douglas, on whose back (at least partly) we felt the Labour Party got into power in 1935.[32]

The desire to 'do something' to alleviate the discontent should not be underestimated. The recollections of many members of the NZL highlight this pressing need. One prominent member recalled that he had joined 'because I was out of work and because I thought that things were in an awful mess and here seemed to be someone who was doing something'.[33] A regular correspondent to the NZL's journal *National Opinion* even used the moniker 'Do Something'.[34]

CHANNELLING THE DISCONTENT

Demand for a populist revolt was clearly present in 1917 and 1933. The twin crises of war and economic depression had given rise to a general feeling of discontent. Long-simmering prejudices against Catholics and party politics – which had been heightened by galvanising events – provided an 'other' against whom this raw discontent could be directed. But demand needed supply if it was to be properly harnessed. The PPA and the NZL provided this supply. They were able to tap into the public's concerns and channel them into unified, well-organised movements. Underpinning this was their conscious desire to attain as large a membership as possible in order to convey an image of size and power – the power to sway governments through the weight of public opinion. Virtually the entirety of their operations, from their organisational structure, their use of public meetings and their production of a significant amount of propaganda material, was designed to build such a mass following.

Both organisations devoted considerable energy to building a robust organisational structure across the country. The efforts of the leading figures in each organisation warrant attention here: Howard Elliott, a Baptist minister and the PPA's full-time National Lecturer, and Robert Campbell Begg, a surgeon and president of the NZL. They were, in many ways, radically different men. Elliott was a fiery character and a galvanising orator, with a long history of zealous anti-Catholicism and a heavy consumption of foreign anti-Catholic literature.[35] Begg, in contrast, was a sober-minded leader who lacked the taste for theatrics and had little experience in politics. While some contemporaries remarked on his 'commanding presence & personality', others observed that his speaking style was wandering and interminable.[36]

Elliott had the considerable backing of the LOI to assist with building an organisation. The LOI resolved at its annual Grand Lodge in April 1916 to form a national Protestant political association, and agreed on the shape and structure of that organisation during the next Grand Lodge a year later. Elliott had spent the intervening months working with a 'Vigilance Committee' appointed by Lodge no. 70 in Auckland (the most militantly anti-Catholic lodge in the LOI) to test the public appetite for anti-Catholic propaganda. By April 1917, he was already a well-known figure on account of the committee's steady stream of pamphlet literature and a series of town hall meetings in Auckland, Wellington, Taranaki and Hamilton.[37]

The PPA itself was not publicly launched until 11 July 1917 – nearly three months after the Grand Lodge. This provided time for the skeleton of the new organisation to be set up. Orange lodges across New Zealand appointed political committees that formed

New Zealand Legion cartoon lamenting the lack of unity between political parties.

National Opinion, vol. 1, no. 4, 21 September 1933, p. 4. DU401.1 NO, J.C. Beaglehole Room, Victoria University of Wellington Library

the foundation of new PPA branches, and began gathering donations and membership fees to underwrite the PPA's initial costs.[38] This provided a solid foundation for Elliott to build upon when he embarked on an extensive public speaking tour after the PPA's launch. From late 1917 to early 1918, Elliott travelled throughout the South Island, the Wellington area, Taranaki and the East Coast of the North Island. After meetings with local 'faithful' in each area – lodge members and other supporters who formed the core of the new branches – he held large town hall events to draw in supporters.[39] By March 1918, he claimed that the PPA had 40,000 members across 60 branches.[40]

The NZL, on the other hand, lacked an existing organisational backer, but made up for it in sheer mileage. Between 17 February and 26 March 1933, Begg and other prominent NZL figures travelled nearly 15,000 kilometres across the country, organising meetings and establishing branches. Begg alone traversed some 8500 kilometres and attended 42 meetings, which led one national newspaper to declare that he 'must have some of St. Paul's qualifications as a missionary'.[41] Begg, an early proponent of flight, joked that he must have flown in every aircraft in New Zealand to keep up with this punishing schedule.[42] These inaugural meetings were by invitation only, to establish the foundations for new branches before the start of a wider recruitment drive. They were also closed to the press, generating an air of mystery about the new organisation. The military and professional backgrounds of many of the NZL's leading figures likely helped to provide the contacts needed for this initial step. Most were well established within their professions, had held positions within local government, and were involved in community service or voluntary organisations such as Rotary.[43] By April 1933, the NZL's foundations were solid enough that its leaders determined it was time to begin holding public meetings to recruit a larger membership. These typically attracted audiences in the thousands in major cities, and in the hundreds in rural areas.[44] By the end of August 1933, the NZL claimed in excess of 20,000 members.[45]

The public meetings held by the PPA and the NZL played an important role in channelling public discontent. They followed the standard protocol for public meetings since the nineteenth century: they were presided over by a prominent local citizen, began with speeches and ended with a vote on pre-written resolutions to be put to elected officials.[46] What set them apart was the size of the audience and the populist nature of the speakers' rhetoric. They were a form of political theatre designed both to reach a wide audience of potential members and to convey the sheer weight of public opinion the two organisations claimed to represent. This was not an entirely new phenomenon – William Massey was known to draw large crowds and engage in a bit of political theatre – but the conscious desire to convey an image of size and power was relatively novel.

The inaugural meeting of the PPA on 11 July 1917 and the first public meeting of the Wellington branch of the NZL on 9 April 1933 provide a useful comparison.[47] Both meetings began with a series of speeches by secondary speakers to warm up the crowd. These speakers raised familiar grievances. For the PPA, it was the agitation by Catholics to exempt the Marist Brothers from conscription and provide public funding to denominational schools. For the NZL, it was the dysfunction of the political system and the parlous economic situation. Then came the main event: speeches by Elliott and Begg, who wove these threads together to convey the overarching vision of their respective organisations. The PPA, stated Elliott, was intended to unite Protestants against the insidious conspiracy being hatched by Catholics to 'control national and civic life in this Dominion'. The NZL would unite the loyal citizens behind candidates who would eliminate party politics, rationalise national and local government, and restore a sense of self-reliance among a public that had become too accustomed to 'sugar plums' funded by the public purse. Both meetings ended with a plea to sign membership forms, which many did.

Both organisations also produced a significant amount of printed material. The PPA produced more than 40 pamphlets and leaflets between 1917 and 1928. Its best-selling item was *Rome's Hideous Guilt in the European Carnage*, a diatribe against the Pope's supposed role in causing the Great War that was initially produced by

Loyal Orange Order cartoon linking anti-Catholic and anti-Bolshevik prejudices into one multifaceted enemy. *New Zealand Truth*, 27 December 1919, p. 5. Source https://paperspast.natlib.govt.nz

the Vigilance Committee and had sold 20,000 copies by August 1917. The PPA also issued its own newsletter, *The New Zealand Sentinel*, and acted as a 'clearing house' for overseas anti-Catholic literature.[48] The NZL's two main pamphlets, *Light on the Legion* and *National Unity in Crisis*, sold well in many bookstores and newsagents.[49] From August 1933 to October 1934 the NZL also issued a journal, *National Opinion*, which contained various public-interest pieces on politics, economics and history, and acted as an unofficial testing ground for the organisation's policy proposals. However, it only ever achieved a circulation of 2400, and its short-lived successor, *Legion*, fared even worse.[50] The NZL also discussed the use of radio broadcasts, but it is unclear whether they made use of them.[51] In addition, prominent figures in both organisations wrote letters to the editors of major newspapers to express their views – and, in the PPA's case in particular, to respond to negative press coverage or the comments of their critics.

DIFFERENCES BETWEEN THE PPA AND THE NZL

A simple outline of the parallels between the PPA and the NZL might imply that they were very much alike. In reality, there were as many differences between the two organisations as there were similarities. Some obvious differences emerge from the comparison outlined above: they were responding to different crises, animated by different prejudices, opposed different 'others' and proposed different solutions. But the PPA was also much more fundamentally conspiratorial in outlook than the NZL – a feature it shared with radical-right groups in the post-World War II period. Elliott and the PPA leadership genuinely believed that Rome was actively working to destroy the British Empire and bring Protestants back into the Catholic fold. They claimed that the Great War had been instigated by Rome to achieve these ends, and that Catholics in New Zealand and the other Dominions were a fifth column whose allegiance lay solely with the Pope. This conspiratorial world-view underpinned the PPA's more general complaints about funding for denominational schools and conscription of the Catholic clergy – sometimes subtly but more often unabashedly overtly. It was summarised in their best-selling pamphlet, *Rome's Hideous Guilt*:

> It is impossible to get the daily Press to publish the great underlying facts of the cause of this present terrible war. Germany is being made the scapegoat to hide an equally guilty party – Rome. Austria is the chief of Rome's representatives. The Papacy has two great objects at the present time, viz:, the restoration of the temporal power of the Pope and the destruction of Protestantism. England has stood in the way of the achievement of these objects. Rome's aim is to crush England, as also is Germany's.[52]

Such was their paranoia about Catholics that members were required to sign a declaration confirming that they were 'not married to a Romanist, nor will I marry one', although this likely reflected the PPA's position on the *Ne Temere* decree as well.[53] While the anti-party rhetoric in the NZL's *National Opinion* occasionally became quite heated, neither the overall movement nor its leaders expressed the same degree of conspiratorial thinking as the PPA. They did not view party politicians as subversives seeking to undermine the state, but rather as expressing a style of government that put sectional and parochial interests above the common good.

The PPA's relationship with the media was also much more strained. While both organisations received a steady stream of negative commentary from those who opposed them – Catholic and Labour newspapers for the PPA, Labour and Douglas Social Credit publications for the NZL – the NZL was received much more warmly by mainstream newspapers.[54] The *New Zealand Herald*, for example, praised it as a movement of 'wholesome ideas' that would 'inspire courage'.[55] The PPA's reception was much more mixed. Media coverage of the Vigilance Committee's early town hall rallies prior to the establishment of the PPA was overwhelmingly negative, with mainstream newspapers criticising Elliott as a fanatic who was unnecessarily stirring up sectarian tensions.[56] The wholly divisive nature of sectarianism likely played a part in this negative reception – the NZL's anti-party rhetoric was largely directed at the system rather than specific politicians, and it packaged it with a much more positive message of national unity. Yet while most newspaper editors disagreed with the PPA's aims and methods, many of their readers were more sympathetic. Letters to the editor published in the *New Zealand Times* and *New Zealand Truth* expressed a mix of support and opposition to the PPA.[57]

The PPA was also willing to court publicity through real and manufactured crises. From early 1917, Elliott began to suspect that mail coming into the post office box used by the Vigilance Committee was being censored – which it was, albeit in a rather intermittent and haphazard fashion. To test his suspicions, Elliott drafted four letters to the committee containing highly salacious rumours about the Catholic Church in New Zealand. When only one of these reached its destination, Elliott believed his suspicions about Catholics in the public service trying to suppress anti-Catholic literature were confirmed. He exposed this at length during the inaugural PPA town hall meeting, and pressured the government into holding a public inquiry into the matter.[58] In an unexpected sequel to the inquiry, Elliott was assaulted in October 1917 by the brother of a deceased Catholic nun who had featured prominently in one of Elliott's salacious letters. The subsequent court case – which exonerated the brother – was used as a further publicity opportunity by the PPA, which published its own pamphlet about the incident shortly thereafter.[59]

The types of people that joined the two organisations differed in some respects. The lack of surviving internal PPA material makes it difficult to gain a comprehensive understanding of its members, their motivations and the organisation's total membership. As a result, studies of the PPA's membership tend to be qualitative rather than quantitative.[60] Historians have suggested that the PPA was evenly split between urban and rural areas, and weighted towards the lower-middle and working classes. Its strongest contingent came from non-conformist Protestant churches: Presbyterians, Baptists and Methodists. Anglicans tended to view the PPA with scepticism and distaste, and the social elite generally shunned it.[61] Max Satchell's quantitative assessment of the PPA leadership in Dunedin makes a persuasive case that the organisation's members were indeed of 'lower' social standing: 42.9 percent were white-collar workers and only one in five were professionals.[62]

To complement this scarce information I have compiled a list of approximately 40 members who held leadership positions within the PPA between 1918 and 1921 (delegates, executive members and regional organisers). This suggests that, among the PPA's leadership at least, there were more figures from the social elite than previously thought. Almost half were professionals, including two accountants, an engineer, a physician, a dentist and two elected officials (a member of the House of Representatives and a member of the Legislative Council). Slightly over 25 percent were clergymen, all of whom were affiliated to non-conformist Protestant churches. In total, just over 70 percent were professional, semi-professionals or businesspeople. The average age of the sample was 43.5 years. While it would be problematic to extrapolate from such a small sample size, this analysis does suggest that the national leadership of the PPA may have been more middle class and respectable than previously suggested. This does not, however, shed any light on front-line members, about whom very little is known.

The amount of NZL source material that has survived – including the complete list of members for the Hawke's Bay division – makes an assessment of the NZL's membership much easier. The average member of the NZL was white, male, in his mid-forties and more likely than not a professional/semi-professional or businessperson, although there were significant minorities of farming and working-class members.[63] Front-line members were younger than the leaders by a few years. A high proportion of the organisation's leaders and front-line members who were old enough to have served in the Great War had done so – 46 percent of leaders versus 38.4 percent of front-line members – but whereas leaders were more likely to have achieved officer rank, almost 60 percent of front-line members did not progress beyond the rank of private or equivalent. While religious affiliation is more difficult to determine, six of the seven Reverends who joined the Hawke's Bay division were Anglican.[64] In sum, the NZL was a movement of the socially respectable: overwhelmingly middle-aged and middle class, with its leaders stretching into the upper-middle and upper class.

The PPA and the NZL also differed in their eventual decline. The NZL burnt brightly but briefly: by the end of 1933 it was largely a spent force, though it managed to limp on for a further two years. It was riven with internal tensions, particularly between those who retained their adherence to laissez-faire principles and those who were willing to entertain unorthodox economic theories like Douglas Credit and the growing global trend of greater economic intervention characterised by President Roosevelt's New Deal. The NZL's decision to field its own political candidates, which raised fears of splitting the centre-right vote in favour of Labour, caused further rifts within the organisation.[65] The PPA, in contrast, managed to remain a significant political force until at least 1921, in part by drawing on the social and economic uncertainty of the immediate postwar years.[66] Indeed, it achieved its most tangible political successes after the war: in the passage of the Marriages Amendment Act 1920, which made it an offence to allege or imply that a lawfully constituted wedding was illegitimate, and the removal of state scholarships for denominational school students in the same year. The PPA's decline was a long and protracted affair as a small coterie of faithful continued to push their message while also folding new 'others' into the grand conspiracy. As Chapter Five reveals, socialism was a key 'other' in the PPA's world-view, and one with wide social traction. Anti-Catholicism, on the other hand, proved increasingly untenable as the 1920s progressed, particularly after the failed sedition trial of Bishop James Liston in 1922 for his remarks on the 1916 Easter Rising and the Anglo-Irish Treaty.[67] The PPA finally folded around 1932 – though James Gerrie, a longstanding leader of the organisation in Otago, joined the NZL one year later.[68]

RADICAL RIGHT OR SIMPLY RADICAL?

Like many radical groups in the interwar period, the PPA and the NZL are difficult to position on the political spectrum. The NZL was founded on a wave of laissez-faire backlash against allegedly undue state interference in the economy. Its world-view was fundamentally conservative, albeit mobilised through a populist rejection of party politics. Its members came from sections of society that typically voted for centre-right parties, at least prior to 1935, and its opponents clearly perceived the NZL as a conservative, anti-labour and perhaps even fascist movement. Yet the NZL ultimately adopted an unorthodox economic position that drove away many of its more traditionally-minded members, one of whom later recalled that 'control had passed in Wellington to an extreme Left Wing group whose aims were directly contrary to our own'.[69] This partly reflected political fluidity in times of crisis – the NZL was merely one manifestation of a shift away from economic orthodoxy that ultimately brought Labour to power in 1935 and presaged the Keynesian consensus of the postwar period.

It also reflected the NZL's dubious claim to be apolitical, combined with its awareness of the growing societal scepticism for orthodox economics. As Begg said of Douglas Credit: 'With the knowledge that Lister, Simpson and Pasteur in my own profession were opposed as cranks by the orthodox school, I am willing to believe that the same error may be made in the sacred realms of economics … That Douglas is opposed by the so-called orthodox school makes the pleasure of listening to him more attractive.'[70]

The PPA is more difficult to classify. Anti-Catholicism was not unique to the right, although anti-communism and anti-socialism were far more commonly employed by centre-right politicians. Unlike the NZL, the PPA was not perceived as right wing by its opponents. The left-leaning *New Zealand Truth* described the PPA as 'disaffected, jaundiced-eyed and minded sectaries' possessed of 'burning zeal and fanatic fancies' from the old world: 'We fail to see what the "superstition of the Romish doctrine of the Mass," or the denial of a Catholic wife, or husband, or an undertaking not to marry either a Roman Catholic wife or husband has to do with New Zealand politics, or in what way such will bring the war to a glorious termination. On the contrary, it seems to be a revival of the bitterness of bygone days in older countries than New Zealand.'[71]

Yet the PPA clearly cleaved most strongly to the centre-right Reform Party, even throwing its weight behind Reform candidates after its support for an independent candidate in the 1918 Wellington Central by-election contributed to splitting the vote in favour of the Labour candidate.[72] This was part of a broader trend in the early twentieth century whereby Protestants generally aligned with Reform, and Catholics aligned with Liberal and Labour.[73] The PPA fundamentally sought to defend traditional values, beliefs and privileges that they believed were under threat by a nefarious 'other'. This made them conservatives by nature and populists in style.

CONCLUSION

How did the PPA and the NZL manage to attract such significant support? Three overarching factors stand out. First, they arose at times of pronounced crisis that generated a general sense of inchoate discontent. The heightened tensions of the Great War and the Great Depression made people more susceptible to radical alternatives: as one former NZL member aptly summarised in the 1970s, '[t]he man in the street felt doubtful – he could easily be sold a pup with so little support.'[74] But discontent also needed an 'other' upon which to focus its frustrations. The second factor behind the PPA and NZL's support was their ability to tap into long-simmering prejudices that in ordinary times did not animate people to the extent they did during times of crisis. Catholics and party politicians were not new 'others' – they had a history that proved much more relevant after certain galvanising events. For Catholics, it was the education question, the Easter Rising and debates about conscripting Catholic clergy; for party politicians, it was the polarising decision to devalue the currency to boost farmers' export returns. The PPA and the NZL were able to channel these concerns through a skilful blend of organisational and promotional techniques designed to build an enthusiastic and committed mass following. They devoted considerable time and energy to building robust organisational structures, they utilised large meetings as a form of public ceremony to recruit and energise members, and they produced a substantial amount of propaganda material. This was the third factor behind their support – they provided the right supply to the right demand. There were, however, many important differences between the two organisations. The PPA was fundamentally conspiratorial in its world-view and deliberately controversial in its strategy. Where the NZL was a movement of the respectable that aimed to unite, the PPA drew widespread criticism for its provocative and divisive rhetoric.

Ultimately, both the PPA and the NZL represented ideological dead-ends. In twenty-first-century New Zealand, anti-Catholicism is arguably no longer a noticeable form of prejudice.[75] And while anti-party griping remains a common pastime of the middle class and minor parties alike, it has not been a major galvanising force since the days of the NZL (although it has resurged among anti-mandate and anti-vaccination groups since August 2021). While the contribution of ex-NZL members to the ranks of the future National Party may have had an impact on the style of centre-right politics in New Zealand, this is difficult to quantify. Yet, despite their failure, the PPA and the NZL remain powerful counterpoints to the popular belief that Kiwis are too apathetic and laid back to be swayed by radical right-wing ideas. Given the right conditions, even the most barren of soils can sprout weeds from time to time.

CHAPTER SEVEN

'The Jews are to blame!' Antisemitic political radicalisation during the 1930s economic crisis

MARINUS LA ROOIJ

AT THE HEIGHT OF THE 1935 ELECTION CAMPAIGN during New Zealand's worst economic crisis, Prime Minister George Forbes, leader of the doomed Coalition government, attended a raucous meeting in Martinborough. Forbes made a spirited, if not desperate, attack on the 'phoney money' solutions to the Great Depression being promoted by the Opposition Labour Party. Forbes pinned his re-election chances on the Coalition's record of sound, orthodox economic management, as opposed to Labour's seemingly radical monetary reform policies. Forbes told the assembled Wairarapa voters that their choice was reasoned fiscal management or a reckless money-printing revolution. But this message was blunted when an animated citizen heckled out his own solution: 'Get rid of the Jews, sir ... The Jews are to blame from the beginning to end. You are in a position to kick them out ... They have all the money and control it.'[1]

Forbes, having heard these sentiments before, retorted that more Scotsmen were likely running banks than Hebrews – much to the crowd's entertainment. Yet by the month's end, Forbes was gone, his United–Reform Coalition losing 31 seats in a Parliament of 80, as the Labour Party doubled its vote and took power for the first time. This political earthquake was the result of five years of economic misery that destroyed public confidence in the political establishment long dominated by the Reform and Liberal–United Parties.[2] Less well known is how this tectonic shift in the political landscape was partly enabled by the rise of antisemitic conspiracy theories that characterised the Coalition as the pawns of international Jewish bankers who had manufactured the economic crisis. Conspiracist thinking was hardwired into the radical monetary reform movement that emerged during New Zealand's 'broken decade' of the 1930s.[3] Reflecting on the disastrous election loss, Gordon Coates, Reform Party leader and former deputy prime minister, estimated that around 200,000 voters had switched to Labour on the basis of its monetary reform policies.[4] These policies were broadly stated across the Labour caucus, from the more centrist and interventionist views of future minister of finance, Walter Nash, to those in the party who espoused more radical monetary reform ideas that rejected basic economic principles.

RISE OF RADICAL MONETARY REFORM AND CONSPIRACY THINKING

The most significant and enduring radical monetary reform movement was Douglas Social Credit (more commonly known in the 1930s as Douglas Credit), which believed the solution to the crisis was to radically overhaul a malfunctioning financial system, take power from the banks and create debt-free credit. This would be achieved by creating (not borrowing) vast amounts of credit to inject purchasing power into the hands of consumers and small producers, thus restarting the economy. Importantly, these radical monetary reformers rejected key precepts of mainstream economics, leading others like John Maynard Keynes, who favoured moderate reform of the financial system, to dismiss C.H. Douglas and his social credit movement as part of 'a brave army of heretics' in economic thinking.[5] But this economic unorthodoxy, particularly the notion that banks create money from nothing, made the movement prone to conspiracy theories that bridged the logical chasms in their belief structures. Many within this broad and diverse radical monetary reform movement believed that such fundamental reform of the financial system would break the power of the malevolent forces who caused the economic crisis by withholding credit. For these 1930s 'truthers', the Great Depression was a deliberate and planned act of economic sabotage by a cabal of malicious and mysterious international Jewish bankers. By 1935, the belief in an international bankers' conspiracy was so widespread that the Associated Banks of New Zealand needed to publicly denounce the idea, complaining in its newsletter that '[i]t is sometimes imagined that there is some hidden hand, some mysterious power dwelling behind the scenes directing the policies of the trading banks'.[6]

The mostly Australian-owned retail banks pleaded that their institutions were completely transparent and run by ordinary and unmysterious people. This appeal to reason had little impact on those who had spent the previous five years nurturing a

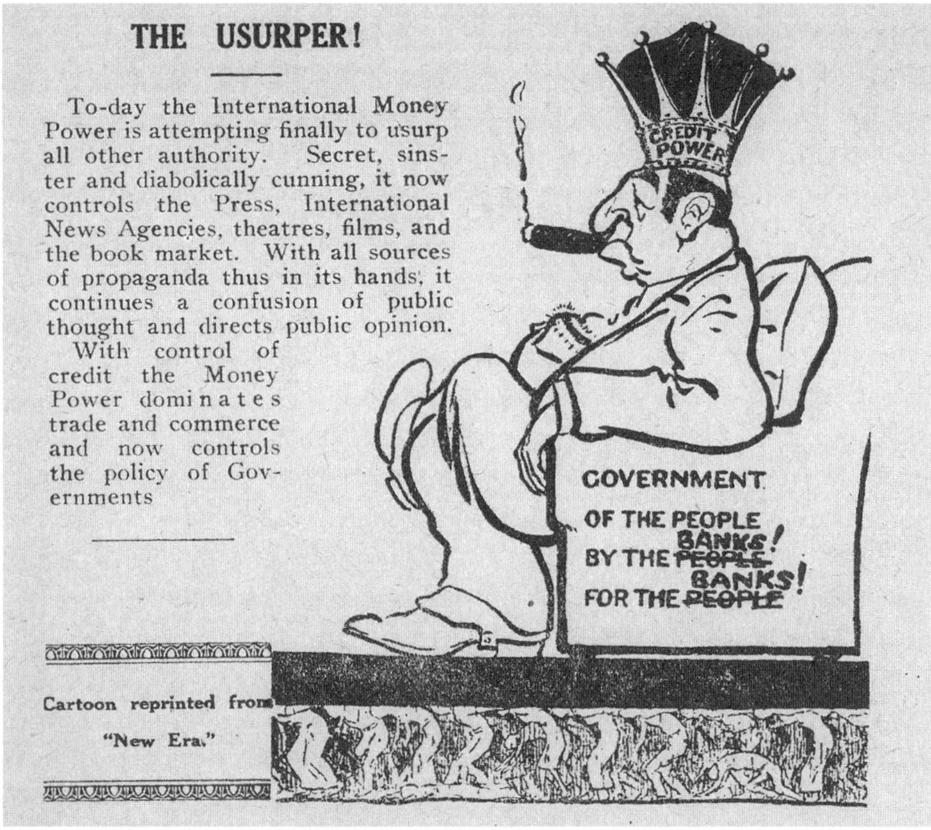

THE USURPER!

To-day the International Money Power is attempting finally to usurp all other authority. Secret, sinster and diabolically cunning, it now controls the Press, International News Agencies, theatres, films, and the book market. With all sources of propaganda thus in its hands, it continues a confusion of public thought and directs public opinion.

With control of credit the Money Power dominates trade and commerce and now controls the policy of Governments

Cartoon reprinted from "New Era."

Central to the notion of a Jewish super-conspiracy was the belief that it controlled the government and coordinated the output of thousands of mainstream media outlets across the globe. *New Zealand Plain Talk*, 18 August 1933, p. 7. S-L-1723-1, Alexander Turnbull Library, Wellington

deep belief in a vast bankers' conspiracy. For them, blame for the international trade collapse, bankruptcies of businesses and farms, and the suffering of the unemployed and of families thrown onto the street was due not to soulless market forces or mechanical failings of the economic system. Rather, the years of misery were caused by a 'super-conspiracy' of international Jewish financiers whose web of power and influence spanned the globe across banks, governments, newspapers, unions, political movements, cultural trends, universities and churches. For believers, all the world's events were connected and consciously coordinated in real time by a cabal that aimed to destroy the British Empire, enslave New Zealand and overthrow Christian civilisation.[7]

ARTHUR NELSON FIELD

While not every radical monetary reformer believed in the Jewish bankers' plot, the notion of a conspiracy by the 'MONEY POWER' was endemic within the movement. The popularity of the Jewish super-conspiracy in New Zealand during the 1930s can be attributed largely to the work of Arthur Nelson Field, the scion of one of Nelson's early Pākehā settler families.[8] His father, T.A.H. Field, owned a successful hardware business in Nelson, and was part of the conservative political establishment, serving as mayor of Nelson (1911–13) and its MP (1914–19).[9] Prior to 1930, A.N. Field had a successful career as a journalist, working mainly for the conservative Wellington newspaper, the *Dominion*, which he helped establish.

Field was known for his passionate loyalty to the British Empire and New Zealand's seemingly unbreakable connection to the United Kingdom. This imperial devotion was common among New Zealanders during the interwar years – they saw themselves first and foremost as 'British', and their small dominion of 1.5 million people as part of a great global empire. This generation was raised during the self-assured height of Britain's imperial power and had watched it spread its 'civilising mission' across the world. At the same time, there was a growing sense of a distinct national identity, even if this gave rise to conflict between national and imperial interests.[10] New Zealand's loyalty to Britain was also grounded in material dependence. International trade was almost exclusively with the 'Mother Country', and dependent on three exported commodities: butter, frozen meat and wool. External government loans were raised in London, most imports came from Britain and the colony depended on Britain's military protection. The relationship was described by the *Dominion* in its first editorial in 1907, possibly penned by Field: 'The Colony has passed into a Dominion under the protection of that Empire which has given us birth – perhaps the greatest in moral grandeur which the world has ever seen. We should strive in loyalty to our great parent to be worthy of our race and lineage.'[11]

This loyalty was put beyond doubt during World War I, when more than 100,000 New Zealanders volunteered or were conscripted to fight for King and Empire. Of these, around 18,000 were killed and 40,000 wounded – including A.N. Field. The distant places of Gallipoli and Flanders became sacred ground where New Zealand's debt to the British Empire was repaid in blood. Field's sacrifice was made at Armentières, France, where he was seriously wounded in June 1916. While recovering in England, he wrote a poem that expressed his feelings about having faced his own test of imperial patriotism. As one of 'England's sons afar', he had answered the call to war, ready to give everything to the Empire: 'all that we have and are we lay on England's shrine'.[12]

For Field and other returned soldiers, victory was promised as their opportunity to build a prosperous life through hard work and enterprise. At a Gallipoli commemoration in Palmerston North in 1929, the Rev. G.T. Brown recalled this promise: the Anzac sacrifice 'had destroyed the external menace and with bloodstained fingers, had handed back an opportunity to make New Zealand a land of light, liberty, peace and prosperity …'[13] Instead, the 1920s proved dispiriting as the British Empire lurched from one crisis to another. Much worse was to come with the global economic slump late in 1929. Like many economic shocks, the Great Depression opened existing fractures within New Zealand society. This included the growing burden of farm debt falling on the thousands of returned servicemen who had purchased Crown land at inflated prices. While assisted by generous government loans, these were often at unsustainable interest rates on marginal or unbroken land, requiring intensive work and ongoing investment without sustainable returns.[14] Despite the marginal economic returns provided by the new farms, the substantial expansion of land settlement in the 1920s also triggered significant infrastructure investment by local and central government, and New Zealand's debt increased year on year.[15]

THE ECONOMIC CRISIS

By 1928, the national debt had grown so large, compared to the size of the economy, that the newly elected United government struggled to convince lenders in the London market to provide more cash to enable its ambitious infrastructure programme.[16] To make matters worse, while the debt to the London market increased in size and cost, the value of New Zealand's exports collapsed by one-third during 1928–30.[17] This massive loss of revenue had a severe, even catastrophic, impact on farmers, many of whom walked off the land. The farmers' woes soon became a crisis for local and central government finances as revenues fell, borrowing costs increased and loan payments came due.

While the outlook was grim, next door in Australia the economic crisis was desperate: 'the lucky country' was even more vulnerable, owing massive debts to the London money market. With the collapse of export prices, Australia faced bankruptcy without drastic economic management. Seeking expert advice, the Australian government invited representatives from the Bank of England, which had a middleman role in Australasia's borrowing, to review the situation. On the basis of this advice, it was hoped an agreement could be reached to calm the London loan market and allow further bridging finance while the economy stabilised.[18]

While a visiting team of economists normally engenders little excitement, the Bank of England's mission radicalised people across Australia and New Zealand. Leading the mission was Sir Otto Niemeyer, the 'world's financial doctor', who spent the 1930s dispensing advice to economically distressed countries. Accompanying him was Professor Theodore Gregory, an expert on banking and monetary policy at the London School of Economics. The mission's timing and Niemeyer's austere and unsweetened advice shocked Australians, who became enraged at the notion that they had lived beyond their means. But the 1920s had seen investment directed into low-value infrastructure projects while the spending stimulus propped up artificially high living standards. Recognising that this debt-financed house of cards could not continue, Niemeyer recommended an austerity programme to balance the books. Borrowing as a strategy to cover the downturn was not a sustainable option, given the growing reluctance of the London loan market to lend more to a country struggling to meet its existing responsibilities.[19]

Many Australians denied there was even a problem, especially as the seriousness of the nation's growing indebtedness had not been acknowledged by its political leadership over the previous decade. The rude awakening of Niemeyer's message was exaggerated by its tactless delivery, and this served to focus public anger on the messenger. By happy chance, Niemeyer's mission coincided with an election in New South Wales, where the opposition Labor Party poised to benefit from the state's severe financial distress. With its long tradition of attacking international bankers and the 'London Jews', Labor called out the austerity plan as a Jewish plot.[20] Labor-leaning newspapers raged against the Bank of England's emissaries, using language that quickly descended into antisemitism. The *Labor Daily* called Niemeyer 'Shylock', and accused him of coming for his 'pound of flesh' on behalf of 'the British branch of International High Finance'.[21] Importantly, the paper argued that Australia and New Zealand – the 'most British' of Dominions – were for some reason being treated worse by Britain than foreign countries receiving debt relief.[22] In making sense of this treachery, Niemeyer was accused of not just acting the role of Shylock, but of being Jewish himself.

Rumours began circulating that Professor Gregory had suspiciously changed his name to conceal his 'alien' identity. Gregory was indeed Jewish, and had changed his name from Gugenheim in 1914 to affirm his Englishness, as King George V would also do three years later, replacing his German surname. Niemeyer too was born in England to German parents from Hanover, but unlike Gregory he was not Jewish. This did not stop Jack Lang, soon to be Labor premier of New South Wales, from making political hay from this clumsy conflation. Before a cheering crowd in the rural Tablelands, Lang thundered: 'Niemeyer sneered at you ... he will kick you and trample on you to-morrow. It is impudent for him to say that we are too well clothed, our children are too highly educated and that our standard of living is too high. He laughed at us.' After condemning Niemeyer's advice as an assault on Australia's sovereignty by sinister alien forces, he went further: 'Anything [Niemeyer] has done in any part of the world has been a curse to the workers – the curse of the Wandering Jew. He has always left plague and disaster behind him. He will not do any Wandering Jew act in Australia if I have a say.'[23]

During September, while Australia seethed over Niemeyer's advice, the delegation arrived in New Zealand at the invitation of Forbes' United administration. For weeks, Niemeyer's mission had been widely reported, with local newspapers noting that Australians were 'stirred and deeply concerned' at the austerity advice received and the need for the country to take 'her medicine'.[24] The political consensus in New Zealand was that a period of austerity was also necessary to balance the government's books, manage down debt and reduce the cost of production (and living) to make the economy more competitive. The main disagreement was over how this reduction in living standards would be spread across the population, with the Labour Party advocating for the rich to make a greater sacrifice. This consensus would soon start to fracture.[25]

THE TRUTH ABOUT THE SLUMP

Niemeyer's brief in New Zealand was narrower, focused more on monetary policy and the question of the exchange rate. But his harsh austerity message to Australia struck a raw nerve. New Zealanders saw Australians not as mere cousins in a neighbouring country but as kindred racial Britons in an empire bound in blood and shared sacrifice. This was certainly the case for A.N. Field. Niemeyer's mission triggered his political radicalisation and made him a committed antisemite. During 1930, Field had spent his time exploring the causes of the economic crisis, driven by the experience of his own family's financial difficulties and the loss of the farm he had hoped to settle on. Recalling his own debt crisis, he later reflected: 'I know all about what it is to be the toad beneath the financial harrow.'[26]

During September 1930, Field penned a series of columns entitled 'Wobbling Money' for his old paper, the *Dominion*.[27] With no formal training as an economist, Field pondered how matters could have become so perilous as to have brought

'Australia to the verge of bankruptcy' and 'leaving a trail of disaster and depression around the whole globe'.[28] He focused on Britain's return to the gold standard in 1925 to determine the value of the pound and, with the benefit of hindsight, wondered why the promised benefits of this monetary stabilisation did not eventuate. He noted the sinister rise of the US as an economic power, seemingly at Britain's expense. Financing the Great War had, he noted, made Britain and France indebted to the US, making that country a significant holder of the world's gold reserves and providing great influence on the world's money supply. This change in the world's economic centre of gravity meant the British economy was more vulnerable to economic shocks in America, like the Wall Street crash of 1929. The economic sinews of Empire meant that Britain's vulnerability to American monetary power flowed on to New Zealand, dependent on a single market to sell its devalued goods.

In 1930, the technical discipline of economics was still being established in Australasia, with expertise mostly confined to the banks and a few universities. In this vacuum, Field's articles reflected popular efforts to find plausible explanations for the systematic failure of the world's complex and entangled financial order. Most importantly, Field's articles avoided the potential for borrowers' remorse, and instead looked for others to blame. In 'Wobbling Money', Field pondered the increasing importance of the US Federal Reserve in setting America's monetary policy and, as a result, the international supply of money. The 'answer' was found on Wellington's Lambton Quay on the same day Niemeyer's picture serendipitously appeared in the *Dominion* along with Field's first column.[29] A banker friend chanced upon him in the street, and asked if Field knew that Professor Gregory's real name was Gugenheim, 'suspiciously' changed during the war to conceal that he was Jewish and not a racial Briton.[30] It was a landmark moment in Field's life, sending him on a 30-year mission to expose what he saw as a global Jewish plot.

Until then, Field had had little interest in the idea of a Jewish conspiracy, having dismissed the idea when exposed to it in England following the war.[31] Prior to 1930, New Zealanders generally were of a similar view, with most ethnic or religious paranoia focused on either the imagined Irish-Catholic conspiracy to break up the Empire and infiltrate the public service, or the existential threat of Asian mass migration.[32] There had been isolated episodes of antisemitism and an ongoing undercurrent of anti-Jewish prejudice that expressed itself in popular culture or was aimed directly at the small Jewish community. But this was minor compared to the coherent political antisemitism that would emerge in the fertile conditions of the 1930s. Field's work over the next five years would prove to be the spark that allowed the idea of a Jewish world conspiracy to jump the metaphorical firebreak from the fringe into the political mainstream. As the astute commentator W.N. Pharazyn observed at the time: 'Ten years ago the idea of anti-Semitism in New Zealand would have been laughed to scorn, but no matter how insignificant its disciples may be, we have it here now.'[33]

While the left-wing Pharazyn dismissed their beliefs as laughable, conditions were ripe enough for Field and other antisemites to find the notion of a globally coordinated, multifaceted super-conspiracy a plausible explanation for the world's economic chaos. Field certainly had remembered enough of the antisemitic conspiracies he'd dismissed 10 years earlier to think there was now something to them. His awakening over Professor Gregory's 'hidden' Jewishness prompted him to re-read the notorious *Protocols of the Learned Elders of Zion*, the plagiarised and fictitious minutes of a supposed meeting of a Jewish world government or 'Sanhedrin' that set out their plan to enslave the world.[34] While researching in the Parliamentary Library, he would chat to A.D. McIntosh, a future senior public servant, who noted that Field seemed compelled to dedicate 'his life to exposing what he considers the nefarious machinations of the Jews in international finance'. McIntosh also observed that Field himself was aware of the psychological changes he was undergoing, and that 'he was becoming obsessed' with the topic.[35]

Nonetheless, Field believed the public had to be warned of the terrible danger they faced. In early 1931, discussion of the economic crisis dominated the newspapers, as one opinion piece observed: 'Almost every paper is reeking with economics, for this is the outstanding subject of the day.'[36] However, Field believed that the mainstream media was reporting an elaborately created or foolishly misguided fiction. The remedy was his self-published book *The Truth About the Slump*, subtitled *What the news never tells*.[37] Field's work explained why the Niemeyer mission was a symptom of a much greater crisis – that a powerful British institution was guilty of treason against the British people of Australia and New Zealand:

> [It] is surely a very extraordinary thing that the Bank of England should send out two agents, both from their names obviously of Teutonic descent. The character of these gentlemen may be beyond reproach, but in view of the German-Jew domination in New York, in view of the way British finance is under the thumb of New York, what feeling can a layman experience but one of disgust at finding a foreign flavour in Bank of England action on this side of the world?[38]

The Truth About the Slump was one of many self-funded books, pamphlets and journals that sought to explain and solve the economic crisis of the 1930s. What set it apart was that Field was a respected mainstream journalist, with an authoritative and objective writing style. But the 'evidence' that gave him his authority was largely from writings by British antisemites like Hilaire Belloc, Nesta Webster, Alan Percy (the eighth Duke of Northumberland and publisher of the aggressively antisemitic *The Patriot*) and, notably, Arthur Kitson, a radical monetary reformer and ardent critic of the gold standard.[39]

PROTOCOLS OF THE LEARNED ELDERS OF ZION

A key objective of Field's book was to convince readers of the 'truth' contained in the *Protocols of the Learned Elders of Zion* by demonstrating the existence of a Jewish bankers' conspiracy and its connection to all the world's problems.[40] But Field's increasingly fanatical beliefs narrowed his research to the tenuous connections linking Jewish people to purportedly interconnected world events that were often decades apart. One example of this confirmation bias is his reliance on the US House of Representatives' 1913 inquiry into the so-called 'Money Trust'.[41] Known as the Pujo Commission, its work was politically motivated, and aimed at trimming the power and influence of a number of notable American millionaires, primarily the legendary J.P. Morgan (of Welsh ancestry).[42] Importantly, the commission's majority report noted that the 'Money Trust' was not a 'consequence of any definite agreement' but rather a tendency for businessmen to make deals and form short-term alliances with people they knew to advance their commercial and political interests. The report also noted the peripheral role within the Money Trust of the Jewish-owned banking firm Kuhn, Loeb & Company, described as 'only qualifiedly allied with the inner group'.[43] But Field's 'research' filtered out the non-Jewish inner group, focusing instead on the connections and actions of Jewish businessmen, notably those associated with the US Federal Reserve and Kuhn, Loeb & Co. Paul Warburg and Jacob Schiff, in particular, become the arch-villains of his book, the so-called 'Men at the Top' of the super-conspiracy.[44] Field later described his approach to conspiracy research: newspapers, he said, must be read through 'Jewish spectacles', as only through the prism of the *Protocols of the Learned Elders of Zion* could one discern the workings of the plot hidden behind the media's misdirection.[45]

OPPOSITE: Front cover of the first of three New Zealand editions of the notorious antisemitic forgery reportedly documenting Jewish plans for world domination.

Protocols of the Learned Elders of Zion: With recent comments from many quarters, Plain Talk, Auckland, 1933. B-K-1431-cover, Alexander Turnbull Library, Wellington

PROTOCOLS

of the

Learned Elders *of* Zion

S.

The Jewish Symbol of the Serpent. See pages 10 and 90.

IS IT A FORGERY?—READ IT AND DECIDE FOR YOURSELF.

Price—2/6 Net.

Professor A.H. Tocker of Canterbury University College reviewed *The Truth About the Slump* for fellow technical experts in banking and economics. He dismissed it and the 'stable money' monetary reform policies it advocated, but noted with some alarm its readability and the superficial credibility of the conspiracist 'cloak and dagger' story it wove. The reader, he wrote, 'is inclined to rub his eyes in wonder whether he is reading a serious contribution to the solution of present economic difficulties or the latest thriller in detective fiction bought from the railway bookstall.'[46] But Field was certainly successful in convincing others without the benefit of technical training in economics. In June 1931, Anglican Archdeacon Taylor, of St Luke's Church in Nelson, preached to his congregation of his hope that the economic crisis would 'lead to the discovery of the arch-criminals' whose 'selfishness and greed' had thwarted God's bounty that should provide enough for all. He drew his flock's attention to A.N. Field's book that 'made definite charges against a group of international financiers. These charges were supported by much documentary evidence and were worthy of careful examination. Either [these charges] must be refuted by the people concerned, or they must be held to discredit those people in the eyes of all decent men.'[47]

The readability and superficial objectivity of *The Truth About the Slump* was complemented by the timing of its release, Field's standing in Wellington and his knowledge of the parliamentary village. He posted copies to every MP at the end of the summer recess, knowing they had plenty of reading time available on the train ride back to Wellington. Once Parliament resumed, the first great debate was on the Finance Bill and the government's intention to embark on an austerity programme. In the House of Representatives, Labour's Bob Semple, an elder statesman of New Zealand's labour movement, lamented the terrible impact that economic austerity was having on workers. Armed with information from Field's 'great book', he claimed that the cause of the economic crisis was the malevolent global control of credit: 'It can safely be said that one of the difficulties facing the world to-day is the money trusts which have developed into a titanic monopoly, which wields a tremendous power over nations.'[48] Later in the day, Minister of Education Harry Atmore encouraged people to read the 'most interesting book' by Field who 'is not only courageous and able, but is painstaking and untiring in research; and, whether one agrees with all his deductions or not, one must recognize that the author has put forward the truth, and a reader can make his own deductions.'[49]

Arguably, *The Truth About the Slump* helped fracture the pre-1931 consensus, with some opposing government policies now using conspiracy theories to argue that the economic crisis was artificially created by international bankers through money manipulation, and that it could simply be undone through massive government credit creation. The political debate became peppered with such allusions. By July 1931, Colonel T.W. McDonald (formerly a pro-government Wairarapa MP) espoused at length on his new-found conviction in conspiracy theory: 'What I have read and studied leads me to the conclusion – and I am not alone in this belief – that the whole monetary policy of the world is in the hands of a few Jewish financiers.'[50]

Outside Parliament, some of the groups opposing austerity used Field's book as more ammunition with which to attack the government. Such was its 'astonishing vogue' that Minister of Finance Downie Stewart told noted economist Horace Belshaw that it was more 'poisonous than anything coming from the Labour Party'.[51] For its part, Labour adopted some of Field's thinking. The *New Zealand Worker* recommended *The Truth About the Slump* as 'a book which all should read', while hedging its bet on whether Field had 'put the blame for the slump on the right shoulders', commenting 'it shows how through the actions of this [US Federal Reserve] board the banking and credit systems not merely of America, but practically of the whole world have come to be controlled by a few men, mostly Jews, and that it is these few men by the control of monetary policy who are the masters of Government'.[52]

INFLUENCE ON DOUGLAS CREDITERS

Field's influence on the burgeoning Douglas Social Credit movement was particularly profound, with *The Truth About the Slump* amplifying the antisemitism located within the theories of its British founder Major C.H. Douglas.[53] This feedback-loop made the mainstream of the movement arguably more openly antisemitic than any other in the world. The swelling ranks of Douglas Crediters heaped praise on Field as a foremost contributor to their thinking – aside from Major Douglas, of course. The influential Auckland Farmers' Union adopted Douglas Credit and became an enthusiastic promoter of anti-Jewish conspiracy theories, stating in 1932 that 'New Zealanders had heard little of the matter before Mr Field forced it to the front.'[54] The effects of this radicalisation lasted for decades: newly migrated English Douglasites in the 1950s were shocked at how antisemitic the New Zealand movement was.[55]

The dramatic growth of the Douglas Credit movement during 1932–33 somewhat horrified Field, who was trying to build his own national emergency movement for radical monetary reform and to cleanse the government of semitic influences.[56] Indeed, he openly despised the movement, stating: 'It is curious that a lot of modern movements seem to induce people to leave their reasoning faculties behind them in taking up with a cult … the Douglas Credit folk are largely this way.'[57] Even so, not long after publishing *The Truth About the Slump*, a steady stream of fan mail from Douglas Crediters began arriving at his Nelson home.

One of those profoundly affected by Field's work was Frank Robson, a Douglas Crediter recently returned from Sydney. Robson too was a journalist, a South Islander who had also been seriously wounded in Flanders in 1916. His fierce hatred of Jews grew out of his reporting on the notorious Sydney auction houses of the 1920s.[58] Operated on the margins of legality, like the mobile truck shops of today, these businesses used tricks like easy loans with high interest rates, rigged auctions, shoddy goods, phoney sale promotions and aggressive salesmanship. Some of these auction houses were run by a small circle of Jewish people from the former Russian Empire, who disproportionately attracted the attention of sensationalist newspapers. A 1927 article, likely authored by Robson, stated that the 'Shylocks' running the auction houses were 'vultures' who through their disreputable practices were 'feeding on the human wreckage of the Great War'.[59]

Robson's dislike of a few small-time Jewish moneylenders and concern for the plight of destitute returned soldiers seems to have metastasised during the economic crisis into a deep antisemitism. He came to believe that global Jewish moneylenders were driving returned soldiers, war widows and their children to ruin. This obsession with 'THE PLOT' would dominate the rest of his life and 'ruin' the lives of his own wife and children.[60] That A.N. Field had a role in Robson's radicalisation is highly likely. In March 1932, Robson wrote to Field, informing him that he had moved to Christchurch and was earning good money from what 'the Jews have so far overlooked'. Noting how widely Field's writings were known, Robson thought it possible to launch an independent newspaper that would promote monetary reform, propagate the Jewish conspiracy and be a profitable concern.[61]

The culmination of Robson's vision appeared in October 1932 with the publication of *New Zealand Plain Talk* and its opening headline: 'Have Shylocks got us Bluffed?'[62] *Plain Talk* was full of the hyperbole and hysterical headlines that Robson was accustomed to from his time in Sydney's populist newspaper culture. But with added antisemitism, the paper attacked the 'Feeble-minded Government' who 'are about to Sell us Finally to the Shylocks!', and warned that the economic crisis and the government's failure to act 'is deliberately planned by a group of International Financiers'.[63] For Douglasites like Robson, the way to end people's suffering was simple: the government should issue 'social credit' printed to match the nation's productive capacity. So straightforward was the Douglas plan to effectively print money and allow every citizen to receive a 'national dividend' to boost their spending power, it raised one profound question: what was stopping this beneficial tsunami of credit now? The answer was a sinister one: hidden forces were preventing such an easy solution to further their own ends. Robson identified the culprit as the 'cabal' of Jews who secretly manipulated the world's financial order and, in their spare time, were also instrumental forces behind every major event in the world – from triggering the Great War to orchestrating the Russian Revolution. Like Field, Robson turned on the mainstream media that consistently failed to report these 'truths', calling them the 'Parrot Press [who are] the Judas Iscariot of to-day' and writing that: 'Much of the Press of the world, together with the news services, have been bought or dominated by the Money Power – a group of International financiers which has long ago conceived the ambition of world domination through currency control.'[64]

In the absence of an official publication, *Plain Talk* became the Douglas Credit movement's unofficial paper by default, and sold thousands of copies around the country. A Wellington confidant of Field reported that the paper was 'getting big sales the newsboys tell me'.[65] But not all Douglas Crediters were pleased with the paper's frank antisemitism. Australian Douglas Credit leader Barclay Smith recalled the paper's apparent desire to 'fill every reader with hatred and loathing of all things Jewish' rather than to win people to Douglasism.[66] Disputes soon broke out across the movement over whether to support *Plain Talk*'s explicit antisemitism, avoid openly discussing the Jewish conspiracy so as to avert controversy, or to dismiss notions of a conspiracy as ludicrous, as some Douglasites did. The dilemma was encapsulated by Wellington Social Credit Association president Norman Taylor in a letter to Raymond Hansen, *Plain Talk*'s Waikato contributor and distributor. Taylor voiced his reluctance to associate openly with the paper's antisemitism but reassured his fellow Douglasite: '[P]lease do not misunderstand me. I agree with you entirely that this Money Menace is mainly Jewish … Yet as a responsible officer of this association I still regard it as my duty to steer a middle course.'[67]

The final straw was when Robson published the first New Zealand edition of the *Protocols of the Learned Elders of Zion* in March 1933.[68] The *New Zealand Herald* was quick to report on the appearance of this 'device for fomenting hostility towards Jews', setting out at length the history of this fraudulent document, fabricated by Tsarist police in 1905 to focus Russian hostility on the Jewish population rather than supporting the revolutionary movement.[69] In her novel about the tribulations of a returned soldier in the years after the war, Robin Hyde (Iris Wilkinson) also noted *Plain Talk*'s polarising impact on the political landscape, describing an Auckland meeting:

> Mr Chairman, I wish to bring a very serious matter under your notice. The faked 'Protocols of Zion,' exposed years ago as a forgery, are being used by men purporting to be Douglas Social Credit advocates, for the purpose of cooking up attacks on the Jews. They've got a paper, and they're advocating hatred and violence. It has to be stopped.[70]

The country's Jewish community also feared that New Zealand could become infected with the same violent intolerance Germany had succumbed to. In April 1933, William Warnock, a trusted employee of the influential Nathan family, contacted the Commissioner of Police in the hope that *Plain Talk* could be shut down. Despite *Plain Talk*'s frequent claims that at any moment it was to be silenced by the minions of the alleged Jewish conspiracy, the legal right to free speech prevailed. This left Robson free to continue publishing until early 1934, when competition from other Douglas Credit papers closed him down.[71]

THE RESERVE BANK AND THE END OF FREEDOM

Despite the divisions, conspiracists across the radical monetary reform movement agreed that the plot was coming to a dramatic climax in 1933. Robson warned his readers that the economic crisis was merely another step in the 'Gigantic Secret Plan for World Domination', with the worst yet to come.[72] For conspiracy believers, the next great step in New Zealand's enslavement was the establishment of the Reserve Bank, a development also recommended by Niemeyer.[73] The economic crisis had created a consensus among economists that every country would benefit from having a central bank to better insulate their economies from overseas financial shocks.[74] Radical monetary reformers, fuelled by a deep mistrust of 'orthodox' economic experts and a paranoia that any Niemeyer proposal was another step in the global plot, saw the creation of a central bank in apocalyptic terms. Country Party leader and MP for the Bay of Islands, Captain H.M. Rushworth warned the influential Auckland Farmers' Union at their annual conference that the move could 'lead to civil war', adding: 'This, in my mind, is part of a ghastly conspiracy to transfer the control of New Zealand, first to the [Reserve] Bank of New Zealand and then to the Bank of International Settlements, and once that is done nothing but bloody revolution will get us back our power of self-governing. And I know of no constitutional means which will stop this bill going through.'[75] The conference needed little convincing and passed a motion against the legislation, with other Farmers' Union branches also flooding government

Referring to the creation of the Reserve Bank – Deputy Prime Minister Gordon Coates and Prime Minister George Forbes are lampooned as bungling crime fighters failing to prevent Jewish bankers from stealing control over New Zealand.

Point Blank, 15 December 1933, p. 5. S-L 62, Alexander Turnbull Library, Wellington buildings with letters of protest.[76] Radical monetary reformers went into overdrive, holding protest meetings, writing hyperbolic letters to editors and printing their own 'media' to argue that the bank would be 'Disastrous to [the] Country'.[77]

As the Reserve Bank legislation went through Parliament, it became clear the extent to which the political debate had become infected by ideas of a Jewish super-conspiracy. Arthur Stallworthy, independent-conservative MP for Eden, argued that behind the 'world-wide oligarchy of finance' stood 'the Judeo-German-American group, the four big D's of Germany, Kuhn, Loeb of New York, J. Henry Schroder of London, and such industrial groups as the Imperial Chemicals, headed by Alfred Mond, now Lord Melchett'. Stallworthy went on, explaining that they were led by the Bleichröder group who (bizarrely) were engaged in a titanic financial struggle with the Rothschilds for control of the world's currencies.[78] Captain Rushworth also weighed in, surmising that world financial power was similarly divided into two feuding Jewish super-conspiracies – 'the Bleichroder-Mendelssohn group and the Rothschild group'.[79]

Significantly, the notion that the creation of the Reserve Bank provided an ultimate mechanism for Jewish financial control over New Zealand was embraced by members of the Labour Party. Rev. Clyde Carr, MP for Timaru, channelled A.N. Field to explain that Paul Warburg's 'manipulation of the [Federal Reserve] legislation as it passed through Congress' allowed that institution to become 'largely responsible' for the Wall Street crash.[80] Frank Langstone, MP for Waimarino, also had nothing good to say about the dangerous machinations of (the now deceased) Paul Warburg and the 'big banking house' of Kuhn Loeb & Co: 'If one reads the written history of Paul Warburg one will find that his brother was head of the German espionage system during the Great War. This is the type of man Paul Warburg is – a man connected with the German Jews and the big banking interests controlling practically the whole of modern finance.'[81]

UNTRUSTED AND UNWANTED

While the Reserve Bank Act was passed, the incoming Labour government in April 1936 kept its promise to bring the bank to heel by nationalising it. But there was one last twist. During the development of the legislation, Field and the Farmers' Union lobbied to insert a clause preventing Jews from sitting on the bank's board. Indeed, the legislation stipulated that board members must be 'a British subject by birth', and one left-wing paper confirmed the clause was inserted as the result of antisemitic pressure on Minister of Finance Gordon Coates, who was 'only too pleased to accede to the wishes of the anti-Semitics [*sic*] among the currency reformers by providing in the original Reserve Bank Act that only natural born British subjects should sit on its board'.[82] While Coates saw the conspiracy theorists' objections to the creation of the bank as ridiculous, he likely conceded the clause simply to allow the legislation to pass and to placate the unreasoning level of opposition to it.

But when the Labour Party wanted to appoint their own man to the bank's board in August 1936, they appeared to have forgotten that they had helped normalise the notion of sinister Jewish influence in the bank. Approving Dunedin socialist Mark Silverstone as a safe choice for the now state-owned bank, Minister of Finance Walter Nash ended up red-faced and forced to defend his appointee, who was Polish-born (and Jewish), so failing the British-by-birth requirement. Getting one back on his political foes, Gordon Coates roared with incredulity on the irony: 'The [Labour] Opposition of the day talked about the Bank of International Settlements and Jewish financiers, and about the necessity for keeping the Reserve Bank in the control of our own race. No Opposition criticism was more fierce or single-minded.'[83] Labour's embarrassment was self-inflicted, as it had been unwilling to amend the British-by-birth clause when it had the chance in April. Removing it would have inflamed the passions of the still vocal radical monetary reformers it counted within its caucus and wider support base.

Silverstone's appointment was retrospectively confirmed through one-off empowering legislation, rather than by amending the original law.[84] But the drama over his appointment illustrated the extent to which, by the mid-1930s, Jewish people were considered suspect by a sizeable and vocal minority of New Zealanders. This was tragically reflected a few years later when Walter Nash, in his capacity as minister of customs, pondered how many Jewish refugees could safely be accepted without triggering an allergic reaction from those who regarded Jews as an existential threat. As Jews desperately tried to flee violent persecution in Europe, Nash wrote that 'anti-Semitism, never far from the surface, was very apt to emerge in the case of the talented race whose members can often beat us at our own game, especially the game of money making'.[85] This meant that New Zealand accepted fewer refugees, compared against population size, than Australia and Canada.[86]

Despite widespread sympathy for the plight of the Jewish community living under Nazi terror, Nash knew there was only political risk from accepting anything but a trickle of Jewish refugees into the country, no matter how desperate their situation. Among those opposed to any loosening of non-British immigration restrictions was the Auckland Returned Soldiers' Association (RSA), which campaigned on the issue before and during World War II. This agitation culminated in a resolution adopted in 1945 by the national RSA that called for the removal of all enemy aliens from New

Zealand within two years.[87] Most of these 'enemy aliens' were Jewish refugees from Germany and Austria. Frank Robson, who was active in the Auckland RSA, argued that returned soldiers feared that the 'economic control and influence of these aliens is out of all reasonable proportion to their numbers'.[88]

CONCLUSION

As the economic crisis eased and New Zealand joined the war against Nazi Germany, the idea of a Jewish world conspiracy lost much of its potency outside the milieu of hardened conspiracists who continued their political activism over the decades, opposing everything from water fluoridation, multiculturalism, democracy in southern Africa, and the establishment of the World Bank and International Monetary Fund. For some, the conspiracist bug that took hold of them in the early 1930s propelled them on a lifetime of activism opposing the supposed super-conspiracy. In one of the last letters A.N. Field received before his death in 1963, W.B. Bray of Leeston, Canterbury, reminisced about his political awakening 30 years earlier: 'It was your book, *The Truth About the Slump* that gave me the first clue that Social Credit was founded on truth and I have worked and written for it ever since.'[89] As late as 1981, when the Social Credit Party was New Zealand's third largest and received 20 percent of the national vote, Michael Sheppard's book on the party exposed the antisemitism that remained ingrained within the movement. Sheppard recalled how when first introduced to Douglasism, he was handed a copy of *All These Things* – Field's magnum opus on the Jewish conspiracy first published in 1936.[90]

What started as a confluence of events at the start of New Zealand's worst economic crisis ended up spawning a radicalising contagion that helped reshape the political landscape. This ideological infection also had life-changing consequences for those consumed by conspiracist thinking. Hundreds of activists were radicalised during the 1930s, including Field and Robson, and they would spend the rest of their lives obsessed with a compulsion to expose a phantom super-conspiracy. They saw this plot everywhere and in everything, yet, inexplicably – as James Meek has observed in modern times – this highly organised, 'marvellously slow' super-conspiracy continued to evolve but never succeeded in establishing the diabolical enslavement its believers continually predicted.[91]

The causes of the 1930s economic crisis were for many complex and seemingly baffling, with some finding it easier to personify the world's financial system into a malevolent Jewish banker. *New Zealand Sunday News*, 24 November 1934, p. 5. PAL NZS, Hocken Collections, Uare Toaka o Hākena, University of Otago

PART 3

The rise of the radical right after World War II

CHAPTER EIGHT

Behind the golden weather

The rightward fringe in New Zealand, 1950–70

STEVEN LOVERIDGE

RECOLLECTIONS OF NEW ZEALAND ACROSS THE 1950–70 PERIOD tend towards visions of a postwar 'golden weather', featuring political stability, rising affluence, and perhaps stifling cultural consensus.[1] Indeed, the major study of the New Zealand far right frames extremism in the following decades as *The Politics of Nostalgia* centred on a longing 'for the untroubled days of the immediate post-war period'.[2] The years of golden weather, however, do contain political events and cultural shifts that reverberated in fringe movements, and New Zealand's first explicitly neo-Nazi organisations emerged in this period. Major context includes local reactions to volatile global developments as the Cold War presented an ongoing threat from international communism, as 'the winds of change' in Africa signalled changing racial politics, particularly after sanctions were placed on Rhodesia following the 1965 declaration of independence and as tensions mounted around sporting contacts with apartheid South Africa, and as Britain's declining global position and turn towards Europe rumbled longstanding pillars of New Zealand's cultural identity and economic orientation.

This chapter provides a tour of consequent reactions on the rightward fringe, and concludes with some assessment of the major legacies and implications of this period. Given that any bright lines delineating the 'centre right', the 'far right' and the 'extreme right' are contentious, the proposed solution is to chart a journey to the fringe. This journey tracks the increasing radicalisation of the moderate conservative impulse to preserve the institutions and traditions taken as sustaining a community's health or existence.[3] Typical symptoms of this radicalisation include heightened, if not obsessive, threat perceptions and the conspiratorial linkage of threats and targets. Typical reactions include the conviction that decisive and potentially authoritarian actions are necessary to preserve the community, and to reassert the traditions, institutions, mores and, in some cases, racial identity taken as underwriting the community's moral and physical bonds.

In the extreme, this radicalisation leads to movements with fascist tendencies and groups openly identifying as neo-Nazi. The question of what constitutes 'fascism' is complicated by both a common vulgarisation of the term and intricate scholarly debate over its essential nature.[4] This chapter approaches fascism as a particular and extreme manifestation of fears of communal decline and prescriptions for regeneration. Certainly, Robert Paxton's study of the essential themes of fascism reads as consistent with the course of radicalisation:

> Fascism may be defined as a form of political behaviour marked by obsessive preoccupation with community decline, humiliation, or victimhood and by compensatory cults of unity, energy, and purity, in which a mass-based party of committed nationalist militants, working in uneasy but effective collaboration with traditional elites, abandons democratic liberties and pursues with redemptive violence and without ethical or legal restraints goals of internal cleansing and external expansion.[5]

Approaching the subject as a journey towards and into an eclectic and frequently bizarre and sinister scene has the advantage of impressing recurring passions and ideas as well as distinct elements. Indeed, the 'far right' was not a monolith and, besides a shared rejection of progressive directions taken as threatening communal cohesion, was hardly ideologically uniform. While the Country Party and the National Socialist Party shared a rejection of political and cultural directions, the former championed a return to a 1930s-vintage, pre-welfare-state individualism: 'We are against concentration and centralisation of power by Government or big business. It will lead to either fascism or Communism.'[6] Conversely, the latter championed fascistic collectivism and a powerful state: 'We demand the Union of all New Zealanders to form a Greater New Zealand'; '… we demand the creation of a strong central power of the State, unquestioned authority of the politically centralised Parliament over the entire Nation.'[7] Even organisations that could be classed as white nationalist groups could flaunt their distinctions. As one neo-Nazi stated: 'Those of us in the National Socialist Movement … consider those in the National Front to be kosher conservatists [*sic*].'[8] In what may well be a peak example of the narcissism of small differences, a 1969 security report noted that the National Socialist Party of New Zealand and the New Zealand National Socialist Party were 'at loggerheads', with the head of the former deeming the latter 'extremist and disruptive'.[9]

POLITICAL THEATRE

Another set of complications arise from the complex position that visions of fascism have within the political theatre and the cultural landscape. Responding to the emergency powers wielded by Prime Minister Sidney Holland's National government during the 1951 waterfront conflict, for example, striker literature made a staple of damning Holland as Hitler, the 'Secret Police' as the Gestapo and the emergency regulations as fascism. In a 1952 essay written with this episode in mind, social critic Bill Pearson pondered whether an observed disposition for conformity and a passive acceptance of authority represented an opening for fascism in New Zealand: '... in countries nominally democratic, fascists have first to prepare the ground. In New Zealand the ground is already prepared, in these conditions: a docile sleepy electorate, veneration of war-heroes, willingness to persecute those who don't conform, gullibility in the face of headlines and radio peptalk ... Fascism has long been a danger potential in New Zealand.'[10]

Evoking fascism as a means of condemnation gained new life during the countercultural skirmishes of the 1960s and 1970s.[11] Hecklers disrupted a 1965 Democratic Society lecture by Ron Gostick, a visiting figure on the Canadian far right, with mocking chants of 'sieg heil'.[12] A 1969 university student stunt, fusing elements of prank and protest, went to further effort, festooning the Wellington headquarters of the Security Intelligence Service with a swastika banner.[13] In 1971, members of Auckland's Progressive Youth Movement protested a visit from Siegfried Westphal, a former Wehrmacht general, by dressing in full SS uniform and posing outside the city's Cenotaph.[14]

This dynamic was distinct from that of social rebels who appropriated Third Reich regalia and rituals during the 1960s to shock rather than mock. This practice gave the Stormtroopers their name, and the gang also adopted swastikas, stahlhelms, sieg heils and fascist salutes.[15] In 1970 investigative reporter Brian Edwards described half of the dozen Stormtroopers he interviewed as wearing 'a uniform' of 'jeans, heavy black boots, Nazi-style helmets (which turned out to be made of fibre-glass or plastic), and leather jackets emblazoned with swastikas, German eagles, the word "Storm Troopers", and in one or two cases stripes indicating office in the gang hierarchy'.[16] A historian of New Zealand gangs describes this penchant as 'flaunting a rejection of social norms' without, necessarily, adopting any political tenets.[17] Many have certainly noted the oddity of Māori and Pasifika gang members donning the trappings of white supremacy; only one of the dozen Stormtroopers Edwards interviewed was white.[18]

Young protester Tim Shadbolt added, 'We were proud of being rejected because we didn't want to be like those who rejected us. That's why we wore swastikas – it really seemed to bug people. The swastika meant as much to us as Napoleon's tricolour meant to our parents.'[19] On his first point Shadbolt was undoubtedly correct, and registrations of apprehension, disgust and outrage (often by refugees and veterans of World War II) formed a theme in commentary on the appearance of Nazi symbolism in New Zealand. As Commissioner of Police C.L. Spencer put it: 'They flaunt the swastika, steel helmet, and the iron cross – symbols of hate, cruelty and brutal death for innocent persons, which thousands of New Zealanders gave their lives to eradicate.'[20]

A rash of neo-Nazi graffiti at the start of the 1960s similarly expressed this power to shock. The first publicised cases appeared in West Germany in late 1959 and soon spawned imitators across Europe and the US.[21] By mid-January the first cases of 'paint-pot Hitlers' were being reported in New Zealand.[22] In Christchurch, the front door of a Jewish-owned restaurant and a synagogue were defaced with reversed swastikas and slogans reading 'Hitler will live forever' and 'Kill more Jews'. A site in Mackworth Street, Woolston, was painted with a swastika superimposed on a Star of David, with 'Jewish swine get out' written underneath in German. Shirley Intermediate School was also vandalised with swastikas and an SS Death's Head insignia. Further examples were reported in February at Victoria University of Wellington, where reversed swastikas and 'no Jews' were painted.[23] On the appearance of swastika graffiti, one correspondent noted: 'We who use public conveniences see it all too often.'[24]

Resulting investigations suggest the phenomena reflected a mix of loutish behaviour and nebulous antisemitism, which might account for regular observations of grammatically flawed German and incorrectly orientated swastikas. A security memo analysing such cases noted the incidents 'appear to be the work of hooligans and odd individuals with strong anti-Semitic feelings. They were probably engendered by the publicity given to the [European] outbreak by the overseas and local press, which has had an effect throughout the world of stirring latent anti-Semitic sentiments and of fostering imitation.'[25] This appraisal matched the circumstances of some of those apprehended. The case at Victoria University of Wellington, for example, was the work of six young men aged between 17 and 23. Judgment attributed their actions more to loutish behaviour and intoxication than to bigotry; all were fined.[26] Likewise, a swastika drawn in lipstick on an Invercargill window was found to be the work of a 20-year-old youth already on probation. His legal counsel denied that there was any sinister motive: his client was too young to understand just what the insignia meant. The magistrate seemed to approach the case as an act of social rebellion and criticised

In May 1969, university students, in a dramatic example of the evocation of fascism to indict authority, secured a swastika banner to the front of 175 Taranaki Street, Wellington (the then headquarters of the NZSIS). *Salient*, 28 May 1969, p. 10

the accused's dress – a shiny silver-threaded sports coat and stove-pipe trousers. He advised him to reconsider the impression he was making, as people would think him 'peculiar' and he would 'start life under a handicap'.[27]

BOUNDARY ISSUES

Adding to the period's complexity were organisations whose reactions to contemporary issues took a step away from the centre. For example, in May 1961 Auckland carpenter M.L. Peers founded the Anti-Communist League in a stated effort to defeat communism via education. Denying any radical intent, he noted 'we have no pseudo-

OPPOSITE: A 1966 newspaper feature of 'gang antics' outside the New Plymouth Police Station. This exhibitionism included a large crucifix and 'public sexual relations', but the flaunting of Nazi regalia was the centrepiece of the gang's 'offensive rebellion'.

Evening Post, 14 June 1966, p. 29. R24881828, Archives New Zealand

military set up, no drilling in secret'.[28] Fairlie Curry, a veteran, businessman and National Party candidate (standing in Island Bay in 1960 and 1963), headed the League's Wellington branch and added: 'Don't mix us up with Nazis or Fascists. We are opposed to them as much as we are to Communists.'[29] By 1962 the League was defunct but was revived under Curry's leadership as the Democratic Society, with the stated aims '[t]o expose and fight Communist infiltration, "Red front" movements and to preserve the Kiwi way of life'.[30] Curry warned that infiltration was apparent in 'the Public Service, local government, and the trade unions' and was working towards supplanting New Zealand democracy with communist totalitarianism.[31] The society took out newspaper advertisements warning of this 'infiltration and misuse of our democratic institutions', sought to counter anti-Vietnam War demonstrations, and invited prominent members of the Australian League of Rights to speak on Vietnam and international communism.[32]

Likewise, the Liberal Party was formed in 1963 and became the Country Party in November 1968, reviving the dispositions of an earlier rural-interest party. Party leader Cliff Emeny was a farmer turned insurance agent who had flown in the Battle of Britain, been a prisoner-of-war in Burma and regarded the National Party as betraying its principles regarding free enterprise.[33] Emeny described his party's mission as 'to regain a New Zealand way of life based on self-reliance ... self-direction ... self-discipline and self-respect'. Another commentator described it as representing the 'Arch-Conservatism of the 1930s'.[34] Certainly, the 1969 national convention championed nineteenth-century style laissez-faire liberalism as the solution to a perceived slide into a tyranny of bureaucracy, socialism and private monopoly.[35] Reactions to cultural directions also informed old-school approaches to order, tradition and discipline. Positions included a warm contemplation of reintroducing birching; opposition to any liberalisation of access to marijuana, abortion or *The Little Red Schoolbook* (a controversial book encouraging young people to question social norms); and a commitment to the principle that, wherever practical, criminals should 'make full restitution to their victims'.[36] Foreign policy similarly embraced a muscular stand against threats to traditional bonds. In regards to 'our own kinsmen' in Rhodesia, Emeny noted: 'Surely if it is right for us to send troops to Vietnam ['an undemocratic Asian country having no connection to New Zealand'] ... for the purpose of repulsing

THIS IS HERE! — NOT COSILY FAR AWAY

Here is what gang antics in New Zealand look like.

"The Post" is not publishing these pictures without deep consideration and soul-searching. They came to "The Post" through unusual channels, but their authenticity is indisputable.

Some will be shocked at them, but you cannot hide the facts for ever.

They show the recent visit to New Plymouth of the Auckland motor-cycle gang, the self-styled "Hell's Angels."

Their arrogance, their contempt for authority and their compulsive exhibitionism are frighteningly evident.

One of the photographs in "The Post's" possession, of public sexual relations, too obscene for publication, has today been passed by "The Post" to the Prime Minister, the Minister of Justice and the Leader of the Opposition.

The gang, seeking the ultimate in offensive rebellion, flaunted Nazi flags, Nazi medals and a large crucifix, posed in front of the New Plymouth Police Station, and taunted constables on duty.

One of the gang, arrested armed with a whip, told a sergeant it was "for hitting nosey cops with." He was fined £20 and castigated by the Magistrate, Mr. A. W. Yortt.

Mr. Yortt commended the Police on eventually running the gang out of town.

On their way home the gang broke into a house near Hamilton and a number of them were arrested and three sent to prison. Six were fined.

The Hell's Angels gang and their ilk thrive on disturbance, rebellion, violence, and, it is true, notice being taken of them, but "The Post," in publishing these pictures, believes that the whole country should take more notice of them—and their blatant endorsement of barbaric behaviour.

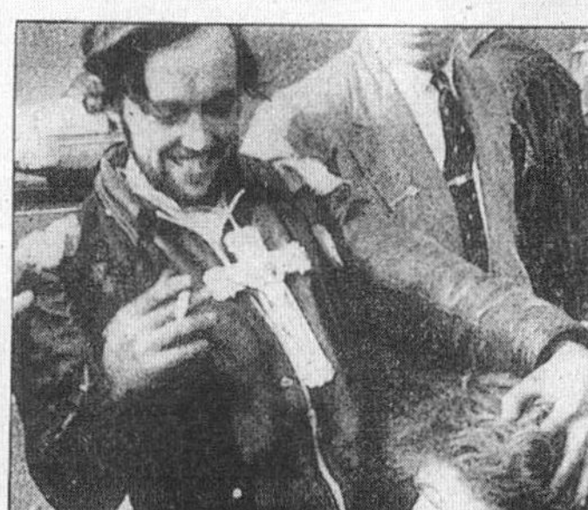

STOP PRESS

...ON: Havelock Hcp., ...(First division), ...rn Lass (11) 1; New- ...) 2. Scr.: Sam Scott, ...and £3/12/6; £2/2/-. ...division): Tobacco- ... 1; Scott's Song (17) ... Rosalie Mora, High- ...£5/10/6 and £2/13/-;

...Hcp.: ... (3) ... Modoro ...Light (10) ... Show- ...; Richard Hanover ...Scr.: Blue Pin, Truly ...£11/1/6 and £3/16/-; ...£2/19/6.

Printed and Published by Blundell Bros., Ltd., Proprietors, at the Registered Office of the Company, 62-68 Willis St., Wellington, Tuesday, June 14, 1966.

Communist infiltration and terrorism, how can anyone defend economic warfare sanctions against Rhodesia.'[37]

As this suggests, the controversies developing around white rule in Africa spurred responses on the right (as discussed in detail in Chapter Nine). Rationales spanned support for sporting contacts, expressions of kinship with white or Christian Africa, active sympathy for apartheid, and arguments that the loss of white governance would bring chaos and advantage international communism.[38] Major examples included the New Zealand Rhodesia Society, founded in 1962 with James Andrew as president. A former farmer and co-founder of the Pahiatua branch of the National Party, Andrew argued for sporting contacts with South Africa and called for a settlement that would see Rhodesia re-join the international community.[39] The Aid Rhodesia Movement, founded in Christchurch during 1966, sought to have the government denounce sanctions against Rhodesia. It was headed by A.C.R. Elderton, a former lieutenant-colonel who had served with the King's African Rifles and claimed apartheid was 'the best solution': 'Whether we like it or not, the Africans are unable to compete with Asiatics or Europeans in business acumen or intelligence.'[40] Later, as the chairman of Christchurch's Southern African Friends Association, established 1970, he was quoted as describing Hitler as 'one of the greatest German leaders ever – with the exception of the gas oven where he went too far'.[41] The Auckland-based Friends of South Africa Association was formed in 1970 '[t]o present the facts about South Africa and maintain sporting contacts'. Co-founder and Rhodesian expat Tony Blake argued that 'some aspects of apartheid should be relaxed … but separate development is necessary'.[42] The Association Defending South African Tours, founded in 1972, was headed by Ashburton schoolteacher Brian Thompson, who actively championed apartheid and warned about the threat of world communism and a Jewish conspiracy.[43]

Other organisations stood within the mainstream while encountering more extreme elements. For example, the Douglas Social Credit movement founded in the 1920s had, in the postwar era, achieved mainstream respectability, with the Social Credit Party effectively representing New Zealand's third political party. However, the movement continually attracted elements with more conspiratorial and antisemitic interpretations of Douglas Credit's theories of financial power.[44] In his 1956 talk on why he supported Douglas Credit, for example, Carey Carrington, a former member of the Legislative Council, noted that the fight against 'the deadly menace of International Communism' was pointless, 'whilst International (Zionist) Control of money and credit continued in power over the governments and people of the world'. In outlining his positions, he acknowledged his 'sincere thanks' for the writings of Arthur Nelson Field.[45]

THE PARANOID STYLE

Another set of anxieties and animosities towards modern developments falls into what Richard Hofstadter memorably termed 'the paranoid style', characterised by 'heated exaggeration, suspiciousness, and conspiratorial fantasy'.[46] The products of this mindset involve bestowing massive explanatory power and diabolical intent on a sinister element – so often a Jewish presence – to explain the state of things. Stephen Bronner described this phenomenon as representing 'the stupid answer to a serious question'.[47]

For example, in the late 1950s the Dunedin-based Christian Campaign for Freedom exhibited a pronounced concern with the fluoridation of drinking water, which it condemned as 'Communism via the Water Tap'. Evoking an urban legend that Nazi scientists had pioneered research into fluoride as a mind-control agent, the group's magazine claimed that fluorine degraded brain tissue and made the subject submissive to authority: 'any person who drinks artificially fluorinated water for a period of one year or more will never again be the same person, mentally or physically'.[48] Other subjects and developments, notably the United Nations and 'the mental health racket', were similarly held as threats to the Christian way of life: 'When we look over the current scene, we see clearly the workings of the diabolic mind. Integration of races, fluoridation of water, confiscatory taxation, "foreign aid", the U.N.O., labour tyranny, forced unionism, atomic bombs – anything, everything – just name it and a little study will prove absolutely that it does NOT come from Christian sources.'[49] In an interview with academic Austin Mitchell, the local organiser also noted that the group's main objective was to 'combat Zionism'.[50] By 1965, the movement had been renamed Co-Resistance, and was promoting literature from the American-based, conspiratorially minded anti-communist John Birch Society while continuing to warn of the march of subversion: 'All the Communists have to do is keep doing the things they have been doing, and all we have to do is keep on doing the same things we have been doing, and their timetable calls for taking us over from within, by 1973.'[51]

Other groups and individuals were much less involved in political campaigning or movement-building. One case began in 1952 when people around New Zealand reported receiving a leaflet purported to transcribe a speech delivered on 12 January 1952 by 'Rabbi Emanuel Rabinovich' to the 'Emergency Council of European Rabbis' in Budapest, Hungary. Melodramatic, and aping *The Protocols of the Learned Elders of Zion*, the exposition-laden speech outlined the progress of a millennia-old, fantastically intricate conspiracy to make 'every Jew a king and every Gentile a slave'. Machinations within this plot included instigating World War II (the result of 'our propaganda campaign during the 1930s'), complying with the Holocaust (a ploy to bring about the execution of national leaders as war criminals) and manufacturing the Cold War superpower standoff. 'Rabinovich' outlined that the council's next step was to provoke World War III, which would devastate all belligerents and clear the way for a 'Pax Judaica'. In this new order, Gentile capacity for resistance would be systematically destroyed by the eradication of Christianity and forced miscegenation: 'I can state with assurance that the last generation of white children is now being born.' Consequent Jewish dominance was presented as a certainty: 'Our superior intelligence will easily enable us to retain mastery over a world of dark peoples.'[52]

Visiting an Auckland address connected to the leaflet as part of an investigation, Senior Detective J.P. Marsh reported that he was greeted enthusiastically by an elderly man who described the leaflet as a 'smasher'.[53] Inquiries revealed that he and another elderly Aucklander had acquired the leaflet from an overseas source and decided to distribute it. After ordering 1000 copies from a printer, the two proceeded in their effort to propagate the leaflet.[54] A confiscated distribution list records that the leaflet was mailed to dozens of politicians, without their solicitation, including James George Barnes, Dean Eyre, James Carroll and Walter Nash. However, the duo also contacted a series of international leaders (Dwight Eisenhower, 'Uncle Joe' [Stalin], Robert Menzies and Winston Churchill); individuals with various levels of authority, influence and prestige (the director of the CIA, Sir Keith Park, the Queen Consort, the Argentine consul-general and the president of the Rotary International), as well as lesser-known figures ('chap in Devonport fruit shop', 'mate on ferry'). One of the two men estimated that they had posted 'about 100' copies to addresses selected randomly from the telephone directory, and had left others in various letterboxes around Auckland.

In assessing motives, Marsh dwelled on the 'mental rating' of the duo, which he described as 'low and not stable'. He noted that both men had spent time in psychiatric hospitals, and described one as 'not as bad mentally as [his colleague]' but as having 'fixed ideas and worries himself about world affairs'. A meeting with this man's son revealed that he had 'been a problem to his family for many years and that his association with [his colleague] had not improved matters'. With reference to the second man, Marsh's report observed a recurring habit of contacting people of influence, including a claimed correspondence with Adolf Hitler, Benito Mussolini and Harry Truman. The report noted: '[E]ventually he will become certifiable for

This cartoon features the major ideas of antisemitic conspiracies of Jewish domination. These include the utilisation of, seemingly opposed, factions, the subversion of religions, nations and movements, and the destruction of racial groups. Miscellaneous radical right organisation papers. R24716778, Archives New Zealand admission to a mental hospital.' Further assessment of the duo's motives observed their perception that their activities represented a civic duty: 'In their own way these two men considered they were being extremely loyal citizens.' The investigation concluded with the duo surrendering the remaining 528 leaflets to the police, who informed them that the pamphlet was a hoax and warned that further distribution could result in prosecution.

DUBIOUS PASTS

Another strand of the rightward fringe derived from elements among European immigrants displaced and resettled after the war.[55] In late 1953, the frequently sensationalist newspaper *New Zealand Truth* began a series of articles claiming that: 'Among the considerable number of European settlers now in New Zealand are members of the former Rumanian Iron Guard, Norwegian Quislings, members of the Slovakian Hlinka Guard and Hungarians who are former members of Nazi organisations.'[56] A particular concern was the content of the Hungarian-language paper *Hidverok*, originally published in Neumarkt, Bavaria, and distributed from a residence in Petone. Among the periodical's content were claims that Anglo-American policy was set by Jewish financiers, that 'Her Majesty the Queen and Sir Winston [Churchill] have Jewish blood in their veins', and that 'the ulcer of Jewry already has nibbled to a skeleton the Christian Hungarian people.'[57]

Official inquiries into the issue saw the secretary for internal affairs note, in a letter to the director of Special Branch:

> For some time it has been fairly clear that the wartime activities of a certain number (probably not a large number) of the displaced persons in New Zealand were highly dubious. Provided, however, the people concerned show by their conduct in New Zealand that they left their political conduct behind them when they came here, it is probably the fair and possibly the only feasible course to accept the position and let by-gones be by-gones.[58]

A Special Branch memorandum for the prime minister likewise questioned the effectiveness of postwar screening procedures for extremists. 'There are now 23,000 aliens in New Zealand. All alien immigrants who have arrived here since 1945 were security screened before their departure from Europe, but the standard of this screening varies a good deal and has proved inadequate in some cases.'[59] This 'inadequacy' was a curiously open secret, and one memoirist recalls Wellington in the 1950s as 'a drab but strangely cosmopolitan town, full of postwar European exiles, escaped Nazis (minor Jew hunters and concentration camp officers – the big boys went to Brazil) and a gaggle of budding poets …'[60]

Subsequent police investigations into *Hidverok* deemed it to 'contain anti-Semitic and anti-British vituperation of the worst possible type' and to be a 'worthy successor of [Julius] Streichers "Der Stuermer" [*sic*]', and noted that any person favouring its political ideology was 'of definite security interest'.[61] Some degree of inquiry into suspected communities continued, and a related 1959 security investigation into one Hungarian man informed him that a complaint noted that he 'was importing and distributing what had been described as seditious literature' and invited him to comment. The subsequent character assessment noted that 'he is so anti-Semitic in his outlook that he is of security interest'.[62]

Ideas of 'dubious pasts' and hidden fascists flared again in the early 1960s, doubtlessly spurred by the aforementioned 'paint-pot Hitlers' and sensational headlines around the Israeli intelligence agency Mossad's abduction of Adolf Eichmann and the consequent trial and execution of 'the architect of the Holocaust'.[63] Some commentators linked outbreaks of antisemitism with a postwar scattering of fascists, and Auckland's Rabbi Astor, for example, asserted that 'anti-semitic hooliganism had its origin in Germany and that easy immigration to Australia and other free and democratic areas had given ample scope for infiltration'. He added that 'New Zealand had fortunately been free of inhuman persecution'.[64] Days later, the first reports of comparable antisemitic vandalism challenged such assertions of New Zealand exceptionalism.

The communist newspaper *People's Voice* claimed that 'there is considerable evidence that not only have ex Nazis and S.S. men been allowed to immigrate, but that they are forming new groups in New Zealand with a strong concentration in Christchurch'.[65] Certainly some resulting security investigations note some generational torch-passing. A January 1960 inquiry into a Hungarian association noted some young members displayed pronounced antisemitism and an interest in neo-Nazism.[66] It reported that two individuals in Christchurch with Hungarian heritage had established a headquarters for a local Nazi Party in their flat. Both were in their twenties and had lost fathers fighting for the Axis during the war.[67] In 1972, a journalistic investigation into neo-Nazism saw one interviewee claim that their group had obtained their swastika banner from 'a former Nazi stormtrooper who has settled here … there are quite a few of them in New Zealand'.[68]

REACTIONARY CONSERVATISM AND FASCISTIC TENDENCIES

As this suggests, the most salient feature within the scene was the emergence of groups that had highly fascistic qualities or openly identified as neo-Nazis. Ironically, it was probably groups in Britain and Australia, rather than former Axis countries, that represented the most potent vectors for fascistic and ultra-reactionary movements.[69] A major example was the League of Empire Loyalists, established in the United Kingdom in April 1954 and headed by Arthur Chesterton, a former leading figure in Oswald Mosley's British Union of Fascists. The league sought to arrest the decline of the British Empire, which it perceived as threatened by Soviet communism and American capitalism, both believed to be headed by a Jewish-led conspiracy.[70] The League reached a peak in 1958, with some 3000 members in Britain and possibly 10,000 worldwide.[71]

A New Zealand branch of the League was active by 1955. Its constitution noted the foremost objective was 'the maintenance, and where necessary, the recovery of the sovereign independence of the British Peoples throughout the world'.[72] The threat to this global British community featured many familiar points. Thus the Rothschild dynasty was said to be manipulating events in striving towards 'the time when each Jew will be a king and each Gentile a slave', and was working through the banks, the universities and via fluoridation (a scheme 'to create mental deterioration in the West').[73] Britain's moves towards the European Economic Community were a betrayal that would 'tear asunder the bonds of trade, loyalties, culture, traditions, and ties of spirit'.[74] Trade and immigration with Asia and collaboration with the US would see New Zealand become 'the 51st state' and/or the British population swamped, and its heritage destroyed by Asian populations hungry for living space.[75]

In 1967 the New Zealand branch of the League evolved into the New Zealand National Front, styled after the recently created British National Front, itself an amalgamation of groups including the League of Empire Loyalists and the British National Party.[76] Brian Thompson, who had a history in the League, served as the national secretary and later deputy chairman. Thompson claimed that British nations were 'under a concerted attack from the evils of international finance and its offspring international communism, which, while seeming to be opposites, are both working to destroy the concepts of national sovereignty and racial integrity'.[77] A security report summarised the stated aims of the Front as allegiance to the British Crown; cooperation in rebuilding a white British Commonwealth; halting non-European immigration; the repatriation of non-European residents; a 'separate development' approach for Māori and Pākehā; an assertive anti-communist foreign policy; and New Zealand's withdrawal from the United Nations, the International Labour Organisation and UNESCO. The report summarised that '[t]he NZNF could best be described as an openly racist pro-white body loosely affiliated to the [British National Front].'[78]

Also indicative of international transmissions was the creation of a New Zealand branch of the Australian League of Rights. The Australian League of Rights was founded by Eric Butler in 1946 and developed out of the Douglas Credit movement. By the 1960s, Butler had an extensive publishing record, including titles like *The International Jew: The truth about 'The Protocols of Zion'* (1946), *Fluoridation or Freedom* (1960); *A Basic Course on the Communist Conspiracy* (1969); *The Fabian Socialist Contribution to the Communist Advance* (1964); and *Australia's Front Line in Southern Africa* (1969). The recurring theme was the threat to white Christian civilisation from a malicious Jewish conspiracy operating through international capitalism and international communism. Activist Ken Gott described Butler as a 'soft-sell anti-Semite', adept at opening conversations with people who 'no doubt would have shunned him had they known of his other activities'.[79] Thus Butler made several speaking tours in New Zealand seeking a common front, or converts, from organisations including Douglas Social Credit, the RSA, the Country Party and the Democratic Society. Typical topics included opposing British entry into the EEC (warning that Westminster would be reduced to 'the status of a municipal council') and supporting Rhodesia (proclaimed as a bastion that had 'thrown one of the biggest spanners into the works of the Communist Global Strategy').[80]

Planning for a New Zealand League of Rights began around 1968, with the body formally established in February 1970 and Tauranga's Sidney Wood as the co-founder and first director.[81] By 1972 it claimed a membership approaching 200, though Harvey Buchman called this into question in his thesis on the League.[82] Its public material proclaimed it was 'a PATRIOTIC non-party Political Association which ACTS to PROTECT and EXPAND individual RIGHTS and FREEDOMS'. This also warned that rights and liberties were being undermined by the centralisation of power, a growing socialist bureaucracy, 'Marxian-socialist financial policies', the growth of monopolies, the erosion of social standards, rising crime and communist infiltration of institutions.[83] Advocating Douglas Credit economics, the League regarded itself as the true heir to C.H. Douglas's teachings and claimed that the Social Credit Party's policies 'bear as much resemblance to Douglas' policies as devil-worship does to

Christianity'.[84] One study of the New Zealand League of Rights outlined its sense that national/Western decline was being wrought by malicious capitalist/communist/ Jewish subversion working through politics, schools and churches, as well as cultural developments, including protesting, fluoridation and music.[85]

NEO-NAZISM

Other groups styled themselves, to varying extents, after the Third Reich, and might be classed as neo-Nazi groups. Many were transitory and have left few, or elusive, traces. For example, in May 1962, a letter sent to the 'Security Police' detailed an encounter with a female Auckland University student who proclaimed a 'hatred for the Jewish race' and claimed membership in an Auckland-based group 'whose avowed aim is to "rid" New Zealand of Jews by fair means or foul'. The student claimed the group was two thousand strong, had the interest of 'people in quite high places', was compiling lists of Jews, and threatened to undertake 'big offensives' within a year.[86] A subsequent investigation concluded, 'While it is possible there is an Anti-Semitic movement in Auckland, it is likely some evidence of its existence would have been brought to light during the course of this enquiry.'[87] Also mysteriously, one early morning in September 1965 a black flag with a 'crudely sewn' single white lightning flash was hoisted on the flagpole outside Parliament. A statement noted that the group responsible was a 'revolutionary organisation' with no official name but described as 'the White Lightning Ideology'. It also noted that the group had 50 members, including former Nazis, and ambitions to overthrow the government and establish a dictatorship.[88]

The earliest example of a New Zealand neo-Nazi party seems to date to 1962, when Dunedin market gardener Alan McKechnie made headlines with his announcement of the formation of a National Socialist Party (aka the New Socialist Party), claiming a nominal membership of 400. The Director of Security noted that 'the operative word may be "nominal"', and notable trade unionist Fintan Patrick Walsh stated that 'the only place Fuehrer McKechie could get 400 members is in a lunatic asylum'.[89] Two years later, Larry Donnell, a 19-year-old warehouse worker, founded a group in Rotorua that would be variously known as the New Zealand Nazi Party, the National Socialist Democratic Workers Party and the New Zealand National Socialist Party. A 1964 police search of Donnell's property seized a variety of fascist pamphlets, correspondence with international neo-Nazi organisations, and a notebook entitled 'My Idea', which briefly outlined his 'Nazi vision' that the state would seize New

Zealand's land and wealth and redistribute it in a more equitable manner. Donnell appeared to conflate Nazism and communism, with the same source noting: 'I will keep Nazism going under the same rule as communist countries' and 'Nazi = National Socialist Communist'.[90] In 1969, another National Socialist Party of New Zealand was launched (McKechnie's party having folded), led by 22-year-old Durward Colin King-Ansell.

Of these groups, King-Ansell's was the most publicly active. It claimed 130 members in 1969 and 150 in 1972, though another source has the membership in this period at 39.[91] King-Ansell's background reads as a case of radicalisation through the fringe. Discharged from the army ('following civil convictions for theft of RNZAF flares and a RNZAF projector'[92]), and associating with a group of friends discussing 'world problems', in 1967 he was sentenced to an 18-month sentence jail term for causing 'malicious damage' to an Auckland synagogue. He would later state of this action: 'In those days I wasn't a National Socialist. I was just an anti-Jew … it was just some stupid thing that we did. I wasn't sober.'[93] While he claimed he was then in correspondence with George Lincoln Rockwell, the founder of the American Nazi Party, in his own telling the malicious damage conviction was formative: 'It made up my mind which way I was heading. I was like a lot of young chaps who were just on the fringes.'[94] In May 1970 he garnered a measure of national publicity and controversy after being interviewed by *Salient*, the Victoria University student magazine, and on Brian Edwards's television show *Gallery*, where he outlined the party's positions, affirmed his sense of the Jewish nature of international capitalism and communism ('They're playing both sides of the paddock') and denied the Holocaust ('I believe there were real concentration camps, but the gas chambers, no').[95]

If the League of Empire Loyalists and the League of Rights largely developed from the traditions of Mosley and Douglas, the National Socialist movements drew heavily on German-style Nazism. King-Ansell and his deputy, Errol Silvester, made appearances adorned with swastika armbands and tie pins. The party recognised anniversaries relating to the original Nazi Party; party secretary W.J. Bergeman literally dated by Adolf Hitler's birthday, signing off a 1970 letter to the *New Zealand Herald* 'YF 81' [Year of the Fuehrer 81].[96] Addressing this tendency, a party FAQ responded to the question, 'Why don't you do yourselves a favour and forget about Hitler? … This is the New Zealand of 1974, not the Germany of 1934' with: 'You might as well ask the Christians to forget about Christ … he's been dead for 2000 years and wasn't a New Zealander either.'[97] A taste for the Germanic also saw King-Ansell title his unpublished memoir, written during his imprisonment in Mount Eden,

Gefangene des Juden (Prisoner of the Jew). Donnell exhibited a similar disposition, noting that 'If I succeed [in seizing power] my flag will be the Swastika and my name Her [*sic*] Franz Fritz Werner Hahn.'[98] In January 1972 it was announced that the party was embracing a 'new look', downplaying 'national socialism' and adopting a kiwi insignia in place of the swastika, with King-Ansell noting: '[W]e're not aping Germans, we're not Germans we're New Zealanders' and 'I've no longer got a portrait of Hitler in my office … I now have one of the Queen … Our motto is God, Queen and Country.'[99] However, this approach was hardly standardised, and posters emblazoned with a swastika and the text 'smash capitalism with National Socialism' appeared in Auckland and Wellington the following month.[100]

Soon after its creation, the party outlined its world-view and plans for a new order in New Zealand. At the core of its manifesto was the belief that communism and capitalism were both anti-national forces that, purposely and with sinister intent, were eroding communal integrity. As King-Ansell put it: '[B]oth Communism and capitalism are of Jewish origin. Both are systems desiring the ultimate enslavement of all mankind for the benefit of a few.'[101] Defence against this threat demanded 'the creation of a strong central power of the State' with 'unquestioned authority' and dedicated to 'the industry and livelihood' of the national community working in conjunction with a committed nation: 'It must be the first duty of each citizen of the State to work with his mind or with his body.'[102]

Race was held as the fundamental basis of community. The party manifesto and other literature stated: 'Our foremost concern is for the maintenance of a homogene ous [*sic*] NATION, moulded from European stock', and: 'We are above all Racial Nationalists.'[103] Within party literature this conception of 'European stock' was used interchangeably with 'Aryan' in a manner remarkably discordant with Nazi conceptions of the Aryan Volk.[104] This racial outlook informed much of the central agenda. Party membership rules stated that the candidate 'must be of European race, free from Jewish blood'.[105] To the proclaimed end of solving 'New Zealand's coloured problem', the party demanded '[t]otal geographic racial separation', to be achieved by the non-violent repatriation of non-European immigrants and outlawing miscegenation. Though it was noted: 'If force is required, however, it will be used.'[106]

Māori represented another point of curiosity within the party's racial world-view. In 1969, the party secretary claimed that '[a] lot of our members are Maoris. We accept them as New Zealanders.'[107] The party application for 'registered supporters', as distinct from full members, noted: 'He or She must be of European or Maori race free from jewish blood.'[108] Policy was stated as standing for 'the self-dignity and emancipation of the Maori People by the way of separate development'. Specifics claimed that Māori would have the same rights as whites, that Māori representation in Parliament would be proportional to the population, that 'Cettain [*sic*] sections of Crown land will be handed over' together with compensation for past land seizures, and that 'Maori Elders would be given more control over their own people.'[109] Donnell, of the New Zealand Nazi Party, would describe this ambition to 'treat Maoris as New Zealanders' as 'ludicrous': '[W]e have never advocated union between the races and we follow Mein Kampf doctrines completely.'[110]

While the party claimed national socialism, or 'Aryan socialism', as an alternative, non-Marxist, socialist model, precise economic and social policies were notably subordinated to the mission of preserving the racial community. Indeed, party literature stated that policies would be evaluated on the question 'What will be the effect of this policy, in long run, on the security the well being and especially on the quality of the Aryan race?'[111] Nonetheless, a series of economic and social policies was advanced. These included the 'abolition of incomes unearned by work'; the 'nationalisation of all business which have been up to the present, formed into Companies'; the 'extensive development of provision for old age'; 'ruthless persecution' of criminal and anti-social elements; economic and housing policies intending to expand the middle class; education and health policies intending to raise public fitness, education and civic spirit; tighter state control of media and the banning of newspapers not conducive to 'the national welfare'; and the promotion of liberty 'for all religious denominations in the State so far as they do not militate against the moral feelings of the New Zealand people'.[112] Stated foreign policies included exiting the United Nations, working towards the liberation of all countries 'suffering under the Communist yoke', and working towards 'closer ties between countries of British race and taditions [*sic*]'.[113]

With respect to methods, King-Ansell publicly claimed that the party did not believe in storm troopers and had no intent to forcefully overthrow the government.[114] However, his proposal for an auxiliary police force to keep public order and his claim that his party had recruited members of the police force clearly raised concerns; the New Zealand Police denied the claim and King-Ansell refused to substantiate it.[115] This discussion led to the prime minister affirming that private armies would not be tolerated in New Zealand.[116] Confirming its effort to win power via the ballot, the party announced its first election bid in the 1972 General Election, standing for Eden.

LEGACIES AND IMPLICATIONS

In summation, New Zealand's era of 'golden weather' possessed a right-wing fringe that spanned rebellious adoption of Nazi regalia, reactionary politicking, antisemitic conspiracy peddling and neo-Nazi designs for New Zealand. The denizens of this scene were diverse, ranging from social rebels to disaffected conservatives, isolated cranks, immigrant fascists and native-born neo-Nazis. Activity was generated by disparate elements driven by their own passions, apolitical rebellions and unstable mental health, and by organised bodies seeking to attract like minds and advance political agendas.

In considering the wider implications of this scene, the salient image would appear to be a failure to achieve mass influence. Internal feuding was a major factor in this outcome. Donnell's Nazi Party imploded in 1969, though the media noted that individual members were still active.[117] In 1970 the Country Party was rocked by factionalism as an unsuccessful coup sought to replace Emeny; the party had a short second wind as the Liberal Reform Party. In 1970 King-Ansell noted a rift with the 'Australian Nazi leader' (Eric Wenberg): 'He seems to have the wild idea that he wants to make New Zealand part of Australia. I'm a nationalist. I won't wear it.' He also claimed an estrangement from the World Union of National Socialists, stating that the 1962 Cotswold Agreement, which laid out the objectives for a National Socialist world revolution and 'the final settlement of the Jewish problem', was 'too binding': 'It is a white extremist policy.'[118] The party deputy Errol Silvester resigned in 1971 after his arrest for burglary, and came into dispute with King-Ansell. Threatening that he would work to get the party outlawed, he taunted: '[R]emember this, Silvester is a Jewish name.'[119] The National Front dissolved in the early 1970s (though another organisation bearing the name emerged in 1977) and the National Socialist Party disbanded in 1980.

Extreme-right movements and ideas were also kept on the fringe by mainstream repulsion. Interviews with neo-Nazis bore headlines like 'There's One in Every Village', and a regional police superintendent noted on the 1952 'Pax Judaica' case: 'It appears likely that these mental bankrupts will cease their activities in this particular field.'[120] Publicity around King-Ansell's politics saw him fired from a bartending job, and the Hotel Association of New Zealand noted that it had 'taken steps to minimise Mr King-Ansell's chances of getting a job in any New Zealand hotel'.[121] Other reactions were more visceral. A 1969 Country Party meeting was disrupted by a group of young men concerned with racial issues. This escalated into a brawl in which '30 persons punched at each other'.[122] The Friends of South Africa's Colonel Elderton reported that his car tyres had been slashed three times and his property vandalised.[123] In February 1971 a number of residents in Ōtara were evacuated after an anonymous caller declared that a bomb had been left on King-Ansell's front porch; an explosives expert subsequently assessed the device, comprised of a rusty defused mortar shell, two batteries, a .303 cartridge and an alarm clock, and reported 'it was unlikely the device could have exploded'.[124] In October 1972 a neo-Nazi meeting in Mount Eden's Methodist church was broken up by members of the Progressive Youth Movement throwing fireworks and borer bombs. A fistfight began outside the church in which two neo-Nazis were 'hopelessly outnumbered' and neither 'seemed keen on continuing the brawl once released'.[125]

However, political rejection, notably by the successes of moderate conservatism, was likely the more effective agent of marginalisation. The Democratic Society, for example, proved unable to mobilise an effective base, and one analysis concluded that it 'was not radical enough to enjoy the support of the ultra-right and many who supported its Vietnam policy found expression of their views through the National Party'.[126] Furthermore, groups seeking to work through the political process achieved negligible results. In the 1969 election the Country Party won 7197 votes (0.5 percent of the popular vote) and no seats.[127] King-Ansell's 1972 contestation of Eden won 35 of the 18,770 votes cast (0.2 percent). A second bid in 1975 netted him 19 of the 19,966 votes cast (0.1 percent).[128]

If these dynamics suggest irrelevance and terminal failure, other implications are of greater concern, and resonate with contemporary worries. Perhaps the most significant is how the failure to thrive locally and overtly directed activities towards subterranean networks and oblique contacts. Indeed, international networks were a significant feature in the scene.[129] Thus McKechie noted he founded his National Socialist Party following contact from a member of 'the British party'.[130] In May 1965, the Director of the Security Service contacted J. Edgar Hoover at the FBI, noting that a police raid on an individual claiming to be the head of the National Socialist Party of New Zealand had revealed a 'brisk correspondence' with National-Socialist movements in the US; he forwarded these addresses for Hoover's consideration.[131] These international links were especially significant in respect of propaganda dissemination. The 1952 distribution of the 'Pax Judaica' leaflet in New Zealand can be traced to the Swedish veteran antisemite Einar Aberg, who had forwarded a copy of the leaflet; in turn, Aberg claimed to have received the leaflet from Eustace Mullins, a veteran US-based antisemite, conspiracy theorist and Holocaust denier. Similarly, in 1962 *Truth* reported that it had received neo-Nazi literature from de Wykeham de Louth, an Australian described as an 'elderly Nazi in a one man crusade', who was distributing material from neo-Nazi groups.[132]

In other cases, international networks prompted visits. In 1969 a security report recounted the activity of 'Geoff', a young Australian, estimated as 18–20 years old, whose father had fought for Germany, and who had come to Christchurch for the expressed mission of recruiting for a National Socialist party.[133] Furthermore, Arthur Chesterton of the League of Empire Loyalists undertook multiple tours of New Zealand, and Eric Butler was a regular visitor in numerous speaking tours.[134] In 1971, King-Ansell visited New South Wales to undertake a training course from the Australian National Socialist Party: 'All we're trying to do is pass on the techniques we've learned so when he goes back he can take New Zealand by storm.'[135]

These links were not one way. Several of A.N. Field's books were re-issued by US right-wing publishers in the 1960s and 1970s, and Arthur Chesterton and Eric Butler both publicly acknowledged a debt to Field. During his visit to New Zealand in the late 1950s, Chesterton also took the time to visit Field in person.[136] In 1977, the New Zealand National Front's Brian Thompson travelled to the UK, where he met with the British National Front and was involved in the infamous Battle of Lewisham, when a provocative National Front march led to a violent clash with counter-demonstrators.[137]

Another dynamic with contemporary resonations was the practice of seeking influence or recruits from less radical causes. The most salient example is Butler and members of the League of Rights. As well as ongoing efforts to work with or within the more mainstream Douglas Credit movement, the League of Rights formed links with less fringe organisations in anti-fluoride campaigns in Dunedin and Tauranga.[138] Butler also gave an address to the Democratic Society, was invited to speak at a 1969 Country Party meeting (highlighting the party's foreign policy regarding Africa), and appears to have had some level of informal access to certain National Party members.[139] It should be noted that some groups made efforts to guard themselves. When publicity was given to Butler's history, the Democratic Society dissociated itself from him.[140] Likewise, at the end of the 1970s the Social Credit Party explicitly stated that League of Rights members were no longer welcome.[141] Similarly, the National Party explicitly rejected any association with the National Front.[142]

In a final sense, if the 'golden weather' of the 1950s and 1960s retains its claim as an era of domestic tranquillity, its rightward fringe demonstrates how the period also included fretful visions of the state of society, and remedies that ventured into weird, sinister and authoritarian places. Likewise, the period provides context for the reactions of subsequent decades. Some of the transgressive appropriation of this era reappeared within punk and skinhead subcultures, Oi! music and a 'swastika chic' aesthetic.[143] Lastly, while many of the era's organisations faltered, many figures cut their teeth in this period and would reappear elsewhere.

CHAPTER NINE

'A bastion of white supremacy'

Southern Africa in the political imagination of New Zealand's radical right

SEBASTIAN POTGIETER AND TYLER WEST

IN THEIR QUEST FOR POLITICAL INFLUENCE, New Zealand's radical right-wing groups have consistently sought ways of propagating their philosophies as legitimate. To do so, they create aspersions about amorphous threats to national security and racial purity. Primarily, it has been the activities of communists, Catholics, Jews and people of colour that they have interpreted as universally threatening, and have sought to locate evidence, both domestically and internationally, to rationalise their fears.[1] In this regard, southern Africa has represented a symbolically important site for New Zealand's radical right. Historical groups and individuals have regarded the white regimes in Rhodesia and South Africa as indicative of the civilising influences Europeans brought to a continent supposedly characterised by tribal politics and violent 'savagery'.[2] Maintaining minority white rule in the region was seen as imperative to secure the superior traditions of the white Anglo-Saxon commonwealth and to offset communist expansion. South Africa, with its formal racial segregation and white domination implemented through the 1948 apartheid policy, was 'seen as something of a model society with strategic and propaganda importance,' noted Paul Spoonley. 'For these reasons every effort is made to ensure that links are maintained with South Africa's white population.'[3] For the local radical right, ensuring South Africa remained 'a bastion of white-supremacy on a black governed continent' was essential.[4]

In this chapter, we map the intersection of southern Africa's white regimes with white supremacist ideologies in New Zealand. Although these regimes were consistently characterised as bastions of civilisation on a hostile frontier, what they were portrayed as defending – and from whom – consistently evolved. We begin our analysis around the time of the South African War, with the perceived threat to racial purity posed by Chinese labour imports working South African mines. Next, we unpack responses to the liberation and decolonisation movements that threatened white rule in southern Africa post-World War II. This section focuses primarily on the anti-apartheid movement and the fears about budding African nationalism coalescing with communist ideologies. Here we also address how ultra-conservative philosophies filtered into seemingly more moderate, libertarian concerns over individual rights following the 1981 Springbok rugby tour of New Zealand. We conclude with a brief discussion of the contemporary 'white genocide' conspiracy.

EARLY INCARNATIONS

The earliest foundations of the role South Africa would play in the imagination of New Zealand's radical right began after the cessation of the South African War (October 1899–May 1902). While New Zealand's contribution of several thousand riflemen and nurses was largely an act of imperial loyalty to demonstrate the colony's value, it was not the only matter of interest in South Africa at the time. During 1903–1904, a public campaign in New Zealand spearheaded by Premier Richard Seddon opposed the importation of Chinese labourers (rather than British workers) to work the Transvaal's Rand gold mines in South Africa's interior.[5] In February 1904, some 500 citizens rallied in Wellington, denouncing the scheme. Seddon spoke at the event and was joined by three Cabinet ministers (for mines, railways and native affairs), Mayor of Wellington John Aitken, the chair of the Wellington Trades and Labour Council, future prime minister Joseph Ward, and former MP and newspaper editor P.J. O'Regan. A letter of support was sent by Chief Justice and former premier Sir Robert Stout.[6] Seddon also recruited Australian Prime Minister Alfred Deakin to contribute joint diplomatic pressure against the scheme, issuing telegrams of protest to London and Pretoria.[7] While the campaign was eventually unsuccessful, for his efforts, Seddon received scores of admiring letters from South Africa, Australia and New Zealand, and his name was cheered at anti-Chinese rallies in South Africa.[8]

Speaking at Kokatahi on the West Coast in January 1904, Seddon declared that the importation of Chinese labour 'would be bitterly resented by the self-governing colonies, who had made great sacrifices' in defeating the hated Boers.[9] He viewed New Zealand as imperially entwined with the newly obtained British possessions in South Africa and at the Wellington rally in February called the scheme a 'great wrong' being enacted on 'the people of South Africa and upon the empire itself'. This 'wrong', he believed, amounted to 'hordes of Asiatics being sent into South Africa … to take the place of the men of our own race, of our own blood'.[10] Seddon's view on Chinese immigration mirrored New Zealand's own prevailing racial prejudices. The intent of the 1896 Asiatic Restriction Act, observes Nigel Robson, was to '"safeguard racial-purity" and prevent an influx of "Persons of Alien Race who are likely to be hurtful to the Public Welfare"'.[11]

The idea that New Zealand had an inherent tie to South Africa by imperial linkage, right of conquest, racial connection and a common abhorrence of Asiatic people was not confined to that campaign. Infamous New Zealand white supremacist and murderer Lionel Terry (discussed in Chapter Three) wrote in his diaries of his anger at the 'importation of 50,000 Chinese coolies to work these "stolen" mines', and addressed the arrival of Chinese labour to South Africa, Canada, Australia and New Zealand in his quasi-manifesto *The Shadow*. Terry's biographer Frank Tod wrote that a great deal of Terry's world-view was influenced by his claimed participation in the failed Jameson Raid and meeting president of the Transvaal Republic Paul Kruger.[12] Two decades later, the White New Zealand League took an interest in the 'Asiatic problem' in South Africa (as well as in the other white colonies, Australia and Canada).[13]

Within a few years of the cessation of the South African War, some of the foundations for how South Africa would weigh in the minds of the postwar radical right had been laid. As the perceived threat of racial degradation from Chinese immigration loomed over the white dominions, New Zealand found in South Africa an ally with shared imperial and racial bonds – though initially Afrikaners were viewed as being outside the fold. Gradually, the anti-Asian hysteria of the late nineteenth and early twentieth centuries subsided. However, the view of South Africa as a keystone of both the Empire and the white race proved influential to how New Zealand's radical right would understand South Africa decades later.

REVIVING INTEREST: CHALLENGING WHITE RULE IN SOUTHERN AFRICA

Significant interest in white-ruled southern Africa – particularly South Africa, Rhodesia (now Zimbabwe) and South West Africa (now Namibia) – re-emerged in New Zealand during the postwar era. Growing instability in the South Rhodesian colony and the protectorates of Northern Rhodesia and Nyasaland in the early to mid-1960s spurred growth in organised support for minority white rule.[14] Two groups formed during this period gave organised form to these sentiments. One, the New Zealand-Rhodesia Society, was formed in 1962 during the final years of the Federation of Rhodesia and Nyasaland before its 1963 dissolution. The society tended toward respectability in its leadership. Founders included Mayor of Dargaville Sam Green and James Andrew, a New Zealand Wool Board member, Federated Farmers dominion councillor and National Party Pahiatua branch founder. Vice-presidents of the society included sitting National Party MPs W.J. Scott and Sir Ronald Algie (former minister of education, broadcasting, and science and industrial research, as well as sitting Speaker of the House).[15] By 1970, the society's *Rhodesia Newsletter* was distributed to some 2000 members. A split in 1971 foreshadowed a decline in society activity, though by 1979, under new chairperson Sten Lawson, the membership was still claimed at 600.[16] The other of these two organisations, the Aid Rhodesia Movement, was founded by Lieutenant-Colonel A.C.R. Elderton in 1966. Elderton was a veteran of the King's African Rifles and the Indian Army, and a former National Party secretary. He began the organisation with a letter sent to all North Island newspapers, which claimed that 55 percent of Africans had an IQ equivalent to a nine-year-old European and that only one in 30 Africans were capable of higher education.[17]

The pro-South African and Rhodesian causes proved initially to be a windfall for the radical right, drawing much greater support than other issues promoted by it at the time. Many New Zealanders had relatives in Rhodesia or felt a sense of racial solidarity towards whites in southern Africa – including, by now, Afrikaners.[18] Others saw Rhodesia and South Africa as bulwarks against the spread of communism and chaos evident elsewhere in Africa.[19] However, the growing instability in southern Africa also offered radical right groups an opportunity for political access and cooperation. For instance, the New Zealand Rhodesia Society drew much of its leadership from the upper echelons of politics, particularly from the National Party. National's Mangere candidate at the 1972 and 1975 elections was Stan Lawson, who was elected chairperson of the New Zealand Rhodesia Society and visited Rhodesia in 1978. In 1972, Minister of Customs George Gair spoke at a League of Rights meeting in Tauranga to attack anti-Springbok tour protesters, which led to a libel case against him.[20]

Gair's comments were not unusual, however. Barry Gustafson noted that a 'bridge building' approach towards South Africa, rather than sanctions or embargos, better reflected opinion within the National Party and that after John (Jack) Marshall replaced Keith Holyoake as prime minister in 1972, the government became more openly sympathetic towards the Republic and to the continuation of All Black-Springbok rugby tours, a trend continued by Robert Muldoon.[21] Others within the National Party, including several of Holyoake's Cabinet ministers, endorsed retaining white rule in southern Africa. Former minister William Sullivan and former Speaker of the House Matthew Oram publicly defended South Africa's apartheid system, arguably suggesting that a considerable dimension of fringe philosophies had faded into, or at least found some sanctuary within, the mainstream politics of the National Party.[22]

Connections between the League of Rights and the National Party had existed for some years by this point. During the 1960s and 1970s, Australian League of Rights founder Eric Butler met National Party ministers during his speaking tours of New Zealand to discuss, among other topics, his pro-South African and pro-Rhodesian views. Butler had a considerable interest in drumming up support for the white governments of southern Africa. In the late 1960s, he arranged for the delivery of a tanker of oil to the Rhodesian government in contravention of a United Nations embargo.[23] Butler's meetings with prominent politicians during his speaking tours included Cabinet ministers and sitting Prime Minister Holyoake. Despite these successes, contact later declined as public pressure mounted on the League.

The National Party was not the only parliamentary party in which sympathisers of the Rhodesian and South African governments found a home. The short-lived Country Party, founded in 1968 by Cliff Emeny, president of the New Zealand Free Enterprise Party, had, as one of its core policies, opposition to sanctions against Rhodesia and official recognition of the white government. This opened the party up to cooperation with others on the radical right, and a public meeting held by the party in Christchurch in 1969 had Eric Butler as a guest to discuss the Rhodesian government.[24] Douglas Credit also proved to be a home for apartheid supporters, with League of Rights activist John Stewart-Menzies a Social Credit candidate for Tauranga in 1969. He travelled to South Africa in 1978 to advocate for an anti-communist pact between South Africa, Australia and New Zealand.[25]

The renewed organisation around, and interest in, southern Africa displayed a historical continuity with themes from the early twentieth century. In this world-view, New Zealand remained a key ally bound by ties of race and imperial loyalty to the white governments of southern Africa. However, distinct new elements also emerged as the situation in the region changed. While a form of white racial solidarity remained the underlying motivation, it was the internal threat to white rule, rather than an external threat from foreign labour, that galvanised radical-right support for the southern African regimes. In the world-view of the radical right, the white Commonwealth governments of southern Africa were transitioning from being outposts of the British

Empire beset by threats to its white residents to a frontier bastion of global, anti-communist white rule.

'WE WANT RUGBY. WE SUPPORT APARTHEID': THE RADICAL RIGHT AND THE SPORTING ISSUE[26]

Amidst an extensive liberation and decolonisation movement, white rule in postwar southern Africa became increasingly untenable. The largest of these, the anti-apartheid movement, developed in the late 1950s and encompassed both domestic revolts and international sanctions pressuring the ruling white Nasionale Party into dismantling its racist practices. Among the most successful sanctions was the boycott and eventual isolation of (white) South African sports. One notable exception, though, was rugby, the pastime most closely aligned with white nationalism. The white South African Rugby Board (SARB) had successfully maintained ties abroad, including with its most revered rival, the New Zealand Rugby Football Union (NZRFU). By the time the All Blacks toured South Africa in 1976, 'the effort to force the severing of New Zealand-South Africa rugby relations was the single-most important driving force behind the extension of sport sanctions internationally'.[27]

In New Zealand, the friendly relations between the two rugby bodies drew significant protests. Malcolm MacLean noted that the campaign against sporting ties with South Africa encompassed one of the biggest political movements in postwar New Zealand and, despite considerable difficulties, developed into the 'largest and most sustained anti-apartheid protests outside South Africa'.[28] By the mid-1970s, some New Zealanders were beginning to link opposition to apartheid with matters on the home front: the effects of colonial dispossession, patriarchal power, a conservative political elite that seemed to endorse apartheid as legitimate (or at least were unwilling to sanction it), and an increasingly racist state that defended the immigration of white Rhodesians and South Africans while Pasifika 'overstayers' were deported, subjected to dawn raids by police and immigration officials, and questioned in the streets.[29] The zenith of the campaign was reached when countless people took to the streets to demonstrate against the 1981 Springbok tour of New Zealand.

The anti-apartheid campaign directly conflicted with the philosophies of New Zealand's radical right. It was internationalist in its ethos and politically altruistic; its values belonged to a postwar postcolonial world; it advocated a bicultural anti-racist society; and it recognised the problems and aspirations of the indigenous cultures in New Zealand and South Africa.[30]

MOBILISING THE RADICAL RIGHT: SUPPORT FOR SPORT

In response to the substantial opposition developing in New Zealand to the white regimes in South Africa and Rhodesia, several significant pro-South African organisations with direct ties to radical right-wing groups were formed. The first of these were the Auckland-based Friends of South Africa Association (FSAA) and Christchurch-based Southern Africa Friends Association (SAFA), founded in 1970. Both were 'focused on events in southern Africa and were a mixture of naïve nostalgia for the "benefits" of being under the influence of Britain and racism towards black Africans and usually anyone non-white'.[31] Among the most vocal leaders of the FSAA, who generally comprised a 'coterie of rabid defenders of the troubled republic's perilous status quo', was Barry Delamore, who claimed that 'en masse the blacks have not reached the genetic level of the European'.[32] When in 1971 Halt All Racist Tours (HART) threatened to disrupt the Centennial Golf Tournament due to the participation of South African golfers, the FSAA announced they would form vigilante gangs to look after South African golfers and were not afraid to use violence to do so.[33] South Africa subsequently withdrew from the tournament.

The SAFA, founded by Lieutenant-Colonel Elderton, claimed up to 5000 members when the 1973 Springbok tour of New Zealand was being debated. Paul Spoonley noted that, typical of a right-wing organisation, the SAFA's ideology included a conspiracy theory that attempts to stop the 1973 tour were part of a communist campaign, based in the United Nations, to undermine white rule in South Africa.[34] Elderton claimed that HART and the Citizens Association for Racial Equality (CARE) were anti-white and that if the news media published more evidence of how separate development benefited 'the South African Bantu' both organisations would collapse.[35] Journalist Bruce Wallace described Elderton's explicitly racist philosophies as 'a reminder of the era of the Indian army, colonialism and fervent anti-communism'.[36] Unsurprisingly, Elderton rigidly endorsed the apartheid system because he saw it as preserving white supremacy.

Two further pro-South African groups were formed in the 1970s. The Association Defending South African Tours (ADSAT), which Trevor Richards called 'the most extreme pro-apartheid group', was formed in Ashburton in 1972, and was chaired by B.B. Thompson, an activist in the New Zealand National Front who served on Elderton's SAFA and founded the pro-Pinochet Friends of Chile in 1976.[37] Thompson displayed all the traits of a radical right-winger: he rigidly supported apartheid, believed modern black emerging nations would challenge white supremacy, and saw communism as part of a global Jewish conspiracy threatening the Western world.[38] Prior to the cancellation of the 1973 tour, ADSAT claimed their intention to instate 'rugby vigilantes' who would serve as nightwatchmen at grounds and assist police at matches to curb potential demonstrations.[39]

Formed shortly after ADSAT in 1972 was the Hastings-based War Against Recreational Disruption (WARD). While it claimed not to be a pro-tour group, most members were fanatical rugby supporters who saw themselves as the guardians of spectator rights.[40] Its founder, Robert Fenton, the National Party MP for Hastings in 1975, claimed that black Africans were the vandals of the twentieth century in their attitude towards sport and culture.[41] He was highly critical of the support black African nations and the World Council of Churches offered to South African liberation movements.[42] Notwithstanding this, soon-to-be prime minister Robert Muldoon regarded Fenton as 'a highly principled New Zealander and one of the few who has been prepared to tackle the extremists who have done so much damage to this country'.[43] Upon returning from a trip to South Africa in 1974, Fenton claimed that even black South Africans had condemned the activities of HART and CARE.

Throughout the 1970s, these groups drew considerable support, sometimes 'from people who did not always understand what or who they were supporting'.[44] Nevertheless, they were largely ineffective in countering the anti-apartheid rhetoric of HART and CARE. The Labour government's decision to direct the NZRFU to call off the 1973 Springbok tour also somewhat doused the efforts of pro-South African groups. It is plausible, too, that the National Party and Robert Muldoon's successful 1975 electoral campaign, which gave significant attention to the freedom of sporting contacts with South Africa, gave these groups what they wanted and thus less reason to continue organising. These pro-South Africa groups likely drew support from people who, while perhaps accepting that apartheid was wrong or were indifferent to it, were eager to see sport with South Africa unhindered by politics restored, or saw such groups as a potential counter to HART and CARE rather than necessarily ascribing to their conservative, right-wing philosophies. Whatever the reason, by the late 1970s, several of these groups had disappeared.

Not even the furore around the 1981 Springbok tour could reignite the same number of pro-South Africa groups that emerged in the early 1970s. Largely, it was the League of Rights who were active in the debate around the 1981 tour and were responsible for establishing the South Africa Friendship Movement.[45] As in most of the country's radical right-wing groups, the belief in white supremacy was the central principle around which the League based its philosophies, and it, therefore, encouraged contact between whites in New Zealand and South Africa. The League interpreted the anti-apartheid campaigns of the 1970s and 1980s as 'a major feature of communist global activity', which sought to undermine law and order in New Zealand.[46] Its official publication, *On Target*, announced in 1984 that there was an 'undeclared war against South Africa, with the forces of International Communism, International Finance [code for the League's belief in antisemitic conspiracy theories] and Western governments all allied against that country. South Africa is in the front line against the Communist totalitarian advance.'[47] In response to what it deemed the threat of 'communist-inspired and directed anti-apartheid activity', the League urged its members to support Robert Muldoon in his stand against communism and government interference in New Zealand's sporting relationship with South Africa.[48] Sustaining sporting ties with South Africa, and rugby ties in particular – alongside the Dutch Reformed Church and the Afrikaner-dominated Nasionale Party, rugby represented the highest expression of white nationalism – intersected (curiously) with the League's pro-Anglo-Saxon views and its support for creating a white Commonwealth.[49]

When it came to the 1981 tour, the League sought to undermine concerns about hosting the Springboks by arguing that New Zealanders had more important things to consider than interfering in the internal affairs of another country. For example, Joy Clapham of the Dunedin chapter of the League (and a regular Social Credit candidate in elections during the 1970s) reasoned that 'New Zealand should be thinking more about the economy and unemployment than the merits of the Springbok tour.'[50] She argued that South Africa would work itself out in a way that suited all its racial groups but added that the 'one-man, one-vote' system was foreign to the tribal politics of blacks.[51] So too, she justified sustaining apartheid because it 'protects blacks, whites, and coloureds from those who are jealous of the country's wealth', a gesture to the League's concerns that communists sought control of South Africa for its strategic position and mineral abundance.[52] Clapham and other League members set about collecting signatures for a countrywide petition in support of the tour that would be presented to Prime Minister Muldoon.

While Spoonley argued that for the League, 'the 1981 Springbok rugby tour of New Zealand was a critical issue', it is not obvious how it – or any other groups from the radical right – went about dealing with the tour.[53] Most newspapers and media outlets were opposed to the tour and gave extensive coverage to the anti-tour movement. The League had traditionally gone about its activities rather quietly, focusing principally on influencing opinion through letter-writing campaigns to the media.[54] Spoonley noted that this tactic 'allows opinion to be expressed publicly without indicating the source or the political attachment of the writer', and that in so doing '[i]t appears that independent citizens are expressing commonly felt views … And newspaper editors are usually unaware that their paper is being used in this way.'[55] A survey of letters to the editor of the *Otago Daily Times* shows there was a concerted effort by apologists for apartheid to influence public opinion in the south. The League had achieved some notoriety in Dunedin for its role in an anti-fluoridation campaign (though as home to New Zealand's only dental school, the city ensured its water remained fluoridated) and now took the opportunity to produce literature supporting the tour.[56]

A common theme among the radical right is the portrayal of black African savagery, with stories of torture and death used to exemplify black people's supposed lack of civilisation. One letter to the *Otago Daily Times* entertained a gruesome future in which black majority rule in South Africa replaced the civilising influence of whites: 'It is time past time [that] HART and the "do-gooders" woke up and thought of our descendants who will be the victims of the blacks once they get control. Remember the Belgian Congo, remember Uganda – I for one am all for apartheid.'[57]

Another letter echoed a similarly common idea that race and nation are 'the basis for specific demarcation and the mixing of separate races or nations … contravene[s] the "natural order"'.[58] For the League, autonomy and self-determination through separate development preserved racial and national purity.[59] This belief is arguably evident in a comment by J. Hill, a frequent author of letters to the editor, who argued: 'What right do New Zealanders have to interfere and bring about the subversion of a government overseas? Have we the right to dictate to these people their safety and future? Separate development means the retention of tribal cultures of incompatible factions.'[60]

A letter written under the pseudonym 'Pro-Apartheid' invoked the right-wing touchstone of the chaos of black-ruled Africa, noting that '[t]he Black African states of Uganda, Angola, and Mozambique [which were also Marxist states] are not exactly shining examples of "Black Power".'[61] The letter is also explicitly racist: 'Apartheid exists in my view in every country in the world. Very few honest parents would say they would prefer their daughters to marry a black man. Most when asked will say "that's different".'[62]

Another frequent contributor, J. McLachlan, endorsed the apartheid 'homelands' policy and expressed a distrust of the United Nations as a communist organisation and a tool of the global conspiracy. The author also cited Robert Fenton's book, *Sinners in the Stadium* (1974), which argued that South Africa and Rhodesia were undeserving of boycotts, as evidence of 'a very undesirable, trained revolutionary element in New Zealand who, given a chance, are out to create chaos'.[63] Challenging the 'usual distortions regarding South Africa' made in a letter written by Mrs H. McInnes, J. McLachlan wrote: 'It is interesting to note she relies for her information on UNESCO sources which in my view is totally committed to downgrading the white man's efforts on the African continent. This, in many respects, is not surprising after a glance at that fearful master, the communist-dominated United Nations of which UNESCO is merely an agency. Anti-communist South Africa could hardly expect praise from such an organization.'[64]

Continuing the anti-communist rhetoric, another letter writer endorsed the League and other groups' assessment of the anti-tour movement as communist inspired. Reflecting on Muldoon's refusal to cancel visas for the Springboks, 'Play it Cool' noted: 'This does not suit the Communist element (working behind the scenes in all free countries), but which knows not the true meaning of freedom and would impose dictatorship on all Western nations if it could. That New Zealand is the only country which has not fallen into this is a credit to our leaders.'[65] Another letter had similar musings: 'The "Bash New Zealand Brigades" are encouraging a sinister force to develop and tear our nation apart. Under the guise of fighting apartheid, the old communist trick of divide and conquer is doing big business here it seems to me.'[66]

Communist subversion has long been seen by New Zealand's right-wing groups as an explanation for opposition to continuing sporting contact with South Africa. Spoonley noted that because the 'enemy is often only an ideology it becomes critical to locate activists or sympathisers who can be labelled communist'.[67] Claims that HART and CARE were communist tended to rely on the fact that members of the pro-Soviet Socialist Unity Party, the Trotskyist Socialist Action League and Workers' Communist League featured in the anti-tour groups (although largely not in leadership positions, and all were sworn ideological enemies).[68]

Numerous representations of the anti-tour protesters attempted to delegitimise the anti-apartheid campaign as communist. Ross Meurant, a member of the 1981 Red Squad police unit, and later National Party MP for Hobson and co-founder in the 1990s of the New Zealand Conservative Party, interpreted most anti-tour activity as communist inspired. 'The type of civil disorder and breakdown in the rule of law New Zealand experienced during the tour', he noted, 'is a classic example of the manner in which communists operate in countries like ours which normally have a stable political environment.'[69] New Zealand 'was the type of society communism is sworn to destroy' and the anti-tour campaign 'exposed the reality of communism, as a threat to the social fabric of our society'.[70]

Rugby, too, was not immune from the anti-communist rhetoric. Perhaps the most explicit example of this came from 1981 All Black and later team captain Andy Haden, who maintained that 'the Soviet Union's southern Africa conquest has been conducted as a crusade in the name of national liberation' and that many members of the 'terrorist' African National Congress, the main liberation party in South Africa, were 'card carrying members of the South African Communist Party'.[71] He feared that black rule in southern Africa represented Soviet expansion and maintained that it was 'difficult to imagine a South Africa under the African National Congress would be able to maintain the economic strengths which are symptomatic of South Africa today'.[72]

Whether the sentiments expressed above indicate support for radical right-wing ideologies or groups is hard to discern, especially as groups like the League thrived on influencing opinion without making political affiliation explicit. Nevertheless, these were ideas shared with numerous radical right groups and extended beyond mere conservatism to align closely with more extreme views on apartheid, race and communism. At the very least, they indicate that the 1981 tour provoked a social and political climate conducive to such philosophies spreading into the mainstream. While radical-right groups were not particularly successful in ensuring sustained ties between the two countries, their ideologies and ideas influenced how some New Zealanders thought about sporting ties with South Africa. The anti-communist rhetoric was particularly effective and shaped much of the thinking for those who endorsed maintaining ties with South Africa. This emphasis on anti-communism and connecting it to the anti-apartheid movement received considerable support in New Zealand during the 1970s and 1980s and represents perhaps the radical right's most successful campaign in recent history.[73]

IN DEFENCE OF INDIVIDUAL RIGHTS: FRENZ, SPIR AND FIS

The only other major pro-South African organisation that emerged around the 1981 tour was the Society for the Protection of Individual Rights (SPIR).[74] The organisation was established in April 1981 in response to HART's disruption of the World Veteran Games in Christchurch. By the time of the Springboks' tour, SPIR claimed 10,000 members, most of whom were New Zealand-based rugby administrators, coaches and former players, and received endorsement from the NZRFU. Primarily SPIR drew support from those who reasoned that sport and politics were separate and who sought to organise against what they saw as the political invasion of sport by the likes of HART. However, Spoonley noted that a prominent member of the New Zealand Nazi Party attended SPIR events in Auckland, and that a student newspaper claimed two key members of SPIR in Christchurch were involved in organising 'extreme right wing groups based on Nazi and white supremacist principles'.[75]

Much like other ultra-conservative groups, SPIR challenged the legitimacy of the anti-apartheid movement and criticised police for not taking a harder line against protestors.[76] A prominent activist, Yvonne Wilcox, claimed that HART was a front for the Communist Party and that communism sought to destabilise New Zealand by provoking violence and social chaos.[77] Ultimately, SPIR had little success. Despite organising some marches in Auckland, it was unable to mobilise support or resources to the same extent as HART and resorted mainly to letter-writing campaigns to put the pro-tour case.[78] In 1982, a group broke away from SPIR and formed the Free Nation New Zealand (FRENZ), led by Wilcox, J. Malone, Norman McKenzie and, later, ex-National Party MP Pat Hunt. FRENZ aligned itself with the British Freedom in Sport (FIS), led by Tommie Campbell, which sought to remove what it deemed to be political interference in sport.

Notwithstanding Wilcox's preoccupation with communism in the anti-tour movement, organisations like SPIR, FRENZ and FIS (and, to an extent, WARD) represented a new type of right-wing group devoid of explicit white supremacy, and that 'used libertarian arguments about the rights of citizens to play with whomever they wanted'.[79] Traditional radical-right concerns over race and communism were more muted, and in their place came 'a seemingly more moderate stance which stressed individual rights'.[80] To the casual onlooker, it may well have seemed that these groups were simply campaigning for individual rights to watch and engage in sport free from political interference. For instance, FRENZ defined itself as 'upholding the right of the individual to have freedom of choice about where a person wishes to pursue a sporting interest, and against whom and to promote non-political and non-racial sport worldwide'.[81] However, FRENZ, as well as SPIR and FIS, appear also to have been stalking horses in support of apartheid and ideologies of white supremacy. In the wake of the 1981 tour, FRENZ sought to educate New Zealanders, particularly youth, on the benefits of maintaining sporting and economic contact with South Africa.[82] It sought to 'breakdown the defensive barriers which government and people set up when one mentions South Africa' and was 'determined to play its part in the strengthening of [New Zealand] ties with South Africa'.[83] In 1982, members of SPIR and FRENZ travelled to South Africa on a fact-finding mission and, upon their return, insisted that there existed no case for denying South Africa its rightful place in world sport.[84]

In 1983, they sought to recruit New Zealand journalists to attend the International Rugby Media Congress in Cape Town, hosted by the SARB and organised by FIS, which attempted to portray South African sporting contacts as a non-racial question.

A recurring argument from SPIR, FRENZ and FIS was the hypocrisy of those who sought to abolish apartheid.[85] Drawing on statistics from Freedom House (an American human rights organisation), FRENZ reasoned that if only 19 percent of the world's population enjoyed full human rights, South Africa should not be singled out for apartheid.[86] Elizabeth Sutherland, chairperson of SPIR in 1984, attempted to convince the England Rugby Football Union to tour South Africa with the following logic: 'What is abnormal about South African society? That her black people have overall, the highest standard of housing, education and welfare on the African continent; that her black people live in relative peace with at least some degree of legal protection and franchise.'[87] FRENZ also regularly and publicly criticised one of apartheid's most vocal opponents, the Organisation of African Unity (OAU), which it regarded as grossly hypocritical and one of the primary propagandists against South Africa. Prime Minister Muldoon rebuked it for doing so, though he had himself come under fire from the OAU for sustaining sporting ties with South Africa.

In the main, none of these groups proved to be particularly effective. Leading up to the proposed 1985 All Black tour of South Africa, both Sutherland and Wilcox resigned their respective chair positions of SPIR and FRENZ. Wilcox resigned from FRENZ because she claimed she did not want a repeat of the death threats and harassment she had faced in 1981 while working for SPIR.[88]

An enduring problem among radical right-wing groups in New Zealand has been their critical lack of resources. SPIR and FRENZ were no different, and both organisations approached the SARB for funding. Norman McKenzie requested that the SARB assist FRENZ in finding South African businesses willing to offer the group up to $100,000 to launch an extensive pro-tour campaign. No such sponsorship emerged, and by 1986, the relationship between the SARB, FRENZ and FIS had petered out. Importantly, Spoonley believed that one of the reasons these organisations were generally unsuccessful was because 'there was not the anger which was generated by the events in 1981 and rugby at least [was] more circumspect about contact with South Africa.'[89] In the wake of the deeply divisive 1981 tour, South Africa came to be considered an 'economic and symbolic liability', and support in New Zealand for pro-South Africa groups no longer held the allure it once had.[90]

Nonetheless, radical pro-South African activity continued for much of the 1980s, although perhaps in a less obvious and public way than in the previous decades.

The Truth About Southern Africa organisation, founded in Christchurch in 1987, emphasised South Africa as a natural ally of New Zealand against communism.[91] This group distributed the Johannesburg-based *Aida Parker Newsletter*, which the League of Rights advertised in a special issue of *On Target Bulletin*.[92] The League of Rights also continued to focus on South Africa throughout the 1980s. The October 1989 issues of *On Target* and *On Target Bulletin* decried the condemnation of South Africa at that year's Kuala Lumpur Commonwealth Heads of Government Conference. Readers were encouraged to write to British Prime Minister Margaret Thatcher to thank her for her opposition to sanctions against South Africa.[93] The League also explored topics beyond the continuation of white rule in the region. *On Target* and *On Target Bulletin* carried numerous articles by South African antisemitic conspiracy theorist and hard-line apartheid supporter Ivor Benson, reprinted from his *Behind the News* publication. The topics covered in these articles spanned Japanese finance capital, the French Revolution, the 1988 French elections, US–Soviet relations, threats to South African trade, the Demjanjuk war crimes trial and the Aids crisis.[94] The League also advertised two of Benson's books, *The Age of Conflict* and *The Zionist Factor*, alongside its other titles.[95]

More recently, with the fight to keep white rule lost, the New Zealand right has picked up on the post-apartheid 'white genocide' hysteria linked to a spate of farm killings. The 'white genocide' conspiracy comprises a paranoid and apocalyptic rhetoric largely fuelled through a small lobbying group called Afri-Forum and what A. Dirk Moses calls semi-clandestine internet communities of conspiracy theorists (such as the *Suidlanders*, meaning South-landers) who believe they are the victims of a plot to replace South Africa's European population.[96] These conspiracists fear that they, like white Zimbabwean farmers who under Robert Mugabe's rule were forcibly removed from their farms in the early 2000s, are part of a protracted campaign to eviscerate whites from southern Africa.

The supposed 'white genocide' in South Africa has been a touchstone for right-wingers. Extremist Anders Breivik, who massacred 76 young Norwegian social democrats and others in 2011, addressed it in his manifesto under the section titled 'The European Afrikaner/Boer genocide in Africa'.[97] Dylann Roof, who murdered nine black churchgoers in Charleston, South Carolina, in 2015, did likewise. Conservative politicians, too, have picked up on this conspiracy. Former US President Donald Trump asked Secretary of State Mike Pompeo to keep abreast of 'land and farm seizures' and the 'killing of farmers' in South Africa. Australian Home Affairs Minister Peter Dutton considered granting white South African farmers fast-tracked visas on humanitarian grounds due to exaggerated reports of farm killings and threats of potential land seizures.

In New Zealand, the 'Boer genocide' conspiracy has garnered attention, partly because of the large size of the South African expatriate community. The white supremacist Dominion Movement, which shut down after the 15 March attack, was preoccupied with claims of 'white genocide' and produced a poster reading 'Boer Refugees Welcome'. At an All Black–Springbok match in Wellington in 2019, members of the group were pictured with a banner reading 'Save the Boer'. In 2018 James Fairburn, a former member of the Army Reserves who has ties to the radical right group Action Zealandia (successor to the Dominion Movement), presented a petition with 41 signatures to Parliament that white South African farmers 'facing systematic land confiscation and murder by their own government' be given priority as refugees. The petition was closed several months later with no ensuing action taken. So too Kerry Bolton, formerly of the National Front and associate of the New Zealand Rhodesia Society and League of Rights, continues to publish explicitly pro-apartheid material and has written on the believed genocide of Afrikaners. Evoking the usual radical-right imagery of Africans as barbarous, Bolton claims (without evidence) that '[s]ince 1994 over 70,000 Whites have been murdered, including over 6000 farmers, plus an unknown number raped, tortured, and mutilated.'[98] Typical of this conspiracy (not only in the South African context), Bolton believes that a 'white genocide' is being undertaken as 'retribution for apartheid' and cites Julius Malema, leader of the far-left South African Economic Freedom Fighters, saying there would be no compensation 'for the criminals who stole our land'.[99] Despite evidence to the contrary, claims of a 'white genocide' in South Africa demonstrate that proponents of this conspiracy elicit a world-view in which they, as white peoples, are the target of a malevolent plan for extermination. For them, this justifies a response, sometimes extreme action, to avert the impending anti-white apocalypse.

CONCLUSION

Reflecting on the activities of the radical right, Spoonley noted that during the 1960s and 1970s 'these individuals were in their element; they could combine their support for whites in South Africa and Zimbabwe with arguments about the communist threat and the need for patriotism and racial pride'.[100] Yet contemporary understandings of this period tend to emphasise it as a time when the country displayed and consolidated its commitment to an anti-racist philosophy.[101] This effectively *forgets* that there was substantial support in New Zealand for sustaining sporting ties with South Africa, and that for radical-right groups it was critical to facilitate closer bonds between whites in New Zealand and southern Africa. In fact, the issue of sporting contacts with South Africa was one of the few to produce a degree of unity between New Zealand's radical right-wing groups, and garnered considerable mainstream support for some of their core concepts.[102]

However, the extent to which support for these groups comprised an endorsement of the racist, antisemitic and anti-communist philosophies associated with the radical right is questionable. Rather, the boost in public profile these groups received around the South African tours issue should be seen as a spectrum of agreement and support, ranging from strong endorsement of their philosophies to more subtle, perhaps even unwitting support. Many of the core arguments of the radical right, particularly about apartheid as a bulwark against communism, featured in mainstream discussion, from letters to editors to public figures and politicians. Meanwhile, of those who supported pro-South African groups that were affiliated with radical right-wing groups in the 1970s and 1980s, it is likely some were influenced mainly by their desire to see sport uninterrupted by political matters or arguments around individual rights, and were perhaps unaware of (or unperturbed by) these groups' radical philosophies. Nevertheless, for a country passionate about its rugby, including the joyful hope of defeating the South African Springboks, the question of supporting minority white rule in southern Africa provided for the most extensive dissemination of the radical right's ideas into the mainstream of public thinking.

CHAPTER TEN

Street racism – skinheads in New Zealand

JARROD GILBERT

AS THE FINAL DECADE OF THE TWENTIETH CENTURY DAWNED, New Zealand's economy was in dire shape, with unemployment peaking at over 10 percent. In many areas, hardship was rife. The anaemic economy, and often the political remedies, significantly influenced developments in New Zealand's existing gang scene. One of these was the advent of new white supremacist – predominantly skinhead – gangs. New Zealand's skinhead gangs had first appeared in the 1970s and 1980s but became more prominent during the 1990s, with numerous groups appearing across the country, although primarily concentrated in the South Island. Like many such groups overseas, these gangs were not especially ideologically rigorous or politically motivated but became known for their blunt racism and violence. This chapter will look at skinhead gangs in New Zealand and discuss the economic, social and political factors that motivated their sudden rise and swift decline in the 1990s.

WHITE SUPREMACY IN NEW ZEALAND

The notion of white supremacy has a long and complex history in New Zealand that arguably dates back to the country's inception as a colonial nation. Its approach to race has often reflected its early status as a 'neo-Britain'.[1] New Zealand advertised itself to potential migrants as being demographically '98.5% British' – a false claim that represents not only a focus on being seen as an ethnically (or at least culturally) homogenous new Britain but also a desire to exclude Māori from the cultural record by overwriting their culture and assimilating them into Pākehā society.[2] The presumption of Pākehā superiority and assertion that New Zealand was British was both implicit and explicit in state-sponsored violence against Māori who failed to accept either the authority of the Crown or the mass confiscation of their lands and the near-ruin of their language and cultural heritage.

New Zealand's immigration policies historically favoured British or, at most, northern European immigrants and discriminated against others. Between the 1880s and 1950s, the country evolved, and then gradually dismantled, an approach to immigration that historians have called a 'white New Zealand policy' whereby a system of taxes, tests and implicit barriers prioritised migrants from Britain, and to a lesser extent other European nations, and obstructed access to those from India, China or the Middle East. A 'preferred-country source' system that prioritised migrants from the United Kingdom and parts of Europe continued until 1986 and, in combination with other exclusionary laws and policies, made it particularly difficult for non-white migrants to come to New Zealand.[3]

During the period following World War I, broadly understood ideas of white supremacy crystallised around fascism, which would later form the basis for numerous types of white supremacist groups worldwide, including those under review here. Following the defeat of fascist Germany and Italy in World War II – and the temporary defeat, therefore, of fascist white supremacy – aspects of New Zealand's institutional racial bias were deliberately softened, and while more subtle elements of racial prejudice remained acceptable among many parts of society, explicitly fascist and far-right groups were relegated to the fringes. A New Zealand Nazi Party was formed in 1969 by Colin King-Ansell, for example, but attracted more media attention than actual interest in membership, and a New Zealand branch of the British National Front was launched in 1967 but folded in the 1970s.[4] These groups and their history have been documented by other scholars and in other chapters of this book.[5] But one key period is of particular interest here because fashion and economics conspired to bring white supremacy in the form of the skinheads temporarily back into vogue in the 1990s.

SKINHEADS

The skinhead subculture first arose in the United Kingdom in the late 1960s and came to prominence in the early 1970s in the street fights associated with football hooliganism.[6] Arising out of London's working class and the same milieu as the mods and rude boys of the 1950s and 1960s, the early skinheads were recognisable by their distinctive dress, which included close-cropped hair, leather boots and braces.[7] While they were generally anti-authoritarian and known for their violence, the skinheads of the 1960s were not initially racist or right wing – and, in fact, originally coalesced around the ska and reggae music brought to the UK by Jamaican immigrants – but became synonymous with racism and the far right by the mid-1980s.

Although they were notionally fascist, these groups were essentially street gangs and, as such, tended to be limited in their ideology and political engagement. Although some individual ideologues attached themselves to groups (in New Zealand, the most visible of these individuals were Kerry Bolton, Colin King-Ansell or Colin Ansell as he became known, and later Kyle Chapman), skinhead groups were rarely interested in articulating their ideas in any form more complex than simple xenophobia. Instead of using political speech, the skinheads primarily expressed themselves through symbols. The symbols used by the far-right skinhead movement included swastikas, Nazi salutes, the numbers 88 (for HH or 'Heil Hitler') and, in the latter end of the 1990s, 14 (for David Lane's infamous 'fourteen words') and various other historical symbols such as the doppelte Siegrune runes used by the Nazi Schutzstaffel (SS).[8] These symbols were often worn as tattoos or badges on clothing and were paired with other skinhead identifiers, such as the shaved head and boots, to create a visual style that was aggressive, confrontational and uniquely recognisable.

Following overseas trends, skinhead groups had been present in New Zealand since the late 1970s and began taking on a racist edge in the 1980s.[9] In Wellington at that time, a skinhead band was established called the Knives of West Eleven who were said to be 'quite serious about their neo-fascism'.[10] Down south in Christchurch, which became a key centre for the skinhead scene because of its relatively high ethnic homogeneity and its reputation for conservatism, a small skinhead music scene thrived in the early 1980s with the advent of skinhead, bootboy or punk bands like Desperate Measures, Unauthorised, Aryan Army and Johnnies.[11] Three significant skinhead gangs soon formed: the Christchurch Skins, the United Skinheads (known as the 'Uniteds') and the Firm. These were not the only skinhead groups in the city. Other less formal groups were simply known by the suburb from which they came – for instance, Papanui skins or Linwood skins – and many of them were not overtly racist.[12] All of them, however, faded away in rather short measure, and it was not until the 1990s that skinhead and white power groups surged to national attention, in large part as a result of the adverse economic conditions and increasing levels of Asian immigration.

Skinheads represented a considerable deviation from the established culture of New Zealand's gangs, the majority of which, among them the large, patched street gangs, wear back patches and follow the organisational structure of outlaw motorcycle clubs. Elements of gang culture in New Zealand first emerged in the 1950s with a subculture of youthful and disorganised motorcycle-riding groups known as bodgies, widgies and milkbar cowboys, and crystallised into a familiar form with the formation of the Auckland Hells Angels chapter in 1960.[13] This chapter of the Hells Angels was the first outside of America, and just the third in the world, and their influence quickly led to the formation of other motorcycle clubs following a similar template. The country's predominantly Māori street gangs formed during the same period, influenced by the rigours of what was called the 'urban drift', taking the unusual step of adopting many of the features of the outlaw clubs, such as the formal structure and back patch. The large influence of Māori gangs made the scene seem to many a 'Māori issue'.

Partially as a result of their divergence from the norm, skinheads and other non-patched gangs have been the subject of comparatively little local research. In 1987, in what appears to be New Zealand's first investigation of non-patched gangs (since the emergence of patched gangs, at least), Paul Spoonley identified the rise of racist skinhead gangs, linking them to social developments – particularly musical influences stemming from Britain.[14] Although few in number, these gangs had been involved in some racially motivated violent activity, and Spoonley warned of their potential dangers. Indeed, his concern proved prescient, and for a time during the 1990s skinheads burst dramatically into national consciousness. Another piece of research came in response to a growing skinhead presence in Christchurch. During the mid-1990s, Rasjad Addison explored the culture and activities of skinhead gangs for his Master of Arts degree at the University of Canterbury.[15] Like Spoonley before him, Addison linked the rise of skinheads in New Zealand to English influences, and examined a form of detached youth work being employed in Christchurch: a scheme run by the controversial Kyle Chapman, who went on to become the leader of a white supremacist faction and the visible face of racial politics in New Zealand.

Skinhead gangs have received similarly little attention overseas, primarily due to a focus on ethnic minority gangs. In 1995, the American sociologist M.W. Klein said, 'the white gang problem, although present, is not in any sense comparable to the size of the minority gang problem'.[16] It is for this reason, perhaps, that there is a paucity of American research on such groups. Jankowski found American white gangs tend to have a hierarchical structure, and Spergel suggested 'some [white gangs] are concerned with protecting turf or territory, less often with expanding it'.[17] Though tiny in number, racist skinhead gangs are evident in America and, unusually, are often from more middle-class backgrounds. These groups are an imported trend from England.[18] With hindsight, the influences and focal concern of New Zealand skinhead gangs become much clearer – and these start with the economic situation of the late 1980s and early 1990s.

THE 1990s: THE DRIVERS AND FOCAL CONCERN OF THE SKINHEADS

As the country went to the polls for the General Election in October 1990, widespread disillusionment with the radical neoliberal policies adopted by the Fourth Labour Government, and which had hit New Zealand's poorest communities hardest, was overwhelming, even among many traditional Labour supporters. Led by the conservative Jim Bolger, whose staid personality added credibility to a more moderate approach, the National Party made a pre-election promise of a return to a 'decent society'.[19] The party won the election in an unprecedented landslide, claiming 67 of the 97 seats on offer. The change of government, however, did not adjust the direction of the country; in fact, it confirmed it. The new minister of finance, Ruth Richardson, adopted the same monetarist policies championed by Labour's Roger Douglas before her – 'Rogernomics' becoming 'Ruthanasia'. Despite the new government making significantly fewer economic changes than the last, economic neoliberalism was confirmed as a bipartisan philosophy during the 1990s.[20]

The Bolger National government continued the previous government's policy of austerity, asset sales and privatisation. Doing business was made easier as compulsory unionism was axed and the Employment Contracts Act 1991 was introduced. The latter removed penal rates and other employment provisions, reducing the ability of workers to collectively negotiate wages and other employment conditions. The changes cut costs for businesses but came at the expense of workers. Those dependent on social welfare fared even worse. In 1991 the government slashed benefit payments equating to a drop in income for beneficiaries of between 2.9 and 24.7 percent.[21] Further affecting many on welfare or low incomes was the decision to charge market rents for state housing. Unsurprisingly, the difference between the rich and poor widened, and the poor became poorer. Between 1987 and 1993, the real spending power of the wealthiest 20 percent of New Zealanders increased by 7 percent, while the poorest quintile dropped by nearly 3 percent.[22] A change of government had not brought respite for those most affected by the dramatic reforms of the 1980s; rather, it brought greater hardship. This enhanced the social conditions identified by international researchers as important to gang formation and maturation.[23] Worse, despite the promise that the post-1984 reforms would make the economy stronger, the country went into recession during 1991 and 1992. Total unemployment soared and eventually peaked at between 10 and 11 percent, and one in four Māori were unemployed.[24] New Zealand was experiencing the most significant rise in unemployment since the Great Depression.[25]

The 'decent society' had seemingly become the 'descent society' and many people felt betrayed by the continuation of monetarist policies. National's support plummeted in the 1993 election, but they clung to power with 50 of the 99 seats on offer. Widespread dissatisfaction with the country's political situation was reflected in a poll from 1992 that showed just 4 percent of people trusted politicians.[26] This distrust was to have significant implications. In a referendum held alongside the General Election of 1993, New Zealanders chose to adopt proportional representation via a Mixed Member Proportional system (MMP), effectively removing unbridled power from the two traditionally dominant parties. The change signalled widespread political dissatisfaction. On the streets, another signal of social stress was the rise and entrenchment of gangs, including those with white supremacist tendencies.

When the economy deteriorated in the 1980s, lower socio-economic communities tended to be the worst affected. These areas were predominately made up of Māori and Pasifika, so it is of little surprise that gangs from these ethnic communities became the most common. However, as the economic conditions worsened in the early 1990s and spread to impact a wider section of the population, large numbers of urban Pākehā were also severely affected. Unemployment and a bleak social and economic outlook fostered a sense of alienation among many Pākehā youth. Perhaps ignorant of the true genesis of their plight, they lashed out at ethnic minorities and immigrants who they felt were saturating the job market or challenging their perceived status as the dominant ethnic group. The gang scene may have been easily dismissed by some as a Māori issue, but the rise of the skinheads showed that when the conditions fitted, Pākehā were just as quick to form gangs as Māori.

Although the anaemic economy provided a foundation for these groups, as they do for all gangs, they were given direction and impetus by other developments. The most obvious of these was immigration. During the 1980s, New Zealand – a migrant nation – had suffered a net outflow of 30,000 people.[27] More New Zealanders were leaving the country – particularly for Australia – than coming to it, and this imbalance was inhibiting economic growth. Consequently, a drive for suitable immigrants was proposed. The strategy of attracting wealthy Asian immigrants began with the Business Immigration Policy of 1986 and yielded immediate results. By 1990, 10,000 middle-class Asian migrants had settled in New Zealand.[28] Census data show that New Zealand's Asian population increased by 74 percent between 1991 and 1996, and then by a further 37 percent between 1996 and 2001 – by which time it totalled nearly 240,000, or 6.6 percent of the total population.[29] By the end of the 1990s, Asian peoples outnumbered those from the Pacific Islands. This demographic change drew antagonism among those who saw immigrants as unwelcome, and became a rallying cry for the skinheads. Similarly, concessions made to Māori by recent governments – in particular, large Treaty settlements beginning in 1992 – created resentment among some Pākehā, who saw Māori as receiving special treatment at a time when white New Zealanders were suffering. The skinheads sought to exploit this tension as well, although this particular concern tended to take a back seat to Asian migration, which was much more visible on the country's streets and, therefore, more tangible.

In the early 1990s there was a surge of white supremacist or reactionary groups worldwide, and the advent of the internet as the decade proceeded meant that their literature was easily spread.[30] In 1991 a book on New Zealand gangs by Bill Payne was published. The work (called *Staunch*) featured extensive photographs and had a section on skinheads, giving the movement a 'minor shot in the arm'.[31] But perhaps the most significant pop-culture influence came in 1992 when an Australian film depicting the struggles of a group of Melbourne skinheads was released. *Romper Stomper*, starring New Zealand-born actor Russell Crowe, became a cult classic for many youths who identified with the characters and sought to mimic their beliefs and lifestyle. The film had a major impact in shaping the skinhead scene in New Zealand.[32] Certainly, the skinhead movement gained greater momentum and wider appeal.

Without question the scene flared in ways never seen before, or since, but the exact number of racist skinhead gang members is difficult to gauge. In 1994, Christchurch's *Press* reported that 'every day brings fresh news of violence involving skinheads', but acknowledged that 'their public image and reputation for intimidation, violence, and aggression has always far exceeded their numbers'.[33] The easily identifiable nature of the skinheads made them highly visible, and their desire to hang around main centres – such as Christchurch's Cathedral Square – made them perhaps seem greater in number than they were. But the scene did begin to extend beyond the strictly skinhead gangs. Many predominately Pākehā motorcycle gangs also went through a dramatic visual change as their traditionally shaggy appearance gave way to close-cropped or shaved heads. Indeed, many skinhead gangs had close links with the predominantly Pākehā outlaw motorcycle clubs, particularly the South Island clubs (except for Highway 61) and the Satan's Slaves and Sinn Féin in the lower North Island.

Perhaps the most significant group to emerge from the white power ranks was Christchurch's Harris Gang, at the core of which were four brothers: Daryl, Ricky, Paul and Russell Harris. Initially, the Harris brothers were associates of the Epitaph Riders and aspired to prospect for that gang, but they were rejected by the Riders for being too dangerous and quick to attract police attention. Striking out on their own, the Harris's established a clubhouse and a staunch group of followers. Their association with the Epitaph Riders had given them a first-class training in the requirements of being a gang, and they quickly gained a reputation as a fearsome group, involving themselves in numerous criminal activities.[34] In October 1990, the Harris Gang was involved in an ongoing war with Highway 61, and 12 members of the group were convicted for shooting – non-fatally – two Highway 61 members at the Brisbane Street periodic detention centre.[35] Only one member pulled the gun's trigger, but none of the group would say who. Their leader, Daryl Harris, told me in 2005 that the fact that everyone 'stuck tight' and refused to speak was a source of pride among the gang and proof of their commitment. Those outsiders who did testify against the gang were terrorised and several houses were bombed or set alight. One woman who testified against the group, and another man, were marched out of the woman's house at gunpoint by two masked men who then proceeded to set it on fire.[36] Although the group looked capable of achieving longevity on its own, in 1993, fulfilling their outlaw club ambitions, the Harris Gang became the Christchurch chapter of the Road Knights.[37]

By this time, the Road Knights in Invercargill and Timaru were being bolstered by a young, staunchly white power-orientated skinhead gang called the Bandenkrieg ('gang war' in German). Also informally known as 'the Germans' or 'Young Germans', the group acted as a feeder club to the Road Knights and was at least partially under the outlaw club's control. The Road Knights were not the only outlaw motorcycle club to have adopted white power ideals: the charter of the Southern Son's Motorcycle Club, fleetingly formed in the 1990s, declared it to be a 'white members only' club, and praised Adolf Hitler as a 'truely [*sic*] amazing man with truth in his heart'.[38] But none wore their far-right affiliation as openly as the skinheads.

Perhaps the most feared of all the skinhead gangs was the Fourth Reich. The Fourth Reich formed in Christchurch Prison in the early 1990s and was a small but hardcore gang that controlled the East Wing of the prison and much of the Invercargill Prison. During the mid-1990s it was said that any skin who was sent to East Wing would be stood over by the Fourth Reich and told 'he must join them, grow his hair back, or "go West" [to the protection wing]'.[39] Formidable within the prison, the Fourth Reich struggled to maintain strong numbers outside of jail, but nevertheless did develop a presence in Christchurch, Nelson, Greymouth, Timaru and Dunedin.[40]

Members of the group were involved in four murders, three of which appear to have been motivated by the group's ideology. Hemi Hutley, who was Māori, was killed in 1997; James Bambrough, who was gay, was murdered in 1999; and Jae Hyeon Kim, who was a Korean tourist, was picked up and killed while hitchhiking in 2003. The murder of Hemi Hutley was of particular interest because one of the killers, Neihana Foster, was himself part-Māori. This seeming anomaly highlights the special – though seldom explicitly discussed – status often given to the few Māori who were members of skinhead gangs. It is unclear, however, why this status did not extend to the Māori victim. Prominent skinhead leader Kyle Chapman, using the words of Robert Mathews – the leader of an American white nationalist group called 'The Order' – put it to me thus: 'If it looks white, acts white, and fights white, then it is white.' For his part, Foster told police that his father was white and his heart was white.[41]

The killings were not the only time the Fourth Reich came to national attention. In 1997 a member of the gang – who described himself as having the rank of 'private' – had his finger cut off. The victim told the Christchurch High Court he was punished for wanting to leave the group, but it is widely known to those close to the gang that the punishment was for theft of the gang's drug supply.[42] Then, in 1998, a conflict between the gang and the Lost Breed of Nelson was exposed when a Lost Breed member was nearly killed in an attack in Christchurch Prison. According to a prison officer, the Fourth Reich member said 'something to the effect that this will teach you for crossing us'.[43]

In response to the growing problem, and in recognition of the reputational damage to the city at the centre of national skinhead activity, the Christchurch City Council helped fund the New Way Trust in 1994. Established, somewhat ironically, by Kyle Chapman, the Trust's objectives were:

1. To enable and assist young people alienated from mainstream society (particularly those known as Skinheads) to participate in rehabilitation programmes
2. To assist young people who are unemployed to increase their skills and obtain useful employment.[44]

In 1995, an evaluation commissioned by the Christchurch City Council and the Police Crime Prevention Unit gave a largely positive view of the work being undertaken by the Trust.[45] Nevertheless, the Trust quickly became controversial when Chapman confessed to numerous historical race-based crimes he had committed as a skinhead in Invercargill, including the firebombing of a marae. Chapman said the confession was to 'ensure he paid his debt to society'.[46] He told me in 2007 that the confessions were part of an Alcoholics Anonymous pledge that he had taken after giving up drugs and alcohol and becoming a Christian. Despite the seriousness of the crimes, Chapman escaped a jail sentence, thanks largely to his positive work at the New Way Trust. The Trust's chairperson and Christchurch city councillor, David Close, said he admired Chapman's courage in confessing, taking it 'as evidence of his commitment to a new way of life'.[47] However, in 1997 Chapman again created headlines when he was linked to the distribution of racist literature that called on 'Young patriots ... for the formation of a fascist youth group'. The pamphlets, which were distributed to many Christchurch mailboxes, carried a picture of a paramilitary figure, and implored: 'If you love your race and nation and have the courage to fight for your homeland ... Join Now!'[48]

Chapman's desire to help motivate disillusioned Pākehā youth had clearly taken a more radical path. His association with the Trust became untenable and he left to establish a new skinhead gang – the Hammerskins – which for a short time became quite prominent and claimed to have chapters across the country.[49] The New Zealand Hammerskins was a chapter of the international Hammerskin Nation movement, which formed in Dallas, Texas, in 1980, and was described by the Jewish Anti-Defamation League as 'the most violent and best-organised neo-Nazi skinhead group in the United States', though appears to have since foundered.[50] Under Chapman's leadership the group shunned drugs, encouraged only moderate use of liquor, and promoted general wellbeing because 'your better fitness may be the deciding factor in battle'. Although a common feature in far-right ideology, the prohibition of alcohol and drugs was not popular among the group's members, most of whom, Chapman later admitted to me, were no less interested in partying than any other young gang members.[51]

A recruitment document distributed by the group claimed that they followed the 'leaderless resistance' strategy, popularised for far-right revolutionary groups by Ku Klux Klan member Louis Beam, in which groups avoid hierarchical or centralised command so that cells do not compromise one another if they are captured by law enforcement.[52] This commitment appears to have been primarily rhetorical, however: the group operated openly, and is not known to have committed any major acts of 'resistance'. Like most skinheads, the members were more concerned with drinking cheap alcohol, doing drugs and sneering at outsiders on public streets than organising any type of political revolution. The Hammerskins soon faded and quickly became defunct.

While the most obvious skinhead and white power activities were reserved for the South Island where there are smaller populations of Māori and Pasifika peoples, one notable exception was a group called Unit 88 that arose in West Auckland in 1997. The group formed under the guidance of long-time white supremacist Colin Ansell (also known as Colin King-Ansell), who had established the New Zealand Nazi Party in the 1960s and was also a founding member of the New Zealand Fascist Union. Unit 88 was overtly racist and established a base in an industrial area in Henderson, West Auckland. The group soon received significant attention in the media – simply for their brash appearance in the heart of an area with a significant Māori and Pasifika population. A co-founder of Unit 88, Karl Warlock, said that attacks on 'black families' had led the public to believe Christchurch was the main centre for white power activities, but '[y]ou might be surprised how many skinheads there are in the Auckland district'.[53] The gang began printing and distributing white supremacist leaflets, and Race Relations Conciliator Rajen Prasad said he would look to take legal action against the gang, as their material 'incites racial disharmony and breaches our anti-discrimination laws'.[54] The gang also elicited comment in Parliament, with Opposition members calling for race-hate laws. Minister of Justice Doug Graham responded that he was satisfied existing legislation was adequate and that the race relations conciliator would act as necessary.[55] But Rajen Prasad was saved any such action as a more immediate deterrent to the gang came from both the Black Power and the Head Hunters gangs who stated that Unit 88 would not be tolerated and that they would be subjected to 'street justice'.[56] The threats were not hollow, and following 'visits' from both gangs, Unit 88 vacated their clubhouse and quickly petered out.

The sudden rise and equally rapid fall of Unit 88 is perhaps an exemplar of skinhead gangs generally. While the skinhead movement flared significantly in the early and mid-1990s, it began to fade by the end of the decade. Even in the stronghold city of Christchurch, the street prominence of skinheads all but disappeared. The wider skinhead fashion had ebbed, and with it the skinhead gangs. Unlike the patched gangs, they were unable to achieve significant longevity. Many of these groups lacked the organisational structure of the patched gangs, and although some skinheads held onto their ideals, the improving economy and lower unemployment – particularly among Pākehā – robbed the scene of recruits and relevance.

A further explanation for the decline was the markedly different social folkways evident within the 1990s. Most of the established gangs were born in a period in the 1960s and 1970s; like the hippies, they prided themselves on shunning private material possessions and had a culture of sharing. The skinheads were of a time when individualism and self-attainment were at the fore. Such an ethos was not as conducive to successfully forming the bonds – or achieving a physical base, such as a clubhouse – that had kept the patched gangs together. Nor did the skinheads formally shun intravenous drug use, as the patched gangs did, meaning many became drug addled and, therefore, liabilities to their gang.

By the 2000s, the skinhead scene had not just come off its peak, it had faded almost entirely from view. Certainly, some old skins remained, and there were some notable features to the scene – such as the creation of the Right Wing Resistance in 2009 – but the overt racism of the street had morphed into something else entirely. As it has elsewhere, the surge in right-wing extremist views that occurred in the mid- to late 2010s has touched New Zealand, but it has tended to overlook the skinhead scene, which is regarded by many in the new movements to be a relic of the past. This more recent 'alternative right' (alt-right) movement has avoided many aspects of skinhead culture, such as the emphasis on violence and gang activity, tending to be much more focused on ideology and politics. Reflecting this broader change, the alt-right-style groups that have formed in New Zealand have a more middle-class membership and have concentrated on maintaining plausible deniability, instead of the skinheads' more overt signals of membership.[57] The largest and most organised of these is Action Zealandia, a group that styles itself as 'a movement of young nationalists dedicated to the revitalisation of our people, culture, environment and community', and which claims to have chapters in most of New Zealand's major centres.[58] These developments, including connections with the skinhead scene, are discussed in the chapters in Part 5.

CONCLUSION

During the 1990s, as racist skinhead gangs surged to the fore, albeit rather briefly, it became clear that the gang scene in New Zealand had changed in important ways. There is no doubt this emergence can largely be understood by looking at the context in which it occurred – a bleak economic environment that impacted harshly on lower socio-economic sectors. It is no coincidence that as unemployment was peaking at double-digit levels in the early 1990s, skinhead gangs – comprised of poor urban Pākehā – became so prominent.

The immediate rise of white supremacist gangs following the economic downturn in the 1990s – and their subsequent decline as the economy regained its footing –

serves to underscore the argument that gang formation is a consequence of negative social conditions, not ethnicity. Ethnic minorities may face 'multiple marginality', the process by which minority groups are subject to a greater number of negative social and economic conditions, and, therefore, may be more susceptible to gang formation.[59] The establishment of gangs by alienated members of a dominant ethnic group is achieved when the necessary conditions of crisis present themselves.

PART 4
Religious and cultural intolerance

CHAPTER ELEVEN

From moral crusaders to new conservatives

the evolution of New Zealand's Christian religious right, 1970–2021

DOLORES JANIEWSKI

THE HISTORY OF THE CHRISTIAN RIGHT in New Zealand deserves attention for its 50-year battle to defend 'family values': the patriarchal family, monogamy, heterosexuality and restrictions on women's reproductive choices. Its defence of a hierarchical and two-gendered model of the 'Christian family' has attracted fervent, although diminishing, support in New Zealand since its emergence in the 1970s.[1] It was during this decade that feminists, lesbians and gay liberationists added patriarchy, gender and sexuality to the 'leftist' agenda, inciting vociferous opposition from the emergent Christian right. Although 'moral conservatism' has been less powerfully articulated in New Zealand than in Australia and the US, it continues to exert an appeal to some New Zealanders, including parts of the Pasifika, Māori, Indian and Chinese communities.[2] What follows will trace the history of groups 'championing Godly values and principles' in opposition to what one scholar has discussed as the 'perceived threat posed by secular humanism, post-modernism and ethical liberalism', which included feminism, gay rights, abortion and other challenges to rigidly defined gender, parental, moral and sexual norms.[3]

THE 'CHRISTIAN' IN 'CHRISTIAN RIGHT'

The Christian right in Aotearoa has engaged religious conservatives from a diverse range of denominations, including evangelicals, Pentecostals, fundamentalists, Mormons, Reformed churches, charismatics and Catholics. For its Protestant members, a belief in the inerrant nature of the Bible as interpreted by their religious leaders offered a religious justification for a family based on male authority, female dedication to motherhood and child-rearing, and the restriction of sexuality to heterosexual marriage. Some subscribe to a dualistic cosmology predicated upon an opposition between 'the spiritual and the worldly', 'good and evil' and 'God and Satan'. This requires primary loyalty to the spiritual realm rather than a secular state, especially when the state's actions violate the moral code that religious leaders insist is God's law.[4] A militant strand of Calvinism espoused by some Reformed ministers advocates the replacement of the secular state by a theocratic one, and refuses to tolerate deviations from an absolutist moral code derived from the Old Testament.[5] As was also the case in the US, the Catholic hierarchy and activist laity have formed a tacit alliance with conservative Protestants in opposition to abortion, and this continues into the present.[6] Catholic bishops expressed more muted opposition to the decriminalisation of homosexuality and civil unions, but Catholic activists undertook vociferous moral campaigns against pornography and euthanasia in the name of 'family values'.[7]

Built upon a new model of 'apostolic' religious leadership, independent congregations have mobilised under the leadership of 'highly influential dynamic individuals who "exude authority"'.[8] Some of these leaders combine pro-family and pro-market positions in what is discussed as 'health-and-wealth', Word of Faith or the Prosperity Gospel.[9] This American import originated in Pentecostal revivals in the US after World War II before spreading around the globe. Offering the promise of economic security and faith healing to marginalised indigenous communities, this theological fusion of Christian, family and market values appeals to New Zealanders in financial hardship, entrepreneurial immigrants, centre-right politicians and corporate executives.[10] Unsurprisingly, this form of religious practice can generate opposition to vaccination and other state-mandated policies that offer alternatives to what pastors and apostles assure their members will happen as they ascend to 'higher levels of faith'.[11]

Moral campaigners in New Zealand have consistently taken inspiration from the US Christian right. Visiting evangelists, including Billy Graham (who hosted revivals in New Zealand and Australia in 1959), helped foster an ideological affinity between Christian and secular libertarianism.[12] Readers of *The Challenge Weekly* in the 1970s and 1980s could learn about prominent leaders of the Moral Majority (Anita Bryant's anti-gay rights campaign), visits from the Accelerated Christian Education (ACE) creator encouraging use of its programme in New Zealand schools, and the warnings from self-appointed textbook censor Norma Gabler.[13] US-based Christian right organisations such as Focus on the Family, Human Life International and Promise Keepers have affiliates in New Zealand, while the New Zealand Business Roundtable (NZBR) and Maxim Institute have ties to American, Australian and British think tanks. Magazines, pamphlets, Radio Rhema, evangelical newspapers, cassettes, books and the internet continue to deliver messages from the American Christian right.[14] Christian radio delivers Focus on the Family programming, and five Christian television networks now feature US televangelists.[15] This combination of inspiration from the American Christian right, diverse religious traditions, and innovations in leadership and organisations has created a dynamic but fragmented Christian right in New Zealand.

SCHOLARLY ANALYSES OF THE CHRISTIAN RIGHT

This chapter builds upon the historical and conceptual framework of 'moral authoritarianism', which was presented by Allanah Ryan in a 1988 co-written study of three major strands in the New Zealand right.[16] My own more recent work brings this history up to 1999, exploring the problems faced by moral conservatives in New Zealand where the dominant political culture favoured a combination of sexual and market liberalism.[17] Bryan Gilling's edited collection on fundamentalism is another key study. John Evans's contribution to Gilling's collection argued that fundamentalists became politically engaged in reaction to what they abhorred as 'permissiveness' in the 1960s. By 1970, the Society for the Protection of Community Standards (SPCS) and the Society for the Protection of the Unborn Child (SPUC – now Voice for Life) formed to campaign against obscenity and abortion respectively. More extensive mobilisation occurred later in the decade and expanded still further in the 1980s. After a failed effort to sway votes to secure a National victory in 1987, Christian Heritage emerged as the first exemplar of a 'Moral Right', 'Authoritarian Right', 'Moral Populist' or 'New Christian Right' political party.[18] This chapter will extend the scholarship another three decades.

Peter Lineham's case study of Destiny Church and its involvement in Christian-right politics from the early 2000s to the early 2010s also provides insights into Christian Heritage, the Christian Democrats (later the religious grouping in United Future) and National's attempts to attract Christian-right constituencies. Lineham outlined the moral agenda put forward by Destiny and its subsequent rebirth as Vision New Zealand. Moral conservatism, anti-smacking, homophobia, anti-Islam, authoritarianism and the 'Prosperity Gospel' combined in a paradoxical mixture inspired by American-style evangelical politics.[19] He detailed how the National Party under Don Brash's leadership took morally conservative positions in a tacit alliance with the Maxim Institute in opposition to the socially liberal policies of the Labour government under Prime Minister Helen Clark. Journalists uncovered additional support for Brash from the Exclusive Brethren, who persuaded him to oppose the Civil Unions legislation in 2004 and circulated pamphlets in the election campaign in 2005.[20] As Lineham makes clear, it was difficult to forge a united Christian coalition between Destiny's mix of Pentecostal and prosperity gospel, the fundamentalist evangelical approach of Christian Democrats, and the Reformed Church-inspired Christian Heritage Party.

In other insightful interpretations, the concept of 'worlds colliding' or 'in collision' focused on the emerging clash between the sacred and the profane, between church and state. Rex Ahdar discussed the conflict between conservative Christian adherents of 'traditional moral values' and the secular, humanist state in areas such as feminism, abortion, gay rights and children's rights.[21] Laurie Guy produced a useful overview of religion and politics in New Zealand, including discussions of gender and sexuality, focusing on the 'gay debate' leading to the decriminalisation of homosexuality in 1986.[22] In these interpretations, New Zealand's religious right resembles the trajectory discussed by Whitney Straub in tracing American conservatives' adoption of 'moralism as a discursive displacement' for overt racism and anti-communism in the 1970s.[23] Signs of a similar awakening of politically engaged religious activists occurred in New Zealand in the same decade. Exploring the image of 'Jesus in Godzone', Bill Cooke looked at heresy in the 1960s and the revival of evangelical religion and Jesus marches in the early 1970s as periods of conflict between a 'waning' and a resurrected Jesus.[24] Jonathan Boston usefully traced the first 'distinctively Christian' political parties in New Zealand with a 'relatively narrow policy focus' on family, marriage, education and sexual ethics.[25] Ahdar explored the question of whether New Zealand was a 'Christian state' in a collection he co-edited with John Stenhouse. He highlighted the difficulties facing militant Christians in combating 'notions of equality, freedom and state neutrality' in an increasingly secular and pluralist society.[26] Read together, the scholarship points to the 1970s – the decade marked by 'resurgent religiosity' and moral conflicts over gay rights, abortion and the emergence of a 'family values' agenda in the US – as a starting point for the New Zealand Christian right.[27]

Scholarship outside of the New Zealand context provides additional insights into the causes of Christian-right mobilisation, particularly transnational influences on domestic issues and strategy. A Canadian-edited collection, *Contesting*

Fundamentalisms, discussed not only fundamentalist religious practices but also the fundamentalist tendencies of indigenous cultural revitalisation processes, neoliberalism and hegemonic masculinity. The editors' description of fundamentalism as a 'process in which a set of binary absolutes are constructed, insiders and outsiders, truth and lies, God and the devil' applies to other constituencies in the Christian right, despite theological and institutional differences.[28] Martin Durham offered a useful discussion of the components of the American Christian right that contribute to an understanding of New Zealand developments.[29] Ann Burlein explored how the Christian-right founder of Focus on the Family seeks to reclaim children, home and church as 'domains of male leadership' from radical feminists, gay rights activists, permissive child-rearing and other perceived threats.[30] Together, these scholars help to explain the factors that make some New Zealanders participants in the Christian right.

'THE WAY WE NEVER WERE' – CONTESTED MEMORIES OF THE 1960s AND 1970s

A Conservative Party candidate in 2014 exemplified the importance of the 1970s as a starting point for a discussion of the New Zealand Christian right. Looking back nostalgically to his childhood, Lachie Ashton (now a New Conservative) expressed his determination 'to stop the slide and restore New Zealand back to the prosperous country it once was back in the 60's when there was virtually no unemployment, people grew up in stable families on one income and housing was affordable'. It was a time without 'racial disharmony, no gangs, no drugs and no teenage suicides'. Ashton had grown up on a large farm in Central Otago before conflict, crime and unstable families disrupted his vision of a moral paradise.[31] Recalling one of the most remote and least ethnically diverse parts of New Zealand (where television only arrived in 1967), Ashton conjured up a whitewashed fantasy, which an American historian has described as 'the way we never were': a 'golden age of family life' which in New Zealand became the Pākehā harmonious paradise.[32]

Age and location shielded Ashton from appreciating that his favoured decade ushered in demands for women's liberation and the arrival of Betty Friedan's *The Feminine Mystique* to receptive readers. The language of gay rights and books like *Lesbian Nation* travelled across the Pacific, along with reports about the American Indian Movement and the Black Panthers that inspired a new generation of Māori and Pasifika activists.[33] The New Conservative dream of a Christian restoration relies upon nostalgia for a time of nationwide social harmony that never existed, as well as the belief that an ancient text offers solutions to contemporary social and personal problems for all who follow its tenets. Participants in the Christian right thus simultaneously engage 'in nostalgia for the past while displaying historical amnesia' about what actually happened.[34]

Feminist recollections of the 1970s reveal realities that a harmonious imagined Christian patriarchy fail to recognise. Christine Dann discussed the founding of women's liberation groups in 1970 with an agenda that included daycare centres, liberalising abortion laws, ensuring access to contraceptives and consciousness-raising for New Zealand women. The claims of female enslavement by being confined to 'housekeeping and reproduction' certainly clashed with a nostalgic vision of happy families and contented housewives, as did the emergence of lesbian organisations in 1973.[35] Ngahuia Te Awekotuku recalled eagerly reading a 'dog-eared' copy of *Notes From the Second Year*, a foundational text from New York's Radical Women in 1970, as an early introduction to her involvement in Māori feminism and struggles against 'queer-bashing homophobia' in the 1970s.[36] In combination with the 'renaissance in Māori awareness', Te Awekotuku's political awakening in the 1970s differed significantly from a Christian-right portrait of the same decade.

The Abortion Law Reform Association of New Zealand formed in response to SPUC in 1971.[37] That same year, Sylvia Baynes joined Auckland Women's Liberation, devoured *The Feminine Mystique*, and 'haunted' bookshops for other feminist publications that arrived from the US, including *Sisterhood is Powerful*, *The Female Eunuch* and *The Dialectic of Sex*.[38] Anne Else read Germaine Greer's *Female Eunuch* and discussed what was, in 1971, becoming known as 'women's liberation' after Greer's declaration of belonging to the 'second feminist wave'.[39] *Broadsheet*, a New Zealand feminist magazine, first appeared in 1972, the same year as the passage of an Equal Pay Act, while Greer called for more revolutionary actions during a visit to New Zealand in March.[40] Marilynn Johnson joined a gay liberation group in Wellington in 1972 before becoming active in She (Sisters for Homophile Equality), which began publishing a magazine called *Circle* in 1973.[41] These recollections present a vastly different image of New Zealand from that painted by the religious right. A culture war had started to emerge between liberation movements and moral conservatives in which the Christian right became a major combatant as its members responded to challenges to their beliefs and nostalgic memories about family, gender and sexuality.

CULTURE WARRIORS AND MORAL CRUSADERS

Many of the battles in New Zealand's version of the culture wars occurred whenever Parliament began to debate moral and sexual issues. Ryan's formulation of 'moral authoritarianism' described a self-defined group of 'moral people' opposing what they termed a 'corrupt power bloc of the state and various progressive groups'.[42] Some battles concerned the kind of conduct that should be criminalised, including abortion, marital rape, homosexuality and corporal punishment. Others revolved around claims to sexual citizenship, such as the inclusion of sexual orientation in the Human Rights Act, civil unions and same-sex marriage. As interpreted through a feminist lens, the issues of sexuality and social control posed the question of the balance of power between church, state, families, men and women.[43] Each of these episodes exemplifies what might be called 'clashes' or tensions between the religious right's commitment to patriarchal 'family values' and an expansive concept of civil, political, social and sexual rights. By examining groups and individuals opposed to abortion, gay rights and the protection of children from 'the use of force for the purpose of correction', this section will trace the history of efforts to defend a divinely organised moral order in opposition to claims for rights rooted in secular ideas about equality.

Alarmed by the passage of the Abortion Reform Act in Britain in 1967 and similar developments in Australian states, Catholics played an active role in the founding of SPUC in 1970. So did Anglicans, Methodists, Jews, the Salvation Army and members of Moral Re-Armament, a group engaged in an international crusade against communism in China, New Zealand and elsewhere.[44] Announcing the formation of a national organisation in 1972, SPUC took direct aim at Greer, the 'Australian whirlwind' who had used 'the abortionist tactics of noise, emotionalism and intimidation' during her New Zealand visit to claim the right to inflict 'violence' on the 'foetus'. It vowed never to 'abandon him to his fate'.[45] SPUC hosted the visit of British Conservative MP Jill Knight, a 'cyclone', who toured New Zealand speaking out against the decriminalisation of abortion in Britain. SPUC imported newsletters from sister organisations in the US, and kept its members aware of Australian morality campaigns, as well as morals campaigner Mary Whitehouse's Festival of Light in Britain and Australia.[46] In the view of a SPUC leader, it was defending 'traditional values' against the 'abortion juggernaut' that was advocating reproductive rights for women around the globe.[47]

Fortunately for SPUC, opposition to abortion attracted significant political support. This included Norman Kirk, the Labour Prime Minister, and Ruth Kirk who became a SPUC patron. When a debate ensued over a private member's Bill seeking to close an Auckland abortion clinic, it received support from leader of the Opposition Robert Muldoon. Bringing the debate to a close, MP for Western Māori Koro Wetere warned that opposing the Bill would allow 'moral standards' to deteriorate 'to a level where our Christian beliefs are being forgotten'.[48] The Bill passed on a vote of 43 to 16.

In 1975 and 1976, a Royal Commission on Contraception, Sterilisation and Abortion provided ample opportunity for the concerns of the religious right to be aired. SPUC testified on behalf of the 'rights of the unborn child' and 'father's rights', declaring that the fertilised zygote was an 'independent person from the moment of conception' in 'command of the whole process of pregnancy'. A later SPUC witness elaborated on this claim by alleging that the 'embryo develops a placenta and a protective capsule of fluid for himself' as though the only active agent in a pregnancy were a male foetus.[49] Catholic bishops, denying accusations that they were 'conservative, reactionary, or narrow-minded', insisted that the central issue was the 'holiness of marriage and the family' that rendered sexual intercourse 'sacred' rather than a 'matter of personal pleasure and fulfilment'.[50] The Family Rights Association defended the family as 'God's plan', and opposed the 'anti-family propaganda' that arose from 'secular humanism' and 'women's liberation'.[51] Another witness introduced an article by an early advocate of men's rights and forerunner to Canadian psychologist Jordan Peterson's more recent expression of the necessity of male dominance and opposition to the legal recognition and protection of 'gender identity and expression'. Writing in *Reader's Digest*, American George Gilder insisted that manhood was a fundamental part of the 'sexual constitution' and that giving in to feminist demands for gender equality would result in the 'suicide of the sexes'.[52] Religious witnesses dominated the proceedings of the Royal Commission, which produced 28 volumes. SPUC's views in particular were extensively documented.

Ultimately, the ongoing conflict between women's liberationists and Christian conservatives produced the Abortion, Sterilisation and Contraception Act 1977. This kept abortion in the Crimes Act 1961, except when pregnancy threatened the mother's mental or physical health as certified by two consultants, while decriminalising abortions for pregnancies of fewer than 20 weeks.[53] The *Challenge Weekly*, an evangelical newspaper, described the result as 'ambiguous'.[54] It was circumvented by the feminist group Sisters Overseas Service, which sent women to Australia for terminations. The Act also failed to prevent legal abortions from increasing after a temporary decline, as consultants proved unwilling to deny most requests. Nevertheless, the campaign against abortion law reform was the most enduring success achieved by the Christian right. Abortion was not fully removed from the Crimes Act until March 2020.

Emerging in parallel to SPUC was another initiative: a crusade against pornography.[55] A member of the Sisters of Mercy, Patricia Bartlett, became horrified by media depictions of nudity, obscenity and explicit sexual acts, including homosexual and lesbian sexual practices. Convinced that such material constituted a threat to the family and morality, she began a personal campaign of letter writing to film censors and newspapers that alarmed her superiors. Leaving her Order in 1969, and inspired by British moral crusader Mary Whitehouse, Bartlett decided that 'indecency' needed to be redefined in the Crimes Act to include nudity, sexual intercourse, bare breasts, and lesbian and homosexual 'love scenes'.[56] She founded the Society for Promotion of Community Standards (SPCS) in November 1970 and built up a membership of 22,000 in the following decades. Her crusade to preserve the 'moral heritage' of New Zealanders and promote the 'public good' included opposition to abortion, sex education, the decriminalisation of homosexuality, and contraception for young teenagers.[57] Referring to 'Bartlett syndrome', a critic accused Parliament of yielding to SPCS pressure by making it a 'criminal offence' to give 'advice and instruction on contraception' in the Abortion, Sterilisation and Contraception Act – even though more New Zealanders subscribed to *Playboy* than signed Bartlett's petitions.[58] SPCS supporters, however, viewed her as a courageous champion of the 'silent majority' who sent 'a charge of moral electricity through the body politic' in a 25-year crusade for 'decency'.[59]

The 1970s made visible the growing strength of a religious reaction to what Christian-right organisers described as a 'determined assault' on 'family life, morality and decency'. Warning about a 'moral landslide', Jesus marches took place in 14 cities. After the formation of the Family Rights Association in 1973, the Concerned Parents' Association took up the fight against sex education as a state-promoted intrusion into family life. Feminists for Life formed in the same year to oppose demands for abortion law reform. SPCS and other groups organised a 'public outcry' against 'perversion and the debasing of manhood' to defeat a private member's Bill decriminalising homosexual acts for adults. Thousands of 'Pro-lifers' marched in 1975. In 1976, a visiting American educator told *Challenge Weekly* readers that 'we should teach our children God's law and cease to allow them to hear instruction that causes them to err' in state schools. A female contributor insisted that men had the 'God-given role of being the head of the house', and another wrote that women had no 'right to be equal to men'. Late in 1977, Save Our Homes formed to instruct women in God's model of true femininity, and Concerned Parents sponsored Texan Norma Gabler's tour in which she warned that secular 'values education' was a 'blasphemous' rejection of the 'God-given difference' between male and female and an unacceptable promotion of 'secular humanism'.[60] Children's education, abortion and gender had become major issues as the American Christian right became a significant influence on receptive New Zealanders.

Another upsurge in Christian-right mobilisation occurred in 1984 when the newly elected Labour government set up a series of forums to develop its policy agenda for New Zealand women. Conservative women poured into Women's Forums to oppose the 'liberal, humanist world-and-lifeview', fearing that the Labour government's ratification of the UN Convention on the Elimination of All Forms of Discrimination against Women would usher in a 'one-world, anti-Christ government'. Unable to prevent the ratification, these groups remained on the alert for the next sign of danger from the Labour government and its contingent of feminist MPs. When Labour MP for Wellington Central Fran Wilde introduced a private member's Bill to decriminalise homosexuality and prevent discrimination based on sexual orientation in early 1985, these forces geared up for a moral Armageddon. Their weapons included SPCS's importation of *The Homosexual Network* from the US, which argued that homosexuality was a 'manifestation of sinful condition that affects mankind'.[61] The battle lasted 18 months, and included a petition against the Bill signed by 800,000 New Zealanders that was delivered during what supporters of the Bill described as a 'Nuremburg rally' when uniformed and flag-wielding ranks of the Salvation Army lined Parliament's steps.[62]

Moral missionaries from the US helped to organise a New Zealand equivalent of the Moral Majority in the battle against the decriminalisation of homosexuality. The Coalition of Concerned Citizens waged discursive battle against the 'gay rights' framework being used by the proponents of the legislation. The Coalition expressed 'great suspicion' about the 'talk of rights, deeming it to be humanistic, egotistical and overly optimistic about human nature'. Rather than accepting the 'sexual citizenship' model that underlay the claims to removing legal prohibition against homosexuality, the opponents rejected the concept of 'consensual non-procreative and recreational sexualities'. They urged New Zealanders to consider themselves not as free and equal sexual citizens but as 'sinners' having 'no rights before God', who restricted sexuality to married, heterosexual couples. Claims to sexual citizenship constituted 'human rebellion against the law of God'. Objecting to the consignment of religion and morality to the 'private sphere', members of the Coalition, and allies like SPCS, took their message into the public realm by adopting tactics from the US Christian right.[63]

My analysis of the submissions to the select committee considering the Bill made apparent the stark difference in world-views. Advocates of homosexual law reform overwhelmingly argued for the right to be protected against discrimination (84 percent), in the name of human rights (71.4 percent), and to a lesser extent stressed the sexual freedom of consenting adults (54.4 percent). The Bill's supporters mostly discussed morality in negative terms, as puritanism based upon outdated Old Testament passages used to justify punitive treatment for homosexuals, rather than New Testament calls for compassion. Opponents' submissions described anal and oral sex as unnatural (88 percent), defined themselves as a moral majority who should be allowed to discriminate against the immoral minority (69.7 percent), and worried about youth being seduced into homosexuality (68 percent). Laurie Guy and Rex Ahdar have argued that this conflict represented 'worlds colliding' due to contradictions between an 'unchanging objective order' based upon 'Judaeo-Christian tradition' and an expanding concept of the sexual rights of citizens in a democratic, secular state.[64]

Scholarly analyses of the Christian right's 'moral conceptual systems' have described 'Christian conservative thinking' as centred around the patriarchal or 'strict father' model of the family, with God also understood as the stern patriarch of the Old Testament. According to Selwyn Dawson, this model could be found in New Zealand in the Coalition of Concerned Citizens, with its vision of 'the traditional family' and belief that sexuality should be 'exclusively heterosexual and confined within marriage'. This model required both an authoritarian masculinity to perform the patriarchal role and a submissive female helpmate. Male sexuality served an important social purpose when subjected to constraints 'by the boundaries of the family' and monogamous marriage, thus making it a 'cause of stability and security'. Aggressive women and homosexuality undermined masculine virility as the crucial energetic source that bound the family together under the divinely instituted paternal authority. This model also required children to submit to parental authority. With human nature prone to sin, children must be 'brought into subjection' through 'instruction and correction' lest evil impulses draw them into a life of sin and immorality, as James Dobson explained in books and films that encouraged parents to 'dare to discipline'.[65] Defining the family as a sacred realm, the adherents of this familial model set themselves apart from the secular world of humanism, universalism and equal rights.

The stark opposition between good and evil was crucial to Christian conservative thinking. Its adherents understood homosexuality as destroying the 'natural order', which presupposed male sexual and personal dominance over women. Because nature was a divine creation, the 'natural order' coincided with the 'moral order' in the family and the nation. Rather than a homosexual minority deserving the same rights as the heterosexual majority, conservative Christians viewed homosexuals as having made an immoral choice and as lacking in self-discipline – something which also applied to women rebelling against male authority. Homosexual law reform undermined the 'moral community', eroded moral standards, and threatened the family and the nation.[66] Much like the 'domino theory' – the belief that, if communism took root in one country, it would cause other states to 'topple' like dominoes to communist forces within their borders – moral conservatives believed that one form of loosening moral controls would inevitably produce an avalanche of moral depravity. Since tolerance for diversity would 'destroy the public expression of values essential to an ordered and honest society' and hasten the 'moral decline of our society' and the 'disintegration of the family', the concept of sexual citizenship must be opposed because there could be no compromise with evil.[67]

Inevitably the culture wars continued into the next decade. In the early 1990s, proposed amendments to the Human Rights Act to extend protection against discrimination based on sexual orientation stirred up yet another battle. After the National caucus had excluded sexual orientation from the Human Rights Amendment Bill in November 1992, Associate Minister of Health Katherine O'Regan introduced a supplementary order paper to amend the Bill. O'Regan defined sexual orientation as including homosexuality, bisexuality and heterosexuality to guard against charges of 'special rights' that had been used in the US to defeat gay rights legislation in 1992. Trying to avoid the 'outbreak of homophobia in Parliament that had occurred in 1986', O'Regan argued for the elimination of discrimination against sexual orientation as necessary to encourage Aids sufferers to seek treatment. The Aids Foundation worked with public relations professionals to develop a media campaign focused on health issues while denying that there were any threats to freedom of expression or association. Advocates of the Bill also pointed out that the 'doom' scenario predicted in the mid-1980s conflict had failed to eventuate. As Helen Clark noted: 'All kinds of fears were left to run in the community about what might happen to the moral fibre of society' but it was 'quite clear that not a single fear has materialised'.[68] Astute management of the messaging sought to secure the necessary support without provoking the religious right, including moral conservatives in O'Regan's National Party.

Opponents and advocates of the inclusion of sexual orientation in human rights legislation debated whether homosexuality was an 'inherent part of the person' or 'learned behaviour' that could be 'cured'. This led to comparisons between homosexuals and other minority groups already recognised as deserving protection. The Credo Society, SPCS, Women for Life, the Coalition of Concerned Citizens, Lion of Judah Ministries, the Christian Heritage Party and some churches made submissions and distributed literature opposing the legislation. They argued against inserting sexual orientation into the Human Rights Act on the grounds of biblical morality, protecting the traditional family, and the rights of Christian businessmen and landlords to refuse to employ or rent to homosexuals. They displayed much less fervour than in 1985, submitting fewer than 25 percent of the total submissions to the select committee. Nonetheless, SPCS warned that 'overt homosexuals dressed in women's clothing' might invade women's toilets, and described homosexuality as a 'disease', a 'biological absurdity' and a 'perversion of proper human sexuality'. A Baptist elder suggested that 'droughts', 'unseasonable snowfalls' and 'the recent contamination of our shellfish' constituted 'God's warnings' about legalising the sin of homosexuality. A Brethren spokesman argued that discrimination against 'evil' was an 'essential part of a Christian's pathway'. Brethren 'can't allow these things in our business any more than we'd allow them in our house'. These submissions labelled homosexuality as a sinful form of sexual deviancy. They described homosexuals as poor role models for children who might imitate their behaviour, and argued that protection against discrimination for sexual orientation would restrict the freedom of those who wished to denounce homosexuality.[69]

Pamphlets, letters to the editor and press statements carried some of the more extreme arguments against the legislation. At Carisbrook the Community Baptist Church distributed pamphlets bearing the title 'They are after your children' that described homosexuals as 'unhygienic walking pieces of human debris' who 'don't reproduce, they recruit!' The co-pastor, when challenged, denied that the church intended to 'convey a bigoted approach', but supporters of the Bill used the pamphlet as evidence that homosexuals needed protection against discrimination. Barbara Faithful, of the conservative Catholic Credo Society, provided a confidential analysis of a 'clandestine', 'undemocratic' and subversive campaign by gay rights supporters. She believed 'the pursuit of homosexual "rights"' was part of a 'wider ideological battle' masterminded by the United Nations. On Radio Rhema, a Christian station, a doctor described Aids as a 'rectal virus' and claimed that the legislation would spread the infection. Graham Capill, leader of the Christian Heritage Party (and later convicted of multiple sex offences against children) opposed the legislation because it 'put homosexuality on a par with heterosexuality', and mistakenly referred to it as a 'crime' until interviewer Kim Hill reminded him that it had been legalised in 1986. National MP Graeme Lee described homosexuality as 'clearly unnatural and immoral' because it could not be found in the 'animal world'. He called the legislation a 'travesty of justice' that was 'not only destructive of the family unit but to the whole of society'. John Banks, minister of police in the National government, told the Police Association that there was no justification for allowing 'these misfits into the police'. Showing his gift for emotive language and his willingness to appeal to prejudice, he added: 'The very last thing we need in this country is policemen walking the beat wearing lipstick and pantyhose.' Banks accused 'gay activists' of forcing opponents like himself 'into a corner where those who don't agree with them are seen as attacking the civil rights of the gay community', and criticised 'our nation's muddled infatuation with tolerance'.[70] Banks and Lee continued their battle against tolerance in opposition to O'Regan and other progressive MPs.

Parliamentary opponents of the inclusion of sexual orientation in the Human Rights Act argued for the need to protect families, warned about the dangers of the permissive society and attacked claims for sexual citizenship. Lee called it 'preposterous to consider sexual behaviour as a basis for rights', which would 'give to a minority certain rights that deny at the same time the freedoms of the majority', and asserted that homosexuals were 'anti-family'. Banks insisted that pandering to the 'perversions of minority groups' struck 'another blow to the sanctity of the home and the family' and asked whether 'bestiality' would soon receive protection. He asserted that the law would encourage the 'permissive society' and the 'anti-family homosexual lobby' who monopolised 'all those good words such as "justice", "inclusive" and "tolerance"' to use against people like himself – part of the 'silent majority of the decent society', he said, in an echo of Richard Nixon (which Bartlett had also used). Lee predicted that a ban on discrimination would lead to an increase in paedophilia. Warning that the legislation debased 'true heterosexual marriage', Grant Thomas asserted that the proposal threatened the family, the 'cornerstone of a healthy nation'. Geoff Braybrooke defended the rights of the Brethren and the Pentecostals to refuse to employ 'open or closet homosexuals'.[71] Endorsing the religious right to discriminate over the right to protection from discrimination for non-heterosexual New Zealanders, these MPs continued to uphold 'family values' and what they asserted was the moral but silent majority of New Zealanders.

Some Māori MPs drew upon the vocabulary of British and US anti-gay activists to oppose the supplementary order paper. Peter Tapsell warned that without discipline the 'wonderful and the terrible power of the sexual drive in man ... leads to perversions that are not seen even among the beasts of the field'. Asking whether 'homosexuality is a sickness, a disorder, a disability, a mild nuisance or an alternative lifestyle', Ian Peters decided that it constituted a 'wrong' and an 'insult' to compare homosexuals to legitimate 'minority groups such as Maori'. Speaking also of the need to protect young children against homosexual influence, these parliamentarians defended a constrained but authoritative masculine sexuality channelled towards the creation of a patriarchal family.[72]

Advocates for the proposed legislation parried these claims. O'Regan stated that 'most paedophiliacs are heterosexual'. Michael Cullen wondered somewhat facetiously about the 'peculiar obsession with sodomy' among 'middle-aged males' in Parliament. He pointed out that the 'vast bulk of people who commit rape, sexual abuse or child abuse are male heterosexuals'. He countered the arguments that homosexuality was a 'learned behaviour' by archly referring to the 'learned behaviour' of 'being a Presbyterian'. Even though Presbyterianism could be unlearned, 'we do not thereby argue that one should discriminate against Presbyterians'. Portraying his opponents as immature, prurient and alarmist, Cullen urged his opponents to 'grow up in respect of these matters and accept that difference is a part of our society'. Richard Prebble hailed the passing of the Bill as a 'statement of tolerance' but argued for a way to exempt the Exclusive Brethren. O'Regan promised a waiver for churches while Jim Anderton insisted that being 'pro-justice' was also being 'pro-family'.[73] The ability to claim the mana of human rights for their cause and deny it to their opponents enabled protection against discrimination on the basis of sexual orientation to be enacted into law. When the votes were tabulated, 26 percent of MPs opposed the inclusion of sexual orientation; another 24 percent avoided casting a vote on a controversial issue with the knowledge that 50 percent of MPs supported the inclusion of sexual orientation in the Human Rights Act.[74]

More battles ensued in the culture war between the Christian right and progressive opponents. Formed in 1998, Destiny Church created a political vehicle, Destiny New Zealand, in 2003 to fight the 'godless liberalism' that had resulted in the decriminalisation of prostitution in 2003 and a Labour-backed Civil Union Bill in 2004.[75] It sponsored protest marches in different New Zealand communities, including a march through Wellington that the Christian Heritage Party also joined, with black T-shirt-wearing men chanting 'Enough is enough' in a protest against civil unions. The unfortunate colour choice reminded journalists of Nazis – an impression reinforced by the presence of the National Front in the Wellington march, as Christopher Slane noted in a *Listener* cartoon in September 2004. The march and the media's framing of its links to a repressive regime aided the Bill's passage.[76] Undeterred by defeat or criticism, Destiny leader Brian Tamaki undertook a national tour to denounce the Labour government as 'evil' and to condemn the 'radical homosexual agenda'. Predicting that Destiny New Zealand would take power in 2008, he prepared for the next conflict in the culture war.[77]

Three years later, an acrimonious debate over Green MP Sue Bradford's private members' Bill to remove the Section 59 exemption for the parental use of force for purposes of correction in the Crimes Act gave Tamaki and other religious-right organisations a popular cause. It also provided a potential alliance with libertarians who shared their opposition to the Labour government. Youth with a Mission, Family Life New Zealand, Home Education Foundation, Family Life International, SPCS, Family Integrity, Family First New Zealand (FFNZ), Destiny's Family Values Network, Voice for Life, the Maxim Institute, and the American imports Focus on the Family and Promise Keepers prepared to defend what they referred to as 'smacking', which the mainstream media adopted in their coverage of the conflict, unintentionally aiding the religious right position.[78]

My quantitative assessment of the arguments used in submissions on the Bill yielded 59 themes. Anti-state intrusion in the family and parents' rights were the most prominent. Destiny's Family Values Network claimed that the Labour government had 'taken it upon itself to invade New Zealand homes to dictate the terms by which parents raise their children today'. This image of a malevolent regime that would require 'parents who choose to smack' to be 'ratted out, Soviet-style' inspired the Coalition against Nanny State's Anti-Smacking Law to march on Parliament as part of a paradoxical combination of libertarian and authoritarian attacks on the Labour government and Prime Minister Clark. The second most frequent claim was the accusation that the change would criminalise 'good' parents. The SPCS described a 'deceitful' Clark and a 'deluded' Bradford as 'hell-bent on stripping parents of the only defence they have in law' for using 'reasonable force in correction' of unruly children.[79] While defending patriarchal family values, the opponents seized the opportunity to attack a progressive, female-headed government and a Green MP. The supporters of smacking used terms laden with the negative gender associations of an 'over-bearing nanny' who interfered with individual freedoms or, in this case, parental rights, wielding unholy power from a dictatorial 'Helengrad'.[80]

Pro-smacking organisations invited so-called experts to prove that removing corporal punishment would increase violence, crime, family breakdown and the rate of imprisonment. Swedish lawyer Ruby Harrold-Claesson and Dr Robert E. Larzelere

Christopher Slane's rendition of the Destiny-sponsored march against the Civil Unions Bill. *Listener*, 4 September 2004. Courtesy of Christopher Slane

from Oklahoma contributed to the debate at the invitation of FFNZ, Sensible Sentencing Trust and For the Sake of Our Children. Harrold-Claesson discussed 'examples of unpunished children who ended up as criminals', reporting on one mother who witnessed her son's execution because 'she had not smacked his bottom when he did wrong' as a child. Arguing that smacking constituted one of 'the tried and true principles of good parenting', Craig Smith of Family Integrity argued for a divinely mandated parental duty described as 'The Christian Foundations of the Institution of Corporal Correction' to keep children 'on the right path'. Bringing together all the major strands of the argument in a Christian libertarian ideological fusion, Family Integrity described its core purposes as 'promoting parental authority, minimal state interference, loving discipline and responsible smacking' while encouraging parents 'to do battle to protect the integrity of their family' from secular forces, female politicians and government bureaucrats.[81]

Communications from these groups often referred to other organisations, suggesting that there was an intention to present a unified movement. Links on web pages and lists of organisations sought to show a breadth of support, as did the claim that polls showed that the majority of New Zealanders agreed with their position. Pro-smacking organisations were aware of the need to separate 'good' parents from 'bad' and acceptably 'mild' smacking from child abuse. Grey Power, for example, assured the public that it did 'not condone beatings' but believed that the passage of the Bradford Bill would result in an 'increase in violent offending' that other 'soft soap legislation' had allegedly produced. Bob McCoskrie, the FFNZ leader, told the *New Zealand Herald* that 'lax discipline' would lead to 'serious youth violence'. The Sensible Sentencing Trust, asserting that 'New Zealand is already locking up more young people than most western nations', warned that 'the anti-smacking bill will condemn thousands more to the journey from cradle to jail'. Instead of the 'politically correct nonsense of children's rights', these groups demanded 'toughened' sentences to act as 'a deterrent and a clear message' of 'disgust' for child abusers who were clearly distinguishable from 'good' parents. These religious-right critics, who argued that the intrusive 'nanny state' was undermining parental authority, predicted the future imprisonment of children whose lack of proper parental discipline would turn them into 'unrestrained agents of evil'.[82] Sparing the rod inevitably spoiled the child for those who relied upon the Bible instead of the state for guidance on the God-mandated parental right to discipline.

Within the discursive construction put forward by the pro-smackers, 'good' parents could be trusted to use 'reasonable force'. Family Integrity accused the 'nanny state and its agents' of treating 'good' parents like 'prime suspects'. Engaging in populist rhetoric and coded attacks on Clark and Bradford, submissions juxtaposed 'sensible' Kiwis against 'pointy-headed ideologues', 'childless bureaucrats' and 'ideologically driven politicians'. The children of 'good' parents did not need 'rights' bestowed by a 'nanny' state and a childless prime minster. References to rights in more than half the submissions carried negative connotations, denying the concept of children's rights – despite the religious right's insistence on the 'right to life' for the unborn child in the battle against abortion.[83]

Although parents failed to retain the legal right to inflict corporal punishment on disobedient children, the smacking controversy contributed to the Labour Party's defeat in the 2008 election. The conflict over smacking also split the United Future Party as Christian conservatives broke away from its 'socially liberal' faction to form what became the Kiwi Party. They sought to defend the 'Judeo-Christian tradition' and to organise a referendum asking whether a 'smack as a part of good parental correction' should be a 'criminal offence' in 2009.[84] Leighton Baker, a future New Conservative leader, gained his first political experience when he was selected as the

Kiwi Party candidate for Waimakariri. Although the Kiwi Party and Tamaki's Destiny New Zealand failed to get any seats, the Christian right could take encouragement from the almost 1.5 million New Zealanders who supported the right to smack in the referendum, and from the election of a more conservative government headed by a male prime minister, as restoring the proper gender balance of power and rescuing New Zealand from the 'nanny state'.[85]

AFTER FIVE DECADES

Despite more defeats in the conflicts over same-sex marriage in 2013, the passage of the End of Life Choice Act in 2019 and the removal of abortion from the Crimes Act in 2020, the Christian right continued with its efforts to secure public support for its positions. By 2020, the FFNZ added other issues to those causes for which it had already experienced defeat. Listing 34 'key family issues' divided into the categories of marriage, abortion, euthanasia, smacking and prostitution, with pornography as a subheading of parenting, FFNZ included opposition to same-sex adoption, marriage as limited to 'one man and one woman', and gender identity as inseparable from 'biological sex'. It also opposed the decriminalisation of cannabis and other drugs, advocated the raising of the drinking age to 20, wanted a change to the tax system to allow income splitting, and rejected Easter Sunday trading. In the case of one 'key family issue', FFNZ defended the 'three strikes' legislation originally passed in 2010, which imposed mandatory sentences based upon a 1994 California law (as indicated by its use of baseball terminology).[86] Imitating the moral scorecard used by the Christian right in the United States in the 1990s, the list demonstrated that the religious right agenda for 2020 in New Zealand closely resembled the 1970s except for the emphasis on only two genders in reaction to transgender activism. Almost five decades of setbacks had only made FFNZ and other participants in the religious right determined to fight against what Bob McCoskrie derided as 'gender ideology' and to remain the guardian of the 'traditional family unit' while refusing to admit defeat.[87]

The electoral results in the 2020 General Election may have given FFNZ encouragement for its consistency when at least 100,000 New Zealanders voted for parties that endorsed significant elements of the FFNZ family values agenda.[88] Vision New Zealand, led by Hannah Tamaki, whose husband Brian had denounced female political leadership as 'the work of the devil' when Helen Clark was prime minister, received 4200 votes for its opposition to immigration, homosexuality and abortion. ONE Party, a 'Christian fundamentalist', 'economically right-wing' and 'socially conservative' party, received nearly double that number.[89] The New Conservative Party received almost twice the total votes given to its smaller Christian-right rivals for policies based on 'family values and Judeo-Christian principles' coupled with 'right-wing' economics.[90] During the election campaign, it received an implicit endorsement from FFNZ whose moral scorecard declared that the New Conservative Party supported all 34 'key family issues'. Finding Labour, the Greens, ACT and the National parties unfriendly to 'traditional marriage' and the family, FFNZ ignored the other two denominationally based parties in support of a broad-church strategy to improve the chances for electoral success that the New Conservatives sought to implement.[91]

The media's fascination with Winston Peters and the anticipation of his potential downfall may at least partially explain the lack of journalistic attention to New Zealand First's support for 20 'key family issues' on the FFNZ agenda, which included the decriminalisation of 'non-abusive smacking' and the insistence on a biologically determined 'gender identity'.[92] The results for that party added another 75,000 voters for the religious right. Billy Te Kahika's short-lived Public Party also attracted a conservative Christian element, but its decision against explicitly promoting a Christian-right policy agenda makes it more difficult to identify as Christian right. Had these parties forged a successful alliance based upon their common commitments to patriarchal family values, 'economic nationalism' and concerns about immigration, political commentators would have been less able to ignore the evidence of a significant Christian-right minority political constituency that gained support from four times as many voters as the more politically successful Māori Party.[93]

The participation of Pasifika, Māori and Chinese New Zealanders in FFNZ, Vision New Zealand, One Party and the New Conservatives – and Māori and Indian New Zealanders in New Zealand First – is another factor that merits attention. It suggests that religious conservatism is also important in understanding support for moral authoritarianism rather than Pākehā racism.[94] Michael Jones, a former All Black of Samoan ancestry, serves on FFNZ's executive board; Rachel Wong spoke against abortion; and Dr Mary English, wife of former National Prime Minister Bill English and a New Zealander with Samoan and Italian ancestry, expressed her opposition to euthanasia at the FFNZ's 2019 New Zealand Forum on the Family.[95] Vision New Zealand discussed 'Mana Motuhake', 'Whakamana Whānau' and 'Tuatahi Tangata' as it declared its opposition to multiculturalism, 'foreign buildings of worship' (such as 'mosques' and 'temples'), mass immigration and the 'socialist, globalist, liberal plan of reshaping our society'. ONE Party pledged its support for Te Tiriti o Waitangi and the preservation of the 'customs, traditions, wairua and values of Tangata Whenua' even while failing to recognise the pledge for religious freedom contained in the unwritten 'fourth article' of the Treaty.[96] New Zealand First chose the expediency of silence about the Treaty in 2020, with an occasional negative reference to the protests against a housing development at Ihumātao, instead of reviving its more inflammatory 2005 references to 'treaty mumbo jumbo and political correctness'.[97] A Māori-inflected, Pasifika, Indian or Chinese version of ethnonationalism might seek to exclude those defined as 'foreign', but culture, religion, morality and immigrant status represent the basis for exclusion rather than white supremacy.[98]

Viewed from the present, it is evident that the Christian religious right has continued to advocate for the 'family values' agenda that the emergent movement initially promoted in the 1970s. Destiny, FFNZ and other organisations continue their moral crusade against egalitarian movements for sexual, gender, reproductive and children's rights. The New Conservative Party, for example, stands for the 'safeguarding of life' from 'the womb to the tomb', claims that crime is due to 'broken families', insists on the 'scientific fact that there are only two biological genders', opposes the teaching of 'gender ideology' in schools, and upholds 'the right to defend one's self and property' with guns.[99] Yet change has also occurred, as exemplified by the combination of multicultural diversity and populist nationalism, anti-Islam sentiments and opposition to immigration. This may be taking Christian-right parties further to the right, depending on the relative strength of competing commitments.

New Conservative deputy leader Elliot Ikilei, for example, describes himself as a 'born again' Christian and 'fair-faced Islander' with a Niuean, English, Tongan and Te Ātiawa/Ngāti Raukawa ancestry. In 2018, Ikilei attended a Free Speech rally in support of alt-right, white supremacist, anti-feminist, anti-socialist and anti-Islamist Canadians Stefan Molyneux and Lauren Southern at which speakers described sharia law as a gateway to Marxism.[100] Briefly the New Conservative leader after Baker's post-election removal, Ikilei's opposition to 'socialism' and defence of the 'greatness' of 'western culture' point to a rightward shift, albeit tempered by the party's multi-ethnic membership.[101] Ikilei's participation in an August 2020 anti-lockdown march presaged the much larger anti-vaccine protests in the second half of 2021. His fellow marchers opposed the United Nations' Sustainable Development goals, the use of 1080 for pest control, and water fluoridation, and claimed that 5G networks spread Covid-19. This hints at a shift towards an anti-statist conspiracy thinking that could result in a congealing of alt-right and religious right politics fuelled by social media influences and algorithms.[102] A similarly eclectic mix of conspiratorial concerns has animated participants in the anti-vaccine protests organised by the Freedoms and Rights Coalition, which was founded by Brian Tamaki as an ostensibly non-religious group, and the parliamentary occupation in 2022 at which Christian-right involvement was visible. While disparate and ineffective, the protests have nevertheless been influenced by far-right ideas from overseas, with some Christian-right elements.[103]

A youthful New Conservative recruit illustrates the potential for a rightward shift in the most popular avowedly religious right party. Dieuwe de Boer campaigned in the Botany electorate as 'an unapologetic nationalist' who defended the 'unborn', 'gun rights', '2 genders' and the restoration of the 'traditional family' to the 'centre of our society and economy'.[104] The creator of the *Right Minds* website and organiser of the Free Speech rally wanted to create a 'broad church right-wing movement for New Zealand conservatives, libertarians, traditionalists, capitalists, and nationalists' who share 'our Christian values, believe in personal responsibility, and want to see government play a lesser role in our lives'.[105] To that blend of family values and opposition to the welfare state, De Boer added vehement opposition to the 'rapid Islamization of New Zealand'. Despite being an immigrant himself, he argued that New Zealand should admit only immigrants 'who will want to integrate and will want to participate in our society'.[106] Coming fourth in Botany, de Boer promised to continue to fight the 'satanic' LGBTQ agenda, assuring his supporters that a 'vocal minority' could exert power notwithstanding the victory of the neoliberal 'messiah of the nation', as he sarcastically described Prime Minister Jacinda Ardern.[107]

The National Party may offer a politically more successful alternative to the New Conservatives. An indication of the strength of its moral conservativism was the vote by a majority of the National caucus, including then leader Simon Bridges, against the removal of abortion from the Crimes Act in March 2020.[108] Alfred Ngaro's comparison of abortion to the Holocaust showed the presence of Christian conservatism among some Pasifika, although he retracted his comment and abandoned rumoured plans to create a conservative Christian party to cooperate with National.[109] Another Pasifika anti-abortion MP, Agnes Loheni, was only briefly in Parliament before losing in the selection process in Botany to Christopher Luxon.[110] The choice of Luxon brought media attention to his opposition to abortion and membership in the evangelical Upper Room Fellowship, which has ties to religious-right organisations including Promise Keepers and Focus on the Family.[111] After the 2020 election, the much-reduced National caucus was more socially conservative and Pākehā. The elevation of Luxon to the National Party leadership in December 2021 made National more attractive to the 120,000 conservative Christians who voted for other parties in 2020.

A punitive stance on crime could also favour closer cooperation with Christian-right groups, including Sensible Sentencing Trust and FFNZ.

Despite scandals and defeats in a succession of culture-war battles in New Zealand, the Christian right has survived for over five decades and may be on the verge of increasing its influence. Despite commitments to moral absolutes and interdenominational rivalries, more pragmatic members of the Christian right are likely to gravitate towards National, as occurred in 1985, 2005 and 2008.[112] National could welcome such support, although Luxon has insisted that his personal faith is a private matter separate from politics. As the Christian right's embrace of Donald Trump indicates, however, the desire for political power can make strange bedfellows even for those committed to heterosexuality, monogamy and patriarchal family values.

CHAPTER TWELVE

The anti-Treatyist response to the recognition of Māori Treaty rights

PETER MEIHANA

IN FEBRUARY 2021, the Local Electoral (Māori Wards and Māori Constituencies) Amendment Bill passed its third and final reading. Since 2001 when Labour made it possible for local authorities to establish Māori wards and constituencies, only three have been successful, despite 24 councils trying to do so. The 2001 legislation was designed to help remedy the chronic and longstanding under-representation of Māori at the governance level of local government, even in areas with sizeable indigenous populations.[1] The legislation also allowed for a poll and referendum that could overturn the decision by local authorities to create a Māori ward if five percent of electors signed a petition; the 2021 amendment removed this provision. Lobby groups such as Hobson's Pledge worked hard to derail the 'wards campaign', claiming they were another example of Māori privilege and a sign that New Zealand's democracy is at peril of becoming an 'apartheid' regime. This chapter places such claims within a longer timeframe and argues that the notion of Māori privilege has been a constant feature of New Zealand politics since the nineteenth century. As the chapter progresses it will become apparent that since the 1970s, many Pākehā have experienced some anxiety about power sharing. They see the supposed privileging of Māori as undermining traditional Western values and beliefs.

THE TREATY'S INCREASING PROFILE SINCE THE 1970s

The historian Richard Hill used the terms 'anti-Treatyist/anti-Treatyism' to describe the 'beliefs and works of opponents of modern developments in Treaty relationships and, more broadly, race/ethnic relations'.[2] Anti-Treatyism thus arose out of a particular local context that was shaped by international events. Globally, in the wake of World War II, colonised peoples in Africa and Asia were agitating for independence, while in ex-settler colonies such as Australia, Canada, the US and New Zealand indigenous peoples demanded that governments recognise their status and rights. As Edward Said wrote, all peoples resisted European imperialism and that resistance took different forms.[3]

The Māori experience of colonisation is both similar and dissimilar to that of other indigenous peoples. First and foremost is that Māori signed a treaty with the British Crown in 1840, which guaranteed them continued self-rule and ownership of their land and other assets. While Māori like other indigenous peoples soon experienced marginalisation, deprivation, and loss of land through shadowy land purchases and wars, the memory of the promises made in the Treaty of Waitangi lingered. Iwi Māori certainly never forgot the Treaty, and generations of indigenous political leaders reminded the colonial powers in New Zealand and their imperial masters in London about the specific rights guaranteed to them in the 1840 agreement. In the last 70 years the Treaty has gained more prominence as the Māori population has grown, become more vocal and drawn attention to the large social and economic gap between them and Pākehā. An important aspect of this campaign has been to note the inability of iwi Māori to make decisions about their lives without government involvement, and their lack of a voice at the table in local and central government.

The migration of Māori people from their traditional rohe (homelands) to larger urban spaces dominated by Pākehā following World War II led to increasing numbers of Māori entering tertiary institutions. This new generation, educated and confident, were more prepared to challenge the status quo, especially in the wake of the 1961 Report on Maori Affairs (Hunn Report) and amendments to the 1967 Maori Affairs Act. The report took stock of the situation that had arisen out of Māori urbanisation, and discussed areas of Māori disadvantage such as health, education, crime, housing and land development. Its author, Secretary of Maori Affairs Jack Hunn, proposed integration as the official intent of Māori policy, and advocated for the elimination of that section of the Māori population deemed unassimilated and unintegrated and 'living a backward life in primitive conditions'. According to Aroha Harris and Melissa Matutina Williams the Hunn Report was the 'single most important mid-twentieth-century document on Māori relations with the state'. Hunn viewed integration as a natural process that was already under way but his 'emphasis on haste and implied compulsion was problematic for some'. The report's recommendations were also reflected in the area of Māori land administration. Against firm Māori opposition, the government passed the Maori Affairs Amendment Act 1967, which strengthened the powers of the Department of Maori Affairs and the Maori Trustee. Now so-called uneconomic interests in Māori land could be compulsorily acquired, while land that had four or fewer owners would be converted to general land. This, wrote Harris and Williams, 'attacked a clearly defined bottom line that Māori land should under no circumstances be dealt with compulsorily'.[4] These issues were seen as examples of ongoing colonisation. The Treaty of Waitangi provided the focus for much of the protest action, which included land occupations, protests at Waitangi and the 1984 land march.[5] The Treaty was also employed in different ways as either a 'fraud' or an agreement to be 'honoured'.

The Waitangi Tribunal, established in 1975, has played a significant role in propelling the Treaty into public discourse. Modern Treaty settlements have seen resources such as forests, fisheries and environmental taonga returned to tribal entities tasked with governing and managing the assets. While iwi settlements have provided a platform for economic growth and cultural development, they are not flawless and often difficult to achieve, and as Martin Fisher noted in the case of Ngāi Tahu, settlements represent a mere fraction of the value of what was lost.[6] Other successes have also contributed to an increasing Māori presence in national life. The Māori language remains in a precarious state; however, Māori language initiatives have grown since the 1980s, including te kōhanga reo and kura kaupapa Māori. Te Matatini o Te Ao is a significant event in the Māori calendar and, despite an initial backlash, the national anthem is now sung in te reo Māori. And, in 2004, Māori Television was launched. Since the inception of MMP in 1996, more Māori have entered Parliament – including from an increase in the number of Māori electorates from four to seven. MMP also opened up space for a distinct Māori Party. Most recently, the government's decision to make New Zealand history compulsory in schools presents an opportunity to retell the country's past divested of its colonial frameworks.

Scholars from numerous disciplines have been researching and writing about these developments. New priorities, methodologies and theories have seen a deeper understanding of the past emerge. The Treaty of Waitangi, in particular, has been the subject of numerous books and articles. Historian Ruth Ross's 1972 article 'Te Tiriti o Waitangi: Texts and translations', 'won the respect of the scholarly community, and it soon became required reading in university courses'.[7] Claudia Orange's *The Treaty of Waitangi*, first published in 1987, still stands as a go-to for students of history.[8] Ranginui Walker's *Listener* articles, later published in *Nga Tau Tohetohe*, placed Māori issues squarely in the public eye.[9] His 1990 publication, *Ka Whawhai Tonu Matou – Struggle without end*, presented an alternative history that challenged New Zealand's colonial foundations.[10] Likewise, James Belich's 1986 publication, *The New Zealand Wars*, questioned longstanding ideas about this conflict and New Zealand history generally.[11]

MĀORI 'PRIVILEGE': THE HISTORICAL ROOTS OF ANTI-TREATYISM

Māori assertiveness and Crown responses have not been universally welcomed. Some New Zealanders have grown restless with what they see as the rewriting of New Zealand history to serve left-wing causes and the privileging of Māori. Treaty claims and settlements, parliamentary seats, government departments dedicated to Māori affairs, affirmative action programmes in universities, and the creation of Māori wards are just a few examples cited of so-called Māori privilege. A notable development since the 1980s has been the growing number of written texts and online blogs criticising work in the Treaty space. As this chapter argues, very few of the ideas expressed in these anti-Treatyist texts are new or original. They appear throughout New Zealand history particularly during times of 'crisis' when settler ambitions were hindered by Māori attempts to retain control of their lands and resources.

Anti-Treatyist texts exhibit several characteristics. For the most part they sit outside of academic scholarship. One exception is Canterbury University law lecturer David Round's *Truth or Treaty?*, published in 1998 by Canterbury University Press. According to the publisher 'this is no right-wing rant against all that is new, but a sensible, refreshing and at times surprising book by an acute commentator on social and political issues'.[12] This may be so, but Round's views are not dissimilar to those of other anti-Treatyists. More recently, Round and others have contributed to texts published by Wellington-based Tross Publishing.[13] *Twisting the Treaty* brought together an eclectic team of New Zealanders including mathematicians, scientists, an architect and a law lecturer. One of the contributors was Hugh Barr, president of the Federated Mountain Clubs and secretary of the Council of Outdoor Recreation Associations of New Zealand Inc. He was also a co-founder of the Coastal Coalition, an entity established to preserve Crown ownership of the foreshore and seabed. What concerns all anti-Treatyists, however, is New Zealand's future.[14]

Despite a declared interest in the future welfare of the nation, anti-Treatyist texts have a near obsession with the 'past'. For them the past is straightforward: Māori lived in a state of ungoverned savagery, and a humanitarian Britain reluctantly intervened by obtaining from Māori the voluntary cession of sovereignty over New Zealand.

Having established a civil government, English law reigned supreme and beneficially, and thereafter the Crown acted consistently and even-handedly within its authority when dealing with Māori. In particular, anti-Treatyists like to dwell on the violence and upheaval of the musket wars, on a narrow interpretation of the Treaty focused on property and citizenship rights, and on recent attempts by historians and so-called radical Māori to reconsider New Zealand history. For the anti-Treatyist, the Treaty guaranteed Māori the 'rights and privileges of British subjects', including private property rights, without retaining any customary authority over their lands, people or resources. The Treaty was thus a great privilege for Māori, particularly given that Māori had previously lived under the constant threat of war, slavery and the (exaggerated) threat of a French invasion.[15] Anti-Treatyists claim that the Treaty was a supreme act of benevolence, especially when compared to the way other indigenous peoples were treated, particularly indigenous Australians.

The anti-Treatyist view of the past is over-simplistic, and draws on a few select government sources and outdated texts, such as William Pember Reeves's *The Long White Cloud*. Reeves's history held sway for much of the twentieth century, but scholars have since deconstructed the assumptions upon which it was built.

The notion of a humanitarian Britain whose job it was to protect the weak and bring them the benefits of British civilisation was at its zenith in the decade leading up to 1840. In 1837, a parliamentary select committee, having acknowledged Britain's past mistakes (slavery and the treatment of native peoples in the colonies), set down the principles upon which Britain would operate in the future.[16] As it would so happen, Māori would be the first 'privileged beneficiaries' of this new and enlightened thinking.

New Zealand's potential as a settlement colony had been recognised well before 1840. James Cook had said as much. In fact, the Cook expeditions were important in the development of Māori privilege discourse. Māori and other Pacific peoples were from then on observed, classified and incorporated into existing racial (and racist) hierarchies and notions of progress. It was determined that Māori, although savages, were a particular type of superior savage. Unlike Australian Aboriginals, they were amenable to civilisation, for they had an identifiable social structure and they engaged in cultivation. This elevated status, however, did not reflect any innate respect for Māori culture; rather, it was taken to mean that Māori could divest themselves of their savage customs and beliefs.[17]

As 1840 approached, interest in New Zealand grew, and so did calls to protect Māori. Cook's observations had lured sealers, whalers and traders. Requests for greater control over wayward Britons began in 1817. In that year, and again in 1823 and 1828, legislation extending the jurisdiction of the New South Wales courts allowed for the prosecution of British subjects for crimes committed in New Zealand. Although ineffectual, it was, according to Orange, 'an indication that the Crown took some responsibility for the actions of British subjects'.[18] Missionary Samuel Marsden also requested that Justices of the Peace be appointed, though as Alan Ward noted they were 'powerless and their magisterial exertions slight and ineffectual'.[19] The appointment of James Busby as Resident was Britain's most significant response to the New Zealand situation, but he too lacked the means of imposing control.[20] By the end of the 1830s, reports of a chaotic and lawless New Zealand had reached Britain; moreover, the New Zealand Company, the brainchild of Edward Gibbon Wakefield, had expressed its intention to establish a colony in New Zealand. Historians now contend that the reports of chaos have been overstated.[21]

Having concluded that colonisation was inevitable, officials in Britain clamoured to develop an appropriate set of policies. Colonial Office Under-Secretary James Stephen stated that 'the Cardinal points to be kept in view in establishing a regular Colony in New Zealand are, first, the protection of Aborigines and, secondly, the introduction among the Colonists of the principle of self-Government'.[22] In this humanitarian moment, the Crown recognised that it had certain obligations to both Māori and settlers. However, reconciling Stephen's 'cardinal points' would prove difficult to achieve. The reality was that Māori had what the settlers most wanted, and as the settler population grew so too did their demands for land and power.

The Treaty of Waitangi was a product of the humanitarian impulse of the 1830s. This impulse also gave rise to a rhetoric of benevolence that was readily deployed by colonial administrators, missionaries and Company officials, despite the latter disavowing the Treaty. To this extent, writing played a fundamental role in shaping political culture and opinion. As Tony Ballantyne noted, this was articulated through 'letters to the editor, private correspondence, sermons, committee meetings and pamphlets'.[23] 'Advice books' were another important medium for promoting New Zealand as an 'ideal society for European settlers'.[24] As well as providing practical information for intending colonists, they helped disseminate important ideological information.

The belief that the colonisation of New Zealand was predestined is a common theme of these books. In his 1840 treatise, Montague Hawtrey applauded the 'great and good' objectives of the New Zealand Company. According to Hawtrey, the Church Missionary Society's New Zealand mission was 'marked out by Providence to become the Great Britain of the Southern hemisphere'.[25] He pointed to the colonisation of

America as an example to be avoided.[26] Māori, he said, were 'a very fine race of human beings, possessing many noble traits of character', but if the colonists hoped to civilise Māori they would have to 'use the same patience and forbearance ... which a parent or wise instructor would use towards a wayward child'. Hawtrey believed that while this was an obstacle to success, it was not insurmountable and could be overcome through recourse to higher ideals.[27] He envisaged a future in which native and colonist would be 'amalgamated' in 'Holy Matrimony'.[28]

The Treaty of Waitangi was how the gifts of civilisation would be made available to Māori. However, the veiled and not so veiled threat of annulment was never far away. At Waimate in September 1844, two months following Hone Heke's felling of the flagstaff at Kororāreka, Governor Robert Fitzroy reminded Māori of the benefits accrued to them through their association with Britain. They were once 'wild barbarians', and in former times 'European nations attacked and conquered countries inhabited by uncivilized men'. However, he assured them 'England acted differently' and that the flag was a 'signal of freedom, liberty, and safety'. Under its protection, Māori were spared 'a fate as that which has since befallen Tahiti and Marquesa'.[29]

Sixteen years later, and facing another crisis in the form of warfare with Taranaki Māori over a disputed land sale at Waitara, Governor Thomas Browne sought to gauge the level of support among Māori for the new King movement (the Kīngitanga) centred on the Waikato. Like his predecessor, he drew on the well-established rhetoric of benevolence by reminding those gathered at a conference in Kohimarama that 'New Zealand is the only Colony where aborigines have been treated with unvarying kindness. It is the only colony where they have been invited to unite with the colonists, and to become one under the law.' The governor was unreserved in his view that Māori should 'avail themselves of this generous policy, and thus save their race from the evils which have befallen others less favoured'.[30] The consequences were not long in coming; in fact, some saw the confiscations as necessary if Māori were to enjoy the benefits of British civilisation.

The idea that Māori were privileged among indigenous peoples rests on the belief that the Treaty afforded them benefits that other indigenous peoples had not received. Article Three was certainly something new in colonial policy. Imparting to Māori the 'rights and privileges of British subjects' implied that they would be amalgamated into settler-colonial society and, in doing so, would enjoy the benefits of English law. Article Three also afforded Māori 'her majesty's royal protection', an idea that has a much longer history. Following its victory over France in 1763, Britain acquired France's former territories and had to develop a policy for the administration of lands west of the Appalachians. The problem was complicated further by speculative interests in the area, including of fur traders and land speculators. When news of a rebellion by a group of American Indian tribes reached the British government, it issued a royal proclamation that, among other things, prohibited the purchase of native land by all parties other than the Crown. This principle of 'royal protection' (pre-emption) would be included in the Treaty of Waitangi 77 years later.[31]

Within a hundred years of settlement, New Zealanders were of the view they had built a country that was an exemplar of race relations. In Governor-General Lord Bledisloe's assessment, Māori had benefited greatly under British sovereignty. The Treaty 'had quenched inter-tribal feuds, softened ancient grudges, and above all it has for ever abolished internecine wars and thus averted race suicide'. The decision to intervene had not been taken lightly, but 'the dictates of humanity' meant that the situation in New Zealand in 1840 could not be ignored. Bledisloe was also of the view that the instructions issued to William Hobson were 'eminently just in spirit, broadly humanitarian in principle, they form a document which any nation might be proud to have enshrined within its archives'.[32]

CHANGING HISTORICAL INTERPRETATIONS OF NEW ZEALAND'S RACE RELATIONS

Today, anti-Treatyists remain committed to a particular version of the past – one reinforced by the work of early New Zealand historians whose highly accessible texts might now be considered 'classics'. William Pember Reeves's *The Long White Cloud* confirmed for New Zealanders that theirs was an exceptional country, and 'gave contour and coherence to the New Zealand past'.[33] Reeves viewed the Treaty of Waitangi as an act of benevolence, writing that 'as a rule civilized nations do not recognize the right of scattered handfuls of barbarians to ownership of immense tracts of soil, only a fraction of which they cultivate or use'.[34] According to Reeves, the average colonist 'likes the Maori, and treats them in many respects as his equals', while he 'regards a Mongolian with repulsion, a Negro with contempt, and looks on an Australian black as very near to a wild beast'.[35] Reeves did not recoil from acknowledging that the colonial government 'made mistakes … yet in the end they came out with credit'; the Māori were a 'beaten race' but 'their gift of citizenship and parliamentary representation' was a demonstration that 'victory in moderation' was not beyond them.[36]

The rhetoric of benevolence certainly had utility in politics, but historians were also influenced. Historians of the 1920s, the first to be professionally trained, studied the 1840s and 1850s through the lenses of Empire and New Zealand's English-ness; colonisation was viewed as both 'inevitable and, if British, benign'.[37] Other historians, while not completely discarding these ideas, built on Reeves's narrative. James Cowan and Lindsay Buick saw New Zealand as a country born out of conflict but one that had become a 'harmonious bi-racial society'.[38]

In 1914, Buick wrote that the Treaty 'was in very truth the foundation of our nationhood'.[39] This assertion led to ongoing academic research. The historiography that emerged has undergone several shifts, reflecting new methodologies and ideas about how the past should be dealt with. Buick espoused the notion, later known as 'fatal impact' theory, that indigenous peoples who came into contact with European nations would eventually be catastrophically overcome.[40] In 1977, Peter Adams also argued along fatal impact lines by pointing to disease and European technology as reasons for the decline in the Māori population.[41] Buick and Adams framed the Treaty in humanitarian terms, viewing British intervention as necessary to prevent the inevitable outcome of colonisation. In 1971, Keith Sinclair argued that while race relations in New Zealand were not perfect, they were certainly better than in other settler societies. For Sinclair, the difference was the 'Anglo-Saxon attitudes at the time New Zealand was annexed'.[42]

Sinclair's claim was quickly challenged by other Pākehā historians. Alan Ward, in *A Show of Justice*, wrote that 'the colonisation of New Zealand, notwithstanding the Treaty of Waitangi and the humanitarian idealism, was substantially an imperial subjugation of a native people'.[43] Paul Clark and Judith Binney also produced works sceptical of earlier accounts of New Zealand history.[44] James Belich's landmark *The New Zealand Wars* was another important revisionist text that highlighted Pākehā racism as the 'main drive wheel for colonization'. As noted, understanding of the Treaty also underwent revision. Ruth Ross's analysis of the Treaty placed emphasis on Te Tiriti, the reo Māori version that was signed by the overwhelming majority of rangatira and would help shape debates for three decades. Ross presented her ideas at Victoria University in 1972, and an expanded version was published in the *New Zealand Journal of History* later that year.[45] Ranginui Walker later commented that hers was the 'most penetrating critique in recent times of the drafting and signing of the Treaty'.[46] Ross looked to historicise the Treaty by understanding the motives and intentions of the parties involved. According to Rachel Bell, by insisting that Te Tiriti *was* the real Treaty, Ross 'moved scholarly focus from the Colonial Office, which had dominated earlier studies, and asked instead what the Treaty meant here, in New Zealand'.[47] In her seminal work, Claudia Orange, in step with her contemporaries and immediate predecessors, wrote that earlier writers 'over emphasised the humanitarian concern in the original Treaty negotiation, at the fair evaluation of the Treaty's role in serving British and settler interests'.[48]

The Waitangi Tribunal has also made a significant contribution to New Zealand's understanding of the Treaty. Established as a standing commission of inquiry in 1975, the Tribunal was initially restricted in its jurisdiction to contemporary Crown actions and omissions. Minister of Maori Affairs Matiu Rata, who introduced the empowering legislation, was disappointed that the Tribunal was not allowed to inquire into historical claims back to 1840; moreover, when National routed Labour in the 1975 elections, it restricted the Tribunal financially for the next nine years to limit its ability to function. Despite initially receiving just 14 claims, many of which related to environmental despoliation and the destruction of mahinga kai (traditional food sources), the findings from early claims were significant in that they charted a course for those that followed.[49]

In the Motunui-Waitara claim, the Tribunal investigated the National government's proposal to build a new outfall at Motunui as part of the Syngas synthetic fuel plant. It found that the pollution would not only threaten the reef but would also prevent Te Ātiawa from carrying out their customary role as kaitiaki (guardians) and fulfilling their manaakitanga obligations (by using potentially polluted seafood as nourishment for guests and other tribes).[50] Early environmental claims highlighted Māori frustration with a system that marginalised them in planning and decision-making processes. As Harris and Williams noted, 'environmental issues have remained central to Treaty claims generally'.[51] Prime Minister Robert Muldoon rejected the Tribunal's findings but was compelled to reverse his decision in the face of public support generated by these environmental claims.[52] He also opposed some historical claims; for example, he contended that Ngāi Tahu had no rights under the Treaty because of Hobson's proclamation of British sovereignty over the South Island by way of 'discovery', and launched a particularly vitriolic diatribe against iwi leader Tipene O'Regan on the *Midevening News* in 1988.[53]

In 1985 Huirangi Waikerepuru and Ngā Whakapūmau i te Reo Incorporated Society argued before the Tribunal that the Crown had breached Article Two of the Treaty because it had failed to protect te reo Māori. Unlike claims relating to specific resources and property, the Te Reo Māori claim concerned, potentially, all Māori. The Tribunal made several recommendations that led to the Māori Language Act 1987, which recognised te reo Māori as an official language of New Zealand. To promote te reo and assist the Crown in carrying out its obligations, Te Taura Whiri i te Reo Māori, the Māori Language Commission, was established. Later claims also focused on te reo Māori. Access to the radio spectrum and television was viewed as important for getting te reo into workplaces, schools and homes.[54]

It is worthwhile noting that Judge Edward Taihakurei Durie presided over the Motunui-Waitara and te reo Māori claims, among others. In 1980 Durie became the first Māori to be appointed Chief Judge of the Māori Land Court, and thus became the chairperson of the Waitangi Tribunal. There he joined Sir Graham Latimer and L.H. Southwick, who retired in 1984 and was replaced by Paul Temm. Durie was instrumental in transforming the Tribunal, in terms of both procedure and 'its philosophical approach to the issues'. Where earlier claims were heard in hotels and halls, they would now be heard on claimant marae. Where legal scholars had once reiterated court decisions that stemmed back to Prendergast's 1877 judgment that the Treaty was a 'legal nullity', the Tribunal under Durie looked to the work of a new generation of scholars who were informed by developments in international law and court decisions in North America as well as a detailed review of historical evidence. This laid the foundation for a new interpretation of the Treaty, and development of its principles and effect in the present day. As M.P.K. Sorrenson writes, this meant examining the context of the time to understand the 'minds of the men who made, negotiated, and signed the Treaty'. This led to an investigation of the historical traditions of both Treaty partners.[55]

Ten years after the passing of the Act, the Labour government made the Tribunal's jurisdiction retrospective to 1840, opening the way for claimants to have historical grievances investigated. Since then, the Tribunal has heard numerous claims, made hundreds of recommendations and produced volumes of research.[56] By acknowledging and including Māori oral tradition and practices in its inquiries, the Tribunal has 'consciously challenged the privileging of written documents that has frequently been at the heart of Western historical practice'. In hearing claims against the Crown, the Tribunal has also assisted in the institutionalisation of the Treaty and has helped to shape a new discourse on Treaty 'principles'.[57]

The Tribunal has come under some scrutiny. In 2001, W.H. Oliver argued that by imposing modern standards on the past in order to hold the Crown to account, the Tribunal ignores the reality of the past.[58] This line of argument was picked up by Giselle Byrnes, who described Oliver's article as 'perhaps the most trenchant and thoughtful criticism of the Tribunal's methods of history writing'.[59] According to Jim McAloon, however, the criticism that the Tribunal 'views the past entirely in the light of present concerns and agendas' is incorrect. He argued that the Tribunal bases its findings on historical context and source material that the Crown had access to at the time in question. Thus, the Tribunal does not so much impose a present agenda on the past; rather it emphasises 'arguments and perspectives that were evident in the nineteenth century and which were at the time marginalized'.[60]

Anti-Treatyists are not much concerned with why and how interpretations of the past change. For them, historiography constitutes part of the rewriting of the past; the 'facts' can be found in unreconstructed primary sources and books written in the nineteenth century. Their rationale is that if it was written at the time, it must be taken as true. There also seems to be an unwillingness to accept that there have always been dissenting views that challenge the 'facts'. Since 1840, hapū and iwi across the country have used various channels to express their views. Having acquired the skills of literacy, Māori began utilising some of the 'rights and privileges' that had been afforded to them under Article Three of the Treaty. Māori became prolific letter writers and petitioners and, in many instances, these efforts led to the appointment of commissions of inquiry.[61] My own hapū petitioned the government in 1883, complaining that the reserves established under an 1856 'sale' were completely inadequate. The investigation that followed confirmed that Ngāti Kuia were, as Teone Hiparaiti stated, 'the poorest tribe under the heavens'. The remedy was in many ways no better than the problem. Some land was found for Ngāti Kuia and Rangitāne in the Marlborough Sounds but it was unfit for European-style farming. To make up the shortfall, they were also given land in Southland and Stewart Island, hundreds of kilometres from their homes.[62] James Carroll (Ngāti Kahungunu) would later declare that it was 'a blot on our colonial reputation to have allowed these claims to remain unsettled and undetermined for so many years'.[63]

Māori also coalesced around kaupapa they believed would advance their interests in the face of colonisation. Land loss and political marginalisation were issues that affected all Māori. Two responses were the Kīngitanga and Kotahitanga, the Māori Parliament. While the Kīngitanga remains an important institution to this day, the Kotahitanga held its final hui in 1902. The decision to disband the Māori Parliament was partly a response to legislation passed in 1900 that saw the establishment of land and health councils. Although the councils granted a degree of autonomy to hapū and iwi, many of the provisions of the legislation – for instance, leasing – were quickly eroded.[64] The four Māori parliamentary seats established in 1867 (prior to which Māori had been unable to vote or stand for Parliament unless they owned land in 'European' freehold title) became increasingly important; however, they were but four in a Parliament overwhelmingly Pākehā in representation. Similarly, Māori were not represented and many could not vote in local government bodies until the 1950s, as participation in elections had similar property-ownership requirements.

ANTI-TREATYIST 'HISTORY' FROM THE 1970s

Reassessment of the past and the increasing demands by Māori for the recognition of their Treaty rights caused great anxiety among some in the general public. South African-born Hilda Phillips went so far as to lobby the publishers to recall unsold copies of Sinclair's *A History of New Zealand*. In 1973 she became aware of Matiu Rata's proposed amendments to the Maori Affairs Amendment Act 1967.[65] The 1974 amendment changed the definition of Māori from a prescribed blood quantum to ancestral descent.[66] Phillips was opposed to the legislation because she believed it would privilege Māori, allowing them to enrol on the Māori parliamentary roll and access funds not available to Pākehā. Past wrongs committed against Māori should, according to Phillips, be ignored for the national good. Upon signing the Treaty, Māori supposedly gave up their sovereignty and received in return the rights of British citizenship. Claims made to the Waitangi Tribunal were simply 'people of mixed-race descent capitalising on their Māori ancestry'. A prolific letter writer, she produced letters to the editor (including a long-running battle with Ranginui Walker in the pages of the *Listener*), pamphlets, and a self-published broadsheet entitled 'Let the Truth be Known'. An abridged version of the latter was published in 1989 by the One New Zealand Foundation as 'Racial Discrimination Violates the Treaty of Waitangi'. Historians at the time addressed Phillips's claims, one describing 'Let the Truth be Known' as 'tedious, repetitive, confused, obsessive, and in places irresponsible and scurrilous'. Others followed in the same vein as Phillips, contributing to a growing body of anti-Treatyist texts. According to Tim Shoebridge they, like Phillips, 'drew on a narrow body of evidence in an attempt to discredit Māori grievances'.[67]

As Māori continued to assert themselves through the 1980s, new forms of accommodation needed to be found. In the public sector, biculturalism saw the Treaty of Waitangi increasingly referenced as New Zealand's founding document, with Cabinet issuing a codified set of Treaty principles in 1989. In 1986, a ministerial advisory committee, chaired by John Rangihau, issued its report on the Department of Social Welfare – *Puao-te-ata-tu*. A key recommendation was the devolution of services to Māori, following on from the overall conclusion that Māori faced institutional racism.[68] The 1987 Report of the Royal Commission on Social Policy acknowledged that the 'Māori dimension is basic to New Zealand society and this must have profound implications for all social policy'.[69] These policy statements helped set the agenda for the 1980s but, as Paul Spoonley writes, 'it also encouraged a response amongst Pākehā'.[70]

Biculturalism implied there were two dominant cultures in New Zealand, Māori and Pākehā. However, even the term 'Pākehā' was problematic for some. Scholars such as Michael King embraced it, interrogating what it meant to be Pākehā, while others rejected it. *Metro* and *North and South* ran articles discussing the ideas expressed by King. Writing in *Metro*, Carroll Wall declared that 'guilty liberals hang bone carvings around their necks, adopt Maori spellings of their names, call New Zealand Aotearoa and flock to the Te Maori exhibition as if it will assuage their guilt ... The Pakeha liberal seems to believe that the wrongs of the past can be righted somehow transmogrifying the Pakeha race into Maori by altering the media, the education system, the courts'.[71] According to Spoonley, 'anything which reflected Māori concerns meant varying degrees of disadvantage to non-Māori and particularly Pākehā'.[72]

The views expressed in *Metro*, *North and South* and other media outlets reached a wide audience. Others continued to write from the margins. Geoff McDonald's best-selling *Shadows over New Zealand* touched on many of the themes discussed by Wall and Phillips but added a conspiracist dimension with communists, bankers and a malevolent world government at work behind the scenes. [73] McDonald, an Australian and a professed 'ex-communist who converted to the far right', visited New Zealand during the 1980s and joined the League of Rights, a far-right group with branches in Australia, Britain, Canada and New Zealand. The League's beliefs combined British racial supremacy with conservative Christianity, and held that a communist conspiracy was financed by Jewish bankers to undermine governments and create a new world order.[74] According to McDonald, the 'whole history of New Zealand is being twisted and distorted'.[75] He went on: 'Academics and teachers have been complicit in the rewriting of history in which the ancestors of the New Zealanders are being subjected to ridicule and smear.'[76] Claims that Māori are oppressed were, he said, unfounded: in his view, New Zealand Māori had more rights than Pākehā. In his books and in speaking tours, McDonald also claimed that communists had co-opted the indigenous rights movement in New Zealand, as they had in Australia.[77]

With the extension of the Tribunal's jurisdiction back to 1840 came a surge in anti-Treatyist texts. In *The Treaty & the Act*, published in the wake of the Ngāi Tahu Waitangi Tribunal claim, Robin Mitchell argued that the Treaty of Waitangi Act should be 'amended to refer to the Treaty itself – its provisions, not its principles – and to set guidelines for its interpretation by the courts'. Mitchell believed the Tribunal would thus be rendered 'superfluous'. Like many anti-Treatyist writers, he adhered to a particular interpretation of the Treaty. For him the Treaty did little more than facilitate the transfer of sovereignty from Māori to the Crown, afford Māori 'the rights and privileges of British subjects' and establish equality for all New Zealanders, and placed no obligation on the part of the Crown to 'protect Maori culture or language'.[78] In Mitchell's view, the Treaty 'is not for Maoris only: it is for everyone', and had been hijacked. He had arrived at this view following the changes to the way the Tribunal operated under Judge Edward Durie in the early 1980s. Hearings held on marae rather than in courts or hotels, speeches and singing in te reo Māori were 'disconcerting'. According to Mitchell, the Act was 'grossly one-sided' and was being built into laws that 'should protect our national unity' but were 'instead being used to invoke sheaves of special rights and privileges for those New Zealanders with Māori blood, irrespective of how small that blood fraction may be'.[79]

Mitchell also spent a considerable amount of time denigrating the Māori world and any attempt to incorporate tikanga Māori into the mainstream of New Zealand society. He undermined biculturalism by labelling it 'Racism's New Clothes'.[80] He constructed a caricature of Māori culture fixed at 1840, the date beyond which, in his view, Māori were incapable of moving. In the typical anti-Treatyist fashion that favours style over substance, he wrote that 'Māori culture is a gramophone record stuck at 1840 – stirring, perhaps, but encouraging no initiative and allowing little progress'.[81]

Stuart C. Scott's 1995 publication, *Travesty of Waitangi*, sold 18,000 copies in six print runs.[82] Like other anti-Treatyists, Scott framed his reality according to assumptions grounded in colonisation. According to him, Māori had become moribund, tied to tradition and endless cycles of violence. With the arrival of Pākehā, savagery gave way to civilisation. Scott alleged that Māori secured many benefits through the Treaty, but that present-day Māori had taken advantage of this generosity. He found this particularly offensive, because Māori were treated remarkably well compared to 'the North American Indians or the Australian Aborigines'.[83] This highlights another theme common to anti-Treatyist texts: the classification of colonisation. Māori, according to the anti-Treatyist, received better treatment than other indigenous peoples; a claim predicated on the notion of humanitarianism and the acquisition of sovereignty by Treaty rather than war. Of course Māori are no strangers to classification. Since the time of James Cook, Māori have been classified according to criteria determined by the coloniser. The noble savage no longer has much utility; however, the trope of the privileged Māori does.

Anti-Treatyists have also called into question the very wording of the Treaty. In 1989, the discovery of what appeared to be an early English draft of the Treaty, the so-called 'Littlewood Treaty', spawned a flurry of activity. Well-known anti-Treatyist Martin Doutré produced a book arguing that the Littlewood Treaty was the English draft upon which Te Tiriti – the reo Māori version – is based.[84] For the anti-Treatyist, the absence of any explicit reference to 'lands, forests, and fisheries' in Te Tiriti, coupled with Littlewood's omission of the same, strengthened the claim that this was a lost draft. In the late 1980s, the Crown was negotiating the settlement of Māori fisheries claims. For anti-Treatyists, this raised the question of why, when both Littlewood and Te Tiriti make no mention of fisheries, Māori were being paid out for their apparent loss.[85]

The historian Donald Loveridge was asked by the Treaty of Waitangi Information Unit to conduct a review of the document. He observed that James Busby, in the three decades following 1840, 'made repeated references to the drafting, the text and the interpretation of the Treaty in books, letters, petitions, speeches and pamphlets'. Loveridge himself had 'never come across a statement by Busby that might be construed as a claim that the "official" English text of the Treaty was not the one which should be treated as the authoritative version'. Likewise, 'one might also ask why Henry Williams made no reference to having used an English text that was different from the "official" one in preparing the Māori text, if that was the case?' Hobson also considered the 6 February text to be 'the official English version of the Treaty', and it was this version that was sent in his despatch to Governor Gipps in Sydney.[86] Moreover, while Te Tiriti does not make specific reference to 'lands, forests, and fisheries', it is implausible to think that Māori would have envisaged such critical resources being lost to them. When one considers the petitions and complaints by Māori concerning forests and fisheries, this point is abundantly clear.[87]

PSEUDO-HISTORY AND PSEUDO-ARCHAEOLOGY

Another dominant anti-Treatyist theme is that Māori are not the indigenous people of New Zealand. Such claims can in part be traced to the longstanding misconception that a Melanesian people known as the Moriori arrived and settled here before the arrival of Polynesians. Although dismissed by scholars, the notion of a pre-Māori race persists in anti-Treatyist writing.

One of the earliest proponents of the more conspiratorial pre-Māori theories was Kerry Bolton, an early supporter of the One New Zealand Foundation established to oppose the return of land to Māori. He also helped found the anti-immigrant and white supremacist New Zealand National Socialist Party and the Nationalist Workers Party. Unlike nativist counterparts in Europe, Bolton had to contend with the dilemma that Pākehā were recent arrivals in Aotearoa. In his 1987 pamphlet 'Lords of the Soil', Bolton resolved this conundrum by co-opting the oral traditions of central North Island iwi Ngāti Hotu. According to Bolton, Ngāti Hotu were a 'white warrior tribe' who settled New Zealand first, and upon the arrival of Polynesians retreated to Taupō where they made their last stand. Scott Hamilton observed that Bolton viewed the arrival of William Hobson in 1840 as an important moment, as he 'was retaking New Zealand for what he [Bolton] calls the "Europoid race"'.[88]

Bolton's work presaged the proliferation of countless other conspiracy theories, some to be found on YouTube, which argued that ancient Europeans had made it to the Pacific and – ignoring other land masses – settled New Zealand first. Martin Doutré, who also has links to the One New Zealand Foundation, argued in his 1999 publication *Ancient Celtic New Zealand* that there are certain stone features in the New Zealand landscape that attest to a pre-Māori civilisation.[89] According to Doutré, ancient Celts with links to the builders of Stonehenge and the Great Pyramid were responsible for the construction of the so-called Bombay Obelisk and other 'astronomical devices'.[90] Others have argued that it was the Greeks who pre-dated Polynesians in New Zealand. Noel Hilliam, co-author of *To the Ends of the Earth*, contended that Greek navigators landed before the Christian era.[91] Hilliam's claims were published uncritically in both the *Northern Advocate* and the *New Zealand Herald*. It was soon found the 'Dargaville historian's' story was unsupported by evidence – but not before the claims received support from renowned British botanist David Bellamy.[92] In 2017 Hilliam claimed that he had discovered skulls that pre-dated Māori, and provided facial reconstructions from the University of Edinburgh to support his claims. The claims again received widespread media coverage before the story was exposed as a fabrication and that Hilliam had plundered the remains from a Māori burial site.[93] Sian Halcrow of the University of Otago said '[t]he statement that the young woman is from Wales is ludicrous. There is no way to find that information out from the skull size and shape nor is it possible to tell that a person has blue eyes and blonde hair from skeletal features.' A spokesperson for the University of Edinburgh said they were not aware of any academic who had been involved in the research. When contacted for comment, Hilliam stated that he, Doutré and Bolton were 'trying to get the true early history of this country'.[94]

THE INFLUENCE OF ANTI-TREATYISM ON MAINSTREAM POLITICS IN THE TWENTY-FIRST CENTURY

Claims of Māori 'privilege' are not new to politics. Historically, those in Opposition or those wanting to initiate a policy change – for instance, to free up more land for settlement – appealed to the idea of Māori privilege. Don Brash's January 2004 Ōrewa speech is an example of how, in recent times, the tenets of anti-Treatyism have occasionally moved from the margins to the mainstream. Brash, then leader of a struggling Opposition National Party, claimed that the Treaty had been 'wrenched out of its 1840s context and became the plaything of those who would divide New Zealanders from one another, not unite us'. According to Brash, governments had encouraged some Māori to 'adopt grievance mode' at the expense of other New Zealanders. Like politicians before him, he appealed to New Zealand's so-called egalitarian foundations and the threat Māori privilege allegedly posed to the nation. 'We are one country', declared Brash, 'with many peoples, not simply a society of Pākehā and Māori where the minority has a birthright to the upper hand.'[95] In its election campaign the National Party subsequently called on people to vote for this homogenous view of national identity, and to choose if they were 'kiwi' or 'iwi'.

The context in which Brash delivered this speech speaks clearly to the way politicians and the public sometimes respond when Māori interests clash with those of Pākehā. The Court of Appeal's June 2003 decision in *Attorney General v Ngāti Apa* found that the Māori Land Court had jurisdiction to determine whether Te Tauihu Iwi (the iwi of the Northern South Island) had retained customary rights in the foreshore and seabed of the Marlborough Sounds. Reaction to the decision varied. The court stated that it would be exceedingly difficult for iwi to establish freehold title and, even then, only in a few areas. The Clark Labour government indicated that it would legislate to ensure public access and uphold Māori customary rights so as to provide certainty. Māori too sprang into action, fearing that their right to have their claims heard in court was going to be removed. Hui were held across the country to plan a coordinated response to the government's proposals. The National Party's 'one law for all' campaign initiated under Bill English failed to gain any traction, and English was replaced as leader by Brash in October 2003.[96]

Brash's Ōrewa speech boosted National 17 percent in the polls, but the party was unable to maintain enough momentum to oust Labour at the 2005 elections. Ōrewa had a long tail, however. Brash had initiated, or at least reignited, debates about race relations, biculturalism and the Treaty. He had, according to Ranginui Walker, 'tapped

For many Don Brash's speech was a call to reverse the increasing role the Treaty of Waitangi, and iwi Māori more generally, were playing in New Zealand society.

Ross P. Kettle, 'Treaty of Orewa', *Stuff*, 1 September 2005. Courtesy of Ross P. Kettle

into public fatigue with and ignorance of the Treaty of Waitangi'. Brash believed 'the principles of the Treaty of Waitangi' were a modern invention and undefined. Walker pointed out that this is incorrect: '[T]here is nothing new about the principles of the Treaty except their belated recognition and application.' Attempts by Māori during the nineteenth century to have the Crown recognise the tino rangatiratanga of the chiefs were denied. The subsequent transfer of land and resources to Pākehā impoverished and marginalised tangata whenua. Moreover, the benefits of British citizenship and royal protection promised to Māori in Article Three were deployed in such a way as to be no more than window dressing. Peter Adams encapsulated this in 1977, writing that 'the belief prevalent today that the Treaty enshrined equality between the races, powerfully illustrates the degree to which a historical myth can serve as a cloak against the cold wind of reality.'[97]

Efforts during the last four decades to 'level the playing field' have been labelled by some as race-based privileges, but it is difficult to deny that affirmative action has been needs based. Māori are disproportionately represented in negative health, justice, housing and education statistics – all of which do not reconcile with the claim that Māori are privileged. A common retort to such statistics is that the privileges Māori apparently receive have made them dependent on the state. Claims of lazy Māori living off the hard work of Pākehā are not new. For instance, at the turn of the twentieth century the Opposition, the Farmers Union and the *New Zealand Herald* campaigned to amend legislation put in place to protect what land remained in Māori ownership. Leasing 'idle' land to hardworking Pākehā, rather than selling the whenua, was seen as a viable option for Māori. For the aspirational farmer, however, leasing reeked of privilege and landlordism. It was also argued that leasing would make Māori indolent. The campaign worked. By 1909 the leasing provisions of the Māori Lands Administration Act 1900 had been nullified, and in the following years a further 2.3 million acres of Māori land would be alienated.[98]

The early twentieth-century stereotype of the indolent Māori has not disappeared. Today, the anti-Treatyist has simply deployed other tropes to restrain Māori development. As part of his 'Colourblind State' and 'Treatygate' campaigns in 2012, John Ansell (the instigator of the iwi/kiwi campaign of 2005) asserted that New Zealand was heading towards 'apartheid' (this fantasy being an inverse of the brutal South African racial laws under which white people are supposedly reduced to the status of second-class citizens), and that successive governments had facilitated 'mass brainwashing with false history'. The aim of the campaign, stated Ansell, was to expose the 'Treatygate fraudsters and for the government to create a colourblind state'.[99] In his view, the 'Treaty grievance industry' is 'crooked', as is the 'appeasement industry which has been propping it up'. Elites in Parliament, academia, the judiciary and the media have all supposedly been involved in a cover-up that has allowed the 'griever Maori' to extort the taxpayer. Like the indolent Māori of a century ago, Ansell's 'griever Maori' feeds the idea that the hard-working New Zealander is being defrauded. The 'griever Maori', stated Ansell, should 'show a bit more gratitude and get their hands back in their pockets and stop expecting money from other people'.[100]

Anti-Treatyists adhere to a common canon derived from historical interpretations bereft of a Māori perspective or from cherry-picked sources that ignore context and scholarly works. Anti-Treatyists have a particular dislike for the Waitangi Tribunal, with lobby groups such as Hobson's Pledge and the New Zealand Centre for Political Research (NZCPR) having called for its abolition.[101] The Treaty of Waitangi Act 1975, the Tribunal's empowering legislation, states that 'the text of the Treaty in the English language differs from the text of the Treaty in the Māori language'.[102] The task of the Tribunal, therefore, is to determine the 'meaning and effect of the Treaty for the purposes of inquiring into Māori claims'.[103] For Hobson's Pledge and NZCPR, this apparent conundrum is a convenient invention; they argue that once the sources are identified and interpreted properly, the reasons for the Tribunal begin to dissipate. For supporters of Hobson's Pledge, the Treaty was simply rendered moot when it was signed, with Governor Hobson saying to each chief, 'We are all now one people' (he iwi tahi tātou). For anti-Treatyists, the implication of Hobson's gesture, if he even uttered the words, is that Māori had no special rights or status under the Treaty separate from any other British subject.

CONCLUSION

Anti-Treatyist writing varies, but there are some common themes and ideas. One is the belief that there is a coordinated drive to defraud Pākehā of the wealth they have accrued from colonisation, and to funnel it to a 'Māori elite' and a cabal of historians, lawyers and officials who are riding the so-called 'Treaty gravy train'. A plethora of books, blogs and websites speak to this. Conspicuous in this space is Wellington-based Tross Publishing whose titles *Twisting the Treaty: A tribal grab for wealth and power*; *The Corruption of New Zealand Democracy: A treaty industry overview*; and *Tribes Treaty Money Power: A guide to New Zealand's treaty issues* typify this genre.[104] A '1Law4All' pamphlet delivered into mailboxes across the country in 2020 declared that it was time 'to clear the air with a few truths'. According to its authors:

> In order for one minority group of New Zealanders – part-Maoris – to get special privileges and ownership of former publicly owned resources like forests and the foreshore and seabed, it has been necessary for the tribal elite and their collaborators in academia, the media, Parliament and the judiciary to misrepresent New Zealand history so that in every situation – past and present – European New Zealanders are portrayed as wrongdoers and 'Maoris' (now part-Maoris) as the so-called victims.[105]

Another theme common to anti-Treatyist texts, and that underpins this great heist, is the apparent rewriting of New Zealand history. For the anti-Treatyist the truth can be found in older historical works or in cherry-picked quotes from Māori leaders. Context often takes a back seat to easily digestible soundbites. Invariably anti-Treatyists begin their analyses of New Zealand history with the 'musket wars', which provide a useful starting point in arguing that Māori were on the verge of total self-destruction before a benevolent Britain intervened at the request of Māori, who voluntarily surrendered their sovereignty. This very simplistic account gives Māori little agency, even though in 1840 they were overwhelmingly dominant, demographically and militarily.

With chaos resolved, the anti-Treaty narrative goes, the main utility of the Treaty of Waitangi was to allow British settlers to build a modern and prosperous nation based on Western values and beliefs. However, the wars, comprehensive land loss and disintegration of Māori society caused by Crown actions that followed the signing of the Treaty sit problematically within this narrative. So too does the fact that prior to this catastrophe Māori were significant contributors to the colonial economy. Waikato, for instance, were major suppliers of food stuffs to Auckland. But anti-Treatyists emphasise the 'justness' of the land confiscations that followed the 'rebellion'.[106] Here they typically cite Tā Āpirana Ngata's 1922 explanation of the Treaty of Waitangi, which claimed that Māori had ceded their sovereignty in exchange for the guarantee of their property rights.[107] Ngata, unfortunately, has become a poster boy for the anti-Treatyist cause, although one does wonder what its adherents make of Ngata's views on, for instance, Māori rights to petroleum, or his negative reflections on the effects of colonisation on Māori at the 1940 Treaty centennial.[108]

Colonisation is at its core a process of dispossession, and it is an ongoing one. Land was essential to the establishment of a British settlement, thus it was taken first. With the loss of land came the subjugation of Māori authority. Operating within the same colonising paradigm, today's anti-Treatyists attempt to dispossess Māori by attacking the validity of the growing recognition of the Treaty of Waitangi over recent decades. They argued, for instance, that the unsigned 'Littlewood Treaty' confirmed what those who drafted the Treaty of Waitangi had originally intended. Expert analysis has concluded that this was not a lost draft from which Te Tiriti was translated, but the Littlewood Treaty continues to feature in anti-Treatyist works, in part to discredit what they call a corrupt Treaty industry. Whereas the Littlewood Treaty was an attempt at extinguishing Māori Treaty rights, pre-Māori conspiracy theories such as those advanced by Bolton, Doutré and Hilliam are deployed to undermine Māori indigeneity. Anti-Treatyism, when infused with pre-Māori conspiracy theories, is an intoxicating mix that appeals to some, even when they are presented with evidence to the contrary. For this reason, it will continue to linger on the margins – although politicians may continue to bring anti-Treatyism into the mainstream when the need arises.

PART 5
The radical right in the twenty-first century

CHAPTER THIRTEEN

Kyle Chapman, the National Front and Right Wing Resistance

MARK DUNICK

IN MAY 2004, far-right activist Kyle Chapman led a group of skinheads into Christchurch's Cathedral Square and called for a ban on Asian immigration. The protest was timed to clash with a larger anti-racism rally, and the controversy generated led to Chapman becoming the public face of the far right in New Zealand for more than a decade. As a high-profile leader of the New Zealand National Front (NZNF), Chapman brought members of the Nazi skinhead subculture into contact with older fascist leaders, and spent more than a decade organising public street marches, leaflet drops and media interviews. Chapman's links with the ageing remnants of the 1990s skinhead subculture provided the older leadership with a ready-made support base of a few dozen activists around the country, but ultimately this was also the movement's greatest weakness. The Nazi skinhead lifestyle and the focus on crude anti-Asian racism repelled others who might have been receptive to far-right ideas, and even the older veterans gave up on the idea of mainstreaming the far right. Their departure left Chapman free to launch a new group with a paramilitary image, the Right Wing Resistance (RWR), which briefly became an international movement before collapsing when Chapman left the group in 2016. Despite his failure to attract mass support, the organisations Chapman led were for a short time the most successful far-right movements New Zealand had seen for many decades.

Race relations dominated mainstream political discourse in 2004 after National Party leader Don Brash gave a speech at Ōrewa that appealed directly to the prejudices of those who felt threatened by the increasing visibility of Māori and Māori concerns (discussed in Chapter Twelve).[1] While overt anti-Asian prejudice had receded since the New Zealand First Party achieved mainstream political success by campaigning against Asian immigration in the 1990s, some voters remained anxious about foreign investments from China.[2] Chapman and the other far-right leaders were not interested in mainstream voters, instead claiming to speak for the alienated white working class and promoting an anti-Asian racism that was far cruder than that of the mainstream political parties.

Chapman saw an opportunity to launch his career as a high-profile far-right leader in May 2004 when the Asian community in Christchurch spoke out against racism. Assaults on young Asians had increased dramatically in that city, and Asian community members responded by calling for a public demonstration against racism. Chapman announced he would lead the National Front in a counter-rally against Asian immigration.[3] It was the first time in years that a far-right organisation had openly announced a street demonstration. Chapman was very willing to take advantage of the media attention, and quickly became a minor public figure. He was supported by veteran far-right activists who helped him package traditional fascist ideas in ways that aimed to appeal to working-class white conservatives in New Zealand.

WHO IS KYLE CHAPMAN?

Kyle Chapman was born in 1971 and became involved in far-right politics in 1980s Invercargill after hearing about the British National Front and discovering the group also existed in New Zealand. At the time, Chapman was leader of a small group of skinheads.[4] During this period, he became addicted to alcohol and other drugs and took part in several racially motivated arson attacks, including the firebombing of a Southland marae. Chapman's responsibility for these crimes remained undetected until he confessed years later.[5]

After giving up alcohol, Chapman moved to Christchurch in his early twenties and became employed as a social worker, receiving local council funding, and founding the New Way Trust to assist and rehabilitate skinhead youth.[6] Recognising that any visible connection with the far right would jeopardise his career and funding, Chapman hid his increasing involvement with right-wing politics and presented himself as solely concerned with providing employment and assistance to skinhead youth in Christchurch.[7] In 1994 the *Press* exposed his links with the New Zealand National Front (NZNF), then run by Anton Foljambe. Chapman denied being a supporter of the group, and was publicly backed by city councillor David Close.[8] In 1995, he confessed to his teenage crimes but escaped a prison sentence due to his record of community work and the continued public backing of Councillor Close.[9]

Eventually, Chapman grew tired of publicly denying his right-wing politics. He ceased working for the New Way Trust in February 1997.[10] Away from the public eye, he established the New Zealand chapter of the Hammerskins, an international white supremacist skinhead organisation.[11] At the same time, some of the elders of the New Zealand far right founded the New Zealand Fascist Union. Auckland-based far-right veteran Colin King-Ansell was national leader, with Kerry Bolton running the Wellington branch.[12] King-Ansell had been convicted under the Race Relations Act 1971 for printing and distributing antisemitic leaflets in 1977, and knew that a few strategically placed offensive leaflets could provoke headline news coverage far beyond the reach of the leaflets themselves.[13] The Fascist Union distributed a series of crude racist leaflets in Christchurch, attracting outrage and national headlines, but most members remained in the shadows.[14] To identify those responsible for the leaflets, the *Press* staked out the Fascist Union mailbox and exposed Kyle Chapman as the man collecting the mail. He could no longer deny he was deeply involved in the fascist movement.[15] The Fascist Union appears to have collapsed a few months later, but it was through this group that Kyle Chapman became involved with the leadership of New Zealand's far right. Unlike the other veterans, Chapman was also very well connected in the skinhead subculture. He would make use of these connections when he became leader of the NZNF in 2004.

REVIVING THE NATIONAL FRONT

The NZNF originated in 1967 with a group of activists who supported the British National Front. The British organisation promoted traditional fascist ideas but distanced itself from German-style national socialism. They opposed non-white immigration and promoted the preservation of the 'British race'. Among the New Zealand activists were members of earlier local far-right groups and migrants who had been active in the British far right, but they remained a fairly informal group until, by the late 1970s, they had evolved into a formal organisation. One of the three founding directors was the young Kerry Bolton, based in Upper Hutt.[16] Born in 1956, Bolton became interested in the far right at high school. He expressed support for racial separation and apartheid and a belief in antisemitic conspiracy theories, and was active in a range of fascist groups through the 1980s.[17]

Christchurch-based activist Anton Foljambe was in his twenties when, in 1989, he became the new leader of the NZNF. He dressed smartly in a suit and tie, and kept a low profile. The group seems to have been inactive when Kyle Chapman approached him, offering to revive the organisation.[18] Chapman became the Christchurch coordinator and by March 2004 had gained the backing of most members.[19] In Wellington, Kerry Bolton became national secretary of the organisation and produced most of its propaganda.

The reorganised NZNF made its public debut on Saturday 8 May 2004 in Christchurch's Cathedral Square, where the city's Asian community had called for a rally to draw attention to the growing number of racist attacks in the city, many of which had been linked with skinheads.[20] In the lead-up to the event, public discussions around racism in Christchurch featured in the pages of the *Press*, and broadened to include not just attacks by violent skinheads but also more subtle manifestations of anti-Asian prejudice right across society.[21] Media interest grew, and Chapman saw the opportunity for easy publicity for the NZNF. He announced plans to hold a counter-demonstration against immigration on the day of the anti-racism march. Aiming for maximum controversy, Chapman told the *Press*: 'If Asian people don't fit into our culture they are going to be abused … If people want to be racist, they have the right to be racist in their own country.'[22]

Christchurch Mayor Garry Moore was becoming increasingly uncomfortable with how discussions about racism were affecting the city's image, and asked the organisers of the anti-racism rally to cancel the event. 'How will this be perceived in Beijing or Kuala Lumpur or Singapore? This will be seen as proving Christchurch is a racist city,' he asked the organisers. Moore worried the march would provide the National Front with 'a perfect opportunity to gain exactly what they are seeking – an opportunity to appear on worldwide television … this would undo any goodwill which you hope to engender.' He angered rally organisers by suggesting they work behind the scenes with various council initiatives rather than organising a public event. Organisers Hock Lee and Lincoln Tan refused to cancel the march. Lee told the *Press* he had been involved with council-sponsored initiatives for several years but nothing had come of them.[23] In the days leading up to the event, Moore continued to criticise the organisers and implied that the march may well turn ugly.[24] Meanwhile, the NZNF promoted their counter-rally by handing out leaflets in town on Friday nights.[25]

As the debate heated up in Christchurch, media organisations outside the city became interested and found Kyle Chapman was eager to offer his opinions. Chapman used these interviews to argue that there were too many Asians in New Zealand and that immigrants who refused to integrate into society should expect to be abused. Chapman debated Lincoln Tan on National Radio, arguing that immigration should be restricted to Europeans only.[26]

The public debate encouraged a large turnout for the anti-racist march, with two thousand people gathered into Cathedral Square to listen to speeches denouncing racism. In one corner, separated from the crowd by police, were a group of 20 black-clad skinheads carrying New Zealand flags and wearing red and white National Front logos on their T-shirts.[27] One member forgot the party line and was filmed boasting to news cameras, 'I'm a nazi and I'm f...g proud of it.'[28] No violence occurred on the day and the NZNF was widely condemned. However, these events turned Kyle Chapman into a high-profile spokesperson for the far right, available whenever the media needed a sensational quote on race or immigration. Media and public interest in more everyday forms of racism were replaced by a fascination with the National Front and its provocative spokesperson.[29] The *Sunday Star Times* ran a full page interview with Chapman the day after the march.[30] He projected an intimidating image while claiming the National Front was merely a nationalist organisation promoting pride in New Zealand. While few believed him, Chapman's strategy of denying the obvious meant he was always in the news.

As Chapman became the public face of the far right, the NZNF organised several protests around the country. A picket of the Chinese Embassy in Wellington, allegedly to criticise a free trade agreement, was opposed by 40 anti-racist protesters.[31] In Auckland, NZNF members picketed the High Court, demanding the death penalty for child molesters.[32] The biggest protest was to be a national event during the Labour Day weekend holiday in October 2004, when the NZNF would converge on Wellington for a rally in support of the New Zealand flag. While this was happening, Chapman announced he would stand for the Christchurch mayoralty. Campaign statements were scarce but he did criticise the tourist industry, claiming most tourism operations were 'owned by foreigners'.[33] He also claimed voters had contacted him about rising crime, and proposed neighbourhood security patrols to be run by National Front members.[34]

In Wellington a series of high-profile racist incidents had taken place in the winter of 2004. In June skinheads attacked a group of Somali teenagers in Newtown following an altercation with a man wearing a National Front shirt. Shortly afterwards, 91 Jewish gravestones at the Mākara cemetery were vandalised; another 19 were desecrated at the Bolton Street cemetery.[35] In August racist letters containing pieces of pork were posted to a number of Wellington Muslim families.[36] Wellington police were reported to have been looking for a Wellington National Front member in connection with the attacks in Newtown and the vandalism of the Jewish headstones, but Chapman denied involvement and claimed anti-racist anarchists or even 'Jewish radicals themselves' might be responsible.[37] No one was convicted for these attacks but police did charge

National Front member Nicholas Miller with planning the assault on the Somali teenagers. He was later acquitted, though had been identified by the victims as being present before the attack.[38]

The racist attacks in Wellington led to a public meeting in Newtown. Hundreds of people attended and decided to organise a march against racism in response to the upcoming NZNF 'flag day' rally. The coalition of anti-racists called itself Multicultural Aotearoa (MCA), and quickly gained community support, including endorsements from unions and migrant groups.[39] Kerry Bolton led a cluster of NZNF members who picketed the meeting, attacking the supposed 'Zionism' of the organisers.[40]

In the days leading up to the march, media and police predicted violent confrontations. While both MCA and the NZNF denied any plans for violence, Chapman promised retaliation if his group was attacked.[41] When Saturday 23 October arrived, the NZNF discovered that its increasingly high profile had triggered more opposition than expected. The day began with NZNF's northern regional leader Sid Wilson speaking for nearly an hour on the so-called 'sell out of NZs heritage' at the cenotaph. Later, the group moved up to Parliament grounds where Kyle Chapman addressed his followers. Anton Foljambe and Kerry Bolton were also present.[42] Two hundred mostly anarchist counter-protesters attempted to drown them out with whistles, drums and chanting.[43] The National Front withdrew to the railway station before the arrival of some two thousand MCA supporters at Parliament at midday. Trouble began later when the right-wing group tried to return to their cars parked just outside Parliament grounds. The MCA rally had just finished and the streets were full of anti-racism protesters. According to an eyewitness, an NZNF supporter threw the first punch before onlookers attacked him. Police were unable to separate the two sides, and a crowd surrounded about 20 NZNF members, including Chapman. Punches and bottles were thrown, and Chapman and his supporters jumped into their cars and fled as best they could. One NZNF supporter and two anti-racist activists were arrested for minor disorder offences. Chapman promised retaliation and blamed police for failing to protect his group. Police were unsympathetic, saying Chapman had misled them about his plans, but admitted the anarchist group 'really did cause most of the trouble'.[44]

Chapman continued with the bravado in the days after the rally, but it was clear the NZNF had suffered a humiliating defeat. He claimed the publicity had led to a huge boost in membership enquiries, and insisted, not for the first time, that the NZNF had the 500 members needed to register as a political party.[45] Bolton, writing in the National Front newsletter, described 23 October as 'a date that, if our nation does

New Zealand National Front supporters at a flag rally in Wellington in 2004. Most members were skinheads but the group discouraged open Nazi insignia in favour of black shirts, bold National Front logos and New Zealand flags.

Stuff, 25 June 2015. Fairfax New Zealand

survive, will be marked on the calendar as the beginning of the patriotic resistance'.[46] He proclaimed the rally to be a total success and that the police had prevented them from leaving 'in good order' – a situation that would never have happened if the 'more than capable' NZNF security team had been free to act.[47]

This bravado was essential to the National Front's aggressive image. Although the Front downplayed or hid overt fascist policies, they tried to appeal to authoritarian and nationalist tendencies that Chapman imagined would resonate with white working-class New Zealanders. Public appearances featured shaven-headed men in black jeans and black T-shirts with bold red and white logos. The most common design featured the letters 'NF' encircled by white fern leaves and the group name, and resembled a gang or biker club patch. Open display of swastikas was discouraged, but as most members were skinheads who commonly incorporated Nazi symbols into their look, indiscretions often occurred. Swastikas tattooed on bald white heads were especially difficult to hide.

THE POLITICS OF THE NATIONAL FRONT

Chapman's public statements usually took the form of soundbites for television or print journalists. He often portrayed himself as the voice of the forgotten working class, or the 'hard-working men', in contrast to middle-class liberal commentators.[48] He claimed his hair was cut short because he favoured 'the working-class look'.[49] During interviews, Chapman repeated the same few talking points. The NZNF stood for a European New Zealand in which Māori were accepted if they gave up any claims to tino rangatiratanga, and Pasifika and Chinese migrants were not welcome. He argued for the return of compulsory military service, capital punishment and traditional gender roles.[50] He claimed multiculturalism and globalisation were threatening New Zealand culture, and the 'foreigners' pouring into the country were undermining traditional 'Kiwi' culture. He told a student newspaper that friendly neighbourhood chats were impossible because too often 'the person over the fence doesn't even speak English'.[51] Chapman denied being racist, but admitted racists were welcome in his group.[52] His supporters were merely 'down-to-earth patriotic New Zealanders'.[53]

Despite his attempts to relate to the 'everyday Kiwi racist', there was no sign of any significant political support. Chapman's campaign for the Christchurch mayoralty in 2004 failed to attract much interest.[54] He received 1665 votes – 2 percent of the turnout – but still much higher than campaign manager Anton Foljambe had been expecting. Foljambe was pleased that many of the mayoral candidates had accepted Chapman as a legitimate rival, including incumbent Garry Moore who had described Chapman as a 'champion' for the little guy.[55] Although Chapman stood repeatedly for election over the next decade, he usually stuck to the usual far-right talking points. Given the usual low turnout in local elections and the variable quality of many of the candidates, he may have had a better chance at success had he instead tried to seriously engage with local issues.

The NZNF produced a range of written material, most of it likely the work of Kerry Bolton, to promote the standard far-right ideas about patriotism, anti-immigration feeling, anti-communism and 'traditional' family values. A leaflet titled 'Our Nationalist Heritage' argued that New Zealand nationalism was 'rooted in the very soil, soul, flesh and blood of our people and our land' and therefore right-wing activists had no need to import foreign ideologies like Nazism or fascism.[56] The leaflet featured a picture of nineteenth-century imperial soldier Gustav Von Tempsky on the cover, and argued that New Zealand nationhood began not with the Treaty of Waitangi but with the formation of colonial settler militias. It contained patriotic quotes from former governor and premier Sir George Grey, and praised Richard Seddon's campaigns against Chinese immigration. Poet Rex Fairburn and rebel Labour politician John A. Lee were dubiously celebrated alongside the New Zealand Legion of the 1930s as forebears of this nationalistic consciousness.

The indigenous status of Māori complicated this nationalist mythmaking. In the 1980s, Kerry Bolton had solved the problem by inventing the myth that New Zealand was settled by ancient Europeans well before Māori arrived. Bolton's pre-Māori civilisation theories were later taken up by the pseudo-historian Martin Doutré with his 'Ancient Celtic New Zealand' theory. Bolton continued to offer his booklets to National Front members in 2006, without much success.[57]

If Chapman believed Bolton's pseudo histories, he never mentioned them in public interviews. Although he claimed Don Brash's Ōrewa speech had boosted the popularity of the NZNF, he avoided talking in detail about Māori issues unless they could be used to make a point in favour of 'Kiwi' nationalism. The NZNF supported the right of Māori to New Zealand citizenship, but opposed any demands for recognition beyond this. Chapman often claimed to have Māori support but never offered evidence.[58] Bolton issued a pamphlet claiming the establishment of the Māori Party in 2004 legitimised the race-based politics of the NZNF. While asserting the two groups had similar approaches in some areas, Bolton warned that the ultimate aim of the Māori Party was to 'dispossess the already powerless white worker'.[59] He believed the meaning of the Treaty of Waitangi had been distorted as part of a foreign agenda driven by the United Nations, which was using the Treaty to 'drag NZ into a UN World Police State'.[60]

Like the earlier fascist groups led by King-Ansell and Bolton, the NZNF opposed free-market capitalism. Traditionally, the broader far-right tradition included small business owners who generally supported free enterprise, but the NZNF attempted to appeal to the disaffected working class.[61] National Front writings rejected neoliberal economic policies, but instead of proposing a more equitable alternative they simply blamed the policies on a vast conspiracy. A leaflet produced for a demonstration against a free trade agreement with China warned that the extreme left was siding with big business to close New Zealand industries and replace Kiwi workers with 'Coolie Labour'.[62]

Despite these attempts to appeal to alienated working-class Pākehā, the NZNF's membership remained predominantly racists and skinheads. Most of those attending NZNF protests appeared to be aged 40 or older – old enough to have been part of the mid-1990s skinhead scene in their youth. As Jarrod Gilbert demonstrates in Chapter

Ten, this subculture had grown when mass unemployment and alienation caused by neoliberal economic and social policies had begun affecting large numbers of young urban Pākehā.[63] By the end of the decade economic conditions had improved to the point where the skinhead scene was unable to recruit in large numbers.[64] The small number of recruits who joined post-2004 were also young men alienated from mainstream society and primarily motived by racism. A recent sociological study interviewed six former members of the NZNF. Five had become involved in the NZNF or other skinhead groups as teenagers between 2005 and 2010, and one had joined a few years earlier. All were from lower-middle-class backgrounds and most had experienced downward social mobility. Four of the six came from single-parent homes. Several had negative perceptions of multiculturalism or 'political correctness', but the most frequently stated reasons for becoming actively involved in the far right were negative (and usually violent) interactions with ethnic minorities.[65]

Those members who were interested in more complex ideas were referred to Kerry Bolton's extensive book catalogues. His 2006 catalogue listed hundreds of titles from authors including Joseph Goebbels, Adolf Hitler, Oswald Spengler, Oswald Mosley and Francis Parker Yockey, as well as lesser-known far-right authors.[66] The New Zealand authors listed included antisemite A.N. Field and racist murderer Lionel Terry (discussed in Chapters Three and Seven) and Bolton himself. The antisemitic forgery *Protocols of the Elders of Zion* was available, with Bolton helpfully offering his own illustrated guide to understanding them. A short section offered a range of Holocaust-denial literature, as well as titles on eugenics and race theory written by 'prominent scientists'.

SPLITS IN THE MOVEMENT, AND CHAPMAN TURNS TOWARDS PARAMILITARISM

The first 18 months of the NZNF's campaign were the most productive, but the pressure of constant media attention and the defeat in Wellington took its toll on the leadership team. Chapman, Bolton and Foljambe all left the NZNF during 2005 and started a range of smaller organisations. Chapman announced his resignation as leader in May. He told newspapers his son was suffering at kindergarten because other parents were refusing to let their children play with him. He had also undertaken several trial periods as a doorman at a local nightclub until complaints were made about his presence. He told newspapers he could handle losing work, 'but as soon as my son suffered, that was too much for me'. Pressure from anti-fascists had also contributed to his decision.[67] Chapman admitted energy was low in the organisation, and that the senior officers needed a rest. While agreeing to help run the NZNF until a new leader was found, he would not be leading any marches.[68]

Eventually, the Front decided 47-year-old unemployed fisherman Sid Wilson would be their new leader.[69] Weeks into Wilson's leadership, two teenage NZNF members were arrested for vandalising mosques in Auckland. Wilson denied any responsibility for the actions of his younger supporters, claiming he had been 'expelling people left right and centre'.[70] The mother of one of the teens did not accept that the NZNF was blameless. 'These are old men running this, and these young ones are like sponges, soaking it all up,' she said.[71] Both teens were both sentenced to a year in prison for the attacks.[72]

Foljambe and Chapman joined the newly formed Direct Democracy Party (DDP) and became list candidates in the 2005 General Election. The party was led by Kelvyn Alp, an ex-soldier who had previously formed a militia called the Armed Intervention Force.[73] The group did not survive the election, obtaining only 783 votes (0.03 percent) nationally.[74] The NZNF claimed a mix-up had prevented them for registering for the election. Sid Wilson reluctantly threw his support behind the DDP for its economic policy but saw Chapman and Foljambe's new party as soft on race issues. 'They support everyone becoming coffee coloured through open border multiculturalism' that would 'destroy the white race', said Wilson.[75] The second annual flag-day rally in Wellington under Wilson's leadership drew only 20 supporters, who were outnumbered by around a hundred counter-protesters.[76]

Meanwhile, Kerry Bolton had also resigned, taking several former Wellington members with him into a group called the New Right. The New Right described itself as 'a non-party protest movement dedicated to the revival of New Zealand as a sovereign nation founded upon the principles of Western Civilisation'.[77] The group produced a one-page newsletter and a range of leaflets, all in Bolton's distinctive style.

In 2006, Chapman began recruiting far-right activists for secret military training in Canterbury. The Phantom Recon Militia was fairly amateurish, with members donning combat gear and replica rifles, but an internal manual directed members to obtain and store ammunition in preparation for armed 'militant action'. Chapman attempted to recruit members of the NZNF to his new group. In turn, Wilson accused Chapman of trying to destabilise his group.[78] Wilson was not a popular leader and was replaced by veteran fascist Colin King-Ansell in 2007.

Chapman, Bolton and Foljambe reunited for the 2007 local body elections, founding the short-lived National Democrats Party. The three far-right veterans constituted the management committee, with Foljambe as chair and Chapman as deputy and Christchurch mayoral candidate. The party described itself as dedicated to saving 'western civilisation' and opposed to the 'liberal agenda of the political establishment, which we view as neo-marxism by stealth'. The party rejected feminism and abortion, and boasted they had the most hard-line law and order policy of any party, supporting increased defence spending and compulsory military training. Policies on race and immigration were notably absent, as were any local Christchurch policies.[79] Voters were unimpressed, and Chapman gained only 673 votes, coming eighth of 10 candidates.[80]

In 2008, with Wilson gone and veteran activists leading all the major groups, Chapman, Foljambe, Bolton and King-Ansell agreed to work together under the banner of the Nationalist Alliance. The NZNF, Bolton's New Right group and the National Democrats signed up, and a new website was designed to promote the Alliance. Representatives from Australia and New Zealand signed a statement blaming the movement's previous disunity on 'unfavourable external political factors and fractious individuals', which had now been overcome, and hoping that '[u]ltimately one nationalist party will emerge'.[81] Chapman, Foljambe and New Right activist Steve Larsen travelled to Sydney in June to attend a meeting of the Australia First Party, led by veteran far-right extremist Jim Saleam. The talks led to the publication of an ANZAC manifesto, which claimed a commonality of interest between Australian and New Zealand nationalists. The declaration said the two nations had both 'wrested civilisations from the wilderness, and built civilised nations out of mere colonies'. It predicted impending war with China and viewed Asian immigration as 'a prelude to our dispossession'. Both nationalist movements saw 'indigenous issues' as 'being stoked by vested interests' aimed at dividing and therefore weakening society, 'leaving us open to foreign takeover'.[82]

This newfound unity led to increased cooperation at the 2008 flag-day rally. Although the demonstration was primarily organised and hosted by the NZNF, all the old far-right leadership were present. Speakers included Colin King-Ansell and Steve Larsen, with Jim Saleam travelling from Australia to speak on behalf of the Australia First Party.[83]

Behind the scenes the same problems remained. Chapman was primarily a skinhead who was attracted to paramilitary imagery and fascist street activism. He and his followers did not have the patience of the older leaders who were attempting to mainstream far-right ideas. Chapman remained interested in survivalism and began planning a 'Nationalist Land Base' in North Canterbury. In a leaked fundraising email to supporters in January 2009, Chapman outlined ambitious plans for a rural far-right community with a school and meeting space. He envisaged survivalist training and sport fighting taking place, and imagined that Europeans from other 'dying countries' could be invited to make use of the base.[84]

A few months later, Chapman announced he was leaving the movement entirely, intending to marry and move to Hamilton. The dramatic change was apparently based on love and a return to the Mormon faith of his mother; he claimed he no longer wished to live the far-right lifestyle. Resigning from his leadership positions, he said that if funds were raised for the land base it would have to go ahead without him. While he still felt 'white people' were disadvantaged, he believed this was irrelevant without God.[85] His retirement (and marriage) did not last long. A few months later he was photographed at the NZNF's October 2009 flag-day rally in Wellington, alongside members of a previously unknown group, the RWR. Chapman had quietly founded the organisation months earlier as the 'street arm' of the Nationalist Alliance, and the group already had five branches across the country.[86] His new wife was unimpressed with this news and threw him out that weekend.[87]

The older veterans were also unhappy with Chapman's new direction. Although Bolton, King-Ansell and Australian Jim Saleam had attended the 2009 rally with him, the Nationalist Alliance was falling apart. A *Press* journalist interviewed many of the leaders and discovered morale was low. King-Ansell was unenthusiastic and admitted he had come out of retirement to save the NZNF from total collapse. At the Front's annual general meeting in 2009, King-Ansell implied previous leaders had been less than honest with group funds, and a financial report was produced for the first time. The former neo-Nazi worried that the NZNF's public image made it unelectable, complaining of the difficulty in convincing skinhead members to hide their swastika tattoos: 'I've told those people to at least stick a flaming hat on it.'[88] King-Ansell was hoping to step down if another leader could be found to replace him.[89]

Bolton told the *Press* he had joined the fascist movement because he believed in its authoritarian philosophy but had always been frustrated by the quality of the movement's supporters. As always, Bolton sought to portray fascism as something more sophisticated than crude bigotry and neo-Nazi imagery. He claimed he had attended the rally only to meet with Jim Saleam, and dismissed most of his previous activism: 'It probably looked like a hell of a lot was going on when bugger all was going on.' Bolton minimised his involvement with the NZNF, claiming he had been inactive for several years.[90] Foljambe had not attended the 2009 rally, claiming he had retired earlier that year. He spoke to the *Press*, though, explaining that while he had been instrumental in forming the Nationalist Alliance, the group was mostly talk and the name was used as a fundraising vehicle for Chapman's land-base project. Foljambe distanced himself from the organisation he had once led, saying he had 'no interest in some of the idiot ideas and idiot people' he had associated with.[91]

Chapman told the *Press* that leading the NZNF was a constant battle to keep members under control. He said that not only had members been arrested for vandalising mosques, assaults, handling stolen explosives and firing airguns at people, but many of the skinhead members were not interested in thinking too much about politics. They treated the group as a social club and found the intellectual fascists too extreme. The intellectuals, on the other hand, would openly insult the 'moderates' in the movement. More recently, Chapman had himself fallen out with many veteran activists who thought his new-found interest in survivalism would damage the cause.[92]

Former members of the NZNF interviewed for a sociology study confirmed that the internal life of the group was dominated by drinking and fighting, and that many members failed to take politics as seriously as the leadership would have liked. One former member described trips to flag-day rallies in Wellington as 'more of a holiday and ... just a time to drink and stuff, you know?'[93] Another described drinking 'every single day', and said while '[t]here is always violence with skinheads drinking', wearing right-wing insignia in public definitely increased the risk of a fight.[94] The same former member described one branch of the NZNF as more like a gang, whose members were 'capable of extreme violence'.[95] Disputes between skinheads within the organisation were 'normally sorted with violence'.[96] The Christchurch skinhead scene was the largest in the country but also the most dysfunctional and violent: 'A lot of it is criminals and druggies and alcoholics.'[97] Another former NZNF member reported being disgusted when he visited the Christchurch branch. He found members of the group were involved in a criminal lifestyle he had previously associated with ethnic minorities, including 'selling drugs to kids and shit'.[98]

THE RISE OF THE RIGHT WING RESISTANCE

As the veteran leaders gave up on public activism, Chapman's RWR became the most active street-level far-right group in New Zealand and soon eclipsed the NZNF. In founding an organisation using insignia and other symbols designed to appeal to Nazi skinheads, Chapman had returned to his roots. The RWR portrayed itself as a 'paramilitary' organisation and aimed to recruit members of the skinhead subculture into fascist street activism. The group logo featured a skull and laurel over a Wolfsangel

Right Wing Resistance members at a white nationalist march in Christchurch, April 2012. Members wore a range of black T-shirts with white ink designs including white pride slogans, codes and group symbols. *Stuff*, 1 April 2012. Fairfax New Zealand

rune, an ancient Germanic symbol adopted by the Nazi regime and used by neo-Nazis around the world as a substitute for the swastika.[99] Most versions of the logo included the number 14, code for a white supremacist slogan.[100] As new branches opened around the country and later overseas, localised versions of the logo were designed and printed on shirts, which appear to have been one of the main attractions of joining the group. Later a dress uniform was added, consisting of a black shirt and tie and a forage cap. Rank insignia and various Nazi-style badges were issued. Chapman held ceremonies where new recruits were 'knighted' with a sword.[101] Members swore an oath to fight for 'Family, Race and Nation'.[102] The ideology of the RWR was crude and openly supportive of white supremacy. A 2010 article on the group's website described skinheads as 'the only true modern revolutionary force' and urged them to become organised and disciplined in fighting the capitalist system.[103]

The strong fascist imagery of the new group attracted immediate interest from racist skinhead groups around the country and internationally. In its first year of existence, the RWR opened chapters in five cities around New Zealand, and by 2013 claimed at least 12 active branches. At its height, the group claimed a further three chapters in Australia, 11 contacts in mainland Europe, and groups in the United Kingdom, and North and South America.[104] In 2015 the RWR became part of the Black & Silver Solution, an apparently short-lived international coalition started by North American neo-Nazi groups.[105] It is difficult to determine how many of these groups were active, but the RWR grew rapidly and became the first group in the history of the New Zealand far right to have an international reach. However, the open fascist imagery also represented an admission that Chapman had given up on attempting to mainstream far-right ideology.

Although the fascist imagery and style had wide appeal in neo-Nazi skinhead subcultures, the evidence suggests very few of the international chapters were involved in serious political organising. In 2015, plans were announced for European branches of the RWR to meet at a UK 'White Man's March' in Liverpool.[106] Organised by National Action, a UK neo-Nazi group, the event was cancelled when marchers were outnumbered by anti-fascists.[107] RWR's European leader, Swedish Nazi Peter Krämer, was trapped in a pub for the day, and it appears the meeting never took place.[108] News coverage of international RWR chapters reveals multiple examples of long-time neo-Nazi skinheads with criminal records for racist violence joining the organisation and often attending events organised by other far-right groups, rather than organising their own public events.[109] The Glasgow chapter appears to have been typical. The leader, Gary Crane, was an ageing skinhead who regularly attended violent right-wing demonstrations around the UK, but the remaining members were teenagers he had recruited locally by offering them alcohol.[110] In the US a former RWR leader in North Carolina, Benjamin McDowell, was charged with illegal possession of a firearm after telling an undercover FBI agent he was interested in carrying out a racist terror attack.[111] In Australia, the Brisbane branch was briefly in the news when one former member was revealed to have spent time fighting in a nationalist militia in the Ukraine. Ethan Tilling was an ex-soldier and committed neo-Nazi when he joined the Brisbane RWR. He attended three meetings in six months before deciding they were 'absolutely useless human beings' and leaving for the Ukraine.[112]

In New Zealand, Chapman's leadership and energy kept the organisation active and in the news. The group carried out 'crimewatch' patrols in the Christchurch suburb of New Brighton. The patrols were apparently directed against 'homie [American rap-style] vandalism and muggings' in East Christchurch, which they claimed had been abandoned by the authorities – 'and it is left to us to sort this out now'. A local resident's association spokesperson said the crime issue was real but criticised the RWR for adding to the problem. The patrols she had seen consisted of skinheads 'hanging around looking menacing'.[113] Chapman used his notoriety to gain national news coverage for the group. He told a current affairs television show they had deliberately leafleted a wealthy Auckland area to provoke complaints and, therefore, media coverage. He was subsequently invited to debate immigration with an Auckland University professor of Asian Studies on a national current affairs show. He denied being a 'White Supremacist', instead describing himself as 'a white nationalist', adding 'what's wrong with that?'.[114] Similar leaflet drops received publicity in provincial towns around the country.

In 2011, the group disrupted an election meeting in Christchurch. About a dozen RWR members wearing camouflage, balaclavas and masks lined up in front of the crowd while Chapman blustered with a megaphone. He told the *Press* the government was 'running the country into the ground' and promised disruption of polling booths across the country. Nothing came of these threats but the incident received national news coverage.[115]

In 2012, Chapman chose World Race Relations Day to stage the biggest far-right march Christchurch had ever seen. He claimed 115 people joined the group's White Pride event. Joining RWR were members of Blood & Honour (a worldwide neo-Nazi organisation that grew out of the skinhead music scene), a few National Front members and various local skinhead groups. Chapman credited the turnout to good weather and 'a scarcity of communists'.[116] Without the guidance of veteran right-wing activists the group's messages were slightly cruder, and when Chapman was asked why he opposed Race Relations Day, he simply replied, 'It's a load of crap.'[117]

Chapman appears to have become exhausted by 2015. Although he retained control of the RWR website, he appointed Peter Krämer as worldwide leader of the RWR, and in New Zealand day-to-day leadership was passed to Masterton scrap dealer Vaughan Tocker. The group continued distributing anti-Asian leaflets in regional towns, but when interviewed Tocker proved to be much less capable than Chapman. Most notably, he was widely mocked after he sat down for an in-depth television piece and failed to realise the interviewer was a comedian making fun of him.[118]

In the process of stepping back, Chapman published a slightly bizarre public apology on the RWR website. He wrote that he regretted his style of leadership and its impact on friends and family, and admitted he had become 'somewhat of a dictator'. He also regretted the move towards military uniforms and intimidating behaviour and asked his followers for forgiveness.[119] The announcement seemed to have been

Kyle Chapman in his Right Wing Resistance leader's dress uniform, early 2013. Note the collar and cuff insignia modelled on the style of Nazi SS uniforms.

Stuff, 23 May 2013. Fairfax New Zealand

triggered by media coverage causing problems in his personal life. It was not the first time Chapman had publicly renounced his previous actions, nor was it likely genuine, but it did spell the end of the RWR. Without Chapman the organisation collapsed. A month after Chapman's letter, the group's last public event, a flag-day rally, was held in Christchurch. A fight broke out at the after party, a man was stabbed, and his attacker was charged with causing grievous bodily harm.[120] The final update on the RWR website, which appeared to still be controlled by Chapman, appeared on 11 January 2017. A series of messages was posted reporting the events that ended the organisation. Firstly, Peter Krämer had stepped down as world leader. He had recently tried to enter New Zealand but had been arrested and deported back to Sweden. The website stated that former leaders had broken away from the group and sought applicants for various newly open leadership positions. RWR distanced itself from drugs, criminal behaviour and 'random drunken violence'. Finally, all remaining T-shirts were available at discount prices and would not be reprinted.[121]

CONCLUSION

The disintegration of the RWR was the final stage of Kyle Chapman's 12-year attempt to build a fascist street movement in New Zealand. In 2017, Chapman turned 46, and many of his skinhead allies were the same age or older. The skinhead subculture was already ageing when Chapman took on the leadership of the NZNF, and the old men of the far right had failed to recruit the new young members necessary for any successful street movement. The few new members who did join were often repelled by the overt criminality within the skinhead scene.

Unlike some of the older leaders, Chapman was willing to be the public face of the far right and organise street protests, an online presence and, with Foljambe's help, run for the mayoralty of a major New Zealand city. Chapman also proved capable of manipulating mainstream media (and even some politicians) into giving him a platform to promote white supremacism as a valid political opinion within a multicultural democracy. This provided an opportunity for Kerry Bolton's efforts to popularise the anti-democratic ideas of the radical-right tradition by linking them to traditional 'Kiwi' patriotism and conservatism. These efforts at breaking into the mainstream, however, were constantly thwarted by the undisciplined behaviour of the neo-Nazi rank and file – despite the leadership's efforts to distance itself from the thuggish movements of the past.

While their greatest impact was perhaps the flag-day rallies organised as a show of strength, participants were almost always heavily outnumbered by anti-fascist protesters. Nonetheless, under Chapman's leadership the NZNF and the RWR provided the far right in New Zealand with experience in political organising – lessons not forgotten, despite the collapse of the organisations they founded. Public revulsion at the 15 March terrorist attack made open white supremacist organising almost impossible for the far right, with the NZNF closing down shortly afterwards.[122] Despite this, Kerry Bolton continues to mentor a younger generation of far-right youth, working behind the scenes with the Dominion Movement until it dissolved after the terror attack, and then with its successor Action Zealandia (these groups are discussed further in Chapter Fourteen). Chapman has backed away from fascist organising but remains active in Christchurch-based right-wing and conspiracy campaigns, and was distributing anti-vaccination flyers in 2021.[123] While seemingly lying dormant, the continued activism of Chapman, Bolton and other leaders in right-wing, populist and conspiracy theorist circles today provides them the opportunity when the time is right to try to introduce white supremacist ideas into New Zealand politics.

CHAPTER FOURTEEN

Identitarianism and the alt-right

A new phase of far-right politics in Aotearoa New Zealand

PAUL SPOONLEY AND PAUL MORRIS

THE MASSACRES OF 15 MARCH 2019 at two Christchurch mosques confirmed that the far right remains a constant threat to public order and safety in New Zealand, and that this threat was largely overlooked by security and intelligence agencies. Both elements were corroborated by the findings of the Royal Commission of Inquiry into the attacks that was released in November 2020.[1] The country was not exempt from such activist, murderous politics, despite widespread complacency. While the perpetrator exhibited many of the longstanding ideological beliefs and violent tactics of white supremacists, his 'manifesto' reflected the influence and rise of the alt-right, with a focus on the 'great replacement', the participation in online subcultures and new versions of conspiracies (as well as old ones). It is these politics and arguments that we canvass in this chapter.

We trace the development of the alt-right as a series of disparate coalitions of far-right and (white) ethnonationalist groups, activists and ideologies – secular and religious – and their use of online platforms to proselytise, recruit and radicalise. We are particularly interested in the rise of identitarian movements and ideologies, and their transnational influence and reach. How has ethnonationalism been (re-)radicalised? How have new motifs and symbols been used to attract and explain, especially in identifying groups – the 'deep state', mass media, groups such as Muslims or Jews – as an existential threat facing the 'white race' or 'European civilisation'? What role does religion play in these new coalitions and their selection of religious enemies and targets? How significant is the neglect of religion in the failure to recognise religious motivations and ideologies by security and intelligence agencies in secular polities?

And how have online platforms and possibilities been utilised in the cause of these new politics?

Ultimately, the question is how have these politics influenced developments in Aotearoa New Zealand? This chapter will explore contemporary expressions of the alt-right in this country, with a particular focus on groups such as the Dominion Movement and Action Zealandia. Some of these ideas and activists can also be found in fringe religio-political parties such as the New Conservatives, the New Zealand Public Party/Advance New Zealand, ONE Party and Vision New Zealand, as well as alternative media such as Counterspin Media. How significant have these politics been in mainstream politics and views?

THE ALT-RIGHT: A NEW STAGE IN FAR-RIGHT POLITICS

The alt-right is a product of the ideological mixing of traditional far-right politics and conservative populist movements. Key elements began to appear with the Tea Party after 2010 in the US: nativist anti-immigrant views, specifically in relation to '"parasitic" minorities and immigrants', a 'hostility towards "liberal" elites' and the 'supposed "tyranny" of the president'.[2] These populist movements have created an '[a]lternative universe [and] a set of alternative explanations … [which are] amplified by a panoply of conspiracy theories [including] a New World order [which is] plotting to enslave all of mankind in a world government that permits no freedom … In this alternative universe, facts and the laws of political gravity do not apply.'[3]

The term 'alt-right' was first coined in 2009 by Richard Spencer, an American white nationalist disillusioned with contemporary conservativism and who became director of the National Policy Institute, a lobby group for race-based policies where 'race is the foundation of identity' – a far-right response to, and version of, contemporary identity politics.[4] A year later (2010), Spencer established his own webzine, *The Alternative Right*.[5] By the 2016 US presidential election, the views and activities of the alt-right had become well established and provided a contrast to more traditional far-right politics – in two particular ways. First, the alt-right were firmly internet-based. Secondly, many followed the Spencer tradition of the 'suit-and-tie image' of white nationalism, the preppy-look of middle America.[6] The term gained traction when Hillary Clinton, as a presidential candidate, used it in a speech in August 2015 to critique white supremacy and her opponent, Donald Trump.

Explanations for the rise of the alt-right vary. Some see it as a 'manifestation of the angry White male who has status anxiety about his declining social and economic power'.[7] There is certainly some evidence of a high degree of disillusionment and feelings of marginalisation in white communities in the US that then translates into support for an angry and exclusive nationalism through the second decade of the twenty-first century. Arlie Hochschild chronicles this in her compelling book, *Strangers in their Own Land*.[8] The second explanation is that it is a product of the echo chambers of the internet – or 'an informal and ill-defined collection of internet-based radicals'.[9] Jessie Daniels goes on to argue that:

> The rise of the alt-right is both a continuation of a centuries-old dimension of racism in the U.S. and part of an emerging media ecosystem powered by algorithms … The ideology of the contemporary alt-right is entirely consistent with earlier manifestations of extremist White supremacy with only slightly [*sic*] modifications in style and emphasis … This iteration is newly enabled by algorithms [which] deliver search results for those who seek confirmation for racist notions and [which] connect newcomers to like-minded racists … providing networked white rage.[10]

The ideological positions of the alt-right are just as likely to be embedded in video games or music videos.

A third component is the demographic profile of the alt-right. Many are young white males, some of whom are university graduates or students. Milo Yiannopoulos, a key US alt-right activist and commentator who, with Allum Bokhari, wrote 'An establishment conservatives guide to the alt-right' (March 2016), described the movement as 'born out of the youthful, subversive underground edges of the internet'.[11] In many ways, this is no different from earlier neo-fascist and neo-Nazi movements, such as skinheads, but the image and membership have changed: more intellectual (or claiming to be), more skilful messaging (by Canadian YouTube activists Stefan Molyneux and Lauren Southern, for example) and a more carefully managed appeal to conservatives, nationalists and populists.

The alt-right had been growing and evolving for some time, but the US presidential campaign in 2016 and the subsequent election of Donald Trump confirmed the presence and influence of the alt-right as a 'mass movement' that hinged on the radicalising potential of the internet, especially of 'disenfranchised and mostly anonymous, young White men'.[12] As David Neiwert noted: 'Alt-righters see [getting red-pilled] as a metaphor for what they consider to be the revelatory power of their ideology, which cuts through the lies of "social justice warriors" (SJWs), "cultural Marxists" and the mainstream media.'[13] A new phase, and a variation on far-right political traditions and activism, had emerged by 2015–16. One element of this, which appeared alongside the alt-right, was identitarianism, which places the threat to the 'white race' or 'European civilisation' at the core of alt-right activism.

IDENTITARIAN POLITICS

This term has been largely defined by Generation Identity, a European-based movement that arose from Bloc Identitaire that was founded in 2002 in Nice. A youth wing was established a decade later, and was most apparent in Austria, Germany and Italy.[14] Generation Identity, one of whose leaders is Martin Sellner, an Austrian and former neo-Nazi, is a European analogue of the largely American alt-right.[15] A core ideological concern is the 'great replacement' and, specifically, the belief that a mix of 'pro-abortion and pro-LGBTQI+ laws had lowered birthrates of native Europeans, and pro-migration policies … have allowed minorities to engage in a "strategic mass breeding"'.[16] American identitarians formed Identity Evropa, which was renamed the American Identity Movement in the US in 2019. It has close links to Generation Identity in Europe and with the alt-right in the US.

European identitarians have adopted some of the strategies of the alt-right, especially the Breitbart belief (a reference to Andrew Breitbart, an influencer of the alt-right and founder of the website that bears his name) that changing cultural narratives precedes political change. In particular, there is the Breitbart argument that activists 'need to create counter-cultures that attract young people [in order] to increase public pressure on mainstream politics'.[17] This is sometimes referred to as 'strategic polarisation' or forcing bystanders to take a position either of support or against alt-right or identitarian ideological positions. The intent is to radicalise individuals or communities and to implement their own local or national campaigns. Here is an example of seeking to alter the 'Overton window' (changing the spectrum of politically-acceptable views) and to move the political spectrum to the right so that alt-right and identitarian ideas become normalised. Julie Ebner infiltrated Generation Identity groups in the United Kingdom and provided an excellent account of how such identitarian politics operate – and how such politics were a major influence on the 15 March terrorist.[18]

Identitarianism is a movement that primarily advocates for a contemporary ethno-nationalism, is typically exclusive (hence, 're-migrating' non-natives and immigrants) and that portrays Islam as the key threat (therefore 'de-Islamisation'). This position was espoused by Renaud Camus in his book, *Le Grand Remplacement* (2011), which introduced the idea of 'white genocide' and 'reverse racism', and has had a major influence on the ideological preoccupations of the alt-right:

> The Great Replacement theory combines all four features of a violence inciting ideology [or] so-called 'crises narratives': conspiracy, dystopia, impurity and existential threat. The idea is that Europeans [sometimes labelled the 'white race'] are being replaced with racially and culturally distinct migrants (impurity) by a cabal of global elites and complicit actors in governments, tech firms and media outlets (conspiracy), leading to the gradual decay of society (dystopia) and the eventual extinction of whites (existential threat).[19]

This theory, along with its four components, is found in a range of contemporary alt-right groups such as Action Zealandia (discussed below). It was also a preoccupation of the 15 March terrorist whose manifesto, 'The Great Replacement', draws heavily on Renaud Camus' *You Will Not Replace Us!* (2018), as well as the earlier work that also provided the rallying call to the Unite the Right rally in Charlottesville, Virginia, in 2017.[20] The terrorist valorised Anders Behring Breivik and referenced the Norwegian's manifesto alongside the justificatory confessions and statements of other terrorists, in particular highlighting the tradition of Christian crusader knights doing God's work defending Christendom and Christianity against their enemies, mainly Muslims and Jews. These precursors provided the symbols, memes, framework, inspiration and pre-emptive-strike strategy for the 15 March attacks. The terrorist identified with Breivik's self-understanding as 'a militant Christian' and 'a cultural Christian' and, like his Nordic hero, promoted the role that Christianity should play in uniting the white race. However, like Breivik, he was not particularly religiously observant and was conflicted about his 'complicated' Christian identity.[21]

If the 'great replacement' provided one of the core themes of contemporary far/alt-right politics, then QAnon provided other elements in the grand conspiracy of the alt-right.

QANON

An important development in the alt-right is the appearance of QAnon in October 2017. 'Q' claims to be an intelligence officer in the US military who has 'access to classified information about the Deep State's agenda'.[22] The initial disclosure claimed a satanic paedophile ring involving political elites (Clinton), along with public personalities such as actor Tom Hanks and billionaire philanthropist George Soros, had begun with meetings in a Washington pizza restaurant (a conspiracy dismissively referred to as 'pizzagate'). QAnon followers saw the 'great awakening' as a period when an understanding of the nature of the 'threat' occurs; it precedes the 'storm' which, it was originally argued, would involve President Trump locking up those involved in the 'deep state'.[23] Since then, QAnon followers have adopted or developed a whole range of new conspiracy theories to explain a range of events, from the killing of John F. Kennedy through to longstanding views about a Jewish conspiracy concerning the Rothschilds (updated to include their use of space-lasers to start forest fires across the US), to seeing the Covid-19 pandemic as part of a plan to take over countries and communities, hence as a 'plandemic'.[24] In this way, QAnon arguments build from a 'fear of the "other" translated into racism and antisemitism; a reactionary response to cultural change; a fight response to feeling out of control during a societal crises'.[25]

QAnon first appeared on 8chan (now 8kun) and 4chan before migrating to more mainline platforms such as Facebook, YouTube, Twitter, Rumble and Parler. The 'bubble communities' that operate on Facebook, combined with the algorithms that draw conspiracy-curious people towards the harder conspiratorial views of the QAnon community, soon generated a significant base of supporters and believers in the US and globally.[26] QAnon 'further erodes the link between what we can see to be true and what we will believe to be true'.[27] By 2020, many of these platforms monitored QAnon posts and either removed the more extreme ones or posted warnings. This did not ease the concern that QAnon was influencing both the alt-right and elements of the conservative media and politics in the US. QAnon followers were strongly supportive of Trump as president, and QAnon views have been associated with members of the Trump administration, with 19 Congressional Republican members appearing to support QAnon, and a further two elected to the House of Representatives.[28] There was also evidence, during the 2020 General Election in New Zealand, that QAnon views were gaining traction in this country, at least among a vocal fringe.

Several QAnon-related organisations were formed. One was Freedom for the Children (FFTC), founded in June 2020 in the US and then emerging as a group in the UK (FFTCUK), which latched onto the belief that children were being kidnapped, trafficked, tortured or even cannibalised on an industrial scale. This mythos repurposed the blood libel (the false accusation that non-Jews were murdered and their blood used in rituals) taken directly from Christian tradition and often linked to the notorious forgery outlining Jewish plans for world domination, the *Protocols of the Learned Elders of Zion*. FFTCUK organised meetings in New Zealand, as well as in the US, Canada and Australia.[29] It is one of a number of 'conspiracy theory-driven protest groups to have emerged during lockdown', which picked up the QAnon beliefs about an international conspiracy that targeted children and sought to develop a 'big tent' approach in public (that is, seeking broad support) while adhering to more extreme conspiratorial QAnon beliefs in private settings.[30] FFTCUK increasingly worked with anti-lockdown and conspiracy-driven groups such as SUX (Stand Up X, founded in May 2020) that combines beliefs about a 'plandemic' with anti-5G and anti-vaccine arguments.[31]

The research group Institute for Strategic Dialogue found that QAnon groups on Facebook increased by 120 percent in March 2020 while the rate of engagement went up by 91 percent, and that between October 2017 and June 2020 QAnon hashtags and phrases appeared in 69 million tweets and nearly half a million Facebook posts.[32] The pandemic appears to have increased the willingness to search for and believe alternative conspiracy theories and to mobilise new groups, activists and online activity. There is certainly evidence of a considerable growth through 2020, fed by the new anxieties associated with a pandemic, Black Lives Matter, critical race theory and a US presidential election.[33] Australia ranks as one of the top five countries in terms of QAnon tweets, and heat maps show that New Zealand is similar – or was at least in certain months of 2018 and 2019.[34]

As gatherings moved to the world of videoconferencing under the lockdown provisions associated with public health measures in a range of countries, a new opportunity was provided to the alt-right to disrupt and proselytise. 'Zoombombing' or 'Zoom raiding' became new ways of trolling others or intruding on Zoom calls to spread a message. The *New York Times* discovered several active message boards on Reddit and 4chan where activists gathered to arrange harassment campaigns that targeted both private and public meetings and involved racism and hate speech.[35]

QAnon has used a mix of platforms – 4chan, 8chan, Facebook, YouTube, Twitter, Parler – to circulate and popularise its messages about the 'deep state', satanic cabals typically involving Democratic politicians and supporters, as well as Jews (often embodied as a specific person – or cypher – such as George Soros, or as some more amorphous group such as Jewish bankers), international agencies (notably the United Nations) and narratives about the threats posed to the 'white race' or 'European civilisation'. Facebook provides 'ready-made digital pathways from public pages to public groups to private groups and finally secret groups that mirror the process of "falling down the rabbit hole or taking the red pill"'.[36] Online platforms provide the means for both recruitment and amplification.

QAnon narratives have become so concerning that in May 2019 the FBI identified it as a potential domestic terrorism threat to the extent that certain individuals and groups were acting out some of the violence discussed online.[37] Certainly, there is evidence that QAnon was a major influencer for many of the groups who judged the 2020 US presidential election to be fraudulent, and has been closely associated with the circulation of anti-vaccine, anti-China (or often, anti-Chinese Communist Party) and anti-5G sentiment. It has also influenced many of those who believe that the Covid-19 pandemic is either false or part of a conspiracy to obtain power and control. The FBI is right to be concerned about these beliefs migrating from an online world into an offline world and violence. There is now evidence that such online worlds do translate into real-world hate and violence.[38] The 15 March terrorist attack is an example.

IDENTITARIAN RELIGION

In the US, religion, specifically Christianity, has played – and continues to play – a central role in the groups that make up these new far-right coalitions, from the Ku Klux Klan and the various Christian militias with their explicit Protestant Christianity, to QAnon with its Christian-Shamanistic 'conspirituality', with most followers across these movements explicitly identifying as Christian.[39] In the wake of the US presidential election in 2020, headlines focused on the coalition of hundreds of insurrectionists, including Oath Keepers, QAnon, Proud Boys, alt-righters and others, displaying antisemitic, Christian and Nordic symbols and motifs as they dramatically attacked and occupied the US Capitol on 6 January 2021. Their aim was to prevent Congress from confirming the electoral college votes and thus overturn the presidential election.[40] Led by Jacob Chansley, aka the 'QAnon shaman', a group stopped to pray inside the US Senate chamber. He shouted, 'Jesus Christ, we invoke your name!' to which the group responded 'Amen'. Chansley, face painted blue, adorned with fur hat and horns, called on the group to 'say a prayer in this sacred place' – and this was exactly what they did, thanking their 'Heavenly Father' for his grace and for 'filling this chamber with those that love you and that love Christ and for allowing the United States to be reborn'. Then another rioter, Leo Kelly, knelt and (re-) 'consecrated the Senate to Jesus', reminiscent of the re-dedication of the defiled biblical temple in the book of Maccabees.

White nationalism and white supremacy have broad support among millions of people in evangelical and Pentecostal churches, especially in countries like the US, and the alt-right coalition actively recruits from these congregations and from others who have had similar Christian upbringings. The mainstream American churches are currently openly combating this support in their ranks. Alongside the coincidence of far-right politics and personal Christian piety are those whose endorsement of Christianity is integral to their identitarian alt-right politics but does not necessarily include a personal or existential spiritual dimension.

The discourse and activist politics of the identitarian alt-right is focused on the recognition, recovery and protection of what they view as the white European legacy of unprecedented and advanced cultural and scientific achievement, a historical legacy underpinned and framed by Christianity. European culture is defined as a white Christian culture, with a (Christian) history that includes antisemitism and a phobic view of Islam and Muslims as manifest in crusades and holy wars. This 'white race', consisting of Europeans and those of European descent, and their 'superior' culture, is seen as under dire existential threat from interracial breeding, multiculturalism, globalism, communism, and an identity politics that prioritises people of colour, LGBQTI+, refugees and other victims, and that demands the dismantling and demise of all white privilege. These threats are seen as consciously, and covertly, led by secret cabals of Jews and others who plan the replacement and destruction of the 'white race', thus removing the final barrier to world domination. Identitarians understand themselves to be an oppressed, pursued and endangered minority who seek only to retrieve their white, Christian culture and to proudly assert their white identity.

Populist nationalist politics in Europe as manifest in France, Hungary, Austria, Poland, Italy and Spain are supported by, and support, parts of the Roman Catholic Church as a principal vehicle for conservative values, European identity and culture, and a bulwark against Islam.[41] This discourse is not readily or necessarily attached to religious practice or personal moralities.[42] In general, European identitarians reflect the continent's dominance of secular discourse, and valorise Christendom and Christian heritage rather than Christian practice or church community. This tension was clearly evident when Dominique Venner, the inspiration behind Bloc Identitaire and Génération Identitaire, committed suicide in the Notre-Dame Cathedral in 2013 in an attempt to raise European awareness of the dangers of Muslim migration to Europe. He was not a practising Christian but professed such huge admiration for Christian culture and its legacy that he chose to shoot himself in this exemplar of Christian culture.

The secular bias of intelligence and security agencies, alongside the orthodoxy of secular scholars and commentators, has led not only to the abject failure to recognise the nature and extent of the threat of white nationalists but also to prioritise the Islamic terrorist threat. They have assumed that religiosity and religious identification are essentially non-Western and pre-modern, and that such religious extremism had been displaced in the West by now dominant secular ideologies. This failure has three major implications. First, just as all Muslims and Islam cannot be held responsible for terrorists who endorse fantastic reconstructions of their Islamic heritage, so all Christians and Christianity cannot be held responsible for white nationalists who endorse their selective and equally fantastical, ahistorical version of Christian culture – or, more accurately, Christendom, a time of absolute Christian rule and European cultural dominance. Secondly, the failure to recognise the religious dimensions of Christian nationalism has obscured the conscious construction of its enemies and targets for murderous violence. White nationalists religiously identified their victims in Halle, Pittsburgh, San Diego and Christchurch. These were not simply racist attacks but attacks on selected religious targets in their places of worship. Finally, the deficiency in recognising and locating the religious dimensions of the identitarian alt-right discourse and actions, and the complex intersectionality of religion and racism, has drastically reduced the capacity to understand the phenomenon, and thus to respond to it strategically and effectively.[43]

ALT-RIGHT AND IDENTITARIAN POLITICS IN AOTEAROA NEW ZEALAND: ACTION ZEALANDIA

Alt-right groups with a strong identitarian focus began to appear in New Zealand during and after the publicity gained by such groups during the 2015–16 US presidential elections. Formed in February 2018, the Dominion Movement described itself as a 'youth-oriented brotherhood of nationalists committed to the revitalisation of European culture and identity in New Zealand. [And] we seek to invigorate our people personally, culturally, and politically'.[44] The Dominion Movement looked like the alt-right groups that appeared in the US and Europe – young, male (typically exclusively so, and the use of the term 'brotherhood' is deliberate), and often involved in tertiary education.

There were key elements of identitarian ideology, especially in the expressed belief in the need to preserve and revitalise 'European culture' and identity in the face of demographic and political displacement by non-whites and Muslims. Members of the Dominion Movement announced that they were 'bound by blood' and were unwilling to 'surrender New Zealand to the "immigrant masses"'.[45] Like the subsequent local group, Action Zealandia, there was an emphasis on community work, especially environmental, and a shared belief in keeping fit. The group and its members became more obvious as they took part in public rallies, specifically free-speech events or events in favour of visiting alt-right activists Stefan Molyneux and Lauren Southern after the private venue they booked in Auckland cancelled the event. They appeared to have members, and to be most active, in Nelson, Wellington and Auckland, with some activity in Palmerston North, Christchurch and Hamilton. Their presence was signalled by stickers and posters such as 'Boer refugees welcome' (repeating Lauren Southern's claims about white South African farmers 'facing genocide') and 'family-community-nation'.

The Dominion Movement faded from view after the 15 March terrorist attacks, especially as the media and security agencies took a great deal more interest in the group and its members – outing them as extremists with connections to international neo-Nazi groups.[46] The Dominion Movement was soon replaced by Action Zealandia, which was formed in July 2019. A leaked manual for the new organisation made it clear that there was significant membership overlap, and provided 'security guidelines' for ex-Dominion Movement members who had, or were about to, join Action Zealandia.[47] The new organisation was active in the same centres as the Dominion Movement.

Action Zealandia continues many of the ideological positions, tactics and appeal to a certain membership that was apparent in the Dominion Movement, and it certainly appears that there was extensive overlap between the two groups. At first glance, Action Zealandia, like the Dominion Movement, appears to involve groups of young men in environmental activities (cleaning up rubbish, planting trees) and outdoor pursuits such as tramping. Their slogan is: 'Building a community for European New Zealanders.' But membership has not been open to women, libertarians and drug addicts. It appears to be concerned with wholesome activities – environmentalism, keeping fit – albeit as a group of young (primarily) men. This impression is reinforced by advice to members.

One of their manuals provides guidance on how members should conduct themselves, and provides extensive details on the activities and powers of the security and intelligence services, how to keep a low profile (get your details removed from the public electoral roll) and how to manage social media accounts. Impression management is designed to maximise the appeal ('big tent' approach), and to avoid labels that might prove to be a barrier to recruitment and online access. But it soon became apparent that the group reflected key ideological elements of its alt-right, and far-right, antecedents.

Soon after it was formed, an American, in an online interaction, advised the group to keep Jews out of the organisation; the reply from an Action Zealandia member was that they would not be bought by 'Jewish money'.[48] The antisemitic material became more obvious through 2020, especially with Kerry Bolton contributing material that drew on his longstanding involvement in far-right political activism (see Chapter Thirteen).[49] Bolton regularly writes for the Action Zealandia website.[50] This is accompanied by a range of other articles that seek to revise New Zealand and global history in ways that reinforce identitarian and alt-right world-views. Others contribute their own conspiracies about Jews. See, for example, 'The Jewish elephant in the room' by Lovecraft's Cat in October 2020, which contains sentences such as: '... it's Jews who have been the most effective creators and propagandists for the progressive dogma of absolute and unequivocal equality between all human groups', and 'The (((fellow-whites))) ... wormed their way through White people's institutions until they subverted the very Cultural assumptions that established and safeguarded our countries as White nations.' (The triple parentheses or echoes are used by the alt-right and others to signal a Jewish person, organisation or community). The article goes on to talk about 'the disproportionate influence Jews have on the media and culture'. Elsewhere, the ethno-nationalism of Action Zealandia is on display: 'Yet again, the liberal-Marxist order has fully disclosed its anti-White, Europhobic hatred for our people.'[51]

Action Zealandia members are active in placing stickers in public places. The University of Auckland is a regular target, as are certain National Party offices. A Chinese National Party MP, Jiang Yang, was one target, and MP Nick Smith's Nelson electorate office another. Members take part in rallies, typically in favour of free speech, and events protesting against the United Nations in general and the United Nations Compact on Migration in particular. They are antagonistic towards China and have marched and placed banners claiming, 'white lives matter'.

Despite advice to its members, and an extensive web presence that seeks to convey that members are considering matters of some intellectual and political importance, Action Zealandia has always struggled to maintain the image of a broad-based 'conservative and nationalist' organisation. At the very moment in March 2020 that an Action Zealandia document talked about a commitment to ensuring activities were within the law, one of its members was arrested in relation to a terror threat against Masjid Al Noor; the organisation posted a leaked Financial Intelligence Unit document from the New Zealand Police on Twitter; and another Action Zealandia member discussed buying firearms and starting a terror cell with the Atomwaffen Division, a violent American neo-Nazi organisation.[52] In mid-2019, reports started to appear about ties between a member of the New Zealand army and Action Zealandia, although the same individual was active on a number of far-right online sites. This activist referenced the 'great replacement' and submitted a petition to Parliament to give priority to white South African farmers for visas to come to New Zealand.[53] He also participated in a rally opposing the United Nations Compact on Migration in Auckland. He subsequently left the army. Other Action Zealandia members were in touch with a range of alt-right and far-right groups such as the Nordic Resistance Movement and the Atomwaffen Division.[54]

Action Zealandia has an extensive online presence with articles on historical and political matters, on-air discussions on issues like 'mass migration', and a clear statement of philosophy and intent. It has published material critical of QAnon, yet shares several alt-right ideological positions and concerns.[55] The anxiety of the 2020 pandemic combined with the uptake of similar arguments during a general election provided it with fellow-travellers. Like other groups in the identitarian–alt-right coalition, Action Zealandia valorises Christendom, Christian militarism and the idealised Christian heritage of European white culture.

Mention should also be made of Wargus Christi (Outlaws of Christ), a far-right identitarian 'martial-monastic order' or 'brotherhood' of 'Christian crusader knights' whose religious purification disciplines include the oppression of the flesh.[56] They have links to military personnel at the Linton military camp, and other members are former service people. The group's Facebook account has posted antisemitic, homophobic and anti-Islamic materials, and subscribes to 'replacement theory', referring to Chinese and other Asian migrants in New Zealand. One member based at Linton, the co-founder of the 'Dominion Movement', was arrested and charged with 'unauthorised disclosure of information' that is 'likely to prejudice the security or defence of New Zealand' and with 'accessing a computer system for a dishonest purpose' in 2020. This group has significant parallels with the Oath Keepers, one of the identitarian alt-right militias that stormed the Capitol in January 2021, among whom are current and former members of the armed forces, police, first responders and security services. The Oath Keepers have similar views on the threat of non-white, particularly Muslim, immigration to white Christian culture and the white race, and conspiratorial views of covert Jewish 'satanic' power, asserting that 'Judaism is a diametrical enemy of Christ'.[57]

QANON AND THE ALT-RIGHT SINCE 2020

As 2020 progressed, and a lockdown to limit the spread of Covid-19 was instituted in March, some New Zealanders began to take more interest in some of the arguments that emerged from the US, including those made by QAnon and other members of the alt-right. Four of the fringe conservative political groups – New Zealand Public Party (NZPP) or Advance New Zealand (who formed an alliance of convenience for the purposes of the election), Vision New Zealand, the New Conservatives and the ONE Party – were explicitly 'Christian' and expressed, to varying levels and with different levels of enthusiasm, a degree of interest and advocacy for conspiratorial arguments, sometimes with a clear identitarian component.[58] Additionally, there are elements of conspiracy in the policies and positions of the New Zealand Outdoors Party, focused on 'community wellbeing', the replacement of agribusiness with personal fishing and hunting, and strong opposition to the use of 1080 poison, mandatory vaccinations, Covid-19 restrictions and 5G technology.

The 2020 General Election was dominated by the uncertainties of the Covid-19 pandemic and the lockdown, exacerbated by the fact the election was delayed. As well as casting their constituency and party votes the public were able to respond to two 'progressive' referendum questions on euthanasia and cannabis. These served to highlight concerns with public morality, and mobilised the minor Christian and conservative parties (and parachurch groups such as Family First with its seemingly effective 'Say No to Dope' campaign) as they proffered alternative futures for New Zealand society to those offered by the major 'secular' political parties. The main opposition National Party leader, Judith Collins, went as far as being filmed by the press praying in church in the attempt to capture some of this 'Christian' vote.

A key activist, Seventh Day Adventist preacher and a prominent public voice for conspiracy theories, was Billy Te Kahika. He began broadcasting on his Facebook page and by March 2020 was becoming more political in his commentary.[59] His claims that the pandemic had been planned and was being used as a justification for the enslavement of populations began to draw more attention. By April, he had an audience of 30,000 online. He then launched the explicitly Christian NZPP in Auckland in June 2020, and a month later joined with Jami-Lee Ross and the Advance New Zealand Party to contest the 2020 General Election (Ross was previously a National Party MP and activist, with links to the party leadership). Te Kahika called on 'God to bless and make New Zealand great again'; his pivotal messages included the claim that the Covid-19 pandemic was a fraud, and that 'billionaires have developed viruses to enslave humanity ... that the government was authorising [the] military to enter people's homes and [was] planning to implement forced vaccinations'. He also pedalled 'misinformation about the facts of fluoridation and 5G'.[60] Radio NZ summed up the rationale for his key beliefs:

> ... 1080 poison is not about competing ideas of pest control, but a plot to poison the rural landscape to concentrate people in cities ... Vaccines and water fluoridation are not about public health, but about numbing the population, increasing their compliance, and reducing intelligence ... 5G is not an iterative evolution of existing technology, but a dangerous weapon ... being used on unsuspecting populations.[61]

In June 2020, there was evidence Te Kahika was deploying some of the more bizarre and racist elements of the conspiracy theories of the alt-right in an online video. He outlined his views about Israel and the role of Jews in creating disarray and new international systems that meet Jewish, and other 'internationalist', agendas. Te Kahika's views were clearly and crudely antisemitic, and involved the repetition of tropes of classical far-right antisemitism.[62] What was concerning were the number of views of this video, the numbers turning up to Te Kahika's public meetings, and the thousands who attended his mid-September anti-lockdown rally in Auckland. There was certainly an audience for his heady mixture of Christian apocalyptic and conspiratorial views. Crowd shots of his audience included 'Q' signs and placards expressing conspiratorial views about a range of topics, from the United Nations through to vaccines.[63] Some commentators noted the links to QAnon.[64] His conspiracy theories, along with his own behaviour towards others, were detailed in an extensive documentary, *The False Prophet*, in mid-2020.[65]

Another interesting parallel between Billy Te Kahika and QAnon can be found in his claim that the pandemic is a Chinese conspiracy in agreement with, and 'sanctioned' by, President Biden and other cabal leaders. Falun Gong/Dafa (a Chinese new religious movement, now with a global following), via their free newspaper *The Epoch Times*, have in recent years intensified their public programmes of awareness-raising and recruitment across the Western world. In New Zealand, Falun Gong/Dafa has been both a source for these campaigns and a widely distributed media outlet for such conspiracies, also serving as an advertising platform for Te Kahika's political campaign.

The reaction to NZPP was varied. Te Kahika was a compelling and charismatic speaker, and in meetings in Tauranga, Whangārei and Auckland he gathered large and enthusiastic audiences. But political pundits and the media were largely critical and often scathing. In one instance, a newspaper editor took it on himself to challenge local NZPP supporters and candidates. The editor of the *Gisborne Herald* published an extremely critical op-ed of NZPP and then, in an editorial, defended its publication.[66] He then followed this up with a dismissal of the key conspiratorial claims made at a meeting of local supporters and more generally by the party. The subsequent online comments illustrated that there was a committed and believing constituency for the party and its beliefs – as well as strong opposition. The editor continued to critique the supporters and their arguments. It was an interesting insight into the role of the media and the mixed reaction to conspiratorial QAnon-style arguments. In February 2021, the NZPP (renamed the Freedom Party) was wound up, although Te Kahika promised to continue his work via social media and still solicits cash donations.

Four other fringe parties that contested the 2020 General Election shared some of the conspiratorial views of the NZPP: Vision New Zealand, the party associated with Destiny Church through its leader Hannah Tamaki; the ONE Party; the New Conservatives; and the New Zealand Outdoors Party (which was under pressure to join with the NZPP at one point, and had its advertising pulled from Facebook because it was deemed to have breached the misinformation guidelines). Vision New Zealand, the ONE Party and the New Conservatives are all explicitly Christian parties subscribing to Christian values, albeit with diverse evangelical and Pentecostal theologies. The degree to which each party articulated conspiratorial views, or ethno-national politics, varied considerably, and rather depended on the inclination and activities of the candidates and, sometimes, the comments of supporters. The New Conservatives, for example, echoed some of the broad themes of the identitarian movement. In a letter to the *Northland Age*, the party's deputy leader, Elliot Ikilei, outlined the core concerns and politics of the New Conservatives. They included:

- the supremacy and core values of 'our Western civilisation', which were seen as under threat;
- the use of fear (at that point, often focused on Covid-19) of 'progressivism' and Marxism that are said to erode 'free speech, our democratic process and our equality'; and
- an 'alignment to other nations and ideologies, including an increasing adherence to the United Nations', which is said to weaken 'our sovereignty, our nationalism and our identity'.[67]

Some of the views expressed by New Conservatives candidates in the 2020 election gave rise to claims in the media that the party had attracted 'far-right' activists. A Radio NZ piece to this effect was subsequently the subject of a complaint to the Media Council. This complaint was rejected, in part because the New Conservative candidate in question had agreed that '"far right" might not be a bad description of his views'.[68]

The ONE Party, co-led by Stephanie Harawira (formerly Māori Party and Mana Party) and Edward Shanly, argued that elected MPs should be answerable to an Apostolic Council of Elders. Echoing Tahupōtiki Wiremu Rātana, founder of the Rātana faith, they visited marae around New Zealand with Te Tiriti o Waitangi and the Bible held high as their dual inspired guides. Their Pentecostal and evangelical theology is focused on wairua, and Harawira claimed that God has spoken directly to her. Their intention is to (re-) establish New Zealand as a moral Christian nation opposed to Covid-19 lockdowns and regulations, which they understand as undermining individual rights and freedoms. They also oppose water fluoridation, would introduce compulsory military service for all over 18, and believe it is a fundamental right to own firearms. Identifying the evangelical and Pentecostal Christian dimensions of these religiously inflected identitarian alt-right parties in New Zealand is vital for understanding their apocalyptic-driven policies, recruitment bases, and national and international sources and linkages.

In the end, voters did not support these fringe conservative political parties, with the NZPP/Advance NZ Party receiving a total of 28,429 votes (1 percent of the total votes cast) and ONE Party 8121 votes (0.3 percent); the New Conservatives did slightly better at 42,613 (1.5 percent). Te Kahika's response was to claim that the voting was rigged.[69]

Several activists, bloggers and protesters have echoed alt-right and QAnon arguments during and since the election. This has been exacerbated by the anti-vaccination politics that have emerged during 2020–21 with clear references to QAnon and far-right arguments.[70] In Christchurch, a group of speakers collected on a regular basis to yell conspiracy theories about a range of topics at a typically small audience and passers-by. Long-time far-right activist Kyle Chapman was one.[71] Recently, he has become very involved in anti-government and anti-vaccination protests and campaigning. Lee Williams was another. Williams has argued that social media companies are 'part of the globalist conspiracy to lie to Western nations, the people of Western nations, because they seem hell-bent on flooding Western nations with mass migration from the Third World'.[72] Williams is strongly opposed to the United Nations, and especially the Migration Pact, and is a believer in the 'great replacement'.[73] He was a speaker at a NZPP anti-lockdown rally in Auckland in September 2020. In mid-2021, Williams was fired by his employer Synlait for making racist comments about Māori MPs and *He Puapua*, a report commissioned by the government to explore options to implement the United Nations Declaration on the Rights of Indigenous Peoples; he subsequently returned to the United Kingdom for several months before returning to New Zealand in early 2022. In November 2020, comments from a blogger, Olivia Pierson, criticised the appointment of Nanaia Mahuta as foreign minister due to her traditional moko kauae, calling it 'the height of ugly, uncivilized wokedom'.[74] Pierson describes herself as a 'free-thought advocate' and has published on Western values and why they ought to be defended – a common theme among identitarians. Vinny Eastwood broadcasts Free America Radio from Auckland. Eastwood helped run the social media activities for the NZPP and regularly interviews conspiracy theorists from around the world on his station. There are also the online sites, including 'We are Q' and 'For the Qulture reports', the latter describing itself as a 'group ... for ANONS from NZ in search of the truth'.[75]

Alternative media such as Counterspin Media – broadcast on American activist Steve Bannon's platform GTV – echoes the QAnon line on the pandemic and the alleged rise of communism in New Zealand and elsewhere. The host of Counterspin Media, Kelvyn Alp, has been involved in peripheral politics for some time, and formed an anti-government militia in the 1990s.[76] Social and other media posts and comments confirm that conspiratorial and anti-government views have drawn inspiration from global influences such as QAnon. The adoption of Islamophobic and antisemitic material, including drawing cynical parallels to the Holocaust, are particularly concerning.[77] There are also specific New Zealand aspects. These include misogynistic attacks on a female prime minister, and the appearance of some identitarian and QAnon views in farmers' protests in 2021.[78] Inevitably, others in the government and media are also subject to attack and threats – ironically likening them to Nazis and/or communists against whom all acts of resistance might be justified.[79]

The year 2020 proved to be a moment when groups from the alt-right such as Action Zealandia existed alongside several political parties that expressed identitarian and, on occasion, QAnon arguments during a general election. The expansion of the audience for such arguments, and the congealment of far-right and conservative activism, have continued since the election. Heightened media interest also introduced the New Zealand public to several activists and bloggers who echoed alt-right and identitarian beliefs. The constituency for these views appears to have grown given the anxieties and anti-government politics associated with the pandemic, although the size of the overall constituency remains limited compared to that in the US or the UK, at least in terms of translating into political support. Perhaps the horror of the 15 March terrorist attacks made New Zealanders more wary of such views and the potential and actual consequences.

CHRISTCHURCH AND THE 15 MARCH TERRORIST ATTACKS

Julie Ebner noted that in the aftermath of the 15 March attacks, it became clear to some people that 'transgressive memes were more than just transgressive jokes to many' and that there was a clear gap between those who were interested in trolling and 'those who were serious about the race war'.[80] The other consequence of Christchurch, for Ebner, was that the 'digital dualism' (the idea that online and offline worlds are separate, a phrase coined by Nathan Jurgenson in 2011) was no longer sustainable. Here was evidence that the two intersected in the self-radicalisation of the shooter and in the ideological universe he inhabited. One was intimately and causally linked with the other. Evidence of this universe and the translation of online hate to offline violence is provided in some detail in the Royal Commission report.[81] There is clear evidence of the influences on the shooter from orthodox white supremacist traditions, as well as more recent ideological and political developments, both alt-right and identitarian. The latter is embodied in the shooter's obsession with the 'great replacement'. It opens his 'manifesto' (which begins with the statement 'It's the birthrates' repeated three times) and is apparent in his financial support for Martin Sellner and Generation Identity.

As the live-streaming and reports of the 15 March attack went around the world, support was expressed by people from across the far-right and white supremacist spectrum (epithets used included 'Invader Crusader', prefixing the terrorist's surname with 'Saint', and a nickname based on his first name for girls 'expressing their admiration' for him').[82] Ebner saw the actions of the 15 March terrorist as boosting the far-right gaming world, or 'gamification', and the inclusion of gaming elements in far-right actions and ideas.[83]

The events in Christchurch on 15 March 2019 made it clear that New Zealanders' complacency, especially the belief that the country is somehow exceptional and does not have far-right activists and groups, or is exempt from white supremacist terrorism, was misplaced. The awful events of that day might have heightened the awareness of many New Zealanders about the consequences of far-right political views. But as the 2020 election, the existence of groups like Action Zealandia, and the actions of those who believe the government's pandemic response is malevolently inspired demonstrate, there are still those prepared to see conspiracies and to believe that there are people, groups, communities and organisations who are covertly doing evil and damaging Christian and 'European' institutions and values. The links between the expression or re-posting of extreme radical racist, nationalist or religious opinions and murderous extreme violence are the subject of intense academic scrutiny – and are just beginning to be understood.[84] But what is already clear is that extreme convictions and ideologies are a pre-condition of extreme violence, although the obverse may not be so.

CHAPTER FIFTEEN

Internationalising white extremism

Far-right networks in New Zealand and beyond

MICHAEL DAUBS

THE 15 MARCH 2019 TERRORIST ATTACK against two mosques in Ōtautahi Christchurch, and the content shared by the perpetrator of that attack, provide cogent examples of how the communicative affordances of online platforms and tools – that is, the 'possibilities for action that emerge from … given technological form' – support the internationalisation of the modern far right.[1] The terrorist not only livestreamed his murderous rampage for an international audience on Facebook but, in his manifesto, which was shared minutes before the attack began on the then-popular 'alt-right' website 8chan (renamed to 8kun after the 15 March attacks), also claimed to have been inspired by previous mass shootings in other countries and incorporated material designed for an internet-savvy audience. Additionally, the Royal Commission of Inquiry report on the terrorist attack detailed how the terrorist was radicalised online, particularly via YouTube, and maintained informal ties to international far-right organisations.[2]

It is increasingly necessary to understand how the far right in New Zealand operates in an era of near-ubiquitous connectivity. The proliferation of information communication technologies (ICTs) makes it possible for content, cultures and ideologies to spread unchecked by geographic space or national borders. These technologies, which include websites, social media platforms, instant messengers and chat systems, enable a flexible, adaptive and international community of white extremists that is difficult to track and regulate.[3] In this chapter, I use the term 'white extremism' as an umbrella term that incorporates white nationalists, white supremacists and other racially motivated far-right groups. Rather than operating independently, white extremists, including those who operate in Aotearoa, are situated within this informal but global international far-right network and contribute to a 'global white identity that transcends local and regional ties'.[4]

The internationalisation of white extremism is demonstrated in this chapter through an examination of the radicalisation and actions of the 15 March terrorist. Central to this discussion is Manuel Castells' concept of the 'network society' in which networks are the predominant organisational form. I begin by providing a brief overview of the network society, summarising what Castells refers to as its four main 'dimensions'. In the next section, I outline how the network society benefits the far right and white extremists. Using examples from the terrorist's manifesto, the Royal Commission report released in December 2020, and interviews with internet experts, anti-extremist activists and deradicalised members of the far right, I detail how white extremists use online platforms to spread extremist ideologies in support of an 'international white nationalism'. The final section discusses how this networked extremism challenges the regulatory powers of individual nation-states, and also highlights some of the more promising developments in ways to challenge the far right both in New Zealand and abroad.

THE FOUR DIMENSIONS OF THE NETWORK SOCIETY

According to Castells, the term 'network society' describes the era resulting from a shift from an industrial age to one centred on information. Castells introduced the concept for two primary reasons. First, he considered calling the post-industrial era an 'information society' to be inaccurate, since 'information, in its broadest sense, e.g. as communication of knowledge, has been critical in all societies'.[5] Second, he suggested that it is the network that is the primary driver of society, starting in the latter half of the twentieth century. The network society is comprised of four 'dimensions of social change' that make possible the new social structure Castells outlined.[6] The first of these dimensions is a 'new technological paradigm, based on the deployment of new information technologies' that 'allow the formation of new forms of social organization and social interaction along electronically based information networks' with their own global logic.[7] He ultimately argued that information networks are now the 'predominant' form of social organisation.[8]

The second dimension Castells highlighted is 'globalisation', which he described as 'the technological, organizational, and institutional capacity of the core components of a given system (like the economy) to work as a unit in real or chosen time on a planetary scale'.[9] As this statement indicates, globalisation affects nearly all facets of human existence, from social structures to the economy. Castells noted, however, that globalisation does not supersede operations at all levels of society. For example, in capitalist systems, 'most production, employment and firms are, and will remain, local and regional'.[10] These local and regional processes, however, support an economic system working on a global scale.

Culture and ideologies can operate in a similar manner in the network society, suggesting the third dimension of social change – the 'enclosing of dominant cultural manifestations in an interactive, electronic hypertext'.[11] Culture is now 'organized primarily around an integrated system of electronic media', which enables a fluid and interactive exchange of cultural content.[12] Interactions between people are key to this dimension, and 'offline' practices, beliefs and processes are stored, replicated and shared via networks.[13]

The fourth dimension, which is a 'consequence' of the three dimensions outlined above, is the 'demise of the sovereign nation-state'.[14] Castells was careful to note that current nation-states will not disappear but, instead, will become 'a network state, a state made out of a complex web of power-sharing, and negotiated decision-making between international, multinational, national, regional, local, and non-governmental, political institutions'.[15] Local or regional influences thus operate in conversation with, and contribute to, global exchanges of ideas and information.

THE FAR RIGHT IN THE NETWORK SOCIETY: INTERNATIONAL INFLUENCES IN THE 15 MARCH TERRORIST ATTACKS

Castells does not overlook potential downsides of the network society. He noted, for example, that power in the network society is dependent upon access to the network and control over informational flows. Those with the means to access the network – often coinciding with the more privileged – are, therefore, granted more power in the network society. The concept of the 'digital divide' between those with access and those without stems from concerns about exclusion from the network society.[16] However, Castells also saw great potential in the network society, arguing: 'This networking logic is needed to structure the unstructured while preserving flexibility, since the unstructured is the driving force of innovation in human activity'.[17] He further asserted that 'the technology of the Internet embodies the culture of freedom, as shown in the historical record of its development'.[18]

The recent activities of white extremists demonstrate that the network society also supports the spread of their ideas and the development of an international far-right community that operates in New Zealand. The 'new technological paradigm' enabled by ICTs allows interactions between individual extremists in ways that were previously limited. These interactions facilitate the 'formation of a trans-local white identity, which is in turn shaped through global information technologies rather than in opposition to them'.[19] This network of extremists operates internationally in line with the second dimension of 'globalisation'. Through social networks, messaging systems, websites and discussion boards, extremists can discuss, spread and share ideas in real time across geographic borders, reflecting Castells' third dimension of a 'fluid exchange' in a networked hypertext. Finally, these three dimensions are contributing to the 'demise' of nation-states, in part because they contribute to a form of white extremism that, even though it often manifests as hyper-nationalism and the pursuit of ethnically 'pure' (i.e. white or European) nation states, often operates across national borders.[20] Kyler Ong and Raffaello Pantucci noted, for example, that '[s]omewhat paradoxically given their tendency to oppose the European Union, these far-right political groups have found themselves networking across the continent.'[21] In addition, because the platforms on which extremists communicate make it difficult for individual nations to regulate or restrict their activities, responses to online extremism tend to comprise (and perhaps necessitate) multinational cooperation. The Christchurch Call, the agreement created in the wake of the 15 March terrorist attack, and signed in May 2019 by 17 countries, the European Commission, and several major technology companies including Amazon, Facebook, Google, Microsoft and Twitter, is just one example of a multinational effort to combat violent extremism online.[22]

Consideration of white extremism in one region or country, including New Zealand, must, therefore, be contextualised within this international extremism. To be clear, as a colonial settler nation, white supremacist and nationalist views existed in New Zealand well before the advent of digital networks, as many of the chapters in this collection demonstrate. These views were normalised and common among those of European descent throughout the nineteenth and early to mid-twentieth centuries. Margaret Mutu argued that British colonists 'imposed a regime of White supremacy in the name of the Crown', resulting in the establishment of a White New Zealand policy that, in addition to informing immigration policies, also involved 'actively encouraging the stigmatisation of being Māori and outlawing Māori language, culture and practices'.[23] The effects of this policy and colonisation 'burden Māori to this day'.[24] Steve Elers demonstrated how this White New Zealand policy also led to discrimination against other racial groups, documenting a series of public anti-Chinese statements made by New Zealand politicians between 1880 and 1920 that 'undeniably articulate an ideology of white supremacy'.[25]

Nor is the operation of groups inspired by the international far right a phenomenon specific to the digital era. In 1933, Frank Robson published *The Hidden Hand Revealed*, a reprint of the antisemitic *Protocols of the Learned Elders of Zion* first published in 1903 in Russia.[26] Robson's version of *The Protocols* included material borrowed from British antisemitic groups the Britons and the Imperial Fascist League. *The Protocols* was distributed throughout the British Commonwealth, Europe and the US over the next few decades, and the notion of a vast Jewish conspiracy remains influential in far-right circles to this day. It is potentially an inspiration for QAnon, which promotes the conspiracy theory that a cabal of politicians and celebrities is working to 'kidnap children, slaughter, and eat them to gain power from their blood'.[27] In 1961, the New Zealand Security Intelligence Service (NZSIS) filed a report about a Wellington man who was a 'recipient and distributor of anti-Jewish literature which he received from Australia and Munich, West Germany'.[28] That same year, the US embassy in Wellington notified the office of the minister of external affairs that the then leader of the American Nazi Party was seeking to visit New Zealand for two weeks to have a 'private meeting with other National Socialists in the area'.[29] In 1964, a 'quantity of Fascist pamphlets from Austria, USA and Great Britain' was seized by New Zealand police in Rotorua, along with notebooks containing, among other things, Nazi propaganda.[30] A 1969 memo from the Ministry of Defence also noted that the number of people connected to extremism in New Zealand 'is infinitesimal but nevertheless during the past eight years or so continuing cases, usually about one or two a year, have come to the attention of individuals communicating with national socialist organisations overseas and professing an interest in the fascist creed'.[31] These are but a few anecdotal examples that demonstrate how far-right groups have operated and networked internationally for decades. Many other examples are discussed in the earlier chapters of this collection.

The capabilities afforded by digital media represent a significant shift in the possibilities for the far right to communicate and organise – and the ease and speed with which they can do so. The informal networks seen today have been in development for well over a decade. Jessie Daniels detailed how white supremacists in the US used websites, such as Stormfront, and social media, such as Facebook, in the first decade of the twenty-first century to develop a global online community and an 'expression of whiteness across national boundaries'.[32] As she argued, 'The Internet enables social movements to cross national boundaries in ways simply not possible in any previous era.'[33] ICTs provide 'more and greater opportunities for international contact'.[34] Thus, while the far right is anti-*globalist* – 'globalist' having antisemitic connotations in far-right circles – Daniels argued that 'in the Information Age white supremacy is global and quite self-consciously so'.[35] Daniels praised Castells' 'farsighted sociological vision' by recognising the role the internet plays in the process of globalisation.[36] However, Daniels critiqued Castells for seeing globalisation as 'allied with tolerance, pluralism and cosmopolitanism whereas identity is implicated in racism, tribalism and ethnic identities'.[37] As a result, she argued that Castells 'misses the extent to which the Internet figures in the formation of a global white identity that transcends local and regional ties'.[38]

This claim does not mean extremists' understanding of whiteness does not have local or regional variances. In a 2000 interview, for example, Peter Coleman, the founder of the KKK in Australia, said that the Klan would be open to Māori members if it expanded to New Zealand again: 'Every country has its different Klans and there's room for Maori.'[39] Similarly, a former member of a white supremacist 'skinhead' group in Christchurch I interviewed, who asked to be referred to only as Alanna, stated that members of her gang openly welcomed Māori members because they believed it would be difficult to expand if Māori were excluded.[40] However, J.M. Berger believed that a recent surge in white extremism is in part attributable to 'the sort of connective tissue that you get from the Internet that wasn't there before that's really making it easier for groups to be influenced and to coordinate, or not necessarily coordinate but synchronize over large geographical distances'.[41]

Released in December 2020, the report of the Royal Commission of Inquiry into the 15 March terrorist attacks provides ample evidence of the increasingly global and networked character of white extremism, and the far right in general. The 15 March terrorist, who is Australian but had lived in New Zealand for almost two years before the attack, said he was radicalised while travelling in Europe.[42] But he explained in interviews after his arrest that 'YouTube was, for him, a far more significant source of information and inspiration.'[43] The way YouTube acts as a pathway to radicalisation is discussed in detail in a 2018 report from Becca Lewis, who demonstrated how 'social networking between influencers makes it easy for audience members to be incrementally exposed to, and come to trust, ever more extremist political positions'.[44] The terrorist subscribed to several right-wing video channels on YouTube and made a financial donation to Freedomain Radio, a 'podcast and YouTube channel created by Canadian Stefan Molyneux, who is a prominent member of the far right'.[45] The terrorist probably watched videos in which Molyneux 'openly promotes scientific racism, advocates for the men's rights movement, critiques initiatives devoted to gender equity and promotes white supremacist conspiracy theories focused on "White Genocide" and "The Great Replacement".[46] These ideas engender a sense of 'white victimisation' that can be 'weaponized for potential political gain'.[47] Exposure to these ideas can often lead to radicalisation. Caleb Cain, an American who was radicalised on YouTube but has since rejected far-right ideologies and shares his experiences to educate others, said that one of the reasons people fall down the 'rabbit hole' is because far-right ideologies are often 'watered down' and coded in 'pseudoscience' and 'pseudohistory'. As he explained, 'I just see it as a lot of marketing and ... it worked on me and I've seen it work on a lot of other people as well.'[48]

While YouTube is frequently mentioned in the Royal Commission of Inquiry report, it also notes that the 15 March terrorist accessed other platforms, including Facebook, where he shared far-right memes, articles and links to YouTube videos; a 'gaming site chat room' where he also frequently shared articles and video links; and far-right discussion boards on websites such as 4chan and 8chan, though he was less active there.[49] He also downloaded the manifesto of another white extremist from Oslo who murdered 77 people in a mass shooting and bombing in 2011. The Royal Commission of Inquiry suggested that the 15 March terrorist 'was significantly influenced by the Oslo terrorist', in part because the latter's manifesto included detailed instructions for 'would-be extreme right-wing terrorists', which the terrorist seems to have followed when preparing for his own attack.[50]

The report details other social, informational and even financial international connections of the terrorist, such as several donations to the French branch of a European far-right movement called Génération Identitaire (Generation Identity), which helped spread the 'Great Replacement' conspiracy theory, and the Identity Movement in Germany, which the terrorist paid in the cryptocurrency Bitcoin.[51] One of the most prominent of these connections was to Martin Sellner, an Austrian far-right politician and leader of the Identitäre Bewegung Österreichs (Austrian Identity Movement). The terrorist donated money to Sellner in January 2018, after which the two exchanged several emails. Sellner invited the terrorist to visit Austria, and the terrorist, in return, invited Sellner to Australia or New Zealand, where he promised people 'would happily have you stay in their homes'.[52] In Facebook posts made before his attack, the terrorist also encouraged others to donate to Sellner, potentially introducing him to a larger international audience.[53]

Many of the elements and people discussed above appear within the 74-page 'manifesto' the terrorist uploaded to 8chan before his attack. The title of the document,

'The Great Replacement', refers to a conspiracy-theory laden anti-immigration book that, despite being available for several years, had not received much attention locally – at least not until the 15 March attacks. It argues that declining birth rates among white or European populations, coupled with immigration and higher birth rates among 'non-Europeans (i.e. non-whites), is leading to the systematic erasure of white people and white culture'.[54] The terrorist refers to this idea repeatedly throughout his manifesto, repeating the phrase 'It's the birthrates' three times at the start of his introduction. He later claims that differences in birth rates amount to 'ethnic replacement', 'cultural replacement', 'racial replacement' and, finally, 'white genocide'. In all, he references the idea of 'replacement' nearly 30 times throughout the manifesto, and references 'genocide' another five. Clearly, the ideas espoused on YouTube by international white extremists such as Molyneux played a significant role in the terrorist's manifesto and were a key motivation for his terrorist attack.

The terrorist also references another idea popular in far-right circles online: accelerationism, which is 'the idea that Western governments are irreparably corrupt. As a result, the best thing white supremacists can do is accelerate their demise by sowing chaos and creating political tension.'[55] The terrorist dedicated a one-page section in his manifesto to accelerationism, advising others who share his beliefs to 'Destabilize, then take control.' The neo-Nazi Atomwaffen Division (AWD) and the US-based white nationalist The Base are among far-right groups in several countries who promote this idea. The Base is notable because it has developed its own international network; despite operating mostly in the US, the group's leader resides in Russia, and The Base recruits internationally for members, including in Australia, where they recruited from a white nationalist group that once invited the terrorist to be a member.[56] Finally, the terrorist referred to other white extremists who committed acts of terrorism as inspiration for his own attack, including a white supremacist who killed nine people in a church in South Carolina in 2015 and the Oslo terrorist whom he calls his 'true inspiration'. Notably, both of these terrorists wrote and distributed their own manifestos before committing their attacks. The terrorist's own manifesto would similarly influence other terrorists, such as the perpetrator of an attack who killed 22 people outside of a Walmart in El Paso, Texas, in August 2019.

While these examples demonstrate how the 15 March terrorist's beliefs and actions were the culmination of his contact with an international network of white extremists, many elements, including the title of the manifesto itself, were carefully planned to motivate readers to access or even participate in the shared hypertext generated there. Other elements were designed to appeal to an international, internet-savvy audience such as those at 8chan, where he posted his manifesto. The document is laced with memes that combine deeply xenophobic hatred with the irony, sarcasm and playfulness common to social media sites. For example, in an early section in which he answered hypothetical questions about himself and his motivations, part of his response to the imagined question 'Who are you?' states that he has 'been working part time as a kebab removalist'. This comment is a reference to a song featured in a video produced by four Bosnian Serb soldiers in 1995 and posted to the internet in 2006, and called either 'Serbia Strong' or 'Remove Kebab'. It is militantly anti-Muslim and has become popular with white extremists.[57] For those in the know, the terrorist's reference to himself as a 'kebab removalist' identifies him as part of the white extremist community dedicated to the removal of Muslims; those who do not understand the reference are either left confused or might perhaps seek out more information and be exposed to the song and its anti-Muslim message.

He answered a later question about whether various media texts such as games or movies had taught him violence and extremism by sarcastically stating, 'Yes, Spyro the dragon 3 taught me ethno-nationalism. Fortnite trained me to be a killer and to floss on the corpses of my enemies.' Finally, in a response to imagined accusations of racism, the terrorist included a block of text that replicates an internet meme known as the 'navy seal copypasta'. The term 'copypasta' simply refers to a segment of text that is frequently copied and pasted on social media and other online platforms. The 'navy seal copypasta' is a satirical response meant to mock those who make grandiose threats online, and includes spelling errors such as 'gorilla warfare', and exaggerated claims such as 'I graduated top of my class in the Navy Seals, and I've been involved in numerous secret raids on Al-Quaeda, and I have over 300 confirmed kills.' Robert Evans said the meme started on 4chan around 2010 and was included in the manifesto to 'distract attention from [the terrorist's] more honest points, and to draw the attention of his real intended audience'.[58] The terrorist even encouraged audiences to generate their own memes in his manifesto.

Other elements are there to sow confusion and garner media attention. This process is known colloquially online as 'shitposting', which Evans defined as 'the act of throwing out huge amounts of content, most of it ironic, low-quality trolling, for the purpose of provoking an emotional reaction in less Internet-savvy viewers. The ultimate goal is to derail productive discussion and distract readers.'[59] The shitposting elements in the manifesto, Evans argued, render the manifesto a 'trap' that is 'laid for journalists searching for the meaning behind this horrific crime'.[60] For example, the 'navy seal copypasta' led some journalists early on to report that the terrorist had military experience.[61] Other references simply brought more attention to the terrorist, his manifesto and the attack. For example, the terrorist claimed a primary inspiration for his attack was African-American conservative media personality Candace Owens but that 'the extreme actions she calls for are too much, even for my tastes'. The reference to Owens was noted by many online, who repeated the assertion that Owens helped radicalise the terrorist. These accusations prompted a Twitter response from Owens, who dismissed the claims as 'reach' by 'the Left'.[62] Evans argued that the manifesto's evocation of Owens 'was "bait", thrown out to attract attention on social media and sow further political division'.[63] In that sense, it was successful and, through her tweet, Owens potentially brought the terrorist and his manifesto to the attention of her over two million worldwide followers. The terrorist thus used the media and the interactive nature of the internet to further his white extremist message.

The livestream video of the attack also included memes and other 'shitposting' content. For example, while driving to commit his attack, the terrorist played the song 'Remove Kebab', as noted by commenters on 8chan who watched the video.[64] In addition, before starting his attack, the terrorist shouted, 'Remember, lads, subscribe to PewDiePie', the screen name of Felix Kjellberg who, at the time, ran YouTube's most subscribed-to channel and coincidentally has faced allegations of antisemitism.[65] The phrase references an internet meme started by Kjellberg's fans when he was omitted from YouTube's 2018 'Rewind' retrospective video.[66] In a now-deleted tweet, Kjellberg publicly disavowed the shooter, saying that he was 'absolutely sickened' to have been mentioned by him.[67] The inclusion of the meme was again a signal, a playful gesture to the terrorist's online audience. However, Taylor Lorenz also noted, 'By forcing Kjellberg to acknowledge the attack, the shooter succeeded in further spreading the word about the crime to Kjellberg's tens of millions of followers.'[68] As in the Candace Owens example, the mention of Kjellberg's name was a 'trap' designed to further the international spread of his message, amplify his notoriety and possibly cause some to seek out the video of his attack.

These elements encourage others to watch the video and, potentially, commit similar acts of terrorism. As Berger explained: 'The video is a powerful tool to get people to emulate [the violence]. If somebody sees a video like this, when you're exposed to violence, it increases the possibility that you might be inclined to take up violence yourself. It doesn't happen to everybody, but for certain people, seeing that kind of example really has a powerful effect.'[69]

There is evidence that 'certain people' were indeed inspired to take up violence. White extremists who attempted or carried out terrorist attacks in Poway, California, and El Paso, Texas; in Bærum, Norway, and Halle, Germany, and in London, all cited the terrorist as an inspiration or emulated his approach.[70] Like the terrorist, the El Paso shooter posted a manifesto to 8chan before his attack and began by praising the manifesto of the terrorist.[71] The Halle terrorist, who attempted to attack a synagogue, livestreamed his attempted attack on Twitch, a platform now owned by Amazon and most known for its use by gamers to livestream their games.[72]

The links between these terrorists and the references they make to each other demonstrate that, rather than encouraging tolerance and pluralism, the globalisation enabled by the network society also supports white extremism by spreading racism and hate, which can inspire some to commit violent acts against minority groups. The Royal Commission of Inquiry report stated that the terrorist's interactions with online white extremist content 'may have contributed to his actions on 15 March 2019 – indeed, it is plausible to conclude that it did. We have, however, seen no evidence to suggest anything along the lines of personalised encouragement or the like.'[73] It thus concluded that he 'is appropriately labelled a lone actor'.[74] Discussing the El Paso terrorist, however, Joan Donovan argued: 'The uptick in these online screeds, which increasingly refer to one another, has made one point clear: It's time to re-evaluate the lone wolf phenomenon.'[75] Donovan is absolutely correct in her assessment. Terrorists may act as individuals but they are hardly lone wolves; instead, they operate as representatives of a loosely networked community of white extremists based on a trans-local white identity. As Heidi Beirich, director of the SPLC's Intelligence Project, argued: '[T]he Christchurch killer didn't see himself as an Australian; he saw himself as part of a white collective ... It has never been the case that these people didn't think in a global way. They may have acted in ways that looked domestic but the thinking was always about building an international white movement.'[76]

Byron Clark, a Christchurch-based anti-extremist activist who monitors far-right groups in New Zealand, has observed a shift from white nationalists focusing on 'their own country' to 'more of an idea of a pan-European nationalism that's about the entirety of Europe or of the Western world, which they said would include North America, Australia, and New Zealand'.[77] This 'pan-European nationalism', which Clark referred to as an 'international white nationalism', reflects the idea of a trans-local, and extremist, whiteness.

While the discussion here focuses mainly on an individual terrorist, far-right groups in Aotearoa also regularly use ICTs to participate in an international network of white extremists. Clark, for example, noted that members of Action Zealandia took part in a group chat with thousands of international members on the encrypted chat app Telegram. This group chat was hosted in the Ukraine but featured members from throughout Europe, North America and elsewhere. Clark believes this chat group acted as a kind of community that 'allows these people to feel that they're part of a, you know, huge movement when in each individual country, probably, there's a very small number of them'.[78] One member, identified only as 'Matt', used Telegram to chat with terrorists in the US, inquire about purchasing black-market weapons and plan terror cells in New Zealand.[79] These limited examples show the ways in which white extremists are communicating, organising and crafting a trans-local white identity via online networks.

REGULATORY CHALLENGES AND POTENTIALITIES

Beirich argued that governments and law enforcement agencies 'conceive of this problem as being a domestic one. But that's not the case.'[80] The development of international white extremist networks presents specific challenges to those working to limit the spread of extremist ideologies and prevent future attacks. One challenge is determining exactly what limits can be placed on content. Proposals for censoring extremist content are fraught with difficulties. David Shanks, the former Chief Censor for New Zealand, who classified both the 15 March terrorist's video and the manifesto as 'objectionable' (and, therefore, illegal to possess or distribute), looked to the work of Susan Benesch, who draws distinctions between 'dangerous' content and simply offensive content when determining what to classify as objectionable, with dangerous speech being that which encourages others to commit acts of violent extremism.[81] Shanks said the goal is to 'have a balance in there and not tip too far into potentially criminalising some bad behaviour and some stuff that probably should be condemned, but shouldn't be criminalised at a level that our legislation provides for'.[82] That approach made classifying the 15 March terrorist's manifesto a challenge, Shanks recalled, in part because the language in many ways replicated that found in 'chan culture' used by 'shitposters'. Ultimately, the manifesto was considered objectionable because the terrorist expressed a 'deadly intent' and his message was aimed at those 'potentially at risk of following down that path'.

The fact that major platforms are usually hosted outside of New Zealand, particularly in the US, presents another set of challenges that reflect the diminishing power of individual nation-states that Castells sees as due to the network society. Regulating content on US-based platforms such as Facebook can be a complex legal issue, though not without precedent. For example, Germany's Netzwerkdurchsetzungsgesetz

(NetzDG), or Network Enforcement Act, which took effect in 2018, is 'designed to clamp down on hate speech and illegal content on the internet'.[83] The law has plenty of critics, however, including journalists worried that 'the government has deliberately left the task of deleting content or blocking users to the internet platforms themselves, rather than having courts make decisions'.[84] Shanks also noted that, when dealing with US-based companies, 'there's this constitutional, almost absolutist mindset that prevails around discourse around … boundaries'. In other words, a US-informed understanding of 'free speech', which is more permissive than that in other liberal democracies, has informed platforms' approaches to regulating content, leading to confusion and frustration when working with governments.

This permissive approach may be changing in the wake of the 6 January 2021 storming of the US Capitol building by Trump supporters, many of whom were QAnon adherents. Following this attack, platforms such as Twitter and YouTube 'vowed to crack down further on misinformation'.[85] Despite this dedication, however, Alex Kaplan of Media Matters noted in April 2021 that YouTube 'is still hosting shows supporting the conspiracy theory – some of which even run ads, meaning both the channel and YouTube make money from them'.[86] While several of the channels and videos Kaplan listed were eventually removed, his analysis highlights the difficulties of regulating online content.

Regulating content can sometimes backfire. Using the example of how attempts to prevent Lauren Southern and Stephen Molyneux from speaking in New Zealand only brought more attention to their message, Paul Moon argued, 'Every time something is banned, or prohibited, or discouraged, it creates an attraction to it.'[87] Moon's argument is a matter of debate, however. While attempts to prevent Molyneux and Southern from speaking did result in a short-term increase in media attention, the subsequent 'deplatforming' of Molyneux – that is, his banning from major online platforms such as YouTube and Twitter – resulted in him complaining that 'he had lost most of his audience, that donations had largely dried up, and that, as a result, he has largely abandoned producing videos about politics'.[88]

The affordances of technologies and platforms themselves are another challenge. Members of the far right were early adopters of ICTs, in part because they 'saw great possibilities for using networked communication technology to circumvent social, physical and legal restrictions on the expression of racism and antisemitism'.[89] Tools such as virtual private networks (VPNs), which allow people to appropriate an IP address from another country, can be used to circumvent blocked or filtered content as well. Nicola Brown, a policy advisor at InternetNZ, a non-profit organisation that advocates for a free and secure internet, said, '[T]he way the internet works, it routes around damage by design and, if someone wants to reach that website, they can pop open a VPN … or change their DNS service settings. You know, there's so many, *so* many ways around it … [it's] not really an effective mechanism.'[90] Clark similarly noted that technologically savvy and insistent extremists have 'no trouble getting the Telegram app or getting the Tor browser, if they need to, to access things that are blocked by their ISP'. Brown believes governments that impose technological solutions like content filters are 'going for the lowest-hanging fruit that they have levers to control'.

The ease and speed at which digital content can be replicated is another challenge, as was seen in the hours after the 15 March terrorist attack, when over 1.5 million copies of the video were shared on Facebook alone. Most were removed, but copies persisted even six months after the attack.[91] Automatic detection algorithms used to identify and remove objectionable content can be easily fooled by marginally altering content: for example, by changing the zoom, speed, or aspect ratio before reposting. While these copies may eventually be detected, any delay is an opportunity for others to copy and redistribute it again. In our discussion, Byron Clark said one New Zealand-based far-right member has shared a 'guide' on Facebook that instructed others on these methods to avoid having content removed. The success of these methods means that platforms rely on users reporting content, and on human content moderators to identify and remove content. However, research by Sarah T. Roberts shows these methods have their own issues, including a reliance on poorly paid contract workers, often located in other countries with differing values and cultural norms, who often experience significant distress from reviewing a constant stream of disturbing content.[92]

Clark also noted that people who run groups on social media such as Facebook 'will deliberately manage two or three pages so that they've got a backup. So, if one does get removed, you know, the other ones will still be there.' He further elaborated:

> And, you know, it's not uncommon to see now, like on YouTube in particular, people say, 'Oh, I'm likely to get banned any time now. Follow me on BitChute.' Or even on Facebook they'll be, like, 'Oh, this page will likely get taken down. Follow me on this Telegram channel.' Or, 'My Twitter's going to get taken down. Follow me on Gab.' So, these mainstream social media platforms sort of funnel people to the platforms where there's more extremist content and blocking the most extreme – the platforms that allow the most extremist content – isn't going to end, sort of, the radicalisation to the far right.

He described attempts to block content as a game of 'whack-a-mole' because of the ease of replicability ICTs provide.

But perhaps the biggest challenge to combating white extremism is changing perceptions of, and approaches to, extremism and terrorism. Current laws and proposals are often reactive, such as requiring the removal of content after it has been posted – itself a difficult task. Another challenge is to overcome a 'sometimes myopic focus on Islamic extremism as the only driver of international terrorism'.[93] The Royal Commission report found that the 'focus of the counter-terrorism resources was on what was seen as the presenting threat of Islamist extremist terrorism'.[94] While the report also states that this focus 'was not to the exclusion of addressing other leads when they arose', and found that 'the concentration of resources on the threat of Islamist extremist terrorism is not why the individual's planning and preparation for his terrorist attack was not detected', it does call this focus 'inappropriate', in part because there were 'no substantial assessments of other potential threats of terrorism'.[95]

Finally, governments and law enforcement agencies tend to focus specifically on combating violent extremism (CVE) rather than a broader spectrum of extremist activities. Berger stated that this focus is understandable, since violence is 'the most destructive, escalatory, and irrevocable expression of the extremist paradigm'.[96] CVE and the elimination of terrorist and violent extremist online content is a primary focus of the Christchurch Call.[97] A report from The Workshop, and funded by the New Zealand Law Foundation's Information Law & Policy Project, argued that 'it is critical that the Prime Minister and her advisors look beyond immediate concerns about extremism and content moderation, and ensure that our government's efforts in this moment take into account the wider structural issues that created the conditions in which a live video of an act of such violence could be shared and viewed so widely'.[98]

The challenges listed above – and they are only some of the many complex issues facing those wishing to prevent extremism in Aotearoa and abroad – led Berger to state: 'There's a huge playground for these people to wreak a lot of havoc. It's going to take us probably several years to really get this under control. So I think we're looking at a pretty extended period of increased extremist activity, probably 10 years at least.'[99] However, there are reasons for optimism. Nicola Brown, for example, noted that while InternetNZ was originally against the establishment of New Zealand's Digital Child Exploitation Filtering System (DCEFS) because the group is against *any* filtering of the internet, one positive feature is that, rather than simply blocking content, users who are trying to access a website with child sexual abuse images are instead presented with an interstitial that informs them of the reason the site is blocked, and provides links to educational resources and places to seek help. She says this system is 'actually really successful [in terms of] how many people click on those links'.[100] The advantage of this system is that it could be a potential model to help prevent people from 'going down the rabbit hole' and becoming radicalised in the first place, without preventing access for researchers and anti-extremist activists.

The Royal Commission report also recognised the need for a broader approach to tackling racism and extremism in New Zealand. It recommended 'the establishment of a new national intelligence and security agency' that would 'deliver a more systematic approach to addressing extremism and preventing, detecting and responding to current and emerging threats of violent extremism and terrorism'.[101] Speaking before the release of the report, Shanks was sceptical of the need for a new agency dedicated to anti-extremism, stating, 'I have a natural aversion whenever someone says, "We need another body to do this." … Well, really? Don't we already have kind of enforcement authorities or a Digital Safety Unit at Internal Affairs who's actually got a mandate and a scope and expertise and kind of some scale in terms of understanding of what it means to look at the internet for material that may be harmful?'[102] However, the proposed new agency would be responsible for 'integrated preventing and countering extremism, violent extremism and terrorism strategy'.[103] This could have the potential advantage of preventing possible radicalisation by better linking the online and offline activities of individuals and groups. More important, perhaps, are recommendations to engage with civil society, local governments and the private sector to address extremism, generate resources to help people better understand and prevent extremism, and improve social cohesion and inclusion, all of which recognise opportunities to prevent radicalisation and limit the propagation of extremist ideology before the threat of violence.[104] As a part of these efforts, the report also recommended 'significantly increasing workforce diversity, including in leadership roles' in the public-sector agencies involved in counter-terrorism.

CONCLUSION

In sum, there seems to be a long-overdue recognition of, and reckoning with, past law enforcement failures, systemic discrimination against minority groups in New Zealand and the threat of white extremism. The network society can be equally damaging by supporting the international spread of the far right and white extremism via the internet. As such, there are still issues to address, and combating white extremism in New Zealand will be an arduous task. Hamimah Ahmat, a New Zealand-based special educator and speech language therapist whose husband Zekeriya Tuyan was among the 51 victims of the 15 March terrorist attack, wrote an op-ed about the Royal Commission report in which she stated:

> After 21 months of waiting patiently for the big reveal, what I ended up reading was mainly an echo of what many in the community have been saying for decades: that aspects of our public services are deficient – even damaging to us … We need to enable our community to heal alongside, and hand-in-hand with, the wider public, organisations and government agencies. There are many great initiatives already underway in the community that need long-term support and coordination to sustain. While there is an opportunity for the community to have some agency in managing the report's recommendations and related outcomes, it is struggling for direction and capacity. We need capable people who have a good understanding of systems, Islam, culture and the contemporary western mentality. The need for competency and capacity-building goes both ways.[105]

Notes

INTRODUCTION

1. 'Ko tō tatou kāinga tēnei: Report of the Royal Commission of Inquiry into the terrorist attack on Christchurch masjidain on 15 March 2019', Royal Commission of Inquiry website, 26 November 2020: https://christchurchattack.royalcommission.nz/the-report/
2. Marc Daalder, 'Man charged after mosque car bomb threat', Newsroom, 4 March 2021: www.newsroom.co.nz/two-arrested-after-car-bomb-threat
3. Jade Hutchinson, 'Far-right terrorism: The Christchurch attack and potential implications on the Asia Pacific Landscape', *Counter Terrorist Trends and Analyses*, vol. 3, no. 5, 2019, pp. 19–28.
4. Jeff Sparrow, *Fascists Among Us: Online hate and the Christchurch massacre* (London: Scribe, 2019), pp. 4, 7.
5. Paul Spoonley, 'Christchurch mosque shootings must end New Zealand's innocence about right-wing terrorism', Conversation, 15 March 2019: https://theconversation.com/christchurch-mosque-shootings-must-end-new-zealands-innocence-about-right-wing-terrorism-113655
6. John Battersby and Rhys Ball, 'Christchurch in the context of New Zealand terrorism and right wing extremism', *Journal of Policing, Intelligence and Counter Terrorism*, vol. 14, no. 3, 2019, p. 204.
7. 'Summary of submissions to the Royal Commission of Inquiry', Royal Commission of Inquiry website, 26 November 2020: https://christchurchattack.royalcommission.nz/assets/Publications/Summary-of-submissions.pdf, paras 9–34.
8. William Ray, 'The story of white supremacy', Radio New Zealand, 26 March 2019: www.rnz.co.nz/programmes/black-sheep/story/2018688225/the-story-of-white-supremacy; Scott Hamilton, 'The land of the long white stain', Spinoff, 20 March 2019: https://thespinoff.co.nz/atea/20-03-2019/the-land-of-the-long-white-stain/
9. Paul Spoonley, *The Politics of Nostalgia: Racism and the extreme right in New Zealand* (Palmerston North: Dunmore Press, 1987).
10. Cas Mudde, *The Far Right Today* (Cambridge: Polity Press, 2019), p. 6; Paul Hainsworth, *The Politics of the Extreme Right: From the margins to the mainstream* (London: Bloomsbury, 2000), p. 8.
11. Jens Rydgren (ed.), *The Oxford Handbook of the Radical Right*, (New York: Oxford University Press, 2018), p. 2. Cas Mudde also distinguished between 'radical' and 'extreme' right, although he uses the term 'far right' as a blanket term for both – see Mudde, *The Far Right Today*, p. 7.
12. Roger Eatwell and Matthew Goodwin, *National Populism: The revolt against liberal democracy* (London: Penguin Random House, 2018); Enzo Traverso, *The New Faces of Fascism: Populism and the far right*, trans. David Broder (London: Verso, 2019); Ruth Wodak, Majib KohsraviNik and Brigitte Mral (eds), *Right-wing Populism in Europe: Politics and discourse* (London: Bloomsbury Academic, 2013).
13. Spoonley, *The Politics of Nostalgia*, p. 13.
14. Marcus Wagner and Thomas Meyer, 'The radical right as niche parties? The ideological landscape of party systems in Western Europe, 1980–2014', *Political Studies*, vol. 65, no. 1, 2016, pp. 84–107.
15. Peter H. Argersinger, *Populism and Politics: William Alfred Peffer and the People's Party* (Lexington: The University Press of Kentucky, 2015); Robert Franklin Durden, *The Climax of Populism: The election of 1896* (Lexington: The University Press of Kentucky, 2015); Matthew Hild, *Greenbackers, Knights of Labor, and*

Populists: Farmer-labor insurgency in the late-nineteenth-century south (Athens: University of Georgia Press, 2007); Franco Venturi, *Roots of Revolution: A history of the populist and socialist movements in 19th century Russia* (New York: Phoenix Press, 2001). Kaltwasser et al. make a persuasive case that Boulangism in 1880s France should also be classified as an early manifestation of populism – see Rovira Kaltwasser et al., 'Populism: an overview of the concept and the state of the art', in Rovira Kaltwasser et al. (eds), *The Oxford Handbook of Populism* (New York: Oxford University Press, 2017), p. 4.

16. This first body of scholarship in the 1950s and 1960s culminated in a cross-disciplinary conference on populism at the London School of Economics in May 1967, which led to a publication – see Ernest Gellner and Ghita Ionescu, *Populism: Its meaning and national characteristics* (New York: Macmillan, 1969).
17. Kaltwasser et al., 'Populism: An overview', pp. 2–10; Mudde, *The Far Right Today*, p. 18.
18. Kaltwasser et al., 'Populism: An overview', pp. 13–14; Benjamin Moffitt, *Populism: Key concepts in political theory* (Oxford: Polity Press, 2020), pp. 10–29.
19. Daniel Woodley, *Fascism and Political Theory: Critical perspectives on fascist ideology* (New York: Routledge, 2010), p. 1.
20. See for example Roger Griffin, *The Nature of Fascism* (London: Routledge, 1993); Stanley G. Payne, *A History of Fascism 1914–1945* (Madison: University of Wisconsin Press, 1995); Zeev Sternhell, *The Birth of Fascist Ideology* (Princeton: Princeton University Press, 1994).
21. See for example Nicos Poulantzas, *Fascism and Dictatorship: The third international and the problem of fascism* (London: NLB, 1974); David Renton, *Fascism: Theory and practice* (London: Pluto Press, 1999).
22. Robert O. Paxton, *The Anatomy of Fascism* (London: Penguin, 2004), p. 218.
23. Payne, *A History of Fascism*, pp. 7–8.
24. Klaus von Beyme, 'Right-wing extremism in post-war Europe', *West European Politics*, vol. 11, no. 2, 1988, p. 14.
25. Mudde, *The Far Right Today*, pp. 11–23.
26. John Stenhouse, '"A disappearing race before we came here": Doctor Alfred Kingcome Newman, the dying Maori, and Victorian scientific racism', *New Zealand Journal of History*, vol. 30, no. 2, 1996, p. 140.
27. Dr Isaac Featherstone quoted in *Grey River Argus*, 23 February 1884, p. 4.
28. Jane Stafford and Mark Williams, *Maoriland: New Zealand literature 1872–1914* (Wellington: Victoria University Press, 2006), pp. 110–33.
29. Diane B. Paul et al., 'Introduction: Eugenics as a transnational subject: The British Dominions', in Diane B. Paul, John Stenhouse and Hamish G. Spencer (eds), *Eugenics at the Edges of Empire: New Zealand, Australia, Canada and South Africa* (London: Palgrave Macmillan, 2018), p. 11.
30. Ibid., p. 2.
31. Erik Olssen, 'Truby King and the Plunket Society: An analysis of a prescriptive ideology', *New Zealand Journal of History*, vol. 15, no. 1, 1981, pp. 3–23; S.K. Wilson, 'The aims and ideology of Cora Wilding and the Sunlight League 1930–36' (MA thesis, University of Canterbury, 1980).
32. Barbara Brookes, '"Aristocrats of knowledge": Māori anthropologists and the survival of the "race"', in Paul et al. (eds), *Eugenics at the Edges of Empire*, pp. 267–88.
33. Jacqueline Leckie, 'In defence of race and Empire: The White New Zealand League at Pukekohe', *New Zealand Journal of History*, vol. 19, no. 2, 1985, pp. 103–29.
34. P.S. O'Connor, 'Keeping New Zealand white, 1908–1920', *New Zealand Journal of History*, vol. 2, no. 1, 1968, pp. 41–65.
35. Brian Moloughney and John Stenhouse '"Drug-besotten, sin-begotten fiends of filth": New Zealanders and the oriental other, 1850–1920', *New Zealand Journal of History*, vol. 33, no. 1, 1999, pp. 47, 50.

36. Philip Ferguson, 'The making of a white New Zealand policy: Nationalism, citizenship and the exclusion of the Chinese, 1880–1920' (PhD thesis, University of Canterbury, 2003), p. 252.
37. *New Zealand Parliamentary Debates* (hereafter *NZPD*), vol. 187, 1920, p. 905.
38. Glynn Barratt, 'The enemy that never was: The New Zealand "Russian scare" of 1870–1885', *New Zealand Slavonic Journal*, vol. 1, 1976, pp. 13–33; Alexander Trapeznik, 'New Zealand's Perceptions of the Russian Revolution of 1917', *Revolutionary Russia*, vol. 19, no. 1, 2006, p. 66; Tony Wilson, 'Defeating the "red menace": "Russophobia" and New Zealand–Russian relations from the Tsars to Stalin', in Alexander Trapeznik and Aaron Fox (eds), *Lenin's Legacy Down Under: New Zealand's Cold War* (Dunedin: University of Otago Press, 2004), pp. 99–102.
39. Sternhell, *The Birth of Fascist Ideology*, chapter 4.
40. Marinus La Rooij, 'Political antisemitism in New Zealand during the Great Depression: A case study in the myth of the Jewish world conspiracy' (MA thesis, Victoria University of Wellington, 1988), pp. 13–14. There were no fewer than 33 different monetary reform organisations represented at an October 1932 conference – see Minutes of special meeting of Hawke's Bay provincial district, 15 October 1932, Hawke's Bay branch minute book 1928–1936, New Zealand Farmers' Union papers, MSY-0288, Alexander Turnbull Library, Wellington (hereafter ATL); circular from Wynford O. Beere c. October 1932, printed matter associated with the Federation of Monetary Reform Associations 1932, Arthur Nelson Field papers, MS-Papers-8615-052 (hereafter Field papers), ATL.
41. Robin Clifton, 'Douglas Credit and the Labour Party, 1930–1935' (MA thesis, Victoria University of Wellington, 1961), pp. 210–16, 265–67.
42. *New World*, 1 June 1933, p. 6; Clifton, 'Douglas Credit and the Labour Party', pp. 97–98; Barry Gustafson, *The First Fifty Years: A history of the New Zealand National Party* (Auckland: Reed Methuen, 1986), p. 4.
43. Baiba Berzins. 'Douglas Credit and the A.L.P.', *Labour History*, vol. 17, 1969, pp. 154–55.
44. Clifton, 'Douglas Credit and the Labour Party', pp. 97–102.
45. Spoonley, *The Politics of Nostalgia*, pp. 17, 54–57.
46. Andrew Moore, *The Secret Army and the Premier: Conservative paramilitary organisations in New South Wales, 1930–32* (Kensington: New South Wales University Press, 1989); Michael Cathcart, *Defending the National Tuckshop: Australia's secret army intrigue of 1931* (Fitzroy: McPhee Gribble, 1988); Andrew Moore, *The Right Road: A history of right-wing politics in Australia* (Melbourne: Oxford University Press, 1995), chapter 3.
47. There is a robust body of literature on the New Guard, which is summarised in Matthew Cunningham, 'Australian fascism? A revisionist analysis of the ideology of the New Guard', *Politics, Religion & Ideology*, vol. 13, no. 3, 2012, pp. 375–93.
48. Matthew Cunningham, *Mobilising the Masses: Populist conservative movements in Australia and New Zealand during the Great Depression* (Canberra: Australian National University Press, 2022), p. 20; Matthew Cunningham, 'Massey's Cossacks reborn? Public and private counterrevolutionary preparations in New Zealand, 1920–1921' (currently seeking publication).
49. Cunningham, *Mobilising the masses*, p. 232.
50. Ibid.
51. Paul Spoonley and Helen Cox, *Report no. 11: Antisemitism in New Zealand since 1945* (Wellington: New Zealand Jewish Council, 1982), p. 4.
52. James Belich, *Paradise Reforged: A history of the New Zealanders from the 1880s to the year 2000* (Auckland: Penguin, 2001), pp. 297–99.
53. Spoonley, *The Politics of Nostalgia*, pp. 23–29.
54. Ibid., pp. 59–61.

55. Marinus La Rooij, 'Arthur Nelson Field: Kiwi theoretician of the Australian radical right?', *Labour History*, vol. 89, 2005, pp. 37–54.
56. For more information on these groups, see Spoonley, *The Politics of Nostalgia*, chapters 5–6; Paul Spoonley, 'New Zealand first!: The extreme right and politics in New Zealand, 1961–1981', *Political Science*, vol. 33, no. 2, 1981, pp. 99–126; Harvey Stephen Buchman, 'The political thought of the New Zealand League of Rights' (MA thesis, University of Waikato, 1983); David Harcourt, *Everyone Wants to be Fuehrer: National socialism in Australia and New Zealand* (Cremorne: Angus & Robertson, 1972), pp. 134–39; *Salient*, 6 May 1970, pp. 10–17.
57. Richard Hill, *Anti-treatyism and Anti-scholarship: An analysis of anti-treatyist writings*, Treaty of Waitangi Research Unit Occasional Paper no. 8 (Wellington: Victoria University of Wellington, 2002).
58. Charlotte Bennett, 'The New Zealand history wars', Hist419 research essay, University of Wellington, 2010, p. 10.
59. Hainsworth, *The Politics of the Extreme Right*, p. 2.
60. Mudde, *The Far Right Today*, pp. 27–40.
61. Ibid., pp. 99–101.
62. Eatwell and Goodwin, *National populism*, pp. xxi–xxv.
63. Rydgren (ed.), *The Oxford Handbook of the Radical Right*, pp. 7–10.
64. Hainsworth, *The Politics of the Extreme Right*, p. 10.
65. Traverso, *The New Faces of Fascism*, p. 6.
66. Ibid., p. 184. Traverso sees Islamic extremism as filling the same utopian need.
67. See for example Gregory Melleuish, 'Populism and conservatism in Australian political thought', in Paul Boreham et al. (eds), *The Politics of Australian Society: Political issues for the new century* (Sydney: Longman, 2000), pp. 51–64; Geoffrey Stokes, 'One Nation and Australian populism', in Michael Leach, Geoff Stokes and Ian M. Ward (eds), *The Rise and Fall of One Nation* (Brisbane: University of Queensland Press, 2000), pp. 23–41; Bligh Grant et al., *The Rise of Right-populism: Pauline Hanson's One Nation and Australian politics* (Singapore: Springer, 2019); Anna Broinowski, *Please Explain: The rise, fall and rise again of Pauline Hanson* (Sydney: Penguin Random House, 2017); Murray Goot, 'Pauline Hanson's One Nation: extreme right, centre party or extreme left?' *Labour History*, vol. 89, 2005, pp. 101–19.
68. Andy Fleming and Aurelian Mondon, 'The radical right in Australia', in Rydgren (ed.), *The Oxford Handbook of the Radical Right*, pp. 650–62.
69. Barry Gustafson, 'Populist roots of political leadership in New Zealand', in Raymond Miller and Michael Mintrom (eds), *Political Leadership in New Zealand* (Auckland: Auckland University Press, 2006), pp. 51–69; Ben Thomas McLachlan, 'In search of a New Zealand populism: Heresthetics, character and populist political leadership' (MA thesis, Victoria University of Wellington, 2013); Raymond Miller, 'New Zealand First', in Hans-Georg Betz and Stefan Immerfall (eds), *The New Politics of the Right: Neo-populist parties and movements in established democracies* (New York: St Martin's Press, 1998); Claire Haeg, *The Cross of Gold Revisited: Neo-populist party emergence in Australia, Canada, and New Zealand* (Berlin: VDM Verlag, 2009).
70. Benjamin Moffitt, 'Populism in Australia and New Zealand', in Kaltwasser et al. (eds), 'Populism: An overview', pp. 121–39.
71. Moffitt, 'Populism in Australia and New Zealand', p. 132.
72. Fleming and Mondon, 'The radical right in Australia', p. 662.
73. Paul Spoonley and Philip Gendall, 'Welcome to our world: Attitudes to immigrants and immigration', in Andrew Trlin et al. (eds), *New Zealand*

and International Migration: A digest and bibliography (number 5) (Auckland: Massey University Press, 2010), p. 136.

74. Murdoch Stevens, 'Refugee resettlement and activism in New Zealand', Forced Migration Review, February 2017: www.fmreview.org/resettlement/stephens
75. Moffitt, 'Populism in Australia and New Zealand', pp. 127–28.
76. Byron Clark, 'The crowded mess on NZ's populist right', Fightback, 22 September 2020: https://fightback.org.nz/2020/09/22/the-crowded-mess-on-nzs-populist-right/
77. Kate Hannah, Sanjana Hattotuwa and Kayli Taylor, 'Working paper: Mis- and disinformation in Aotearoa New Zealand from 17 August to 5 November 2021', The Disinformation Project, November 2021: www.tepunahamatatini.ac.nz/2021/11/09/mis-and-disinformation/
78. Ibid., pp. 3, 5.
79. 'A protest where voices united, but agendas diverged', Stuff, 10 November 2021: www.stuff.co.nz/national/politics/opinion/126932706/a-protest-where-voices-united-but-agendas-diverged
80. Spoonley, *The Politics of Nostalgia*, pp. 29–44.
81. Ibid., p. 13.
82. Moore, *The Right Road*, pp. 2–4.
83. Dr Muriel Newman, 'Merry Christmas and Happy New Year!', New Zealand Centre for Political Research, 22 December 2021: https://nzcpr.com/merry-christmas-and-happy-new-year/
84. Stephanie Coontz, *The Way We Never Were: American families and the nostalgia trap* (New York: Basic Books, 2000), p. x.
85. Richard Hofstader, 'The paranoid style in American politics', Harper's Magazine, November 1964: https://harpers.org/archive/1964/11/the-paranoid-style-in-american-politics/
86. Harold Moores, 'The rise of the Protestant Political Association: Sectarianism in New Zealand during World War One' (MA thesis, University of Auckland, 1966), p. 106; Buchman, 'The political thought of the New Zealand League of Rights', p. 151; 'Who we are', New Conservatives Party: www.newconservative.org.nz/who-are-new-conservative/
87. T.H. Marshall, *Citizenship and Social Class: And other essays* (Cambridge: Cambridge University Press, 1950), pp. 1–85.
88. See for example Peter Gourevitch, *Politics in Hard Times: Comparative responses to international economic crises* (New York: Cornell University Press, 1986); Manuel Funke et al., 'Going to extremes: Politics after financial crises, 1870–2014', *European Economic Review*, vol. 88, 2016, pp. 227–60.
89. David Scott, 'Impacts of the Global Financial Crisis on earnings of tertiary graduates in New Zealand', Education Counts, May 2020: www.educationcounts.govt.nz/publications/tertiary_education_all/impacts-of-the-global-financial-crisis-on-earnings-of-tertiary-graduates-in-new-zealand
90. 'The social report 2016: Te pūrongo orange ngā tangata – unemployment', Ministry of Social Development, June 2016: https://socialreport.msd.govt.nz/paid-work/unemployment.html
91. Spoonley, *The Politics of Nostalgia*, pp. 41–44.
92. Ibid., p. 114.
93. Jarrod Gilbert and Ben Elley, 'Shaved heads and sonnenrads: Comparing white supremacist skinheads and the alt-right in New Zealand', *Kōtuitui: New Zealand Journal of Social Sciences online*, vol. 15, no. 2, 2020, pp. 280–94.
94. Byron Clark, 'The genocide that inspired the Christchurch terrorist', Fightback, 24 March 2021: https://fightback.org.nz/2021/03/24/the-genocide-that-inspired-the-christchurch-terrorist/
95. A relatively recent summary of the literature to date can be found in Claire Frances Gray, 'White privilege: Exploring the (in)visibility of Pākehā whiteness' (MA thesis, University of Canterbury, 2012), chapter 2.

CHAPTER ONE

1. Translated by Merimeri Penfold in Anne Salmond, *Two Worlds: First meetings between Māori and Europeans 1642–1772* (Auckland: Viking, Penguin, 1991), p. 62.
2. Waitangi Tribunal, *Hauora: Report on stage one of the health services and outcomes kaupapa inquiry* (Wellington: Legislation Direct, 2019).
3. Waitangi Tribunal, *Haumaru: The COVID-19 priority report* (Wellington: Waitangi Tribunal, 2021).
4. Gustav Jahoda, *Images of Savages: Ancient roots of modern prejudice in western culture* (London: Routledge, 1999).
5. C.W. Smith, 'Kimihia te maramatanga: Colonisation and iwi development' (MA thesis, University of Auckland, 1994).
6. Steven Newcomb, *Pagans in the Promised Land: Decoding the doctrine of Christian discovery* (Golden: Fulcrum Publishing, 2008).
7. Linda Tuhiwai Smith, *Decolonising Methodologies: Research and indigenous peoples*, 2nd edn, (London: Zed Books, 2012); Roxanne Dunbar-Oritz, *An Indigenous Peoples' History of the United States* (Boston: Beacon Press, 2014); Glen Sean Coulthard, *Red Skin, White Masks: Rejecting the colonial politics of recognition* (Minneapolis: University of Minnesota Press, 2014).
8. Leonie Pihama, 'Tihei Mauri Ora, honouring our voices: Mana wahine as a kaupapa Māori theoretical framework' (PhD thesis, University of Auckland, 2001), p. 167.
9. David Bedggood, *Rich and Poor in New Zealand* (Auckland: George Allen & Unwin, 1980).
10. Ibid., p. 24.
11. Paul Spoonley, *Racism and Ethnicity: Critical issues in New Zealand society* (Auckland: Oxford University Press, 1988).
12. Ranginui Walker, *Ka Whawhai Tonu Matou: Struggle without end* (Auckland: Penguin, 1990, 1996); Paul Spoonley et al., *Ngā Patai: Racism and ethnic relations in Aotearoa/New Zealand* (Palmerston North: Dunmore Press, 1996); Dunbar-Oritz, *An Indigenous Peoples' History of the United States.*
13. Bronwen Douglas, 'Climate to crania: Science and the racialization of human difference', in Bronwen Douglas and Chris Ballard (eds), *Foreign Bodies: Oceania and the science of race 1750–1940* (Canberra: Australian National University Press, 2008), p. 33.
14. Stephen Jay Gould, *The Mismeasure of Man* (New York: W.W. Norton & Company, 1981).
15. Ranginui Walker, 'Reclaiming Maori education', in Jessica Hutchings and Jenny Lee-Morgan (eds), *Decolonisation in Aotearoa: Education, research and practice* (Wellington: NZCER Press, 2006), p. 19.
16. D.T. Goldberg, *Anatomy of Racism* (Minneapolis: University of Minnesota Press, 1990).
17. Steve Newcomb, 'Five hundred years of injustice: The legacy of fifteenth century religious prejudice', *Shaman's Drum Journal*, Fall, 1992, p. 18.
18. O. Lyons, '400 years of hostility to Native Americans', Albany Times Union, 9 August 2009: www.onondaganation.org/mediafiles/pdfs/un/Doctrine%20of%20Discovery.pdf, p. B1.
19. 'Iwi at forum urges repudiation of doctrine of discovery', Radio New Zealand, 1 November 2019: www.rnz.co.nz/news/national/402309/iwi-at-forum-urges-repudiation-of-doctrine-of-discovery
20. Charles Darwin, *The Origin of Species by Means of Natural Selection* (London: J. Murray, 1859).
21. Adrian Desmond and James Moore, *Darwin* (London: Penguin, 1991).
22. Darwin, *The Origin of Species.*
23. Elazar Barkan, 'Reevaluating progressive eugenics: Herbert Spencer Jennings and the 1924 immigration legislation', *Journal of the History of Biology*, vol. 24, no. 1, 1991, pp. 91–112.
24. Desmond and Moore, *Darwin*, p. 580.
25. G.E. Allen, 'Essays on science and society. Is a new eugenics afoot?', *Science*, vol. 294, no. 5540, 2001, p. 59.

26. J. Daniels and V. Houghton, 'Jensen, Eysenck and the eclipse of the Garlton paradigm', in K. Richardson and D. Spears (eds), *Race, culture and intelligence* (London: Penguin, 1972).
27. Clyde Chitty, *Eugenics, Race and Intelligence in Education* (London: Bloomsbury, 2009).
28. Daniels and Houghton, 'Jensen, Eysenck and the Eclipse of the Garlton paradigm', p. 76.
29. Cited in Desmond and Moore, *Darwin*, pp. 174–75.
30. Salmond, *Two Worlds*.
31. Desmond and Moore, *Darwin*.
32. Ibid.
33. A.S. Thomson, *The Story of New Zealand: Past and present, savage and civilized* (London: J. Murray, 1859), p. 81.
34. Leonie Pihama, 'Tungia te Ururua, Kia Tupu Whakaritorito Te Tupu o te Harakeke: A critical analysis of parents as first teachers' (MA thesis, University of Auckland, 1993).
35. C. Dalli, 'Policy agendas for children's lives', *New Zealand Journal of Educational Studies*, vol. 27, no. 1, 1992, pp. 53–67.
36. Hilary Stace, 'Moving beyond love and luck: Building right relationships and respecting lived experience in New Zealand autism policy' (PhD thesis, Victoria University of Wellington, 2011), p. 106.
37. Cited in Erik Olssen, 'Truby King and the Plunket Society: An analysis of a prescriptive ideology', *New Zealand Journal of History*, vol. 15, no. 1, 1981, p. 6.
38. Ibid., p. 5.
39. Cherryl Smith and Paul Reynolds, *To Tatou Hokakatanga: Action and intervention in sexual and reproductive health. A report prepared for the Health Research Council of New Zealand* (Wellington: Te Puawai Tapu, 2006).
40. T. Taylor, 'Thomas Hunter and the campaign against eugenics', *New Zealand Journal of History*, vol. 29, no. 2, 2005, pp. 194–214.
41. *New Zealand Truth*, 3 March 1917, p. 8.
42. Elsdon Best, *The Maori as He Was: A brief account of Maori life as it was in pre-European days* (Wellington: Dominion Museum, 1924), p. 6.
43. Quoted in Elsdon Best, *Maori Religion and Mythology, Part One* (Wellington, Dominion Museum, 1924), p. 35.
44. Edward Markham, *New Zealand or Recollections of It* (Wellington: R.E. Owen, 1963), p. 83.
45. P.J. Fleming, 'Eugenics in New Zealand 1900–1940' (MA thesis, Massey University, 1981); Hilary Stace, 'Statement of Hilary Stace to the Royal Commission of Inquiry into historical abuse in state care and in the care of faith-based institutions', Royal Commission, October/November 2019: www.abuseincare.org.nz/assets/Uploads/Documents/Public-Hearings/Contextual/12.-Hilary-Stace.pdf
46. Stace, 'Moving beyond love and luck'.
47. Ibid.
48. Barbara Brookes, '"Aristocrats of knowledge": Māori anthropologists and the survival of the "race"', in Diane B. Paul, John Stenhouse and Hamish G. Spencer (eds), *Eugenics at the Edges of Empire: New Zealand, Australia, Canada and South Africa* (London: Palgrave Macmillan, 2018), p. 269.
49. Mason Durie, *Whaiora: Maori health development*, 2nd edn (London: Oxford University Press, 1998), p. 44.
50. Taylor, 'Thomas Hunter and the campaign against eugenics', pp. 196–97.
51. Quoted in Smith et al., *To Tatou Hokakatanga*, p. 58.
52. Cited in Emma Gattey, 'Sir Robert Stout as freethinker and eugenics enthusiast', in Paul, Stenhouse and Spencer (eds), *Eugenics at the Edges of Empire*, p. 205.
53. Quoted in Smith and Reynolds, *To Taou Hakakatanga*, p. 58.
54. Report of the Committee of Inquiry appointed by the Hon. Sir Maui Pomare, K.B.E., C.M.G., Minister of Health, *Appendices to the Journals of the House of Representatives* (hereafter *AJHR*), 1925 Session I, H-31a, p. 23.

55. Helen Smyth, *Rocking the Cradle: Contraception, sex and politics in New Zealand* (Wellington: Steele Roberts, 2000), p. 15.
56. J. Forster and P. Ramsay, 'Migration, Education and Occupation: The Maori population 1936–66', in J. Forster (ed.), *Social Process in New Zealand: Readings in sociology* (Auckland: Longman Paul, 1969); Department of Education, 'The education of Maori children: A review', *Education*, vol. 20, no. 4, 1971.
57. Cited in Smyth, *Rocking the Cradle*, p. 122.
58. Leonie Pihama, *Overview of Māori Teen Pregnancy* (Wellington: Families Commission, 2011), pp. 10–11.
59. Pihama, 'Tungia te Ururua'.
60. L.J. Woodward et al., 'Teenage pregnancy: Cause for concern', *New Zealand Medical* Journal, vol. 114, no. 1135, 2001, pp. 301–3.
61. 'Te Kuku O Te Manawa – Ka puta te riri, ka momori te ngākau, ka heke ngā roimata mo tōku pēpi', Office of the Childrens Commissioner, 2020: www.occ.org.nz/assets/Uploads/TKTM-JUNE2020-Final.pdf
62. Ian Pool, *Colonisation and Development in New Zealand Between 1769 and 1900: The seeds of Rangiatea* (Auckland: Springer, 2015), p. 14.
63. R. Tinirau et al., *Whakatika: How does racism impact on the health of Māori: A national literature review for the Whakatika Research Project* (Whanganui: Te Atawhai o Te Ao Charitable Trust, 2021), p. 28.
64. Waitangi Tribunal, *Hauora*.
65. R. Harris et al., 'Racism and health: The relationship between experience of racial discrimination and health in New Zealand', *Social Science and Medicine*, vol. 63, no. 6, 2006, pp. 1428–41; B. Robson and R. Harris (eds), *Hauora: Maori standards of health IV. A study of the years 2000–2005* (Wellington: Te Rōpū Rangahau Hauora a Eru Pōmare, 2007); B.A. Borell et al., '"It's hard at the top but it's a whole lot easier than being at the bottom": The role of privilege in understanding disparities in Aotearoa/New Zealand', *Race / Ethnicity: Multidisciplinary Global Contexts*, vol. 3, no. 1, 2009, pp. 29–30; Leonie Pihama et al., *He Oranga Ngākau: Māori approaches to trauma informed care. Report to Health Research Council* (Hamilton: Te Kotahi Research Institute, 2020).
66. Waitangi Tribunal, *Hauora*.
67. Ian Pool, 'The effects of the 1918 pandemic of Influenza on the Maori population of New Zealand', *Bulletin of the History of Medicine*, vol. 47, no. 3, 1973, pp. 273–81; Geoffrey Rice, *Black November: The 1918 influenza pandemic in New Zealand* (Christchurch: Canterbury University Press, 2005); Emma Espiner, 'New Zealand must learn lessons of 1918 pandemic and protect Māori from Covid-19', The Guardian, 25 March 2020: www.theguardian.com/commentisfree/2020/mar/26/new-zealand-must-learn-lessons-of-1918-pandemic-and-protect-maori-from-covid-19; New Zealand Māori Council, 'Covid-19: Guidance for Māori and Māori communities/organisations', National Digital Heritage Archive, March 2020: https://ndhadeliver.natlib.govt.nz/delivery/DeliveryManagerServlet?dps_pid=IE53334142
68. Leonie Pihama and Marjorie Lipsham, 'Noho Haumaru: Reflecting on Māori approaches to staying safe during Covid-19 in Aotearoa', *Journal of Indigenous Social Development*, vol. 9, no. 3, 2020, p. 93.
69. Mark Mosley, 'Viewpoint: COVID-19 and eugenics in 2020', *Emergency Medicine News*, vol. 42, 2020, p. 3.
70. P. Reid, 'About our rōpū', Te Rōpū Whakakaupapa Urutā, 2020: www.uruta.maori.nz/about; Pihama and Lipsham, 'Noho Haumaru'.
71. Nicholas Steyn et al., 'Estimated inequities in COVID-19 infection fatality rates by ethnicity for Aotearoa New Zealand', *New Zealand Medical Journal*, vol. 133, no. 1521, 2020, pp. 28–39.

72. Waitangi Tribunal, *Haumaru*.
73. Borell et al., '"It's hard at the top"'; P. King et al., 'COVID-19 and Māori health – when equity is more than a word', Te Rōpu Whakakaupapa Urutā, 2020: www.uruta.maori.nz/when-equity-is-more-than-a-word; R. Jones, 'Why equity for Māori must be prioritised during the Covid-19 response', University of Auckland website, 20 March 2020: www.auckland.ac.nz/en/news/2020/03/20/equity-maori-prioritised-covid-19-response.html

CHAPTER TWO

1. Stevan Eldred-Grigg and Zeng Dazheng, *White Ghosts, Yellow Peril: China and New Zealand 1790–1950*, (Dunedin: Otago University Press, 2014).
2. These seven colonies being New South Wales, New Zealand, Queensland, South Australia, Tasmania, Victoria and Western Australia.
3. Judith Bassett, 'Sir Harry Atkinson and the conservative faction in New Zealand politics, 1879–1890', *New Zealand Journal of History*, vol. 2, no. 2, 1968, pp. 130–47.
4. *NZPD*, vol. 38, 1881, p. 68.
5. When as premier in 1880 he was petitioned by the Christchurch Knight of Labour movement in the midst of a depression, he reportedly lectured them on their moral obligations and told them that 'you must depend upon yourselves and look to yourselves more than you do' as he had done. His was the last of the conservative 'Continuous Ministry' before the Liberal era. James Drummond, *The Life and Work of Richard John Seddon* (Christchurch: Whitcombe & Tombs, 1907), p. 92.
6. *NZPD*, vol. 38, 1881, pp. 208–9.
7. Ibid., p. 239.
8. Ibid., p. 213.
9. Ibid., p. 216.
10. Ibid., p. 212.
11. Ibid., pp. 74–75.
12. Ibid., pp. 212–34.
13. Ibid., p. 69.
14. *NZPD*, vol. 36, 1880, p. 95.
15. Ibid., p. 94.
16. *NZPD*, vol. 38, 1881, p. 123.
17. Ibid., p. 244.
18. Ibid., pp. 241–42.
19. Ibid., p. 210.
20. Philip Ferguson, 'The making of a white New Zealand policy: nationalism, citizenship and the exclusion of the Chinese, 1880–1920' (PhD thesis, University of Canterbury, 2003).
21. A. Mondon and Aaron Winter, 'Whiteness, populism and the racialisation of the working class in the United Kingdom and the United States', *Identities*, vol. 26, no. 5, 2019, pp. 510–28.
22. *Evening Post*, 12 July 1879, p. 3.
23. *Evening Post*, 29 July 1879, p. 2.
24. Ibid.
25. *Grey River Argus*, 21 October 1879. p. 2.
26. Nevertheless, there was still political capital to be made against the influx of the immigrants from Germany and Sweden who were, like the Chinese, willing to work for small remuneration and reduce wages for the others.
27. *NZPD*, vol. 38, 1881, p. 115.
28. Alastair Bonnett, 'How the British working class became white: The symbolic (re) formation of racialized capitalism', *Journal of Historical Sociology*, vol. 11, no. 3, 2002, pp. 316–40. Bonnett also noted in the late nineteenth century 'a hardening, an increased literalness, of interpretations of the catholic Irish as racially other to, and as darker in complexion to other Britons, more especially the English'.
29. This strategy echoes the political rhetoric of the 'freeborn Englishman', which simply assumes as a 'birthright' the revolutionary demand for a new right to livelihood and to democratic participation. E.P. Thompson, *The Making of the English Working Class* (London: Penguin, 1991), pp. 84–111.
30. *Lyttelton Times*, 7 January 1879, cited by Ferguson, 'The making of a white New Zealand policy', pp. 91–92.

31. *South Canterbury Times*, 23 May 1881, p. 2.
32. *Daily Telegraph*, 28 April 1881, p. 2.
33. Ferguson, 'The making of a white New Zealand policy', pp. 167–70.
34. *NZPD*, vol. 38, 1881, p. 248.
35. Ibid., p. 215.
36. Ibid., pp. 211, 241.
37. Ibid., p. 215.
38. Ibid., pp. 242–43.
39. Ibid., p. 245.
40. Ibid., p. 70.
41. *Press*, 13 June 1887, p. 2.
42. *NZPD*, vol. 38, 1881, p. 244.
43. *NZPD*, vol. 57, 1887, p. 239.
44. *Press*, 25 April 1895, p. 6.
45. *NZPD*, vol. 92, 1896, p. 4.
46. *NZPD*, vol. 94, 1896, p. 312.
47. *NZPD*, vol. 92, 1896, p. 373.
48. Ibid., p. 449.
49. *Evening Star*, 18 April 1896, p. 2.
50. *Press*, 25 April 1895, p. 4.
51. *NZPD*, vol. 92, 1896, pp. 255, 378–79.
52. Ibid., p. 246.
53. Frances Porter, 'Chinese immigration to New Zealand in the nineteenth century' (MA thesis, University of New Zealand, 1948), quoted in Ferguson, 'The making of a white New Zealand policy', p. 23.
54. *Star*, 12 July 1907, p. 2.
55. *Otago Witness*, 31 July 1907, p. 12.
56. Ibid.
57. *NZPD*, vol. 142, 1907, p. 963.
58. *NZPD*, vol. 137, 1906, p. 34.
59. *NZPD*, vol. 187, 1920, pp. 905–8.
60. *Press*, 13 August 1890, p. 5.
61. *New Zealand Mail*, 28 May 1896, p. 31.
62. *Lyttleton Times*, 15 March 1912, p. 5.
63. *Franklin Times*, 22 January 1926, p. 5; also Jacqueline Leckie, 'In defence of race and empire: The White New Zealand League at Pukekohe', *New Zealand Journal of History*, vol. 19, no. 2, 1985, pp. 103–29.
64. *Star*, 24 April 1895, p. 2.
65. *Evening Post*, 14 September 1897, p. 5; *Wairarapa Daily Times*, 12 June 1897, p. 3.
66. Lynette Shum, 'Remembering Chinatown', in Manying Ip (ed.), *Unfolding History, Evolving Identity*, (Auckland: Auckland University Press, 2003), pp. 82–83.
67. *Evening Post*, 7 September 1888, p. 3.
68. *Inangahua Times*, 9 September 1891, p. 2.
69. *New Zealand Truth*, 24 December 1910, p. 1.
70. *Cyclopedia of New Zealand* (Wellington: Cyclopedia Co., 1897), p. 551.
71. *Otago Daily Times*, 18 April 1896, p. 6.
72. *New Zealand Times*, 5 August 1895, p. 3.
73. *Evening Star*, 18 April 1896, p. 2.
74. Ibid.
75. *Dominion*, 1 April 1914, p. 7.
76. *Press*, 19 November 1913, p. 9.
77. *Maoriland Worker*, 1 December 1920, p. 2. The editorial was written seven years later, but looking back at the 1913 industrial dispute.
78. Ibid., 12 April 1912, p. 1.
79. *NZPD*, vol. 185, 1920, p. 533.
80. Ferguson argued that this was not because of the spread of international socialism, but 'because the labour movement had largely achieved what it wanted' with the passing of the 1920 law. Ferguson, 'The making of a white New Zealand policy', p. 248.
81. *Maoriland Worker*, 31 August 1921, p. 10.
82. Jarrod Gilbert, *Patched: The history of gangs in New Zealand* (Auckland: Auckland University Press, 2013), p. 140.

CHAPTER THREE

1. See Julie Ebner, *Going Dark: The secret social lives of extremists* (London: Bloomsbury, 2020), p. 236.
2. See 'Two years ago, they marched in Charlottesville. Where are they now?', ADL, 8 August 2019: www.adl.org/blog/two-years-ago-they-marched-in-charlottesville-where-are-they-now
3. For example, the victims of the 2011 far-right terror attack in Norway were predominantly ethnic Norwegians – see 'Foreløpig navneliste etter terroren mot Norge 22. Juli', NRK: www.nrk.no/norge/savnede-og-drepte-etter-22.-juli-1.7724498
4. These main biographical sources are entertaining accounts of Terry's life by

someone who knew him in later life, but are uncritical, unreferenced and exclude important material – see Frank Tod, *Lionel Terry: The Making of a Madman* (Dunedin: Otago Foundation Books, 1977); Frank Tod, 'Terry, Edward Lionel', Te Ara – the Encyclopaedia of New Zealand: https://teara.govt.nz/en/biographies/3t27/terry-edward-lionel/sources

5. *Daily Mirror*, 13 November 1905, p. 5.
6. Edward Lionel Terry, Regimental number: 390, WO 400/279/390, The National Archives, United Kingdom.
7. Tod, *Lionel Terry*, p. 13.
8. *Daily Mirror*, 31 October 1905, p. 3.
9. For the origins of the war see Denis Judd and Keith Surridge, *The Boer War – A history* (London: I.B. Tauris, 2013), pp. 32ff.
10. Dr Edgar Strong to Chief Inspector, Southern Rhodesian Constabulary, 16 November 1905, 'Murder of Joe Kum Yung by Lionel Terry', R20119991, ANZ.
11. *Otago Witness*, 3 January 1906, p. 14.
12. Terry, 'Making of a Madman', reprinted in *Lionel Terry*, p. 198.
13. See A. Ross McCormack, *Reformers, Rebels, and Revolutionaries: The western Canadian radical movement 1899–1919* (Toronto: University of Toronto Press, 1977).
14. See Patricia E. Roy, *A White Man's Province: British Columbia politicians and Chinese and Japanese immigrants 1858–1914* (Vancouver: UBC Press, 1989).
15. *Hamilton Times* (Ontario), 9 October 1905, p. 153; *Victoria Daily Colonist*, 24 December 1905, p. 16; *Victoria Daily Colonist*, 24 November 1906, p. 7.
16. Terry Reksten, *The Dunsmuir Saga* (Vancouver: Douglas & McIntyre, 1991), p. 166.
17. *Victoria Daily Times* (British Columbia), 21 December 1900, p. 4.
18. Quoted in John Hinde, *When Coal Was King: Ladysmith and the coal-mining industry on Vancouver Island* (Vancouver: University of British Columbia Press, 2003), p. 34.
19. *Nanaimo Free Press* (British Columbia), quoted in ibid., pp. 28–29.
20. Mark Leier, 'Ralph Smith', Dictionary of Canadian Biography: www.biographi.ca/en/bio/smith_ralph_14E.html
21. *Nanaimo Free Press*, 11 February 1901, p. 6.
22. Reksten, *The Dunsmuir Saga*, p. 167; *Victoria Daily Times*, 23 January 1901, p. 4.
23. *Nanaimo Free Press*, 7 February 1901, p. 3.
24. *Vancouver Daily World*, 16 March 1901, p. 5.
25. Clarence Karr, 'James Dunsmuir', Dictionary of Canadian Biography: www.biographi.ca/en/bio/dunsmuir_james_14E.html
26. Ross, *Reformers, Rebels and Revolutionaries*, pp. 9, 27.
27. *Nanaimo Free Press*, 1 March 1901, p. 1.
28. *Nanaimo Free Press*, 11 May 1901, p. 2.
29. *Victoria Daily Colonist*, 16 April 1901, p. 4.
30. See Roy, *A White Man's Province*, pp. 104ff.
31. Ibid., pp. 109ff.
32. *Nanaimo Free Press*, 13 April 1901, p. 4.
33. Submission of the Alexandra Miner's Union, Report of the Royal Commission on Chinese and Japanese Immigration, Sessional Paper 54, 1902, pp. 85–86.
34. Roy, *A White Man's Province*, p. 118.
35. *Nanaimo Free Press*, 25 March 1901, p. 2.
36. *Nanaimo Free Press*, 9 May 1901, p. 4.
37. *Nanaimo Free Press*, 4 May 1901, p. 1.
38. *Nanaimo Free Press*, 7 May 1901, p. 3.
39. Ibid., p. 2.
40. *Daily Colonist* (British Columbia), 11 June 1901, p. 1.
41. *Vancouver Daily World*, 27 June 1901, p. 6.
42. *Nanaimo Free Press*, 11 April 1901, p. 4.
43. Roy, *A White Man's Province*, p. 192.
44. See Tom Brooking, *Richard Seddon: King of God's own* (Auckland: Penguin, 2014), pp. 163ff.
45. See G.R. Warburton, 'The attitudes and policies of the New Zealand labour movement towards non-European immigration' (MA thesis, University of Canterbury, 1982), pp. 17ff.

46. See David C. Atkinson, *The Burden of White Supremacy: Containing Asian migration in the British Empire and the United States* (Chapel Hill: University of North Carolina Press, 2017), pp. 23–34.
47. See Matthew 6:19–21, 24.
48. Lionel Terry, *God or Mammon?* (Auckland: Herald, 1902), pp. 2–3.
49. Ibid., p. 4.
50. Ibid., p. 7, his emphasis.
51. *New Zealand Herald*, 21 June 1902 (supplement), p. 5. The 'Britains' refers to the 'home country' and its offshoot settler colonies.
52. *Evening Star*, 13 June 1903, p. 4.
53. *New Zealand Illustrated Magazine*, 1 June 1903, pp. 192–93.
54. Terry, *God or Mammon?*, p. 3.
55. See Atkinson, *The Burden of White Supremacy*, pp. 49–75.
56. See Jeremy Martens, 'Richard Seddon and popular opposition in New Zealand to the introduction of Chinese labour into the Transvaal, 1903–1904', *New Zealand Journal of History*, vol. 42, no. 2, 2008, pp. 176–95.
57. *Wairarapa Daily Times*, 26 September 1899, p. 2.
58. Seddon's interpretation of imperial policy, speaking at Hokitika, *New Zealand Mail*, 20 January 1904, p. 22.
59. *Lyttelton Times*, 24 February 1903, p. 2.
60. Seddon's opposition to Asian immigration was used in the victorious British Liberal Party's 1906 election campaign. For the empire-wide mourning at Seddon's death in 1906 – see Brooking, *Richard Seddon*, pp. 405ff.
61. *New Zealand Times*, 12 January 1904, p. 4.
62. Warburton, 'The attitudes and policies of the New Zealand labour movement', p. 71.
63. Ibid., p. 75.
64. *New Zealand Times*, 27 January 1904, p. 4.
65. Claire Hirshfield, 'The Anglo-Boer War and the issue of Jewish culpability', *Journal of Contemporary History*, vol. 15, 1980, pp. 619–31.
66. Ibid., pp. 620–21.
67. *New Zealand Free Lance*, 24 January 1903, p. 14.
68. *New Zealand Free Lance*, 16 January 1904, p. 6.
69. *New Zealand Mail*, 10 February 1904, p. 23.
70. *New Zealand Times*, 8 February 1904, p. 7.
71. *New Zealand Times*, 2 February 1904, p. 6.
72. *New Zealand Mail*, 10 February 1904, p. 5 (supplement).
73. See, for example, A.N. Field's journey to radical antisemitism in 1930s New Zealand: Marinus La Rooij, 'From colonial conservative to international antisemite: The life and work of Arthur Nelson Field', *Journal of Contemporary History*, vol. 37, no. 2, April 2002, pp. 223–39.
74. *Free Lance*, 11 June 1904, p. 6.
75. J.A. Hobson, *The War in South Africa* (London: James Nisbet & Co., 1900), pp. 189–97.
76. *Otago Daily Times*, 11 April 1904, p. 5.
77. *Herald* (South Australia), 30 January 1904, p. 4.
78. *Munsey's Magazine*, November 1903, pp. 229–41.
79. *New Zealand Herald*, 2 January 1904, p. 4.
80. *Christchurch Star*, 13 February 1904, p. 2; *Lyttelton Times*, 16 February 1904, p. 4.
81. See G.C. Lebzelter, *Political Anti-Semitism in England 1918–1939* (London: Macmillan, 1978).
82. Lionel Terry, *The Shadow* (Auckland: Wilson & Horton Printers, 1904), p. 8.
83. Ibid., p. 9.
84. Ibid., pp. 6, 9.
85. Ibid., p. 8.
86. *Daily Colonist*, 14 April 1901, p. 1; *Province*, 15 April 1901, p. 2.
87. Terry, *The Shadow*, p. 11.
88. *Mangonui County Times*, 29 November 1904, p. 2.
89. *Waikato Times*, 19 December 1904, p. 2.
90. *Sheffield Daily Telegraph*, 12 April 1905, p. 3.
91. *Gundagai Independent and Pastoral, Agricultural and Mining Advocate*, 26 July 1905, p. 4.
92. *Sydney Mail and New South Wales Advertiser*, 7 June 1905, p. 1406.

93. *Evening Star*, 22 July 1905, p. 11.
94. *Waikato Independent*, 17 August 1905, p. 4.
95. Terry, *The Shadow*, p. 11 refers directly to the protests of the Australasian premiers, led by Seddon.
96. The letter was published in most New Zealand newspapers – see *Southland Times*, 26 September 1905, p. 2.
97. *New Zealand Times*, 22 November 1905, p. 4.
98. Lionel Terry, 'A message to men', unpublished manuscript (*c.* 1913), Lionel Terry papers, Misc-MS-0313/001, Hocken Collections, Dunedin.
99. *New Zealand Worker*, 18 October 1905, p. 4.
100. *New Zealand Worker*, 4 October 1905, p. 2.
101. *New Zealand Worker*, 22 November 1905, p. 5.
102. *Vanguard* (East Sussex), January 1988, p. 7.
103. Kerry Bolton, *The Shadow of Lionel Terry* (Kapiti, Renaissance Press, 2011).

CHAPTER FOUR

1. Keegan Hankes, senior analyst, Southern Poverty Law Centre, quoted in E.J. Dickson, 'The Gilroy Garlic Fest shooter plugged a white power manifesto on Instagram', *Rolling Stone*, 30 July 2019: www.rollingstone.com/culture/culture-news/gilroy-garlic-fest-shooting-santino-legan-864594/
2. Kitty Shropshire, doctoral fellow, Centre for Analysis of the Radical Right, Carnegie Mellon University, personal communication with the author, 31 March 2020.
3. CBS News, 29 July 2019: www.cbsnews.com/news/santino-william-legan-what-we-know-about-the-gilroy-garlic-festival-shooter/
4. www.redbeardright.com
5. This chapter draws on my earlier work, *Ragnar Redbeard: The Antipodean origins of radical fabulist Arthur Desmond* (Paraparaumu: Steele Roberts, 2017), but has been supplemented with additional research.
6. *Vanguard* (East Sussex), 7 July 1884, p. 4.
7. *Daily Telegraph*, 16 December 1884, p. 2.
8. *Hawke's Bay Herald*, 3 October 1887, p. 2.
9. *Poverty Bay Herald*, 18 February 1889, p. 2.
10. *Auckland Star*, 1 March 1889, p. 2.
11. *Bulletin* (Sydney), 23 March 1889, p. 8.
12. *Zealandia*, vol. 1 no. 12, June 1890, pp. 715–22.
13. *Auckland Star*, 26 August 1890, p. 2.
14. Darrell W. Conder, *I Beheld Desmond as Lightening Fall: To Chicago, the story of Arthur Desmond, 'Ragnar Redbeard' and Might Is Right* (Port Townsend: Eluciddomain, 2007), fn. 57.
15. 'Douglas H. Handyside, PhD', preface to 1896 edition of *Might Is Right*, quoted in D. Conder, introduction to D. Conder (ed.), *Might Is Right* (Missouri: Dil Pickle Press, 2005), p. iii, fn. 6 (hereafter 2005 edition of *Might Is Right*).
16. Letters from W.W. Tanner and clippings related to Arthur Desmond, MS-0985-002/062, Hocken Collections, Dunedin (hereafter HC). I am grateful to Marinus La Rooij for providing this research material.
17. W.M. Hughes, *Crusts and Crusades – Tales of bygone days* (Sydney: Angus, 1947), p. 149.
18. *Hard Cash*, vol. 2, no. 3, *c.* 1893, p. 1.
19. *Australian Worker*, 11 May 1927, p. 13.
20. *Daily Standard* (Brisbane), 20 December 1921, p. 8.
21. J.T. Lang, *I Remember* (Sydney: Invincible Press, 1956), p. 9.
22. Conder, 2005 edition of *Might Is Right*, p. 17.
23. Ibid., p. 2.
24. Ibid.
25. Leo Tolstoy, *What is Art? And other essays on art*, trans Aylmer Maude (London: Oxford University Press, 1930), p. 258.
26. *Voice of the People* (New Orleans), IWW, 18 December 1913: https://ecology.iww.org/PDF/VOP/No.23.pdf?bot_test=1
27. Rachel Barrowman 'Desmond, Arthur,' the Dictionary of New Zealand Biography: https://teara.govt.nz/en/biographies/2d9/desmond-arthur

28. Geo. G. Reeve, 'Ragnar Redbeard', *Ross's Monthly* (Melbourne), March–April 1920, p. 4; 'Ragnar Redbeard article 2', *Ross's Monthly*, 6 August 1921, p. 1.
29. A.S. LaVey, *The Satanic Bible* (New York: Avon, 1969).
30. J.A. Lewis, 'Infernal legitimacy', in J.A. Petersen (ed.), *Contemporary Religious Satanism: A critical anthology* (Milton Park: Routledge, 2016).
31. W.R. van Leeuwen, 'Dreamers of the dark: Kerry Bolton and the Order of the Left Hand Path: A case study of a satanic/neo-nazi synthesis' (MA thesis, Waikato University, 2008), pp. 6–7.
32. *The Heretic: Incorporating The Watcher and The Realist*, no. 1, July 1992, Petone, New Zealand.
33. Quoted in van Leeuwen, 'Dreamers of the dark', p. 17.
34. Ibid., p. 14.
35. *The Heretic* [unpaginated].
36. Kerry Bolton, comment on Counter Currents, 27 March 2020: https://counter-currents.com/2020/03/damned-by-amazon/
37. Reeve, 'Ragnar Redbeard part 2', *Windsor and Richmond Gazette*, 10 December 1926, p. 7.
38. R. Jacobs, 'Running with the wolves: Jack London, the cult of masculinity, and "Might is Right"', July 1999: https://web.archive.org/web/20140816012844/, http://london.sonoma.edu/Bibliographies/redbeard.html
39. The 15 March terrorist's manifesto contains allusions to the writings of David Lane, among other far-right ideologues.
40. K. Lane, introduction to *Might Is Right*, Millennial Wotansvolk edition 1999, p. xi: https://archive.org/details/MightIsRight/page/n3/mode/2up
41. Jacobs, 'Running with the wolves'.
42. Ibid.
43. Conder, 2005 edition of *Might Is Right*, p. 41.
44. Ibid., p. 75.
45. Kitty Shropshire, 'The influence of Might is Right in the Gilroy shooting', Centre for Analysis of the Radical Right, Carnegie Mellon University, 16 August 2019: www.radicalrightanalysis.com/2019/08/16/the-influence-of-might-is-right-in-the-gilroy-shooting/
46. https://underworldamusements.com/collections/egoism-individualist-anarchism/products/might-is-right-ragnar-redbeard
47. Shropshire, pers. comm. 31 March 2020. For the National Alliance, see: https://natall.com
48. K. Lane, introduction to *Might Is Right*, p. x.
49. This information is drawn from Dr Shropshire's 2019 article referenced above.
50. Conder, 2005 edition of *Might Is Right*, p. 56.
51. 'Gilroy gunman shared our facebook post', Redbeard Right: http://www.redbeardright.com/2019/08/02/gilroy-gunman-shared-our-facebook-post/

CHAPTER FIVE

1. *Light and Liberty*, 30 June 1914, p. 1.
2. *Dominion*, 18 November 1913, p. 6.
3. James Belich describes the unusually strong loyalty that New Zealand felt towards the Empire as recolonisation – see James Belich, *Paradise Reforged: A history of the New Zealanders from the 1880s to the year 2000* (Auckland: Penguin Press, 2001), pp. 76–85.
4. See *Auckland Star*, 12 July 1916, p. 7; *Press*, 12 July 1916, p. 6; *Otago Daily Times*, 13 July 1916, p. 4; *Free Lance*, 14 July 1916, p. 6.
5. For example: Reform Candidate Handbook 1919, pp. 26–30, Field Pam, NZ REF 1919, ATL details how Reform is a 'workers party'; General Election 1919: A record of the Reform Party in connection with the session on 1919 and other matters, pp. 21–28, Field Pam, NZ REF 1919, ATL lists the ways in which Reform is a 'labour party'. Less of the Liberal Party's election

material has survived; for a summary of why 'moderate labour' should vote for the Liberals see *New Zealand Times*, 15 December 1919, p. 13.

6. The Liberal Party was still active under various names during the period covered in this chapter. However, there was not enough surviving material to judge how much anti-socialist propaganda influenced it.
7. Coates to Stewart, 7 November 1936, MS-0985-002/046, William Downie Stewart Papers, Hocken Collections (here after HC). This letter mentions the destruction of the papers; Michael Bassett advised the author in a discussion that it was Masters.
8. M.A. Noonan, 'The aims of the New Zealand Welfare League 1919–1922', *The University of Auckland Historical Society Annual*, 1969, pp. 28–46; H.S. Moores, 'The rise of the Protestant Political Association' (MA thesis, University of Auckland, 1966).
9. Matthew Cunningham, 'The reactionary and the radical: A comparative analysis of mass sonservative mobilisation in Australia and New Zealand during the Great Depression' (PhD thesis, Victoria University of Wellington, 2015), pp. 61–69; Marinus La Rooij, 'Political antisemitism in New Zealand during the Great Depression: A case study in the myth of the Jewish world conspiracy' (MA thesis, Victoria University of Wellington, 1998), pp. 46–53; Barry Gustafson, *Labour's Path to Political Independence: The origins and establishment of the New Zealand Labour Party, 1900–19* (Auckland: Auckland University Press, 1980), pp. 126–29, 146.
10. P.S. O'Connor, 'Sectarian conflict in New Zealand, 1911–1920', *Political Science*, vol. 19, no. 1, 1967, p. 12; Rory Sweetman, 'New Zealand Catholicism and the Irish issue 1914–1922', *Studies in Church History*, vol. 25, 1989, p. 383.
11. Mark Dunick 'Making rebels: The New Zealand Socialist Party 1901–1913' (MA thesis, Victoria University of Wellington, 2016); Grant Duncan, *Society and Politics: New Zealand social policy*, 2nd edn (Auckland: Person Prentice Hall, 2007), pp. 83–88 has a good summary of the various socialist groups active during this period.
12. D.A. Hamer, *The New Zealand Liberals: The years of power, 1891–1912* (Auckland: Auckland University Press, 1988), pp. 40–43.
13. 'Industrial Unionist: Background', Papers Past website: https://paperspast.natlib.govt.nz/newspapers/industrial-unionist; Peter Clayworth, 'Patrick Hodgens Hickey and IWW: A transnational relationship', in Peter Cole, David Struthers and Kenyon Zimmer (eds), *Wobblies of the World: A global history of the IWW* (London: Pluto Press, 2017), p. 235 points out it was short-lived.
14. Cole, Struthers and Kenyon (eds), 'Introduction', *Wobblies of the World*, p. 14.
15. Ibid.
16. R.M. Burdon, *The New Dominion: A social and political history of New Zealand, 1918–39* (London: Allen & Unwin, 1965), p. 36.
17. Elizabeth Ward, '"For light and liberty": The origins and early development of the Reform Party 1887–1915' (PhD thesis, Massey University, 2018), p. 120.
18. Peter Franks and Jim McAloon, *The New Zealand Labour Party 1916–2016* (Wellington: Victoria University Press, 2016), pp. 51–53.
19. Hamer, *The New Zealand Liberals,* pp. 220–307.
20. *New Zealand Herald*, 17 February 1908, p. 6.
21. Gustafson, *Labour's Path to Political Independence*, pp. 30–31; *Evening Post*, 17 February 1921, p. 7 contains a report of the second Welfare League annual conference which outlines many of these events as the impetus behind the formation of the League.
22. Gustafson, *Labour's Path to Political Independence*, p. 57.
23. *Lyttleton Times*, 28 May 1912, p. 6.
24. *Press*, 6 June 1912, p. 6.
25. Peter Franks, 'Chronology of events', in Melanie Nolan (ed.), *Revolution: The 1913 Great Strike in New Zealand* (Christchurch: Canterbury University Press, 2005), pp. 9–19.

26. For example, the term 'mob rule' was used 200 times in newspapers between 1 October 1913 and 31 December 1913. However, James Taylor argues that public opinion was more split over the strike than many newspapers portrayed: see Taylor, 'Contemporary media portrayals of the 1913 dispute', in Nolan (ed.) *Revolution*, pp. 142–63.
27. *Dominion*, 4 November 1913, p. 9. Also see *Free Lance*, 8 November 1913, p. 1, the cover illustration of which has 'New Zealand' handing a special constable a baton and asking him to defend New Zealand towns from 'mob rule'.
28. Ward, '"For light and liberty"', p. 208.
29. *Light and Liberty*, 21 November 1914, p. 8; James Watson, 'The continuation of politics: Parliamentarians and the Great War', in Steven Loveridge (ed.), *New Zealand Society at War 1914–1918* (Wellington: Victoria University Press, 2016), p. 52.
30. *Press*, 12 July 1916, p. 6.
31. Antony Wood, 'The origins of the first National government: A study in New Zealand wartime politics, 1914–15' (MA thesis, University of Canterbury, 1963), p. 212.
32. Franks and McAloon, *The New Zealand Labour Party 1916–2016*, p. 72.
33. *Manawatu Standard*, 19 June 1917, p. 2.
34. Tony Wilson, 'Defining the "red menace": "Russophobia" and New Zealand-Russian relations from the Tsars to Stalin', in Alexander Trapeznik and Aaron Fox (eds), *Lenin's Legacy Down Under: New Zealand's Cold War* (Dunedin: Otago University Press, 2004), pp. 96–97.
35. Ibid., p. 97.
36. *Dominion*, 16 December 1918, p. 6.
37. *Manawatu Standard*, 13 December 1918, p. 6. For more on Galbraith's later political career see Kerry Taylor, 'The old Bolshevik: Alex Galbraith, the Communist Party and the New Zealand revolution', in Rachael Bell (ed.), *New Zealand Between the Wars* (Auckland: Massey University Press, 2017); *Evening Post*, 16 December 1919, p. 2.
38. Franks and McAloon, *The New Zealand Labour Party 1916–2016*, p. 73.
39. Cunningham, 'The reactionary and the radical', p. 63.
40. *Sun*, 15 March 1919, p. 9.
41. Ibid.
42. Ibid.
43. Graham Langton, 'Harper, Arthur Paul', Dictionary of New Zealand Biography: https://teara.govt.nz/en/biographies/4h17/harper-arthur-paul
44. For Wellington see *Auckland Star*, 31 March 1919, p. 6; for Auckland see *Auckland Star*, 7 May 1919, p. 4; for Christchurch see *Sun*, 2 July 1919, p. 5; for Dunedin see *Otago Daily Times*, 22 October 1919, p. 8. Some other places where Welfare League branches were formed were New Plymouth (*Taranaki Daily Times*, 25 April 1919, p. 4), Palmerston North (*Manawatu Times*, 10 May 1919, p. 4) and Napier (*Hastings Standard*, 24 May 1919, p. 4). A branch was formed in Motueka, possibly the only provincial one in the South Island (*Colonist*, 14 June 1919, p. 4). It is also possible that Harper was aided by some members of the League having been involved in the Federation of New Zealand Patriotic War Relief Societies, which would have given him contacts throughout New Zealand. For a summary of the work of this group, see L.O.H. Tripp, 'War relief and patriotic societies', in H.T.B. Drew (ed.), *The War Effort in New Zealand* (Auckland: Whitcombe & Tombs, 1923).
45. *Maoriland Worker*, 10 December 1919, p. 2. Given the strong anti-Welfare League stance taken by the *Maoriland Worker*, it is difficult to know if this was a business decision or the editor had another motive. For examples of anti-Welfare League material, see *Maoriland Worker*, 16 July 1919, p. 4; *Maoriland Worker*, 10 March 1920, p. 5; *Maoriland Worker*, 29 June 1921, p. 7; *Maoriland Worker*, 11 October 1922, p. 10.
46. See *Sun* 17 March 1919, p. 4; *Evening Post*, 17 March 1919, p. 6; *Taranaki Herald*, 18

March 1919, p. 2; *Marlborough Express*, 21 March 1919, p. 4.

47. *New Zealand Times*, 15 March 1919, p. 6. This was a real issue for Massey – see P.S. O'Connor, 'Some political preoccupations of Mr Massey, 1918–20', *Political Science*, vol. 18, no. 2, 1966, pp. 22–25.
48. Charles Skerrett was a prominent Wellington lawyer and in a law partnership with Harper's cousin, Leonard Tripp – see G.P. Barton, 'Skerrett, Charles Perrin', Dictionary of New Zealand Biography: https://teara.govt.nz/en/biographies/3s21/skerrett-charles-perrin; *Sun*, 15 March 1919, p. 9.
49. *Dominion*, 20 September 1919, p. 6.
50. The first located appeared in *Observer*, 4 October 1919, p. 23.
51. Although the beginning of the Welfare League is well documented, its end is not. The last mention of the League in newspapers appeared in *Evening Post*, 12 July 1941, p. 11, and *Otago Daily Times*, 18 July 1941, p. 2; both articles are drawing on the same material about national savings during a period of war. There is evidence that they may have tried to produce their own newspaper called *Freedom*. However, only the first edition has survived, so it is difficult to know if any more were published beyond this. See New Zealand Welfare League, A.G. Bagnall papers, 89-249-7/04, ATL.
52. *Hastings Standard*, 5 November 1920, p. 3.
53. *Sun*, 22 April 1920, p. 6; *Grey River Argus*, 30 October 1920, p. 2; *Dominion*, 26 November 1920, p. 7; *Evening Post*, 23 February 1922, p. 7.
54. *Dominion*, 22 December 1920, p. 8.
55. Although the number of Welfare League articles drop off in Papers Past from 1921, this is likely caused by some of the regular publishing newspapers not being digitised beyond 1920 at the time this chapter was written, e.g. *Dominion*, *Wairarapa Age*, *Southland Times*, *Wanganui Herald*, *Sun*, *Taranaki Herald* and *Hastings Standard*.
56. *Evening Post*, 17 February 1921, p. 7.
57. New Zealand Welfare League General Report for year ending 31 December 1931, 73-148-089, MS-Group-1543, Field papers.
58. New Zealand Welfare League General Report for year ending 31 December 1931, 73-148-089, MS-Group-1543, Field papers; New Zealand Welfare League General Report for year ending 31 December 1932, 73-148-089, MS-Group-1543, Field papers both mention this. This practice was very noticeable in the early 1930s – for example, the League kept up a long-running letter exchange in the *Otago Daily Times* between July and September 1932.
59. For example, *Marlborough Express*, 15 July 1920, p. 5; *Otago Daily Times*, 16 September 1922, p. 12; *Otago Daily Times*, 12 May 1923, p. 2; *Evening Post*, 4 October 1926, p. 15.
60. For example, *Hastings Standard*, 17 July 1920, p. 5; *Otago Daily Times*, 19 November 1921, p. 7; *Evening Post*, 2 December 1922, p. 9; *Evening Post*, 23 May 1925, p. 13; *Manawatu Standard*, 1 March 1930, p. 4.
61. *Evening Post*, 20 October 1923, p. 13.
62. For example, *Manawatu Standard*, 8 March 1924, p. 12; *Evening Post*, 7 August 1924, p. 10; *Manawatu Standard*, 14 March 1925, p. 3; *Evening Post*, 31 July 1926, p. 15; *Otago Daily Times*, 12 November 1927, p. 26; *Evening Post*, 23 June 1928, p. 17; *Manawatu Standard*, 16 March 1929, p. 4; *Manawatu Standard*, 31 October 1931, p. 10; *Otago Daily Times*, 28 January 1935, p. 11; *Otago Daily Times*, 26 November 1935, p. 8.
63. *Evening Post*, 26 October 1920, p. 6.
64. *Southland Times*, 3 August 1920, p. 7.
65. *Evening Post*, 17 December 1922, p. 2; *Evening Post*, 3 November 1922, p. 8.
66. *Evening Post*, 5 March 1924, p. 9.
67. *Manawatu Standard*, 8 September 1928, p. 2.
68. *Wairarapa Age*, 25 August 1920, p. 6; *Hastings Standard*, 30 August 1920, p. 3. These are samples as these articles appeared in up to seven other newspapers.
69. *Wanganui Herald*, 10 September 1920,

p. 4; *Evening Post*, 20 September 1920, p. 7; *Sun*, 22 September 1920, p. 8; *Hawera and Normanby Star*, 22 September 1920, p. 4; *Evening Post*, 25 September 1920, p. 9. Some of these articles were very popular, appearing in up to nine other newspapers.

70. *Otago Daily Times*, 20 November 1926, p. 9; *Evening Post*, 20 August 1932, p. 12.
71. Taylor, 'The old Bolshevik', pp. 123–24.
72. Franks and McAloon, *The New Zealand Labour Party 1916–2016*, p. 87.
73. *Evening Post*, 9 February 1928, p. 12.
74. *Manawatu Standard*, 1 March 1930, p. 4.
75. H. Roth, 'The Communist vote in New Zealand', *Political Science*, vol. 17, no. 2, September 1965, pp. 26–35.
76. *Manawatu Standard*, 6 June 1928, p. 11.
77. As an example, the Welfare League published no anti-Labour articles after 1931.
78. *Manawatu Standard*, 7 November 1931, p. 2.
79. *Manawatu Standard*, 16 June 1931, p. 3.
80. This is reflected in the 1932 annual report, which listed organisations in New Zealand it believed to be a front for communists. See New Zealand Welfare League General Report for year ending 31 December 1932, 73-148-089, MS-Group-1543, Field papers.
81. *Manawatu Standard*, 27 June 1931, p. 8.
82. *New Zealand Herald*, 25 January 1932, p. 11; *Evening Post*, 20 August 1932, p. 12; *Evening Post*, 24 February 1933, p. 10; *Evening Post*, 23 January 1931, p. 8. The Red International Labour Union was formed in 1920 with the aim of promoting communist activity in trade unions. It was more active in the Pacific region from 1927 until 1933 – see Reiner Tosstorff, *The Red International of Labour Unions 1920–1937*, trans. Ben Fowkes (Boston: Brill, 2016), p. 776.
83. *Evening Post*, 31 May 1933, p. 20.
84. *New Zealand Herald*, 6 October 1932, p. 15; *New Zealand Herald*, 15 October 1932, p. 15.
85. *Manawatu Standard*, 4 March 1933, p. 8; *Evening Post*, 12 July 1933 p. 11. The 'twisted teaching' controversy played out in the *Evening Post* over the second half of 1933 and led to an inquiry by the University Council – see Rachel Barrowman, *Victoria University of Wellington 1899–1999: A history* (Wellington: Victoria University Press, 1999), pp. 93–94.
86. *Evening Post*, 8 September 1923, p. 8; *Evening Post*, 22 September 1923, p. 11.
87. *Manawatu Standard*, 22 March 1930, p. 14; *Evening Post*, 28 June 1930, p. 15; *Evening Post*, 14 August 1934, p. 8; *Manawatu Standard*, 19 January 1935, p. 8. Although the Welfare League began to fade into obscurity in the mid-1930s, there were groups that continued its message. For example, the New Zealand Freedom Association led by Ronald Algie, which became closely associated with the National Party – see 'Algie, Ronald Macmillan', Dictionary of New Zealand Biography: https://teara.govt.nz/en/biographies/4a8/algie-ronald-macmillan
88. *New Zealand Herald*, 1 February 1938, p. 13.
89. For example, *Manawatu Standard*, 16 March 1940, p. 6; *Otago Daily Times*, 24 May 1940, p. 5; *Manawatu Standard*, 10 July 1940, p. 2. This needs to be seen against the backdrop of the German–Soviet non-aggression pact, which had effectively placed the Soviet Union on the opposing side to New Zealand.
90. *Otago Daily Times* 18 July 1941, p. 2 is the last League article. Why they faded is unclear; possibly key personnel were ageing. It is also probable that the war had an influence in the League's ability to get its message published, and that it may have seemed inappropriate alongside war news.
91. Matthew Cunningham, 'Massey's Cossacks reborn? Public and private counterrevolutionary preparations in New Zealand, 1920–1921' (currently seeking publication).
92. Ibid.
93. Ibid.
94. Ibid.
95. Ibid.
96. Loyal Citizens League, Wellington Branch, MS-Papers-0682, ATL.
97. *Manawatu Standard*, 5 October 1920, p. 5.

98. *Evening Post*, 30 September 1920, p. 6.
99. Loyal Citizens League, Wellington Branch, MS-Papers-0682, ATL.
100. Ibid.
101. Cited in Anthony Dreaver, *An Eye for Country* (Wellington: Victoria University Press, 1997), p. 127.
102. *Taranaki Herald*, 9 October 1920, p. 2; *Wairarapa Age*, 7 October 1920, p. 5; Cunningham, 'Massey's Cossacks'.
103. Cunningham, 'Massey's Cossacks'.
104. *Evening Star*, 20 April 1923, p. 5.
105. It is more likely they were linked to the Welfare League as it mentions in its 1921 interim report that it supported action to get men elected to local bodies to counter socialist candidates. See New Zealand Welfare League, Interim report for Period Ending May 31st, 1921, MHE 14:114, Australian National Library, Canberra (hereafter ANL).
106. A good account of the formation of the PPA is contained in Christopher van der Krogt, 'Elliott, Howard Leslie', Dictionary of New Zealand Biography: https://teara.govt.nz/en/biographies/3e5/elliott-howard-leslie
107. R.P. Davis, 'The New Zealand Labour Party's "Irish Campaign" 1916–1921', *Political Science*, vol. 19, no. 2, 1967, pp. 13–14 has more details.
108. Ibid., pp. 16, 19.
109. Roman Catholic Articles of War on the British Empire and the Protestant People, p. 11, box 3 folder 4, Harold Moores research papers, A-188, Auckland University Library Special Collections Auckland (hereafter Moores papers). This details how the Roman Catholic Church was using socialist ideas to encourage world revolution. The pamphlets in this collection are undated, but there are two, 4th and 7th edition. There is also a copy on the National Library dated 1923 which is the 2nd edition. This suggests that this pamphlet may have had a long life.
110. Protestant Political Association of NZ: Political Platform, box 3 folder 6, Moores papers.
111. *Evening Post*, 1 May 1922, p. 10.
112. *Evening Star*, 19 February 1925, p. 4. Further examples include *Otago Daily Times*, 23 May 1923, p. 4; *Otago Daily Times*, 10 October 1923, p. 4; *Hawera Star*, 29 October 1924, p. 5; *Hawera Star*, 4 April 1925, p. 6.
113. See remits from the 1927 annual conference, *Evening Star*, 2 July 1927, p. 3.
114. *Manawatu Standard*, 9 June 1925, p. 7.
115. *What is the Red Menace? The secret history of the forces behind socialism and communism: An exposure of the so-called 'Labour' Party* (Wellington: Loyalty League, 1925).
116. There are several newspaper reports about '*What is the Red Menace?*' – see *Evening Star*, 5 October 1925, p. 6; *Manawatu Standard*, 17 October 1925, p. 8; *Western Star*, 23 October 1925, p. 2; *Franklin Times*, 28 October 1925, p. 3.
117. Particularly box 6, Moores papers.
118. Communist Germ, box 6 folder 3, Moores papers. Elliot gave some talks entitled 'The Roman Octopus and the Communist Germ' in 1927 – see *Otago Daily Times*, 29 April 1927, p. 12; *Hawera Star*, 5 May 1927, p. 1; *Stratford Evening Post*, 14 May 1927, p. 7.
119. This happened at the 1925 Labour Party conference – see Franks and McAloon, *The New Zealand Labour Party 1916–2016*, p. 87.
120. *Evening Post*, 6 February 1929, p. 13; *Otago Daily Times*, 3 September 1929, p. 10.
121. *Evening Post*, 12 September 1929, p. 11.
122. Boxes 4, 5 and 6 of the Moores papers contain material from overseas groups.
123. van der Krogt, 'Elliott, Howard Leslie'.
124. *Nelson Evening Mail*, 29 April 1922, p. 5. For a report of Detterich's speech, see *Press*, 3 May 1922, p. 12; *New Zealand Herald*, 25 May 1922, p. 8. Howard was also influential in Australia, he spoke to anti-Catholic groups there, and PPA material was used by those groups.
125. Matthew Cunningham, *Mobilising the Masses: Populist conservative movements in*

Australia and New Zealand during the Great Depression (Canberra: Australian National University Press, 2022), chapter 1.

126. *Dominion*, 26 November 1920, p. 7.
127. Dave McLaren had been a member of the Labour movement until World War I. He had begun life as a bootmaker and was an independent Labour MP from 1908 to 1911. He was writing for the Welfare League from 1920. See Ernest James to William Massey, 21 June 1920, R22281270, PM9 3, Archives New Zealand, Wellington (hereafter ANZ); Kerry Taylor, 'McLaren, David', Dictionary of New Zealand Biography: https://teara.govt.nz/en/biographies/3m22/mclaren-david; *Stratford Evening Post*, 31 January 1921, p. 5.
128. New Zealand Welfare League, Interim report for Period Ending May 31st, 1921, MHE 14:114, ANL.
129. *Otago Daily Times*, 14 February 1922, p. 6.
130. *Evening Post*, 21 January 1922, p. 6. This is not an exhaustive list. Over the length of its life the League had contact with other groups as they formed or morphed into other groups.
131. New Zealand Welfare League General Report for year ending 31 December 1932, 73-148-089, MS-Group-1543, Field Papers.
132. New Zealand Welfare League, Interim report for Period Ending May 31st, 1921, MHE 14:114, ANL.
133. Ibid.
134. New Zealand Welfare League General Report for year ending 31 December 1931, 73-148-089, MS-Group-1543, Field papers.
135. *Evening Post*, 3 April 1926, p. 6 mentions this organisation and the League's contacts with it.
136. Markku Ruostslia, 'International anti-communism before the Cold War: Success and failure of building a transnational right', in Margaret Power and Martin Durham (eds), *New Perspectives on the Transnational Right* (New York: Palgrave Macmillan, 2010), pp. 26–27.
137. *Evening Post*, 4 October 1926, p. 15; *Evening Post*, 28 February 1927, p. 3; *Evening Post*, 12 May 1927, p. 17; *Otago Daily Times*, 16 June 1927, p. 15.
138. *Evening Post*, 20 February 1928, p. 8; *Evening Post*, 22 February 1928, p. 3.
139. There were between three and four political parties in the New Zealand Parliament in the interwar period. However, Reform dominated, and Labour became the second party in 1925 and eventually became the dominant party after the 1935 election. See Michael Bassett, *Three Party Politics in New Zealand, 1911–1931* (Auckland: Historical Publications, 1982).
140. *The Newsletter* began sometime during World War I as a two-page publication. Two survived and are in the Alexander Turnbull Library. It is probable that it was written by E.A. James who had been the Reform organiser prior to the war. In October 1920 it switched to a magazine-style format. This coincided with James' re-employment by the party. See James to Massey, 21 August 1920, Reform Party Correspondence September 1919–March 1921, PM9 2/9, R22281271, ANZ; *Newsletter*, no. 58, 31 July 1926, p. 2.
141. *Newsletter*, no. 1, 30 October 1920, pp. 5–7.
142. For example, *Newsletter*, no. 4, 11 December 1920, pp. 3–4; *Newsletter*, no. 7, 26 March 1921, p. 4; *Newsletter*, no. 14, 29 October 1921, pp. 1–3; *Newsletter*, no. 18, 25 February 1922, pp. 1–3; *Newsletter*, no. 21, 27 May 1922, pp. 1–4.
143. *Newsletter*, no. 13, 24 September 1921, p. 3.
144. *Newsletter*, no. 37, 29 March 1924, p. 10.
145. *Newsletter*, no. 44, 29 November 1924, pp. 9–10.
146. *Newsletter*, no. 54, 27 February 1926.
147. For example, *Newsletter*, no. 67, 31 March 1928, p. 6; *Newsletter*, no. 70, 30 June 1928, p. 1; *Newsletter*, no. 71, 28 July 1928, p. 2; *Newsletter*, no. 74, 27 October 1928, p. 8.
148. As the 1930s progressed the League encountered more letters rebutting its articles. For example, an article entitled 'Russia and capitalism' published in *Auckland Star*, 29 June 1936, p. 6 received four letters to the editor rebutting it.

149. *Otago Daily Times*, 10 December 1935, p. 11.
150. Wilson, 'Defining the "red menace"', p. 113–14 covers anti-communism in the postwar period. Althought the Labour Party was openly anti-communist it did not stop them from being targeted, the best known example being the 'Dancing Cossacks' National Party advertisement for the 1975 election – see 'Dancing Cossacks political TV ad', NS History online: https://nzhistory.govt.nz/media/video/dancing-cossacks

CHAPTER SIX

1. *Press*, 20 August 1920, p. 8; Letter from J.B. Wilson to Hawke's Bay members, 22 August 1933, file 5 folder 1, Hawke's Bay division of the New Zealand Legion papers, A-38, Auckland University Library Special Collections, Auckland (hereafter NZL papers).
2. Michael Pugh, 'The New Zealand Legion and conservative protest in the Great Depression' (MA thesis, University of Auckland, 1969), pp. 195–99.
3. Cas Mudde, *The Far Right Today* (Cambridge: Polity Press, 2019), pp. 20–23.
4. The PPA switched tactic to supporting Reform Party candidates after its support for an independent in the 1918 Wellington Central by-election contributed to splitting the vote in favour of the Labour candidate – see Harold Moores, 'The rise of the Protestant Political Association: sectarianism in New Zealand during World War One' (MA thesis, University of Auckland, 1966), pp. 309–10. The NZL's aspiration to run its own candidates in the 1935 General Election never materialised due to a lack of funds and manpower, along with the declining relevance of the organisation – see Matthew Cunningham, *Mobilising the Masses: Populist conservative movements in Australia and New Zealand during the Great Depression* (Canberra: Australian National University Press, 2022), chapter 6.
5. Jens Rydgren, 'The sociology of the radical right', *Annual Review of Sociology*, vol. 33, 2007, p. 242.
6. Daniele Albertazzi and Duncan McDonnell, 'Introduction: The sceptre and the spectre', in Daniele Albertazzi and Duncan McDonnell (eds), *Twenty-first Century Populism: The spectre of western European democracy* (New York: Palgrave Macmillan, 2008), p. 3.
7. The PPA's National Lecturer Howard Elliott had ministered to a number of Baptist congregations in Australia (his home country) before moving to New Zealand in 1909. Both he and H.H. Seabrook (a leading figure in the PPA) were avid collectors of international anti-Catholic literature. Several early anti-Catholic organisations in New Zealand were based on Australian groups such as the Protestant Defence Association. See Moores, 'The rise of the Protestant Political Association', pp. 30–32, 99–106.
8. Ibid., pp. 19–24; Brad Patterson, '"We stand for the Protestant religion, the (Protestant) King and the Empire": The rise of the Protestant Political Association in World War One', in Steven Loveridge (ed.), *New Zealand Society at War 1914–1918* (Wellington: Victoria University Press, 2016), p. 237.
9. James Watson, 'Were Catholics over-represented in the public service during the early twentieth century?' *Political Science*, vol. 42, no. 2, 1990, pp. 20–34.
10. P.S. O'Connor, 'Sectarian conflict in New Zealand, 1911–1920', *Political Science*, vol. 19, no. 1, 1967, pp. 3–4.
11. Moores, 'The rise of the Protestant Political Association', p. 49.
12. Rory Sweetman, 'New Zealand Catholicism, war, politics and the Irish issue 1912–1922' (PhD thesis, University of Cambridge, 1990), pp. 97–100.
13. Moores, 'The rise of the Protestant Political Association', pp. 60–67.

14. In addition to the 62 Marist Brothers engaged in teaching in New Zealand in 1917, there were also five Christian Brothers. Cited in Sweetman, 'New Zealand Catholicism, war, politics and the Irish issue', p. 128.
15. P.S. O'Connor, 'Storm over the clergy – New Zealand 1917', *Journal of Religious History*, vol. 4, no. 2, 1966–1967, pp. 129–48.
16. Dan Coward, 'The impact of war on New South Wales: Some aspects of social and political history, 1914–1917' (PhD thesis, Australian National University, 1974), p. 367; Robert Bollard, '"The active chorus": The mass strike of 1917 in eastern Australia' (PhD thesis, Victoria University, 2007).
17. Moores, 'The rise of the Protestant Political Association', p. 268. Elliott was invited to give a speech to the Loyalty League in October 1921, which they reprinted in pamphlet form under the title 'How New Zealand defeated the Roman menace'. See *Daily Telegraph*, 4 October 1921, p. 6; Series 21 item 79, Papers of Herbert and Ivy Brookes, 1869-1970, MS 1924, National Library of Australia.
18. Cunningham, *Mobilising the Masses*, pp. 36–37.
19. *Otago Daily Times*, 8 May 1895, p. 2.
20. Elizabeth Ward, 'For light and liberty: The origins and early development of the Reform Party, 1887–1915' (PhD thesis, Massey University, 2018), pp. 156–57; David Lindsey, 'Conscience voting in New Zealand' (PhD thesis, University of Auckland, 2011), p. 122.
21. *Marlborough Express*, 26 May 1919, p. 5
22. *Colonist*, 15 March 1919, p. 6.
23. Cunningham, *Mobilising the Masses*, pp. 95–96.
24. P.S. Tait, *In the Chair: The public life of Sir John Ormond* (Waipukurau: CHB Print, 1989), pp. 12–17.
25. Cunningham, *Mobilising the Masses*, pp. 116–17.
26. Noel G. Butlin, 'Colonial socialism in Australia, 1860–1900', in Hugh Aitken (ed.), *The State and Economic Growth* (New York: Social Science Research Council, 1959), pp. 26–78; James Belich, *Making Peoples: A history of the New Zealanders from Polynesian settlement to the end of the nineteenth century* (Auckland: Penguin, 1996), p. 375.
27. Pugh, 'The New Zealand Legion and conservative protest', pp. 11–16; B.D. Graham, 'The Country Party idea in New Zealand politics, 1901–1935', in Robert Chapman and Keith Sinclair (eds), *Studies of a Small Democracy* (Auckland: Auckland University Press, 1963), p. 183; Michael Bassett, *Coates of Kaipara* (Auckland: Auckland University Press, 1995), pp. 91–129.
28. Peter Gourevitch, *Politics in Hard Times: Comparative responses to international economic crises* (New York: Cornell University Press, 1986), pp. 10, 21–22, 160–61.
29. Patterson, '"We stand for the Protestant religion"', p. 236; Andrew Francis, '"To be truly British we must be anti-German": Patriotism, citizenship and anti-alienism in New Zealand during the Great War' (PhD thesis, Victoria University of Wellington, 2009), p. 108.
30. Steven Loveridge, 'Introduction', in Steven Loveridge (ed.), *New Zealand Society at War 1914–1918* (Wellington: Victoria University Press, 2016), pp. 30–33; Steven Loveridge and James Watson, *The Home Front: New Zealand society and the war effort, 1914–1919* (Palmerston North: Massey University Press, 2019), pp. 189–215.
31. J.B. Condliffe, *New Zealand in the Making: A study of economic and social development* (London: Allen & Unwin, 1936), p. 45; Gary Hawke, *The Making of New Zealand: An economic history* (Cambridge: Cambridge University Press, 1985), pp. 124, 127, 134, 148, 155; Malcolm McKinnon, *The Broken Decade: Prosperity, depression and recovery in New Zealand, 1928–39* (Dunedin: Otago University Press, 2016), p. 12.
32. Letter from Sir Douglas Robb, 29 September 1972, Transcripts of taped interviews with

various people for Tony Simpson's 'The Sugar Bag Years', MS-Papers-9902, ATL (hereafter Simpson papers).

33. Letter from L.E. Earle, 27 August 1972, Simpson papers.
34. *National Opinion*, vol. 2, no. 16, 29 March 1934, p. 12; *National Opinion*, vol. 2, no. 23, 5 July 1934, p. 13.
35. Elliott's impressive collection of international anti-Catholic material was preserved by Harold Moores when writing his thesis on the PPA – see Moores papers boxes 3–7 in particular.
36. Letters from W. Bright and H.L. Paterson, 26 and 28 August 1972, Simpson papers.
37. Patterson, '"We stand for the Protestant religion"', pp. 241–43.
38. Moores, 'The rise of the Protestant Political Association', pp. 209–10.
39. Ibid., pp 212–15, 240.
40. *Ellesmere Guardian*, 20 March 1918, p. 3.
41. Itinerary in forming the NZ Legion, file 1 folder 1, NZL papers; *Evening Post*, 6 April 1933, p. 10.
42. Robert Campbell Begg, *The Secret of the Knife* (Norwich: Jarrold & Sons, 1966), pp. 84–85.
43. Cunningham, *Mobilising the Masses*, pp. 175–84.
44. Pugh, 'The New Zealand Legion and conservative protest', pp. 97–98.
45. Letter from J.B. Wilson to Hawke's Bay members, 22 August 1933, file 5 folder 1, NZL papers.
46. Damen Ward, 'Colonial communication: creating settler public opinion in Crown colony South Australia and New Zealand', in Simon J. Potter (ed.), *Imperial Communication: Australia, Britain, and the British Empire c. 1830–50* (London: Menzies Centre for Australian Studies, 2004), pp. 12–21.
47. Detailed reports of these meetings are contained in *New Zealand Herald*, 12 July 1917, p. 6 and *Evening Post*, 20 April 1933, p. 12.
48. Moores, 'The rise of the Protestant Political Association', pp. 145, 210–12.
49. Letter from Begg to all Divisions and Centres, 3 February 1934, file 1 folder 2, NZL papers.
50. Ref. 6/12/17, 15 May 1933, file 1 folder 2; Letter from A.S. Tonkin to J.R.V. Sherston, 6 June 1933, file 2 folder 3, NZL papers.
51. Minutes of Meeting of the Provisional National Council, 4–5 April 1933, file 1 folder 1, NZL papers.
52. *Rome's Hideous Guilt in the European Carnage* (Auckland: Free Press Print, 1916).
53. *Constitution and Rules of the PPA* (Auckland: J.F. Leighton Printer, 1917).
54. Pugh, 'The New Zealand Legion and conservative protest', pp. 77, 112–14.
55. *New Zealand Herald*, 17 March 1933, p. 8.
56. Moores, 'The rise of the Protestant Political Association', pp. 156–57.
57. Dickon John Milnes, 'The church militant: Dunedin churches and society during WW1' (PhD thesis, University of Otago, 2015), pp. 290–93.
58. Moores, 'The rise of the Protestant Political Association', pp. 174–207.
59. *The Truth about the Elliott Assault Case* (Auckland: Auckland PPA Committee, 1917).
60. The key secondary sources on the PPA are Moores, 'The rise of the Protestant Political Association'; Patterson, '"We stand for the Protestant religion"', pp. 235–51; Max Satchell, 'Pulpit politics: The Protestant Political Association in Dunedin from 1917 to 1922' (BA (Hons) diss., University of Otago, 1983); P.S. O'Connor, 'Sectarian conflict in New Zealand, 1911–1920', pp. 3–16; O'Connor, 'Storm over the clergy – New Zealand 1917', pp. 129–48; P.S. O'Connor, 'Mr Massey and the PPA – a suspicion confirmed', *New Zealand Journal of Public Administration*, vol. 28, no. 2, 1966, pp. 69–74; Christopher John van der Krogt, 'More a part than apart: The Catholic community in New Zealand society, 1918–1940' (PhD thesis, Massey, 1994); Milnes, 'The church militant', chapter 5; Sweetman, 'New Zealand Catholicism, war, politics and the Irish issue 1912–1922'.

61. Patterson, '"We stand for the Protestant religion"', p. 250.
62. Satchell, 'Pulpit politics', pp. 68–70, Appendix 4.
63. Especially in rural regions – see for example Elizabeth Ward's analysis of the NZL in the Manawatū: Elizabeth Ward, 'The New Zealand Legion in Manawatu-Wanganui, 1933–1935' (BA (Hons) thesis, Massey University, 2011), p. 20.
64. Cunningham, 'The reactionary and the radical', Appendix B.
65. Cunningham, *Mobilising the Masses*, pp. 248–49.
66. Moores, 'The rise of the Protestant Political Association', p. 311.
67. van der Krogt, 'More a part than apart', p. 355.
68. Gerrie, a grain salesman born in 1884, appears to have served as an Otago delegate for the PPA or a member of the national executive every year from 1918 until at least 1927. See *New Zealand Herald*, 1 July 1927, p. 12.
69. Letter from Peter Hall, 24 August 1972, Simpson papers.
70. *National Opinion*, vol. 2, no. 13, 15 February 1934, pp. 14–15.
71. *New Zealand Truth*, 22 September 1917, p. 1.
72. Moores, 'The rise of the Protestant Political Association', pp. 312–13.
73. Ibid., pp. 40–46.
74. Letter from N. Tilley, 26 August 1972, Simpson papers.
75. Although it does rear its head from time to time – see, for example, the widespread distribution of A. Jan Marcussen's 'National Sunday Law' to letterboxes across New Zealand in early 2021. See Matthew Tso, 'Mother disgusted 11-year-old daughter being asked to deliver "extreme" religious publication on paper round', Stuff, 9 March 2021: www.stuff.co.nz/national/124465378/mother-disgusted-11yearold-daughter-being-asked-to-deliver-extreme-religious-publication-on-paper-round

CHAPTER SEVEN

1. *New Zealand Herald*, 12 November 1935, p. 13.
2. See Malcolm McKinnon, *The Broken Decade: Prosperity, depression and recovery in New Zealand 1928–1939* (Dunedin: Otago University Press, 2016), pp. 326ff.
3. This chapter is based partly on Marinus La Rooij, 'Political antisemitism in New Zealand during the Great Depression: A case-study in the myth of the Jewish world conspiracy' (MA thesis, Victoria University of Wellington, 1998).
4. Barry Gustafson, *The First Fifty Years: A history of the New Zealand National Party* (Auckland: Reed Methuen, 1986), p. 4.
5. John Maynard Keynes, *The General Theory of Employment Interest and Money* (London: Macmillan & Co, 1936), pp. 370–71.
6. *Auckland Star*, 4 September 1935, p. 10.
7. On these beliefs see Marinus La Rooij, 'Arthur Nelson Field: Kiwi theoretician of the Australian radical right?', *Labour History*, no. 89, 2005, pp. 37–54.
8. On Field's life see Marinus La Rooij, 'From colonial conservative to international antisemite: the life and work of Arthur Nelson Field', *Journal of Contemporary History*, vol. 37, no. 2, 2002, pp. 223–39.
9. Paul Spoonley, 'Field, Arthur Nelson', Dictionary of New Zealand Biography: https://teara.govt.nz/en/biographies/4f8/field-arthur-nelson/sources
10. See P.J. Gibbons, 'The climate of opinion', in Geoffrey W. Rice (ed.), *The Oxford History of New Zealand* (Auckland: Oxford University Press, 1992), pp. 308–36.
11. *Dominion*, 26 September 1907, p. 4.
12. *Spectator*, 15 July 1916, p. 13.
13. *Manawatu Times*, 26 April 1929, p. 8.
14. Philip M. Coupland, *Farming, Fascism and Ecology: A life of Jorian Jenks* (Oxon: Routledge, 2016), pp. 42–49.
15. Michael Bassett, *The State in New Zealand 1840–1984* (Auckland: Auckland University Press, 1998), p. 167.

16. Michael Bassett, *Sir Joseph Ward: A political biography* (Auckland: Auckland University Press, 1993), pp. 272–73.
17. McKinnon, *The Broken Decade*, pp. 58ff.
18. Alex Millmow, *The Power of Economic Ideas: The origins of Keynesian macroeconomic management in interwar Australia 1929–39* (Canberra: Australian National University Press, 2011), pp. 43–44.
19. C.B. Schedvin, *Australia and the Great Depression* (Sydney: Sydney University Press, 1970), p. 131.
20. Peter Love, *Labour and the Money Power: Australian labour populism 1890–1950* (Melbourne: Melbourne University Press, 1984), pp. 91–107.
21. Shylock is a Jewish moneylender and the principal character in William Shakespeare's *Merchant of Venice.*
22. *The Labor Daily* (Sydney), 20 August 1930, p. 4.
23. *Goulburn Evening Penny Post*, 3 October 1930, pp. 4–5.
24. *Evening Post*, 23 August 1930, p. 9.
25. See McKinnon, *The Broken Decade*, pp. 75ff.
26. Field to A.K. Chesterton, 29 February 1960, p. 1, 73-148-049, Field papers, ATL.
27. *Dominion*, 9 September 1930, p. 7; 10 September, p. 7; 11 September, p. 7.
28. *Press*, 5 September 1930, p. 12.
29. *Dominion*, 9 September 1930, p. 7.
30. Field to H.H. Beamish, 28 January 1938, Field papers, MS-Papers-12550, ATL.
31. See G.C. Lebzelter, *Political Anti-Semitism in England 1918–1939* (London: Palgrave Macmillan UK, 1978), pp. 13–27.
32. See P.S. O'Connor, 'Sectarian conflict in New Zealand, 1911–1920', *Political Science*, vol. 19, no. 1, 1967, pp. 3–16; P.S. O'Connor, 'Keeping New Zealand white 1908–1920', *New Zealand Journal of History*, vol. 2 no. 1, 1968, p. 41; Jacqueline Leckie, 'In defence of race and empire: The white New Zealand League at Pukekohe', *New Zealand Journal of History*, vol. 19, no. 2, 1985, pp. 103–29.
33. *Tomorrow*, 30 January 1935, pp. 4–5.
34. See N. Cohn, *Warrant for Genocide: The myth of the Jewish world conspiracy and the protocols of the elders of Zion* (Harmondsworth: Penguin, 1970).
35. A.D. McIntosh, Secretary External Affairs to NZ Legation Washington, 24 December 1943, p. 1, External Affairs Files, Subversion – General file, series 1, 84/10/1 pt.1a, ANZ.
36. *Hokitika Guardian*, 3 March 1931, p. 6.
37. Arthur Nelson Field, *The Truth About the Slump* (Nelson: Okiwi Books, 1931).
38. Ibid., p. 107.
39. David Hammes and Douglas Wills, 'Thomas Edison's "except one" – the monetary views of Arthur Kitson revisited', *Journal of Economic Studies*, vol. 32, no. 1, 2005, pp. 33–46.
40. See Field, *The Truth About the Slump*, pp. 139–53.
41. See ibid., pp. 78ff.
42. *Record-Journal* (Meriden, Connecticut), 1 March 1913, p. 5.
43. *Springville Journal* (Springville, New York), 13 March 1913, p. 6.
44. Field, *The Truth About the Slump*, pp. 33ff.
45. Field to W.H.W. Young, 10 September 1935, 73-148-124, Field papers.
46. *Gisborne Times*, 28 September 1931, p. 5.
47. *Nelson Evening Mail*, 23 June 1931, p. 8.
48. *NZPD*, vol. 227, 1931, p. 314.
49. Ibid., p. 320.
50. Ibid., vol. 228, 1931, p. 136.
51. Downie Stewart to Horace Belshaw, 16 July 1931, Downie Stewart Papers, MS-0985-002/026, HC.
52. *New Zealand Worker*, 29 April 1931, p. 4.
53. Douglas first argued in 1924 that the monetary question would only be understood within the context of the 'Jewish Question', See C.H. Douglas, *Social Credit* (London: Eyre & Spottiswoode, 1935), p. 29.
54. *Farming First*, 10 April 1932, p. 21.
55. Albert E, Willyams to Dorothy Graham, 10 August 1955, box 6 '1957' folder, Hislop papers, 85-145-06, ATL.
56. See A.N. Field, *The money spider* (Auckland: Mirror Publishing Company, 1933).

57. Field to M.E. Collingridge, 31 August 1938, 73-148-050, Field papers.
58. *Truth* (Sydney), 24 November 1929, p. 16.
59. *Truth* (Sydney), 10 July 1927, p. 10.
60. See Frank Robson (junior), 'My father, the fascist', Good Weekend – Sydney Morning Herald, 8 March 2019: www.smh.com.au/national/my-father-the-fascist-20190305-p511rp.html
61. Frank Robson to A.N. Field, 28 March 1932, 73-148-096, Field papers.
62. *New Zealand Plain Talk*, October 1932, p. 1.
63. Ibid., p. 2.
64. Ibid.
65. Michael Ryan to Field, 16 March 1933, 73-148-103, Field papers.
66. Barclay Smith to Dorothy Graham, 22 December 1952, p. 2, box 8, Hislop papers, 85-145-08, ATL.
67. Norman Taylor to Raymond Hansen, 23 April 1933, box 5, Raymond E. Hansen papers, 84-204, ATL.
68. *Protocols of the Learned Elders of Zion* (Auckland: Plain Talk, 1933).
69. *New Zealand Herald*, 16 March 1933, p. 10.
70. Robin Hyde, *Nor the Years Condemn* (Auckland: New Women's Press, 1986), p. 288. The novel was first published in 1938.
71. William Warnock to Police Commissioner W.G. Wohlmann, 28 April 1933, box 2, Miscellaneous Organisations: Fascist, Anti-Semitic, Extreme Right-Wing: 1933–1966, R24716778, ANZ (hereafter miscellaneous radical right organisation papers).
72. *Plain Talk*, October 1932, pp. 5–6.
73. O.E. Niemeyer, 'Banking and currency in New Zealand', 19 February 1931, *AJHR*, 1931 Session I-II, B-03.
74. See G.R. Hawke, *Between Government and Banks: A history of the Reserve Bank of New Zealand* (Wellington: Reserve Bank, 1973).
75. *Northern Advocate*, 24 May 1933, p. 4.
76. A swag of protest letters is held in the Treasury Files, New Zealand Farmers' Union, series 1-52/589, ANZ.
77. *Auckland Star*, 6 January 1933, p. 5.
78. *NZPD*, vol. 236, 1933, p. 822.
79. Ibid., p. 800.
80. Ibid., p. 673.
81. Ibid., p. 810.
82. *Tomorrow*, 14 October 1936, p. 3.
83. *New Zealand Herald*, 9 October 1936, p. 13.
84. See Finance Act (1936 no. 2), section 27(1).
85. Quoted in Ann Beaglehole, *A Small Price to Pay: Refugees from Hitler in New Zealand 1936–46* (Wellington: Allen & Unwin, 1988), p. 16.
86. Ibid., p. 7.
87. *Auckland Star*, 13 July 1945, p. 7.
88. *Auckland Star*, 24 July 1945, p. 4.
89. W.B. Bray to Field, 8 July 1961, p. 1, 73-148-045, Field papers.
90. Michael Sheppard, *Social Credit, Inside and Out* (Dunedin: Caveman, 1981), p. 30.
91. James Meek, 'Red Pill, Blue Pill', London Review of Books, 22 October 2020: www.lrb.co.uk/the-paper/v42/n20/james-meek/red-pill-blue-pill

CHAPTER EIGHT

1. James Belich, *Paradise Reforged: A history of the New Zealanders from the 1880s to the year 2000* (Auckland: Penguin, 2001), pp. 297–321. Colin James recalls postwar New Zealand as 'a place of no choice and none needed. Small, rich and complete. Bland beyond boredom. The most comfortable place in the world to grow up in.' Colin James, *The Quiet Revolution: Turbulence and transition in contemporary New Zealand* (Wellington: Allen & Unwin, 1986), p. 30.
2. Paul Spoonley, *The Politics of Nostalgia: Racism and the extreme right in New Zealand* (Palmerston North: Dunmore Press, 1987), blurb.
3. Jonathan Haidt, *The Righteous Mind: Why good people are divided by politics and religion* (London: Penguin, 2012), pp. 356–61.

4. Daniel Woodley provides a critical summary of competing schools of thought. Daniel Woodley, *Fascism and Political Theory: Critical perspectives on fascist ideology* (New York: Routledge, 2009).
5. Robert O. Paxton, *The Anatomy of Fascism* (London: Penguin, 2004), p. 218.
6. *New Zealand Herald*, 15 June 1970, p. 2.
7. Copy of the National Socialist Party of New Zealand Manifesto, 31 January 1969, Organisations: Fascist, Anti-Semitic, Extreme Right-Wing: National Socialist Party of NZ, R24881828, Archives New Zealand (hereafter National Socialist Party papers).
8. 'Kosher' here denotes opposition that is controlled or acceptable to 'Jewish power'. Vetting inquiry, 22 August 1979, Organisations: Fascist, Anti-Semitic, Extreme Right-Wing: NZ National Front, R24881827, Archives New Zeaand (hereafter National Front papers).
9. Security reports on the National Socialist Party of New Zealand, October 1969 and 12 November 1969, National Socialist Party papers.
10. Bill Pearson, 'Fretful sleepers: A sketch of New Zealand behaviour and its implications for the artist', *Landfall*, vol. 23, September 1952, pp. 203–04. Similar trepidations of an authoritarian turn in New Zealand informed C.K. Stead's novel *Smith's Dream* (1971) and provided the basis for the film *Sleeping Dogs* (1977).
11. For examples of protest literature evoking fascism see Government and Public Order – Strikes: 1951 Strike: Pamphlets 1951-1951, R10074976, ANZ. For examples post-1951 see Security Intelligence Service – Cuttings and articles, MS-Papers-6218-06, ATL.
12. *New Zealand Monthly Review*, July 1968, pp. 19–20.
13. For further commentary see *Salient*, 28 May 1969, p. 10 and *Cock*, 16 February 1972.
14. *PYM Rebel*, vol. 30, 1971.
15. *Evening Post*, 14 June 1966, p. 29.
16. Brian Edwards, *The Public Eye* (Wellington: Alister Taylor, 1972), p. 177.
17. Jarrod Gilbert, *Patched: The history of gangs in New Zealand* (Auckland: Auckland University Press, 2013), p. 30.
18. Edwards, *The Public Eye*, pp. 177, 182. A segment of the interview is available at https://teara.govt.nz/en/video/28246/stormtroopers-interview
19. Tim Shadbolt, *Bullshit & Jellybeans* (Wellington: Alister Taylor, 1971), p. 36.
20. *Evening Post*, 15 June 1966, p. 32.
21. Peter Novick, *The Holocaust and Collective Memory* (London: Bloomsbury, 2001), p. 128.
22. Further details on this vandalism are covered in Paul Spoonley and Helen Cox, *Report no. 11: Antisemitism in New Zealand since 1945* (Wellington, New Zealand Jewish Council, 1982), p. 4.
23. Further incidents were reported on the Hutt Road, Ngauranga, and in Napier. *New Zealand Truth*, 19 January 1960, p. 12.
24. Report dated 18 January 1960, Miscellaneous radical right organisation papers.
25. Memorandum for Director, 4 April 1960, Miscellaneous radical right organisation papers.
26. *New Zealand Truth*, 2 February 1960, p. 32.
27. Report dated 20 January 1960, Miscellaneous radical right organisation papers.
28. National Socialist Party publications and newsclippings.
29. Ibid.
30. Ibid.
31. *Salient*, 10 May 1970, p. 15. Curry also warned about the communist history of undermining churches and religion. See Fairlie Fergus Curry, *Some Facts About – communism and the churches* (Wellington: Fairlie, Fergus, Curry, 1966).
32. *New Zealand Truth*, 19 January 1966, p. 4; *Salient*, 6 May 1970, p. 15; *New Zealand Monthly Review*, July 1968, pp. 19–21.
33. *New Zealand Weekly News*, 31 May 1971, p. 13.
34. *Sunday Times*, 18 June 1972, p. 6; *Dominion*, 14 December 1968, p. 14.

35. *Salient*, 6 May 1970, p. 10. For further platform positions, see *The Aims, Objects, and Basic Policy for the N.Z. Country Party* (Stratford: The Society, 1969).
36. *New Zealand Truth*, 23 September, 1969, p. 16; Newspaper clipping, New Zealand Country Party, MS-Papers-4442-32, ATL.
37. *New Zealand Herald*, 22 January 1969, p. 8.
38. In 1976 some 20 New Zealanders were believed to have enlisted to fight in Rhodesia. *New Zealand Herald*, 22 July 1976, p. 1.
39. *New Zealand Listener*, 22 May 1972, p. 9.
40. *Press*, 19 April 1969, p. 21.
41. Press statement from the National Anti-Apartheid Committee, NZ Rhodesia Society/Southern Africa Friends Association/Aid Rhodesia, MS-Papers-4442-34, ATL.
42. *New Zealand Listener*, 22 May 1972, p. 9.
43. Ibid.; NZ Rhodesia Society/Southern Africa Friends Association/Aid Rhodesia, Papers relating to Aid Rhodesia Movement (NZ), 82-381-14, MS-Papers-4442-34, ATL; *Aid Rhodesia: the battle for Rhodesia – the facts* (Christchurch: Aid Rhodesia Movement, 1967).
44. Michael Sheppard, *Social Credit: Inside and out* (Dunedin: Caveman, 1981), pp. 28–47.
45. Carey John Carrington, *New Zealand's Greatest Need* (Tauranga: Publicity Printing, 1956), pp. 1, 8.
46. Richard Hofstadter, *The Paranoid Style in American Politics, and Other Essays* (London: Cape, 1966), p. 3.
47. Stephen Eric Bronner, *A Rumour About the Jews: Reflections on antisemitism and the protocols of the learned elders of Zion* (New York: St Martin's Press, 2000), p. 140.
48. *Wetherbys Visions of A Nobler Day*, September 1958, pp. 4–5; January 1959, p. 1.
49. Ibid., January 1959, p. 5.
50. Austin Mitchell, 'Fluoridation in Dunedin: A study of pressure groups and public opinion', *Political Science*, vol. 12, no. 1, March 1960, p. 72.
51. *Salient*, 18 July 1965, p. 12.
52. Leaflet entitled 'Speech of Rabbi Emanuel Rabinovich', Miscellaneous radical right organisation papers.
53. Subsequent case details are taken from Miscellaneous radical right organisation papers.
54. A subsequent inquiry to the printer saw the manager submit that he had not previously examined the leaflet, and that he would not have printed it had he done so: 'the subject matter of the pamphlet is contrary to my convictions and if necessary I am prepared to publish my disbelief of the correctness of the contents of the pamphlet. I have many Jewish friends whom I would not like to offend.'
55. The issue attracted some renewed attention in the early 1990s. An overview is available in Anthony Hubbard, 'Murderers among us', *New Zealand Listener*, 21–27 May 1990, pp. 10–13 and Hubbard, 'Sanctuary: How we let in the war criminals', *New Zealand Listener*, 28 May–3 June 1990, pp. 24–28.
56. For example, *New Zealand Truth*, 25 November 1953, p. 3. See also *New Zealand Truth*, 9 December 1953, p. 17 and 6 January 1954, p. 3.
57. *New Zealand Truth*, 25 November 1953, p. 3.
58. Memorandum for the Director, 4 December 1953, Miscellaneous radical right organisation papers.
59. The Work of Special Branch, 5 November 1953, p. 137, Richard S. Hill security papers (private collection), 1st tranche.
60. Peter Bland, *Sorry I'm a Stranger Here Myself: A memoir* (Auckland: Vintage, 2004), p. 98.
61. Memorandum for [redacted], 24 March 1954, Miscellaneous radical right organisation papers.
62. Report to the District Officer, 1 May 1959, Miscellaneous radical right organisation papers.
63. Novick, *The Holocaust and Collective Memory*, pp. 127–34.
64. *New Zealand Herald*, 8 January 1960, p. 8.
65. *People's Voice*, 24 February 1960, p. 1.

66. Counter subversion report, 25 February 1960, Miscellaneous radical right organisation papers.
67. Newspaper clipping, National Socialist Party publications and newsclippings.
68. Ibid.
69. Evan Smith, 'Exporting fascism across the Commonwealth: The case of the National Front of Australia', in Nigel Copsey and Matthew Worley (eds), *Tomorrow Belongs to Us: The British far right since 1967* (New York: Routledge, 2018), pp. 69–89.
70. David Barker, *Ideology of Obsession: A.K. Chesterton and British fascism* (London: I.B. Tauris, 1996).
71. Joe Mulhall, 'From apathy to obsession: the reactions of A.K. Chesterton and the British far right to imperial decline', *Patterns of Prejudice*, vol. 50, no. 4–5, 2016, p. 466.
72. Constitution and rules for the League of Empire Loyalists, League of Empire Loyalists papers, MS-Papers-4442-24, ATL.
73. NZSIS report for Christchurch district officer, 1 July 1958, National Front papers.
74. Poster entitled 'announcing ... operation protest', National Front papers.
75. It's a Sell-out! Eph-B-politics 1960s, ATL; Joe Hartley, *New Zealand's Asian destiny* (Christchurch: League of Empire Loyalists, 1960).
76. Richard Thurlow, *Fascism in Britain: A history, 1918–1985* (New York: Basil Blackwell, 1987), pp. 275–97.
77. Newspaper clipping, National Socialist Party publications and newsclippings.
78. Report on the National Front of New Zealand, August 1978, National Front papers.
79. K.D. Gott, *Voices of Hate: A study of the Australian League of Rights and its director, Eric D. Butler* (Melbourne: Dissent Pub. Association, 1965), p. 5.
80. Newspaper clipping, National Socialist Party publications and newsclippings; *Salient*, 17 March 1967, p. 3; *Salient*, 9 September 1966, p. 1.
81. Nicola Legat, 'The small but insistent voice of the far right', *Auckland Metro*, September 1985, pp. 80–85.
82. Harvey Buchman, 'The political thought of the New Zealand League of Rights' (MA thesis, University of Waikato, 1983), p. 28.
83. Pamphlet entitled 'a personal message to every loyal Kiwi!', New Zealand League of Rights – Publications, 94-106-17/09, ATL.
84. Buchman, 'The political thought of the New Zealand League of Rights', p. 56.
85. Ibid., p. 78.
86. Letter to 'Officer in charge, Security Police', 1 May 1962, Miscellaneous radical right organisation papers.
87. Security report, 3 August 1962, Miscellaneous radical right organisation papers.
88. *Dominion*, 13 September 1965, p. 1.
89. *Dominion*, 13 September 1962, p. 10; *New Zealand Truth*, 18 September 1962, p. 33.
90. Report on property seized by the Police, 20 October 1964, Miscellaneous radical right organisation papers.
91. Newspaper clipping, National Socialist Party publications and newsclippings; Paul Spoonley private collection.
92. NZSIS report on national socialism, 5 December 1969, National Socialist Party papers.
93. *Salient*, 6 May 1970, pp. 12–13.
94. Ibid., p. 13.
95. Ibid., p. 12. A transcript of the interview is available at https://theicebloc.wordpress.com/2017/04/15/reprint-salient-interviews-colin-king-ansell-1970/
96. Newspaper clipping, National Socialist Party publications and newsclippings.
97. *Questions & Answers for National Socialists* (Auckland: National Socialist Party of N.Z. 1974), p. 2.
98. A security assessment of King-Ansell's memoir noted it as '... a reiteration of all the old themes – the need for white racial purity, national unity, and subordination of ego to the requirements of the party. The emphasis is on youth and the need for discipline, but KING-ANSELL'S plans are ethereal, and contain no practical guide to organisation or Party activity. The writer seems to be living out fantasies in print ...'

Counter subversion report, 20 October 1969, National Socialist Party papers. For Donnell see report on property seized by the Police, 20 October 1964, Miscellaneous radical right organisation papers.

99. Newspaper clipping, National Socialist Party publications and newsclippings.
100. Ibid.
101. *New Zealand Truth*, 19 January 1971, p. 16.
102. Policy and Constitution of the National Socialist Party, National Socialist Party papers.
103. National Socialist Party of New Zealand manifesto, point 2, MS-Papers-4442-33, ATL; *Questions & answers*, p. 1.
104. Michael Burleigh and Wolfgang Wippermann, *The Racial State: Germany 1933–1945* (New York: Cambridge University Press, 1991).
105. Policy and Constitution of the National Socialist Party, National Socialist Party papers.
106. *Questions & Answers*, p. 3; National Socialist Party of New Zealand manifesto, 'Immigration and race', MS-Papers-4442-33, ATL.
107. *Sunday News*, 11 May 1969, p. 5.
108. Policy and Constitution of the National Socialist Party, National Socialist Party papers.
109. National Socialist Party of New Zealand manifesto, point 22, MS-Papers-4442-33, ATL.
110. *Sunday News*, 18 May 1969, p. 8.
111. *Questions & Answers*, pp. 4–5.
112. Policy and Constitution of the National Socialist Party, National Socialist Party papers.
113. Ibid.
114. *Salient*, 6 May 1970, p. 13.
115. Newspaper clipping, National Socialist Party publications and newsclippings.
116. *NZPD*, vol. 366, 1970, p. 1179.
117. *Sunday News*, 18 May 1969, p. 8.
118. *Salient*, 6 May 1970, p. 11. On the Cotswold Agreement, see Travis Morris, *Dark Ideas: How neo-nazi and violent jihadi ideologues shaped modern terrorism* (London: Lexington, 2016), p. 82.
119. Newspaper clipping, National Socialist Party publications and newsclippings; David Harcourt, *Everyone Wants to be Fuehrer* (Wellington: Alister Taylor, 1972), p. 138.
120. *Critic*, 25 June 1970, p. 7. A footnote in the 'Pax Judaica' investigation articulates its rationale. Several months after the case was closed, a letter written to the minister of police inquired under what authority the distribution of literature had been stopped. The response from W.H. Fortune, the minister in charge of police, described the material as 'lying, scurrilous anti-semitic propaganda of the worst type calculated to arose feelings of ill-will against the Jewish community', and that the police would have been failing their duty to preserve peace and order had they not advised the distributors of the probable consequences of activities 'likely to encourage disorder, violence or lawlessness.'
121. Harcourt, *Everyone Wants to be Fuehrer*, p. 137.
122. *Press*, 11 March 1969, p. 1.
123. *Christchurch Star*, 31 May 1976, p. 1.
124. Newspaper clipping, National Socialist Party publications and newsclippings.
125. Ibid.
126. *Salient*, 6 May 1970, p. 15.
127. *New Zealand Year Book*, 1970, pp. 1135–37.
128. *New Zealand Year Book*, 1973, p. 958; *New Zealand Year Book*, 1976, p. 941.
129. For further thoughts on international connections in the far right and 'political-antisemitism', see Graham Macklin, 'Transatlantic connections and conspiracies: A.K. Chesterton and "The New Unhappy Lords"', *Journal of Contemporary History*, vol. 47, no. 2, 2012, pp. 270–90; Evan Smith, 'Keeping the nazi menace out: George Lincoln Rockwell and the border control system in Australia and Britain in the early 1960s', *Social Sciences*, vol. 9, no. 9, 2020, pp. 1–13.

130. *Dominion*, 13 September 1962, p. 10.
131. Letter from H.E. Gilbert to J. Edgar Hoover, 27 May 1965, Miscellaneous radical right organisation papers.
132. *New Zealand Truth*, 13 November 1962, p. 5.
133. NZSIS report on national socialism in Christchurch, 6 July 1969, National Socialist Party papers.
134. Spoonley, *The Politics of Nostalgia*, p. 117.
135. Harcourt, *Everyone Wants to be Fuehrer*, p. 138.
136. Marinus La Rooij, 'From colonial conservative to international antisemite: The life and work of Arthur Nelson Field', *Journal of Contemporary History*, vol. 37, no. 2, April 2002, pp. 236, 238; La Rooij, 'Arthur Nelson Field: Kiwi theoretician of the Australian radical right?', *Labour History*, vol. 89, November 2005, pp. 38, 47–48.
137. Report on the National Front of New Zealand, August 1978, National Front papers.
138. Spoonley, 'New Zealand first!: The extreme right and politics', *Political Science*, vol. 33, no. 2, December 1981, p. 120.
139. *Press*, 11 March 1969, p. 1; Buchman, 'The political thought of the New Zealand League of Rights', pp. 29, 38–39.
140. *Salient*, 23 September 1966, p. 1.
141. *New Zealand Truth*, 13 November 1979, p. 11.
142. Newspaper clipping, National Socialist Party publications and newsclippings.
143. Spoonley, The Politics of Nostalgia, p. 154.

CHAPTER NINE

1. Paul Spoonley, *The Politics of Nostalgia: Racism and the extreme right in New Zealand* (Palmerston North: Dunmore Press, 1987), p. 101.
2. Ibid., pp. 128–29.
3. Paul Spoonley, 'New Zealand first!: The extreme right and politics in New Zealand, 1961–1981', *Political Science*, vol. 33, no. 2, 1981, p. 110.
4. Ibid.
5. *Star*, 8 February 1904; *Southland Times*, 8 February 1904.
6. Philip Ferguson, 'The making of the white New Zealand policy: Nationalism, citizenship and the exclusion of the Chinese, 1880–1920' (PhD thesis, University of Canterbury, 2003), p. 198.
7. Jeremy Martens, 'Richard Seddon and popular opposition in New Zealand to the introduction of Chinese labour into the Transvaal, 1903–1904', *New Zealand Journal of History*, vol. 42, no. 2, 2008, p. 177.
8. Ibid.
9. Ibid., p. 186.
10. Ibid., pp. 176–77.
11. Nigel Robson, *Our First Foreign War: The impact of the South African War 1899–1902 on New Zealand* (Auckland: Massey University Press, 2021), p. 172.
12. The Jameson Raid was a failed incursion by Leander Starr Jameson on 29 December 1895 to invade the Transvaal and trigger a rebellion which would give the British High Commissioner in Cape Town the pretext to proclaim British sovereignty over the Transvaal. See Hermann Giliomee, *The Afrikaners: Biography of a people* (Cape Town: Tafelberg, 2009), pp. 241–43; Frank Tod, *The Making of a Madman: Lionel Terry* (Dunedin: Otago Foundation Books, 1977), pp. 19–20.
13. Jacqueline Leckie, 'In defence of race and empire: The White New Zealand League at Pukekohe', *New Zealand Journal of History*, vol. 19, no. 2, 1985, p. 112.
14. Then unified as the three-territory Federation of Rhodesia and Nyasaland, also known as the Central African Republic, which existed as a colonial entity within the British Empire from 1953–1963. It dissolved shortly before Northern Rhodesia and Nyasaland gained independence as Zambia and Malawi respectively, and Southern Rhodesia unilaterally declared independence in 1965.

15. Spoonley, 'New Zealand first!', p. 111.
16. Ibid.
17. Bruce Jesson, Allanah Ryan and Paul Spoonley, *Revival of the Right: New Zealand politics in the 1980s* (Auckland: Heinemann Reed, 1988), p. 96; Spoonley, 'New Zealand first!', p. 111.
18. Barry Gustafson, *Kiwi Keith: A biography of Keith Holyoake* (Auckland: Auckland University Press, 2007), p. 193.
19. Ibid.
20. Spoonley, 'The politics of racism', in Paul Spoonley (ed.), *Tauiwi: Racism and ethnic conflict in New Zealand* (Palmerston North: Dunmore Press, 1984), p. 75.
21. Gustafson, *Kiwi Keith*, p. 200.
22. Ibid., p. 193.
23. Spoonley, *The Politics of Nostalgia*, p. 132.
24. Ibid., pp. 77–78, 111.
25. Ibid., p. 113.
26. Trevor Richard cites an instance where in Eltham, rural Taranaki, in 1981 anti-tour protesters were accosted in the street by a man shouting 'We want rugby. We support apartheid. We support racist teams. Give us rugby.' See Trevor Richards, *Dancing on Our Bones: New Zealand, South Africa, rugby and racism* (Wellington: Bridget Williams Books, 1999), p. 213.
27. John Nauright and David Black, *Rugby and the South African Nation: Sport, cultures, politics, and power in the old and new South Africas* (Manchester: Manchester University Press, 1998), p. 87.
28. Malcolm MacLean, '"Almost the same, but not quite … almost the same, but not white": Maori and Aotearoa/New Zealand's 1981 Springbok Tour', *Kunapipi*, vol. 23, no. 1, 2001, p. 70.
29. Malcolm MacLean, 'Football as social critique: Protest movements, rugby and history in Aotearoa/New Zealand', *International Journal of the History of Sport*, vol. 17, no. 2–3, 2000, p. 256; MacLean, '"Almost the same, but not quite … almost the same, but not white"', pp. 77–78.
30. Richards, *Dancing on Our Bones*, pp. 187–88, 239, 244.
31. Spoonley, *The Politics of Nostalgia*, p. 88.
32. Chris Laidlaw, *Mud in Your Eye: A worm's eye view of the changing rugby world* (Wellington: Reed, 1973), p. 195; *New Zealand Listener*, 22 May 1972.
33. Richards, *Dancing on Our Bones*, p. 65.
34. Spoonley, 'New Zealand first!', p. 111.
35. Ibid.; Richards, *Dancing on Our Bones*, p. 82.
36. *New Zealand Listener*, 22 May 1972.
37. Richards, *Dancing on Our Bones*, p. 82.
38. *New Zealand Listener*, 22 May 1972.
39. Laidlaw, *Mud in your Eye*, p. 195.
40. Ibid., p. 196.
41. *Hawke's Bay Herald Tribune*, 12 January 1976.
42. Richards, *Dancing on Our Bones*, p. 82.
43. Robert Muldoon, *Muldoon* (Christchurch: A.H. & A.W. Reed, 1977), p. 193.
44. Spoonley, 'Right of way: The far right in New Zealand', *Kaea*, 1 September 1980.
45. Spoonley, 'New Zealand first!', p. 112.
46. Ibid., p. 117; Spoonley, *The Politics of Nostalgia*, p. 122.
47. Spoonley, *The Politics of Nostalgia*, p. 99.
48. Spoonley, 'New Zealand first!', p. 117.
49. Laidlaw, *Mud in your Eye*, p. 187.
50. *Otago Daily Times*, 30 April 1981.
51. Ibid.
52. Ibid.
53. Spoonley, *The Politics of Nostalgia*, p. 110.
54. Ibid., p. 113.
55. Ibid., p. 114.
56. Spoonley, 'New Zealand first!', p. 120.
57. *Otago Daily Times*, 29 April 1981.
58. Spoonley, 'New Zealand first!', p. 100.
59. Spoonley, *The Politics of Nostalgia*, p. 121.
60. *Otago Daily Times*, 30 July 1981.
61. *Otago Daily Times*, 17 July 1981.
62. Ibid.
63. *Otago Daily Times*, 30 July 1981.
64. *Otago Daily Times*, 28 July 1981.
65. Ibid.
66. *Otago Daily Times*, 21 July 1981.
67. Spoonley, 'New Zealand first!', p. 106.
68. Malcolm MacLean, 'From old soldiers to old youth: Political leadership and New Zealand's 1981 Springbok Rugby tour', *Football Studies*, vol. 1, no. 1, 1998, p. 31.

69. Ross Meurant, *The Red Squad Story* (Auckland: Harlen Publishing, 1982), p. 173.
70. Ibid., pp. 171–72.
71. Andy Haden, *Lock, Stock 'n Barrel* (Auckland: Rugby Press, 1988), pp. 124–25.
72. Ibid., pp. 128–29.
73. Spoonley, 'New Zealand first!', p. 114.
74. After the 1981 tour SPIR changed its name to SPIR-New Zealand: Organization for Sporting Freedom. Throughout this section, though, we continue to use the abbreviation SPIR.
75. Spoonley, 'New Zealand first!', p. 112.
76. *Otago Daily Times*, 28 July 1981.
77. *Auckland Star*, 18 July 1981, cited in Spoonley, *The Politics of Nostalgia*, p. 96.
78. Stephanie Gibson, Matariki Williams and Puawai Cairns, *Protest Tautohetohe: Objects of resistance, persistence and defiance* (Wellington: Te Papa Press, 2019), p. 180.
79. Spoonley, *The Politics of Nostalgia*, p. 96.
80. Ibid.
81. Letter from Yvonne Willcox of Free Nation New Zealand to Ces Blazey, 15 February 1982, Box: Politics in Sport/Apartheid, Collection VII: SARB Business, South African Rugby Board papers, History department, Stellenbosch University (hereafter SARB papers).
82. Report from Free Nation New Zealand to Danie Craven outlining their objectives for 1982, 31 October 1981, Box: Politics in Sport/Apartheid, Collection VII: SARB Business, SARB papers.
83. Ibid.
84. Letter from Elizabeth Sutherland to G. Craig of the New Zealand Olympic and Commonwealth Games Association, 13 September 1982, Box: Politics in Sport/ Apartheid, Collection VII: SARB Business, SARB papers.
85. This is also a recuring theme in numerous of the letters written to the editor of the *Otago Daily Times* during the tour and may be indicative of support for these groups. One letter challenged the 'blatant hypocrisy' of Shridath Ramphal, Commonwealth Secretary-General in 1981, for rebuking New Zealand for the tour when 'extreme poverty and other serious problems exist in the country of Mr Ramphal's own origin, India. Advocating the caste system India practices its own brand of apartheid.' (*Otago Daily Times*, 25 July 1981). Another letter reads: 'The record of human rights of many of these [Commonwealth countries] is, again, nothing to be proud of and that they should point the finger of judgment and accusation against New Zealand is the last word in hypocrisy'. (*Otago Daily Times*, 28 July 1981). J. Hill similarly maintained that 'most New Zealanders won't be conned by professional agitators into mob violence or by threats of other countries whose record of human rights Mr Muldoon has rightly criticized'. (*Otago Daily Times*, 17 July 1981).
86. Letter from Elizabeth Sutherland to G. Craig of the New Zealand Olympic and Commonwealth Games Association, 13 September 1982, Box: Politics in Sport/ Apartheid, Collection VII: SARB Business, SARB papers.
87. Letter from Elizabeth Sutherland to the England Rugby Football Union, 12 March 1984, Box: Politics in Sport/Apartheid, Collection VII: SARB Business, SARB papers.
88. Correspondence with Norman McKenzie. Letter from Norman McKenzie to Danie Craven, 26 February 1985, SARB Archive, Collection B, Box: B3, SARB papers.
89. Spoonley, *The Politics of Nostalgia*, p. 98.
90. Rob Nixon, 'Apartheid on the run: The South African sports boycott', *Transition*, vol. 58, no. 1, 1992, p. 81.
91. Jesson, Ryan and Spoonley, *Revival of the right*, pp. 98–99.
92. *On Target Bulletin*, vol. 11, no. 3, 13 February 1989.
93. *On Target*, vol. 11, no. 18, 30 October 1989; *On Target Bulletin*, vol. 11, no. 18, 30 October 1989.
94. *On Target*, vol. 11, no. 18, 30 October 1989; *On Target Bulletin*, vol. 11, no. 16, 29 September 1989; *On Target*, vol. 10, no. 19,

31 October 1988; *On Target*, vol. 10, no. 15, 8 August 1988; *On Target*, vol. 10, nos. 10-11, 13 June 1988; *On Target Bulletin*, vol. 10, no. 8, 2 May 1988.

95. *On Target*, vol. 11, no. 11, 3 July 1989; *On Target Bulletin*, vol. 11, no. 8, 15 May 1989; *On Target*, vol. 11, no. 2, 13 February 1989.
96. A. Dirk Moses, '"White genocide" and the ethics of public analysis', *Journal of Genocide Research*, vol. 21, no. 2, 2019, p. 209.
97. Ibid., p, 207. Moses draws this from Breivik's manifesto, pp. 1200–01.
98. 'Boer Lives Matter', Kerry Bolton's website: www.kerrybolton.com
99. Ibid. Bolton proceeds to explain why white farms were not stolen lands.
100. Spoonley, 'Right of way'.
101. See Sebastian J.S. Potgieter, '(Re)presenting 1981: Narrating the Springbok tour' (PhD thesis, University of Otago, 2020).
102. Paul Spoonley, 'Right of way'.

CHAPTER TEN

1. James Belich, *Paradise Reforged: A history of the New Zealanders* (Auckland: Penguin Press, 2001), p. 17.
2. Ibid, p. 189.
3. Paul Spoonley, 'The Asianisation of Aotearoa: Immigration impacts', in Avril Bell, Vivienne Elizabeth, Tracey McIntosh and Matt Wynyard (eds), *A Land of Milk and Honey? Making sense of Aotearoa New Zealand* (Auckland: Auckland University Press, 2017).
4. Paul Spoonley, 'Boots and bristle: Skinhead music and politics as resistance', *Sites*, vol. 14, 1987, pp. 103–4.
5. See, for example, ibid.
6. John Pollard, 'Skinhead culture: The ideologies, mythologies, religions and conspiracy theories of racist skinheads', *Patterns of Prejudice*, vol. 50, no. 4–5, 2016, pp. 398–419.
7. Jack B. Moore, *Skinheads Shaved for Battle: A cultural history of American skinheads* (Ohio: Bowling Green State University Popular Press, 1993), p. 34.
8. The 14 words are: 'We must secure the existence of our people and a future for white children'. Lane wrote the slogan while serving a 190-year prison sentence for his part in an antisemitic murder, and it is derived from a passage in Adolf Hitler's *Mein Kampf*.
9. R. Addison, 'Alienation and skinheads: An exploratory study into the attitudes of an antisocial subgroup of society' (MA thesis, University of Canterbury, 1996); M.S. Hamm, *American Skinheads: The criminology and control of hate crime* (Westport: Praeger Publishers, 1993); J.O. Jefferson, 'Cultural responses of the teds: The defence of space and status', in S. Hall and T. Jefferson (eds), *Resistance Through Rituals* (London: Hutchinson, 1976).
10. Spoonley, 'Boots and bristle', p. 105.
11. 'Estimated resident population (ERP), subnational population by ethnic group, age, and sex, at 30 June 1996, 2001, 2006, 2013 and 2018 2018 Information on table', NZ.Stat: http://nzdotstat.stats.govt.nz/WBOS/Index.aspx?DataSetCode=TABLECODE7512; Addison, 'Alienation and skinheads', pp. 93–101.
12. Chapman, 1997, pers. comm.
13. Jarrod Gilbert, *Patched: The history of gangs in New Zealand* (Auckland: Auckland University Press, 2013).
14. Ibid.
15. Addison, 'Alienation and skinheads'.
16. M.W. Klein, *The American Street Gang: Its nature, prevalence and control* (New York: Oxford University Press, 1995), p. 106.
17. M.S. Jankowski, *Islands in the Street: Gangs and American urban society* (Berkeley: University of California Press, 1991); I.A. Spergel, *The Youth Gang Problem: A community approach* (New York: Oxford University Press, 1995), p. 65.
18. Hamm, *American skinheads*, chapters 2–3.

19. *National Party Policies: Creating a decent society* (Wellington: New Zealand National Party, 1990).
20. Belich, *Paradise Reforged*, p. 410.
21. P. Dalziel and R. Lattimore, *The New Zealand Macroeconomy: A briefing on the reforms* (Melbourne: Oxford University Press, 1996), p. 90.
22. J. Kelsey, *The New Zealand Experiment: A world model for structural adjustment?* (Auckland: Auckland University Press, 1995), p. 258.
23. J.M. Hagedorn, *People and Folks: Gangs, crime and the underclass in a rustbelt city* (Chicago: Lake View Press, 1988); Jankowski, *Islands in the Street*; J.F.J. Short, 'Forward: Diversity and change in U.S. gangs', in C.R. Huff (ed.), *Gangs in America*, 2nd edn (Thousand Oaks: Sage Publications, 1990); C.S. Taylor, *Dangerous Society* (East Lansing: Michigan University Press, 1989); J.D. Vigil, *A Rainbow of Gangs: Street cultures in the mega-city* (Austin: University of Texas Press, 2002).
24. *New Zealand Year Book*, 1993, p. 272.
25. Patrick Massey, *New Zealand: Market liberalisation in a developed economy* (Basingstoke: Palgrave Macmillan, 1995), p. 161.
26. Michael King, *The Penguin History of New Zealand* (Auckland: Penguin, 2003), p. 493.
27. W. Kasper, *Populate or Languish? Rethinking New Zealand's immigration policy* (Wellington: New Zealand Business Roundtable, 1990).
28. Belich, *Paradise Reforged*, p. 537.
29. *New Zealand Year Book*, 2002, p. 11.
30. Glennis Dennehy and Greg Newbold, *The Girls in the Gang* (Auckland: Reed, 2001), p. 188.
31. Addison, 'Alienation and skinheads', p. 103.
32. Ibid., pp. 102–3; Dennehy and Newbold, *The Girls in the Gang*, p. 188.
33. *Press*, 2 April 1994.
34. Dennehy and Newbold, *The Girls in the Gang*, p. 188.
35. *New Zealand Herald*, 2 December 1991.
36. Ibid.; *Press*, 23 September 1992.
37. Sometime before this, the group either had, or were seeking to form, an outlaw club called the 'Last Rebels'. Many years later, I saw the back patch that they had designed for this purpose.
38. Letter attached to the Charter and Rules of the Southern Sons Motorcycle Club (held by the author).
39. Addison, 'Alienation and skinheads', p. 197.
40. Dennehy and Newbold, *The Girls in the Gang*, p. 189.
41. *Sunday Star Times*, 29 June 2008.
42. *New Zealand Herald*, 8 May 1998.
43. *Press*, 3 April 1999.
44. *The New Way Trust: Establishment of office system and employment strategy – 2 August 1994* (New Way Trust, 1994), p. 1.
45. R. Addison, *Evaluation of the New Way Trust Skinhead Project* (Christchurch: Christchurch City Council and the Crime Prevention Unit, 1995).
46. *Press*, 2 April 1994.
47. *New Zealand Herald*, 11 January 1995.
48. A copy of the pamphlet is held by the author.
49. *Health and Fitness, Hammer* (New Zealand Hammerskins, *c.* 2003).
50. 'The Hammerskin Nation', Anti-Defamation League, www.adl.org/education/resources/profiles/hammerskin-nation
51. Jarrod Gilbert and Benn Elley, 'Shaved heads and sonnenrads: Comparing white supremacist skinheads and the alt-right in New Zealand', *Kōtuitui: New Zealand Journal of Social Sciences online*, vol. 15, no. 2, 2020, pp. 280–94; Chapman 2015 personal communication.
52. *Hammerskin Nation: What we are and what we stand for* (New Zealand Hammerskins, *c.* 2003); Jeffrey Kaplan, 'Leaderless resistance', *Terrorism and Political Violence*, vol. 9, no. 3, 1997, pp. 80–95.
53. *New Zealand Herald*, 17 November 1997.
54. Ibid., 19 November 1997.
55. *New Zealand Parliamentary Debates*, vol. 565, 1997, p. 5458.
56. *New Zealand Herald*, 20 November 1997.
57. Gilbert and Elley. 'Shaved heads and sonnenrads', p. 286.

58. Action Zealandia website: https://action-zealandia.com/
59. J.D. Vigil, Barrio Gangs (Austin: University of Texas Press, 1988).

CHAPTER ELEVEN

1. Dolores Janiewski and Paul Morris, *New Rights New Zealand: Myths, moralities and markets* (Auckland: University of Auckland Press, 2005), pp. 5–7. A popular book about the 'Christian Family' circulating in conservative Christian circles described the husband as the 'head' and counselled women to fulfil their 'primary responsibility' as the 'helpmeet' relying upon *Genesis* 2:18 – see Larry Christensen, *The Christian Family* (Minneapolis: Bethany Fellowship, 1970), p. 17, as discussed in Rex J. Ahdar, *Worlds Colliding: Conservative Christians and the law* (Aldershot: Ashgate Publishing, 2001), pp. 187–88; 'Advance the Kingdom', One Party: https://oneparty.net/; 'Moral Issues', Vision NZ 2020 Policy Platform: www.vision.org.nz/2020-policy.
2. Janiewski and Morris, *New rights New Zealand*, p. 108; Bruce Jesson, Allanah Ryan and Paul Spoonley, *Revival of the Right: New Zealand politics in the 1980s* (Auckland: Heinemann Reed, 1988), pp. 18–29, 84–85.
3. Jonathan Boston, 'Christian political parties and MMP', in Rex Ahdar and John Stenhouse (eds), *God and Government: The New Zealand experience* (Dunedin: University of Otago Press, 2000), pp. 105–24, p. 115.
4. Fraser Macdonald, 'Spirit of resistance: Why Destiny Church and other New Zealand Pentecostalists oppose lockdowns and vaccination', The Conversation, 29 October 2021: https://theconversation.com/spirit-of-resistance-why-destiny-church-and-other-new-zealand-pentecostalists-oppose-lockdowns-and-vaccination-170193
5. Gary North and Gary DeMar, *Christian Reconstructionism: What it is, what it isn't* (Tyler: Institute for Christian Economics, 1994); Glenn H. Utter and John W. Storey, 'Chalcedon Foundation', in Glenn H. Utter and John W. Storey (eds), *The Religious Right: A reference handbook* (Santa Barbara: ABC-Clio, 2001); Kenneth L. Gentry, 'Appointed for the defense of the gospel: The life and ministry of Greg L. Bahnsen', Chalcedon Foundation, 1 February 2004: https://chalcedon.edu/magazine/appointed-for-the-defense-of-the-gospel-the-life-and-ministry-of-greg-l-bahnsen; David K. Watson, 'The Christian reconstruction/theonomy movement', Christian Library: www.christianstudylibrary.org/article/christian-reconstruction-theonomy-movement; John Haverland, 'Theonomy: What have we learned?' OPC: www.opc.org/OS/html/V4/2b.html/
6. 'Family Life International's Story', Family Life International, https://fli.org.nz/about_fli/;PK; 'Inspiring Men', Promise Keepers: www.promisekeepers.org.nz/links/; Laurie Guy, *Shaping Godzone: Public issues and church voices in New Zealand 1840–2000* (Wellington: Victoria University Press, 2011), pp. 408–09. For evidence of the continuing alliance, see National March for Life New Zealand whose sponsors include the NZ Catholic Bishops Conference, Family First, Focus on the Family, Promise Keepers, Voice for Life, Right to Life, and National March for Life New Zealand; Megan Cook, 'Abortion – opposition and support from the 1960s', Te Ara – The Encyclopedia of New Zealand: https://teara.govt.nz/en/abortion/page-3
7. *Otago Daily Times*, 6 December 2004.
8. Brad Christerson and Richard Flory, *The Rise of Network Christianity: How independent leaders are changing the religious landscape* (New York: Oxford University Press, 2017), p. 7.
9. Kate Bowler, *Blessed: A history of the American prosperity gospel* (New York: Oxford University Press, 2013), pp. 6–8.
10. Greta Bond, 'Evangelistic performance in New Zealand: The word and what is not

said' (PhD thesis, University of Canterbury, 2008), p. 155; Donald E. Miller and Tetsunao Yamamori, *Global Pentecostalism: The new face of Christian social engagement* (Berkeley: University of California Press, 2007), p. 29; John Laidler, 'Try hard, find God, get rich', *Harvard Gazette,* 24 October 2017; Ben Mack, 'Villainesse goes inside ultraconservative New Zealand churches', Villainesse, 19 May 2017: www.villainesse.com/no-filter/villainesse-goes-inside-ultraconservative-new-zealand-churches; Harkanwal Singh and Lincoln Tan, 'Money and faith', New Zealand Herald, 29 September 2016: https://insights.nzherald.co.nz/article/money-and-faith/; Bowler, *Blessed*, p. xx.

11. Bowler, *Blessed*, p. 68.
12. T. Jeremy Gunn, *Spiritual Weapons: The Cold War and the forging of an American national religion* (Westport, CT: Praeger, 2009), pp. 107, 121–28; Michael G. Long, *Billy Graham and the Beloved Community: America's evangelist and the dream of Martin Luther King, Jr.* (New York: Palgrave, 2006); Darren E. Grem, *The Blessings of Business: Corporate America and the rise of conservative evangelicalism* (New York: Oxford University Press, 2016); D.W. Brogan, 'God and the juke-box: Religion in the United States,' *Manchester Guardian*, vol. 5 October 1954, p. 6; Singh and Tan, 'Money and faith'.
13. 'USA corrupt and corrupting', 'Pastors and teachers return to school!', *Challenge Weekly*, vol. 11, September 1976; John Massam, 'U.S. report', *Challenge Weekly*, 27 September 1985; 'Enthusiastic response to Christian schools', *Challenge Weekly*, 7 February 1976; 'Christian schools dedicated', *Challenge Weekly*, 7 May 1977; 'Textbook battle is on', 'Bouquets and brickbats for Anita Bryant', *Challenge Weekly*, 30 July 1977.
14. The papers of John Stafford and Elizabeth Agnes O'Neill are replete with anti-abortion pamphlets, newsletters and reports from the US but also from Australia and Canada. See AG-582, Hocken Collections.
15. 'Statement on religious diversity', Te Ara – The Encyclopedia of New Zealand: https://teara.govt.nz/en/document/32297/statement-on-religious-diversity. Brian Houston, a New Zealander, has also influenced the Christian right in Australia by creating the politically influential and controversial Hillsong Church – see Riza Casidy, 'The rise and rise of Hillsong, and what other Australian churches should learn from them', *The Conversation*, 11 July 2018: https://theconversation.com/the-rise-and-rise-of-hillsong-and-what-other-australian-churches-should-learn-from-them-94487; Jennifer Butler, *Born Again: The Christian right globalized* (London: Pluto Press, 2006); Jennifer Wright, 'The politics of fertility: The global emergence of "pro-family" organisations' (PhD thesis, Victoria University of Wellington, 2009); Doris Buss and Didi Herman, *Globalizing Family Values: The Christian right in international politics* (Minneapolis: University of Minnesota Press, 2003); Michael Wilkinson, *Global Pentecostalism: Migration, mission and public religion* (Leiden: Brill, 2012). The Christian television networks available in New Zealand include Shine, Daystar, SBN, Hope and Firstlight. New Zealanders can view James Robison, Kenneth Copeland, T.D. Jakes, Jimmy Swaggert (and his wife and son), and can also see Brian Houston on TV 3 and Shine.
16. Jesson, Ryan and Spoonley, *Revival of the Right,* pp. 56–85,
17. Janiewski and Morris, *New Rights New Zealand,* pp. 119–30, 153–68.
18. Bryan Gilling, 'Introduction', in Bryan Gilling (ed.), *'Be Ye Separate': Fundamentalism and the New Zealand experience,* Waikato Series in Religion vol. 3 (Hamilton: University of Waikato and Colcum Press, 1992), pp. xi–xiv, xi; John Evans, 'The new Christian right in New Zealand', in Gilling (ed.), *'Be ye separate'*, pp. 69–106.

19. Peter Lineham, *Destiny: The life and times of a self-made apostle* (Auckland: Penguin, 2013), pp. 12–22; 127–58, 184–98.
20. Kevin List, 'Don Brash, civil unions and the Exclusive Brethren', Scoop: www.scoop.co.nz/stories/HL0509/S00237/don-brash-civil-unions-the-exclusive-brethren.htm
21. Rex John Ahdar, 'Worlds colliding: Aspects of New Zealand conservative Christians' encounter with the law' (PhD thesis, University of Otago, 2000).
22. Guy, *Shaping Godzone,* pp. 357–460; Laurie Guy, *Worlds in Collision: The gay debate in New Zealand, 1960–1986* (Wellington: Victoria University Press, 2002).
23. Whitney Straub, *Perversion for Profit: The politics of pornography and the rise of the new right* (New York: Columbia University Press, 2011), p. 2. See also Paul Boyer, 'The evangelical resurgence in 1970s American Protestantism', in Bruce J. Schulman and Julian E. Zelizer (eds), *Rightward Bound: Making America conservative in the 1970s* (Cambridge: Harvard University Press, 2008), pp. 29–51; Joseph D. Harper, '"Heal their land": Evangelical political theology from the great awakening to the moral majority' (PhD diss., University of Nebraska-Lincoln, 2014).
24. Bill Cooke, *Kernel and Husk: The waning of Jesus in Godzone* (Wellington: Steele Roberts, 2014).
25. Boston, 'Christian political parties and MMP', p. 115.
26. Rex Ahdar, 'New Zealand: The idea of a Christian state', in Rex Ahdar and John Stenhouse (eds), *God and Government: The New Zealand experience*(Dunedin: University of Otago Press, 2000), pp. 59–76; Allan Davidson, 'Chaplain to the nation or prophet at the gate? The role of the church in New Zealand society', in John Stenhouse (ed.) assisted by G.A. Wood, *Christianity, Modernity and Culture: New perspectives on New Zealand history* (Adelaide: ATF Press, 2005), pp. 311–31.
27. Straub, *Perversion for profit*, p. 179; Seth Dowland, *Family Values and the Rise of the Christian Right* (Philadelphia: University of Pennsylvania Press, 2015).
28. Carol Schick, JoAnn Jaffe and Ailsa M. Watkinson (eds), *Contesting Fundamentalisms* (Halifax: Fernwood, 2004), p. 14.
29. Martin Durham, *The Christian Right, the Far Right and the Boundaries of American Conservatism* (Manchester: Manchester University Press, 2000).
30. Ann Burlein, *Lift High the Cross: Where white supremacy and the Christian right converge* (Durham: Duke University Press, 2002).
31. 'Get to know four more candidates', Stuff, 12 September 2014: www.stuff.co.nz/southland-times/10489238/Get-to-know-four-more-candidates
32. Stephanie Coontz, *The Way We Never Were: American families and the nostalgia trap* (New York: Basic Books, 2000), p. x.
33. Christine Dann, *Up from Under: Women and liberation in New Zealand, 1970–1985* (Wellington: Allen & Unwin, 1985), pp. 3, 15–16; Anne Else, 'On shifting ground: Self-narrative, feminist theory and writing practice' (PhD thesis, Victoria University, 2006), pp. 45, 48; Gareth Watkins, 'Birth of the gay movement', New Zealand History online: https://nzhistory.govt.nz/politics/further-information-homosexual-law-reform; Aroha Harris, *Hīkoi: Forty years of Māori protest* (Auckland: Penguin, 2004).
34. Schick, Jaffe, and Watkinson, *Contesting Fundamentalisms*, p. 9.
35. Dann, *Up from Under,* pp. 4–15, 28–39.
36. Ngahuia Te Awekotuku, 'Mana wahine: Seeking meanings for ourselves', in Maud Cahill and Christine Dann (eds), *Changing Our Lives: Women working in the women's liberation movement, 1970–1990* (Wellington: Bridget Williams Books, 1991), pp. 25–33; Ngahuia Te Awekotuku, 'Dykes & queers: Facts, fairytales and fictions'; 'He wāhine, he whenua, e ngaro ai te tangata: By women, by land, men are lost', in Ngahuia Te Awekotuku (ed.), *Mana wāhine Māori: selected writings on Māori women's art,*

culture and politics (Auckland: New Women's Press, 1991), pp 36–47.

37. 'Chronology', in Pat Rosier (ed.), *Been Around for Quite a While: Broadsheet: twenty years of Broadsheet magazine* (Auckland: New Women's Press, 1992), p. 18.
38. Sylvia Baynes, 'Waiting for the suffragettes' in Cahill and Dann (eds), *Changing our Lives*, pp. 35–41.
39. Germaine Greer, *The Female Eunuch* (London: Paladin, 1971), p. 11; Else, 'On shifting ground', pp. 55–57; Anne Else and Rosslyn Noonan, 'Unfinished business', in Sue Kedgley and Mary Varnham (eds), *Heading Nowhere in a Navy Blue Suit and Other Tales From the Feminist Revolution* (Wellington: Daphne Brasell Associates, 1993), pp. 190–203.
40. W.B. Sutch, *Women With a Cause* (Wellington: New Zealand University Press, 1973), pp. 156–225; 'Chronology', in Rosier (ed.), *Been Around for Quite a While,* p. 18; Germaine Greer as quoted in Sue Kedgley, 'Heading nowhere in a navy blue suit', in Kedgley and Varnham (eds), *Heading Nowhere in a Navy Blue Suit and Other Tales From the Feminist Revolution*, pp. 13–31.
41. Marilynn Johnson, 'Lesbian and feminist: Invisible among the invisible', in Cahill and Dann (eds), *Changing our Lives*, pp. 65–69.
42. Else and Noonan, 'Unfinished business', pp. 194–95; Jesson, Ryan and Spoonley, *Revival of the Right*, p. 84.
43. Penny Fenwick, 'Fertility, sexuality and social control in New Zealand', in Phillida Bunkle and Beryl Hughes (eds), *Women in New Zealand Society* (Auckland: George Allen & Unwin, 1980), pp. 77–98; Judith Aitken, 'Women in the political life of New Zealand', in Bunkle and Hughes (eds), *Women in New Zealand Society*, pp. 11–33.
44. James Baynard-Smith, 'What is moral re-armament?' *Salient*, 12 April 1956; H.B.R., 'Holyoake and moral re-armament', *Salient*, 1 June 1965; Society for the Protection of the Unborn Child, 'Birth of the society', *SPUC Newsletter*, 1 May 1970; Marilyn Pryor, *The Right to Live: The abortion battle of New Zealand* (Parnell: Harlen Publishing, 1986), pp. 31–32.
45. 'National conference'; 'Germaine Greer and abortion', *SPUC Newsletter*, 10 May 1972.
46. *SPUC Newsletter*, August 1972; Australian Right to Life newsletters, Human Life International, *HLI Reports,* papers of John Stafford and Elizabeth Agnes O'Neill, Hocken Collections.
47. Pryor, *Right to Live*, pp. 28, 36.
48. Ibid., pp. 39–44.
49. B.D. Inglis, Society for the Protection of the Unborn Child, N.Z. Royal Commission on Contraception, Sterilisation & Abortion, Submissions & Hearings, vol. 7, Parliamentary Library, Wellington (hereafter RCCSA papers); Comments of William Liley, SPUC, vol. 14, RCCSA papers.
50. Contraception and sterilisation from Catholic Bishops, 2 February 1976, vol. 8, RCCSA papers.
51. Very Rev. O.J. Rymer, Family Rights Association, vol. 10, RCCSA papers.
52. George Gilder, 'The suicide of the sexes', *Reader's Digest*, February 1975, pp. 52–57, vol. 12, RCCSA papers; Pankaj Mishra, *Bland Fanatics: Liberals, race and empire* (London: Verso, 2020), pp. 121–27; Nellie Bowles, 'Jordan Peterson, custodian of the patriarchy', *New York Times*, 18 May 2018: www.nytimes.com/2018/05/18/style/jordan-peterson-12-rules-for-life.html
53. Abortion, Sterilisation and Contraception Act (1977 no. 112); Dann, *Up from Under*, pp. 59–63.
54. 'Royal report ambiguous', *Challenge Weekly*, 14 May 1977.
55. Straub, *Perversion for profit*, pp. 179–212; Carolyn Moynihan, *A Stand for Decency: Patricia Bartlett and the Society for Promotion of Community Standards, 1970–1995* (Wellington: SPUC, 1995).
56. Moynihan, *A Stand for Decency*, pp. 14–15, 27.
57. Ibid., pp. 9–12, 43–44, 62–64, 126–43.
58. Gordon Tait, *The Bartlett Syndrome: Censorship in New Zealand* (Christchurch:

Freedom to Read, 1979), pp. 1, 11, 13.

59. Moynihan, *A Stand for Decency,* pp. 12, 202, p. 12; Angela Ots, 'Retired Bartlett promises to keep society on its toes', *Evening Post,* 14 November 1995, p. 9; Richard Nixon, 'Address to the nation on the War in Vietnam ('Silent Majority speech')', MIT, 3 November 1969: http://web.mit.edu/21h.102/www/Primary%20source%20collections/Vietnam/Nixon,%20Silent%20Majority.htm
60. Evans 'The new Christian right in New Zealand', pp. 74–76; Cooke, *Kernel and Husk,* pp. 80–81, 90; 'Thousands march for life', *Challenge Weekly,* 16 September 1975; 'Pro-lifers fill Queen Street', *Challenge Weekly,* 30 September 1976; 'Enthusiastic response to Christian schools'; Pat Blane, 'To lib or not to lib?' *Challenge Weekly,* 17 July 1976; Mrs Margaret Robertson, Blenheim, *Challenge Weekly,* 11 February 1977; 'Textbook battle is on'; Dowland, *Family Values and the Rise of the Christian Right,* pp. 35, 54–64, 70, 74–77; Moynihan, *A Stand for Decency,* pp. 127–28.
61. Moynihan, *A Stand for Decency,* pp. 129–36. Enrique Rueda, the author of *The Homosexual Network,* was a priestly associate of a right-wing think tank in Washington, DC who had also written *Roman Catholicism and American capitalism*; clipping, advertisement for 'The homosexual network', *National* Review, 22 July 1983, Resource Center LGBT Collection, UNT Digital Library, University of Texas, Austin: https://digital.library.unt.edu/ark:/67531/metadc177449/m1/1/
62. Janiewski and Morris, *New Rights New* Zealand, pp. 122–29; Moynihan, *A Stand for Decency,* pp. 7–8. See also Laurie Guy, *Worlds in Collision.*
63. 'Concerned Group Form Coalition', 'John Massam's US Report', *Challenge Weekly,* 27 September 1985; Moynihan, *A Stand for Decency,* p. 9; Janiewski and Morris, *New Rights New Zealand,* p. 124. The most prominent moral missionary was the Rev. Louis Sheldon, then head of Californians for Traditional Values, and later head of the Traditional Values Coalition and author of *The Agenda: The homosexual plan to change America* (Lake Mary: Frontline, 2005).
64. Based upon an analysis of submissions to the Select Committee on the Homosexual Law Reform Bill. This included 255 individuals and 50 institutions supporting the Bill and 459 individuals and 140 institutions opposing the Bill, out of a total of approximately 960 submissions. These are held in the lesbian and gay archives of New Zealand (LAGANZ) hosted at the ATL. See also Guy, *Worlds in Collision*; Ahdar, *Worlds Colliding,* p. 10.
65. Selwyn Dawson, 'God's bullies,' *Metro,* July 1985, pp. 170–76; Michael Lienesch, *Redeeming America: Piety and politics in the new Christian right* (Chapel Hill: University of North Carolina Press, 1993), pp. 23, 56, 57, 73, 78, for more extensive discussion see pp. 52–93; 'New Dobson films', *Challenge Weekly,* 13 June 1986; George Lakoff, *Moral Politics: How liberals and conservatives think,* 2nd edn (Chicago: University of Chicago Press, 2002), pp. 40, 65, for a more extended discussion see pp. 65–107.
66. Lakoff, *Moral politics,* pp. 225–26; Evans, *Sexual citizenship,* p. 78.
67. Moynihan, *A Stand for Decency,* p. 7; Dowland, *Family Values and the Rise of the Christian Right,* pp. 5–12.
68. Katherine O'Regan, Associate Minister Public Health Rationale, Ministry of Health, 27 July 1993; Katherine O'Regan to My Colleagues, 21 July 1993; Associate Minister: Documents to Colleagues; Aids Foundation Responds to John Banks, 11 December 1992; Kevin Hague to Vic Francis and John Massam, Editor & Publisher, *Challenge Weekly,* 27 November 1992; NZ Aids Foundation Media Releases; Helen Clark, First Reading of the Human Rights Act, 15 December 1992, all contained in Katherine O'Regan papers, LAGANZ, MS-Papers-0082, ATL (hereafter O'Regan papers).

69. Submissions on Human Rights Amendment Bill, 1992; 'Society says anti-discrimination law would mean gay toilets', 28 April 1993, O'Regan papers.
70. 'Foundation says anti-gay pamphlets stir up prejudice', 25 January 1993, NZPA Coverage; Barbara Faithful, Credo Society to Warren Kyd, 6 December 1992, Confidential; Barbara Faithful, Credo Society to the Editor, *North Shore Times Advertiser*, 5 December 1992; Arthur Wilder-Smith, 'Variety Hour', Radio Rhema, 14 November 1992; Graham Capel and Kim Hill, 'Morning Report', 11 November 1992; Miscellaneous press releases; Graeme Lee, radio discussion, 10 November 1992, NZPA Coverage; Graeme Lee, 10 June 1993, 28 July 1993, Graeme Lee Press Statements; Media Release for the Hon. John Banks, 21 October 1992, 10 November 1992; John Banks, Media Release, Conviction of Peter Ellis 9 June 1993; minister of police press statements, all contained in O'Regan papers.
71. Select Committee Report Back 22 July 1993; John Banks, Second Reading Supplementary Paper to Human Rights Amendment Act, 27 July 1993; 'Banks says public support outweighs threats'; 'No evidence homosexuals abuse more, Shipley says', 10 June 1993; Graeme Lee Press Statements, 10 June 1993, 28 July 1993; Grant Thomas, Geoff Braybrooke, Second Reading Supplementary Paper to Human Rights Amendment Act, 27 July 1993, all contained in O'Regan papers; Moynihan, *A Stand for Decency*, p. 202.
72. Peter Tapsell, Ian Peters, Grant Thomas, Second Reading Supplementary Paper to Human Rights Amendment Act, 27 July 1993, O'Regan papers.
73. 'Homosexuals not child abusers, says O'Regan', 9 June 1993; Michael Cullen, Richard Prebble, Jim Anderton, Third Reading of Supplementary Paper, 27 July 1993, O'Regan papers.
74. Moynihan, *A Stand for Decency*, p. 141.
75. Ann Hardy, 'Destiny breaks through media screens', in Peter Horsfield (ed.), *Papers from the Trans-Tasman Research Symposium: Emerging research in media, religion and culture* (Melbourne: RMIT Publishing, 2005), pp. 40–56; Lineham, *Destiny*, pp. 141–58.
76. 'Five thousand protest against civil unions bill', New Zealand Herald, 23 August 2004: www.nzherald.co.nz/nz/five-thousand-protest-against-civil-unions-bill/KIZCADYO7OWMMU7QUEIQHCJUDA/; Ben Schrader, 'Parades and protest marches – protest marches, 1980s to 2000s', Te Ara: The Encyclopedia of New Zealand: https://teara.govt.nz/en/photograph/21123/enough-is-enough-march; Kevin List, 'Images: Enough (civil unions) is or isn't enough', Scoop, 23 August 2004: www.scoop.co.nz/stories/HL0408/S00233.htm; Leah Haines, 'Black shirts take to the streets', *Dominion Post*, 24 August 2004; Leah Haines, 'March arouses Nazi fears', *Christchurch Press*, 24 August 2004; 'Civil unions bill passed', New Zealand Herald, 4 December 2004: www.nzherald.co.nz/nz/civil-unions-bill-passed/AEJSQ3XMMJCBJ4TZVXK5F5BBHQ/; Lineham, *Destiny*, pp. 12–22; Mike Mawson, 'Enough is enough! Civil unions, religious prejudice and the limits of secular tolerance', *Australian Religion Studies Review*, vol. 19, no. 1, 2006, pp. 53–75.
77. Bishop Brian Tamaki press release, 'Bishop Tamaki's nation under siege tour launched', Scoop, 22 June 2005: www.scoop.co.nz/stories/PO0506/S00236/bishop-tamakis-nation-under-siege-tour-launched.htm; Lineham, *Destiny*, pp. 184–98.
78. Family First press release, 'Organisations opposing "anti-smacking" bill', Family First website, 27 March 2007: https://familyfirst.org.nz/2007/03/27/organisations-opposing-anti-smacking-bill/. Focus on the Family and Promise Keepers were both imported from the United States – see Dowland, *Family Values and the Rise of the Christian Right*, pp. 43, 86–89, 157, 162, 200, 207–27, 231.

79. Destiny New Zealand press release, 'NZ traditional family values in jeopardy', Scoop, 23 March 2007: www.scoop.co.nz/stories/PO0703/S00305/nz-traditional-family-values-in-jeopardy.htm; SPUC press release, 'Dishonesty and u-turns in anti-smacking campaign', Scoop, 20 March 2007: www.scoop.co.nz/stories/PO0703/S00238/dishonesty-and-u-turns-in-anti-smacking-campaign.htm
80. R.S. Magnusson, 'Case studies in nanny state name-calling: What can we learn?', *Public Health*, 2 July 2015; 'Helengrad', 'Story: English language in New Zealand', Te Ara: The Encyclopedia of New Zealand: https://teara.govt.nz/en/cartoon/40313/helengrad
81. Ruby Harrold-Claesson press release, 'Bradford's bill will create new criminals', Scoop, 28 March 2007: www.scoop.co.nz/stories/PO0703/S00360.htm; Coalition against Nanny State's Anti-Smacking Law press release, 'March on parliament to protest anti-smacking', Scoop, 19 March 2007: www.scoop.co.nz/stories/PO0703/S00226.htm; Marc Alexander, 'Children do not belong to the state', Scoop, 16 March 2007: www.scoop.co.nz/stories/PO0703/S00206/children-do-not-belong-to-the-state.htm; Craig Smith, *The Christian Foundations of the Institution of Corporal Correction* (Palmerston North: Family Integrity, 2005).
82. Grey Power New Zealand press release, 'Elderly concerned about Bradford's bill', Scoop, 20 March 2007: www.scoop.co.nz/stories/PO0703/S00237/elderly-concerned-about-bradfords-bill.htm; Sensible Sentencing Trust, 'Ban smacking – build more prisons', Scoop, 24 March 2007: www.scoop.co.nz/stories/PO0703/S00315.htm; 'Rising violence in schools "due to lax discipline"', *New Zealand Herald*, 29 July 2007; Family First press release, '5-point action plan to tackle child abuse', Scoop, 29 July 2007: www.scoop.co.nz/stories/PO0707/S00350.htm; Smith, *The Christian Foundations*.
83. Alexander, 'Children do not belong to the state'; Family Integrity press release, 'Selling out', Scoop, 25 March 2007: www.scoop.co.nz/stories/PO0703/S00320.htm. For a discussion of the Christian right in the United States and the Doha Declaration see Butler, *Born again*, pp. 70–76.
84. Maggie Tait, 'United Future MP quits party over smacking bill', New Zealand Herald, 16 May 2007: www.nzherald.co.nz/nz/united-future-mp-quits-party-over-smacking-bill/CZA4NTSFQY3HBPAFLNDMP472S4/; Gordon Copeland press release: 'Copeland steps down as co-leader of Future New Zealand', Scoop, 25 January 2008: www.scoop.co.nz/stories/PA0801/S00184.htm; Michael Fox, 'Smacking referendum: No vote wins', Stuff, 27 August 2009: www.stuff.co.nz/national/politics/2776567/Smacking-referendum-No-vote-wins
85. Tony Wall, 'Is Tamaki's empire crumbling?' Stuff, 7 March 2010: www.stuff.co.nz/national/3414336/Is-Tamakis-empire-crumbling
86. 'Where do party leaders stand on key family issues?' Family First website: www.familyfirst.org.nz/wp-content/uploads/2020/07/Leaders-page-with-Judith.pdf;
87. Bob McCoskrie, 'A message from Bob McCoskrie – founder and CE,' Family First website: https://familyfirst.org.nz/2022/03/23/update-16-years-of-family-first/
88. Sara Diamond, *Roads to Dominion: Right-wing movements and political power in the United States* (New York: Guilford Press, 1995); Esther Kaplan, *With God on their Side: How Christian fundamentalists trampled science, policy and democracy in George W. Bush's White House* (New York: New Press, 2004); Gunn, *Spiritual Weapons*.
89. Scott Kara and NZPA, '"Devil" talk loses pastor TV slot', New Zealand Herald, 30 June 2000: www.nzherald.co.nz/nz/devil-talk-loses-pastor-tv-slot/HMSJYHFQJSACA2FMLQJQ7VKMMY/; 'Vision NZ policy: NZ Election 2020', Spinoff: https://policy.nz/parties/Vision-NZ; Audrey Young, 'Family First say

the men in black', New Zealand Herald, 24 August 2004; '2020 General Election and Referendums – Official Result – Nationwide Party Votes Results', Electoral Commission: https://electionresults.govt.nz/electionresults_2020/; 'One Party policy: NZ Election 2020', Spinoff: https://policy.nz/parties/One-Party

90. 'New Conservative policy: NZ Election 2020', Spinoff: https://policy.nz/parties/New-Conservative
91. '2020 General Election and Referendums – Official Result'; 'Where do party leaders stand on key family issues?' Family First website: www.familyfirst.org.nz/wp-content/uploads/2020/07/Leaders-page-with-Judith.pdf; Ron Capshaw, 'Crossing the rubicon: a review of Rich Perlstein's "Reaganland: America's Rightward Turn, 1976–1980"', Liberty, November-December 2020: http://libertymagazine.org/article/crossing-the-rubicon
92. 'Where do party leaders stand on key family issues?'; 'NZ First policy: NZ Election 2020', Spinoff: https://policy.nz/parties/NZ-First; '2020 General Election and Referendums – Official Result'.
93. 'Economic policy', New Conservative Party website: www.newconservative.org.nz/policy/economic-policy/; Dowland, *Family Values and the Rise of the Christian Right*, pp. 6, 11–12, 43, 84–89.
94. Alex Braae, 'A night in Gore with New Zealand's most formidable conservative campaigners', Spinoff, 25 September 2020: https://thespinoff.co.nz/politics/25-09-2020/a-night-in-gore-with-new-zealands-most-formidable-conservative-campaigners; Alex Braae, 'A revelation in Marton: The Spinoff meets New Zealand's newest Christian party', Spinoff, 18 August 2020: https://thespinoff.co.nz/politics/18-08-2020/a-revelation-in-marton-the-spinoff-meets-new-zealands-newest-christian-party/; 'Our people', One Party website: https://oneparty.net/our-team/; 'Our team', Vision New Zealand website: www.vision.org.nz/; 'New Conservative policy: NZ Election 2020', Spinoff: https://policy.nz/parties/New-Conservative; 'The NZ First team', New Zealand First website: www.nzfirst.nz/team
95. 'Board of Reference', Family First website: www.familyfirst.org.nz/about-us/board-of-reference/; 'NZ Forum on the Family', Family First website: www.familyfirst.org.nz/wp-content/uploads/2019/04/Forum-Poster-2019.pdf
96. 'Our Values', One Party website: https://oneparty.net/our-values/
97. Jon Stokes, 'Peters unveils NZ First treaty policy', New Zealand Herald, 22 June 2005: www.nzherald.co.nz/nz/peters-unveils-nz-first-treaty; policy/EAIPFTBFPFN4EKMNU4VTRYLVFM/; 'Our policies', New Zealand First, www.nzfirst.nz/our_policies
98. '2020 policy platform', Vision New Zealand website: www.vision.org.nz/2020-policy; Mark Quinlivan, 'Hannah Tamaki's Vision NZ says it will ban the construction of mosques, temples and other "foreign buildings"', Newshub, 11 November 2019: www.newshub.co.nz/home/politics/2019/11/hannah-tamaki-s-vision-nz-says-it-will-ban-the-construction-of-mosques-temples-and-other-foreign-buildings.html
99. 'Are you conservative?', New Conservative Party website, www.newconservative.org.nz/wp-content/uploads/2020/09/nc_brouchure-2.pdf; 'New Conservative congratulates Family First', New Conservative Party website: www.newconservative.org.nz/2020/07/13/new-conservative-congratulates-family-first/; Farida Master, 'From darkness to light: Journey of youth worker turned politician', Times Online, 23 June 2020: www.times.co.nz/news/from-darkness-to-light-journey-of-youth-worker-turned-politician/; 'Our values', New Conservative Party website: www.newconservative.org.nz/our-values/
100. Kevin Roose, 'The making of a youtube radical,' New York Times, 9 June 2019: www.nytimes.com/interactive/2019/06/08/technology/youtube-radical.html;

Tamara Khandaker, 'Lauren Southern is the alt-right's not-so-secret weapon', Vice, 3 November 2017: www.vice.com/en/article/8xmyaa/lauren-southern-is-the-alt-rights-not-so-secret-weapon; Nick Truebridge and Todd Niall, 'Auckland's powerstation owner apologises for booking controversial speakers', Stuff, 3 August 2018: www.stuff.co.nz/auckland/106002242/aucklands-powerstation-owner-apologises-for-booking-controversial-speakers; Gyles Beckford, 'New alt-right groups hiding in plain sight – investigation', Radio New Zealand, 28 April 2019: www.rnz.co.nz/national/programmes/insight/audio/2018692368/new-alt-right-political-groups-hiding-in-plain-sight-investigation; John Weekes, 'Lauren Southern and Stefan Molyneux: "Thugs" veto canned visit, court told', Stuff, 4 August 2020: www.stuff.co.nz/national/politics/300073301/lauren-southern-and-stefan-molyneux-thugs-veto-canned-visit-court-told

101. Alex Braae, 'Coup conservatives? Leader ousted to make way for "outspoken" Elliot Ikilei', Spinoff, 19 November 2020: https://thespinoff.co.nz/politics/19-11-2020/coup-conservatives-leader-ousted-to-make-way-for-outspoken-elliot-ikilei/; Corazon Miller, 'New Conservatives defend western culture as "greatest in the world", warn NZ "sliding toward socialism"', Newshub, 7 July 2020: www.newshub.co.nz/home/shows/2020/07/new-conservatives-defend-western-culture-as-greatest-in-the-world-warn-nz-sliding-toward-socialism.html; Julia Alexander, 'YouTube bans Stefan Molyneux, David Duke and Richard Spencer for hate speech', Verge, 29 June 2020: www.theverge.com/2020/6/29/21307303/youtube-bans-molyneux-duke-richard-spencer-conduct-hate-speech

102. 'Hundreds protest against lockdowns, vaccines while unmasked in Auckland', TVNZ, 29 August 2020: www.tvnz.co.nz/one-news/new-zealand/hundreds-protest-against-lockdowns-vaccines-while-unmasked-in-auckland

103. Kate Hannah, Sanjana Hattotuwa and Kayli Taylor, 'Working Paper: Mis- and disinformation in Aotearoa New Zealand from 17 August to 5 November 2021', The Disinformation Project, November 2021: www.tepunahamatatini.ac.nz/2021/11/09/mis-and-disinformation/

104. Dieuwe de Boer, 'Doing what works: My speech at New Conservative campaign launch', Right Minds, 22 June 2020: www.rightminds.nz/articles/doing-what-works-my-speech-new-conservative-2020-campaign-launch. Dieuwe de Boer was the New Conservative candidate for Botany – see 'Our team', New Conservative Party website: www.newconservative.org.nz/team/dieuwe-de-boer/; Matthew Theunissen, 'Far right activist's house raided over suspected illegal firearm', RNZ, 11 January 2020: www.rnz.co.nz/news/national/407097/far-right-activist-s-house-raided-over-suspected-illegal-firearm; 'New Conservative Party promotes Dieuwe de Boer for Botany seat', Times Online, 7 May 2020: www.times.co.nz/news/new-conservative-party-promotes-dieuwe-de-boer-for-botany-seat/; Dieuwe de Boer, 'From the ashes: New Conservative public meeting in Botany', Right Minds, 19 February 2019: www.rightminds.nz/articles/ashes-new-conservative-public-meeting-botany

105. Qama Qukula, 'SA expat runs for office in New Zealand, calling himself an "apartheid survivor"', Capetalk 567 AM: www.capetalk.co.za/articles/398876/martin-frauenstein-former-da-member-runs-for-office-in-nz-calling-himself-apartheid-survivor; Dieuwe de Boer, 'About us and our mission', Right Minds: www.rightminds.nz/about-us-our-mission; Beckford, 'New alt-right groups hiding in plain sight'; '"Hope NZ enjoys shariah" – alt-right speakers' agent responds to having their Auckland event at the Powerstation cancelled last-minute', One News, 4 August 2018: www.1news.co.nz/2018/08/03/hope-nz-enjoys-shariah-alt-right-speakers-agent-responds-to-

having-their-auckland-event-at-the-powerstation-cancelled-last-minute/; David Fisher, 'Andrew Little happy "insidious" alt-right pair leaving the country as bomb threat emerges', New Zealand Herald, 4 August 2018: www.nzherald.co.nz/nz/andrew-little-happy-insidious-alt-right-pair-leaving-the-country-as-bomb-threat-claim-emerges/MLQJOQGTHE2WET6ZADPH2NFDAI/

106. Beckford, 'New alt-right groups hiding in plain sight'.
107. 'Botany – Official Result', Electoral Commission: www.electionresults.govt.nz/electionresults_2020/electorate-details-04.html; Dieuwe de Boer, 'Life goes on', Right Minds, 19 October 2020: www.rightminds.nz/articles/life-goes-on
108. Dr Stuart Lange, 'It's a matter of life and death', New Zealand Christian Network, 11 March 2020: https://nzchristiannetwork.org.nz/its-a-matter-of-life-and-death/; Dowland, *Family Values and the Rise of the Christian Right*, p. 127.
109. Henry Cooke, 'National Party MP Alfred Ngaro says number of abortions in New Zealand is a "tragedy"', Stuff, 21 May 2019: www.stuff.co.nz/national/politics/112876936/national-party-mp-alfred-ngaro-says-number-of-abortions-in-new-zealand-is-a-tragedy
110. Agnes Loheni, 'Read MP Agnes Loheni's minority report on Labor's Abortion Bill', *Voice for Life*, 15 February 2020.
111. 'National's Fundamentals', Standard, 6 November 2019: https://thestandard.org.nz/nationals-fundamentals/; Chris Trotter, 'Chosen to rule? What sort of Christian is Chris Luxon?' Daily Blog, 8 November 2019: https://thedailyblog.co.nz/2019/11/08/chosen-to-rule-what-sort-of-christian-is-chris-luxon/; Andrea Stepnick, 'Making Godly men: The social construction of masculinities in Promise Keepers' (PhD thesis, Florida State University, 1999); Mary Stricker, 'A new racial ideology for the new Christian right? The meaning(s) of racial reconciliation within the Promise Keepers movement' (PhD thesis, Temple University, 2001); Susan Ridgley, 'Conservative Christianity and the creation of alternative news: An analysis of Focus on the Family's multimedia empire', *Religion & American Culture*, vol. 30, no.1, winter 2020, pp. 1–25.
112. Annie Laurie Gaylor, 'The hands that prey on Sunday morning', Freedom from Religion Foundation, November 1996: https://ffrf.org/component/k2/item/18525-hands-that-prey-on-sunday-morning; Daniel K. Williams, *God's Own Party: The making of the Christian right* (New York: Oxford University Press, 2010); Dowland, *Family Values and the Rise of the Christian Right*, pp. 2–3, 7, 17, 127, 152–53, 231.

CHAPTER TWELVE

1. J. Hayward, *The Treaty Challenge: Local government and Māori – a scoping report* (Wellington: Crown Forestry Rental Trust, 2002).
2. Richard Hill, *Anti-treatyism and Anti-scholarship: An analysis of anti-Treatyist writings* (Wellington: Treaty of Waitangi Unit, 2002).
3. Edward Said, *Culture and Imperialism* (London: Vintage, 1994), p. xiv.
4. Atholl Anderson, Judith Binney and Aroha Harris, *Tangata Whenua: A history* (Wellington: Bridget Williams Books, 2015).
5. Aroha Harris, *Hīkoi: Forty years of Māori protest* (Wellington: Huia Publishers, 2004).
6. Martin Fisher, *A Long Time Coming: The Story of Ngāi Tahu's treaty settlement negotiations with the Crown* (Christchurch: Canterbury University Press, 2020).
7. Rachael Bell, 'Texts and translations: Ruth Ross and the Treaty of Waitangi', *New Zealand Journal of History*, vol. 43, no. 1, 2009, pp. 39–58.
8. Claudia Orange, *The Treaty of Waitangi* (Wellington: Bridget Williams Books, 1987).
9. Ranginui Walker, *Ngā tau Tohetohe: Years of anger* (Auckland: Penguin, 1987).

10. Ranginui Walker, *Ka Whawhai Tonu Matou – Struggle without end*, 2nd edn (Auckland, Penguin, 2004).
11. James Belich, *The New Zealand Wars and the Victorian Interpretation of Racial Conflict* (Auckland: Penguin, 1986).
12. 'Truth or Treaty', University of Canterbury website: www.canterbury.ac.nz/engage/cup/catalogue/books/truth-or-treaty-commonsense-questions-about-the-treaty-of-waitangi.html
13. Hemopereki Hōani Simon, 'A political-cultural textual critique of ALT/far-right anti-indigenous thought on indigenous issues in Aotearoa New Zealand', *SITES*, vol. 17, no. 2, 2020, pp. 97–128.
14. Hugh Barr, Mike Butler, Peter Cresswell, Bruce Moon, John Robinson and David Round, *Twisting the Treaty: A tribal grab for wealth and power* (Wellington: Tross Publishing, 2013).
15. Ibid.
16. *Report of the Parliamentary Select Committee on Aboriginal Tribes* (London: William Bell, Chambers, Paternoster Row and Hatchard & Son, 1837).
17. Peter N. Meihana, 'The paradox of Māori privilege: Historical constructions of Māori privilege circa 1769 to 1940' (PhD thesis, Massey University, 2015).
18. Orange, *The Treaty of Waitangi*, p. 18.
19. Alan Ward, *A Show of Justice: Racial 'amalgamation' in nineteenth century New Zealand* (Auckland: Auckland University Press, 1995), pp. 13–14.
20. Ward, *A Show of Justice*, p. 24.
21. Meihana, 'The paradox of Māori privilege', pp. 92–93.
22. James Stephen cited in 'The Colonial Office and the New Zealand Company', in W. David McIntyre and W.J. Gardner (eds), *Speeches and Documents on New Zealand History* (London: Oxford University Press, 1971), pp. 8–9.
23. Tony Ballantyne, 'The state, politics and power, 1769–1893', in Giselle Byrnes (ed.), *The New Oxford History of New Zealand* (South Melbourne: Oxford University Press, 2009), p. 109.
24. Miles Fairburn, *The Ideal Society and its Enemies: The foundations of modern New Zealand society 1850–1900* (Auckland: Auckland University Press, 1989), pp. 19–20.
25. Montague Hawtrey, *An Earnest Address to the New Zealand Colonists* (London: John W. Parker, 1840), pp. 3–6.
26. Ibid., pp. 7–9.
27. Ibid. pp. 10–12.
28. Ibid., pp. 96–97.
29. *Nelson Examiner*, 12 October 1844, p. 3.
30. Thomas Gore Browne, Minutes of Proceedings of Kohimarama Conference, *AJHR*, 1860 Session I, E-09, pp. 3–5.
31. Meihana, 'The paradox of Māori privilege', pp. 51–52.
32. T. Lindsay Buick (ed.), *Ideals of Nationhood: A selection of Lord Bledisloe's addresses in New Zealand* (New Plymouth: Thomas Avery & Sons Limited, 1935), pp. 146–48.
33. Peter Gibbons, 'Non-fiction', in Terry Sturm (ed.), *The Oxford History of New Zealand Literature*, 1st edn, (Auckland: Oxford University Press, 1991), pp. 56–57.
34. William Pember Reeves, *The Long White Cloud – Aotearoa*, 2nd edn (Auckland: Golden Press, 1950), p. 146.
35. Ibid., p. 62.
36. Ibid., pp. 270–72.
37. Erik Olssen, 'Where to from here? Reflections on the twentieth-century historiography of nineteenth-century New Zealand', *New Zealand Journal of History*, vol. 26, no. 1, 1992, p. 55.
38. Ibid., p. 57.
39. T. Lindsay Buick, *The Treaty of Waitangi: How New Zealand became a British colony* (New Plymouth: T. Avery, 1936), p. xiv.
40. Ibid., pp. 33, 35.
41. Peter Adams, *Fatal Necessity: British intervention in New Zealand 1830–1849* (Auckland: Auckland University Press), 1977, pp. 36–45.
42. Keith Sinclair, 'Why are race relations in New Zealand better than in South Africa, South Australia or South Dakota', *New*

Zealand Journal of History, vol. 5, no. 2, 1971, p. 121.
43. Ward, *A Show of Justice*, p. 308.
44. Paul Clark, *Hauhau: The Pai Marire search for Maori identity* (Auckland: Auckland University Press, 1975); Judith Binney, Gillian Chaplin and Graig Wallace, *Mihaia: The prophet Rua Kenana and his community at Maungapohatu* (Wellington: Bridget Williams Books, 1979).
45. Ruth Ross, 'Te Tiriti o Waitangi: Texts and translations', *New Zealand Journal of History*, vol. 6, no. 2, 1972, pp. 152–53.
46. Ranginui Walker, *Ka whawhai tonu matou*, p. 90.
47. Bell, 'Texts and translations', p. 39.
48. Orange, *The Treaty of Waitangi*, p. 228.
49. Martin Fisher, 'Balancing rangatiratanga and kāwanatanga: Waikato-Tainui and Ngāi Tahu's Treaty settlement and negotiations with the Crown' (PhD thesis, Victoria University of Wellington, 2015), pp. 15–16.
50. Anderson, Binney and Harris, *Tangata Whenua*, pp. 360–61.
51. Ibid., pp. 380–81.
52. Claudia Orange, *The Treaty of Waitangi / Te Tiriti o Waitangi: An illustrated history* (Wellington: Bridget Williams Books, 2020), pp. 184–85.
53. Tipene O'Regan, 'Impact on Māori – a Ngāi Tahu perspective', in Jacinta Ruru (ed.), *'In Good Faith': Symposium proceedings marking the 20th anniversary of the lands case* (Dunedin: University of Otago Press, 2008), p. 47.
54. Anderson, Binney and Harris, *Tangata Whenua*, pp. 380–81.
55. M.P.K. Sorrenson, 'Towards a radical reinterpretation of New Zealand history: The role of the Waitangi Tribunal', in I.H. Kawharu (ed.), *Waitangi-Māori and Pākehā perspectives of the Treaty of Waitangi* (Auckland, Oxford University Press, 1989), pp. 158–61.
56. Alan Ward, *An Unsettled History: Treaty claims in New Zealand today* (Wellington: Bridget Williams Books, 1999).
57. Tony Ballantyne, 'On place, space, and mobility in nineteenth-century New Zealand', *New Zealand Journal of History*, vol. 45, no. 1, 2011, p. 52.
58. W.H. Oliver, 'The future behind us: The Waitangi Tribunal's retrospective utopia', in Andrew Sharp and Paul McHugh (eds), *Histories, Power and Loss: Uses of the past: a New Zealand commentary* (Wellington: Bridget Williams Books, 2001), pp. 9–29.
59. Giselle Byrnes, *The Waitangi Tribunal and New Zealand History* (South Melbourne: Oxford University Press, 2004).
60. Jim McAloon, 'By which standards? History and the Waitangi Tribunal', *New Zealand Journal of History*, vol. 40, no. 2, 2006, p. 195.
61. See Michael Belgrave, *Historical Frictions, Maori Claims and Reinvented Histories* (Auckland: Auckland University Press, 2005).
62. Waitangi Tribunal, *Te Tau Ihu o te Waka a Maui: Report on the Northern South Island claims*, vol. 2 (Wellington: Legislation Direct, 2008), p. 658.
63. *NZPD*, 1906, vol. 137, 138, pp. 323–25.
64. John A. Williams, *Politics of the New Zealand Maori: Protest and cooperation, 1891–1909* (Seattle: University of Washington Press, 1969), pp. 119–23.
65. Tim Shoebridge, 'Phillips, Hilda', from the Dictionary of New Zealand Biography: https://teara.govt.nz/en/biographies/6p3/phillips-hilda/print
66. Tiopira McDowell, '"Ka Hoki a Kupe?" The political career of Matiu Rata, 1963–1979', *New Zealand Journal of History*, vol. 49, no. 1, 2015, p. 144.
67. Shoebridge, 'Phillips, Hilda'.
68. Anderson, Binney and Harris, *Tangata whenua*, p. 376.
69. Janine Hayward, 'Biculturalism', Te Ara – the Encyclopedia of New Zealand: https://teara.govt.nz/en/biculturalism/print#3
70. Paul Spoonley, 'Pākehā ethnicity: A response to Māori sovereignty', in Paul Spoonley, David Pearson and Cluny Macpherson (eds), *Nga Take – Ethnic relations and racism in Aotearoa/New*

Zealand (Palmerston North: Dunmore Press, 1991), p. 159.
71. Cited in Spoonley, 'Pākehā ethnicity', pp. 160–62.
72. Paul Spoonley, 'Migration and the reconstruction of citizenship in late twentieth century Aotearoa', in Stephen Castles and Paul Spoonley (eds), *Migration and Citizenship* (Auckland: Department of Sociology, Massey University, 1997).
73. Geoff McDonald, *Shadows Over New Zealand: Defence, land rights and multiculturism* (Christchurch: Chaston Publishers, 1985).
74. 'The birth of a modern far right in New Zealand: The post-war years, 1950s–1980s', The Ice Bloc: https://theicebloc.wordpress.com/2020/07/14/the-birth-of-a-modern-far-right-in-new-zealand-the-post-war-years-1950s-1980s/
75. McDonald, *Shadows Over New Zealand*, p. 7.
76. Ibid., p. 3.
77. Ibid., p. 17.
78. Robin Mitchell, *The Treaty and the Act: The Treaty of Waitangi, 1940 and the Treaty of Waitangi Act, 1975* (Christchurch: Cadsonbury, 1990), p. 6.
79. Ibid., pp. 32–33.
80. Ibid., p. 97.
81. Ibid., p. 114.
82. Stuart C. Scott, *Travesty After Travesty* (Christchurch: Certes Press, 1996), p. 8.
83. Stuart C. Scott, *Travesty of the Treaty: Towards anarchy* (Dunedin: The Campbell Press, 1995), p. 149.
84. Ian Wishart, *The Great Divide: The story of New Zealand and its Treaty* (Auckland: Howling at the Moon Publishing, 2012), pp. 152–63.
85. Mike Butler, 'Littlewood treaty to disappear', Breaking Views: https://breakingviewsnz.blogspot.com/2016/08/mike-butler-littlewood-treaty-to.html
86. Donald Loveridge, *The 'Littlewood Treaty': An appraisal of the texts and interpretations* (Wellington: Treaty of Waitangi Research Unit, 2006), pp. 12–14.
87. Waitangi Tribunal, *Muriwhenua Fishing Report* (Wellington: GP Publications, 1988), pp. 88–90.
88. Scott Hamilton, 'The white tangata whenua and other bullshit from the One New Zealand crew'. The Spinoff, 22 May 2017: https://thespinoff.co.nz/society/22-05-2017/the-white-tangata-whenua-and-other-bullshit-from-the-one-new-zealand-crew/
89. Martin Doutré, *Ancient Celtic New Zealand* (Auckland: De Danann Publishers, 1999).
90. K.R. Howe, *The Quest for Origins: Who first discovered and settled New Zealand and the Pacific Islands?* (Auckland: Penguin, 2003), p. 148.
91. 'Greeks got here first', Stuff, 29 February 2012: www.stuff.co.nz/auckland/local-news/northland/dargaville-districts/6497943/greeks-got-here-first
92. *Northern Advocate*, 24 March 2015; *New Zealand Herald*, 30 May 2012.
93. 'Northland historian admits grave-robbing Māori burials', Newshub: www.newshub.co.nz/home/new-zealand/2017/05/northland-historian-admits-grave-robbing-maori-burials.html
94. Tess McClure, 'Far-right grave robbers could be stealing ancestral Māori skull', VICE, 18 May 2017: www.vice.com/en/article/kb4yjw/a-group-of-far-right-grave-robbers-could-be-digging-up-sacred-maori-sites
95. Don Brash, 'Nationhood': Scoop: www.scoop.co.nz/stories/PA0401/S00220/nationhood-don-brash-speech-orewa-rotary-club.htm
96. Meihana, 'The paradox of Māori privilege', pp. 247–49.
97. Adams, *Fatal Necessity*, p. 15.
98. Meihana, 'The paradox of Māori privilege', pp. 194–99.
99. 'Rotary Club pulls pin on Ansell', Stuff, 6 October 2012: www.stuff.co.nz/national/politics/7776094/Rotary-Club-pulls-pin-on-Ansell
100. Rod Vaughan, 'Ad man Ansell unveils "Treatygate" and declares war on racial

favouritism', National Business Review, 11 July 2018: www.nbr.co.nz/article/ad-man-ansell-unveils-treatygate-and-declares-war-racial-favouritism-

101. 'Why the Waitangi Tribunal must go', Hobson's Pledge: www.hobsonspledge.nz/why_the_waitangi_tribunal_must_go; Mike Butler, 'Seven reasons why the Waitangi Tribunal must go', New Zealand Centre for Political Research, 2 June 2013: www.nzcpr.com/seven-reasons-why-the-waitangi-tribunal-must-go/
102. Treaty of Waitangi Act (1975 no. 114).
103. See 'Meaning of the Treaty', Waitangi Tribunal: www.waitangitribunal.govt.nz/treaty-of-waitangi/meaning-of-the-treaty/
104. John Robinson, *The Corruption of New Zealand democracy: A Treaty overview* (Wellington: Tross Publishing, 2011); Mike Butler, *Tribes Treaty Money Power: A guide to New Zealand's Treaty issues* (Wellington: Tross Publishing, 2014).
105. 'Are we being conned by the Treaty industry', 1Law4All: www.1Law4All.kiwi.nz
106. James Belich, *Making Peoples: A history of the New Zealanders from Polynesian settlement to the end of the nineteenth century* (Auckland: Penguin, 1996), pp. 214–15.
107. Apirana Ngata, *The Treaty of Waitangi, An Explanation: Te Tiriti o Waitangi, he whakamarama* (Christchurch: Maori Purposes Board, 1963), p. 16.
108. *NZPD*, vol. 249, 1937, p. 1044; Waitangi Tribunal, *The Petroleum Report* (Wellington: Legislation Direct, 2003); 'The 1940 Centennial', New Zealand History online: https://nzhistory.govt.nz/culture/centennial/the-centennial-and-the-treaty-of-waitangi

CHAPTER THIRTEEN

1. Jon Johansson, 'Brash, Orewa and the politics of race', in Steven Levine and Nigel S. Roberts (eds), *The Baubles of Office: The New Zealand general election of 2005* (Wellington: Victoria University Press, 2007), pp. 67–68.
2. Andrew Butcher, Paul Spoonley and Phil Gendall, 'New Zealanders' attitudes to Asia and Asian peoples', *Political Science*, vol. 67, 2015, pp. 44–47.
3. *New Zealand Herald*, 4 May 2004.
4. Jim Saleam, 'Interview with Kyle Chapman', Australia First Party, 28 February 2005: http://ausfirst.alphalink.com.au/nznfinterview.html
5. 'National Front's ex-leader marries Mormon', Waikato Times, 11 May 2009: www.stuff.co.nz/waikato-times/news/2379655/National-Fronts-ex-leader-marries-Mormon
6. *Press*, 23 March 1994, p. 1; *Press*, 24 March 1994.
7. Saleam, 'Interview with Kyle Chapman'.
8. *Press*, 24 March 1994.
9. Jarrod Gilbert, *Patched: The history of gangs in New Zealand* (Auckland: Auckland University Press, 2013), pp. 144–45.
10. *Press*, 18 December 1997, p. 1.
11. Gilbert, *Patched*, p. 145.
12. *New Zealand Herald*, 16 December 1997; *Kapiti Observer*, 25 May 1998.
13. 'The 1977 hate speech attack on Jews in Auckland's Remuera', Stuff, 6 February 2021: www.stuff.co.nz/pou-tiaki/our-truth/300216192/our-truth-t-mtou-pono-the-1977-hate-speech-attack-on-jews-in-aucklands-remuera
14. *New Zealand Herald*, 16 December 1997.
15. *Press*, 18 December 1997, p. 1.
16. Paul Spoonley, *The Politics of Nostalgia: Racism and the extreme right in New Zealand* (Palmerston North: Dunmore Press, 1987), pp. 157–59.
17. Ibid., pp. 168–71.
18. Saleam, 'Interview with Kyle Chapman'.
19. *Press*, 18 March 2004, p. 4.
20. Ibid., 3 May 2004, p. 1.
21. Audrey Kobayashi, '"Here we go again": Christchurch's antiracism rally as a discursive crisis', *New Zealand Geographer*, vol. 65, 2009, pp. 59–72.
22. *Press*, 30 April 2004, p. 5.
23. Ibid., 3 May 2004, p. 1.
24. Ibid., 7 May 2004, p. 1.

25. Ibid., 10 May 2004, p. A5.
26. Kobayashi, '"Here we go again"'.
27. *Press*, 10 May 2004, p. A5.
28. One News, 23 October 2004, item F83644, Ngā Taonga Sound &Vision, Wellington.
29. Kobayashi, '"Here we go again"'.
30. *Sunday Star Times*, 9 May 2004, p. A11.
31. 'National Front thwarted in Wellington', Scoop, 8 June 2004: www.scoop.co.nz/stories/PO0406/S00065/national-front-thwarted-in-wellington.htm
32. *Weekend Herald*, 18 Sept 2004.
33. *Press*, 14 August 2004, p. 5.
34. Radio New Zealand Newswire, 26 Sept 2004:16.44, Newztext News Archive.
35. *Manawatu Standard*, 11 August 2004, p. 1.
36. *Dominion Post*, 28 September 2004, p. 1.
37. *Manawatu Standard*, 11 August 2004, p. 1.
38. *Dominion Post*, 13 April 2006, p. 4.
39. Daphne Lawless, 'Nazis humiliated in Wellington, November 2004', Fightback: https://fightback.org.nz/2018/05/05/flashback-nazis-humiliated-in-wellington-november-2004/
40. *Dominion Post*, 16 August 2004, p. A3.
41. *New Zealand Herald*, 23 October 2004, p. A7.
42. *National Front News*, no. 3, November 2004.
43. *New Zealand Herald*, 25 October 2004, p. A5.
44. *Herald on Sunday*, 24 October 2004; *New Zealand Herald*, 25 October 2004, p. 1; *Sunday Star Times*, 24 October 2004, p. 3; *Press*, 30 October 2004, p. 20; Lawless, 'Nazis humiliated in Wellington'.
45. *Press*, 30 October 2004, p. 20.
46. *National Front News*, no. 3, November 2004, pp. 1–3.
47. Ibid.
48. For example, *Sunday Star Times*, 9 May 2004, p. A11; *Manawatu Standard*, 22 October 2004.
49. *Manawatu Standard*, 22 October 2004.
50. *Weekend Herald*, 18 September 2004.
51. *Magneto*, August 2004, vol. 11, no. 4.
52. Ibid.
53. *Dominion Post*, 30 October 2004, p. A9.
54. *Press*, 7 Sept 2004, p. 4.
55. *National Front News*, no. 3, November 2004, p. 3.
56. 'Our nationalist heritage', undated leaflet, New Zealand National Front, personal collection.
57. Kerry Bolton, Renaissance Press 2006 Catalogue, personal collection; Scott Hamilton, 'The white tangata whenua, and other bullshit from the "One New Zealand crew"', Spinoff, 22 May 2017: https://thespinoff.co.nz/society/22-05-2017/the-white-tangata-whenua-and-other-bullshit-from-the-one-new-zealand-crew/
58. *Sunday Star Times*, 9 May 2004, p. A11.
59. *Waikato Times*, 28 July 2004, p. 3.
60. 'Equal rights for kiwi whites', undated leaflet, New Zealand National Front, personal collection.
61. Spoonley, *The Politics of Nostalgia*, pp. 162, 172–74.
62. 'NZ workers sacrificed to coolie labour', undated leaflet, New Zealand National Front, personal collection.
63. Gilbert, *Patched*, pp. 139–42.
64. Ibid., p. 146.
65. Hayden Crosby, 'Right-wing extremism in New Zealand: Dialogues with those who left' (MA thesis, Auckland University, 2017), pp. 74–76, 106.
66. Bolton, Renaissance Press 2006 Catalogue.
67. *Sunday Star Times*, 29 May 2005, p. 6.
68. Ibid; *Press*, 2 June 2005, p. 7.
69. *Western Leader*, 21 July 2005.
70. *Weekend Herald*, 3 December 2005, p. A13.
71. *Sunday Star Times*, 27 November 2005, p. A6.
72. *New Zealand Herald*, 30 November 2005, p. A2.
73. *Press*, 7 July 2005, p. 2.
74. 'Official count results – overall status', Electoral Commission: www.electionresults.govt.nz/electionresults_2005/partystatus.html
75. *Manawatu Standard*, 1 September 2005, p. 1.
76. Indymedia, 22 October 2006: http://de.indymedia.org/2006/10/159843.html
77. *Western Destiny*, no. 40, October 2005, p. 27.
78. *Sunday Star Times*, 11 June 2006, p. A4.

79. National Democrats Party: www.nationaldemocrats.org, archived 10 September 2007 by the National Digital Heritage Archive, NLNZ.
80. *Press*, 15 October 2007, p. 1.
81. 'The ANZAC declaration: Australia First Party and New Zealand Nationalist Alliance: declaration of common interests and future relations April 25 2008 and the ANZAC manifesto of the Australia First Party and the New Zealand Nationalist Alliance June 14 2008': http://ausfirst.alphalink.com.au/anzacdeclaration.html
82. Ibid.
83. Jim Saleam, 'Report: NZ flag day was a great success for the nationalists: ANZAC ties strengthened between NZ and Australian nationalists!', Australia First Party: http://ausfirst.alphalink.com.au/nzflagday.html
84. 'European only mini-state planned', Stuff, 31 January 2009: www.stuff.co.nz/national/804603/European-only-mini-state-planned
85. *Waikato Times*, 2 May 2009, pp. A1-A2.
86. *Sunday Star Times*, 25 October 2009, p. 2.
87. *Press*, 28 October 2009, p. A11.
88. Ibid., 5 December 2009, pp. C2–C3.
89. Ibid.
90. Ibid.
91. Ibid.
92. Ibid.
93. Eric, in Crosby, 'Right-wing extremism in New Zealand', p. 86.
94. Frank, in ibid., p. 87.
95. Ibid., p. 88.
96. Ibid.
97. Ibid., p. 89.
98. Eric, in ibid., p. 96.
99. Anti-Defamation League: www.adl.org/education/references/hate-symbols/wolfsangel
100. Anti-Defamation League: www.adl.org/education/references/hate-symbols/14-words
101. *Sunday Star Times*, 25 October 2009, p. 2.
102. 'Oaths', Right Wing Resistance, 28 October 2009: http://rwrnz.blogspot.com/2009/10/right-wing-resistance-oaths.html, harvested 18 July 2017 by the National Digital Heritage Archive, NLNZ.
103. 'Skinheads', Right Wing Resistance, 2 Nov 2010: http://rwrnz.blogspot.com/2010/11/skinheads.html
104. 'New Year plan', Right Wing Resistance, 1 Jan 2013: http://rwrnz.blogspot.com/2013/01/new-year-plan.html
105. 'Support for Vaughan', Right Wing Resistance, 17 August 2015: http://rwrnz.blogspot.com/2015/08/support-for-vaughan.html; 'Ahead of the black & silver solution fall conference, questions linger about leadership', Southern Poverty Law Centre, 12 October 2016: www.splcenter.org/hatewatch/2016/10/12/ahead-black-silver-solution-fall-conference-questions-linger-about-leadership
106. 'Right Wing Resistance euro meeting August', Right Wing Resistance, 22 June 2015: http://rwrnz.blogspot.com/2 015/06/rwr-euro-meeting-august.html
107. 'White man march in Liverpool cancelled as protest marches take over city', Liverpool Echo, 16 August 2015: www.liverpoolecho.co.uk/news/liverpool-news/re-read-white-man-march-9862384
108. 'Meet the Swede who went to Liverpool dressed as a turnip', Hope not Hate,18 August 2015: www.hopenothate.org.uk/2015/08/18/meet-the-swede-who-went-to-liverpool-dressed-like-a-turnip/
109. Andy Fleming, 'Right Wing Resistance, Ricky White & slackbastard', Slackbastard, 20 December 2018: https://slackbastard.anarchobase.com/?p=44245
110. 'Unmasked: neo-nazi racist brainwashing young Scots in bid to lure them into his sick gang of hate', Daily Record, 29 March 2016: www.dailyrecord.co.uk/news/scottish-news/unmasked-neo-nazi-racist-brainwashing-7652460
111. 'Anti-Defamation League reveals extremist background of alleged plotter', Anti-Defamation League, 17 February 2017: www.adl.org/blog/anti-defamation-league-reveals-extremist-background-of-alleged-plotter

112. 'From neo-nazi to militant: The foreign fighters in Ukraine who Australia's laws won't stop', ABC News, 1 May 2018: www.abc.net.au/news/2018-05-01/foreign-fighters-return-to-australia-with-military-training/9696784
113. 'Right-wing vigilantes on patrol in Christchurch', Stuff, 29 October 2009: www.stuff.co.nz/national/2999197/Right-wing-vigilantes-on-patrol-in-Christchurch
114. Shot list for Close Up, broadcast on *Television New Zealand* on 11 May 2011, Item TZP398148, Ngā Taonga Sound & Vision, Wellington.
115. '"Guerillas" in camo gear "spoil" meeting', Stuff, 23 November 2011: www.stuff.co.nz/the-press/news/election-2011/6015012/Guerrillas-in-camo-gear-spoil-meeting
116. 'White power movement delivers "warning"', Sunday Star Times, 1 April 2012: www.stuff.co.nz/sunday-star-times/latest-edition/6673662/White-power-movement-delivers-warning
117. '"White pride" marches in Riccarton', Press, 26 March 2012: www.stuff.co.nz/the-press/editors-picks/6635604/White-pride-marches-in-Riccarton
118. 'Masterton – seat of the fourth reich', The Civilian, 8 March 2016: www.hauraki.co.nz/video/hauraki-tv/the-civilian-masterton-seat-of-the-fourth-reich/
119. Right Wing Resistance: http://rwrnz.blogspot.com/2016/
120. 'Man stabbed at Right Wing Resistance party in Christchurch', Stuff, 24 October 2016: www.stuff.co.nz/national/crime/85672679/man-stabbed-at-right-wing-resistance-party-in-christchurch
121. Right Wing Resistance: http://rwrnz.blogspot.com/2017
122. 'Far right groups dispersing after mosque attacks – ex-leader Kyle Chapman', Radio New Zealand, 27 March 2019: www.rnz.co.nz/news/national/385647/far-right-groups-dispersing-after-mosque-attacks-ex-leader-kyle-chapman
123. 'Former far-right leader plans leaflet drop of Covid-19 vaccine disinformation', Stuff, 15 April 2021: www.stuff.co.nz/national/health/coronavirus/124831801/former-farright-leader-plans-leaflet-drop-of-covid19-vaccine-disinformation

CHAPTER FOURTEEN

1. 'Ko tō tatou kāinga tēnei: Report of the Royal Commission of Inquiry into the terrorist attack on Christchurch masjidain on 15 March 2019', Royal Commission of Inquiry website, 26 November 2020: https://christchurchattack.royalcommission.nz/the-report/
2. David Neiwert, *Alt-America: The rise of the radical right in the age of Trump* (London: Verso, 2018), p. 4.
3. Ibid., pp. 4–5.
4. Richard Spencer, quoted in Christopher Caldwell, 'What the alt-right really means', New York Times, 2 December 2016: https://nyti.ms/2gujZCX
5. Neiwert, *Alt America*, pp. 236–37.
6. Ibid., p. 237.
7. Jessie Daniels, 'The algorithmic rise of the "alt-right"', *Contexts*, vol. 17, no. 1, 2018, p. 61.
8. Arlie Hochschild, *Strangers in their Own Land: Anger and mourning on the American right* (New York: The New Press, 2016).
9. Daniels, 'The algorithmic rise of the "alt right"', p. 61; Caldwell, 'What the alt-right really means'.
10. Daniels, 'The algorithmic rise of the "alt-right"', pp. 62, 64.
11. 'An establishment conservative's guide to the alt-right', Breitbart, 29 March 2016: www.breitbart.com/tech/2016/03/29/an-establishment-conservatives-guide-to-the-alt-right/; Caldwell, 'What the alt-right really means'.
12. Quoted in Neiwert, *Alt America*, p. 257.
13. Ibid., p. 257.
14. Julie Ebner, *Going Dark: The secret social lives of extremists* (London: Bloomsbury, 2020), p. 28.

15. Ibid., pp. 28–29.
16. Ibid., pp. 29–30.
17. Ibid., p. 44.
18. Ibid.
19. Ibid., p. 236.
20. Renaud Camus, *You Will Not Replace Us!* (Paris: Chez l'auteur, 2018). This is Camus' first attempt to directly address his audience in English and offers a brief summary of *Le Grand Remplacement* (2011), *Le petit remplacement* (2018), *Du sens* (2002) and *La seconde carrière d'Adolf Hitler* (2017). Some of the videos of the Charlottesville rally indicate that this chant alternated with 'Jews will not replace us!'
21. Anders Breivik, '2083 – a European Declaration of Independence', pp. 1137, 1361.
22. Ebner, *Going Dark*, p. 156. See also Kevin Roose, 'What is QAnon, the viral pro-Trump conspiracy theory?' New York Times, 19 August 2020: www.nytimes.com/article/what-is-qanon.html; Aoife Gallagher, Jacob Davey and Mackenzie Hart, *The Genesis of a Conspiracy Theory* (London: ISD, 2020).
23. Ebner, *Going Dark*, p. 154; 'What is the QAnon conspiracy theory?' CBS News: www.cbsnews.com/news/what-is-the-qanon-conspiracy-theory/
24. Jamie Doward, '"Quite frankly terrifying": How the QAnon conspiracy is taking over', The Guardian, 20 September 2020: www.theguardian.com/world/2020/sep/20/the-qanon-conspiracy
25. Sue Greenwood, 'How have QAnon's conspiracies gained traction in the UK?' The Guardian, 27 October 2020: www.theguardian.com/commentisfree/2020/oct/27/how-qanons-conspiracies-gained-traction-uk-social-media
26. Ibid.
27. Ibid.
28. 'What is the QAnon conspiracy theory?' CBS News.
29. David Lawrence, 'The UK's emerging conspiracy theory street movements', Hope Not Hate, 28 August 2020: www.hopenothate.org.uk/2020/08/28/the-uks-emerging-conspiracy-theory-street-movements/
30. Ibid.
31. Ibid.
32. Ibid.
33. Gallagher, Davey and Hart, *The Genesis of a Conspiracy Theory*.
34. Ibid.
35. Taylor Lorenz and Davey Alba, '"Zoombombing" becomes a dangerous organized effort', New York Times, 3 April 2020: https://nyti.ms/348wWgl
36. Julia Carrie Wong, 'Down the rabbit hole: How QAnon conspiracies thrive on Facebook', The Guardian, 25 June 2020: www.theguardian.com/technology/2020/jun/25/qanon-facebook-conspiracy-theories-algorithm
37. Ibid.
38. Manoel Horta Ribeiro, Raphael Ottoni, Robert West, Virgilio Almeida and Wagner Meira Jr, 'Auditing radicalization pathways on YouTube', arXiv: https://arxiv.org/abs/1908.08313. See also Karsten Müller and Carlo Schwarz, 'From hashtag to hate crime: Twitter and anti-minority sentiment', SSRN, posted 28 March 2018, revised 24 July 2020: https://papers.ssrn.com/sol3/papers.cfm?abstract_id=3149103
39. While some of the intellectual leaders of the alt-right, such as Ricard Spencer, are Nietzschean and reject Christianity as a slave morality of polluted Jewish origin, most of their followers are Christian. Other groups identify with the hero-warrior followers of the pagan Norse gods, although in these movements too many of the followers still explicitly identify with Christianity. Debates about Christianity and its historical significance and contemporary role are central across these groups. See, for example, https://www.stormfront.org/forum/t1331943/; also Dawn Araujo-Hawkins ('The making of the QAnon conspiracy cult', *The Christian Century*, vol. 137, no. 6, 16 December 2020) where the author links adherents of evangelical and Pentecostal 'rapture theology' to QAnon.

On QAnon recruitment of Christians and its growth among churches, see Daniel Burke, 'How QAnon uses religion to lure unsuspecting Christians', CNN, 15 October 2020: https://edition.cnn.com/2020/10/15/us/qanon-religion-churches/index.html; Ari Shapiro, 'How QAnon conspiracy is spreading in Christian communities across the US', NPR, 21 August 2020: /www.npr.org/2020/08/21/904798097/how-qanon-conspiracy-is-spreading-in-christian-communities-across-the-u-s; Katelyn Beaty, 'QAnon: the alternative religion that's coming to your church', Religious News Service, 17 August 2020: https://religionnews.com/2020/08/17/qanon-the-alternative-religion-thats-coming-to-your-church/

40. 'American Jewish Congress report ties Capitol storming to nei-nazi, QAnon and antisemitic activity', American Jewish Congress, 11 January 2021: https://ajcongress.org/statements/american-jewish-congress-report-ties-capitol-storming-to-neo-nazi-qanon-and-antisemitic-activity/
41. Julien Langella, *Catholic and Identitarian: From protest to reconquest* (Budapest: Arktos, 2020).
42. Olivier Roy, *Is Europe Christian?* (London: Hurst, 2019). Anti-abortion campaigns drawing on Christian values are interpreted as enhancing white birth rates necessary to ensure white survival.
43. The following studies focus competently and helpfully on ideology and challenges to democracy but neglect to explore religion, either in terms of Christianity or Christendom: Benjamin R. Teitelbaum, *Lions of the North: Sounds of the new Nordic radical nationalism* (Oxford: Oxford University Press, 2017); David Lawrence, Joe Mulhall, Simon Murdoch and Patrik Hermansson, *The International Alt-right: Fascism for the 21st Century?* (New York: Routledge, 2020); José Pedro Zúquete, *The Identitarians: The movement against globalism and Islam in Europe* (South Bend: University of Notre Dame Press, 2018); Jean-Yves Camus and Nicolas Lebourg, *Far-right Politics in Europe* (Cambridge: Harvard University Press, 2017); Cas Mudde, *The Far Right Today* (Hoboken: John Wiley, 2019); Pierre-André Taguieff, *La Revanche du Nationalisme: Néopopulistes et xénophobes à l'assaut de l'Europe* (Paris: Presses Universitaires de France, 2015); Patricia Anne Simpson and Helga Druxes (eds), *Digital Media Strategies of the Far Right in Europe and the United States* (Lanham, Maryland: Lexington Books, 2015).
44. Dominion Movement Facebook page, 2018.
45. Thomas Manch, 'The "growing" white nationalist group with a "harmful and violent" ideology', Stuff, 26 March 2020: www.stuff.co.nz/national/christchurch-shooting/111415544/the-growing-white-nationalist-group-with-a-harmful-and-violent-ideology
46. Marc Daalder, 'Action Zealandia linked to Dominion Movement', Newsroom, 13 March 2020: www.newsroom.co.nz/action-zealandia-linked-to-dominion-movement
47. Ibid.
48. Ibid.
49. Paul Spoonley, *The Politics of Nostalgia: Racism and extreme right in New Zealand* (Palmerston North: Dunmore Press, 1987).
50. Kerry Bolton, 'Action Zealandia within the context of the right', Action Zealandia website, 31 May 2020: https://action-zealandia.com/articles/action-zealandia-within-the-context-of-the-right
51. Action Zealandia, 'Rebuke of NZ Herald: in defence of children', Action Zealandia website, 28 August 2020: https://action-zealandia.com/articles/rebuke-of-nz-herald-in-defense-of-children
52. Marc Daalder, 'Action Zealandia linked to Dominion Movement'. Also see 'Atomwaffen Division', Southern Poverty Law Centre: www.splcenter.org/fighting-hate/extremist-files/group/atomwaffen-division
53. Marc Daalder, 'Army reservist linked to far-right group', Newsroom, 25 June 2020:

www.stuff.co.nz/national/300042525/army-reservist-linked-to-new-zealand-farright-group

54. See 'Max Newsome ("Matt") and Action Zealandia', The White Rose Society, 10 March 2020: https://thewhiterosesociety.writeas.com/max-newsome-matt-and-action-zealandia
55. Action Zealandia, 'QAnon debunked', Action Zealandia website, 27 August 2020: https://action-zealandia.com/articles/qanon-debunked
56. Wargus Christi was founded in 2019 by Daniel Waring, who has neo-nazi links.
57. Marc Daalder, 'Soldier with far-right ties arrested at Linton Military Camp', Newsroom, 18 December 2019: www.stuff.co.nz/national/crime/118280866/soldier-with-farright-ties-arrested-at-linton-military-camp
58. The Outdoors New Zealand party could be added to this list as prone to conspiracies although less evidently morally conservative.
59. Charlie Mitchell, 'The conspiracists' election: How the farthest fringes of politics are making a play for the centre', RadioNZ, 1 August 2020: www.stuff.co.nz/national/politics/300070891/the-conspiracists-election-how-the-farthest-fringes-of-politics-are-making-a-play-for-the-centre
60. 'Billy Te Kahika – the conspiracy theorist with a hidden following', Radio New Zealand, 13 October 2020: www.rnz.co.nz/programmes/the-detail/story/2018767978/billy-te-kahika-the-conspiracy-theorist-with-a-hidden-following
61. Mitchell, 'The conspiracists' election'.
62. 'A darker truth; The anti-Semitism behind Billy Te Kahika's conspiracy theories', Stuff, October 2020: https://interactives.stuff.co.nz/2020/10/a-darker-truth-anti-semitism-billy-tk-jr-conspiracy
63. See photos at David Farrier, 'Why are conspiracy theories dripping in racism?' Webworm, 16 September 2020: http://webworm.substack.com/p/why-are-conspiracy-theories-dripping
64. Maxine Boag, 'QAnon … NZ style', Bay Buzz, August 2020: www.baybuzz.co.nz/2020/08/22/qanon-nz-style
65. 'False profit: Full and unedited video with Advance NZ co-leader Billy Te Kahika', Stuff, 13 October 2020: www.stuff.co.nz/national/stuff-circuit/300131103/false-profit-full-and-unedited-video-with-advance-nz-coleader-billy-te-kahika
66. Jeremy Milne, 'Responding to some Covid claims', Gisborne Herald, 19 August 2020: www.gisborneherald.co.nz/editorial/20200819/responding-to-some-covid-claims/
67. Letter from Elliot Ikilei, *Northern Age*, 10 September 2020.
68. Media Council quoted in Byron Clark, 'How the far-right found a home in the New Conservative Party', Fightback, 12 June 2020: https://fightback.org.nz/2020/06/12/how-the-far-right-found-a-home-in-the-new-conservative-party
69. Matt Burrows, 'Electoral Commission rubbishes Te Kahika claims Advance NZ a victim of "rigged election", "disqualified votes"', Newshub, 19 October 2020: www.newshub.co.nz/home/politics/2020/10/electoral-commission-rubbishes-billy-te-kahika-s-claims-advance-nz-a-victim-of-rigged-election-disqualified-votes.html
70. 'Antipodean anti-vaxxers are learning from America's far right', The Economist, 27 November 2021: www.economist.com/asia/2021/11/27/antipodean-anti-vaxxers-are-learning-from-americas-far-right; David Farrier, 'New Zealand goes loopy: A summary of Aotearoa's top anti-vax and conspiracy theory nitwits', Webworm, 25 October 2021: www.webworm.co/p/loopy; Kate Hannah, Sanjana Hattotuwa and Kayli Taylor, 'Working Paper: Mis- and disinformation in Aotearoa New Zealand from 17 August to 5 November 2021', The Disinformation Project, November 2021: www.tepunahamatatini.ac.nz/2021/11/09/mis-and-disinformation/
71. Spoonley, *The Politics of Nostalgia*.
72. Marc Daalder, 'Far-right speakers features

at anti-lockdown march', Newsroom, 15 September 2020: www.newsroom.co.nz/far-right-speakers-featured-at-anti-lockdown-march

73. Clark, 'How the far-right found a home in the New Conservative Party'.
74. Eleanor Ainge Roy, 'NZ website withdraws author's works after she criticises Māori foreign minister', The Guardian, 4 November 2020: www.theguardian.com/world/2020/nov/04/nz-website-withdraws-authors-works-after-she-criticises-maori-foreign-minister
75. David Farrier, '"I'm just outlining facts"; watching New Zealand getting red-pilled, in real time', Webworm, 13 August 2020: https://webworm.substack.com/im-just-outlining-facts-watching
76. Byron Clark, 'Counterspin Media', Webworm, 4 June 2021: www.webworm.co/p/fakenews2. Alp founded and led the Direct Democracy Party whose candidates in the 2005 General Election included members of the white nationalist National Front. In 2011 he was an OurNZ parliamentary candidate.
77. Miriam Bell, 'Anti-vaxxers get ugly', Australia/Israel Review, 27 October 2021: https://1.org.nz/anti-vaxxers-get-ugly/; Hannah Moritz, 'Playing the nazi card', *Listener,* 18 December 2021.
78. Toby Manhire, 'The protest that revealed a new, ugly, dangerous side to our country', The Spinoff, 10 November 2021: www.nzherald.co.nz/nz/covid-19-delta-outbreak-toby-manhire-the-protest-that-revealed-a-new-ugly-dangerous-side-to-nz/3YYMC2BYNK66WVXO6AYU4WMXLI/
79. Marc Daalder, 'On the internet, nobody knows you're a terrorist', Newsroom, 21 December 2020: www.newsroom.co.nz/on-the-internet-nobody-knows-youre-a-terrorist
80. Ebner, *Going Dark*, p. 240.
81. 'Ko tō tatou kāinga tēnei: Report of the Royal Commission of Inquiry into the terrorist attack on Christchurch masjidain on 15 March 2019', Royal Commission of Inquiry website, 26 November 2020: https://christchurchattack.royalcommission.nz/the-report/
82. Ebner, *Going Dark*, p. 240.
83. Ibid., p. 238.
84. Milo Comerford, Jakob Guhl and Carl Miller, 'Understanding the New Zealand online extremist ecosystem', ISD/Department of Internal Affairs, 2021: www.isdglobal.org/isd-publications/understanding-the-new-zealand-online-extremist-ecosystem/

CHAPTER FIFTEEN

1. Ian Hutchby, *Conversation and Technology: From the telephone to the internet* (Cambridge: Polity Press, 2001). As other contributions in this collection make clear, however, the far right has long operated internationally. See also Tony Ballantyne, *Webs of Empire: Locating New Zealand's colonial past* (Wellington: Bridget Williams Books, 2012).
2. 'Ko tō tatou kāinga tēnei: Report of the Royal Commission of Inquiry into the terrorist attack on Christchurch masjidain on 15 March 2019', vol. 2, Royal Commission of Inquiry website, 26 November 2020: https://christchurchattack.royalcommission.nz/the-report/
3. See, for example, Kevin Veale, *Gaming the Dynamics of Online Harassment*, 1st edn (Cham: Springer International Publishing, 2020).
4. Jessie Daniels, *Cyber Racism: White supremacy online and the new attack on civil rights* (New York: Rowman & Littlefield, 2009), p. 42.
5. Ibid., pp. 21, 31.
6. Manuel Castells, 'Toward a sociology of the network society', *Contemporary Sociology*, vol. 29, no. 5, 2000, p. 693.
7. Ibid.
8. Manuel Castells, 'Materials for an exploratory theory of the network society',

British Journal of Sociology, vol. 51, no. 1, 2000, p. 16.
9. Castells, 'Toward a sociology of the network society', p. 694. Globalisation is not specific to the network society, of course, but has a long and contested history. For more, see Kevin H. O'Rourke and Jeffrey G. Williamson, 'Once more: When did globalisation begin?', *European Review of Economic History*, vol. 8, no. 1, 2004, pp. 109–17; Robbie T. Robertson, *The Three Waves of Globalization: A history of a developing global consciousness* (New York: Zed Books, 2003).
10. Manuel Castells, *The Rise of the Network Society* (Cambridge: Blackwell Publishers, 2000), p. 101.
11. Castells, 'Toward a sociology of the network society', p. 694.
12. Ibid., p. 12.
13. Ibid., p. 6.
14. Ibid., p. 694.
15. Castells, 'Materials for an exploratory theory of the network society', p. 14.
16. Sarah T. Roberts, *Behind the Screen: Content moderation in the shadows of social media* (New Haven: Yale University Press, 2019), p. 54.
17. Castells, *The Rise of the Network Society*, p. 71.
18. Manuel Castells, *Networks of Outrage and Hope: Social movements in the internet age* (Malden: Polity Press, 2012), p. 231.
19. Daniels, *Cyber racism*, p. 46.
20. For example, far-right political parties have won an increasing number of seats in a number of European counties in recent years, including Austria, Germany, Hungary and Poland, to name just a few.
21. Kyler Ong and Raffaello Pantucci, 'From fringe to mainstream: The extreme rightwing in Europe', Observer Research Foundation: www.orfonline.org/expert-speak/fringe-mainstream-extreme-rightwing-europe-68848/
22. 'The Christchurch Call to eliminate terrorist and violent extremist online content', The Ministry of Foreign Affairs and Trade: www.christchurchcall.com
23. Margaret Mutu, 'Behind the smoke and mirrors of the Treaty of Waitangi claims settlement process in New Zealand: No prospect for justice and reconciliation for Māori without constitutional transformation', *Journal of Global Ethics*, vol. 14, no. 2, 2018, p. 210.
24. Ibid. Adequately addressing the long history of racism and white extremism in New Zealand is beyond the scope of this contribution, but for more information see Paul Spoonley, *Racism and Ethnicity: Critical issues in New Zealand society*, rev. edn (Auckland: Oxford University Press, 1993).
25. Steve Elers, 'A "White New Zealand": anti-Chinese racist political discourse from 1880 to 1920', *China Media Research*, vol. 14, no. 3, 2018, p. 88.
26. Miscellaneous radical right organisation papers.
27. Gregory Stanton, 'QAnon is a nazi cult, rebranded', Just Security: www.justsecurity.org/72339/qanon-is-a-nazi-cult-rebranded/
28. New Zealand Security Intelligence Service, Miscellaneous radical right organisation papers.
29. National Socialist Party papers.
30. New Zealand Security Intelligence Service, Miscellaneous radical right organisation papers.
31. New Zealand Security Intelligence Service, National Socialist Party papers.
32. Daniels, *Cyber Racism*, p. 4.
33. Ibid., p. 39.
34. Ibid., pp. 76–77.
35. Ibid., p. 42.
36. Ibid., p. 45.
37. Ibid., p. 40.
38. Ibid., p. 45.
39. Darrel Mager, 'Klan claims to have room for Māori', New Zealand Herald: www.nzherald.co.nz/nz/klan-claims-to-have-room-for-maori/4HBLLMVOFSLZKZJSMG7P2L5WEQ/
40. 'Alanna' (former white power member) in discussion with the author, March 2020.
41. Quoted in Weiyi Cai and Simone Landon,

'Attacks by white extremists are growing. So are their connections', New York Times: www.nytimes.com/interactive/2019/04/03/world/white-extremist-terrorism-christchurch.html
42. Ibid.
43. 'Ko tō tatou kāinga tēnei', p. 193.
44. Rebecca Lewis, 'Alternative influence: Broadcasting the reactionary right on youtube', Data & Society Research Institute, 2018, pp. 36-37: https://datasociety.net/wp-content/uploads/2018/09/DS_Alternative_Influence.pdf
45. 'Ko tō tatou kāinga tēnei', p. 180.
46. Lewis, 'Alternative influence', p. 37.
47. Jason Stanley, *How Fascism Works* (New York: Random House, 2018), p. 102.
48. Caleb Cain (former far-right member) in discussion with the author, March 2020.
49. 'Ko tō tatou kāinga tēnei', pp. 189–93.
50. Ibid., p. 197.
51. Ibid., p. 194.
52. Ibid., p. 195.
53. Ibid., p. 189.
54. A. Dirk Moses, '"White genocide" and the ethics of public analysis', *Journal of Genocide Research*, vol. 21, no. 2, 2019, p. 3.
55. Zack Beauchamp, 'Accelerationism: The obscure idea inspiring white supremacist killers around the world', Vox, 11 November 2019: www.vox.com/the-highlight/2019/11/11/20882005/accelerationism-white-supremacy-christchurch
56. Jason Wilson, 'The Base: Exporting accelerationist terror', Southern Poverty Law Center: www.splcenter.org/hatewatch/2020/08/12/base-exporting-accelerationist-terror
57. Robert Coalson, 'Christchurch attacks: Suspect took inspiration from former Yugoslavia's ethnically fueled wars', Radio Free Europe/Radio Liberty: www.rferl.org/a/christchurch-attacks-yugoslavia-tarrant-inspiration-suspect-new-zealand/29823655.html
58. Robert Evans, 'Shitposting, inspirational terrorism, and the Christchurch mosque massacre', bellingcat, 15 March 2019: www.bellingcat.com/news/rest-of-world/2019/03/15/shitposting-inspirational-terrorism-and-the-christchurch-mosque-massacre/
59. Ibid.
60. Ibid.
61. Aja Romano, 'How the Christchurch shooter used memes to spread hate', Vox, 16 March 2019: www.vox.com/culture/2019/3/16/18266930/christchurch-shooter-manifesto-memes-subscribe-to-pewdiepie
62. See twitter.com/realcandaceo/status/1106391443457888257
63. Evans, 'Shitposting'.
64. Ibid.
65. Taylor Lorenz, 'The shooter's manifesto was designed to troll', The Atlantic: www.theatlantic.com/technology/archive/2019/03/the-shooters-manifesto-was-designed-to-troll/585058/
66. Aja Romano, 'Youtube's 2018 "Rewind" is the site's most disliked video ever. The implications are huge', Vox, 14 December 2018: www.vox.com/culture/2018/12/14/18138916/pewdiepie-vs-t-series-youtube-rewind-2018
67. Lorenz, 'The shooter's manifesto was designed to troll'.
68. Quoted in ibid.
69. Quoted in Jen Kirby, 'The New Zealand shooter wrote a manifesto: An extremism expert explains what it means', Vox, 18 March 2019: www.vox.com/2019/3/18/18267682/new-zealand-christchurch-shooter-manifesto-online-extremism
70. Lizzie Dearden, 'Man who stormed mosque "armed with shotguns" was inspired by Christchurch and El Paso attackers, messaging board post suggests', The Independent: www.independent.co.uk/news/world/europe/norway-mosque-shooting-attack-suspect-philip-manshaus-christchurch-el-paso-4chan-a9052106.html
71. Yasmeen Abutaleb, 'What's inside the hate-filled manifesto linked to the alleged

El Paso shooter', The Washington Post: www.washingtonpost.com/politics/2019/08/04/whats-inside-hate-filled-manifesto-linked-el-paso-shooter/

72. Julia Carrie Wong, 'Germany shooting suspect livestreamed attempted attack on synagogue', The Guardian" www.theguardian.com/world/2019/oct/09/germany-shooting-synagogue-halle-livestreamed
73. 'Ko tō tatou kāinga tēnei', p. 234.
74. Ibid.
75. Joan Donovan, 'El Paso shooter wasn't a "lone wolf" – and his so-called online "manifesto" proves why', NBC News: www.nbcnews.com/think/opinion/el-paso-shooter-wasn-t-lone-wolf-his-so-called-ncna1039201
76. Quoted in Cai and Landon, 'Attacks by white extremists are growing'.
77. Byron Clark (anti-extremist activist) in discussion with the author, March 2020.
78. Ibid.
79. Marc Daalder, 'Action Zealandia member planned terror cell', Newsroom, 9 March 2020: www.newsroom.co.nz/2020/03/09/1072195/action-zealandia-member-planned-terror-cell
80. Quoted in Cai and Landon, 'Attacks by white extremists are growing'.
81. David Shanks (Chief Censor of New Zealand) in discussion with the author, March 2020. For an example of Benesch's work, see Susan Benesch, 'Dangerous speech: A proposal to prevent group violence' (Voices That Poison: Dangerous Speech Project, 2012).
82. Ibid.
83. Ben Knight, 'Germany implements new internet hate speech crackdown', Deutsche Welle: www.dw.com/en/germany-implements-new-internet-hate-speech-crackdown/a-41991590
84. Ibid.
85. Jason Lemon, 'QAnon influencers on youtube remain online despite promotion of Capitol riot', Newsweek: www.newsweek.com/qanon-influencers-youtube-remain-online-despite-promotion-capitol-riot-1582152
86. Alex Kaplan, 'Despite cracking down on QAnon, youtube continues to profit from content supporting the conspiracy theory', Media Matters: www.mediamatters.org/google/despite-cracking-down-qanon-youtube-continues-profit-content-supporting-conspiracy-theory
87. Marianne Elliott et al., 'Digital threats to democracy', The Workshop, 2019: www.digitaldemocracy.nz/
88. Eyes on the Right, 'Stefan Molyneux mourns the loss of his audience after youtube and twitter bans', Angry White Men, 29 March 2021: www.angrywhitemen.org/2021/03/29/stefan-molyneux-mourns-the-loss-of-his-audience-after-youtube-and-twitter-bans
89. Joan Donovan, Becca Lewis and Brian Friedberg, 'Parallel ports: Sociotechnical change from the alt-right to alt-tech', in Maik Fielitz and Nick Thurston (eds), *Post-digital Cultures of the Far Right: Online actions and offline consequences in Europe and the US* (Bielefeld: Transcript, 2019), p. 49.
90. Nicola Brown (InternetNZ policy adviser) in discussion with the author, February 2020.
91. Olivia Solon, 'Six months after Christchurch shootings, videos of attack are still on facebook', NBC News: www.nbcnews.com/tech/tech-news/six-months-after-christchurch-shootings-videos-attack-are-still-facebook-n1056691
92. Roberts, *Behind the Screen*.
93. Cai and Landon, 'Attacks by white extremists are growing'.
94. 'Ko tō tatou kāinga tēnei', vol. 1, p. 14.
95. Ibid., pp. 14–15.
96. J.M. Berger, *Extremism* (Cambridge: MIT Press, 2018), p. 47.
97. 'The Christchurch Call'.
98. Elliott et al., 'Digital threats to democracy', p. 8.
99. Quoted in Kirby, 'The New Zealand shooter wrote a manifesto'.

100. Ibid.
101. 'Ko tō tatou kāinga tēnei', vol. 4, p. 731.
102. David Shanks (Chief Censor of New Zealand) in discussion with the author, March 2020.
103. 'Ko tō tatou kāinga tēnei', p. 735.
104. Ibid., pp. 736–57.
105. Hamimah Ahmat, 'Christchurch attack inquiry: Survivors need systemic change', Middle East Eye: www.middleeasteye.net/opinion/christchurch-report-survivors-we-need-systemic-change

Bibliography

ABBREVIATIONS

AJHR: *Appendices to the Journal of the House of Representatives*
ANZ: Archives New Zealand, Wellington
ATL: Alexander Turnbull Library, Wellington
HC: Hocken Collections Uare Taoka o Hākena, Dunedin
NLNZ: National Library of New Zealand, Wellington
NZPD: *New Zealand Parliamentary Debates*

ARCHIVES

ALEXANDER TURNBULL LIBRARY

Eph-B-politics 1960s

Field Papers: 73-148-045; 73-148-049; 73-148-050; 73-148-096; 73-148-103; 73-148-089, MS-Group-1543

Raymond E. Hansen Papers: 84-204

Hislop Papers: 85-145-06; 85-145-08

League of Empire Loyalists Papers: MS-Papers-4442-24

New Zealand League of Rights – Publications: 94-106-17/09

New Zealand National Socialist Party Publications and Newsclippings: 94-106-17/12; MS-Papers-4442-33

NZ Rhodesia Society/Southern Africa Friends Association/Aid Rhodesia, MS-Papers-4442-34

O'Regan Papers: LAGANZ, MS-Papers-0082

Security Intelligence Service – Cuttings and Articles: MS-Papers-6218-06

Simpson Papers: MS-Papers-9902

ARCHIVES NEW ZEALAND

External Affairs Files, Subversion – General file, series 1, 84/10/1 pt.1a

Government and Public Order – Strikes: 1951 Strike: Pamphlets 1951-1951, R10074976

Miscellaneous radical right organisation papers: Fascist, Anti-Semitic, Extreme Right-Wing: 1933–1966, R24716778; R24881827; R24881828

Reform Party Correspondence September 1919–March 1921, PM9 2/9, R22281271

Treasury Files, New Zealand Farmers' Union, series 1-52/589

Miscellaneous letters

Ernest James to William Massey, 21 June 1920, R22281270, PM9 3

Dr Edgar Strong to Chief Inspector, Southern Rhodesian Constabulary, 16 November 1905, R20119991

AUCKLAND UNIVERSITY LIBRARY SPECIAL COLLECTIONS

Harold Moores Papers: A-188

Hawke's Bay division of the New Zealand Legion Papers, A-38

HOCKEN COLLECTIONS

William Downie Stewart Papers: MS-0985-002/046; MS-0985-002/026

Letters from W.W. Tanner and clippings related to Arthur Desmond: MS-0985-002/062

John Stafford and Elizabeth Agnes O'Neill Papers: AG-582

OTHER

Australian National Library, Canberra: New Zealand Welfare League, Interim report for Period Ending May 31st, 1921, MHE 14:114

National Library of Australia: Herbert and Ivy Brookes Papers, MS 1924

Ngā Taonga Sound & Vision, Wellington: Item TZP398148

Parliamentary Library, Wellington: Society for the Protection of the Unborn Child, N.Z. Royal Commission on Contraception, Sterilisation & Abortion, Submissions & Hearings, vol. 7

Richard S. Hill security papers

South African Rugby Board papers, History department, Stellenbosch University: Box: Politics in Sport/Apartheid, Collection VII: SARB Business

The National Archives, United Kingdom: Edward Lionel Terry, Regimental number: 390, WO 400/279/390

NEWSPAPERS AND PERIODICALS

Auckland Metro
Auckland Star
Australian Worker
Bulletin (Sydney)
Challenge Weekly
Christchurch Star
Colonist (Nelson)
Critic (student magazine)
Daily Mirror
Daily Standard (Brisbane)
Daily Telegraph
Daily Telegraph (Victoria)
Dominion
Ellesmere Guardian
Evening Post
Evening Star
Farming First
Franklin Times
Gisborne Times
Goulburn Evening Penny Post (NSW)
Grey River Argus
Gundagai Independent and Pastoral, Agricultural and Mining Advocate
Hamilton Times (Ontario)
Hastings Standard
Hawera and Normanby Star
Hawke's Bay Herald Tribune
Herald (South Australia)
Herald on Sunday
Hokitika Guardian
Inangahua Times
Kapiti Observer
Light and Liberty (Reform Party newspaper)
Lyttelton Times
Magneto (student newspaper)
Manawatu Standard
Mangonui County Times
Maoriland Worker
Marlborough Express
Munsey's Magazine
Nanaimo Free Press (British Columbia)
National Front News
Nelson Evening Mail
Nelson Examiner
New Zealand Free Lance
New Zealand Geographer
New Zealand Herald
New Zealand Illustrated Magazine
New Zealand Listener
New Zealand Mail
New Zealand Monthly Review
New Zealand Plain Talk
New Zealand Times
New Zealand Truth
New Zealand Weekly News
New Zealand Worker
New Zealand Year Book
North Shore Times Advertiser
Northern Advocate
Otago Daily Times
Otago Witness
People's Voice
Press
Province (British Columbia)
Record-Journal (Meriden, Connecticut)
Ross's Monthly (Melbourne)
Salient (student magazine)
Sheffield Daily Telegraph
South Canterbury Times
Southland Times
Spectator
Springville Journal (Springville, New York)
Star
Stratford Evening Post
Sun (Christchurch)
Sunday News
Sunday Star Times
Sunday Times
Sydney Mail and New South Wales Advertiser
Taranaki Daily Times
The Labor Daily (Sydney)
The Newsletter (Reform Party)
Tomorrow
Truth (Sydney)
Vancouver Daily World
Vanguard (East Sussex)
Victoria Daily Colonist (British Columbia)
Victoria Daily Times (British Columbia)
Waikato Independent
Waikato Times
Wairarapa Age
Wairarapa Daily Times
Weekend Herald
Western Star
Wetherbys Visions of A Nobler Day (Dunedin)

BOOKS AND REPORTS

Adams, Peter, *Fatal Necessity: British intervention in New Zealand 1830–1849* (Auckland: Auckland University Press), 1977

Addison, R., *Evaluation of the New Way Trust Skinhead Project* (Christchurch: Christchurch City Council and the Crime Prevention Unit), 1995

Ahdar, Rex J., *Worlds Colliding: Conservative Christians and the law* (Aldershot: Ashgate Publishing, 2001)

Albertazzi, Daniele and Duncan McDonnell (ed.), *Twenty-first Century Populism: The spectre of Western European democracy* (New York: Palgrave Macmillan, 2008)

Anderson, Atholl, Judith Binney and Aroha Harris, *Tangata Whenua: A history* (Wellington: Bridget Williams Books, 2015)

Argersinger, Peter H., *Populism and Politics: William Alfred Peffer and the People's Party* (Lexington: The University Press of Kentucky, 2015)

Atkinson, David C., *The Burden of White Supremacy: Containing Asian migration in the British Empire and the United States* (Chapel Hill: University of North Carolina Press, 2017)

Ballantyne, Tony, *Webs of Empire: Locating New Zealand's colonial past* (Wellington: Bridget Williams Books, 2012)

Barker, David, *Ideology of Obsession: A.K. Chesterton and British fascism* (London: I.B. Tauris, 1996)

Barr, Hugh, Mike Butler, Peter Cresswell, Bruce Moon, John Robinson and David Round, *Twisting the Treaty – A tribal grab for wealth and power* (Wellington: Tross Publishing, 2013)

Barrowman, Rachel, *Victoria University of Wellington 1899–1999: A history* (Wellington: Victoria University Press, 1999)

Bassett, Michael, *Coates of Kaipara* (Auckland: Auckland University Press, 1995)

Bassett, Michael, *Sir Joseph Ward: A political biography* (Auckland: Auckland University Press, 1993)

Bassett, Michael, *The State in New Zealand 1840–1984* (Auckland: Auckland University Press, 1998)

Bassett, Michael, *Three Party Politics in New Zealand, 1911–1931* (Auckland: Historical Publications, 1982)

Beaglehole Ann, *A Small Price to Pay: Refugees from Hitler in New Zealand 1936–46* (Wellington: Bridget Williams Books, 1988)

Bedggood, David, *Rich and Poor in New Zealand* (Auckland: George Allen & Unwin, 1980)

Begg, Robert Campbell, *The Secret of the Knife* (Norwich: Jarrold and Sons, 1966)

Belgrave, Michael, *Historical Frictions, Māori Claims and Reinvented Histories* (Auckland: Auckland University Press, 2005)

Belich, James, *Making Peoples: A history of the New Zealanders from Polynesian settlement to the end of the nineteenth century* (Auckland: Penguin, 1996)

Belich, James, *The New Zealand Wars and the Victorian Interpretation of Racial Conflict* (Auckland: Penguin, 1986)

Belich, James, *Paradise Reforged: A history of the New Zealanders from the 1880s to the year 2000* (Auckland: Penguin, 2001)

Berger, J.M., *Extremism* (Cambridge: MIT Press, 2018)

Best, Elsdon, *The Maori as He Was: A brief account of Maori life as it was in pre-European days* (Wellington: Dominion Museum, 1924)

Best, Elsdon, *Maori Religion and Mythology, Part One* (Wellington: Dominion Museum, 1924)

Binney, Judith, Gillian Chaplin and Graig Wallace, *Mihaia: The prophet Rua Kenana and his community at Maungapohatu* (Wellington: Bridget Williams Books, 1979)

Binney, Judith, *Redemption Songs: A life of Te Kooti Arikirangi Te Turuki* (Wellington: Bridget Williams Books, 1979)

Bland, Peter, *Sorry I'm a Stranger Here Myself: A memoir* (Auckland: Vintage, 2004)

Bowler, Kate, *Blessed: A history of the American prosperity gospel* (New York: Oxford University Press, 2013)

Brantlinger, P. *Taming Cannibals: Race and the Victorians* (Ithaca: Cornell University Press, 2011)

Broinowski, Anna, *Please Explain: The rise, fall and rise again of Pauline Hanson* (Sydney: Penguin Random House, 2017)

Bronner, Stephen Eric, *A Rumour About the Jews: Reflections on antisemitism and the protocols of the learned elders of Zion* (New York: St Martin's Press, 2000)

Brooking, Tom, *Richard Seddon: King of God's own* (Auckland: Penguin, 2014)

Buick, T. Lindsay (ed.), *Ideals of Nationhood – A selection of Lord Bledisloe's addresses in New Zealand* (New Plymouth: Thomas Avery & Sons, 1935)

Buick, T. Lindsay, *The Treaty of Waitangi: How New Zealand became a British colony* (New Plymouth: T. Avery, 1936)

Burdon, R.M., *The New Dominion: A social and political history of New Zealand 1918–1939* (Wellington and London: A.H. & A.W. Reed and Allen & Unwin, 1965)

Burgmann, Verity, *In Our Time – socialism and the rise of Labor, 1885–1905* (Sydney: Allen & Unwin, 1985)

Burleigh, Michael and Wolfgang Wippermann, *The Racial State: Germany 1933–1945* (New York: Cambridge University Press, 1991)

Burlein, Ann, *Lift High the Cross: Where white supremacy and the Christian right converge* (Durham: Duke University Press, 2002)

Buss, Doris and Didi Herman, *Globalizing Family Values: The Christian right in international politics* (Minneapolis: University of Minnesota Press, 2003)

Butler, Jennifer, *Born Again: The Christian right globalized* (London: Pluto Press, 2006)

Butler, Mike, *Tribes Treaty Money Power: A guide to New Zealand's Treaty issues* (Wellington: Tross Publishing, 2014).

Byrnes, Giselle, *The Waitangi Tribunal and New Zealand History* (South Melbourne: Oxford University Press, 2004)

Camus, Jean-Yves and Nicolas Lebourg, *Far-right Politics in Europe* (Cambridge: Harvard University Press, 2017)

Camus, Renaud, *You Will Not Replace Us!* (Paris: Chez l'auteur, 2018)

Carrington, Carey John, *New Zealand's Greatest Need* (Tauranga: Publicity Printing, 1956)

Castells, Manuel, *Networks of Outrage and Hope: Social movements in the internet age* (Malden: Polity Press, 2012)

Castells, Manuel, *The Rise of the Network Society*, 2nd edn (Cambridge: Blackwell, 2000).

Cathcart, Michael, *Defending the National Tuckshop: Australia's secret army intrigue of 1931* (McPhee Gribble, Fitzroy, 1988)

Chapple, Geoff, *1981: The tour* (Wellington: A.H. & A.W. Reed, 1984)

Christensen, Larry, *The Christian Family* (Minneapolis: Bethany Fellowship, 1970)

Christerson, Brad and Richard Flory, *The Rise of Network Christianity: How independent leaders are changing the religious landscape* (New York: Oxford University Press, 2017)

Clark, Paul, *Hauhau: The Pai Marire search for Maori identity* (Auckland: Auckland University Press, 1975)

Cohn, N., *Warrant for Genocide: The myth of the Jewish world conspiracy and the protocols of the elders of Zion* (Harmondsworth: Penguin, 1970)

Conder, D.W. (ed.), *Ragnar Redbeard's Might Is Right or The Survival of the Fittest* (Missouri: Dil Pickle Press, 2005)

Condliffe, J.B., *New Zealand in the Making: A study of economic and social development* (London: Allen & Unwin, 1936)

Cooke, Bill, *Kernel and Husk: The waning of Jesus in Godzone* (Wellington: Steele Roberts, 2014)

Coontz, Stephanie, *The Way We Never Were: American families and the nostalgia trap* (New York: Basic Books, 2000)

Coulthard, Glenn Sean, *Red Skin, White Masks: Rejecting the colonial politics of recognition* (Minneapolis: University of Minnesota Press, 2014)

Coupland P.M., *Farming, Fascism and Ecology: A life of Jorian Jenks* (Oxon: Routledge, 2016)

Cunningham, Matthew, *Mobilising the Masses: Populist conservative movements in Australia and New Zealand during the Great Depression* (Canberra: Australian National University Press, 2022)

Curry, Fairlie Fergus, *Some Facts About – communism and the churches* (Wellington: Fairlie, Fergus, Curry, 1966)

Dalziel, P. and R. Lattimore, *The New Zealand Macroeconomy: A briefing on the reforms* (Melbourne: Oxford University Press, 1996)
Daniels, Jessie, *Cyber Racism: White supremacy online and the new attack on civil rights* (New York: Rowman & Littlefield, 2009)
Dann, Christine, *Up from Under: Women and liberation in New Zealand, 1970–1985* (Wellington: Allen & Unwin, 1985)
Darwin, Charles, *The Origin of Species by Means of Natural Selection* (London: J. Murray, 1859)
Dennehy, Glennis and Greg Newbold, *The Girls in the Gang* (Auckland: Reed, 2001)
Derby, Mark, *Ragnar Redbeard – the antipodean origins of radical fabulist Arthur Desmond* (Wellington: Steele Roberts Aotearoa, 2017)
Desmond, Adrian and James Moore, *Darwin* (London: Penguin, 1991)
Diamond, Sara, *Roads to Dominion: Right-wing movements and political power in the United States* (New York: Guilford Press, 1995)
Doutré, Martin, *Ancient Celtic New Zealand* (Auckland: De Danann Publishers, 1999)
Dowland, Seth, *Family Values and the Rise of the Christian Right* (Philadelphia: University of Pennsylvania Press, 2015)
Dreaver, Anthony, *An Eye for Country* (Wellington: Victoria University Press, 1997)
Drummond, James, *The Life and Work of Richard John Seddon* (Christchurch: Whitcombe & Tombs, 1907)
Duncan, Grant, *Society and Politics: New Zealand social policy*, 2nd edn (Auckland: Person Prentice Hall, 2007)
Dunbar-Oritz, Roxanne, *An Indigenous Peoples' History of the United States* (Boston: Beacon Press, 2014)
Durden, Robert Franklin, *The Climax of Populism: The election of 1896* (Lexington: The University Press of Kentucky, 2015)
Durie, Mason, *Whaiora: Maori health development*, 2nd edn (London: Oxford University Press, 1998)
Durham, Martin, *The Christian Right, the Far Right and the Boundaries of American Conservatism* (Manchester: Manchester University Press, 2000)
Eatwell, Roger and Matthew Goodwin, *National Populism: The revolt against liberal democracy* (London: Penguin Random House, 2018)
Ebner, Julie, *Going Dark: The secret social lives of extremists* (London: Bloomsbury, 2020)
Edwards, Brian, *The Public Eye* (Wellington: Alister Taylor Publisher, 1972)
Eldred-Grigg, Stevan with Zeng Dazheng, *White Ghosts, Yellow Peril: China and New Zealand 1790–1950* (Dunedin: Otago University Press, 2014)
Fairburn, Miles, *The Ideal Society and its Enemies: The foundations of modern New Zealand Society 1850–1900* (Auckland: Auckland University Press, 1989)
Fisher, Martin, *A Long Time Coming: The Story of Ngāi Tahu's treaty settlement negotiations with the Crown* (Christchurch: Canterbury University Press, 2020)
Franks, Peter and Jim McAloon, *The New Zealand Labour Party 1916–2016* (Wellington: Victoria University Press, 2016)
Gallagher, Aoife, Jacob Davey and Mackenzie Hart, *The Genesis of a Conspiracy Theory* (London: ISD, 2020)
Gellner, Ernest and Ghita Ionescu, *Populism: Its meaning and national characteristics* (New York: Macmillan, 1969)
Gibson, Stephanie, Matariki Williams and Puawai Cairns, *Protest Tautohetohe: Objects of resistance, persistence and defiance* (Wellington: Te Papa Press, 2019)
Gilbert, Jarrod, *Patched: The history of gangs in New Zealand* (Auckland: Auckland University Press, 2013)
Giliomee, Hermann, *The Afrikaners: Biography of a people* (Cape Town: Tafelberg, 2009)
Gilling, Bryan (ed.), *'Be Ye Separate': Fundamentalism and the New Zealand experience,* Waikato Series in Religion vol. 3 (Hamilton: University of Waikato and Colcum Press, 1992)
Goldberg, D.T., *Anatomy of Racism* (Minneapolis: University of Minnesota Press, 1990)
Gott, K.D., *Voices of Hate: A study of the Australian League of Rights and its director,*

Eric D. Butler (Melbourne: Dissent Pub. Association, 1965)

Gould, Stephen Jay, *The Mismeasure of Man* (New York: W.W. Norton & Co., 1981)

Gourevitch, Peter, *Politics in Hard Times: Comparative responses to international economic crises* (New York: Cornell University Press, 1986)

Grant, Bligh et al., *The Rise of Right-populism: Pauline Hanson's One Nation and Australian politics* (Singapore: Springer, 2019)

Greer, Germaine, *The Female Eunuch* (London: Paladin, 1971)

Grem, Darren E., *The Blessings of Business: Corporate America and the rise of conservative evangelicalism* (New York: Oxford University Press, 2016)

Griffin, Roger, *The Nature of Fascism* (London: Routledge, 1993)

Gunn, T. Jeremy, *Spiritual Weapons: The Cold War and the forging of an American national religion* (Westport, CT: Praeger, 2009)

Gustafson, Barry, *Kiwi Keith: A biography of Keith Holyoake* (Auckland: Auckland University Press, 2007)

Gustafson Barry, *Labour's Path to Political Independence: The origins and establishment of the New Zealand Labour Party, 1900–19* (Auckland: Auckland University Press, 1980)

Gustafson, Barry, *The First Fifty Years: A history of the New Zealand National Party* (Auckland: Reed Methuen, 1986)

Guy, Laurie, *Shaping Godzone: Public issues and church voices in New Zealand 1840–2000* (Wellington: Victoria University Press, 2011)

Guy, Laurie, *Worlds in Collision: The gay debate in New Zealand, 1960–1986* (Wellington: Victoria University Press, 2002)

Haden, Andy, *Lock, Stock 'n Barrel* (Auckland: Rugby Press, 1988)

Haeg, Claire, *The Cross of Gold Revisited: Neo-populist party emergence in Australia, Canada, and New Zealand* (Berlin: VDM Verlag, 2009)

Hagedorn, J.M, *People and Folks: Gangs, crime and the underclass in a rustbelt city* (Chicago: Lake View Press, 1988)

Haidt, Jonathan, *The Righteous Mind: Why good people are divided by politics and religion* (London: Penguin, 2012)

Hainsworth, Paul, *The Politics of the Extreme Right: From the margins to the mainstream* (London: Bloomsbury, 2000)

Hamer, D.A., *The New Zealand Liberals: The years of power, 1891–1912* (Auckland: Auckland University Press, 1988)

Hamm, M.S., *American Skinheads: The criminology and control of hate crime* (Westport: Praeger Publishers, 1993)

Harcourt, David, *Everyone Wants to be Fuehrer: National socialism in Australia and New Zealand* (Cremorne: Angus & Robertson, 1972)

Harris, Aroha, *Hīkoi: Forty years of Māori protest* (Wellington: Huia, 2004)

Hawke G.R., *Between Government and Banks: A history of the Reserve Bank of New Zealand* (Wellington: New Zealand Government Printer, 1973)

Hawke, Gary, *The Making of New Zealand: An economic history* (Cambridge: Cambridge University Press, 1985)

Hawtrey, Montague, *An Earnest Address to the New Zealand Colonists* (London: John W. Parker, 1840)

Hayward, J., *The Treaty Challenge: Local government and Maori – a scoping report* (Wellington: Crown Forestry Rental Trust, 2002)

Hild, Matthew, *Greenbackers, Knights of Labor and Populists: Farmer-labor insurgency in the late-nineteenth-century south* (Athens: University of Georgia Press, 2007)

Hill, Richard, *Anti-treatyism and Anti-scholarship: An analysis of anti-treatyist writings*, Treaty of Waitangi Research Unit Occasional Paper no. 8 (Wellington: Victoria University of Wellington, 2002)

Hinde, John, *When Coal Was King: Ladysmith and the coal-mining industry on Vancouver Island* (Vancouver: University of British Columbia Press, 2003)

Hobson, J.A., *The War in South Africa* (London: James Nisbet & Co., 1900)

Hochschild, Arlie, *Strangers in their Own Land: Anger and mourning on the American right* (New York: The New Press, 2016)
Hofstadter, Richard, *The Paranoid Style in American Politics, and Other Essays* (London: Cape, 1966)
Howe, K.R., *The Quest for Origins: Who first discovered and settled New Zealand and the Pacific Islands?* (Auckland: Penguin, 2003)
Hughes, William M., *Crusts and Crusades – tales of bygone days* (Sydney: Angus, 1947)
Hutchby, Ian, *Conversation and Technology: From the telephone to the internet* (Cambridge: Polity Press, 2001)
James, Colin, *The Quiet Revolution: Turbulence and transition in contemporary New Zealand* (Wellington: Allen & Unwin, 1986)
Jahoda, Gustav, *Images of Savages: Ancient roots of modern prejudice in western culture* (London: Routledge, 1999)
Janiewski, Dolores and Paul Morris, *New Rights New Zealand: Myths, moralities and markets* (Auckland: University of Auckland Press, 2005)
Jankowski, M.S., *Islands in the Street: Gangs and American urban society* (Berkeley: University of California Press, 1991)
Jesson, Bruce, Allanah Ryan and Paul Spoonley, *Revival of the Right: New Zealand politics in the 1980s* (Auckland: Heinemann Reed, 1988)
Judd, Denis and Keith Surridge, *The Boer War – a history* (London: I.B. Tauris, 2013)
Kaltwasser, Rovina et al. (eds), *The Oxford Handbook of Populism* (New York: Oxford University Press, 2017)
Kaplan, Esther, *With God on their Side: How Christian fundamentalists trampled science, policy and democracy in George W. Bush's White House* (New York: New Press, 2004)
Kasper, W., *Populate or Languish? Rethinking New Zealand's immigration policy* (Wellington: New Zealand Business Roundtable, 1990)
Kedgley, Sue and Mary Varnham (eds), *Heading Nowhere in a Navy Blue Suit and Other Tales From the Feminist Revolution* (Wellington: Daphne Brasell Associates, 1993)
Kelsey, Jane, *The New Zealand Experiment: A world model for structural adjustment?* (Auckland: Auckland University Press, 1995)
Keynes, John Maynard, *The General Theory of Employment Interest and Money* (London: Macmillan and Co. 1936)
King, Michael, *The Penguin History of New Zealand* (Auckland: Penguin, 2003)
Klein, M.W., *The American Street Gang: Its nature, prevalence and control* (New York: Oxford University Press, 1995)
Laidlaw, Chris, *Mud in Your Eye: A worm's eye view of the changing rugby world* (Wellington: A.H. & A.W. Reed, 1973)
Lakoff, George, *Moral Politics: How liberals and conservatives think*, 2nd edn (Chicago: University of Chicago Press, 2002)
Lang, Jack T., *I Remember* (Sydney: Invincible Press, 1957)
Langella, Julien, *Catholic and Identitarian: From protest to reconquest* (Budapest: Arktos, 2020)
Lawrence, David, Joe Mulhall, Simon Murdoch and Patrik Hermansson, *The International Alt-right: Fascism for the 21st Century?* (New York: Routledge, 2020)
Lebzelter, G.C., *Political Anti-Semitism in England 1918–1939* (London: Macmillan, 1978)
Lienesch, Michael, *Redeeming America: Piety and politics in the new Christian right* (Chapel Hill: University of North Carolina Press, 1993)
Lineham, Peter, *Destiny: The life and times of a self-made apostle* (Auckland: Penguin, 2013)
Long, Michael G., *Billy Graham and the Beloved Community: America's evangelist and the dream of Martin Luther King, Jr* (New York: Palgrave, 2006)
Love, P., *Labour and the Money Power: Australian labour populism, 1890–1950* (Melbourne: Melbourne University Press, 1984)
Loveridge, Donald, *The 'Littlewood Treaty': An appraisal of the texts and interpretations* (Wellington: Treaty of Waitangi Research Unit, 2006)
Loveridge, Steven (ed.), *New Zealand Society at War 1914–1918* (Wellington: Victoria University Press, 2016)

Loveridge, Steven and James Watson, *The Home Front: New Zealand society and the war effort, 1914–1919* (Palmerston North: Massey University Press, 2019)
Markham, E., *New Zealand, or Recollections of It* (Wellington: R.E. Owen, 1963)
Marshall, T.H., *Citizenship and Social Class: And other essays* (Cambridge: Cambridge University Press, 1950)
Massey, Patrick, *New Zealand: Market liberalisation in a developed economy* (Houndmills: Macmillan Press, 1995)
McCormack, A. Ross, *Reformers, Rebels, and Revolutionaries: The western Canadian radical movement 1899–1919* (Toronto: University of Toronto Press, 1977)
McDonald, Geoff, *Shadows Over New Zealand: Defence, land rights, and multiculturalism* (Christchurch: Chaston Publishers, 1985)
McIntyre, W. David and W.J. Gardner (eds), *Speeches and Documents on New Zealand History* (London: Oxford University Press, 1971)
McKinnon, Malcolm, *The Broken Decade: Prosperity, depression and recovery in New Zealand, 1928–39* (Dunedin: Otago University Press, 2016)
Meurant, Ross, *The Red Squad Story* (Auckland: Harlen Publishing, 1982)
Miller, Donald E. and Tetsunao Yamamori, *Global Pentecostalism: The new face of Christian social engagement* (Berkeley: University of California Press, 2007)
Millmow, A., *The Power of Economic Ideas: The origins of Keynesian macroeconomic management in interwar Australia 1929–39* (Canberra: Australian National University Press, 2011)
Mishra, Pankaj, *Bland Fanatics: Liberals, race and empire* (London: Verso, 2020)
Mitchell, Robin, *The Treaty and the Act: The Treaty of Waitangi, 1940 and the Treaty of Waitangi Act, 1975* (Christchurch: Cadsonbury, 1990)
Moffitt, Benjamin, *Populism: Key concepts in political theory* (Oxford: Polity Press, 2020)
Moore, Andrew, *The Right Road: A history of right-wing politics in Australia* (Melbourne: Oxford University Press, 1995)
Moore, Andrew, *The Secret Army and the Premier: Conservative paramilitary organisations in New South Wales, 1930–32* (Kensington: New South Wales University Press, 1989)
Moore, Jack B., *Skinheads Shaved for Battle: A cultural history of American skinheads* (Ohio: Bowling Green State University Popular Press, 1993)
Morris, Travis, *Dark Ideas: How neo-nazi and violent jihadi ideologues shaped modern terrorism* (London: Lexington, 2016)
Moynihan, Carolyn, *A Stand for Decency: Patricia Bartlett and the Society for Promotion of Community Standards, 1970–1995* (Wellington: SPUC, 1995)
Mudde, Cas, *The Far Right Today* (Cambridge: Polity Press, 2019)
Muldoon, Robert, *Muldoon* (Christchurch: A.H. & A.W. Reed, 1977)
Nauright, John and David Black, *Rugby and the South African Nation: Sport, cultures, politics, and power in the old and new South Africas* (Manchester: Manchester University Press, 1998)
Neiwert, David, *Alt-America: The rise of the radical right in the age of Trump* (London: Verso, 2018)
Newcomb, Steven, *Pagans in the Promised Land: Decoding the doctrine of Christian discovery* (Golden: Fulcrum Publishing, 2008)
Ngata, Apirana, *The Treaty of Waitangi, An Explanation; Te Tiriti o Waitangi, He Whakamarama* (Christchurch: Maori Purposes Board, 1963)
Nolan, Melanie (ed.), *Revolution: The 1913 Great Strike in New Zealand* (Christchurch: Canterbury University Press, 2005)
North, Gary and Gary DeMar, *Christian Reconstructionism: What it is, what it isn't* (Tyler: Institute for Christian Economics, 1994)
Novick, Peter, *The Holocaust and Collective Memory* (London: Bloomsbury, 2001)
Pihama, L., L.T. Smith, N. Cameron, R. Te Nana, H. Kohu-Morgan, H. Skipper and T. Mataki, *He Oranga Ngākau: Māori approaches to*

trauma informed care. Report to Health Research Council (Hamilton: Te Kotahi Research Institute, 2020)

Pihama, L., *Overview of Māori Teen Pregnancy* (Wellington: Families Commission, 2011)

Pool, I., *Colonisation and Development in New Zealand Between 1769 and 1900: The seeds of Rangiatea* (Auckland: Springer, 2015)

Olssen, Erik, *The Red Feds: Revolutionary industrial unionism and the New Zealand Federation of Labour, 1908–14* (New York: Oxford University Press, 1988)

Orange, Claudia, *The Treaty of Waitangi* (Wellington: Bridget Williams Books, 1987)

Orange, Claudia, *The Treaty of Waitangi / Te Tiriti o Waitangi – an illustrated history* (Wellington: Bridget Williams Books, 2020)

Paul, Diane B., John Stenhouse and Hamish G. Spencer (eds), *Eugenics at the Edges of Empire: New Zealand, Australia, Canada and South Africa* (London: Palgrave Macmillan, 2018)

Paxton, Robert O., *The Anatomy of Fascism* (London: Penguin, 2004)

Payne, Stanley G., *A History of Fascism 1914–1945* (Madison: University of Wisconsin Press, 1995)

Poulantzas, Nicos, *Fascism and Dictatorship: The Third International and the problem of fascism* (London: NLB, 1974)

Pryor, Marilyn, *The Right to Live: The abortion battle of New Zealand* (Parnell: Harlen Publishing, 1986)

Reeves, William Pember, *The Long White Cloud – Aotearoa*, 2nd edn (Auckland: Golden Press, 1950)

Reksten, Terry, *The Dunsmuir Saga* (Vancouver: Douglas & McIntyre, 1991)

Renton, David, *Fascism: Theory and practice* (London: Pluto Press, 1999).

Rice, Geoffrey, *Black November: The 1918 influenza pandemic in New Zealand* (Christchurch: Canterbury University Press, 2005)

Rice, G.W. (ed.), *The Oxford History of New Zealand* (Auckland: Oxford University Press, 1992)

Richards, Trevor, *Dancing on Our Bones: New Zealand, South Africa, rugby and racism* (Wellington: Bridget Williams Books, 1999)

Roberts, Sarah T., *Behind the Screen: Content moderation in the shadows of social media* (New Haven: Yale University Press, 2019)

Robertson, Robbie T., *The Three Waves of Globalization: A history of a developing global consciousness* (New York: Zed Books, 2003)

Robinson, John, *The Corruption of New Zealand democracy – a Treaty overview* (Wellington: Tross Publishing, 2011)

Robson, B. and R. Harris (eds), *Hauora: Māori standards of health IV. A study of the years 2000–2005* (Wellington: Te Rōpu Rangahau Hauora a Eru Pōmare, 2007)

Robson, Nigel, *Our First Foreign War: The impact of the South African War 1899–1902 on New Zealand* (Auckland: Massey University Press, 2021)

Rosier, Pat (ed.), *Been Around for Quite a While: Broadsheet: twenty years of Broadsheet magazine* (Auckland: New Women's Press, 1992)

Roy, Olivier, *Is Europe Christian?* (London: Hurst, 2019)

Roy, Patricia E., *A White Man's Province: British Columbia politicians and Chinese and Japanese immigrants 1858–1914* (Vancouver: UBC Press, 1989)

Rydgren, Jens (ed.), *The Oxford Handbook of the Radical Right* (New York: Oxford University Press, 2018)

Said, Edward, *Culture and Imperialism* (London: Vintage, 1994)

Salmond, Anne, *Two Worlds: First meetings between Māori and Europeans 1642–1772* (Auckland: Viking Penguin, 1991)

Schedvin, C.B., *Australia and the Great Depression* (Sydney: Sydney University Press, 1970)

Scott, Stuart C., *Travesty After Travesty* (Christchurch: Certes Press, 1996)

Scott, Stuart C., *Travesty of the Treaty – towards anarchy* (Dunedin: The Campbell Press, 1995)

Shadbolt, Tim, *Bullshit & Jellybeans* (Wellington: Alister Taylor, 1971)

Sheppard, Michael, *Social Credit: Inside and out* (Dunedin: Caveman, 1981)

Simpson, Patricia Anne and Helga Druxes (eds), *Digital Media Strategies of the Far Right in Europe and the United States* (Lanham, Maryland: Lexington Books, 2015)

Smith, Craig, *The Christian Foundations of the Institution of Corporal Correction* (Palmerston North: Family Integrity, 2005)

Smith, Cherryl and Paul Reynolds, *To Tatou Hokakatanga: Action and intervention in sexual and reproductive health. A report prepared for the Health Research Council of New Zealand* (Wellington: Te Puawai Tapu, 2006)

Smith, Linda Tuhiwai, *Decolonising Methodologies: Research and indigenous peoples*, 2nd edn (London: Zed Books, 2012)

Smyth, Helen, *Rocking the Cradle: Contraception, sex and politics in New Zealand* (Wellington: Steele Roberts, 2000)

Sparrow, Jeff, *Fascists Among Us: Online hate and the Christchurch massacre* (London: Scribe, 2019)

Spergel, I.A., *The Youth Gang Problem: A community approach* (New York: Oxford University Press, 1995)

Spoonley, Paul, D. Pearson and C. MacPherson (eds), *Nga Patai: Racism and ethnic relations in Aotearoa/New Zealand* (Palmerston North: Dunmore Press, 1996)

Spoonley, Paul, *The Politics of Nostalgia: Racism and the extreme right in New Zealand* (Palmerston North: Dunmore Press, 1987)

Spoonley, Paul, *Racism and Ethnicity: Critical issues in New Zealand society* (Auckland: Oxford University Press, 1988)

Spoonley, Paul and Helen Cox, *Report no. 11: Antisemitism in New Zealand since 1945* (Wellington, New Zealand Jewish Council, 1982)

Spoonley, Paul (ed.), *Tauiwi: Racism and ethnic conflict in New Zealand* (Palmerston North: Dunmore Press, 1984)

Stanley, Jason, *How Fascism Works* (New York: Random House, 2018)

Stafford, Jane and Mark Williams, *Maoriland: New Zealand literature 1872–1914* (Wellington: Victoria University Press, 2006)

Sternhell, Zeev, *The Birth of Fascist Ideology* (Princeton: Princeton University Press, 1994)

Straub, Whitney, *Perversion for Profit: The politics of pornography and the rise of the new right* (New York: Columbia University Press, 2011)

Sutch, W.B., *Women With a Cause* (Wellington: New Zealand University Press, 1973)

Taguieff, Pierre-André, *La Revanche du Nationalisme: Néopopulistes et xénophobes à l'assaut de l'Europe* (Paris: Presses Universitaires de France, 2015)

Tait, Gordon, *The Bartlett Syndrome: Censorship in New Zealand* (Christchurch: Freedom to Read, 1979)

Tait, P.S., *In the Chair: The public life of Sir John Ormond* (Waipukurau: CHB Print, 1989)

Taylor, C.S., *Dangerous Society* (East Lansing: Michigan University Press, 1989)

Teitelbaum, Benjamin R., *Lions of the North: Sounds of the new Nordic radical nationalism* (Oxford: Oxford University Press, 2017)

Thomson, A.S., *The Story of New Zealand: Past and present, savage and civilized* (London: J. Murray, 1859)

Thurlow, Richard, *Fascism in Britain: A history, 1918–1985* (New York: Basil Blackwell, 1987)

Tinirau, R., C. Smith and M. Haami, *Whakatika: How does racism impact on the health of Māori: A national literature review for the Whakatika Research Project* (Whanganui: Te Atawhai o Te Ao Charitable Trust, 2021)

Tod, Frank, *The Making of a Madman: Lionel Terry* (Dunedin: Otago Foundation Books, 1977)

Tosstorff, Reiner, *The Red International of Labour Union 1920–1937*, trans. Ben Fowkes (Boston: Brill, 2016)

Trapeznik, Alexander and Aaron Fox (eds), *Lenin's Legacy Down Under: New Zealand's Cold War* (Dunedin: University of Otago Press, 2004)

Traverso, Enzo, *The New Faces of Fascism: Populism and the far right*, trans. David Broder (London: Verso, 2019)

Veale, Kevin, *Gaming the Dynamics of Online Harassment* (Cham: Springer International Publishing, 2020)

Venturi, Franco, *Roots of Revolution: A history of the populist and socialist movements in 19th century Russia* (New York: Phoenix Press, 2001)

Vigil, J.D., *Barrio Gangs* (Austin: University of Texas Press, 1988)

Vigil, J.D., *A Rainbow of Gangs: Street cultures in the mega-city* (Austin: University of Texas Press, 2002)

Waitangi Tribunal, *Haumaru: The COVID-19 priority report* (Wellington: Waitangi Tribunal, 2021)

Waitangi Tribunal, *Hauora: Report on stage one of the health services and outcomes kaupapa inquiry* (Wellington: Legislation Direct, 2019)

Waitangi Tribunal, *Muriwhenua Fishing Report* (Wellington: GP Publications, 1988)

Waitangi Tribunal, *The Petroleum Report* (Wellington: Legislation Direct, 2003)

Waitangi Tribunal, *Te Tau Ihu o te Waka a Maui: Report on the Northern South Island claims*, vol. 2 (Wellington: Legislation Direct, 2008)

Walker, Ranginui, *Ka Whawhai Tonu Matou – Struggle without end*, 2nd edn (Auckland: Penguin, 2004)

Walker, Ranginui, *Ngā tau Tohetohe: Years of anger* (Auckland: Penguin, 1987)

Ward, Alan, *A Show of Justice: Racial 'amalgamation' in nineteenth century New Zealand* (Auckland: Auckland University Press, 1995)

Ward, Alan, *An Unsettled History: Treaty claims in New Zealand today* (Wellington: Bridget Williams Books, 1999)

Wilkinson, Michael, *Global Pentecostalism: Migration, mission and public religion* (Leiden: Brill, 2012)

Williams, Daniel K., *God's Own Party: The making of the Christian right* (New York: Oxford University Press, 2010)

Williams, John A., *Politics of the New Zealand Maori: Protest and cooperation, 1891–1909* (Seattle: University of Washington Press, 1969)

Wishart, Ian, *The Great Divide: The story of New Zealand and its Treaty* (Auckland: Howling at the Moon Publishing, 2012)

Wodak, Ruth, Majib Kohsravinik and Brigitte Mral (eds), *Right-wing Populism in Europe: Politics and discourse* (London: Bloomsbury Academic, 2013)

Woodley, Daniel, *Fascism and Political Theory: Critical perspectives on fascist ideology* (New York: Routledge, 2010)

Zúquete, José Pedro, *The Identitarians: The movement against globalism and Islam in Europe* (South Bend: University of Notre Dame Press, 2018)

BOOK CHAPTERS

Ahdar, Rex, 'New Zealand: The idea of a Christian state', in Rex Ahdar and John Stenhouse (eds), *God and Government: The New Zealand experience* (Dunedin: University of Otago Press, 2000), pp. 59–76

Aitken, Judith, 'Women in the political life of New Zealand', in Phillida Bunkle and Beryl Hughes (eds), *Women in New Zealand Society* (Auckland: George Allen & Unwin, 1980), pp. 11–33

Ballantyne, Tony, 'The state, politics and power, 1769–1893', in Giselle Byrnes (ed.), *The New Oxford history of New Zealand* (South Melbourne: Oxford University Press, 2009), chapter 6

Boston, Jonathan, 'Christian political parties and MMP', in Rex Ahdar and John Stenhouse (eds), *God and Government: The New Zealand experience* (Dunedin: University of Otago Press, 2000), pp. 105–24

Boyer, Paul, 'The evangelical resurgence in 1970s American Protestantism', in Bruce J. Schulman and Julian E. Zelizer (eds), *Rightward Bound: Making America conservative in the 1970s* (Cambridge: Harvard University Press, 2008), pp. 29–51

Brookes, Barbara, '"Aristocrats of knowledge": Māori anthropologists and the survival of the "race"', in Diane B. Paul, John Stenhouse and Hamish G. Spencer (eds), *Eugenics at the Edges of Empire: New Zealand, Australia, Canada and South Africa* (London: Palgrave Macmillan, 2018), chapter 13

Butlin, Noel G., 'Colonial socialism in Australia, 1860–1900', in Hugh Aitken (ed.), *The State and Economic Growth* (New York: Social Science Research Council, 1959), pp. 26–78

Clayworth, Peter, 'Patrick Hodgens Hickey and IWW: A transnational relationship', in Peter Cole, David Struthers and Kenyon Zimmer (eds), *Wobblies of the World: A global history of the IWW* (London: Pluto Press, 2017)

Cole, Peter, David Struthers and Kenyon Zimmer, 'Introduction', in Peter Cole, David Struthers and Kenyon Zimmer (eds), *Wobblies of the World: A global history of the IWW* (London: Pluto Books, 2017)

Daniels, J. and V. Houghton, 'Jensen, Eysenck and the Eclipse of the Garlton paradigm', in K. Richardson and D. Spears (eds), *Race, Culture and Intelligence* (London: Penguin, 1972)

Davidson, Allan, 'Chaplain to the nation or prophet at the gate? The role of the church in New Zealand society', in John Stenhouse (ed.) assisted by G.A. Wood, *Christianity, Modernity and Culture: New perspectives on New Zealand history* (Adelaide: ATF Press, 2005), pp. 311–31

Donovan, Joan, Becca Lewis and Brian Friedberg, 'Parallel ports: Sociotechnical change from the alt-right to alt-tech', in Maik Fielitz and Nick Thurston (eds), *Post-digital Cultures of the Far Right: Online actions and offline consequences in Europe and the US* (Bielefeld: Transcript, 2019), pp. 49–66

Douglas, Bronwen, 'Climate to crania: Science and the racialization of human difference', in Bronwen Douglas and Chris Ballard (eds), *Foreign Bodies: Oceania and the science of race 1750–1940* (Canberra: Australian National University Press, 2008), pp. 33–96

Fenwick, Penny, 'Fertility, sexuality and social control in New Zealand', in Phillida Bunkle and Beryl Hughes (eds), *Women in New Zealand Society* (Auckland: George Allen & Unwin, 1980), pp. 77-98

Forster, J. and P. Ramsay, 'Migration, Education and Occupation: The Maori population 1936–66', in J. Forster (ed.), *Social process in New Zealand: Readings in sociology* (Auckland: Longman Paul, 1969)

Franks, Peter, 'Chronology of events', in Melanie Nolan (ed.), *Revolution: The 1913 Great Strike in New Zealand* (Christchurch: Canterbury University Press, 2005)

Gattey, Emma, 'Sir Robert Stout as freethinker and eugenics enthusiast', in Diane B. Paul, John Stenhouse and Hamish G. Spencer (eds), *Eugenics at the Edges of Empire: New Zealand, Australia, Canada and South Africa* (London: Palgrave Macmillan, 2018), chapter 10

Gibbons, Peter, 'Non-fiction', in Terry Sturm (ed.), *The Oxford History of New Zealand Literature*, 1st edn (Auckland: Oxford University Press, 1991)

Graham, B.D., 'The Country Party idea in New Zealand politics, 1901–1935', in Robert Chapman and Keith Sinclair (eds), *Studies of a Small Democracy* (Auckland: Auckland University Press, 1963), pp. 175–200

Gustafson, Barry, 'Populist roots of political Leadership in New Zealand', in Raymond Miller and Michael Mintrom (eds), *Political Leadership in New Zealand* (Auckland: Auckland University Press, 2006), pp. 51–69

Hardy, Ann, 'Destiny breaks through media screens', in Peter Horsfield (ed.), *Papers from the Trans-Tasman Research Symposium: Emerging research in media, religion and culture* (Melbourne: RMIT Publishing, 2005), pp. 40–56

Jefferson, J.O., 'Cultural responses of the teds: The defence of space and status', in S. Hall and T. Jefferson (eds), *Resistance Through Rituals* (London: Hutchinson, 1976)

Johansson, Jon, 'Brash, Orewa and the politics of race', in Steven Levine and Nigel S. Roberts (eds), *The Baubles of Office: The New Zealand General Election of 2005* (Wellington: Victoria University Press, 2007), pp. 62–82

McAloon, Jim, 'The making of the New Zealand ruling class', in Melanie Nolan (ed.), *Revolution: The 1913 Great Strike in*

New Zealand (Christchurch: Canterbury University Press, 2005)

Melleuish, Gregory, 'Populism and conservatism in Australian political thought', in Paul Boreham, Geoffrey Stokes and Richard Hall (eds), *The Politics of Australian Society: Political issues for the new century* (Sydney: Longman, 2000), pp. 51–64

Miller, Raymond, 'New Zealand First', in Hans-Georg Betz and Stefan Immerfall (eds), *The New Politics of the Right: Neo-populist parties and movements in established democracies* (New York: St Martin's Press, 1998)

Short, J.F.J., 'Forward: Diversity and change in U.S. gangs', in C.R. Huff (ed.), *Gangs in America*, 2nd edn (Thousand Oaks: Sage Publications, 1990)

Shum, Lynette, 'Remembering Chinatown', in Manying Ip (ed.), *Unfolding History, Evolving Identity* (Auckland: Auckland University Press, 2003)

Smith, Evan, 'Exporting fascism across the Commonwealth: The case of the National Front of Australia', in Nigel Copsey and Matthew Worley (eds), *Tomorrow Belongs to Us: The British far right since 1967* (New York: Routledge, 2018), pp. 69–89

Oliver, W.H., 'The future behind us: The Waitangi Tribunal's retrospective utopia', in Andrew Sharp and Paul McHugh (eds), *Histories, Power and Loss: Uses of the past: a New Zealand commentary* (Wellington: Bridget Williams Books, 2001)

O'Regan, Tipene, 'Impact on Māori – a Ngāi Tahu perspective', in Jacinta Ruru (ed.), *'In Good Faith': Symposium proceedings marking the 20th anniversary of the lands case*, (Dunedin: University of Otago Faculty of Law / The New Zealand Law Foundation, 2008)

Ruostslia, Markku, 'International anti-communism before the Cold War: Success and failure of building a transnational tight', in Margaret Power and Martin Durham (eds), *New Perspectives on the Transnational Right* (New York: Palgrave Macmillan, 2010)

Sorrenson, M.P.K., 'Towards a radical reinterpretation of New Zealand history: The role of the Waitangi Tribunal', in I.H. Kawharu (ed.), *Waitangi-Maori and Pakeha Perspectives of the Treaty of Waitangi* (Auckland, Oxford University Press, 1989), pp. 158–61

Spoonley, Paul and Helen Cox, 'Antisemitism in New Zealand since 1945', in *New Zealand Jewish Council Report and Educational Papers*, 11, 7 June 1982

Spoonley, Paul, 'Migration and the reconstruction of citizenship in late twentieth century Aotearoa', in Stephen Castles and Paul Spoonley (eds), *Migration and Citizenship* (Auckland: Department of Sociology, Massey University, 1997)

Spoonley, Paul, 'Pākehā ethnicity: A response to Māori sovereignty', in Paul Spoonley, David Pearson and Cluny Macpherson (eds), *Nga Take – Ethnic relations and racism in Aotearoa/New Zealand* (Palmerston North: Dunmore Press, 1991)

Spoonley, Paul, 'The Asianisation of Aotearoa: immigration impacts', in Avril Bell, Vivienne Elizabeth, Tracey McIntosh and Matt Wynyard (eds), *A Land of Milk and Honey? Making sense of Aotearoa New Zealand* (Auckland: Auckland University Press, 2017)

Spoonley, Paul and Philip Gendall, 'Welcome to our world: Attitudes to immigrants and immigration', in Andrew Trlin et al., *New Zealand and International Migration: A digest and bibliography, number 5* (Auckland: Massey University, 2010)

Stokes, Geoffrey, 'One Nation and Australian populism', in Michael Leach, Geoff Stokes and Ian M. Hall (eds), *The Rise and Fall of One Nation* (Brisbane: University of Queensland Press, 2000), pp. 23–41

Taylor, James, 'Contemporary media portrayals of the 1913 dispute', in Melanie Nolan (ed.), *Revolution: The 1913 Great Strike in New Zealand* (Christchurch: University of Canterbury Press, 2005)

Taylor, Kerry, 'The Old Bolshevik: Alex Galbraith, the Communist Party and the New Zealand revolution', in Rachael Bell (ed.), *New Zealand Between the Wars* (Auckland: Massey University Press, 2017)

Te Awekotuku, Ngahuia, 'Dykes & queers: facts, fairytales and fictions'; 'He wahine, he whenua, e ngaro ai te tangata: By women, by land, men are lost', in Ngahuia Te Awekotuku (ed.), *Mana Wahine Maori: Selected writings on Maori women's art, culture and politics* (Auckland: New Women's Press, 1991), pp 36–47

Te Awekotuku, Ngahuia, 'Mana wahine: Seeking meanings for ourselves', in Maud Cahill and Christine Dann (eds), *Changing Our Lives: Women working in the women's liberation movement, 1970–1990* (Wellington: Bridget Williams Books, 1991), pp. 25–33

Tripp, L.O.H., 'War relief and patriotic societies', in H.T.B. Drew (ed.), *The War Effort in New Zealand* (Auckland: Whitcombe & Tombs, 1923)

Utter, Glenn H. and John W. Storey, 'Chalcedon Foundation', in Glenn H. Utter and John W. Storey (eds), *The Religious Right: A reference handbook* (Santa Barbara: ABC-Clio, 2001)

Walker, Ranginui, 'Reclaiming Māori education', in Jessica Hutchings and Jenny Lee-Morgan (eds), *Decolonisation in Aotearoa: Education, research and practice* (Wellington: NZCER Press, 2006), pp. 19–38

Ward, Damen, 'Colonial communication: Creating settler public opinion in Crown colony South Australia and New Zealand', in Simon J. Potter (ed.), *Imperial Communication: Australia, Britain, and the British Empire c. 1830–50* (London: Menzies Centre for Australian Studies, 2004), pp. 7–46

Watson, James, 'The continuation of politics: Parliamentarians and the Great War', in Steven Loveridge (ed.), *New Zealand Society at War 1914–1918* (Wellington: Victoria University Press, 2016)

Wilson, Tony, 'Defining the "Red Menace": "Russophobia" and New Zealand–Russian relations from the Tsars to Stalin', in Alexander Trapeznik and Aaron Fox (eds), *Lenin's Legacy Down Under: New Zealand's Cold War* (Dunedin: Otago University Press, 2004)

JOURNAL ARTICLES

Araujo-Hawkins, Dawn, 'The making of the QAnon conspiracy cult', *Christian Century*, vol. 137, no. 6, 16 December 2020

Ballantyne, Tony, 'On place, space, and mobility in nineteenth-century New Zealand', *New Zealand Journal of History*, vol. 45, no. 1, 2011, pp. 50–70

Barkan, Elazar, 'Reevaluating progressive eugenics: Herbert Spencer Jennings and the 1924 immigration legislation', *Journal of the History of Biology*, vol. 24, no. 1, 1991, pp. 91–112

Barratt, Glynn, 'The enemy that never was: The New Zealand "Russian scare" of 1870–1885', *New Zealand Slavonic Journal*, vol. 1, 1976, pp. 13–33

Bassett, Judith, 'Sir Harry Atkinson and the conservative faction in New Zealand politics, 1879–1890', *New Zealand Journal of History*, vol. 2, no. 2, 1968, pp. 130–47

Battersby, John and Rhys Ball, 'Christchurch in the context of New Zealand terrorism and right wing extremism', *Journal of Policing, Intelligence and Counter Terrorism*, vol. 14, no. 3, 2019, pp. 191–207

Bell, Rachael, 'Texts and translations – Ruth Ross and the Treaty of Waitangi', *New Zealand Journal of History*, vol. 43, no. 1, 2009, pp. 39–58

Berzins, Baiba, 'Douglas Credit and the A.L.P.', *Labour History*, vol. 17, 1969, pp. 148–60

Bonnett, Alastair, 'How the British working class became white: The symbolic (re) formation of racialized capitalism', *Journal of Historical Sociology*, vol. 11, no. 3, 2002, pp. 316–40

Borell, B.A., A.S Gregory et al., '"It's hard at the top but it's a whole lot easier than being at the bottom": The role of privilege in understanding disparities in Aotearoa/New Zealand', *Race / Ethnicity: Multidisciplinary Global Contexts*, vol. 3, no. 1, 2009, pp. 29–50

Brickell, Chris, 'Psychiatry, psychology and homosexual prisoners in New Zealand, 1910–1960', *Medical History*, vol. 65, no. 1, 2021, pp. 1–17

Brogan, D.W., 'God and the juke-box: Religion in the United States,' *Manchester Guardian*, vol. 5, October 1954

Butcher, Andrew, Paul Spoonley and Phil Gendall, 'New Zealanders' attitudes to Asia and Asian peoples', *Political Science*, vol. 67, 2015, pp. 38–55

Castells, Manuel, 'Materials for an exploratory theory of the network society', *The British Journal of* Sociology, vol. 51, no. 1, 2000, pp. 5–24

Castells, Manuel, 'Toward a sociology of the network society', *Contemporary* Sociology, vol. 29, no. 5, 2000, pp. 693–98

Chan, Charles, 'New Zealand last to repeal Chinese poll tax but first to apologise', *New Zealand Legacy*, vol. 23, no. 2, 2011, pp. 18–22

Cunningham, Matthew, 'Australian fascism? A revisionist analysis of the ideology of the New Guard', *Politics, Religion & Ideology*, vol. 13, no. 3, 2012, pp. 375–93

Cunningham, Matthew, 'Massey's Cossacks reborn? Public and private counterrevolutionary preparations in New Zealand, 1920–1921' (currently seeking publication)

Dalli, C., 'Policy agendas for children's lives', *New Zealand Journal of Educational Studies*, vol. 27, no. 1, 1992, pp. 53–67

Daniels, Jesse, 'The algorithmic rise of the "alt-right"', *Contexts*, vol. 17, no. 1, 2018, pp. 60–65

Davis, R.P., 'The New Zealand Labour Party's "Irish Campaign" 1916–1921', *Political Science*, vol. 19, no. 2, 1967, pp. 13–23

Dawson, Selwyn, 'God's bullies,' *Metro*, July 1985, pp. 170–76

Elers, Steve, 'A "White New Zealand": Anti-Chinese racist political discourse from 1880 to 1920', *China Media* Research, vol. 14, no. 3, 2018, pp. 88–98

Funke, Manuel et al., 'Going to extremes: Politics after financial crises, 1870–2014', *European Economic Review*, vol. 88, 2016, pp. 227–60

Garland, A.E., 'Is a new eugenics afoot?', *Science*, vol. 294, no. 5540, 2001, pp. 59–61

Gilbert, Jarrod and Ben Elley, 'Shaved heads and sonnenrads: Comparing white supremacist skinheads and the alt-right in New Zealand', *Kōtuitui: New Zealand Journal of Social Sciences online*, vol. 15, no. 2, 2020, pp. 280–94

Goot, Murray, 'Pauline Hanson's One Nation: Extreme right, Centre Party or extreme left?' *Labour* History, vol. 89, 2005, pp. 101–19

Harris, R. et al., 'Racism and health: The relationship between experience of racial discrimination and health in New Zealand', *Social Science and Medicine*, vol. 63, no. 6, 2006, pp. 1428–41

Hirshfield, Claire, 'The Anglo-Boer War and the issue of Jewish culpability', *Journal of Contemporary History*, vol.15, 1980, pp. 619–31

Hutchinson, Jade, 'Far-right terrorism: The Christchurch attack and potential implications on the Asia Pacific landscape', *Counter Terrorist Trends and* Analyses, vol. 11, no. 6, 2019, pp. 19–28

Kaplan, Jeffrey, 'Leaderless resistance', *Terrorism and Political Violence*, vol. 9, no. 3, 1997, pp. 80–95

Kobayashi, Audrey, '"Here we go again': Christchurch's antiracism rally as a discursive crisis', *New Zealand Geographer*, vol. 65, 2009, pp. 59–72

Laidler, John, 'Try hard, find God, get rich', *Harvard Gazette,* 24 October 2017

La Rooij, Marinus F., 'Arthur Nelson Field: Kiwi theoretician of the Australian radical right?' *Labour History*, vol. 89, 2005, pp. 37–54

La Rooij, Marinus F., 'From colonial conservative to international antisemite: The life and work of Arthur Nelson Field', *Journal of Contemporary History*, vol. 37, no. 2, April 2002, pp. 223–39

Leckie, Jacqueline, 'In defence of race and Empire: The White New Zealand League at Pukekohe', *New Zealand Journal of* History, vol. 19, no. 2, 1985, pp. 103–29

Macklin, Graham, 'Transatlantic connections and conspiracies: A.K. Chesterton and the new unhappy Lords', *Journal of Contemporary History*, vol. 47, no. 2, 2012, pp. 270–90

MacLean, Malcolm, '"Almost the same, but not quite … Almost the same, but not white": Māori and Aotearoa/New Zealand's 1981 Springbok Tour', *Kunapipi*, vol. 23, no. 1, 2001, pp. 69–82

MacLean, Malcolm, 'Football as social critique: Protest movements, rugby and history in Aotearoa New Zealand', *International Journal of the History of Sport*, vol. 17, no. 2–3, 2000, pp. 255–77

MacLean, Malcolm, 'From old soldiers to old youth: Political leadership and New Zealand's 1981 Springbok Rugby Tour', *Football Studies*, vol. 1, no. 1, 1998, pp. 22–36

Magnusson, R.S., 'Case studies in nanny state name-calling: What can we learn?', *Public Health*, 2 July 2015

Martens, Jeremy, 'Richard Seddon and popular opposition in New Zealand to the introduction of Chinese Labour into the Transvaal, 1903–1904', *New Zealand Journal of History*, vol. 42, no. 4, 2008, pp. 176–95

Mawson, Mike, 'Enough is enough! Civil unions, religious prejudice and the limits of secular tolerance', *Australian Religion Studies Review*, vol. 19, no. 1, 2006, pp. 53–75

McAloon, Jim, 'By which standards? History and the Waitangi Tribunal', *New Zealand Journal of History*, vol. 40, no. 2, 2006, pp. 194–213

McDowell. Tiopira, '"Ka Hoki a Kupe?" The political career of Matiu Rata, 1963–1979', *New Zealand Journal of History*, vol. 49, no. 1, 2015, pp. 105–25

Mitchell, Austin, 'Fluoridation in Dunedin: A study of pressure groups and public opinion', *Political Science*, vol. 12, no. 1, March 1960, pp. 71–93

Moloughney, Brian and John Stenhouse '"Drug-besotten, sin-begotten fiends of filth": New Zealanders and the oriental other, 1850–1920', *New Zealand Journal of History*, vol. 33, no. 1, 1999, pp. 43–64

Mondon, A. and Aaron Winter, 'Whiteness, populism and the racialisation of the working class in the United Kingdom and the United States', *Identities*, vol. 26, no. 5, 2019, pp. 510–28

Moritz, Hannah, 'Playing the Nazi card', *Listener*, 18 December 2021

Moses, A. Dirk, '"White genocide" and the ethics of public analysis', *Journal of Genocide* Research, vol. 21, no. 2, 2019, pp. 201–13

Mosley, Mark, 'Viewpoint: COVID-19 and eugenics in 2020', *Emergency Medicine* News, vol. 42, 2020, pp. 1–3

Mulhall, Joe, 'From apathy to obsession: The reactions of A.K. Chesterton and the British far right to imperial decline', *Patterns of Prejudice*, vol. 50, no. 4–5, 2016, pp. 458–77

Mutu, Margaret, 'Behind the smoke and mirrors of the Treaty of Waitangi claims settlement process in New Zealand: No prospect for justice and reconciliation for Māori without constitutional transformation', *Journal of Global Ethics*, vol. 14, no. 2, 2018, pp. 208–21

Newcomb, Steve, 'Five hundred years of injustice: The legacy of fifteenth century religious prejudice', *Shaman's Drum Journal*, Fall 1992, pp. 18–20

Nixon, Rob, 'Apartheid on the run: The South African sports boycott', *Transition*, vol. 58, no. 1, 1992, pp. 68–88

Noonan, M.A., 'The aims of the New Zealand Welfare League 1919–1922', *The University of Auckland Historical Society Annual*, 1969, pp. 28–46

O'Connor, P.S., 'Keeping New Zealand white, 1908–1920', *New Zealand Journal of History*, vol. 2, no. 1, 1968, pp. 41–65

O'Connor, P.S., 'Mr Massey and the PPA – a suspicion confirmed', *New Zealand Journal of Public Administration*, vol. 28, no. 2, 1966, pp. 69–74

O'Connor, P.S., 'Sectarian conflict in New Zealand, 1911–1920', *Political Science*, vol. 19, no. 1, 1967, pp. 13–16

O'Connor, P.S., 'Some political preoccupations of Mr Massey, 1918–20', *Political Science*, vol. 18, no. 2, 1966, pp. 16–38

O'Connor, P.S., 'Storm over the clergy – New Zealand 1917', *Journal of Religious History*, vol. 4, no. 2, 1966–1967, pp. 129–48

O'Rourke, Kevin H. and Jeffrey G. Williamson, 'Once more: When did globalisation begin?',

European Review of Economic History, vol. 8, no. 1, 2004, pp. 109–17
Olssen, Erik, 'Truby King and the Plunket Society: An analysis of a prescriptive ideology', *New Zealand Journal of History*, vol. 15, no. 1, 1981, pp. 3–23
Olssen, Erik, 'Where to from here? Reflections on the twentieth-century historiography of nineteenth-century New Zealand', *New Zealand Journal of History*, vol. 26, no. 1, 1992, pp. 54–77
Pearson, Bill, 'Fretful sleepers: A sketch of New Zealand behaviour and its implications for the artist', *Landfall*, vol. 23, September 1952, pp. 201–30
Pihama, Leonie and Marjorie Lipsham, 'Noho Haumaru: Reflecting on Māori approaches to staying safe during Covid-19 in Aotearoa', *Journal of Indigenous Social Development*, vol. 9, no. 3, 2020, pp. 92–101
Pollard, John, 'Skinhead culture: The ideologies, mythologies, religions and conspiracy theories of racist skinheads', *Patterns of Prejudice*, vol. 50, no. 4–5, 2016, pp. 398–419
Pool, Ian, 'The effects of the 1918 pandemic of influenza on the Maori population of New Zealand', *Bulletin of the History of Medicine*, vol. 47, no. 3, 1973, pp. 273–81
Ridgley, Susan, 'Conservative Christianity and the creation of alternative news: An analysis of Focus on the Family's multimedia empire', *Religion & American Culture*, vol. 30, no.1, winter 2020, pp. 1–25
Ross, Ruth, 'Te Tiriti o Waitangi texts and translations', *New Zealand Journal of History*, vol. 6, no. 2, 1972, pp. 129–57
Roth, H., 'The communist vote in New Zealand', *Political Science*, vol. 17, no. 2, September 1965, pp. 26–35
Rydgren, Jens, 'The sociology of the radical right', *Annual Review of Sociology*, vol. 33, 2007, pp 241–62
Simon, Hemopereki Hōani, 'A political-cultural textual critique of ALT/far-right anti-indigenous thought on indigenous issues in Aotearoa New Zealand', *SITES*, vol. 17, no. 2, 2020, pp. 97–128
Sinclair, Keith, 'Why are race relations in New Zealand better than in South Africa, South Australia or South Dakota?' *New Zealand Journal of History*, vol. 5, no. 2, 1971, pp. 121–27
Smith, Evan, 'Keeping the Nazi menace out: George Lincoln Rockwell and the border control system in Australia and Britain in the early 1960s', *Social Sciences*, vol. 9, no. 9, 2020, pp. 1–13
Spoonley, Paul, 'Boots and bristle: Skinhead music and politics as resistance', *Sites*, vol. 14, 1987, pp. 103–4
Spoonley, Paul, 'New Zealand first! The extreme right and politics in New Zealand, 1961–1981', *Political Science*, vol. 33, no. 2, 1981, pp. 99–126
Stenhouse, John, '"A disappearing race before we came here": Doctor Alfred Kingcome Newman, the dying Māori, and Victorian scientific racism', *New Zealand Journal of* History, vol. 30, no. 2, 1996, pp. 124–40
Steyn, Nicholas et al., 'Estimated inequities in COVID-19 infection fatality rates by ethnicity for Aotearoa New Zealand', *New Zealand Medical Journal*, vol. 133, no. 1521, 2020, pp. 28–39
Sweetman, Rory, 'New Zealand Catholicism and the Irish issue 1914–1922', *Studies in Church History*, vol. 25, 1989.
Taylor, T., 'Thomas Hunter and the campaign against eugenics', *New Zealand Journal of History*, vol. 39, no. 2, 2005, pp. 194–214
Trapeznik, Alexander, 'New Zealand's perceptions of the Russian Revolution of 1917', *Revolutionary Russia*, vol. 19, no. 1, 2006, pp. 63–77
von Beyme, Klaus, 'Right-wing extremism in post-war Europe', *West European Politics*, vol. 11, no. 2, 1988, pp. 1–18
Watson, James, 'Were Catholics over-represented in the public service during the early twentieth century?', *Political Science*, vol. 42, no. 2, 1990, pp. 20–34
Wagner, Marcus and Thomas Meyer, 'The radical right as niche parties? The ideological landscape of party systems

in Western Europe, 1980–2014', *Political Studies*, vol. 65, no. 1, 2016, pp. 84–107

Woodward, L.J., L.J. Horwood and D.M. Fergusson, 'Teenage pregnancy: Cause for concern', *New Zealand Medical Journal*, vol. 114, no. 1135, 2001, pp. 301–3

THESES

Addison, R., 'Alienation and skinheads: An exploratory study into the attitudes of an antisocial subgroup of society' (MA thesis, University of Canterbury, 1996)

Ahdar, Rex John, 'Worlds colliding: Aspects of New Zealand conservative Christians' encounter with the law' (PhD thesis, University of Otago, 2000)

Bennett, Charlotte, 'The New Zealand history wars' (Hist419 research essay, University of Wellington, 2010)

Bollard, Robert, '"The active chorus": The mass strike of 1917 in eastern Australia' (PhD thesis, Victoria University, 2007)

Bond, Greta, 'Evangelistic performance in New Zealand: The word and what is not said' (PhD thesis, University of Canterbury, 2008)

Buchman, Harvey Stephen, 'The political thought of the New Zealand League of Rights' (MA thesis, University of Waikato, 1983)

Clifton, Robin, 'Douglas Credit and the Labour Party, 1930–1935' (MA diss., Victoria University of Wellington, 1961)

Coward, Dan, 'The impact of war on New South Wales: Some aspects of social and political history, 1914–1917' (PhD thesis, Australian National University, 1974)

Crosby, Hayden, 'Right-wing extremism in New Zealand: Dialogues with those who left' (MA thesis, Auckland University, 2017)

Cunningham, Matthew, 'The reactionary and the radical: A comparative analysis of mass conservative mobilisation in Australia and New Zealand during the Great Depression' (PhD thesis, Victoria University of Wellington, 2015)

Dunick, Mark, 'Making rebels: The New Zealand Socialist Party 1901–1913' (MA thesis, Victoria University of Wellington, 2016)

Else, Anne, 'On shifting ground: Self-narrative, feminist theory and writing practice' (PhD thesis, Victoria University of Wellington, 2006)

Ferguson, Philip, 'The making of a white New Zealand policy: Nationalism, citizenship and the exclusion of the Chinese, 1880–1920' (PhD thesis, University of Canterbury, 2003)

Fisher, Martin, 'Balancing rangatiratanga and kāwanatanga: Waikato-Tainui and Ngāi Tahu's Treaty settlement and negotiations with the Crown' (PhD thesis, Victoria University of Wellington, 2015)

Fleming, P.J., 'Eugenics in New Zealand 1900–1940' (MA thesis, Massey University, 1981)

Francis, Andrew, '"To be truly British we must be anti-German": Patriotism, citizenship and anti-alienism in New Zealand during the Great War' (PhD thesis, Victoria University of Wellington, 2009)

Gray, Claire Frances, 'White privilege: Exploring the (in)visibility of Pakeha whiteness' (MA thesis, University of Canterbury, 2012)

Harper, Joseph D., '"Heal their land": Evangelical political theology from the great awakening to the moral majority' (PhD diss., University of Nebraska-Lincoln, 2014)

La Rooij, Marinus, 'Political antisemitism in New Zealand during the Great Depression: A case study in the myth of the Jewish world conspiracy' (MA thesis, Victoria University of Wellington, 1998)

Lindsey, David, 'Conscience voting in New Zealand' (PhD thesis, University of Auckland, 2011)

McLachlan, Ben Thomas, 'In search of a New Zealand populism: Heresthetics, character and populist political leadership' (MA thesis, Victoria University of Wellington, 2013)

Meihana, Peter N., 'The paradox of Māori privilege: Historical constructions of Māori

privilege circa 1769 to 1940' (PhD thesis, Massey University, 2015)
Milnes, Dickon John, 'The church militant: Dunedin churches and society during WW1' (PhD thesis, University of Otago, 2015)
Moores, Harold, 'The rise of the Protestant Political Association: Sectarianism in New Zealand during World War One' (MA thesis, University of Auckland, 1966)
Moriarty-Patten, Stuart, 'A world to win, a hell to lose: The Industrial Workers of the World in early twentieth century New Zealand' (MA thesis, Massey University, 2012)
Pihama, Leonie, 'Tihei Mauri Ora, honouring our voices: Mana wahine as a kaupapa Maaori theoretical framework' (PhD thesis, University of Auckland, 2001)
Pihama, Leonie, 'Tungia te Ururua, Kia Tupu Whakaritorito Te Tupu o te Harakeke: A critical analysis of parents as first teachers' (MA thesis, University of Auckland, 1993)
Porter, Frances, 'Chinese immigration to New Zealand in the nineteenth century' (MA thesis, University of New Zealand, 1948)
Potgieter, Sebastian J.S., '(Re)presenting 1981: Narrating the Springbok Tour' (PhD thesis, University of Otago, 2020)
Pugh, Michael, 'The New Zealand Legion and conservative protest in the Great Depression' (MA thesis, University of Auckland, 1969)
Satchell, Max, 'Pulpit politics: The Protestant Political Association in Dunedin from 1917 to 1922' (BA (Hons) diss., University of Otago, 1983)
Smith, C.W., 'Kimihia te maramatanga: Colonisation and iwi development' (MA thesis, University of Auckland, 1994)
Stace, H., 'Moving beyond love and luck: Building right relationships and respecting lived experience in New Zealand autism policy' (PhD thesis, Victoria University of Wellington, 2011)
Stepnick, Andrea, 'Making godly men: The social construction of masculinities in Promise Keepers' (PhD diss., Florida State University, 1999)
Stricker, Mary, 'A new racial ideology for the new Christian right? The meaning(s) of racial reconciliation within the Promise Keepers movement' (PhD diss., Temple University, 2001)
Sweetman, Rory, 'New Zealand Catholicism, war, politics and the Irish issue 1912–1922' (PhD thesis, University of Cambridge, 1990)
van der Krogt, Christopher John, 'More a part than apart: The Catholic community in New Zealand society, 1918–1940' (PhD thesis, Massey, 1994)
Warburton, G.R., 'The attitudes and policies of the New Zealand labour movement towards non-European immigration' (MA thesis, University of Canterbury, 1982)
Ward, Liz, 'For light and liberty: The origins and early development of the Reform Party, 1887–1915' (PhD thesis, Massey University, 2018)
Ward, Liz, 'The New Zealand Legion in Manawatu-Wanganui, 1933–1935' (BA (Hons) diss., Massey University, 2011)
Wilson, S.K., 'The aims and ideology of Cora Wilding and the Sunlight League 1930–36' (MA diss, University of Canterbury, 1980)
Wright, Jennifer, 'The politics of fertility: The global emergence of "pro-family" organisations' (PhD thesis, Victoria University of Wellington, 2009)

ONLINE SOURCES

'A darker truth: The anti-Semitism behind Billy Te Kahika's conspiracy theories', Stuff, October 2020: https://interactives.stuff.co.nz/2020/10/a-darker-truth-anti-semitism-billy-tk-jr-conspiracy
'A protest where voices united, but agendas diverged', Stuff, 10 November 2021: www.stuff.co.nz/national/politics/opinion/126932706/a-protest-where-voices-united-but-agendas-diverged
'American Jewish Congress report ties Capitol storming to nei-nazi, QAnon and antisemitic activity', American Jewish Congress,

11 January 2021: https://ajcongress.org/statements/american-jewish-congress-report-ties-capitol-storming-to-neo-nazi-qanon-and-antisemitic-activity/

'An establishment conservative's guide to the alt-right', Breitbart, 29 March 2016: www.breitbart.com/tech/2016/03/29/an-establishment-conservatives-guide-to-the-alt-right/

'Antipodean anti-vaxxers are learning from America's far right', The Economist, 27 November 2021: www.economist.com/asia/2021/11/27/antipodean-anti-vaxxers-are-learning-from-americas-far-right

'Atomwaffen Division', Southern Poverty Law Centre: www.splcenter.org/fighting-hate/extremist-files/group/atomwaffen-division

'Billy Te Kahika – the conspiracy theorist with a hidden following', Radio NZ, 13 October 2020: www.rnz.co.nz/programmes/the-detail/story/2018767978/billy-te-kahika-the-conspiracy-theorist-with-a-hidden-following

'Estimated resident population (ERP), subnational population by ethnic group, age, and sex, at 30 June 1996, 2001, 2006, 2013, and 2018 Information on table', Stats New Zealand. n.d.: http://nzdotstat.stats.govt.nz/WBOS/Index.aspx?DataSetCode=TABLECODE7512

'False profit: Full and unedited video with Advance NZ co-leader Billy Te Kahika', Stuff, 13 October 2020: www.stuff.co.nz/national/stuff-circuit/300131103/false-profit-full-and-unedited-video-with-advance-nz-coleader-billy-te-kahika

'Get to know four more candidates', Stuff, 12 September 2014: www.stuff.co.nz/southland-times/10489238/Get-to-know-four-more-candidates

'Iwi at forum urges repudiation of Doctrine of Discovery', Radio New Zealand News: www.rnz.co.nz/news/national/402309/iwi-at-forum-urges-repudiation-of-doctrine-of-discovery

'Ko tō tatou kāinga tēnei: Report of the Royal Commission of Inquiry into the terrorist attack on Christchurch masjidain on 15 March 2019', Royal Commission of Inquiry website, 26 November 2020: https://christchurchattack.royalcommission.nz/the-report/

'Max Newsome ("Matt") and Action Zealandia', The White Rose Society, 10 March 2020: https://thewhiterosesociety.writeas.com/max-newsome-matt-and-action-zealandia

'Reprint: Salient interview Colin King-Ansell, 1970', The Ice Bloc: https://theicebloc.wordpress.com/2017/04/15/reprint-salient-interviews-colin-king-ansell-1970/

'Stefan Molyneux mourns the loss of his audience after YouTube and Twitter bans', Angry White Men: www.angrywhitemen.org/2021/03/29/stefan-molyneux-mourns-the-loss-of-his-audience-after-youtube-and-twitter-bans

'Stormtroopers interview', Te Ara: The Encyclopedia of New Zealand: https://teara.govt.nz/en/video/28246/stormtroopers-interview

'Story: English language in New Zealand', Te Ara: The Encyclopedia of New Zealand: https://teara.govt.nz/en/cartoon/40313/helengrad

'Summary of submissions to the Royal Commission of Inquiry', Royal Commission of Inquiry website, 26 November 2020: https://christchurchattack.royalcommission.nz/assets/Publications/Summary-of-submissions.pdf

'Te Kuku O Te Manawa - Ka puta te riri, ka momori te ngākau, ka heke ngā roimata mo tōku pēpi', Office of The Childrens Commissioner: www.occ.org.nz/publications/reports/te-kuku-o-te-manawa/

'The 1940 Centennial', New Zealand History online: https://nzhistory.govt.nz/culture/centennial/the-centennial-and-the-treaty-of-waitangi

'The birth of a modern far right in New Zealand: The post-war years, 1950s–1980s', The Ice Bloc: https://theicebloc.wordpress.com/2020/07/14/the-birth-of-a-modern-far-right-in-new-zealand-the-post-war-years-1950s-1980s/

'The Christchurch call to eliminate terrorist and violent extremist online content', The Ministry of Foreign Affairs and Trade: www.christchurchcall.com

'The social report 2016: Te pūrongo orange ngā tangata – unemployment', from Ministry of Social Development, June 2016: https://socialreport.msd.govt.nz/paid-work/unemployment.html

'Two years ago, they marched in Charlottesville. Where are they now?', ADL, 8 August 2019: www.adl.org/blog/two-years-ago-they-marched-in-charlottesville-where-are-they-now

'What is the QAnon conspiracy theory?' CBS News: www.cbsnews.com/news/what-is-the-qanon-conspiracy-theory/

Abutaleb, Yasmeen. 'What's inside the hate-filled manifesto linked to the alleged El Paso shooter', The Washington Post: www.washingtonpost.com/politics/2019/08/04/whats-inside-hate-filled-manifesto-linked-el-paso-shooter/

Ahmat, Hamimah. 'Christchurch attack inquiry: Survivors need systemic change', Middle East Eye: www.middleeasteye.net/opinion/christchurch-report-survivors-we-need-systemic-change

Alchorn, William, 'From gangs to groupuscules and solo-actor terrorism: New Zealand radical right narratives and counter-narratives in the context of the Christchurch attack', Hedayah, April 2021: www.hedayahcenter.org/wp-content/uploads/2021/04/2021APR1_FINAL_NewZealand_Country-Report.pdf

Barton, G.P., 'Skerrett, Charles Perrin', from the Dictionary of New Zealand Biography: https://teara.govt.nz/en/biographies/3s21/skerrett-charles-perrin

Beaty, Katelyn, 'QAnon: The alternative religion that's coming to your church', Religious News Service, 17 August 2020: https://religionnews.com/2020/08/17/qanon-the-alternative-religion-thats-coming-to-your-church/

Beauchamp, Zack. 'Accelerationism: The obscure idea inspiring white supremacist killers around the world', Vox: www.vox.com/the-highlight/2019/11/11/20882005/accelerationism-white-supremacy-christchurch

Beckford, Gyles, 'New alt-right groups hiding in plain sight – investigation', Radio New Zealand, 28 April 2019: www.rnz.co.nz/national/programmes/insight/audio/2018692368/new-alt-right-political-groups-hiding-in-plain-sight-investigation

Bell, Miriam, 'Anti-vaxxers get ugly', Australia/Israel Review, 27 October 2021: https://1.org.nz/anti-vaxxers-get-ugly/

Boag, Maxine, 'QAnon ... NZ style', Bay Buzz, August 2020: www.baybuzz.co.nz/2020/08/22/qanon-nz-style

Bowles, Nellie, 'Jordan Peterson, custodian of the patriarchy', New York Times, 18 May 2018: www.nytimes.com/2018/05/18/style/jordan-peterson-12-rules-for-life.html

Braae, Alex, 'A night in Gore with New Zealand's most formidable conservative campaigners', Spinoff, 25 September 2020: https://thespinoff.co.nz/politics/25-09-2020/a-night-in-gore-with-new-zealands-most-formidable-conservative-campaigners

Braae, Alex, 'A revelation in Marton: The Spinoff meets New Zealand's newest Christian party', Spinoff, 18 August 2020: https://thespinoff.co.nz/politics/18-08-2020/a-revelation-in-marton-the-spinoff-meets-new-zealands-newest-christian-party/

Burke, Daniel, 'How QAnon uses religion to lure unsuspecting Christians', CNN, 15 October 2020: https://edition.cnn.com/2020/10/15/us/qanon-religion-churches/index.html

Burrows, Matt, 'Electoral Commission rubbishes Te Kahika claims Advance NZ a victim of "rigged election", "disqualified votes"', Newshub, 19 October 2020: www.newshub.co.nz/home/politics/2020/10/electoral-commission-rubbishes-billy-te-kahika-s-claims-advance-nz-a-victim-of-rigged-election-disqualified-votes.html

Cai, Weiyi and Simone Landon, 'Attacks by white extremists are growing. So are their connections', The New York Times, 3 April 2019: www.nytimes.com/interactive/2019/04/03/world/white-extremist-terrorism-christchurch.html

Caldwell, Christopher, 'What the alt-right really

means', New York Times, 2 December 2016: https://nyti.ms/2gujZCX

Capshaw, Ron, 'Crossing the rubicon: A review of Rich Perlstein's "Reaganland: America's Rightward Turn, 1976-1980"', Liberty, November-December 2020: http://libertymagazine.org/article/crossing-the-rubicon

Casidy, Riza, 'The rise and rise of Hillsong, and what other Australian churches should learn from them', The Conversation, 11 July 2018: https://theconversation.com/the-rise-and-rise-of-hillsong-and-what-other-australian-churches-should-learn-from-them-94487

Clark, Byron, 'Counterspin Media', Webworm, 4 June 2021: www.webworm.co/p/fakenews2

Clark, Byron, 'Encounters with the far-right: Part 1', Webworm, 9 December 2020: www.webworm.co/p/alt-right-pt1

Clark, Byron, 'How the far-right found a home in the New Conservative Party', Fightback, 12 June 2020: https://fightback.org.nz/2020/06/12/how-the-far-right-found-a-home-in-the-new-conservative-party

Clark, Byron, 'The crowded mess on NZ's populist right', Fightback, 22 September 2020: https://fightback.org.nz/2020/09/22/the-crowded-mess-on-nzs-populist-right/

Clark, Byron, 'The genocide that inspired the Christchurch terrorist', Fightback, 24 March 2021: https://fightback.org.nz/2021/03/24/the-genocide-that-inspired-the-christchurch-terrorist/

Coalson, Robert, 'Christchurch attacks: Suspect took inspiration from former Yugoslavia's ethnically fueled wars', Radio Free Europe/Radio Liberty: www.rferl.org/a/christchurch-attacks-yugoslavia-tarrant-inspiration-suspect-new-zealand/29823655.html

Comerford, Milo, Jakob Guhl and Carl Miller, 'Understanding the New Zealand online extremist ecosystem', Institute for Strategic Dialogue, June 2021: www.isdglobal.org/wp-content/uploads/2021/06/NZ-Online-Extremism-Findings-Report.pdf

Cook, Megan, 'Abortion – opposition and support from the 1960s', Te Ara: The Encyclopedia of New Zealand: https://teara.govt.nz/en/abortion/page-3

Daalder, Marc, 'Action Zealandia linked to Dominion Movement', Newsroom, 13 March 2020: www.newsroom.co.nz/action-zealandia-linked-to-dominion-movement

Daalder, Marc. 'Action Zealandia member planned terror cell', Newsroom, 9 March 2020: www.newsroom.co.nz/2020/03/09/1072195/action-zealandia-member-planned-terror-cell

Daalder, Marc, 'Army reservist linked to far-right group', Newsroom, 25 June 2020: www.stuff.co.nz/national/300042525/army-reservist-linked-to-new-zealand-farright-group

Daalder, Marc, 'Far-right speakers features at anti-lockdown march', Newsroom, 15 September 2020: www.newsroom.co.nz/far-right-speakers-featured-at-anti-lockdown-march

Daalder, Marc, 'Man charged after mosque car bomb threat', Newsroom, 4 March 2021: www.newsroom.co.nz/two-arrested-after-car-bomb-threat

Daalder, Marc, 'On the internet, nobody knows you're a terrorist', Newsroom, 21 December 2020: www.newsroom.co.nz/on-the-internet-nobody-knows-youre-a-terrorist

Daalder, Marc, 'Soldier with far-right ties arrested at Linton Military Camp', Newsroom, 18 December 2019: www.stuff.co.nz/national/crime/118280866/soldier-with-farright-ties-arrested-at-linton-military-camp

Dearden, Lizzie, 'Man who stormed mosque "armed with shotguns" was inspired by Christchurch and El Paso attackers, messaging board post suggests', The Independent: www.independent.co.uk/news/world/europe/norway-mosque-shooting-attack-suspect-philip-manshaus-christchurch-el-paso-4chan-a9052106.html

Donovan, Joan, 'El Paso shooter wasn't a "lone wolf" – and his so-called online "manifesto" proves why', NBC News: www.nbcnews.com/think/opinion/el-paso-shooter-wasn-t-lone-wolf-his-so-called-ncna1039201

Doward, Jamie, '"Quite frankly terrifying": How the QAnon conspiracy is taking over', The Guardian, 20 September 2020: www.theguardian.com/world/2020/sep/20/the-qanon-conspiracy

Elliott, Marianne, Jess Berentson-Shaw, Kathleen Kuehn and Leon Salter, 'Digital Threats to Democracy', The Workshop, 2019: www.digitaldemocracy.nz/

Espiner, Emma, 'New Zealand must learn lessons of 1918 pandemic and protect Māori from Covid-19', Guardian, 25 March 2020: www.theguardian.com/commentisfree/2020/mar/26/new-zealand-must-learn-lessons-of-1918-pandemic-and-protect-maori-from-covid-19

Evans, Robert. 'Shitposting, inspirational terrorism and the Christchurch mosque massacre', bellingcat: www.bellingcat.com/news/rest-of-world/2019/03/15/shitposting-inspirational-terrorism-and-the-christchurch-mosque-massacre/

Farrier, David, '"I'm just outlining facts"; watching New Zealand getting red-pilled, in real time', Webworm, 13 August 2020: https://webworm.substack.com/im-just-outlining-facts-watching

Farrier, David, 'New Zealand goes loopy: A summary of Aotearoa's top anti-vax and conspiracy theory nitwits', Webworm, 25 October 2021: www.webworm.co/p/loopy

Farrier, David, 'Why are conspiracy theories dripping in racism?' Webworm, 16 September 2020: http://webworm.substack.com/p/why-are-conspiracy-theories-dripping

Fleming, Andy, 'Right Wing Resistance, Ricky White & slackbastard', Slackbastard, 20 December 2018: https://slackbastard.anarchobase.com/?p=44245

Gaylor, Annie Laurie, 'The hands that prey on Sunday morning', Freedom from Religion Foundation, November 1996: https://ffrf.org/component/k2/item/18525-hands-that-prey-on-sunday-morning

Gentry, Kenneth L., 'Appointed for the defense of the gospel: The life and ministry of Greg L. Bahnsen', Chalcedon Foundation, 1 February 2004: https://chalcedon.edu/magazine/appointed-for-the-defense-of-the-gospel-the-life-and-ministry-of-greg-l-bahnsen

Greenwood, Sue, 'How have QAnon's conspiracies gained traction in the UK?' The Guardian, 27 October 2020: www.theguardian.com/commentisfree/2020/oct/27/how-qanons-conspiracies-gained-traction-uk-social-media

Hamilton, Scott, 'The land of the long white stain', Spinoff, 20 March 2019: https://thespinoff.co.nz/atea/20-03-2019/the-land-of-the-long-white-stain/

Hamilton, Scott, 'The white tangata whenua, and other bullshit from the 'One New Zealand 'crew', Spinoff, 22 May 2017: https://thespinoff.co.nz/society/22-05-2017/the-white-tangata-whenua-and-other-bullshit-from-the-one-new-zealand-crew/

Hannah, Kate, Sanjana Hattotuwa and Kayli Taylor, 'Working Paper: Mis- and disinformation in Aotearoa New Zealand from 17 August to 5 November 2021', The Disinformation Project, November 2021: www.tepunahamatatini.ac.nz/2021/11/09/mis-and-disinformation/

Haverland, John, 'Theonomy: What have we learned?' OPC: www.opc.org/OS/html/V4/2b.html/

Hayward, Janine, 'Biculturalism', Te Ara – the Encyclopedia of New Zealand: https://teara.govt.nz/en/biculturalism/print#3

Hofstader, Richard, 'The paranoid style in American politics', Harper's Magazine, November 1964: https://harpers.org/archive/1964/11/the-paranoid-style-in-american-politics/

Jones, R., 'Why equity for Māori must be prioritised during the Covid-19 response', University of Auckland website, 20 March 2020: www.auckland.ac.nz/en/news/2020/03/20/equity-maori-prioritised-covid-19-response.html

Kaplan, Alex, 'Despite cracking down on QAnon, youtube continues to profit from content supporting the conspiracy theory', Media Matters: www.mediamatters.org/google/despite-cracking-down-qanon-youtube-continues-profit-content-supporting-conspiracy-theory

Karr, Clarence, 'James Dunsmuir', Dictionary of Canadian Biography: www.biographi.ca/en/bio/dunsmuir_james_14E.html

Khandaker, Tamara, 'Lauren Southern is the alt-right's not-so-secret weapon', Vice, 3 November 2017: www.vice.com/en/article/8xmyaa/lauren-southern-is-the-alt-rights-not-so-secret-weapon

King, P. et al, 'COVID-19 and Māori health – when equity is more than a word', Te Rōpu Whakakaupapa Urutā, 2020: www.uruta.maori.nz/when-equity-is-more-than-a-word

Kirby, Jen, 'The New Zealand shooter wrote a manifesto. An extremism expert explains what it means', Vox, 18 March 2019: www.vox.com/2019/3/18/18267682/new-zealand-christchurch-shooter-manifesto-online-extremism

Knight, Ben, 'Germany implements new internet hate speech crackdown', Deutsche Welle: www.dw.com/en/germany-implements-new-internet-hate-speech-crackdown/a-41991590

Langton, Graham, 'Harper, Arthur Paul', from the Dictionary of New Zealand Biography: https://teara.govt.nz/en/biographies/4h17/harper-arthur-paul

Lawrence, David, 'The UK's emerging conspiracy theory street movements', Hope Not Hate, 28 August 2020: www.hopenothate.org.uk/2020/08/28/the-uks-emerging-conspiracy-theory-street-movements/

Leier, Mark, 'Ralph Smith', Dictionary of Canadian Biography: www.biographi.ca/en/bio/smith_ralph_14E.html

Lemon, Jason, 'QAnon influencers on youtube remain online despite promotion of Capitol riot', Newsweek: www.newsweek.com/qanon-influencers-youtube-remain-online-despite-promotion-capitol-riot-1582152

Lewis, Rebecca, 'Alternative influence: Broadcasting the reactionary right on youtube', Data & Society Research Institute, 2018, pp. 36-37: https://datasociety.net/wp-content/uploads/2018/09/DS_Alternative_Influence.pdf

List, Kevin, 'Don Brash, Civil Unions and the Exclusive Brethren', Scoop: www.scoop.co.nz/stories/HL0509/S00237/don-brash-civil-unions-the-exclusive-brethren.htm

Lorenz, Taylor, 'The shooter's manifesto was designed to troll', The Atlantic: www.theatlantic.com/technology/archive/2019/03/the-shooters-manifesto-was-designed-to-troll/585058/

Lorenz, Taylor and Davey Alba, '"Zoombombing" becomes a dangerous organized effort', New York Times, 3 April 2020: https://nyti.ms/348wWgl

Lyons, O., '400 years of hostility to Native Americans', Albany Times Union, 9 August 2009: www.onondaganation.org/mediafiles/pdfs/un/Doctrine%20of%20Discovery.pdf, p. B1

Macdonald, Fraser, 'Spirit of resistance: why Destiny Church and other New Zealand Pentecostalists oppose lockdowns and vaccination', The Conversation, 29 October 2021: https://theconversation.com/spirit-of-resistance-why-destiny-church-and-other-new-zealand-pentecostalists-oppose-lockdowns-and-vaccination-170193

Mack, Ben, 'Villainesse goes inside ultraconservative New Zealand churches', Villainesse, 19 May 2017: www.villainesse.com/no-filter/villainesse-goes-inside-ultraconservative-new-zealand-churches

Mager, Darrel, 'Klan claims to have room for Maori', New Zealand Herald: www.nzherald.co.nz/nz/klan-claims-to-have-room-for-maori/4HBLLMVOFSLZKZJSMG7P2L5WEQ/

Manch, Thomas, 'The "growing" white nationalist group with a "harmful and violent" ideology', Stuff, 26 March 2020: www.stuff.co.nz/national/christchurch-shooting/111415544/the-growing-white-nationalist-group-with-a-harmful-and-violent-ideology

Manhire, Toby, 'The protest that revealed a new, ugly, dangerous side to our country', The Spinoff, 10 November 2021: www.nzherald.co.nz/nz/covid-19-delta-outbreak-toby-manhire-the-protest-that-revealed-a-new-ugly-dangerous-side-to-nz/3YYMC2BYNK66WVXO6AYU4WMXLI/

Master, Farida, 'From darkness to light: Journey of youth worker turned politician', Times Online, 23 June 2020: www.times.co.nz/news/from-darkness-to-light-journey-of-youth-worker-turned-politician/

Milne, Jeremy, 'Responding to some Covid claims', Gisborne Herald, 19 August 2020: www.gisborneherald.co.nz/editorial/20200819/responding-to-some-covid-claims/

Mitchell, Charlie, 'The conspiracists' election: How the farthest fringes of politics are making a play for the centre', RadioNZ, 1 August 2020: www.stuff.co.nz/national/politics/300070891/the-conspiracists-election-how-the-farthest-fringes-of-politics-are-making-a-play-for-the-centre

Müller, Karsten and Carlo Schwarz, 'From hashtag to hate crime: Twitter and anti-minority sentiment', SSRN, posted 28 March 2018, revised 24 July 2020: https://papers.ssrn.com/sol3/papers.cfm?abstract_id=3149103

New Zealand Māori Council, 'Covid-19: Guidance for Māori and Māori communities/organisations', National Digital Heritage Archive, March 2020: https://ndhadeliver.natlib.govt.nz/delivery/DeliveryManagerServlet?dps_pid=IE53334142

Ong, Kyler, and Raffaello Pantucci, 'From fringe to mainstream: The extreme rightwing in Europe', Observer Research Foundation: www.orfonline.org/expert-speak/fringe-mainstream-extreme-rightwing-europe-68848/

Ray, William, 'The story of white supremacy', Radio New Zealand, 26 March 2019: www.rnz.co.nz/programmes/black-sheep/story/2018688225/the-story-of-white-supremacy

Ribeiro, Manoel Horta, Raphael Ottoni, Robert West, Virgilio Almeida and Wagner Meira Jr, 'Auditing radicalization pathways on YouTube', arXiv: https://arxiv.org/abs/1908.08313

Romano, Aja, 'How the Christchurch shooter used memes to spread hate', Vox: www.vox.com/culture/2019/3/16/18266930/christchurch-shooter-manifesto-memes-subscribe-to-pewdiepie

Romano, Aja, 'Youtube's 2018 "Rewind" is the site's most disliked video ever. The implications are huge', Vox, 14 December 2018: www.vox.com/culture/2018/12/14/18138916/pewdiepie-vs-t-series-youtube-rewind-2018

Roose, Kevin, 'The making of a youtube radical,' New York Times, 9 June 2019: www.nytimes.com/interactive/2019/06/08/technology/youtube-radical.html

Roose, Kevin, 'What is QAnon, the viral pro-Trump conspiracy theory?' New York Times, 19 August 2020: www.nytimes.com/article/what-is-qanon.html

Roy, Eleanor Ainge, 'NZ website withdraws author's works after she criticises Māori foreign minister', The Guardian, 4 November 2020: www.theguardian.com/world/2020/nov/04/nz-website-withdraws-authors-works-after-she-criticises-maori-foreign-minister

Schrader, Ben, 'Parades and protest marches – protest marches, 1980s to 2000s', Te Ara: The Encyclopedia of New Zealand: https://teara.govt.nz/en/photograph/21123/enough-is-enough-march

Scott, David, 'Impacts of the Global Financial Crisis on earnings of tertiary graduates in New Zealand', Education Counts, May 2020: www.educationcounts.govt.nz/publications/tertiary_education_all/impacts-of-the-global-financial-crisis-on-earnings-of-tertiary-graduates-in-new-zealand

Shapiro, Ari, 'How QAnon conspiracy is spreading in Christian communities across the US', NPR, 21 August 2020: www.npr.org/2020/08/21/904798097/how-qanon-conspiracy-is-spreading-in-christian-communities-across-the-u-s

Shoebridge, Tim, 'Phillips, Hilda', from the Dictionary of New Zealand Biography: https://teara.govt.nz/en/biographies/6p3/phillips-hilda/print

Singh, Harkanwal and Lincoln Tan, 'Money and faith', New Zealand Herald, 29 September

2016: https://insights.nzherald.co.nz/article/money-and-faith/

Solon, Olivia, 'Six months after Christchurch shootings, videos of attack are still on facebook', NBC News: www.nbcnews.com/tech/tech-news/six-months-after-christchurch-shootings-videos-attack-are-still-facebook-n1056691

Spoonley, Paul, 'Christchurch mosque shootings must end New Zealand's innocence about right-wing terrorism', The Conversation, 15 March 2019: https://theconversation.com/christchurch-mosque-shootings-must-end-new-zealands-innocence-about-right-wing-terrorism-113655

Stace, Hilary, 'Statement of Hilary Stace to the Royal Commission of Inquiry into historical abuse In State care and in the care of faith-based institutions', Royal Commission website, October / November 2019: www.abuseincare.org.nz/assets/Uploads/Documents/Public-Hearings/Contextual/12.-Hilary-Stace.pdf

Stanton, Gregory, 'QAnon is a nazi cult, rebranded', Just Security: www.justsecurity.org/72339/qanon-is-a-nazi-cult-rebranded/

Stevens, Murdoch, 'Refugee resettlement and activism in New Zealand', Forced Migration Review, February 2017: www.fmreview.org/resettlement/stephens

Taylor, Kerry, 'McLaren, David', from the Dictionary of New Zealand Biography: https://teara.govt.nz/en/biographies/3m22/mclaren-david

Tod, Frank, 'Terry, Edward Lionel', Te Ara – the Encyclopaedia of New Zealand: https://teara.govt.nz/en/biographies/3t27/terry-edward-lionel/sources

Trotter, Chris, 'Born to rule? What sort of Christian is Chris Luxon?' Daily Blog, 8 November 2019: https://thedailyblog.co.nz/2019/11/08/chosen-to-rule-what-sort-of-christian-is-chris-luxon/

Tso, Matthew, 'Mother disgusted 11-year-old daughter being asked to deliver 'extreme' religious publication on paper round', Stuff, 9 March 2021: www.stuff.co.nz/national/124465378/mother-disgusted-11yearold-daughter-being-asked-to-deliver-extreme-religious-publication-on-paper-round

van der Krogt, Christopher, 'Elliott, Howard Leslie', from the Dictionary of New Zealand Biography: https://teara.govt.nz/en/biographies/3e5/elliott-howard-leslie

Wall, Tony, 'Is Tamaki's empire crumbling?' Stuff, 7 March 2010: www.stuff.co.nz/national/3414336/Is-Tamakis-empire-crumbling

Watkins, Gareth, 'Birth of the gay movement', New Zealand History online: https://nzhistory.govt.nz/politics/further-information-homosexual-law-reform

Watson, David K., 'The Christian reconstruction/theonomy movement', Christian Library: www.christianstudylibrary.org/article/christian-reconstruction-theonomy-movement

Wilson, Jason, 'The base: Exporting accelerationist terror', The Southern Poverty Law Center: www.splcenter.org/hatewatch/2020/08/12/base-exporting-accelerationist-terror

Wong, Julia Carrie, 'Down the rabbit hole: How QAnon conspiracies thrive on Facebook', The Guardian, 25 June 2020: www.theguardian.com/technology/2020/jun/25/qanon-facebook-conspiracy-theories-algorithm

Wong, Julia Carrie, 'Germany shooting suspect livestreamed attempted attack on synagogue', The Guardian, 9 October 2019: www.theguardian.com/world/2019/oct/09/germany-shooting-synagogue-halle-livestreamed

INDEX

Bold denotes illustrations and tables.